Frommer's®

1st Edition

Oregon

by Karl Samson & Jane Aukshunas

Macmillan • USA

ABOUT THE AUTHORS

Husband-and-wife travel-writing team **Karl Samson** and **Jane Aukshunas** live in Oregon where they spend their time juggling their obsessions with traveling, outdoor sports, and gardening. Each winter, to dry out their webbed feet, they flee the soggy Northwest to update the *Frommer's Arizona* guide, but always look forward to their return to the land of good coffee. Karl is also the author of *Outside Magazine's Adventure Guide to the Pacific Northwest* and *Frommer's Nepal.*

MACMILLAN TRAVEL

A Simon & Schuster Macmillan Company
1633 Broadway
New York, NY 10019

Find us online at **www.frommers.com**

ISBN 0-02-861829-7
ISSN 1093-7455

Editor: Suzanne Roe Jannetta
Production Editor: Carol Sheehan
Design by Michele Laseau
Digital Cartography by Roberta Stockwell, John Decamillis, and Ortelius Design

SPECIAL SALES

Bulk purchases (10+ copies) of Frommer's and selected Macmillan travel guides are available to corporations, organizations, mail-order catalogs, institutions, and charities at special discounts, and can be customized to suit individual needs. For more information write to Special Sales, Macmillan General Reference, 1633 Broadway, New York, NY 10019.

Manufactured in the United States of America

Contents

List of Maps

AN INVITATION TO THE READER

In researching this book, we discovered many wonderful places—hotels, restaurants, shops, and more. We're sure you'll find others. Please tell us about them, so we can share the information with your fellow travelers in upcoming editions. If you were disappointed with a recommendation, we'd love to know that, too. Please write to:

Frommer's Oregon, 1st Edition
Macmillan Travel
1633 Broadway
New York, NY 10019

AN ADDITIONAL NOTE

Please be advised that travel information is subject to change at any time—and this is especially true of prices. We therefore suggest that you write or call ahead for confirmation when making your travel plans. The authors, editors, and publisher cannot be held responsible for the experiences of readers while traveling. Your safety is important to us, however, so we encourage you to stay alert and be aware of your surroundings. Keep a close eye on cameras, purses, and wallets, all favorite targets of thieves and pickpockets.

WHAT THE SYMBOLS MEAN

✪ Frommer's Favorites

Our favorite places and experiences—outstanding for quality, value, or both.

The following abbreviations are used for credit cards:

AE	American Express	EURO	EuroCard
CB	Carte Blanche	JCB	Japan Credit Bank
DC	Diners Club	MC	MasterCard
DISC	Discover	V	Visa
ER	enRoute		

FIND FROMMER'S ONLINE

Arthur Frommer's Outspoken Encyclopedia of Travel (www.frommers.com) offers more than 6,000 pages of up-to-the-minute travel information—including the latest bargains and candid, personal articles updated daily by Arthur Frommer himself. No other Web site offers such comprehensive and timely coverage of the world of travel.

The Best of Oregon

Planning a trip to Oregon involves making lots of decisions about where to go and what to see, so we've tried to give you some direction. We've traveled the state extensively and have chosen what we feel are the very best that the state has to offer in a variety of categories. These are the places and experiences you won't want to miss. Most are described in more detail elsewhere in this book; this chapter will give you an overview and get you started.

1 The Best Natural Attractions

- **The Oregon Coast:** Rocky headlands, offshore islands and haystack rocks, natural arches, sea caves full of sea lions, giant sand dunes, and dozens of state parks make this one of the most spectacular coastlines in the country. See chapter 5.
- **Columbia Gorge National Scenic Area:** Carved by ice-age floods that were as much as 1,200 feet deep, the Columbia Gorge is a unique feature of the Northwest landscape. Waterfalls by the dozen cascade from the basalt cliffs of the gorge. Highways on both the Washington and the Oregon sides of the Columbia River provide countless memorable views. See chapter 8.
- **Mount Hood:** As Oregon's tallest mountain and the closest Cascade peak to Portland, Mount Hood is a recreational mecca par excellence. Hiking trails, lakes and rivers, even year-round snow skiing make this quite simply the most appealing natural attraction in the state. See chapter 9.
- **Crater Lake National Park:** Crater Lake, at 1,932 feet deep, is the deepest lake in the United States, and its sapphire-blue waters are a bewitchingly beautiful sight when seen from the rim of the volcanic crater that forms the lake. See chapter 9.
- **Central Oregon Lava Lands:** Throughout central Oregon and the central Cascades region, from the lava fields of McKenzie Pass to the obsidian flows of Newberry National Volcanic Monument, you'll find dramatic examples of the volcanic activity that gave rise to the Cascade Range. See chapters 9 and 11.
- **Hells Canyon:** Deeper than the Grand Canyon, this massive gorge along the Oregon-Idaho border is remote and inaccessible, and that is just what makes it fascinating. You can gaze down into it from on high, float its waters, and hike its trails. See chapter 12.

2 The Best Outdoor Activities

- **Bicycling the Oregon Coast:** With U.S. 101 clinging to the edge of the continent for much of its route through Oregon, this road has become the most popular cycling route in the Northwest. The entire coast can be done in about a week, but there are also plenty of short sections that make good day trips. See chapter 5.

- **Windsurfing at Hood River:** Winds that rage through the Columbia Gorge whip up whitecapped standing waves and have turned this area into the windsurfing capital of the United States, attracting boardsailors from around the world. See chapter 8.

- **Fly-Fishing for Steelhead on the North Umpqua River:** Made famous by Zane Grey, the North Umpqua is the quintessential steelhead river (though it's open to fly-fishing only for part of its length). The river and the elusive steelhead offer a legendary fishing experience. See chapter 9.

- **Rafting the Rogue River:** Of all the white-water rafting rivers, none is more famous than the Rogue. Meandering through remote wilderness in the southern part of the state, this river has been popular with anglers since early in this century and attracted Zane Grey with its beauty and great fishing. Today, you can splash through roaring white water by day and spend your nights in remote lodges that are inaccessible by car. See chapter 10.

- **Mountain Biking in Bend:** Outside the town of Bend, in central Oregon, dry ponderosa pine forests are laced with trails that are open to mountain bikes. Routes pass by several lakes and along the way you'll get great views of the Sisters, Broken Top, and Mount Bachelor. See chapter 11.

- **Skiing Mount Bachelor:** With ski slopes dropping off the very summit of this extinct volcano, Mount Bachelor Ski Area, in drier and sunnier central Oregon, is the state's premier ski area. Seemingly endless runs of all levels of ability make this a magnet for skiers and snowboarders from around the state, and lots of high-speed quad chairs keep people on the snow instead of standing in line. See chapter 11.

3 The Best Beaches

- **Cannon Beach/Ecola State Park:** With the massive monolith of Haystack Rock rising up from the low-tide line and the secluded beaches of Ecola State Park just south of town, Cannon Beach offers all the best of the Oregon coast. See chapter 5.

- **Oswald West State Park:** It's a 15-minute walk down to the beach at this state park south of Cannon Beach, which keeps the sands from ever getting too crowded. The crescent-shaped beach is on a secluded cove backed by dense forest. This also happens to be a favorite surfing spot. See chapter 5.

- **Sunset Bay State Park:** Almost completely surrounded by sandstone cliffs, this little beach near Coos Bay is on a shallow cove. The clear waters here get a little bit warmer than unprotected waters elsewhere on the coast, so it's sometimes possible to actually go swimming. See chapter 5.

- **Bandon:** It's difficult to imagine a more picturesque stretch of coastline than the beach in Bandon. Haystack rocks rise up from sand and sea as if strewn there by some giant hand. Motels and houses front this scenic beach, which ensures its popularity no matter what the weather. See chapter 5.

- **The Beaches of Samuel H. Boardman State Park:** Within this remote south coast state park are to be found some of the prettiest, most secluded, and least visited beaches on the Oregon coast. Ringed by rocky headlands, the many little crescents of sand in this park provide an opportunity to find *the* perfect beach. See chapter 5.

4 The Best Hikes

- **Cape Lookout Trail:** Leading 2¹/₂ miles through dense forests to the tip of this rugged cape on the north Oregon coast, this trail ends high on a cliff above the waters of the Pacific. Far below, gray whales can often be seen lolling in the waves, and the view to the south takes in miles and miles of coastline. See chapter 5.
- **Umpqua Dunes Trail:** If you've ever dreamed of joining the French Foreign Legion or simply want to play at being Lawrence of Arabia, then the Oregon Dunes National Recreation Area is the place for you. Within this vast expanse of sand dunes you'll find the highest dunes on the Oregon coast—some 500 feet tall. See chapter 5.
- **Eagle Creek Trail:** This trail in the Columbia Gorge follows the tumbling waters of Eagle Creek and passes two spectacular waterfalls in the first 2 miles. Along the way, the trail climbs up the steep gorge walls, and in places, is cut right into the basalt cliffs. See chapter 8.
- **Timberline Trail:** As the name implies, this trail starts at the timberline, near the famous lodge of the same name. Because this route circles Mount Hood, you can start in either direction and make a day, overnight, or multiday hike of it. Paradise Park, its meadows ablaze with wildflowers in July and August, is a favorite for both day hikes and overnight trips. See chapter 9.
- **McKenzie River Trail to Tamolitch Pool:** The McKenzie River Trail stretches for 26 miles along the banks of this aquamarine river, but by far the most rewarding stretch of trail is the 2-mile hike to Tamolitch Pool, an astounding pool of turquoise waters formed as the McKenzie River wells up out of the ground after flowing underground for several miles. The trail leads through rugged, old lava fields. See chapter 9.
- **Deschutes River Trail:** The Deschutes River, which flows down from the east side of the Cascades, passes through open ponderosa pine forest to the west of Bend. Paralleling the river, and passing tumultuous waterfalls along the way, is an easy trail that's popular with hikers, mountain bikers, and joggers. See chapter 11.

5 The Best Scenic Drives

- **Gold Beach to Brookings:** No other stretch of U.S. 101 al[...] is more breathtaking than the segment between Gold Beach [...] remote coastline is dotted with offshore islands, natural rock arches, sea caves, bluffs, and beaches. Take your time, stop at the many pull-offs, and make this a leisurely all-day drive. See chapter 5.
- **Historic Columbia River Highway:** Opened in 1915 to allow automobiles access to the wonders of the Columbia Gorge, this narrow, winding highway east of Portland climbs up to the top of the gorge for a scenic vista before diving into forests where waterfalls, including the tallest one in the state, pour off of basalt cliffs. See chapter 8.
- **The McKenzie Pass–Santiam Pass Scenic Byway:** This loop drive, which crosses the Cascade crest twice, takes in views of half a dozen major Cascade peaks, negotiates a bizarre landscape of lava fields, passes several waterfalls, and skirts the aptly named Clear Lake, the source of the McKenzie River. This is one of the best drives in the state for fall color. See chapter 9.
- **Crater Lake Rim Drive:** This scenic drive circles the rim of the massive caldera that holds Crater Lake. Along the way are numerous pull-offs where you can gasp in astonishment at the sapphire-blue waters and the ever-changing scenery. See chapter 9.

- **Cascade Lakes Highway:** This road, formerly known as Century Drive, covers roughly 100 miles as it loops out from Bend along the eastern slope of the Cascades. Views of Broken Top and the Three Sisters are frequent, and along the way are numerous lakes, both large and small. See chapter 11.

6 The Best Museums

- **American Advertising Museum** (Portland): Though it's small, this museum in Portland's Old Town neighborhood taps into the American national psyche like few museums can. Advertising touches us all, and commercial jingles are some of the most unforgettable sound bites lodged in our minds. See chapter 6.
- **Favell Museum of Western Art and Indian Artifacts** (Klamath Falls): This museum houses an absolutely amazing assortment of Native American artifacts, including thousands of arrowheads, spear points, and other stone tools. See chapter 10.
- **The Museum at Warm Springs** (Warm Springs Reservation): Set in a remote valley in Central Oregon, this modern museum houses an outstanding collection of artifacts from the area's Native American tribes. See chapter 11.
- **The High Desert Museum** (Bend): With its popular live-animal exhibits, this is more a zoo than a museum, but exhibits also offer glimpses into the history of the vast and little-known desert that stretches from the Cascades eastward to the Rocky Mountains. See chapter 11.
- **Oregon Trail Interpretive Center** (Baker City): The lives of pioneers, who gave up everything to venture overland to the Pacific Northwest, are documented at this evocative museum. Set atop a hill in sagebrush country, the museum overlooks wagon ruts left by pioneers. See chapter 12.

7 The Best Family Attractions

- **Oregon Coast Aquarium** (Newport): This modern aquarium is the biggest attraction on the coast. While Keiko, the killer whale star of the movie *Free Willy*, steals the show, tufted puffins and sea otters are equally entertaining. Tide pools, jellyfish tanks, and a giant octopus also contribute to the appeal of this very realistically designed public aquarium. See chapter 5.
- **Sea Lion Caves** (north of Florence): This massive cave is home to hundreds of Steller sea lions that lounge on the rocks of this protected cave beneath busy U.S. 101. See chapter 5.
- **West Coast Game Park** (Bandon): The opportunity to pet wild baby animals, including leopards and bears, doesn't come often, so it's hard to pass up this roadside attraction on the southern Oregon coast. See chapter 5.
- **Oregon Museum of Science and Industry** (Portland): With an OMNIMAX theater, planetarium, a submarine, and loads of hands-on exhibits, this Portland museum is fun for kids and adults alike. See chapter 6.
- **Wildlife Safari** (Winston): Giraffes peer in your window and rhinoceroses thunder past your car doors as you drive the family through this expansive wildlife park. The savannah-like setting is even reminiscent of the African plains. See chapter 10.

8 The Best Historical Sites

- **Fort Clatsop National Memorial** (Astoria): This small log fort is a reconstruction of the fort that explorers Lewis and Clark built during the winter of 1805–06. Costumed interpreters bring the history of the fort to life. See chapter 5.

- **Jacksonville:** With more than 80 buildings listed on the National Register of Historic Places, this 19th-century gold-mining town is the most historic community in Oregon. In fact, the brick buildings of Jacksonville's main street are the oldest in the state. Here you'll also find two inns housed in buildings constructed in 1861, which makes these Oregon's oldest buildings being used as inns. See chapter 10.
- **Granite** (near Baker City): This weather-beaten ghost town in the Blue Mountains is left over from a gold rush that brought miners to this region in the late 1800s. The schoolhouse, general store, and bordello are still standing and are identified with signs. See chapter 12.
- **Oregon Trail Wagon Ruts** (Baker City): It's hard to believe that something as ephemeral as a wagon rut can last more than 150 years, but the trail left by the thousands of pioneers who followed the Oregon Trail cut deep into the land. Among other places, you can see ruts near the Oregon Trail Interpretive Center. See chapter 12.
- **Kam Wah Chung & Co. Museum** (John Day): This unusual little museum is way off the beaten track, but is well worth a visit if you're anywhere in the vicinity. The museum preserves the home, office, and apothecary of a Chinese doctor who ministered to the local Chinese community in the early part of this century. See chapter 12.

9 The Best Bed-and-Breakfast Inns

- **Sandlake Country Inn** (Tillamook County; ☎ 503/965-6745): Located just off the scenic Three Capes Loop, this romantic inn offers some of the largest and most sumptuous rooms of any B&B on the coast. The inn's grounds are filled with flower gardens, and for those seeking extra privacy, there is a small cottage. See chapter 5.
- **Channel House** (Depoe Bay; ☎ 800/447-2140 or 541/765-2140): Situated on the cliff above the channel into tiny Depoe Bay, this B&B offers one of the most striking settings on the Oregon coast. The contemporary design includes guest rooms made for romance—a hot tub on the balcony, a fire in the fireplace, and an unsurpassed view out the windows. See chapter 5.
- **Ziggurat** (Yachats; ☎ 541/547-3925): A boldly styled contemporary pyramid-shaped home built right on the beach, this is the Oregon coast's most visually stunning B&B. Its setting, near one of the most breathtaking stretches of coast, simply makes the inn even more recommendable. See chapter 5.
- **Bandon Beach House** (Bandon; ☎ 541/347-1196): Set atop a 50-foot bluff overlooking the beach, this large new inn offers only two bedrooms, but both are huge. Wood floors, river-rock fireplaces, lots of windows, and classically elegant furnishings make this a great place to hole up for a few days. See chapter 5.
- **Heron Haus** (Portland; ☎ 503/274-1846): Located in the trendiest neighborhood in Portland, this elegant old mansion is surrounded by lush grounds and has a view out over the city. If you want to sample the epitome of bathroom luxury, circa 1920, ask for the room with the multiple-head shower. See chapter 6.
- **The Lion and the Rose** (Portland; ☎ 800/955-1647 or 503/287-9245): Victorian elegance within a block of one of Portland's upscale inner-city neighborhoods is the attraction of this luxurious B&B. The home is an ornate confection of late 19th-century excess, and for a truly memorable stay, you should try to get the turret room. See chapter 6.
- **Springbrook Hazelnut Farm** (Newberg; ☎ 800/793-8528 or 503/538-4606): Set in the midst of the Yamhill County wine country, this working hazelnut farm

captures the essence of rural Oregon and distills it into a tranquil and restorative retreat. You can opt to stay in the main house, a carriage house, or a cottage. See chapter 7.

- **The Secret Garden** (Eugene; ☎ 888/484-6755 or 541/484-6755): Housed in what was once a sorority house and before that the home of one of Eugene's founding families, this very elegant inn is utterly tasteful and filled with family heirlooms and original art. The garden, though still young, does have some very interesting secrets. See chapter 7.
- **Lakecliff Estate Bed & Breakfast** (Hood River; ☎ 541/386-7000): Located not far from the famous Columbia Gorge Hotel, this inn is in a home built about the same time the hotel was. The view from the cliff-top location is superb, and the shady forest setting lends the feel of the deep woods. Basically, what you get here is an upscale historic atmosphere without the crowds. See chapter 8.
- **Mt. Ashland Inn** (Ashland; ☎ 800/830-8707 or 541/482-8707): Set in the forest high on the slopes of Mount Ashland, this huge log inn is a pleasantly rustic, yet luxurious, alternative to the abundant Victorian and country-flavored B&Bs in Ashland proper. While this inn is still close enough for going to the theater, it also happens to have the Pacific Crest Trail running through its front yard. See chapter 10.

10 The Best Small Inns

- **Stephanie Inn** (Cannon Beach; ☎ 800/633-3466 or 503/436-2221): Combining the look of a mountain lodge with a beachfront setting in Oregon's most artistic town, the Stephanie Inn is a romantic retreat that surrounds its guests with unpretentious luxury. See chapter 5.
- **The Inn at Manzanita** (Manzanita; ☎ 503/368-6754): Although small enough to be a B&B and lacking a restaurant of its own, this inn, in what just might be the second-quaintest town on the Oregon coast, is designed for romantic getaways. Within a block you'll find both the beach and two of the state's best restaurants. See chapter 5.
- **Sylvia Beach Hotel** (Newport; ☎ 541/265-5428): Taking literature as its theme and decorating its rooms to evoke different authors—from Edgar Allan Poe to Dr. Seuss—the Sylvia Beach Hotel is the most original small inn in the Northwest. The fact that it's only a block from the beach is just icing on the cake. See chapter 5.
- **Tu Tu Tun Lodge** (Gold Beach; ☎ 541/247-6664): Though some might think of this as a fishing lodge, it's far too luxurious for anglers to keep to themselves. A secluded setting on the lower Rogue River guarantees tranquillity, and choice guest rooms provide the perfect setting for forgetting about your everyday stress. The dining room serves excellent meals. See chapter 5.
- **Steamboat Inn** (Steamboat; ☎ 800/840-8825 or 541/498-2230): Oregon's North Umpqua River is legendary for its steelhead fishing, and this is where you stay if you want to return to elegance and comfort after a day of fishing. The word is out on this inn, and many guests now show up with no intention of casting a fly into the river's waters. They'd rather just sit back and watch the river flow. See chapter 9.
- **The Winchester Country Inn** (Ashland; ☎ 800/972-4991 or 541/488-1113): Located only 2 blocks from the theaters of the Oregon Shakespeare Festival, this inn has the feel of a country inn though it's located right in town. Rooms are in three different buildings, including a modern Victorian cottage that has four

spacious suites. The first floor of the main building is taken up by one of Ashland's best restaurants. See chapter 10.

- **Pine Ridge Inn** (Bend; ☎ **800/600-4095** or 541/389-6137): This luxurious inn is located on the outskirts of Bend on a bluff overlooking the Deschutes River. With its spacious rooms and suites, antiques, and regional art, it provides both elegance and a Northwest flavor. See chapter 11.
- **Pine Valley Lodge** (Halfway; ☎ **541/742-2027**): Set in the tiny hamlet of Halfway just outside Hells Canyon National Recreation Area, this lodge is everything that contemporary rustic Western lodges wish they could be. Owned and operated by two artists, the lodge conjures up the image of an old stage stop with its unusual architecture, while unique details add very personal touches. See chapter 12.

11 The Best Historic Hotels & Lodges

- **The Benson** (Portland; ☎ **800/426-0670** or 503/228-2000): With its crystal chandeliers and Circassian walnut paneling in the lobby, this 1912 vintage hotel is the lodging of choice of presidents, dignitaries, and celebrities visiting Portland. See chapter 6.
- **Columbia Gorge Hotel** (Hood River; ☎ **800/345-1921** or 541/386-5566): Built in 1915 to handle the first automobile traffic up the Columbia Gorge, this mission-style hotel commands a stunning view across the gorge and is surrounded by colorful gardens. The breakfasts are legendary. See chapter 8.
- **Timberline Lodge** (Mount Hood; ☎ **800/547-1406** or 503/231-7979): Built by the WPA during the Great Depression, this stately mountain lodge is a showcase for the skills of the craftspeople who created it, with a grand stone fireplace, exposed beams, and wide plank floors. The views of Mount Hood's peak, and of the Oregon Cascades to the south, are superb. See chapter 9.
- **Crater Lake Lodge** (Crater Lake National Park; ☎ **541/830-8700**): Though only a small portion of the original structure was salvaged during its reconstruction, this place still maintains the feel of a classic mountain lodge, with a stone fireplace and ponderosa pine-bark walls in the Great Hall. The setting, high above jewel-like Crater Lake, is breathtaking. See chapter 9.
- **Geiser Grand Hotel** (Baker City; ☎ **888/GEISERG** or 541/523-1889): Opened in 1889 at the height of the Blue Mountains gold rush, this Baker City grand dame reopened in 1997 after a three-year renovation. With its corner turret, stained-glass ceiling, and abundance of crystal chandeliers, the hotel succeeds in capturing the feel of a Wild West luxury hotel without sacrificing any modern conveniences. See chapter 12.

12 The Best Resorts

- **Salishan Lodge** (Gleneden Beach; ☎ **888/725-4742** or 541/764-2371): Even if it weren't the only real full-service resort on the Oregon coast, Salishan Lodge would likely still be the best. Set amid lush coastal forests and with plenty of holes of golf, this has long been *the* quintessential Oregon coast resort. The only drawback is that the beach is a bit of a hike. See chapter 5.
- **The Resort at the Mountain** (Mount Hood; ☎ **800/669-7666** or 503/622-3101): Located at the foot of Mount Hood, this golf resort is surrounded by dark Northwest woods and offers almost year-round golfing, yet come winter (and summer for that matter), you can ski in the morning and play a round of golf in the afternoon. See chapter 9.

- **Black Butte Ranch** (Sisters; ☎ 800/452-7455 or 541/595-6211): This former ranch offers wide-open views and a world unto itself. The Three Sisters peaks are the backdrop for golf, horseback riding, canoeing, tennis, and numerous other activities, and in the autumn, aspen trees splash the resort with bursts of golden yellow. See chapter 11.
- **Kah-Nee-Ta Resort** (North Central Oregon; ☎ 800/554-4SUN or 541/553-1112): Located miles from the nearest town yet within 90 minutes of Portland, this resort on the Warm Springs Indian Reservation is remarkable primarily for its remote sagebrush canyon setting. However, it also has an 18-hole golf course and a swimming pool fed by a natural warm spring. See chapter 11.
- **Sunriver Lodge & Resort** (Bend; ☎ 800/547-3922 or 541/593-1000): With the Three Sisters for a backdrop and the Deschutes River winding through the property, this resort is something of an institution for Oregonians. In summer, there are golf courses and miles of bike paths, and in winter, the ski slopes of Mount Bachelor (Oregon's best ski area) are just up the road. This resort is really more of a town than just a vacation getaway spot, and once people check in, they usually decide this is just the sort of town where they'd like to live. See chapter 11.

13 The Best Portland Restaurants

For more details on all of the restaurants listed below, see chapter 6.

- **Assaggio** (☎ 503/232-6151): This small neighborhood restaurant in the Sellwood district of southeast Portland captures the essence of an Italian trattoria. With a cozy lounge area, a counter overlooking the kitchen, and a dining room full of closely spaced tables, Assaggio stays packed with not only neighborhood locals but diners from all over the city who come for the perfectly prepared pasta dishes.
- **Caprial's Bistro and Wine** (☎ 503/236-6457): Chef Caprial Pence, though a Portlander, first made a name for herself in Seattle, where she helped pioneer a distinctive regional style of cooking. Here, in her casual bistro and wine shop, she continues her culinary experimentation for a loyal following of patrons from both Portland and Seattle.
- **Couvron** (☎ 503/225-1844): This tiny French restaurant has taken Portland by storm of late with its oh-so-Gallic decor and utterly French menu. Don't let the unpretentious exterior of this converted home dissuade you, the menu boasts the finest of ingredients in dishes of uncompromising complexity.
- **Fiddleheads** (☎ 503/233-1547): With a menu and interior decor that draw somewhat on Native American influences, Fiddleheads offers one of Portland's most distinctive dining experiences. No, you won't be eating pemmican or dried salmon, but you might find buffalo stew or fiddleheads (fern shoots) on the menu.
- **Genoa** (☎ 503/238-1464): Genoa serves Italian fare the likes of which you may never have tasted before, and many a Mediterranean restaurant could take a few lessons here. The seven-course dinners are feasts for the eyes and mouth, and the handful of tables assure very personal service.
- **Higgins** (☎ 503/222-9070): Chef Greg Higgins, first made a name for himself just down the street at the Heathman Hotel. Now he has taken on the Portland restaurant scene with his eponymous restaurant, which features classic styling and a contemporary menu. Located adjacent to the Portland Center for the Performing Arts, Higgins is a favorite of theatergoers.
- **Pazzo Ristorante** (☎ 503/228-1515): While dozens of upscale contemporary Italian restaurants have crowded the Portland dining scene in the past few years,

Pazzo remains one of the best and most reliable. The restaurant is in the wine-themed Hotel Vintage Plaza; not surprisingly, Pazzo has a very good wine list.

- **Toulouse Restaurant & Bar 71** (☎ 503/241-4343): Toulouse is a big hit with Portlanders, offering luscious light meals in the bar, perfectly done rotisseried meats in the main dining room, and even, during the summer, dancing under the stars on the back patio. The crowd is eclectic and stylish, and martinis are the drink of choice in the bar.

- **Wildwood** (☎ 503/248-WOOD): With a menu that draws on the latest culinary trends, Wildwood has been the hippest restaurant in town for several years now. The *Architectural Digest* interior is divided into a variety of different spaces to fit your mood, whether you're looking for a light bar meal or a lavish celebratory feast.

- **Zefiro Restaurant & Bar** (☎ 503/226-3394): With its chic contemporary decor, its Mediterranean-influenced menu, and its impeccably prepared dishes, Zefiro consistently ranks as one of Portland's top restaurants. The tightly packed lounge is also one of *the* places in the city to be seen sipping a martini.

14 The Best Restaurants Outside Portland

- **Jarboe's in Manzanita** (Manzanita; ☎ 503/368-5113): With limited seating and a limited menu, this tiny restaurant, located in one of the coast's quintessential laid-back villages, serves memorable multicourse dinners with an emphasis on creatively prepared seafoods. See chapter 5.

- **Tina's** (Dundee; ☎ 503/538-8880): Located at the base of the Red Hills, which produce some of Oregon's finest wines, this restaurant has long been the favorite wine country dining spot for lunch or dinner. At press time, Tina's was in the process of building a large, new restaurant just up the street from the original tiny place that has stayed packed all these years. See chapter 7.

- **Zenon Café** (Eugene; ☎ 541/343-3005): Hip decor, cases filled with desserts to tempt even the most dedicated dieter, and a long, internationally inspired menu make this the most reliable and gratifying restaurant in Eugene. See chapter 7.

- **Cascade Dining Room** (Mount Hood; ☎ 503/272-3700): Located inside the historic Timberline Lodge, the Cascade Dining Room is Oregon's premier mountain-lodge restaurant and has long kept skiers and other hotel guests happy. Since the windows here are small, it isn't the view that keeps diners content, but rather the creative cuisine that emanates from the kitchen. See chapter 9.

- **Steamboat Inn** (North Umpqua Valley; ☎ 800/840-8825): Set on the bank of the North Umpqua River, this is ostensibly a fishing lodge dining room, but the multicourse gourmet meals served here have become the stuff of legends (and have even spawned a cookbook). See chapter 9.

- **Chateaulin** (Ashland; ☎ 541/482-2264): Though the *raison d'etre* of Ashland may be Shakespeare, it is the French cuisine at Chateaulin that lingers longest in the memories of theatergoers. The dishes are hearty, and the decor is theatrically country French. See chapter 10.

- **New Sammy's Cowboy Bistro** (Ashland, ☎ 541/535-2779): Without even a sign out front to announce that you're at the right place, this Ashland restaurant is something of an underground institution. Although it's a casual place, you cannot just drop by and expect to get a table. Advance reservations are a must. See chapter 10.

- **Kokanee Café** (Camp Sherman; ☎ 541/595-6420): Located amid the ponderosa pines on the bank of the Metolius River near the Western theme town of Sisters, this rustic restaurant has the look of an upscale fishing lodge, but its clientele is much broader than just the foolish fly anglers who come to test the waters of the Metolius. The trout is, of course, always a good bet here. See chapter 11.

- **Wildflower Bakery** (Enterprise; ☎ 541/426-2086): This tiny restaurant on the edge of Enterprise is by far the best restaurant on the north side of the Wallowa Mountains. However, don't come expecting gourmet meals. The menu is usually limited to a couple of simple dishes, which, if you're lucky, might be based on the chef's Caribbean family recipes. See chapter 12.
- **The Halfway Supper Club** (Halfway; ☎ 541/742-2027): Halfway is an unlikely town for a restaurant that can rank among the top in the state, but the imaginative, rustic Western decor combined with the chef/co-owner's love of cooking always make a meal here a highlight of a trip to the Wallowa Mountains region. See chapter 12.

15 The Best Brew Pubs

- **Pelican Pub & Brewery** (☎ 503/965-7007): This brew pub, which overlooks Cape Kiwanda and is right on the beach, has the best view of any brew pub in the state. It also has a good selection of ales, including Tsunami Stout and our personal favorite, the Doryman's Dark Ale. See chapter 5.
- **Bridgeport Brewery & Brew Pub** (Portland; ☎ 503/241-7179): Since it's the oldest brew pub in Portland, you could say this is the place that got the Northwest taps flowing. It's housed in the oldest industrial building in the city, a warehouse with a very medieval look. Don't miss the cask-conditioned ales or, in winter, the Old Knucklehead barleywine ale. See chapter 6.
- **Cornelius Pass Roadhouse** (Hillsboro; ☎ 503/640-6174): Located 15 miles west of Portland, this brew pub is part of the Portland-based McMenamin brothers' brew pub empire and is housed in an old farmhouse. On summer afternoons and evenings, the picnic tables all around the big shady yard are packed with people happily downing pints and noshing on pub grub. See chapter 6.
- **Ringlers Pub** (Portland; ☎ 503/225-0543): Yet another McMenamin brothers brew pub, Ringlers is a cavernous and fantastical place filled with big old signs, Indonesian antiques, mosaic pillars, and big booths. A block away are two other associated pubs, one is a below-street-level joint with a beer cellar feel and the other is in a flat-iron building. Together these three pubs offer the most atmospheric ale houses in town. See chapter 6.
- **Eugene City Brewery** (Eugene; ☎ 541/345-8489): Sharing space with both an Italian restaurant and a barbecue joint, this basement brew pub is best when brewing lighter ales and lagers. With the unusual dining options, this a great choice when you need a pint as well as a meal. See chapter 7.
- **Edgefield Brewery** (in the McMenamins Edgefield Bed & Breakfast Resort, Troutdale; ☎ 503/669-8610): Housed in the former county poor farm, this pub is part of a sprawling complex that includes a B&B, a hostel, restaurants, a beer garden, and a movie theater. There's always a wide selection of McMenamin brothers ales on tap. Don't miss the little shed that now serves as a tiny pub. See chapter 8.
- **Deschutes Brewery and Public House** (Bend; ☎ 541/382-9242): Whether you drop by après-ski, après-hike, après-fly fishing, or après-mountain bike ride, this is definitely Bend's best brew pub for downing a pint or two at the end of the day. See chapter 11.

Getting to Know Oregon 2

Oregon, once the promised land of 19th-century pioneers, is an amalgam of American life and landscapes. Within its boundaries, the state reflects a part of almost every region of the country. Take a bit of New England's rural beauty: covered bridges, steepled churches, and familiar place-names such as Portland and Springfield. Temper the climate with that of the upper South to avoid harsh winters. Now bring in some low rolling mountains like the Appalachians; rugged, glaciated mountains like the Rockies; and even volcanoes, as in Hawaii. Add a river as large and as important as the Mississippi, complete with paddle wheel steamers, and toss in a coastline as rugged as California's. Of course, there would have to be sagebrush and cowboys and Indians. Even the deserts of the Southwest and the wheat fields of the Midwest could be added. A little wine country would be a nice touch, and so would some long sandy beaches. On top of all this, there should be a beautiful city, one whose downtown skyscrapers are framed by high forested hills and whose gardens are so full of roses that the city's nickname is The City of Roses. Mix these things together and you have a portrait of Oregon.

1 The Natural Environment

Oregon, at 97,073 square miles (roughly $1\,^1/_2$ times the size of New England) is the tenth largest state in the Union and encompasses within its vast area an amazing diversity of natural environments—not only lush forests, but also deserts, glacier-covered peaks, grasslands, alpine meadows, and sagebrush-covered hills. Together, these diverse environments support a surprisingly wide variety of natural life.

The **Oregon coast** stretches for nearly 300 miles from the redwood country of Northern California to the mouth of the Columbia River, and much of this length is only sparsely populated. Consequently, this coastline provides habitat not only for large populations of seabirds, such as cormorants, tufted puffins, and pigeon guillemots, but also for several species of marine mammals, including Pacific gray whales, Steller sea lions, California sea lions, and harbor seals.

Each year between December and April, more than 20,000 **Pacific gray whales** pass by the Oregon coast as they make their annual migration south to their breeding grounds off Baja California. These whales can often be seen from shore at various points along the coast, and numerous whale-watching tour boats operate out of different ports. In recent years, more and more gray whales have been choosing to spend the summer in Oregon's offshore waters, and it is now possible to spot these leviathans any month of the year. More frequently spotted, however, are **harbor seals** and Steller and California **sea lions,** which are frequently seen lounging on rocks. Sea Lion Caves and Cape Arago State Park, both on the Oregon coast, are two of the best places to spot sea lions. Off the remote beaches of the Olympic Peninsula, there's also a small population of sea otters.

The **Coast Range,** which in places rises directly from the waves, gives the coastline its rugged look. However, even more than the mountains, it is **rain** that gives this coastline its definitive character. As moist winds from the Pacific Ocean rise up and over the Coast Range, they drop their moisture as rain and snow. The tremendous amounts of rain that fall on these mountains have produced dense forests that are home to some of the largest trees on earth. Although the south coast is the northern limit for the coast redwood, the **Douglas firs,** which are far more common and grow throughout the region, are almost as impressive in size, sometimes reaching 300 feet tall. Other common trees of these coastal forests include sitka spruce, western hemlocks, Port Orford cedars, western red cedars, and the evergreen myrtle trees. The wood of these latter trees is used extensively for carving, and myrtle wood shops are ubiquitous along the southern Oregon coast where myrtle trees grow.

More than a century of intensive **logging** has, however, left the state's forests of centuries-old trees shrunken to remnant groves scattered in largely remote and rugged areas. How much exactly is still left is a matter of hot debate between the timber industry and environmentalists, and the battle to save the remaining old-growth forests continues, with both sides claiming victories and losses with each passing year.

Among this region's most celebrated and controversial wild residents is the **northern spotted owl,** which, because of its requirements for large tracts of undisturbed old-growth forest and its listing as a federally endangered species, brought logging of old-growth forests to a virtual halt several years ago. Today, concern is also focusing on the **marbled murrelet,** a small bird that feeds on the open ocean but nests exclusively in old-growth forests. Destruction of forests is also being partially blamed for the demise of trout, salmon, and steelhead populations throughout the region.

Roosevelt elk, the largest commonly encountered land mammal in the Northwest, can be found throughout the Coast Range, and there are even designated elk-viewing areas along the coast (one off U.S. 26 near Jewell and one off Ore. 38 near Reedsport).

Behind the northern section of the Coast Range lies the **Willamette Valley,** which because of its mild climate and fertile soils, was the first region of the state to be settled by pioneers. Today, the Willamette Valley remains the state's most densely populated region and is home to Oregon's largest cities. However, it is also contains the most productive farmland in the state.

To the east of the Willamette Valley rise the mountains of the 700-mile-long **Cascade Range,** which stretches from Northern California to southern British Columbia. The most prominent features of the Cascades are its **volcanic peaks:** Hood, Jefferson, Three Fingered Jack, Washington, the Three Sisters, Broken Top, Thielsen, and McLoughlin. The eruption of Washington's Mount St. Helens on May 18, 1980, reminded Northwesterners that this is still a volcanically active region. The remains of ancient Mount Mazama, which erupted with great violence 7,700 years ago, are today preserved as **Crater Lake National Park.** Near the town of Bend, geologically recent volcanic activity is also visible in the form of cinder cones, lava flows, lava caves, and craters. Much of this volcanic landscape is now preserved as **Newberry National Volcanic Monument.**

Oregon

WASHINGTON

IDAHO

NEVADA

CALIFORNIA

Pacific Ocean

Boise

Caldwell

Hells Canyon National Recreation Area

Snake River

Joseph

Baker City

La Grande

Wallowa-Whitman National Forest

Malheur National Wildlife Refuge

Malheur Lake

Harney Lake

Pendleton

Columbia River

The Dalles

Mt. Hood

Hood River

John Day

Burns

Cascade Range

Bend

Sisters

Deschutes River

Deschutes National Forest

Mt. Bachelor

Crater Lake National Park

Fort Klamath

Upper Klamath Lake

Klamath Falls

Goose Lake

Longview

Vancouver

Portland

Salem

Corvallis

Springfield

Eugene

Roseburg

Umpqua River

Medford

Ashland

Jacksonville

Grants Pass

Oregon Caves Nat'l Monument

Siskiyou National Forest

Rogue River

Coast Range

Astoria

Seaside

Cannon Beach

Tillamook

Lincoln City

Depoe Bay

Newport

Yachats

Siuslaw National Forest

Florence

Oregon Dunes National Recreational Area

Winchester Bay

North Bend

Coos Bay

Bandon

Port Orford

Gold Beach

Brookings

3
82
11
84
82
26
6
18
22
20
126
58
20
126
101
38
42
138
62
140
66
5
238
199
97
97
97
26
26
395
395
20
20
78
95
95
140
31
5

N

0   100 km
    60 mi

1-0895

13

How to Speak Northwestern

All across Oregon there are dozens of linguistic land mines waiting to trip up visitors to the region—place-names that aren't pronounced the way they're spelled or that simply are so strange that no one could ever figure out how to pronounce them without a little coaching. So we include here an Oregon primer of place-names to help nonnatives speak like locals and thus blend into the Oregon landscape. Think of the following knowledge as verbal camouflage.

Deschutes River	Duh-*shoots Riv*-ur
Heceta	Huh-*see*-tuh
Oregon	*Ore*-uh-gun
Siuslaw	Sigh-*oos*-law
The Dalles	The Dals
Umatilla	You-muh-*til*-uh
Wallowa Mountains	Wuh-*lou*-uh *Moun*-tuns
Willamette River	Wuh-*la*-mit *Riv*-ur
Yachats	*Yah*-hots

The same moisture-laden clouds that produce the near–rain forest conditions in the Coast Range leave the Cascades with frequently heavy snows and, on the highest peaks (Mount Hood, Mount Jefferson, the Three Sisters), numerous glaciers. The most readily accessible glaciers are on **Mount Hood,** where ski lifts keep running right through the summer, carrying skiers and snowboarders to slopes atop the Palmer Glacier, high above the historic Timberline Lodge. It is the winter snowpack in these mountains that provides the water for the state's largest cities. This snowpack can also be the source of floodwaters, as was the case in February 1996 when downtown Portland came within inches of flooding and many other communities along the Willamette River incurred millions of dollars of damage.

East of the Cascades, less than 200 miles from the damp Coast Range forests, the landscape becomes a desert. The **Great Basin,** which reaches its northern limit in central and eastern Oregon, comprises a vast, high desert region that stretches to the Rockies. Through this desolate landscape flows the **Columbia River,** which, together with its tributary the Snake, forms the second-largest river drainage in the United States. During the last Ice Age, roughly 13,000 years ago, glaciers repeatedly blocked the flow of the Columbia, forming huge lakes behind these ice dams. These vast prehistoric lakes repeatedly burst the ice dams, sending massive and devastating walls of water flooding down the Columbia. These floodwaters were sometimes 1,000 feet high and carried with them ice and rocks, which scoured out the **Columbia Gorge.** Today the gorge's many waterfalls are the most evident signs of such floods.

Today, the Columbia is dammed not by ice, but by numerous large, modern **dams** that have become the focus of one of the region's hottest environmental battles. Though many of these dams have fish ladders to allow **salmon** to return upriver to spawn, salmon must still negotiate an obstacle course of degraded spawning grounds in often-clear-cut forests, slower river flows in the reservoirs behind the dams, turbines that kill fish by the thousands, and irrigation canals that often confuse salmon into swimming out of the river and into farm fields. Overfishing for salmon canneries in the late 19th century struck the first major blow to salmon populations, which have been steadily dwindling ever since. Today, the large dams, mostly built during the middle part of this century, create further barriers both to returning adults and to young salmon headed downstream to the Pacific. Compounding the problem has been the use of fish hatcheries to supplement wild salmon populations (hatchery fish tend to be less vigorous than wild salmon). A salmon recovery plan was adopted several years ago to attempt to save threatened runs of native salmon, but farmers, electricity producers, shipping companies, and major users of hydroelectric power have continued to fight the requirements of the recovery plan, which includes lowering water levels in reservoirs to speed the downstream migration of young salmon.

South-central and southeastern Oregon are the most remote and unpopulated regions of the state. However, this vast desert area does support an abundance of wildlife. The **Hart Mountain National Antelope Refuge** shelters herds of pronghorn antelope, which are the fastest land mammal in North America. This refuge also protects a small population of California bighorn sheep. At **Malheur National Wildlife Refuge,** more than 300 species of birds frequent large shallow lakes and wetlands, and at the **Lower Klamath National Wildlife Refuge** large numbers of bald eagles gather. Several other of the region's large lakes, including Summer Lake and Lake Abert, attract large populations of birds.

2 The Regions in Brief

Both geography and climate play important roles in dividing Oregon into its various discernible regions.

The Oregon Coast   Stretching for nearly 300 miles, the Oregon coast is one of the most spectacular coastlines in the country. Backed by the Coast Range mountains and alternating sandy beaches with rocky capes and headlands, this mountainous shoreline provides breathtaking vistas at almost every turn of the road. Haystack rocks—large monoliths just offshore—give the coast an unforgettable drama and beauty. Along the central coast, huge dunes, some as much as 500 feet high, have been preserved as the Oregon Dunes National Recreation Area. Small towns, some known as fishing ports and some as artists' communities, dot the coast. Unfortunately, waters are generally too cold for swimming, and a cool breeze often blows even in summer.

The Willamette Valley   This is Oregon's most densely populated region and site of the state's largest cities, including Portland, Eugene, and the state capital of Salem. The valley's fabled farmland, which once enticed people to walk across 2,000 miles of rugged terrain, grows the greatest variety of crops of any region of the United States. Among these crops are hops, mint, grass seed, berries, hazelnuts, irises, tulips, Christmas trees, and an immense variety of landscape plants. The Willamette Valley is also one of the nation's finest wine regions, with vineyards cropping up along its entire length.

The Columbia Gorge   Beginning just east of Portland, the Columbia Gorge is one of the region's most breathtaking sites. Declared a national scenic area to preserve its beauty, the Gorge is the site of numerous waterfalls, including Multnomah Falls, which are the fourth highest in the United States. Winds regularly blast through the Gorge and have attracted boardsailing enthusiasts to the area. The town of Hood River is now one of the world's top boardsailing spots. Rising above the Gorge on the south side is Mount Hood, the tallest peak in Oregon.

The Cascade Range   Stretching from the Columbia River in the north to the California state line in the south, this mountain range is a natural dividing line between eastern and western Oregon. Dominated by conical peaks of volcanic origin (currently none are active), the Cascades are almost entirely encompassed by several national forests that serve both as sources of timber and year-round recreational playgrounds. Throughout these mountains are several designated wilderness areas in which all mechanized travel is prohibited. Among these, the Mount Hood Wilderness, the Mount Jefferson Wilderness, and the Three Sisters Wilderness are the most scenic and heavily visited. In the southern Cascades, an entire mountain once blew its top, leaving behind a huge caldera that is now filled by the sapphire-blue waters of Crater Lake, Oregon's only national park.

Southern Oregon   Lying roughly midway between San Francisco and Portland, southern Oregon is a jumbled landscape of mountains and valleys through which flow two of the state's most famous rivers. The North Umpqua and the Rogue rivers have been fabled among anglers ever since Zane Grey popularized these waters in his writings. A climate much drier than that of the Willamette Valley to the north gives this region the look of parts of northern California, and in fact, several towns in the region are very popular with retired Californians. Among these are Ashland, site of the Oregon Shakespeare Festival, and Jacksonville, a historic gold-mining town that is now the site of the Britt Festivals, an annual summer festival of music and modern dance.

Central Oregon   Consisting of the east side of the Cascade Range from the Columbia River to just south of Bend, this region is as much a physiological region as a geographical region. Spanning the eastern foothills and the western edge of the high desert of the Great Basin, this region is primarily known for its lack of rain and proximity to the cities of the Willamette Valley. Together, these two factors make this the second most popular summer vacation destination (after the coast), with resorts clustered around Sisters and Bend. However, with Mount Bachelor ski area providing the best skiing in the Northwest, this region is also quite popular in winter. A volcanic legacy has left this region with some of the most fascinating geology in the state.

Eastern Oregon   Large and sparsely populated, eastern Oregon is primarily high desert interspersed with small mountain ranges. Despite the desert climate, the region is also the site of several large, shallow lakes that serve as magnets for a wide variety of migratory birds. In the northeast corner of the region rise the Blue and Wallowa mountains, which are remote, though popular, recreation areas. Carving North America's deepest gorge, and partially forming the border with Idaho, are the Snake River and Hells Canyon. Throughout this region, signs of the Oregon Trail can still be seen.

3 Oregon Today

Perhaps you've heard how Oregonians have webbed feet and how they don't tan—they rust. Most people unfamiliar with Oregon can at least tell you that it rains a lot here. They're absolutely right. There's no getting around the fact that few states receive as much rain or cloudy weather as Oregon (and its northern neighbor, Washington). However, the state's rainfall has changed in the past few years. It no longer has the effect it once had. Sure, it still keeps the landscape green, but it's no longer keeping people from moving here as it once did. The word is out that the Northwest is a beautiful place despite the rain.

For the past decade, Oregon has been one of the fastest-growing states in the nation as high-tech industries have moved manufacturing here and Californians, fed up with that state's pollution, crime, congestion, and high cost of living, have moved north in search of a better quality of life. Oregon is today riding a boom that has fueled rapid growth, especially in the high-tech industries. Intel, the microchip maker that has found its way inside almost everyone's computer, has several large plants in the Portland area, and the presence of these factories has attracted dozens of other high-tech companies to locate there and elsewhere in the Willamette Valley. This economic growth has, however, begun to undermine the very values that have allowed people living in Oregon to ignore the weather. Urban sprawl, congested roads, and sky-rocketing housing costs are all changing the character of the state. However, Oregonians are working hard to preserve the state's unique character and to keep Portland as livable as it has always been. To see what it is that Oregonians want to preserve, it's only necessary to lift one's eyes to the far horizons. From almost any-where in the state, it's possible to look up and see green forests and snow-capped mountains, and a 2-hour drive from any Willamette Valley city will get you to the mountains or the Pacific Ocean's beaches.

Oregonians don't let the weather stand between them and the outdoors. The temp-tation is too great to head for the mountains, the river, or the beach, no matter what the weather. Consequently, life in Northwest cities tends to revolve less around cultural venues and other urban pastimes such as shopping, than around parks, gar-dens, waterfronts, rivers, mountains, and beaches. Portland has its Forest Park, Rose Gardens, Japanese Gardens, and Waterfront Park. Eugene has its miles of riverside parks, bike paths, even a park just for rock climbing. In Hood River, the entire Columbia River has become a playground for boardsailors, and when the wind doesn't blow, there are always the nearby mountain-bike trails and rivers for kayaking. In Bend, mountain biking and downhill skiing are a way of life. These outdoor areas are where people find tranquillity, where summer festivals are held, where locals take their visiting friends and relatives, and where locals tend to live their lives when the fun isn't being interrupted by such inconveniences as work and sleep.

This is not to say, however, that the region is a cultural wasteland. Both Portland and Eugene have large, modern, and active performing arts centers. During the sum-mer months numerous festivals take music, theater, and dance outdoors. Most impressive of these are the Oregon Shakespeare Festival and the Britt Festivals, both of which are staged in southern Oregon. However, there are also many other festi-vals featuring everything from chamber music to alternative rock.

With urban areas of the Willamette Valley experiencing a very rapid population growth in recent years, politics have developed a very pronounced urban-rural split in Oregon. Citizens from the eastern part of the state argue that Salem and Portland are dictating to rural regions that have little in common with the cities, while urban dwellers, who far outnumber those living outside the Willamette Valley, argue that majority rule is majority rule. This split has pitted almost-conservative voters (usually rural) and liberal voters (usually urban) on a wide variety of issues, and the reality of Oregon politics is now quite a bit different from the often-held perception that the state is dominated by liberal, forward-thinking environmentalists and former hippies. In 1997, the state legislature recriminalized possession of small amounts of marijuana (Oregon had been the first state to decriminalize pot), prompting a well-financed campaign to have this new legislation overturned. Oregon was also the first state to make physician-assisted suicide legal, but as this book went to press, voters were being asked a second time to vote on whether or not Oregonians have a right to die.

4 Oregon History 101

EARLY HISTORY   Native Americans inhabiting the various regions that would eventually become the state of Oregon developed very distinct cultures depending on the food-gathering constraints of their territory. The oldest known inhabitants of the state lived along the shores of the huge lakes in the

Dateline

■ **13,000 B.C.** Massive floods, as much as 1,000 feet deep, rage down Columbia River

continues

and carve the Columbia Gorge.

- **10,000 B.C.** Earliest known human inhabitation of Oregon.
- **5,000 B.C.** Mount Mazama erupts violently creating the caldera that will later fill with water and be known as Crater Lake.
- **A.D. 1542** Spanish exploratory ship reaches what is now the southern Oregon coast.
- **1579** Englishman Sir Francis Drake reaches the mouth of the Rogue River.
- **1602** Spain's Martìn de Aguilar explores the coast of Oregon, probably as far as Coos Bay.
- **1792** Robert Gray becomes the first explorer to sail a ship into a great river he names the Columbia, in honor of his ship the *Columbia Rediviva.*
- **1805–06** Expedition led by Meriwether Lewis and William Clark crosses the continent and spends the winter at the mouth of the Columbia River.
- **1810** Americans attempt first settlement at the Columbia River's mouth.
- **1819** Spain cedes all lands above 42° north latitude.
- **1824–25** Russia gives up claims to land south of Alaska; Fort Vancouver founded by Hudson's Bay Company on Columbia River near present-day Portland.
- **1834** Methodist missionary Jason Lee founds Salem, which will later become the state capital.
- **1840** First settlers move to what is now Oregon.
- **1842** Jason Lee founds first school of higher learning west of the Mississippi.
- **1843** First wagons cross the continent on the Oregon Trail; Asa Lovejoy and

continues

Klamath Lakes Basin some **10,000 years ago.** Here they fished and hunted ducks and left records of their passing in several caves. These peoples would have witnessed the massive eruption of **Mount Mazama,** which left a hollowed out core of a mountain that eventually filled with water and was named Crater Lake. Along the coast, numerous small tribes subsisted on salmon and shellfish. In the northeast corner of the state, the **Nez Percé Indians** became experts at horse breeding even before Lewis and Clark passed through the region at the start of the 19th century. In fact, the appaloosa horse derives its name from the nearby Palouse Hills of Washington.

However, it was the **Columbia River tribes** that became the richest of the Oregon tribes through their control of **Celilo Falls,** the richest salmon fishing area that ever existed in the Northwest. These massive falls on the Columbia River east of present-day The Dalles witnessed the annual passage of millions of **salmon,** which were speared and dip-netted by Native Americans who then smoked the fish to preserve it for the winter. Today, Native Americans still fish for salmon as they once did, perched on precarious wooden platforms with dip-nets in hand. However, Celilo Falls are gone, inundated by the pooling water behind **The Dalles Dam,** which was completed in 1957. Today little remains of what was once the Northwest's most important Native American gathering ground, a place where tribes from hundreds of miles away congregated each year to fish and trade. At the **Columbia Gorge Discovery Center** in The Dalles, you can see film footage of people fishing at Celilo Falls before its inundation.

Even before this amazing fishing ground was lost, a far greater tragedy had been visited upon Northwest tribes. Between the 1780s, when white explorers and traders began frequenting the Northwest coast, and the 1830s, when the first settlers began arriving, the Native American population of the Northwest was reduced to perhaps a tenth of its historic numbers. It was not war that wiped out these people, but European **diseases**—smallpox, measles, malaria, and influenza. The Native Americans had no resistance to these diseases and entire tribes were soon wiped out by fast-spreading epidemics.

THE AGE OF EXPLORATION   Though a Spanish ship reached what is now southern Oregon in **1542,** the Spanish had no interest in the gray and rainy coast. Nor did famed British buccaneer **Sir Francis Drake,** who in 1579 sailed his ship the *Golden Hind* as far north as the mouth of the Rogue

River. Drake called off his explorations in the face of what he described as "thicke and stinking fogges."

Though the Spanish laid claim to all of North America's west coast, they had little interest in the lands north of Mexico. However, when the Spanish found out that Russian fur traders were establishing themselves in Alaska and along the North Pacific coast, Spain took a new interest in the Northwest. Several Spanish expeditions sailed north from Mexico to reassert the Spanish claim to the region. In **1775,** Spanish explorers **Bruno de Heceta** and **Francisco de la Bodega y Quadra** charted much of the Northwest coast and though they found the mouth of the Columbia River, they did not enter it. To this day four of the coast's most scenic headlands—Cape Perpetua, Heceta Head, Cape Arago, and Cape Blanco—bear names from these early Spanish explorations.

It was not until **1792** that an explorer, American trader **Robert Gray,** risked a passage through treacherous sandbars that guarded the mouth of the long-speculated-upon Great River of the West. Gray named this newfound river **Columbia's River,** in honor of his ship, the *Columbia Rediviva.* This discovery established the first American claim to the region. When news of the Columbia's discovery reached the United States and England, both countries began speculating on a northern water route across North America. Such a route, if it existed, would facilitate trade with the Northwest.

In **1793,** Scotsman **Alexander MacKenzie** made the first overland trip across North America north of New Spain. Crossing British Canada on foot, MacKenzie arrived somewhere north of Vancouver Island. After reading MacKenzie's account of his journey, Thomas Jefferson decided that the United States needed to find a better route overland to the Northwest. To this end, he commissioned **Meriwether Lewis** and **William Clark** to lead an expedition up the Missouri River in hopes of finding a single easy portage that would lead to the Columbia River.

Beginning in **1804,** the members of the Lewis and Clark expedition paddled up the Missouri, crossed the Rocky Mountains on foot, and then paddled down the Columbia River to its mouth. A French Canadian trapper and his Native American wife, Sacajawea, were enlisted as interpreters, and it was the presence of Sacajawea that helped the expedition gain acceptance among western tribes. After spending a very dismal, wet winter of **1805–06** at

William Overton stake claim on land that will soon become Portland.

- **1844** Oregon City becomes the first incorporated town west of the Mississippi.
- **1846** The 49th parallel is established as the boundary between American and British territories in the Northwest.
- **1848** Oregon becomes first U.S. territory west of the Rockies.
- **1851** Portland is incorporated; gold is discovered in southern Oregon.
- **1860** Gold discovered in eastern Oregon.
- **1905** Lewis and Clark Exposition attracts worldwide attention to Oregon.
- **1915** Columbia Gorge scenic highway is constructed.
- **1935** Angus Bowmer stages *As You Like It* in Ashland and plants the seed of the Oregon Shakespeare Festival.
- **1940s** Kaiser shipyards in the Portland area become the world's foremost shipbuilders.
- **1945** Oregon becomes the only state to have civilian war casualties when six children are killed by a Japanese balloon bomb.
- **1957** The Dalles Dam completed; backwaters inundate Celilo Falls, the most productive Native American salmon-fishing grounds.
- **1974** In a bold step toward making Portland a more livable city, a freeway along the city's downtown waterfront is removed.
- **1980s** Oregon's timber industry suffers a severe economic downturn.
- **1995** Sen. Bob Packwood resigns after the Senate Ethics Committee recommends his

continues

expulsion for sexual misconduct.

■ **1996** February flood waters come within inches of spilling out of the Willamette River and into downtown Portland.

the mouth of the Columbia, the expedition headed back east. Discoveries made by the expedition added greatly to the scientific and geographical knowledge of the continent. A reconstruction of **Fort Clatsop,** the expedition's dreary winter camp at the mouth of the Columbia, is now a national memorial and one of the most interesting historical sites in the state. Outside of The Dalles, a campsite used by Lewis and Clark has also been preserved.

In **1819,** the Spanish relinquished all claims north of the present California-Oregon state line, and the Russians gave up their claims to all lands south of Alaska. This left only the British and Americans dickering for control of the Northwest.

SETTLEMENT—Fur Traders, Missionaries & the Oregon Trail   Only 6 years after Lewis and Clark spent the winter at the mouth of the Columbia, employees of John Jacob Astor's Pacific Fur Company managed to establish themselves at a nearby spot they called Fort Astoria. This was the first permanent settlement in the Northwest, but with the War of 1812 being fought on the far side of the continent, the fur traders at **Fort Astoria,** with little protection against the British military presence in the region, chose to relinquish control of their fort. However, in the wake of the war, the fort returned to American control, though the United States and Britain produced no firm decision about possession of the Northwest. The British still dominated the region, but American trade was tolerated.

With the decline of the sea-otter population, British fur traders turned to beaver and headed inland up the Columbia River. For the next 30 years or so, fur-trading companies would be the sole authority in the region. Fur-trading posts were established throughout the Northwest, though most were on the eastern edge of the territory in the foothills of the Rocky Mountains. The powerful **Hudson's Bay Company** (HBC) eventually became the single fur-trading company in the Northwest.

In 1824, the HBC established its Northwest headquarters at **Fort Vancouver,** 100 miles up the Columbia near the mouth of the Willamette River, and in 1829, the HBC founded Oregon City at the falls of the Willamette River. Between 1824 and 1846, when the 49th parallel was established as the boundary between British and American northwestern lands, Fort Vancouver was the most important settlement in the region. A reconstruction of the fort now stands outside the city of Vancouver, Washington, across the Columbia River from Portland. In Oregon City, several homes from this period are still standing, including that of John McLoughlin, who was chief factor at Fort Vancouver and aided many of the early pioneers who arrived in the area after traveling the Oregon Trail.

By the **1830s,** the future of the Northwest had arrived in the form of American **missionaries.** The first was Jason Lee, who established his mission in the Willamette Valley near present-day Salem (today the site is Willamette Mission State Park). Two years later, in 1836, Marcus and Narcissa Whitman, along with Henry and Eliza Spaulding, made the overland trek to Fort Vancouver, then backtracked into what is now eastern Washington and Idaho, to establish two missions. This journey soon inspired other settlers to make the difficult overland crossing.

In 1840, a slow trickle of American settlers began crossing the continent, a 2,000-mile journey. Their destination was the Oregon country, which had been promoted as a veritable Eden where land was waiting to be claimed. In 1843, **Marcus Whitman,** after traveling east to plead with his superiors not to shut down his mission, headed back west, leading 900 settlers on the **Oregon Trail.** Before these settlers ever arrived, the small population of retired trappers, missionaries, and HBC employees who were living at Fort Vancouver and in nearby Oregon City had formed a provisional government in anticipation of the land-claim problems that would arise with the influx of settlers to the region. Today, the best places to learn about the experiences of the Oregon Trail emigrants are at the **Oregon Trail Interpretive Center** outside Baker City and the **End of the Oregon Trail Interpretive Center** in Oregon City. In many places in the eastern part of the state, Oregon Trail wagon ruts can still be seen.

In **1844,** Oregon City became the first incorporated town west of the Rocky Mountains. This outpost in the wilderness, a gateway to the fertile lands of the Willamette Valley, was the destination of the wagon trains that began traveling the Oregon Trail, each year bringing more and more settlers to the region. As the land in the Willamette Valley was claimed, settlers began fanning out to different regions of the Northwest so that during the late 1840s and early 1850s many new towns, including Portland, were founded.

Though the line between American and British land in the Northwest had been established at the 49th parallel (the current Canadian-American border) in 1846, Oregon was not given U.S. territorial status until **1848.** It was the massacre of the missionaries at the Whitman mission in Walla Walla (now in Washington state) and the subsequent demand for territorial status and U.S. military protection that brought about the establishment of the first U.S. territory west of the Rockies.

The discovery of **gold** in eastern Oregon in **1860** set the stage for one of the saddest chapters in Northwest history. With miners pouring into eastern Oregon and Washington, conflicts with Native Americans over land were inevitable. Since 1805, when Lewis and Clark had first passed this way, the **Nez Percé tribes** had been friendly to the white settlers. However, in 1877 a disputed treaty caused friction. Led by **Chief Joseph,** 700 Nez Percé, including 400 women and children, began a march from their homeland to their new reservation. Along the way, several angry young men, in revenge for the murder of an older member of the tribe, attacked a white settlement and killed several people. The U.S. Army took up pursuit of the Nez Percé, who fled across Idaho and Montana, only to be caught 40 miles from the Canadian border and sanctuary.

INDUSTRIALIZATION & THE 20TH CENTURY   From the very beginning of white settlement in the Northwest, the region based its growth on an extractive economy. Lumber and salmon were exploited ruthlessly. The history of the timber and salmon-fishing industries have run parallel for more than a century and have each led to similar results in the 1990s.

The trees in Oregon grew to gigantic proportions. Nurtured on steady rains, such trees as Douglas fir, Sitka spruce, western red cedar, Port Orford cedar, and hemlock grew tall and straight, sometimes as tall as 300 feet. The first sawmill in the Northwest began operation near present-day Vancouver, Washington, in 1828. Between the 1850s and 1870s Northwest sawmills supplied the growing California market as well as a limited foreign market. When the transcontinental railroads arrived in the 1880s, a whole new market opened up and mills began shipping to the eastern states.

Lumber companies developed a **cut-and-run policy** that leveled the forests. By the turn of the century, the government had gained more control over public forests in an attempt to slow the decimation of forest lands, and sawmill owners were buying up huge tracts of land. At the outbreak of World War I, more than 20% of the forest land in the Northwest was owned by three companies—Weyerhaeuser, the Northern Pacific Railroad, and the Southern Pacific Railroad—and more than 50% of the workforce labored in the timber industry.

The timber industry has always been extremely susceptible to fluctuations in the economy and has experienced a roller-coaster ride of boom and bust throughout the 20th century. Boom times in the 1970s brought on record-breaking production that came to a screeching halt in the 1980s, first with a nationwide recession and then with the listing of the **northern spotted owl** as a threatened species. When the timber industry was born in the Northwest, there was a belief that the forests of the region were endless. However, by the latter half of this century, big lumber companies had realized that the forests were dwindling. Tree farms were planted with increasing frequency, but the large old trees continued to be cut faster than they could be replenished by younger trees. By the 1970s, **environmentalists,** shocked by the vast clear-cuts, began trying to save the last old-growth trees. The battle between the timber industry and environmentalists is today still one of the state's most heated debates.

Salmon was the mainstay of the Native Americans' diet for thousands of years before the first whites arrived in the Oregon country, but within 10 years of the opening of the first salmon cannery in the Northwest, the fish population was decimated. In 1877, the first fish hatchery was developed to replenish dwindling runs of salmon. Salmon canning reached a peak on the Columbia River in 1895. Later, in the 20th century, salmon runs would be further decimated by the construction of numerous dams on the Columbia and Snake rivers. Though fish ladders help adult salmon make their journeys upstream, the young salmon heading downstream have no such help and a large percentage are killed by the turbines of hydroelectric dams. One solution to this problem has been barging and trucking young salmon down river. Today the salmon population of the Northwest is so diminished that entire runs of salmon have been listed as threatened or endangered under the Endangered Species Act.

The **dams** that have proved such a detriment to salmon populations have, however, provided irrigation water and cheap electricity that have fueled both industry and farming. Using newly available irrigation water, potato and wheat farms flourished in northeastern Oregon after the middle of this century. The huge reservoirs behind the Columbia and Snake River dams have also turned these rivers into waterways that can be navigated by huge barges, which often carry wheat downriver from ports in Idaho. Today, the regional salmon recovery plan is attempting to strike a balance between saving salmon runs and meeting all the other needs that have been created since the construction of these dams.

Manufacturing began gaining in importance during and after World War II. In the Portland area, the **Kaiser Shipyards** employed tens of thousands of people in the construction of warships, but the postwar years saw the demise of the Kaiser facilities. Recent years have seen a diversification into **high-tech industries,** with such major manufacturers as Intel, NEC, Epson, Hewlett-Packard, and Hyundai operating manufacturing facilities in the Willamette Valley.

However, it is in the area of **sportswear** manufacturing that Oregon businesses have gained the greatest visibility. With outdoor recreation a way of life in this state, it comes as no surprise that a few regional companies have grown into international giants. Chief among these is **Nike,** which is headquartered in the Portland suburb of Beaverton. Other familiar names include Jantzen, one of the nation's oldest swimwear manufacturers; Pendleton Woolen Mills, maker of classic plaid wool shirts, Indian-design blankets, and other classic wool fashions; and more recently Columbia Sportswear, which in recent years has become one of the country's biggest sports-related outerwear manufacturers. If you like to play outside, chances are you own some article of clothing that originated here in Oregon.

5 Eat, Drink & Be Merry

While there is no specifically Oregon cuisine, there is a regional cooking style that, while somewhat diluted by various international influences in recent years, still can be distinguished by its pairings of meats and seafood with local fruits and nuts. This cuisine features such regional produce as salmon, oysters, halibut, raspberries, blackberries, apples, pears, and hazelnuts. A classic Northwest dish might be raspberry chicken or oysters with a hazelnut crust. In the state's hinterlands, this is often labeled "Portland-style food" to distinguish it from far less creative meat-and-potatoes meals.

Salmon is king of Oregon fish and has been for thousands of years, so it isn't surprising that in one shape or another, it shows up on plenty of menus throughout the state. It's prepared in seemingly endless ways, but the most traditional method is what's known as alder-planked salmon. Traditionally, this Native American cooking style entailed preparing a salmon as a single fillet, splaying it on readily available alder wood, and slow cooking it over an open fire. The result is a cross between grilling and smoking. Today, however, it's hard to find salmon prepared this traditional way, except at powwows such as the one held each August on the Siletz Indian Reservation between Lincoln City and Newport. Much more readily available, especially along the Oregon coast, is traditional smoked salmon. You'll find such smoked salmon for sale at gourmet food shops (often vacuum-packed so that it doesn't need refrigeration until opened), at better grocery stores, and prepared a variety of ways in restaurants. However, for freshness and quality, coastal smokehouses can't be beat. We make it a point of never passing a smokehouse without stopping to sample the wares. Smoked oysters are usually also available.

With plenty of clean cold waters in many of its bays and estuaries, Oregon raises large numbers of **oysters,** especially in Tillamook Bay and South Slough on Coos Bay. Then there are the mussels and clams. Of particular note are **razor clams,** which can be tough and chewy if not prepared properly, but which are eagerly sought after along north coast beaches when the clamming season is open. However, after salmon, **Dungeness crab** is the region's other great seafood offering. Though not as large as an Alaskan king crab, the Dungeness is usually big enough to make a meal for one person. Crab cakes have become a staple of seafood menus across the state in recent years.

The Northwest's combination of climate and abundant irrigation waters has helped make this one of the nation's major fruit-growing regions. Hood River Valley and the Medford area are two of the nation's top pear-growing regions, and just a few miles east of Hood River, around The Dalles, cherries are supreme, with the blushing Rainier cherry a regional treat rarely seen outside the Northwest. The Willamette Valley, south of Portland, has become the nation's center for the production of berries. **Strawberries, raspberries,** and numerous varieties of **blackberries** are grown. All these fruits show up in the summer months at farm stands all over the state, making a drive through the Northwest at that time of year a real treat. Pick-your-own farms are also fairly common throughout the Northwest. So famed are the fruits of Oregon that the Harry and David's company has become a mainstay of the mail-order gift industry, shipping regional produce all over the country.

When hunger strikes on the road, Oregon offers what seems to be a regional potato preparation that just might be the only truly Northwestern cuisine. **Jo-jos** are potato wedges that are first baked then dipped in batter and fried. Traditionally served with a side of ranch dressing for dipping, these belly bombs are usually purchased as an accompaniment to fried chicken.

One last Northwest food that we should mention is the **wild mushroom.** As you'd expect in such a rainy climate, mushrooms abound in this region. The most common wild mushrooms are morels, which are harvested in spring, and chanterelles, which are harvested in the autumn. In recent years, Oregon has been the site of modern-day range wars as armed mushroom hunters have combed the state's forests for these often valuable fungi. Gun battles that have ensued over control of prime mushroom-picking grounds have drawn national attention to this lucrative trade. In hopes of turning the outlaw lifestyle of the mushroom hunter into a more law-abiding pursuit, the National Forest Service, which oversees much of the land from which mushrooms are harvested, has been imposing stricter controls on pickers.

We don't suggest heading out to the woods to pick your own unless you or a companion are experienced mushroom hunters. However, you will find wild mushrooms showing up on menus of better restaurants throughout the region, so by all means try to have some while you're here.

Oregon's thriving **wine** industry has for quite a few years now been producing award-winning varietal wines. Oregon is on the same latitude as the French wine regions of Burgundy and Bordeaux and produces similar wines. Oregon **Pinot Noirs** are ranking up there with those from France, and Chardonnays, Rieslings, and other varietals are getting good press as well. Unfortunately, the wet autumn weather in western Oregon, where most of the state's wine grapes are grown, can adversely affect wines here, so it pays to know your vintages (and your wineries, for that matter). **Wineries** throughout the state are open to the public for tastings, with the greatest concentrations to be found southwest of Portland in Yamhill County, just west of Salem, and northwest of Roseburg. Better restaurants throughout the state tend to stock plenty of Oregon wines. Fruit-flavored wines are also produced here, and contrary to what most people think are not always cloyingly sweet. Fruit-based distilled liqueurs are an up and coming product in the state, and some of the apple brandies are excellent.

With more **microbreweries** per capita than in any other state in the nation, Oregon is at the center of the national obsession with craft beers, and while some trend-watchers claim microbrews are already on the way out, supplanted by a resurgence in popularity of the martini, new brew pubs continue to open across the state. Such local breweries as Bridgeport, Full Sail, and Widmer, which have long been at the forefront of the state's craft brewing industry, have grown so large that the term "microbrewery" no longer applies to them. While Portland is still the state's (and the nation's) microbrewery mecca, brew pubs can now be found throughout the state. From the tiny northeastern town of Enterprise to Cave Junction down in the southwest corner of the state, brew meisters are crafting distinctive lagers, ales, and stouts. Perhaps partly responsible for the popularity of brewing in Oregon is that much of the nation's hops vines are grown here in the Willamette Valley.

While local wines may be the state's preferred accompaniment to dinner and microbrews the favorite social drink, it is **coffee** that keeps Oregonians going through long gray winters—and even through hot sunny summers, for that matter. Coffee in Oregon is no longer always the same bottomless cup of insipid black liquid that's passed off as coffee in most of the rest of the country. The coffee that has become an Oregon obsession is rich, dark, flavorful espresso, often served as a latte, with a generous portion of steamed milk. While there are still a few small towns in the state where you can't get an espresso, you certainly don't have to worry about falling asleep at the wheel for want of a decent cup of java.

6 Recommended Books

GENERAL   The single best introduction to the Northwest, both past and present, is Timothy Egan's *The Good Rain* (Vintage Departures, 1991), which uses a long-forgotten Northwest explorer as the springboard for an exploration of all the forces that have made the Northwest what it is today. In *Stepping Westward* (Henry Holt and Company, 1991), Sallie Tisdale blends memoir, travel, and history in an evocation of the landscapes and life of Washington, Oregon, and Idaho.

The Journals of Lewis and Clark (Mentor, 1964), compiled by Meriwether Lewis and William Clark during their 1804–06 journey across the continent, is a fascinating account of a difficult journey and includes a wealth of observations on Native Americans and North American flora and fauna. David Freeman Hawke's *Those Tremendous Mountains: The Story of the Lewis and Clark Expedition* (W.W. Norton and Company, 1980) is a more readable form of the journals and also has a considerable amount of background information.

For a complete history of the Northwest, try *The Pacific Northwest: An Interpretive History* by Carlos A. Schwantes (University of Nebraska Press, 1989) or *The Great Northwest: The Story of a Land and Its People* (America West Publishing, 1973).

The pioneer period is the subject of *Women's Diaries of the Westward Journey* (Schocken Books, 1992), a collection of writings of women pioneers moving west compiled by Lillian Schlissel. *The Well-traveled Casket: A Collection of Oregon Folklife* by Tom Nash and Twilo Scofield (University of Utah Press, 1992) captures the folk and folklore of the Northwest's African American, Hispanic, Chinese, Native American, and Basque immigrants who came here as farmers, miners, loggers, and fishermen.

FICTION   Oregon has not inspired a great deal of fiction. However, Vince Kohler set his Eldon Larkin mysteries *Rainy North Woods* (St. Martin's Press, 1990) and *Rising Dog* (St. Martin's Press, 1992) in Oregon. Ernest Callenbach's *Ecotopia* (Bantam, 1975) is a novel of the near future in which the Northwest secedes from the United States to pursue its own environmentally conscious beliefs (unfortunately much has changed in the Northwest since the idealistic early 1970s when this novel was written). In *The River Why* (Sierra Club, 1983), David J. Duncan writes of the search for self along the rivers of Oregon. This could best be described as a sort of "Zen and the Art of Fly-Fishing."

Oregon resident Ken Kesey has, over the years, set a couple of his novels in this state. *Sometimes a Great Notion* (Viking Penguin, 1977) presents an evocative portrayal of a logging family and was made into a feature film starring Paul Newman and Henry Fonda. More recently, Kesey set his novel *The Last Go Round* (Viking Penguin, 1994) among the cowboys and bucking broncos of the Pendleton Round-Up circa 1911. The life of a 19th-century mountain man is the subject of Don Berry's *Trask* (Comstock Editions, 1984).

TRAVEL & THE OUTDOORS   The outdoors is a way of life in Oregon and enjoying it might require a specialized guidebook to get you to the best places. If you're a generalist when it comes to the outdoors, *Outside Magazine's Adventure Guide to the Pacific Northwest* (Macmillan, 1997), by this book's coauthor Karl Samson, is a very useful and usable guide to a wide variety of outdoor activities in western Oregon and western Washington.

3   Planning a Trip to Oregon

Before any trip, you need to do a bit of advance planning. When should I go? What is this trip going to cost me? Can I catch a festival during my visit? And where should I head to pursue my favorite sport? We'll answer these and other questions for you in this chapter.

1 Visitor Information & Money

SOURCES OF INFORMATION

Contact the **Oregon Tourism Division,** 775 Summer St. NE, Salem, OR 97310 (☎ **800/547-7842**), or the **Portland Oregon Visitor Association,** Three World Trade Center, 26 SW Salmon St., Portland, OR 97204 (☎ **800/345-3214** or 503/222-2223).

Also keep in mind that most cities and towns in Oregon have either a tourist office or a chamber of commerce that can provide you with information. When approaching cities and towns, watch for signs along the highway directing you to these information centers. See the individual chapters for specific addresses.

CityNet keeps excellent hot lists of many city and some regional Web sites. Log into **www.city.net/countries/united_states/oregon** for cities in Oregon. For Oregon regional Web sites, try Oregon Reference at **www.teleport.com/~samc/index1.html** or the Oregon Tourism Division's Web site at **www.traveloregon.com**.

You can also get travel information covering Oregon from the American Automobile Association (AAA) if you're a member.

To get information on outdoor recreation in national forests of Oregon, contact the **U.S. Forest Service Recreational Information Center,** 800 NE Oregon St., Room 177, Portland, OR 97232 (☎ **503/731-4444**). To make reservations to camp at a national forest, call ☎ **800/280-CAMP.** For information on Crater Lake, the only national park in Oregon, call the park at ☎ **541/594-2211.** Crater Lake National Park does not accept camping reservations.

For information on camping in Oregon state parks, call the state parks information line at ☎ **800/551-6949;** to make a camping reservation at an Oregon state park, contact **Reservations Northwest,** 2501 SW First St., Suite 100, Portland, OR 97201 (☎ **800/452-5687** or 503/731-3411).

What Things Cost in Portland	U.S.$
Taxi from the airport to the city center	22.00–25.00
Bus or tram ride between downtown points	Free
Local telephone call	.25
Double at the Heathman Hotel (very expensive)	180.00–205.00
Double at Mallory Inn (moderate)	70.00–110.00
Double at Super 8 Portland/Airport (inexpensive)	61.00–73.00
Lunch for one at B. Moloch (moderate)	10.00
Lunch for one at Mayas Taqueria (inexpensive)	6.00
Dinner for one, without wine, at the Heathman (expensive)	32.00
Dinner for one, without wine, at Ristorante Pazzo (moderate)	21.00
Dinner for one, without wine, at Caswell (inexpensive)	8.00
Pint of beer	3.25
Coca-Cola	1.00
Cup of espresso	1.50
Roll of ASA 100 Kodacolor film, 36 exposures	6.00
Admission to the Portland Art Museum	6.00
Movie ticket	6.00–6.50
Oregon Symphony ticket at Arlene Schnitzer Concert Hall	10.00–50.00

MONEY

What will a vacation in Oregon cost? That depends on your tastes. If you drive an RV or carry a tent, you can get by very inexpensively and find a place to stay almost anywhere in Oregon. On the other hand, you can easily spend a couple of hundred dollars a day on a room at one of Oregon's resorts. However, if you want to stay in clean, modern motels at Interstate highway off-ramps, expect to pay $50 to $65 a night for a double room in most places. When it comes time to eat, you can get a great meal almost anywhere in the Oregon for under $25, but if you want to spend more, or less, that's also possible

Automatic teller machines (ATMs) (with Cirrus, Visa, Plus, and Star networks widely available) are nearly ubiquitous throughout Oregon, so you can get cash as you travel; however, some small town banks still do not have ATMs.

2 When to Go

Though gray skies and mild temperatures are what Oregon is known for, the state is characterized by a range of climates almost unequaled in the United States for its diversity. For the most part, moist winds off the Pacific Ocean keep temperatures west of the Cascade Range mild year-round. Summers in the Willamette Valley and southern Oregon can see temperatures over 100° Fahrenheit, but on the Oregon coast you're likely to need a sweater or light jacket at night even in August. The Oregon rains that are so legendary fall primarily as a light, but almost constant, drizzle between October and early July. There are windows of sunshine during this period, but they usually last no more than a few days. There are also, unfortunately, occasional wet summers, so be prepared for wet weather whenever you plan to visit. Winters usually include one or two blasts of Arctic air, usually right around Christmas or New Years, that bring snow and freezing weather to the Portland area.

There are several exceptions to Oregon's mild and rainy climate. If you visit the coast, expect grayer, wetter weather than in the Portland area. The Oregon coast can be quite cool in the summer and is often foggy or rainy throughout the year. In fact, when the Willamette Valley is at its hottest in July and August, you can be sure that the coast will be fogged in. The best month at the coast is usually September, with good weather often holding on into October.

In the Cascades and eastern Oregon's Blue Mountains and Wallowa Mountains, snowfall is heavy in the winter and skiing is a popular sport. Summer doesn't come until late in the year here, with snow lingering into July at higher elevations (for instance, the Timberline Lodge area at Mount Hood and the Eagle Cap Wilderness in the Wallowas). At such elevations, late July and on through August are the best times to see the wildflower displays in alpine meadows.

The region east of the Cascades is characterized by lack of rain and temperature extremes. This high desert area can be very cold in the winter, and at higher elevations receives considerable amounts of snow. In summer, the weather can be blazingly hot at lower elevations, though nights are often cool enough to require a sweater or light jacket.

Portland's Average Monthly Temperatures & Rainfall

	Jan	Feb	Mar	Apr	May	June	July	Aug	Sept	Oct	Nov	Dec
Temp. (°F)	40	43	46	50	57	63	68	67	63	54	46	41
Temp. (°C)	4	6	8	10	14	17	20	20	17	12	8	5
Days of Rain	18	16	17	14	12	10	4	5	8	13	18	19

OREGON CALENDAR OF EVENTS

February

- **Portland International Film Festival,** various theaters around the city. Mid-February until early March (☎ **503/221-1156**).

○ **Oregon Shakespeare Festival,** Ashland. The repertory company features a dozen plays—some by Shakespeare and others by classical and contemporary playwrights—in three unique theaters. Backstage tours, a museum, and lectures round out the festival. Call the festival box office at ☎ **541/482-4331** for details and ticket information. February to October.

- **Newport Seafood and Wine Festival,** Newport. Taste local seafood dishes and wines at the Newport Marina. ☎ **800/262-7844.** Third weekend in February.

March

- **Oregon Dune Mushers' Mail Run,** Florence. An endurance dog run over the varied terrain of the Florence coastline commemorates routes that were once used before roads were constructed. ☎ **541/269-1269.** First weekend in March.

- **Winter Games of Oregon,** Mt. Hood. Competitions in five winter sports events are held at Ski Bowl and Timberline ski areas, including snowboarding, skiing, and extreme skiing. ☎ **503/520-1319.** First weekend in March.

- **Spring Whale Watch Week,** Lincoln City. Interpreters are on hand at whale watching sites to help visitors spot migrating gray whales; there's also a beach clean-up. ☎ **800/452-2151.** Third weekend in March.

April
- **Hood River Blossom Festival,** Hood River. Celebration of the blossoming of the orchards outside the town of Hood River. ☎ **800/366-3530.** Third weekend in April.

May
- **Cinco de Mayo Festival,** downtown Portland at Waterfront Park. Hispanic celebration with food and entertainment honoring Portland's sister city, Guadalajara, Mexico. ☎ **503/823-4572** or 503/222-9807. Early May.
- **Mother's Day Rhododendron Show,** Crystal Springs Rhododendron Gardens, Portland. Blooming rhodies and azaleas transform this tranquil garden into a mass of blazing color. There's also a plant sale. ☎ **503/771-8386.** Mother's Day.
- **Rhododendron Festival,** Florence. Viewing of native rhododendrons, a carnival, a car show, and a slug race are some of the festival events. ☎ **541/997-3128.** Mid-May.
- **Azalea Festival,** Brookings. Attractions include foods booths, a craft fair, and of course the colorful native azaleas, which are the main reason for this festival. ☎ **800/535-9469.** Memorial Day weekend.
- **Boatnik,** Grants Pass. Jet boats and hydroplanes race on the Rogue River, and there's also a parade and carnival. ☎ **541/476-8282.** Memorial Day weekend.

June
- **Cannon Beach Sand Castle Festival,** Cannon Beach. Artistic sand-sculpted creations appear along the beach. ☎ **503/436-2623.** Early June.
- **American Musical Jubilee,** Ontario. A talent competition and other musical events comprise this jubilee. ☎ **503/436-2623.** Early June.
- **Sisters Rodeo and Parade,** Sisters. A celebration of the West in this duded-up Western town near Bend. ☎ **800/827-7522.** Mid-June.
- ✪ **Portland Rose Festival.** From its beginnings back in 1888, when the first rose show was held, the Rose Festival has blossomed into Portland's biggest celebration. The festivities have now spread throughout Portland and the surrounding communities and include a rose show, floral parade, rose-queen contest, music festival, car races, footrace, boat races, and even an air show.

  Hotel rooms can be hard to come by; plan ahead. Contact the **Portland Rose Festival Association,** 220 NW Second Ave., Portland, OR 97209 (☎ **503/ 227-2681**), for information on tickets to specific events. Most events take place during the first three weeks of June.
- ✪ **Britt Festivals,** Jacksonville. Multiarts festival that offers world-class jazz, classical, folk, country, dance, musical theater, and pop performances in a beautiful natural setting. Bring a blanket and have a picnic supper before the performance. Call ☎ **800/88-BRITT** or 541/773-6077 for details and ticket information. June to September.
- **Oregon Bach Festival,** Eugene. One of the biggest Bach festivals around serves up Bach's big oratorio works such as the B Minor Mass, but also a variety of other concerts including chamber music and a program for kids. ☎ **800/457-1486.** Late June to early July.
- **Concours D'Elegance Antique Car Show,** Forest Grove. People come from all around to show off their shiny vintage cars. ☎ **503/357-2300.** Last Saturday in June.

July
- **Fourth of July Fireworks,** Vancouver, Washington. Vancouver, which is part of the Portland metropolitan area, hosts the biggest fireworks display west of the Mississippi. ☎ **360/693-5481**. July 4.
- **World Championship Timber Carnival,** Albany. Logging events, parade, food, and fireworks. ☎ **800/526-2256.** Fourth of July weekend.
- **Oregon Country Fair,** Eugene. Counterculture craft fair and festival for Deadheads young and old. ☎ **541/343-4298.** Second weekend in July.
- **Da Vinci Days,** Corvallis. Three-day celebration of science and technology with performances, art, interactive exhibits, children's activities, food, and wine. ☎ **541/757-6363.** Mid-July.
- **Sister Quilt Show,** Sisters. The entire town gets decked out in colorful handmade quilts. ☎ **541/549-5454.** Mid-July.
- **Salem Arts Festival,** Salem. The largest juried art fair in Oregon, under the trees in Bush Park, with musical entertainment and food booths. ☎ **503/581-2228.** Third weekend in July.
- **Chief Joseph Days,** Joseph. Rodeo plus exhibits and demonstrations by local Native Americans. ☎ **541/432-1015.** Last full weekend in July.
- **Oregon Brewers Festival,** Waterfront Park, Portland. Microbreweries show off their suds. ☎ **503/778-5917.** Last weekend in July.

August
- **Mount Hood Festival of Jazz,** Mount Hood Community College, Gresham. For the serious jazz fan, this is the highlight of the summer. It features the greatest names in jazz. ☎ **503/232-3000.** First full weekend of August.
- **Astoria Regatta,** Astoria. See a fleet of boats in full sail in the historic harbor. ☎ **503/325-6311.** Third weekend in August.
- **Oregon State Fair,** Salem. A typical agricultural state fair. ☎ **800/833-0011** in Oregon, or 503/378-3247. The 12 days before and including Labor Day.
- **Cascade Festival of Music,** Bend. Classical and popular music in a park setting. ☎ **541/382-8381.** Last weekend in August.

September
- **Mt. Angel Oktoberfest,** Mount Angel. Biergarten, Bavarian-style oompah bands, food booths. ☎ **503/845-9440.** Mid-September.
- **Cycle Oregon.** Bicyclists get a unique opportunity to appreciate the beauty of Oregon as they cycle across the state on a route that changes annually. ☎ **800/ CYCLEOR.** Mid-September.
- **Pendleton Round-Up and Happy Canyon Pageant,** Pendleton. Rodeo, Native American pageant, country-music concert. ☎ **800/457-6336** or 541/276-2553. Mid-September.
- **Bandon Cranberry Festival,** Bandon. Cranberry bog tours, arts and crafts. ☎ **541/347-9616.** Mid-September.
- **Eugene Celebration,** Eugene. Street party celebrating the diversity of the community. Festivities include the crowning of a Slug Queen. ☎ **541/687-5215.** Third weekend in September.

October
- **Hood River Valley Harvest Fest,** Hood River. At the Hood River Expo Center, enjoy fruit products of the region, crafts, and entertainment; drive the Fruit Loop to visit farm stands and wineries. ☎ **800/366-3530.** First weekend in October.

Serious Reservations

Once upon a time on a sunny Friday morning, it was possible to simply listen to the weekend weather forecast and then decide whether or not you wanted to head to the beach or to the mountains for the weekend. If you think you can still pull off this sort of weekend trip, be prepared to sleep in your car. The days of spontaneous summer weekends are a thing of the past in Oregon. If you want to be assured of getting a room or a campsite at the coast or at some of the busier destinations in the mountains, you'll need to make your reservations months in advance, especially if you're going on a weekend.

To be sure that you get the state park campsite, yurt, cabin, teepee, houseboat, or covered wagon you want, you'll need to make your reservations as much as 11 months in advance (that's the earliest you can reserve) through **Reservations Northwest** (☎ 800/233-0321), which handles reservations at both Oregon and Washington state parks. Reservations are accepted for dates between April 1 and September 30, with Memorial Day, the Fourth of July, and Labor Day weekends, of course, requiring the most advance planning. A $6 reservation fee is charged.

While National Forest Service campgrounds are generally less developed and less in demand than state park campgrounds, many do stay full throughout the summer months, especially those at the beach. For reservations at forest service campgrounds, call the **National Forest Reservation Service** (☎ 800/280-CAMP), which charges a $7.50 reservation fee. These sites can be reserved up to 240 days (8 months) in advance.

The same sort of advance planning also applies to such accommodations as Crater Lake Lodge, Timberline Lodge, and just about any lodging on the coast on a summer weekend. Making rooms even more difficult to come by are the many festivals scheduled around the state throughout the summer months. When planning an itinerary, be sure to check to see whether your schedule might coincide with some event that just might cause all the rooms in town to fill up that particular weekend.

Good luck, and remember, it's still possible to be spontaneous, even when you made your reservation months in advance.

- **International Kite Festival,** Lincoln City. Kite carnival including the world's largest spinning wind sock and lighted night kite flights. ☎ 800/452-2151. Early October.

November
- **Holiday Festival of Lights,** Ashland. A thousand points of light decorate the town. ☎ 541/488-5495. Thanksgiving to New Year's Eve.
- **Yamhill County Wine Country Thanksgiving,** Yamhill County. About 30 miles outside of Portland, more than two dozen wineries open their doors for tasting new releases, food, and entertainment. ☎ 503/434-5814. End of November.
- **Festival of Lights at The Grotto,** The Grotto, Portland. Lighting displays and one of the largest choral festivals in the Northwest. ☎ 503/254-7371. End of November to end of December.

December
- **Holiday Parade of Ships,** Willamette and Columbia rivers. Boats decked out in holiday lights parade and circle on the rivers after nightfall. For more information, call ☎ 503/282-0159. Month of December.

- **Winter Solstice Festival,** Oregon Museum of Science and Industry, Portland. In a 4,000-year-old tradition, the lengthening of the days is celebrated with entertainment, arts and crafts, and special events. ☎ **503/797-4000.** December 20 or 21.
- **Holiday Lights and Open House at Shore Acres State Park,** Coos Bay. Extravagantly decorated gardens near dramatic cliffs at the Oregon coast. ☎ **541/ 756-5401.** Late December to early January.
- **Winter Whale Watch Week,** Lincoln City. Interpreters are on hand at whale watching sites to help visitors spot migrating gray whales; beach clean-up. ☎ **800/ 452-2151.** Last week in December.

3 The Active Vacation Planner

The abundance of outdoor recreational activities is one of the reasons people choose to live in and visit Oregon. With both mountains and beaches within an hour's drive of the major metropolitan areas, there are numerous choices for the active vacationer. For more in-depth coverage on outdoor activities in Oregon, check out the Frommer's new *Outside Magazine's Adventure Guide to the Pacific Northwest.*

OUTDOOR CLASSES & ORGANIZED TRIPS

In addition to the information listed below under different activity categories, there are some places to know about that offer a wide variety of classes and outings.

In the Portland area, **Portland Community College** (☎ **503/977-4933**) offers classes in rock climbing, white-water kayaking, and sea kayaking. **Portland Parks & Recreation** (☎ **503/823-5132**) also offers a wide variety of seasonal outdoor sports classes and trips. Guided hikes, canoe trips, and bird watching excursions are offered throughout the year by **Metro Regional Parks and Greenspaces** (☎ **503/ 797-1850**). The **Tualatin Hills Parks & Recreation District** (☎ **503/644-3855**) also offers similar outings, as well as canoe classes and guided rafting trips.

In the Eugene area, **Lane Community College** (☎ **541/726-2252**) offers a wide variety of outdoor skills classes and tours throughout the year and throughout the region. Everything from sea kayaking to rock climbing to canoeing to cross-country skiing are covered. Call for a current listing of classes. The **City of Eugene Library, Recreation, and Cultural Services** (☎ **541/687-5333**) offers a similar variety of classes and trips.

Outdoors enthusiasts with Web access will want to check out **GORP's** (Great Outdoors Recreation Pages) resource listings for on-line information on area parks and activities from fishing to skiing to kayaking. Head for **www.gorp.com/gorp/ location/or/or.htm** to get to the Oregon hot list.

SOME USEFUL RESOURCES
GOVERNMENT AGENCIES

- **Bureau of Land Management (OR/WA Office),** 1515 SW Fifth Ave. (P.O. Box 2965), Portland, OR 97208 (☎ **503/952-6024**).
- **Oregon Parks and Recreation Department,** 1115 Commercial St. NE, Salem, OR 97310-1001 (☎ **503/378-6305**).
- **National Park Service, Pacific Northwest Region,** 909 First Ave., Suite 546, Seattle, WA 98104-1060 (☎ **206/220-4013**).

OUTDOORS ORGANIZATIONS

- **The Mazamas,** 909 NW 19th Ave., Portland, OR 97209 (☎ **503/227-2345**); a hiking and climbing club.

- **The Mountaineers,** Club Headquarters, 300 Third Ave. W., Seattle, WA 98119 (☎ **206/284-6310**); the Northwest's biggest outdoors organization.
- **Trails Club of Oregon,** P.O. Box 1243, Portland, OR 97207 (☎ **503/233-2740**); a hiking, skiing, snowshoeing, and bicycling club.

ACTIVITIES A TO Z

BICYCLING/MOUNTAIN BIKING   The Oregon coast is one of the most popular bicycling locales in the nation, and each summer attracts thousands of dedicated pedalers. Expect to spend about a week to pedal the entire coast if you're in good shape and are traveling at a leisurely pace. During the summer months, it's best to travel from north to south along the coast because of the prevailing winds. Also keep in mind that many state parks have designated hiker/biker campsites. You can get a free Oregon coast bicycle map, as well as other bicycle maps for the state of Oregon, by contacting the **Oregon Bicycle/Pedestrian Program,** Oregon Department of Transportation, 210 Transportation Building, Salem OR 97310 (☎ **503/986-3556**).

Other regions growing in popularity with cyclists include the wine country of Yamhill County and other parts of the Willamette Valley. Portland and Eugene both have easy bicycle trails that are either in parks or connect parks. The region's national forests provide miles of logging roads and single-track trails for mountain biking. Among the most popular mountain-biking areas are the east side of Mount Hood, the Oakridge area southeast of Eugene, the Ashland area, and the Bend and Sisters areas of central Oregon.

Backroads, 801 Cedar St., Berkeley, CA 94710-1740 (☎ **800/462-2848** or 510/527-1555; fax 510/527-1444), offers road-bike trips on the Oregon coast. Tour prices range from $798 to $1,455. **Bicycle Adventures,** P.O. Box 11219, Olympia, WA 98508 (☎ **800/443-6060** or 360/786-0989; fax 360/786-9661), offers road-bike trips in the Oregon Cascades, the Columbia Gorge, and on the Oregon coast. Tour prices range from $1,360 to $1,798.

BIRD WATCHING   With a wide variety of habitats, Oregon offers many excellent bird-watching spots. Malheur National Wildlife Refuge, in central Oregon, is that state's premier bird-watching area and attracts more than 300 species of birds over the course of the year. Nearby Summer Lake also offers good bird watching, with migratory waterfowl and shorebirds most prevalent. There's also good bird watching on Sauvie Island, outside Portland, where waterfowl and eagles can be seen, and along the coast, where you can see tufted puffins, pigeon guillemots, and perhaps even a marbled murrelet. The Klamath Lakes region of south-central Oregon is well known for its large population of bald eagles.

Throughout the year, the National Audubon Society sponsors expeditions and field seminars. For more information, contact the **Audubon Society of Portland** (☎ **503/292-6855**). To find out what birds are where, you can call the **Audubon Society's Birding Hotline** (☎ **503/292-0661**).

BOARDSAILING (WINDSURFING)   The Columbia River Gorge is one of the most renowned windsurfing spots in the world. Here, high winds and a strong current come together to produce radical sailing conditions. As the winds whip up the waves, skilled sailors rocket across the water and launch themselves skyward to perform aerial acrobatics. On calmer days and in spots where the wind isn't blowing so hard, there are also opportunities for novices to learn the basics. Summer is the best sailing season, and the town of Hood River is the center of the boarding scene with plenty of windsurfing schools and rental companies. The southern Oregon coast also has some popular spots, including Floras Lake just north of Port Orford and Meyers Creek in Pistol River State Park, south of Gold Beach.

CAMPING   Public and private campgrounds abound all across Oregon, with those along the coast among the most popular. Campgrounds on lakes also stay particularly busy. During the summer months, campground reservations are almost a necessity at many state parks, especially those along the coast. To make a camping reservation at a state park, contact **Reservations Northwest,** 2501 SW First St., Suite 100, Portland, OR 97201 (☎ **800/452-5687** or 503/731-3411). Campsite reservations are taken 11 months in advance of the date you wish to stay. To make reservations to camp at a national forest, call ☎ **800/280-CAMP.** Camping is on a first-come, first-served basis at **Crater Lake National Park** (for information, call the park at ☎ **541/594-2211**).

Various state parks also offer a variety of camping alternatives. Tops among these are yurts (circular domed tents with electricity, plywood floors, and beds), which can be found at nine coastal parks as well as at Champoeg and Valley of the Rogue state parks ($25 per night). Yurts have made camping in the rain a bit easier. At Cove Palisades and Prineville Reservoir state parks in central Oregon, there are log cabins for rent, and at Farewell Bend and Emigrant Springs state parks, there are covered wagons for rent ($25 per night). At Farewell Bend and Lake Owyhee, there are teepees for rent ($25 per night). On Lake Billy Chinook, the state even rents houseboats ($1,050 to $1,590 per week). Make reservations through Reservations Northwest.

FISHING   The fish of Oregon enjoy near legendary status, and while there may be few streams in the region of national importance among anglers, there are still plenty of great rivers. Salmon of half a dozen species, steelhead, and sturgeon are the favored game fish among dedicated anglers. However, wild cutthroat and redside rainbow trout also have their fans. If your idea of a great fishing trip is a skillet full of frying rainbow trout, the state's many stocked streams and mountain lakes will keep you content. Scattered throughout the state are also the odd fisheries that become the obsessions of some anglers—mackinaw trout, kokanee salmon, Atlantic salmon. Even bass anglers have plenty of places to fish for both small-mouth and large-mouth. Offshore fishing for salmon, tuna, and bottom fish is also popular, and up and down the coast you'll find numerous charter boat companies that will take you for a day of fishing.

The most important thing to know about fishing in Oregon is that the rules are complicated and they're always changing. It is absolutely essential that you know all the regulations for whatever body of water you happen to be fishing in. To find out what the current regulations are, you'll need to pick up a copy of *Oregon Sport Fishing Regulations.* This publication is free and is available at sporting goods stores and bait-and-tackle shops. Alternatively you can order copies by contacting the **Oregon Department of Fish & Wildlife,** 2501 SW First Ave. (P.O. Box 59), Portland, OR 97207 (☎ **503/229-5403**). For more information on freshwater fishing in Oregon, contact the **Oregon Department of Fish and Wildlife** (☎ **503/229-5222**) or the **Oregon Sport Fishing Info Line** (☎ **800/ASK-FISH**).

GOLFING   Oregon has nearly 200 private and public golf courses, including several resort courses. The majority of courses are clustered in the Portland metropolitan area and in the Bend-Redmond area where numerous resorts are to be found. There are also quite a few excellent courses along the coast.

GUEST RANCHES   Though this is the Northwest, it's still the West and cowboys and Indians are as much a part of life here as they are in the Southwest. You'll find several guest ranches around the region, including the Flying M Ranch in Yamhill, Oregon (see chapter 7), and Minam Lodge, near Joseph, Oregon (see chapter 12).

HANG GLIDING & PARAGLIDING   Lakeview, in south-central Oregon near the California state line, is Oregon's premier hang-gliding location. Strong steady winds and high bluffs provide perfect conditions for experienced hang gliders. Hang gliding and paragliding (using what looks like a parachute) are also popular at Cape Kiwanda on the northern Oregon coast, where a huge sand dune and steady winds create ideal conditions for learning this sport.

HIKING & BACKPACKING   Oregon has an abundance of hiking trails, including the Pacific Crest Trail, which runs along the spine of the Cascades from Canada to the California line (and onward all the way to Mexico). The state's thousands of miles of hiking trails are concentrated primarily in national forests, especially in wilderness areas, in the Cascade Range. Along the length of the Pacific Crest Trail are such scenic hiking areas as the Mount Hood Wilderness, the Mount Jefferson Wilderness, the Three Sisters Wilderness, the Diamond Peak Wilderness, the Mount Thielsen Wilderness, and the Sky Lakes Wilderness. However, many state parks also have extensive hiking-trail systems.

The Oregon Coast Trail is a designated route that runs the length of the Oregon coast. In most places it travels along the beach, but in other places it climbs up and over capes and headlands through dense forests and windswept meadows. The longest stretches of the trail are along the southern coast in Samuel H. Boardman State Park. There's also a long beach stretch in the Oregon Dunes National Recreation Area.

Other coastal parks with popular hiking trails include Saddle Mountain State Park, Ecola State Park, Oswald West State Park, and Cape Lookout State Park. Silver Falls State Park, east of Salem, is also a popular hiking spot. The many trails of the Columbia Gorge National Scenic Area are also well trodden, with Eagle Creek Trail being a longtime favorite. For a quick hiking fix, Portlanders often head for the city's Forest Park. The trails leading out from Timberline Lodge on Mount Hood lead through forests and meadows at the tree line and are particularly busy on summer weekends.

KAYAKING & CANOEING   While Puget Sound, up in Washington, is the **sea kayaking** capital of the Northwest, Oregonians are also taking to this sport. However, sea kayaks in Oregon very rarely make it to the sea, where waters are usually far too rough for kayaks. There are, however, numerous protected bays along the Oregon coast that are popular paddling spots. Also, the Lewis & Clark National Wildlife Refuge on the Columbia River not far from Astoria offers miles of quiet waterways to explore. For more information on paddling in this area, contact the **Lower Columbia Canoe Club,** 7905 SW Canyon Lane, Portland, OR 97225 (Web site: **www.teleport.com/nonprofit/LCCC**) or the **Willamette Kayak & Canoe Club,** P.O. Box 1062, Corvallis, OR 97339.

White-water kayaking is popular on many of the rivers that flow down out of the Cascade Range in Oregon, including the Deschutes, the Clackamas, the Mollala, and the Sandy. Down in southern Oregon, the North Umpqua and the Rogue provide plenty of white-water action.

Sundance Expeditions (☎ **541/479-8508**), which is located near Grants Pass, is one of the premier kayaking schools in the country. They offer a 4-day instructional trip down the wild-and-scenic section of the Rogue River as well as a 9-day beginner's program that does a 4-day trip down the river after 5 days of initial instruction. Sundance also leads kayaking trips down the nearby Illinois River.

Canoeing is popular on many of Oregon's lakes. Some of the best are Hosmer and Sparks Lakes west of Bend, Clear Lake south of Santiam Pass, Waldo Lake near Willamette Pass southeast of Eugene, and Upper Klamath Lake (where there's a canoe trail).

MOUNTAINEERING   Mount Hood and several other Cascades peaks offer challenging mountain climbing and rock climbing for both the novice and the expert.

If you're interested in learning some mountain climbing skills or want to hone your existing skills, contact **Timberline Mountain Guides,** P.O. Box 340, Gov't Camp, OR 97028 (☎ **800/464-7704;** fax 503/272-3677), a company that offers snow, ice, and rock climbing courses. They also lead summit climbs on Mount Hood. A 2-day Mount Hood mountaineering course with summit climb costs $245. Rates for other courses range from $95 for a day-long rock climbing class at Smith Rock to $750 for a 5-day mountaineering seminar.

ROCK CLIMBING   Smith Rocks State Park, near Redmond in central Oregon, is a rock-climbing mecca of international renown. Some of the routes here are among the toughest in the world, and so numerous are the routes that an entire book has been written about these climbs titled *Climber's Guide to Smith Rock,* by Alan Watts (Chockstone Press, 1992). Many climbers claim that sport climbing got its American start here.

SCUBA DIVING   Although Oregon has hundreds of miles of coastline, scuba diving is not as popular a sport as it would at first seem. This is because there are very few places along the coast where shore dives are possible. Consequently, most Oregon divers head offshore to rocky reefs to do their diving, and this entails chartering a boat. You might be able to join such a dive by contacting the **Eugene Dive Club** (☎ **541/998-8104**). Popular destinations include Tacklebuster Reef off Depoe Bay and North Pinnacle and Arch Rock off Newport.

If conditions are just right, there are a few shore dive spots along the coast. Try the jetties at the mouth of Yaquina Bay in Newport, at Sunset Bay State Park outside Coos Bay, and in Port Orford Harbor. For more information, for air, or to find a dive buddy, contact **Doug's Diving,** 609 Commercial Ave., Garibaldi (☎ **503/322-2200**); **Garibaldi Aqua Sports,** 108 Seventh Ave., Garibaldi (☎ **503/322-0113**); **Newport Water Sports,** South Jetty Road, Newport (☎ **541/867-3742**); or **Central Coast Watersports,** 1560 Second St., Florence (☎ **800/789-3483**). It's a good idea to have an advanced open water or rescue diver certification in these often rough waters.

SKIING   Because the winter weather in the Oregon is so unpredictable, the state is not known as a ski destination. Most of the state's ski areas are relatively small and cater primarily to local skiers. Mount Bachelor, in central Oregon outside of Bend, is the one exception. Because of its high elevation and location on the drier east side of the Cascades, it gets a more reliable snowpack and isn't as susceptible to midwinter warming spells, which tend to bring rain to west side ski slopes with irritating regularity.

Ski areas in Oregon include Mount Hood Meadows, Mount Hood Ski Bowl, Timberline Ski Area, Cooper Spur Ski Area, and Summit Ski Area, all of which are on Mount Hood outside Portland. Farther south, there are Hoodoo Ski Bowl, east of Salem, and Willamette Pass, east of Eugene. In the eastern part of the state, Anthony Lakes and Spout Springs provide a bit of powder skiing. Down in the south, Ski Ashland is the only option. There's also snow-cat skiing north of Crater Lake on Mount Bailey.

Many downhill ski areas also offer groomed **cross-country ski trails.** Cross-country skiers will find an abundance of trails up and down the Cascades. Teacup Lake, Trillium Basin, and Mount Hood Meadows, all on Mount Hood, offer good groomed trails. Near Mount Bachelor, there are also plenty of groomed trails. Crater Lake is another popular spot for cross-country skiing. Backcountry skiing is also popular in the Wallowa Mountains in eastern Oregon.

WHALE WATCHING   Gray whales, which can reach 45 feet in length and weigh up to 35 tons, migrate annually between Alaska and Baja California, and pass close by the Oregon coast between December and May. However, with more and more whales stopping to spend the summer off the Oregon coast, it is now possible to see these behemoths of the deep just about any month of the year.

Depoe Bay, north of Newport, is not only the smallest harbor in the world, but it's also home port for several whale-watching boats that head out throughout the year to look for gray whales. It's also possible to whale watch from shore, with Cape Lookout, Cape Meares, Devil's Punchbowl, Cape Perpetua, Sea Lion Caves, Shore Acres State Park, Face Rock Wayside (in Bandon), Cape Blanco, Cape Sebastian, and Harris Beach State Park being some of the better places from which to watch.

WHITE-WATER RAFTING   Plenty of rain and lots of mountains combine to produce dozens of good white-water rafting rivers in Oregon, depending on the time of year and water levels. The Deschutes, which flows through central Oregon, and the Rogue, which is in southern Oregon and was featured in the movie *The River Wild,* are the two most popular rafting rivers. Other popular rafting rivers include the Clackamas outside Portland, the McKenzie outside Eugene, and the North Umpqua outside Roseburg. Out in the southeastern corner, the remote Owyhee River provides adventurers with still more white water. See the respective chapters for information on rafting companies operating on these rivers.

4 Educational & Volunteer Vacations

Older travelers who want to learn something from their trip to Oregon or who simply prefer the company of like-minded older travelers should look into programs by **Elderhostel,** 75 Federal St., Boston, MA 02110 (☎ **617/426-7788**). To participate in an Elderhostel program, either you or your spouse must be 55 years old or older. In addition to 1-week educational programs, Elderhostel offers short getaways with interesting themes.

The **Nature Conservancy** is a nonprofit organization dedicated to the global preservation of natural diversity, and to this end it operates educational field trips and work parties to their own nature preserves and those of other agencies. For information about field trips in Oregon, contact the Nature Conservancy, 821 SE 14th Ave., Portland, OR 97214 (☎ **503/230-1221**).

If you enjoy the wilderness and want to get more involved in preserving it, consider a **Sierra Club Service Trip.** These trips are for the purpose of building, restoring, and maintaining hiking trails in wilderness areas. It's a lot of work, but it's also a lot of fun. For more information on Service Trips, contact the **Sierra Club Outing Department,** 85 Second St., Second Floor, San Francisco, CA 94105 (☎ **415/977-5630;** fax 415/977-5795). Or call the local chapters of the Sierra Club. In Oregon, the Portland Chapter is at ☎ **503/238-0442.**

Earth Watch, P.O. Box 9104, Watertown, MA 02172 (☎ **617/926-8200**), sends volunteers on scientific research projects. Contact them for a catalog listing trips and costs. Projects have included studies of orca whales, chimpanzee communication, and Oregon caves.

The **Northwest School of Survival,** P.O. Box 1465, Sandy, OR 97055 (☎ **503/668-8264**), can teach you everything from how to start a fire with a stick to how to build a snow cave to evaluate avalanche hazard.

5 Travel Insurance

Before going out and spending money on various sorts of travel insurance, check your existing policies to see if they'll cover you while you're traveling. Make sure your health insurance will cover you when you're away from home. Most credit and charge cards offer automatic flight insurance when you purchase an airline ticket with that card. These policies insure against death or dismemberment in the case of an airplane crash. Also, check your cards to see if any of them pick up the loss-damage waiver (LDW) when you rent a car. The LDW can run as much as $15 a day and can add 50% or more to the cost of renting a car. Check your automobile insurance policy too; it might cover the LDW as well. If you own a home or have renter's insurance, see if that policy covers off-premises theft and loss wherever it occurs. If you're traveling on a tour or have prepaid a large chunk of your travel expenses, you might want to ask your travel agent about trip-cancellation insurance.

If, after checking all your existing insurance policies, you decide that you need additional insurance, a good travel agent can give you information on a variety of different options. **Travelex,** P.O. Box 9408, Garden City, NY 11530-9408 (☎ **800/ 228-9792**), offers several different types of travel insurance policies for 1 day to 6 months. These policies include medical, baggage, trip-cancellation or interruption insurance, and flight insurance against death or dismemberment.

6 Tips for Travelers with Special Needs

FOR TRAVELERS WITH DISABILITIES   When making airline reservations, always mention your disability. Airline policies differ regarding wheelchairs and Seeing Eye dogs. Almost all hotels and motels in Oregon, aside from bed-and-breakfast inns and older or historic lodges, offer accommodations accessible for travelers with disabilities. However, when making reservations be sure to ask. Oregon lodgings that are accessible are listed in the *Oregon Traveler's Guide to Accommodations.* To get a copy of this magazine, contact the Oregon Tourism Division, 775 Summer St. NE, Salem, OR 97310 (☎ **800/547-7842**).

The public transit systems found in most Oregon cities either have regular vehicles that are accessible for riders with disabilities or offer special transportation services for people with disabilities.

Oregon State Parks has a TDD (Telephone Device for the Deaf) information line (☎ **800/858-9659**) that provides recreation and camping information.

If you plan to visit any national parks or monuments, you can avail yourself of the Golden Access Passport. This lifetime pass is issued free to any U.S. citizen or permanent resident who has been medically certified as disabled or blind. The pass permits free entry into national parks and monuments.

Rick Crowder of the **Travelin' Talk Network,** P.O. Box 3534, Clarksville, TN 37043-3534 (☎ **615/552-6670** Monday through Friday between noon and 5pm central time), organizes a network for travelers with disabilities. A directory listing people and organizations around the world who are networked to provide travelers with disabilities with firsthand information about a chosen destination is available for $35.

FOR GAY & LESBIAN TRAVELERS   Gay and lesbian travelers visiting Portland should be sure to pick up a free copy of *Just Out* (☎ **503/236-1252**), a monthly newspaper for the gay community. You can usually find copies at **Powell's Books,** 1005 W. Burnside St. The newspaper covers local news of interest to gays. They also publish a resource guide for lesbians and gays called the *Just Out Pocket Book.* Call the above number to find out where you can get a copy. The guide is a free directory of Portland businesses that welcome gay customers.

FOR SENIORS   When making airline reservations, always mention that you're a senior citizen—many airlines offer discounts. You should also carry some sort of photo ID card (driver's license, passport) to avail yourself of senior-citizen discounts on attractions, hotels, motels, and public transportation, as well as another good deal for senior citizens: the Golden Age Passport, which is available for $10 to U.S. citizens and permanent residents age 62 and older. This federal government pass allows lifetime entrance privileges. You can apply in person for this passport at a national park, national forest, or other location where it's honored, and you must show reasonable proof of age.

If you aren't a member of the **American Association of Retired Persons (AARP),** 601 E. St. NW, Washington, DC 20077-1214 (☎ **800/424-3410**), you should consider joining. For a very reasonable membership fee, this association provides discounts at many lodgings and attractions, although you can sometimes get a similar discount simply by showing your ID.

If you'd like to do some studying while on vacation, consider Elderhostel (see "Educational and Volunteer Vacations," earlier in this chapter).

7 Getting There

BY PLANE   Portland International Airport is Oregon's main airport. All the major car-rental companies have locations here. Due to major reconstruction going on at the Portland Airport until the year 2000, it is sometimes difficult to get between the terminal to the parking areas, although shuttle buses run frequently to help expedite movement. Leave plenty of time in your schedule when dealing with the airport. See section 1, "Orientation," in chapter 6 for information on how to get from the airport to downtown Portland.

Portland is served by the following airlines: **Alaska Airlines** (☎ 800/426-0333), **America West** (☎ 800/235-9292), **American Airlines** (☎ 800/433-7300), **Continental** (☎ 800/525-0280), **Delta** (☎ 800/221-1212), **Horizon Air** (☎ 800/547-9308), **Northwest** (☎ 800/225-2525), **Southwest** (☎ 800/435-9792), **TWA** (☎ 800/221-2000), **United** (☎ 800/241-6522), and **US Airways** (☎ 800/428-4322).

If you're searching for a great deal, you may be able to fly for less than the standard fare by contacting a **ticket broker** (also known as a bucket shop or consolidator). These companies advertise in the Sunday travel sections of major city newspapers with small ads listing numerous destinations and ticket prices. You won't always be able to get the low price they advertise, but you're likely to save a bit of money off the regular fare. Call a few and compare prices, making sure you find out about all the taxes and surcharges that may not be included in the initial fare quote. In general, the more restrictions there are attached to an airfare, the lower it will be. However, when an airline runs a special deal, you won't always do better at the ticket brokers. Several companies which may be able to get you tickets at significantly less than full fare include **UniTravel** (☎ 800/325-2222), **A Better Airfare** (☎ 800/FLY-ASAP or 800/454-7700), and **Cheap Tickets** (☎ 800/377-1000).

Also try surfing the **Internet** for bargains on tickets. Services such as America OnLine list ticket discounts in their travel sections, and airlines are beginning to auction seats that they can't unload otherwise. You can be the beneficiary of greatly reduced fares. Use electronic reservation and tracking services, such as **Travelocity** (www.travelocity.com) and **Microsoft Expedia** (www.expedia.com), to keep abreast of fare changes and give your travel agent and dialing finger a break.

BY CAR   The distance to Portland from Seattle is 175 miles; from Spokane, 350 miles; from Vancouver, B.C., 285 miles; from San Francisco, 640 miles; and from Los Angeles, 1,015 miles.

If you're driving up from California, I-5 runs up through the length of the state and continues up toward the Canadian border; it will take you through both Portland and Seattle. If you're coming from the east, I-84 runs from Idaho and points east into Oregon, eventually ending in Portland.

BY TRAIN   Portland is served by **Amtrak** (☎ **800/872-7245**). Several trains serve the region: The *Coast Starlight* operates between Los Angeles and Seattle with stops in San Francisco and Portland, as well as at smaller towns and cities. The *Empire Builder* connects Oregon with Chicago, following the northern route through North Dakota and Montana. Pacific Northwest Corridor trains connect Eugene, Oregon, with Vancouver, B.C., with stops that include Portland and Seattle. At press time, the one-way fare between San Francisco and Portland was between $77 and $142. This trip takes about 19 hours.

BY BUS   **Greyhound Lines** buses (☎ **800/231-2222**) offer service to the Northwest from around the country. These buses operate primarily along the Interstate corridors (I-5, I-84, I-90, and I-82) and to a few other towns and cities on major highways. At press time, the fare between San Francisco and Portland was $46 one way.

8 Getting Around

BY CAR   A car is by far the best way to see Oregon. There just isn't any other way to get to the more remote natural spectacles or to fully appreciate such regions as the Oregon coast or eastern Oregon.

Rentals   Portland has dozens of car-rental agencies, including branches at Portland International Airport. Prices at rental agencies elsewhere in the state tend to be higher, so if at all possible, try to rent your car in a large city such as Portland or Eugene.

For the very best deal on a rental car, make your reservation at least 1 week in advance. It also pays to shop around and call the same companies a few times over the course of a couple of weeks. If you decide on the spur of the moment to rent a car, check to see whether there are any weekend or special rates available. If you're a member of a frequent-flyer program, be sure to mention it: You might get mileage credit for renting a car. Keep asking about special promotions and try different combinations of where to pick up and drop off your car—rental-car agencies, like airlines, don't tell you about the cheapest deals unless you ask, and they have a maze of different offerings and rates.

Major car-rental companies with offices in Portland and the airport area include **Alamo** (☎ 800/327-9633), **Avis** (☎ 800/831-2847), **Budget** (☎ 800/527-0700), **Dollar** (☎ 800/800-4000), **Hertz** (☎ 800/654-3131), **National** (☎ 800/227-7368), and **Thrifty** (☎ 800/367-2277). Because of construction at the Portland International Airport, which is expected to be completed in the year 2000, it's necessary to take a courtesy airport shuttle to Budget, Avis, Hertz, National, and Dollar car rental agencies. To get to others, the traveler must take an additional shuttle.

Gasoline   Oregon is a big state, so keep your gas tank as full as possible when traveling in the mountains or on the sparsely populated east side of the Cascades. There are no self-service gas stations in the state.

Maps   Maps are available at most highway tourist information centers, at the tourist information offices listed earlier in this chapter and throughout this book, and at gas stations throughout the region. For a map of Oregon, contact the **Oregon Tourism Division** (☎ **800/547-7842**). Members of the AAA can get detailed road maps of Oregon by calling their local AAA office.

Driving Rules   A right turn on red is permitted after first coming to a complete stop. You may also turn left on a red light if you're in the far-left lane of a one-way street and are turning onto another one-way street. Seat belts are required, as are car seats for children.

Breakdowns/Assistance   In the event of a breakdown, stay with your car, lift the hood, turn on your emergency flashers, and wait for a police patrol car. *Do not leave your vehicle.* If you're a member of the American Automobile Association and your car breaks down, call ☎ **800/AAA-HELP** for 24-hour emergency road service.

Driving Times   It takes about 1¹/₂ hours to drive from Portland to Canon Beach on the Oregon coast; from Portland to Mt. Hood, about 1 hour; and from Portland to Bend, about 3 hours. Portland to Seattle is about a 3¹/₂-hour trip, depending on traffic conditions.

BY TRAIN   Though there is **Amtrak (☎ 800/872-7245)** passenger rail service linking southern Oregon, Seattle, and Vancouver, B.C., and from Portland eastward along the Columbia River and north from there to Spokane, service is not very frequent. We don't recommend the train for getting around the region except perhaps for the run between Portland and Seattle, which takes about 4 hours and costs between $15.50 and $29, depending on availability (reservations are required).

BY RECREATIONAL VEHICLE (RV)   An economical way to tour Oregon is with a recreational vehicle. If you're considering renting an RV, look under "Recreational Vehicles—Rent and Lease" in the Yellow Pages of your local phone book. They can be rented for a weekend, a week, or longer. In Portland, you might try **Cruise America Motorhome Rental,** 2032 NW 23rd Ave., Portland, OR 97210 (☎ **503/775-0538**). If you're going to be traveling in the peak season of summer, it's important to make reservations for your RV at least 3 months ahead of time. The rest of the year, a couple of weeks lead time is usually sufficient.

9   Cruising the Columbia River

Paddle-wheel steamboats played a crucial role in the settling of Oregon, shuttling people and goods down the Columbia River before railroads came to the region. Today, the *Queen of the West,* a paddle-wheel cruise ship operated by the **American West Steamboat Company,** 601 Union St., Suite 4343, Seattle, WA 98101 (☎ **800/434-1232**), is cruising the Columbia offering a luxury never before known in Columbia River paddlewheelers. Fares for the 7-night cruise range from $1,050 to $4,050 per person. Shorter cruises are also available.

If you'd rather cruise aboard a smaller vessel, consider a trip with **Alaska Sightseeing Cruise West,** Fourth and Battery Building, Suite 700, Seattle (☎ **800/ 426-7702** or 206/441-8687), which offers an 8-day cruise from Portland on the Columbia and Snake Rivers. Fares range from $795 to $3,395 per person. Similar trips, though with naturalists and historians on board, are offered by **Special Expeditions** (☎ **800/762-0003** or 212/765-7740) at similar rates.

FAST FACTS: Oregon

AAA   If you're a member of the American Automobile Association and your car breaks down, call ☎ **800/AAA-HELP** for 24-hour emergency road service.

Accommodations   It is always a good idea to make hotel reservations as soon as you know your trip dates. Reservations require a deposit of one night's payment. Portland and the Oregon coast are particularly busy during summer months, and hotels book up in advance—especially on weekends when there is a festival on. If you do not have reservations, it is best to look for a room in the midafternoon. If you wait until evening, you run the risk that hotels will be filled. Major downtown hotels, which cater primarily to business travelers, commonly offer weekend discounts of as much as 50% to entice vacationers to fill up the empty rooms. However, resorts and hotels near tourist attractions tend to have higher rates on weekends.

American Express   In Portland, their office is at 1100 SW Sixth Ave. (☎ **503/ 226-2961**), open Monday through Friday from 9am to 5pm. Call the Portland office for information on American Express services in other outlying towns. To report lost or stolen traveler's checks, call ☎ **800/221-7282.**

Area Code   The telephone area code for Portland and the northwest part of Oregon is 503. Other parts of Oregon use the area code 541.

Banks and ATM Networks   Automatic teller machines (ATMs) (with Cirrus, Visa, Plus, and Star networks widely available) are nearly ubiquitous throughout Oregon, so you can get cash as you travel; however, some small town banks still do not have ATMs.

Car Rentals   See "Getting Around," earlier in this chapter.

Climate   See "When to Go," earlier in this chapter.

Embassies and Consulates   See "Fast Facts: For the Foreign Traveler," in chapter 4.

Emergencies   Call ☎ **911** for fire, police, and ambulance.

Information   See "Visitor Information & Money," earlier in this chapter, and individual city chapters for local information offices.

Liquor Laws   The legal drinking age in Oregon is 21. Bars can legally stay open until 2am.

Maps   See "Getting Around," earlier in this chapter.

Pets   Many hotels and motels in Oregon accept small, well-behaved pets. However, there's often a small fee charged to allow them into guest rooms. Many places, in particular bed-and-breakfast inns, don't allow pets at all. On the other hand, many bed-and-breakfasts have their own pets, so if you have a dog or cat allergy, be sure to mention it when making a bed-and-breakfast reservation. Two good resources for dog owners are *Frommer's On the Road Again with Man's Best Friend: Northwest* and *Frommer's America on Wheels: Northwest* (both from Macmillan), which will steer you toward dog-friendly accommodations. Pets are usually restricted in national parks for their own safety, so call each park's ranger station to check before setting out.

Police   To reach the police, dial ☎ **911.**

Taxes   Oregon is a shopper's paradise—there's no sales tax.

Time Zone   With the exception of far eastern Oregon near Ontario, the state is on Pacific standard time (PST) and observes daylight saving time from the first Sunday in April to the last Sunday in October, making it consistently 3 hours behind the East Coast.

Weather   In Portland, call ☎ **503/243-7575.**

For Foreign Visitors **4**

This chapter will provide some specifics about getting to the United States as economically and effortlessly as possible, plus some helpful information about how things are done in Oregon, from receiving mail to making a local or long-distance telephone call.

1 Preparing for Your Trip

ENTRY REQUIREMENTS

DOCUMENT REGULATIONS   Citizens of Canada and Bermuda may enter the United States without visas, but they will need to show proof of nationality, the most common and hassle-free form of which is a passport.

The U.S. State Department has a Visa Waiver Pilot Program allowing citizens of certain countries to enter the United States without a visa for stays of fewer than 90 days of holiday travel. At press time these included Andorra, Argentina, Australia, Austria, Belgium, Brunei, Denmark, Finland, France, Germany, Iceland, Ireland, Italy, Japan, Liechtenstein, Luxembourg, Monaco, the Netherlands, New Zealand, Norway, San Marino, Spain, Sweden, Switzerland, and the United Kingdom. (The program as applied to the United Kingdom refers to British citizens who have the "unrestricted right of permanent abode in the United Kingdom," that is, citizens from England, Scotland, Wales, Northern Ireland, the Channel Islands, and the Isle of Man; and not, for example, citizens of the British Commonwealth of Pakistan.)

Citizens from these countries need only a valid passport and a round-trip air or cruise ticket in their possession upon arrival. If they first enter the United States, they may then visit Mexico, Canada, Bermuda, and/or the Caribbean islands and return to the United States without needing a visa. Further information is available from any U.S. embassy or consulate.

Citizens of countries other than those specified above, or those traveling to the United States for reasons or length of time outside the restrictions of the Visa Waiver program, or those who require waivers of inadmissibility must have two documents:

- A valid passport, with an expiration date at least 6 months later than the scheduled end of the visit to the United States. (Some countries are exceptions to the 6-month validity rule. Contact any U.S. embassy or consulate for complete information.)

• A tourist visa, available from the nearest U.S. consulate. To obtain a visa, the traveler must submit a completed application form (either in person or by mail) with a 1^1/$_2$-inch square photo and the required application fee. There may also be an issuance fee, depending on the type of visa and other factors. Usually you can obtain a visa right away or within 24 hours, but it may take longer during the summer rush period (June to August). If you cannot go in person, contact the nearest U.S. embassy or consulate for directions on applying by mail. Your travel agent or airline office may also be able to provide you with visa applications and instructions. The U.S. consulate or embassy that issues your visa will determine whether you will be issued a multiple- or single-entry visa. The Immigration and Naturalization Service officers at the port-of-entry in the United States will make an admission decision and determine your length of stay.

MEDICAL REQUIREMENTS   No inoculations are needed to enter the United States unless you are coming from, or have stopped over in, areas known to be suffering from epidemics, particularly of cholera or yellow fever.

If you have a disease requiring treatment with medications containing narcotics or drugs requiring a syringe, carry a valid signed prescription from your physician to allay any suspicions that you are smuggling drugs.

CUSTOMS   Every adult visitor may bring in free of duty: 1 liter of wine or hard liquor; 200 cigarettes or 100 cigars (but no cigars from Cuba) or 3 pounds of smoking tobacco; $100 worth of gifts. These exemptions are offered to travelers who spend at least 72 hours in the United States and who have not claimed these exemptions within the preceding 6 months. It is altogether forbidden to bring into the country foodstuff (particularly cheese, fruit, cooked meats, and canned goods) and plants (vegetables, seeds, tropical plants, and so on). Foreign tourists may bring in or take out up to $10,000 in U.S. or foreign currency with no formalities; larger sums must be declared to Customs on entering or leaving.

INSURANCE

There is no national health system in the United States. Because the cost of medical care is extremely high, we strongly advise every traveler to secure health coverage before setting out.

You may want to take out a comprehensive travel policy that covers (for a relatively low premium) sickness or injury cost (medical, surgical, and hospital); loss or theft of your baggage; trip-cancellation costs; guarantee of bail in case you are arrested; costs of accident, repatriation, or death. Such packages (for example, "Europe Assistance" in Europe) are sold by automobile clubs at attractive rates, as well as by insurance companies and travel agencies.

MONEY

CURRENCY & EXCHANGE   The U.S. monetary system has a decimal base: 1 American dollar ($1) = 100 cents (100¢).

Dollar bills commonly come in $1 ("a buck"), $5, $10, $20, $50, and $100 denominations (the last two are not always welcome when paying for small purchases and are not accepted in taxis or subway ticket booths). There are also $2 bills (seldom encountered).

There are six denominations of coins: 1¢ (one cent, or "a penny"), 5¢ (five cents, or "a nickel"), 10¢ (ten cents, or "a dime"), 25¢ (twenty-five cents, or "a quarter"), 50¢ (fifty cents, or "a half dollar"), and the rare $1 piece.

Note: The "foreign-exchange bureaus" so common in Europe are rare except at airports in the United States, and nonexistent outside major cities. Try to avoid having to change foreign money or traveler's checks not denominated in U.S. dollars at a small-town bank, or even a branch in a big city; in fact, leave any currency other than U.S. dollars at home—it may prove to be more of a nuisance to you than it's worth.

CREDIT & CHARGE CARDS   The method of payment most widely used is the credit card: Visa (BarclayCard in Britain), MasterCard (EuroCard in Europe, Access in Britain, Chargex in Canada), American Express, Diners Club, Discover Card, and Carte Blanche. You can save yourself trouble by using "plastic money," rather than cash or traveler's checks in most hotels, motels, and retail stores (a growing number of food and liquor stores now accept credit cards). You must have a credit card to rent a car. It can also be used as proof of identity (often carrying more weight than a passport), or as a "cash card," enabling you to draw money from banks that accept them.

TRAVELER'S CHECKS   Traveler's checks in U.S. dollar denominations are readily accepted at most hotels, motels, restaurants, and large stores.

But the best place to change traveler's checks is at a bank. Do not bring traveler's checks denominated in other currencies, with the possible exception of those in Canadian dollars. Because of the proximity of the Canadian border, many hotels, restaurants, and shops will accept Canadian currency.

SAFETY

GENERAL   While tourist areas are generally safe, crime is on the increase everywhere, and U.S. urban areas tend to be less safe than those in Europe or Japan. Visitors should always be alert. This is particularly true of large U.S. cities. It is wise to ask the city's or area's tourist office if you are in doubt about which neighborhoods are safe.

Avoid deserted areas, especially at night. Don't enter a city park at night unless there is an event that attracts crowds—for example, a concert in a park. Generally speaking, you can feel safe in areas where there are many people, and many open establishments.

Avoid carrying valuables with you on the street, and don't display expensive cameras or electronic equipment. Hold on to your pocketbook, and place your billfold in an inside pocket. In restaurants, theaters, and other public places, keep your possessions in sight.

Remember also that hotels are open to the public, and in a large hotel, security personnel may not be able to screen everyone entering. Always lock your room door—don't assume that once inside your hotel you are automatically safe and need no longer be aware of your surroundings.

DRIVING   Safety while driving is particularly important. Question your car-rental agency about personal safety, or ask for a brochure of traveler safety tips when you pick up your car. Obtain written directions, or a map with the route marked in red, from the agency showing how to reach your destination. And, if possible, arrive and depart during daylight hours.

Recently, more and more crime has involved cars and drivers. If you drive off a highway into a neighborhood that seems threatening, leave the area as quickly as possible. If you have an accident, even on a highway, remain inside your car with the doors locked until you assess the situation, or until the police arrive. If you are bumped from behind on the street or are involved in a minor accident with no injuries and the situation appears to be suspicious, motion to the other driver to follow you to the nearest police precinct, a well-lighted service station, or an all-night store. Never get out of your car in such situations. You can also keep a premade sign in your car that reads: PLEASE FOLLOW THIS VEHICLE TO REPORT THE ACCIDENT.

If you see someone on the road who indicates a need for help, do not stop. Take note of the location, drive on to a well-lighted area, and telephone the police by dialing ☎ 911.

Park in well-lighted, well-traveled areas if possible. Always keep your car doors locked, whether attended or unattended. Look around you before you get in or out of your car, and never leave packages or valuables in sight. If someone attempts to rob you or steal your car, do not try to resist the thief/carjacker—report the incident to the police department immediately.

2 Getting to & Around the United States

GETTING TO THE UNITED STATES

Travelers from overseas can take advantage of **APEX** (advance purchase excursion) fares offered by all major U.S. and European carriers. Aside from these, attractive values are offered by **Virgin Atlantic Airways** from London to New York/Newark.

From Toronto, there are flights to Portland on **Air Canada** (☎ **800/268-7240** in Ontario, or **800/776-3000** in the U.S.), American, Delta, Northwest, TWA, and United.

There are flights **from Vancouver, B.C.,** to Portland on Air Canada and Horizon. In addition, Portland is served by **Amtrak** (☎ **800/872-7245**) Pacific Northwest Corridor trains, which connect Vancouver, B.C., with Seattle and Portland.

Airlines traveling **from London** to Seattle and Portland are American, Delta, Northwest, TWA, and United. British Airways flies directly from London to Seattle (which is 3^1/2 hours north of Portland by car).

You can make reservations by calling the following numbers in Britain: **American** (☎ 0181/572-5555), **British Airways** (☎ 0345/222-111), **Delta** (☎ 0800/ 414-767), **Northwest** (☎ 0990/56-1000), **TWA** (☎ 0181/814-0707), and **United** (☎ 0181/990-9900).

From Ireland, you can also try **Aer Lingus** (☎ 01/705-3154 in Ireland).

From New Zealand and Australia, there are flights to Los Angeles on **Qantas** (☎ 131211 in Australia) and **Air New Zealand** (☎ 0800/737-000 in Auckland, or 3/379-5200 in Christchurch). **United** flies to Seattle from New Zealand and Australia, with a stop in Los Angeles or San Francisco.

The visitor arriving by air, no matter what the port of entry, should cultivate patience and resignation before setting foot on U.S. soil. Getting through immigration control may take as long as 2 hours on some days, especially summer weekends. Add the time it takes to clear Customs and you'll see that you should make very generous allowance for delay in planning connections between international and domestic flights—an average of 2 to 3 hours at least.

In contrast, travelers arriving by car, rail, or ferry from Canada will find border-crossing formalities streamlined to the vanishing point. And air travelers from Canada, Bermuda, and some places in the Caribbean can sometimes go through Customs and Immigration at the point of departure, which is much quicker and less painful.

For further information about travel to and around Oregon, see "Getting There" and "Getting Around" in chapter 3.

GETTING AROUND THE UNITED STATES

BY PLANE   Some large airlines (for example, **American, Delta, Northwest, TWA,** and **United**) offer transatlantic and transpacific travelers special discount tickets under the name **Visit USA,** allowing travel between many U.S. destinations at minimum rates. These tickets are not on sale in the United States and must therefore be purchased before you leave your foreign point of departure. This system is the best, easiest, and fastest way to see the United States at low cost. You should obtain information well in advance from your travel agent or the office of the airline concerned, since the conditions attached to these discount tickets can be changed without advance notice.

BY CAR   The United States is a nation of cars and the most cost-effective, convenient, and comfortable way to travel through the country is by driving. The interstate highway system connects cities and towns all over the country, and in addition to these high-speed, limited-access roadways, there is an extensive network of federal, state, and local highways and roads. Another convenience of traveling by car is the easy access to inexpensive motels at interstate highway off-ramps. Such motels are almost always less expensive than hotels and motels in downtown areas.

If your driver's license isn't in English, check with your foreign auto club to see if they can provide you with an International Driving Permit validating your foreign license in the United States.

For more information on getting around Oregon by car, see the "Getting Around" section in chapter 3.

BY TRAIN   International visitors can buy a **USA Railpass,** good for 15 or 30 days of unlimited nationwide travel on **Amtrak** (☎ **800/872-7245**). The pass is available through many foreign travel agents and at any staffed Amtrak station in the United States. The price at press time for a 15-day peak period pass was $375, and for a 15-day off-peak period pass, $260; a 30-day peak period pass cost $480, and a 30-day off-peak period pass was $350. (With a foreign passport, you can also buy passes at major Amtrak offices in the United States, including locations in San Francisco, Los Angeles, Chicago, New York, Miami, Boston, and Washington, D.C.) Reservations are generally required and should be made for each part of your trip as early as possible. Amtrak also offers a program called **Amtrak Vacations,** which allows you to travel both by train and plane and includes hotel bookings; for information call ☎ **800/321-8684.**

Visitors should also be aware of the limitations of long-distance rail travel in the United States. With a few notable exceptions (for instance, the Northeast Corridor line between Boston and Washington, D.C.), service is rarely up to European standard: delays are common, routes are limited and often infrequently served, and fares are rarely significantly lower than discount airfares. Thus, cross-country train travel should be approached with caution.

BY BUS   The cheapest way to travel the United States is by bus. **Greyhound** (☎ **800/231-2222**), the nation's nationwide bus line, offers an Ameripass for unlimited travel for 7 days (for $179), 15 days (for $289), and 30 days (for $399). Bus travel in the United States can be both slow and uncomfortable, so this option is not for everyone.

FAST FACTS: For the Foreign Traveler

Accommodations   It is always a good idea to make hotel reservations as soon as you know your trip dates. Reservations require a deposit of one night's payment. Portland and the Oregon coast are particularly busy during summer months, and hotels book up in advance—especially on weekends when there is a festival on. If you do not have reservations, it is best to look for a room in the midafternoon. If you wait until evening, you run the risk that hotels will be filled. Major downtown hotels, which cater primarily to business travelers, commonly offer weekend discounts of as much as 50% to entice vacationers to fill up the empty rooms. However, resorts and hotels near tourist attractions tend to have higher rates on weekends.

Automobile Organizations   Auto clubs will supply maps, suggested routes, guidebooks, accident and bail-bond insurance, and emergency road service. The major auto club in the United States, with 955 offices nationwide, is the American Automobile Association (AAA). Members of some foreign auto clubs have reciprocal arrangements with the AAA and enjoy its services at no charge. If you belong to an auto club, inquire about AAA reciprocity before you leave. You may be able to join the AAA even if you are not a member of a reciprocal club. To inquire, call ☎ **800/ AAA-HELP.** In addition, some automobile rental agencies now provide these services, so you should inquire about their availability when you rent your car.

Automobile Rentals   To rent a car you need a major credit card and a valid driver's license. Sometimes a passport or an international driver's license is also required if your driver's license is in a language other than English. You usually need to be at least 25, although some companies do rent to younger people but may add a daily surcharge. Be sure to return your car with the same amount of gasoline you started out with, as rental companies charge excessive prices for gas. Keep in mind that a separate motorcycle-driver's license is required in most states. See "Getting Around," in chapter 3 for specifics on auto rental in Oregon.

Business Hours   Banks are open weekdays from 9am to 5pm, with later hours on Friday; many banks are now open on Saturday also. There is also 24-hour access to banks through automatic teller machines (ATMs) at most banks and other outlets. Most offices are open weekdays from 9am to 5pm. Most post offices are open weekdays from 8am to 5pm, with shorter hours on Saturday. In general, stores open between 9 and 10am and close between 5 and 6pm, Monday through Saturday; stores in malls generally stay open until 9pm; some department stores stay open till 9pm on Thursday and Friday evening; and many stores are open on Sunday from 11am to 5 or 6pm.

Climate   See "When to Go," in chapter 3.

Currency   See "Money" in "Preparing for Your Trip," above.

Currency Exchange   You will find currency exchange services in major airports with international service (including Portland International Airport). Elsewhere, they may be quite difficult to come by.

   To exchange money in Portland, go to **American Express,** 1100 SW Sixth Ave. (☎ 206/226-2961), or **Thomas Cook at Powell's Travel Store,** 701 SW Sixth Ave. (☎ 206/222-2665).

Drinking Laws   The legal drinking age in Oregon is 21. The penalties for driving under the influence of alcohol are stiff.

Electricity   The United States uses 110 to 120 volts AC (60 cycles), compared to 220 to 240 volts AC (50 cycles), in most of Europe. In addition to a 110-volt converter, small appliances of non-American manufacture, such as hair dryers or shavers, will require a plug adapter with two flat, parallel pins.

Embassies & Consulates   All embassies are located in the national capital, Washington, D.C. Some consulates are located in major cities, and most nations have a mission to the United Nations in New York City. Listed here are embassies and consulates of some major English-speaking countries. If you are from another country, you can obtain the telephone number of your embassy or consulate by calling Information in Washington, D.C. (☎ **202/555-1212**).

The **Australian embassy** is at 1601 Massachusetts Ave. NW, Washington, DC 20036 (☎ **202/797-3000**). The nearest consulate is in San Francisco at 1 Bush St., San Francisco, CA 94104-4425 (☎ 415/362-6160).

The **Canadian embassy** is at 501 Pennsylvania Ave. NW, Washington, DC 20001 (☎ **202/682-1740**). The regional consulate is at 412 Plaza 600 Building, Sixth Avenue and Stewart Street, Seattle, WA 98101-1286 (☎ 206/443-1777).

The **Irish embassy** is at 2234 Massachusetts Ave. NW, Washington, DC 20008 (☎ **202/462-3939**). The nearest consulate is in San Francisco at 44 Montgomery St., Suite 3830, San Francisco, CA 94104 (☎ 415/392-4214).

The **New Zealand embassy** is at 37 Observatory Circle NW, Washington, DC 20008 (☎ **202/328-4800**). The nearest consulate is in Los Angeles at 12400 Wilshire Blvd., Suite 1150, Los Angeles, CA 90025 (☎ 310/207-1605).

The **British embassy** is at 3100 Massachusetts Ave. NW, Washington, DC 20008 (☎ **202/462-1340**). There is a consulate in Seattle at 999 Third Ave., Suite 820, Seattle, WA 98104 (☎ 206/622-9255).

Emergencies   Call ☎ **911** to report a fire, call the police, or get an ambulance. This is a toll-free call (no coins are required at a public telephone).

Gasoline (Petrol)   One U.S. gallon equals 3.75 liters, while 1.2 U.S. gallons equals one Imperial gallon. You'll notice there are several grades (and price levels) of gasoline available at most gas stations. And you'll also notice that their names change from company to company. The unleaded ones with the highest octane are the most expensive (most rental cars take the least expensive "regular" unleaded) and leaded gas is the least expensive, but only older cars can take this any more, so check if you're not sure. In Oregon you are not allowed to pump your own gasoline.

Holidays   On the following legal national holidays, banks, government offices, post offices, and many stores, restaurants, and museums are closed: January 1 (New Year's Day), third Monday in January (Martin Luther King Jr. Day), third Monday in February (Presidents' Day, Washington's Birthday), last Monday in May (Memorial Day), July 4 (Independence Day), first Monday in September (Labor Day), second Monday in October (Columbus Day), November 11 (Veterans Day/Armistice Day), fourth Thursday in November (Thanksgiving Day), December 25 (Christmas Day).

The Tuesday following the first Monday in November is Election Day, and is a legal holiday in presidential-election years.

Languages   Major hotels may have multilingual employees. Unless your language is very obscure, they can usually supply a translator on request.

Legal Aid   If you are stopped for a minor driving infraction (for example, of the highway code, such as speeding), never attempt to pay the fine directly to the police officer; you may wind up arrested on the much more serious charge of attempted bribery. Pay fines by mail, or directly into the hands of the clerk of the court. If accused of a more serious offense, it is wise to say and do nothing before consulting a lawyer. Under U.S. law, an arrested person is allowed one telephone call to a party of his or her choice. Call your embassy or consulate.

Mail   If you want to receive mail on your vacation and you aren't sure of your address, your mail can be sent to you, in your name, c/o General Delivery at the main post office of the city or region where you expect to be. The addressee must pick it up in person and produce proof of identity (driver's license, credit card, passport).

Generally to be found at intersections, mailboxes are blue with a red-and-white stripe and carry the inscription U.S. MAIL. If your mail is addressed to a U.S.

destination, don't forget to add the five-figure postal code, or zip (zone improvement plan) code, after the two-letter abbreviation of the state to which the mail is addressed (OR for Oregon, WA for Washington, CA for California, and so on).

Medical Emergencies   Dial ☎ **911** for an ambulance.

Newspapers/Magazines   National newspapers include *The New York Times, USA Today,* and the *Wall Street Journal.* National news weeklies include *Newsweek, Time,* and *U.S. News and World Report.* For local news publications, see "Fast Facts: Portland" in chapter 6 for Portland.

Radio & Television   Radio and TV, with four coast-to-coast networks—ABC, CBS, NBC, and Fox—joined by the Public Broadcasting System (PBS) and the cable network CNN, play a major part in American life. In big cities, viewers have a choice of about a dozen channels (including the UHF channels), most of them transmitting 24 hours a day, without counting the pay-TV channels showing recent movies or sports events. All options are usually indicated on your hotel TV set. You'll also find a wide choice of local radio stations, each broadcasting particular kinds of talk shows and/or music—classical, country, jazz, pop, gospel—punctuated by news broadcasts and frequent commercials.

Safety   See "Safety" in "Preparing for Your Trip," above.

Taxes   In the United States there is no VAT (value-added tax) or other indirect tax at a national level. Every state, and each city in it, can levy a local tax on all purchases, including hotel and restaurant checks, airline tickets, and so on. In Portland and the rest of Oregon, there is no sales tax.

Telephone, Telegraph, Telex & Fax   The telephone system in the United States is run by private corporations, so rates, especially for long distance service, can vary widely, even on calls made from public telephones. Local calls from a **public pay telephone** in the United States usually cost 25¢.

Generally, hotel surcharges on **long-distance** and local calls are astronomical. You are usually better off using a public pay telephone, which you will find clearly marked in most public buildings and private establishments as well as on the street. Outside metropolitan areas, public telephones are more difficult to find. Stores and gas stations are your best bet.

Most **long-distance** and **international calls** can be dialed directly from any phone. For calls to Canada and other parts of the United States, dial 1 followed by the area code and the seven-digit number. For international calls, dial 011 followed by the country code, city code, and the telephone number of the person you wish to call.

For **reversed-charge** or **collect calls,** and for person-to-person calls, dial 0 (zero, not the letter "O"), followed by the area code and number you want; an operator will then come on the line, and you should specify that you are calling collect, or person-to-person, or both. If your operator-assisted call is international, ask for the overseas operator.

For **local directory assistance** ("information"), dial ☎ **555-1212;** for long-distance information, dial 1, then the appropriate area code and 555-1212.

Like the telephone system, **telegraph** and **telex services** are provided by private corporations like ITT, MCI, and, above all, Western Union. You can take your telegram to the nearest **Western Union** office (there are hundreds across the country), or dictate it over the phone (a toll-free call, ☎ **800/325-6000**). You can also telegraph money, or have it telegraphed to you very quickly over the Western Union system.

If you need to send a fax, almost all shops that make photocopies offer fax service as well. Many hotels also offer faxing service.

Telephone Directory   There are two kinds of telephone directories available to you. The general directory is the so-called White Pages, in which private and business subscribers are listed in alphabetical order.

The inside front cover lists emergency numbers for police, fire, and ambulance, as well as other vital numbers (coast guard, poison control center, crime-victims hot line, and so on). The first few pages are devoted to community-service numbers, including a guide to long-distance and international calling, complete with country codes and area codes.

The second directory, printed on yellow paper (hence its name, Yellow Pages), lists local services, businesses, and industries by type, with an index at the back. The listings cover not only such obvious items as automobile repair services by make of car, or drugstores (pharmacies), often by geographical location, but also restaurants by type of cuisine and geographical location, bookstores by special subject and/or language, places of worship by religious denomination, and other information that the tourist might otherwise not readily find. The Yellow Pages also include city plans or detailed area maps, often showing postal zip codes and public transportation.

Time   The United States is divided into four time zones (six, if Alaska and Hawaii are included). From east to west, these are: eastern standard time (EST), central standard time (CST), mountain standard time (MST), Pacific standard time (PST), Alaska standard time (AST), and Hawaii standard time (HST). Always keep changing time zones in mind if you are traveling (or even telephoning) long distance in the United States. For example, noon in Portland (PT) is 1pm in Denver (MT), 2pm in Chicago (CT), 3pm in New York City (ET), 11am in Anchorage (AT), and 10am in Honolulu (HT). Daylight saving time is in effect from 2am on the first Sunday in April until 2am on the last Sunday in October except in Arizona, Hawaii, part of Indiana, and Puerto Rico. Daylight saving time moves the clock 1 hour ahead of standard time.

Tipping   This is part of the American way of life, on the principle that you must expect to pay for any service you get. Here are some rules of thumb: bartenders: 10% to 15%; bellhops: at least 50¢ per piece, $2 to $3 for a lot of baggage; cab drivers: 15% of the fare; cafeterias, fast-food restaurants: no tip; chambermaids: $1 a day; checkroom attendants (restaurants, theaters): $1 per garment; cinemas, movies, theaters: no tip; doormen (hotels or restaurants): not obligatory; gas-station attendants: no tip; hairdressers: 15% to 20%; redcaps (airport and railroad stations): at least 50¢ per piece, $2 to $3 for a lot of baggage; restaurants, night-clubs: 15% to 20% of the check; sleeping-car porters: $2 to $3 per night to your attendant; and valet parking attendants: $1.

Toilets   Foreign visitors often complain that public toilets (or "rest rooms") are hard to find in most U.S. cities. True, there are none on the streets, but the visitor can usually find one in a bar, restaurant, hotel, museum, department store, or service station and it will probably be clean (although the last-mentioned sometimes leaves much to be desired).

Note, however, that some restaurants and bars display a notice that TOILETS ARE FOR THE USE OF PATRONS ONLY. You can ignore this sign, or better yet, avoid arguments by ordering a cup of coffee or a soft drink, which will qualify you as a patron. The cleanliness of toilets at railroad stations and bus depots may be questionable; some public places are equipped with pay toilets, which require you to insert one or more coins into a slot on the door before it will open.

5 The Oregon Coast

Stretching from the mouth of the Columbia River in the north to California's redwood country in the south, the Oregon coast is a shoreline of stunning natural beauty. In many spots along the coast, the mountains of the densely forested Coast Range rise straight from the ocean's waves to form rugged, windswept headlands still bearing the colorful names given them by early explorers—Cape Foulweather, Cape Blanco, Cape Perpetua. Offshore lie hundreds of monoliths and tiny islands that serve as homes to sea birds, sea lions, and seals. Lying between these rocky points are miles of sandy beaches. On the central coast there's so much sand that sand dunes rise as high as 500 feet.

To allow visitors to enjoy all this beauty, the state has created nearly 80 **state parks** and **waysides** between Fort Stevens State Park in the north and Winchuck Wayside in the south. Among the more popular activities at these parks are kite flying and beachcombing, but not swimming (the water is too cold). For information on **camping** in area state parks, call the state parks information line at ☎ **800/551-6949;** to make a camping reservation, contact **Reservations Northwest,** 2501 SW First St., Suite 100, Portland, OR 97201 (☎ **800/452-5687** or 503/731-3411).

Wildlife is abundant along the coast, and sea lions and seals can often be seen sunning themselves on rocks. The best places to observe these sea mammals are at Sea Lion Caves north of Florence and at Cape Arago State Park outside of Coos Bay. Gray whales are also regular visitors to the Oregon coast. Twice a year, during their migrations between the Arctic and the waters off Baja California, Mexico, the whales pass close by the coast and can be easily spotted from headlands such as Tillamook Head, Cape Meares, Cape Lookout, and Cape Blanco. The best time to spot whales is in late winter and early spring, although some stick around all summer. At the Oregon Coast Aquarium in Newport, you can learn more about these and all the myriad other animals and plants that inhabit the diverse aquatic environments of the Oregon coast. Near the town of Reedsport, the Dean Creek meadows have been set aside as an elk preserve, and it's often possible to spot 100 or more elk grazing here.

Rivers, bays, and offshore waters are also home to some of the best **fishing** in the country. The rivers, though depleted by a century of overfishing, are still home to salmon, steelhead, and trout, most of which are now hatchery raised. Several charter-boat marinas up and down the coast offer saltwater fishing for salmon and bottom fish, and few anglers return from these trips without a good catch. **Crabbing** and **clamming** are two more productive coastal pursuits that can turn a trip to the beach into a time for feasting.

As we've already mentioned, it rains a lot here. Bring a raincoat, and don't let a little moisture prevent you from enjoying one of the most beautiful coastlines in the world. In fact, the mists and fogs add an aura of mystery to the coast's dark, forested mountain slopes. Contrary to what you might think, the hot days of July and August are not always the best time to visit this coast. When it's baking inland, the coast is often shrouded in fog. The best months to visit are often September and October, when the weather is often fine and the crowds are gone.

1 Astoria

95 miles NW of Portland; 20 miles S of Long Beach, WA; 17 miles N of Seaside

As the oldest American community west of the Mississippi, Astoria abounds in history. In the winter of 1805–06, Lewis and Clark, having crossed the continent by boat and on foot, built a fort nearby and established an American claim to the region. Five years later, in 1811, fur traders working for John Jacob Astor arrived at the mouth of the Columbia River to set up a fur-trading fort that was named Fort Astoria. During the War of 1812, the fort was turned over to the British, but by 1818, it had reverted to American hands. By the mid–19th century, the town boasted the state of Oregon's first brewery. When the salmon-canning boom hit in the 1880s, Astoria became a bustling little city, and wealthy merchants began erecting ornate, Victorian-style homes.

Today, with no beach to call its own, Astoria's greatest attraction lies in its many blocks of restored Victorian homes and its riverfront setting near the mouth of the mighty Columbia River. These Victorian homes date from the 1870s when salmon canneries turned the town into the state's second-largest city, and while Astoria still has its seamy sections of waterfront, it is also developing something of a tourist-oriented waterfront character. However, fish-packing plants still outnumber ice cream parlors.

ESSENTIALS

GETTING THERE   From Portland, take U.S. 30 west. From the north or south, take U.S. 101.

Air service to Astoria from Seattle and Portland is provided by **Harbor Air** (☎ **800/359-3220**), which is an Alaska Airlines commuter service. Astoria is also served by **Pacific Transit System** buses (☎ **360/642-9418**) from the Washington coast as far north as Raymond, Washington. **Pacific Pierce Stages** (☎ **503/436-1859** or 503/717-1651) provides bus service from Portland, Seaside, and Cannon Beach. **Sunset Empire Transit** (☎ **800/776-6406** or 503/325-0563) provides public bus service from Astoria to Seaside and Cannon Beach.

VISITOR INFORMATION   Contact the **Astoria-Warrenton Area Chamber of Commerce,** 111 W. Marine Dr. (P.O. Box 176), Astoria, OR 97103-0176 (☎ **503/325-6311**).

GETTING AROUND   Car rentals are available through Enterprise Rent-a-Car (☎ **800/RENTACAR** or 503/325-6500). If you need a taxi, contact **Yellow Cab** (☎ **503/325-3131**).

FESTIVALS   The **Astoria Regatta,** held each year in early August, is the city's biggest festival and includes lots of sailboat races. As part of the festival you can catch a performance of the Astor Street Opry Company's *Shanghaied in Astoria,* a musical melodrama staged at the Astoria Eagles Lodge, Ninth and Commercial streets (☎ **503/325-6104**). This usually runs from early July to late August.

EXPLORING ASTORIA'S HISTORY

Columbia River Maritime Museum. 1792 Marine Dr. ☎ **503/325-2323.** Admission $5 adults, $4 seniors, $2 children 6–17. Daily 9:30am–5pm. Closed Thanksgiving and Dec 25.

The Columbia River, the second-largest river in the United States, was the object of centuries of exploration in the Northwest, and since its discovery in 1792, this river has become as important to the region as the Mississippi is to the Midwest. This boldly designed museum, built to resemble waves on the ocean, tells the story of the river's maritime history. Displays on shipwrecks, lighthouses, and lifesaving are all testament to the dangerous waters at the mouth of the Columbia. Here, high seas and the constantly shifting sands of the Columbia Bar conspire to make this one of the world's most difficult rivers to enter (over the centuries hundreds of ships have sunk here). Fishing, navigation, and naval history are also subjects of museum exhibits. Docked beside the museum and open to museum visitors is the lightship *Columbia,* the last seagoing lighthouse ship to serve on the West Coast.

✪ **Fort Clatsop National Memorial.** Off U.S. 101, 5 miles southwest of Astoria. ☎ **503/ 861-2471.** Admission $3 per person or $5 per car (not charged in winter months). Labor Day to mid-June daily 8am–5pm; mid-June to Labor Day daily 8am–6pm. Closed Dec 25.

During the winter of 1805–06, Meriwether Lewis, William Clark, and the other members of the Corps of Discovery, having crossed the continent from St. Louis, camped at a spot near the mouth of the Columbia River. They built a log stockade and named their encampment Fort Clatsop after the local Clatsop Indians who had befriended them. Today's Fort Clatsop is a reconstruction of Lewis and Clark's winter encampment and is built near the site of the original fort. The 50-foot-square compound contains seven rooms, each of which is furnished much as it may have been during Lewis and Clark's stay. On weekends in late spring and daily during the summer, park rangers clad in period clothing give demonstrations of activities pursued by the explorers, from candlemaking and firearms use to buckskin sewing and food preparation. In the visitor center you can learn the history of the Corps of Discovery and Fort Clatsop before visiting the stockade itself.

Flavel House Museum. 441 Eighth St. ☎ **503/325-2203.** Admission $5 adults, $2.50 children. May–Sept daily 10am–5pm; October–April daily 11am–4pm.

The Flavel House, owned and operated by the Clatsop County Historical Society, is the grandest and most ornate of Astoria's many Victorian homes. This Queen Anne-style Victorian mansion was built in 1885 by Capt. George Flavel, who made his fortune operating the first pilot service over the Columbia River Bar and was Astoria's first millionaire. When constructed, this house was the envy of every Astoria resident. The high-ceilinged rooms are filled with period furnishings that accent the home's superb construction, and throughout the house there is much ornate woodworking.

Admission to the Flavel House also gets you into the nearby **Heritage Museum,** 1618 Exchange St., which is housed in Astoria's former city hall and chronicles the history of Astoria and surrounding Clatsop County. Native American and pioneer artifacts comprise the main exhibits, but there are also an art gallery and a collection of historic photos dating from the 1880s to the 1930s.

Flavel House tickets also get you into the **Uppertown Fire Fighters Museum,** on the corner of 30th Street and Marine Drive. Housed in a former brewery building that was closed by Prohibition, the museum includes fire-fighting equipment dating from between 1877 and 1921.

The Northern Oregon Coast

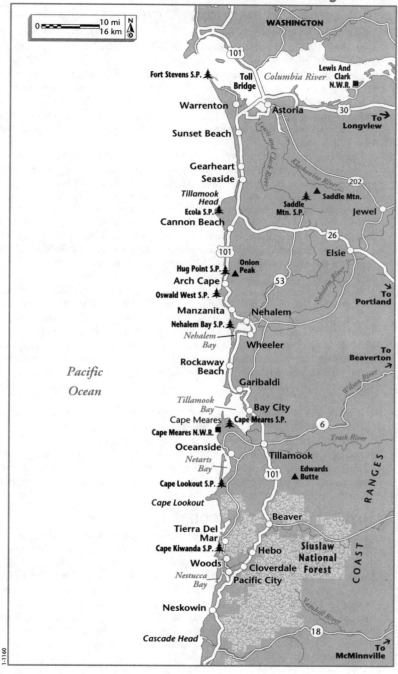

0 ___ 10 mi
___ 16 km
N

WASHINGTON

Fort Stevens S.P.

Toll
Bridge

Columbia River

Lewis And
Clark
N.W.R.

Warrenton

Astoria

30

To
Longview

Sunset Beach

Lewis and Clark River

Klaskanine River

202

Gearheart

Seaside

Saddle Mtn.

*Tillamook
Head*

Ecola S.P.

Cannon Beach

Saddle
Mtn. S.P.

Jewel

26

Elsie

101

Hug Point S.P.

Onion
Peak

Nehalem River

Arch Cape

53

Oswald West S.P.

To
Portland

Manzanita

Nehalem

Nehalem Bay S.P.

*Nehalem
Bay*

Wheeler

To
Beaverton

Rockaway
Beach

Garibaldi

Wilson River

*Tillamook
Bay*

Bay City

Cape Meares

Cape Meares S.P.

*Pacific
Ocean*

Cape Meares N.W.R.

6

Trask River

Oceanside

*Netarts
Bay*

Tillamook

Edwards
Butte

101

R
A
N
G
E
S

Cape Lookout S.P.

Cape Lookout

Beaver

Tierra Del
Mar

Cape Kiwanda S.P.

Hebo

Siuslaw
National
Forest

Woods

Cloverdale

C
O
A
S
T

*Nestucca
Bay*

Pacific City

Neskowin

Yamhill River

Cascade Head

18

To
McMinnville

1-1160

55

OTHER ASTORIA ATTRACTIONS & ACTIVITIES

Atop Coxcomb Hill, which is reached by driving up 16th Street and following the signs, you'll find the **Astoria Column.** Built in 1926, the column is patterned after Trajan's Column in Rome and stands 125 feet tall. On the exterior wall of the column a mural depicts the history of this area. It's 164 steps up to the top of the column, and on a clear day the view is well worth the effort. The column is open daily from dawn to dusk and admission is free. On the way to the Astoria Column, stop by **Fort Astoria,** on the corner of 15th and Exchange streets. A log blockhouse and historical marker commemorate the site of the trading post established by John Jacob Astor's fur traders.

There are several places in downtown where you can linger by the riverside atop the docks that once comprised much of the city's waterfront. Stop by the **Sixth Street Viewing Dock,** where there is a raised viewing platform as well as a fishing dock. From here you can gaze out at the massive Astoria-Megler Bridge, which stretches for more than 4 miles across the mouth of the Columbia River. Also keep an eye out for sea lions, which like to feed in the waters here. A few blocks away, you'll also find the **14th Street River Park.** If you'd like to see the waterfront from a different perspective, you can book a river cruise through **Tiki Charters** (☎ **503/325-7818**). Cruises of the Astoria waterfront are $15 per person, and trips upriver to Cathlamet are $60 per person.

Right in downtown Astoria, you'll find one of the most unusual wineries in the state. **Shallon Winery,** 1598 Duane St. (☎ **503/325-5978**), specializes in fruit wines including vintages made from Himalayan blackberries, evergreen blackberries, black raspberries, and apples. However, it is the winery's unique whey wines that are the greatest achievement of winemaker Paul van der Veldt. The Cran du Lait, made with local cranberries and whey from the Tillamook cheese factory, is a surprisingly smooth and drinkable wine. However, the most amazing wine here is the chocolate-orange wine, a thick nectar that will make a chocoholic of anyone.

If you'd like to see what area artists are up to, stop by the **Ricciardi Gallery,** 108 Tenth St. (☎ **503/325-5450**), which also has an espresso bar.

Over the past decade, quite a few popular movies have been shot in Astoria, including *Kindergarten Cop, Free Willy, Goonies, Short Circuit,* and *Teenage Mutant Ninja Turtles III.* If you're interested in seeing some of the sites where these films were shot, you can pick up the "Shot In Astoria" booklet ($1) at the chamber of commerce visitor center.

ENJOYING THE GREAT OUTDOORS

Fort Stevens State Park, 8 miles from Astoria at the mouth of the Columbia (☎ **503/861-1671**), preserves a fort that was built during the Civil War to protect the Columbia River and its important port cities. Though Fort Stevens had the distinction of being the only mainland military reservation to be fired on by the Japanese, the fort was deactivated after World War II. Today the fort's extensive grounds include historic buildings and gun emplacements, a museum housing military artifacts, miles of bicycle paths and beaches, and a campground and picnic area. Admission is $3. At the north end of the park you can climb to the top of a viewing tower and get a good look at the South Jetty, which was built to make navigating the mouth of the Columbia easier. Also within the park you can see the wreck of the *Peter Iredale,* one ship that did not make it safely over the sandbars at the river's mouth. Bicycle rentals are available just outside the park from **Fort Stevens Bicycle Rentals,** 316 Russell Dr., Hammon (☎ **503/861-0937**).

One of the most unusual bicycle excursions in the country can be had in downtown Astoria from **Railbike Tours of Astoria** (☎ **800/994-5590, ext. 90**), which operates specially designed bicycles on abandoned railroad tracks in the Astoria area. Trips along this track provide a chance to see the Astoria waterfront from a unique perspective, and along the way you cross several trestles, pass a colony of sea lions, and skirt several wetlands and sloughs. Tours are $12 per person.

If you're interested in exploring the waters of the Astoria area, you can rent a kayak from **Pacific Wave Kayaks,** 2021 U.S. 101, Premarq Centre, Warrenton (☎ **503/861-0866**), which also offers classes and guided tours.

Several charter fishing boats operate out of nearby Warrenton. Trips can be arranged through **Tiki Charters** (☎ **503/325-7818**) and **Charlton Deep Sea Charters** (☎ **503/861-2429**). Expect to pay around $65.

A few miles outside of town on Ore. 30, bird watchers will find a roadside viewing platform overlooking the marshes of the **Twilight Creek Eagle Sanctuary.** Take Burnside Road off Ore. 30 between the John Day River and Svenson.

WHERE TO STAY

Clementine's Bed and Breakfast. 847 Exchange St., Astoria, OR 97103. ☎ **800/521-6801** or 503/325-2005. 5 rms. $55–$80 double. AE, DISC, MC, V.

Located across the street from the Flavel House Museum, this eclectic little inn is surrounded by a beautiful flower garden and has its own cafe next door. The inn, built in 1888 in the Italianate Victorian style, is now filled with Asian arts and antiques, and in summer is always filled with fresh cut flowers from the gardens. Rooms vary considerably in size. Two rooms have their own little balconies, and several have expansive views of the river and town. Guests also can use the inn's sit-on-top sea kayaks at no extra charge. With backgrounds in music and river guiding on the Colorado River, innkeepers Judith and Cliff Taylor keep guests entertained and informed about what there is to see and do in the area.

Columbia River Inn Bed & Breakfast. 1681 Franklin Ave., Astoria, OR 97103. ☎ **800/953-5044** or 503/325-5044. 4 rms. $75–$125 double. Rates include full breakfast. MC, V.

With a classic pink-and-blue "painted lady" exterior, this Victorian house overlooks downtown Astoria and the Columbia River and is surrounded by colorful gardens in summer. Inside, reproduction Victorian-era furnishings set the stage for a stay with friendly proprietor Karen Nelson. Much of the inn's country decor was done by the owner, and if you see something you like, you just might be able to buy a similar item at the inn's Krafty's Korner gift shop. Each room is decorated differently, but they all have a little refrigerator and an electric teapot. The Victorian Rose and River Queen rooms have the best views. In order to get private bathrooms into every room, some strange remodeling had to be done. In Amanda's Room, an odd little shower was tucked into one corner.

Crest Motel. 5366 Leif Erickson Dr. (about 2 miles east of town on U.S. 30), Astoria, OR 97103. ☎ **800/421-3141** or 503/325-3141. Fax 503/325-3141. 40 rms. TV TEL. $52.50–$82.50 double. AE, CB, DC, DISC, MC, V.

Located a few miles from downtown Astoria, the Crest Motel sits high on a hillside overlooking the town and the river. The views, congenial atmosphere, and comfortable refurbished rooms have made this motel immensely popular. Keep in mind that the lower-priced rooms have no views—and since the views are the main reason to stay here, it's worth a bit of a splurge for a better room even if you're on a tight budget. The deluxe-view rooms are very large and have sliding glass doors and a patio or balcony. You'll also find a coffeemaker in your room and a whirlpool tub in a gazebo overlooking the river.

⊗ **Franklin Street Station Bed and Breakfast Inn.** 1140 Franklin St., Astoria, OR 97103. ☎ **800/448-1098** or 503/325-4314. Fax 503/325-2275. 5 rms. $68–$120 double. Rates include full breakfast. AE, DISC, MC, V.

Owned and operated by Renée Caldwell, the daughter of the Columbia River Inn's hostess, this bed-and-breakfast is 3 blocks from downtown Astoria. Though from the exterior this house doesn't seem to epitomize Victorian ornateness, inside you'll find rich wood accents and trim in every room. Built in 1900, the large house has been completely renovated and each of the guest rooms now has a private bathroom. The best room in the house, if you don't mind the climb, is the attic Captain's Quarters, which has a great view of the Columbia, a claw-foot tub, TV, VCR, stereo, and wet bar. The Columbia Room is another of our favorites because of its river-view deck.

Officer's Inn Bed and Breakfast. 540 Russell Place, Hammond, OR 97121. ☎ **800/ 377-2524** or 503/861-0884. 9 rms. $75–$95 double. MC, V.

Housed in the former Fort Stevens officers' quarters built in 1905, this sprawling 8,000-square-foot B&B is located just around the corner from the Fort Stevens Museum. Once a duplex, the inn captures the essence of small town America with its long front porch overlooking the old parade grounds. Inside, you'll find simple, classic decor. However, it is the perfectly preserved pressed-tin ceilings of the parlors and dining rooms that are the inn's finest feature. Guest rooms vary in size, and come with king, queen, or double beds. There are even two rooms set up for families. Any time of year, but especially in spring and fall, you might see elk grazing in the field behind the inn.

Rosebriar Hotel. 636 14th St., Astoria, OR 97103. ☎ **800/487-0224** or 503/325-7427. Fax 503/325-6937. 10 rms, 1 cottage. TV TEL. $39–$155 double. Rates include full gourmet breakfast. AE, CB, DC, MC, V.

Originally built as a private home, the Rosebriar became a convent in the 1950s before being renovated and turned into a small hotel in the 1990s. In its current incarnation, the Rosebriar is decorated in the style of a 1920s hotel. Ornate wainscoting, scrollwork ceilings, and lots of wood trim show the quality of workmanship that went into this home when it was built in 1902. The grand old Georgian mansion sits high above the river and high above the street, with commanding views from the two front rooms. If you're seeking that extra bit of privacy for a special occasion, ask for the carriage-house cottage, which has its own fireplace, whirlpool tub, and private patio.

CAMPGROUNDS

Fort Stevens State Park, on the beach at the mouth of the Columbia River, is one of the largest and most popular state park campgrounds on the Oregon coast. For reservations, contact **Reservations Northwest** (☎ **800/452-5687**).

WHERE TO DINE

In addition to the restaurants listed below, you might also want to check out **Josephson's,** 106 Marine Dr. (☎ **503/325-2190**), which is a local seafood-smoking company that sells smoked salmon by the pound, but that also has a take-out deli counter where you can get clam chowder, crab melts, and the like. If you're looking for some local ale, stop by **The Wet Dog Cafe,** 144 11th St. (☎ **503/325-6975**), the town's only brew pub. If it's ice cream you need, try the **Riverside Ice Cream & Candy Parlour,** 1 Sixth St., Pier B (☎ **503/325-5218**), which is the oldest ice cream parlor in town.

MODERATE

Ira's. 915 Commercial St. ☎ **503/338-6192.** Reservations recommended. Main dishes $13–$18; lunch main dishes $6–$7. DISC, MC, V. Mon 11am–3pm, Tues–Thurs 11am–3pm and 5:30–9pm, Fri–Sat 11am–3pm and 5:30–10pm, Sun 5:30–9pm. NORTHWEST.

Located on Astoria's main downtown commercial street (thus the street name), this is the town's most upscale restaurant and draws a very urban and affluent crowd. For a starter, try the home-cured gravlax (salmon), which is made with maple syrup and served with cucumbers, onion, crème fraîche, and capers. Smoked salmon also shows up in an intriguing salad with a ginger-orange vinaigrette. If you haven't yet had your fill of salmon, the salmon in parchment with mango chutney is one of the restaurant's most reliable entrees. At lunch, there are some interesting sandwiches to be had, although the smoked salmon burrito is a definite winner.

Pier 11 Feed Store Restaurant. At the foot of Tenth St. ☎ **503/325-0279.** Reservations recommended. Main dishes $12–$19; lunch main dishes $4.50–$9.75. DISC, MC, V. Daily 11am–10pm. SEAFOOD.

Originally a freight depot for river cargo and one of the few buildings in town that was not destroyed by a fire in 1922, Pier 11 now houses a few small shops and this popular, though touristy, seafood restaurant. Nearly everyone gets a good view of the river through the restaurant's wall of glass, and if you're lucky you might spot some seals or sea lions frolicking just outside the window. Meals are simply prepared and are usually quite good, although the restaurant does have an occasional off night. The blackened prime rib is excellent.

INEXPENSIVE

The Cannery Cafe. Sixth St. at the Columbia River. ☎ **503/325-8642.** Reservations recommended. Main dishes $7–$18; lunch main dishes $4.50–$8. MC, V. Mon 11am–3pm, Tues–Sat 11am–9pm, Sun 9:30am–2:30pm. SEAFOOD/NORTHWEST.

Housed in a restored salmon cannery, this small, bright restaurant provides a more contemporary dining alternative to the aging Pier 11. You get the same views and are just as likely to see sea lions out the window, but the food is much more creative. For nightly specials, chefs draw upon world cuisines for inspiration, and on a recent evening it included North African stew, pork loin rolled with pesto, and lime-marinated prawns. Lunches are mostly grilled sandwiches, salads, and good chowder.

✪ **Columbian Café.** 1114 Marine Dr. ☎ **503/325-2233.** Breakfast or lunch $3.25–$6.50; dinner $5–$10. No credit cards. Mon–Tues 8am–2pm, Wed–Thurs 8am–2pm and 5–8pm, Fri 8am–2pm and 5–9pm, Sat 10am–2pm and 5–9pm, Sun 9am–4pm. VEGETARIAN/SEAFOOD.

This tiny place looks a bit like a cross between a college hangout and a seaport diner, and indeed the clientele reflects this atmosphere. There are only three or four booths and a lunch counter, and the cafe's reputation for good vegetarian fare keeps the seats full throughout the day. Crepes are the house specialty and come with a variety of fillings, including black beans or curried bananas. Dinner offers a bit more variety, and there are always a few specials. If you should see anything on the menu made with *mole* sauce, be sure to order it; it's sure to be great. Even the condiments here, including pepper jelly and garlic jelly, are homemade.

Lagniappe Cafe. 847 Exchange St. ☎ **503/325-5181.** Reservations recommended. Main courses $9–$12; 5-course dinners $14–$17. DISC, MC, V. Mon–Thurs 11am–3pm, Fri–Sat 11am–9pm. NORTHWEST/CAJUN.

Located beside and affiliated with Clementine's Bed & Breakfast, this garden cafe is housed in the oldest building in Astoria (built 1852). Today the tiny cottage is surrounded by beautiful flower gardens, and cut flowers grace the tables in summer. At lunch the menu consists of sandwiches (including New Orleans's standby muffaletta) and salads. At dinner, you'll find a handful of entrees listed on a board. These dinner specials are offered either à la carte or as very reasonably priced five-course dinners. On a recent evening, there was an excellent

Bicycling the Oregon Coast

The Oregon coast is one of the nation's most fabled bicycle tour routes, ranking right up there with the back roads of Vermont, the Napa Valley, and the San Juan Islands. Its fame is in no way overrated. Cyclists will find not only breathtaking scenery, but interesting towns, parks and beaches to explore, wide shoulders, and well-spaced places to stay. Cyclists have the option of staying in campgrounds (all state park campgrounds have hiker/biker campsites) or hotels. If you can afford it, an inn-to-inn pedal down this coast is the way to go (as you slowly grind your way up yet another seemingly endless hill, you'll appreciate the lack of camping gear weighing you down).

The entire route, from Astoria to California, covers between 368 and 378 miles (depending on your route) and includes a disheartening 16,000 total feet of climbing. While most of the route is on U.S. 101, which is a 55 mph highway for most of its length, the designated coast route leaves the highway for less crowded and more scenic roads whenever possible.

During the summer, when winds are generally out of the northwest, you'll have the wind at your back if you ride from north to south. In the winter (when you'll likely get very wet pedaling this coast), you're better off riding from south to north to take advantage of winds out of the southwest. However, planning a trip along this coast in winter is not advisable because although there is less traffic, winter storms frequently blow in with winds of up to 100 mph.

For a map and guide to bicycling the Oregon coast, contact the **Oregon Bicycle/ Pedestrian Program,** Oregon Department of Transportation, 210 Transportation Building, Salem OR 97310 (☎ **503/986-3556**). You might also want to get a copy of the *Umbrella Guide to Bicycling the Oregon Coast* (1990, Umbrella Books) by Robin Cody.

---

blue-cheese stuffed halibut being offered. Other courses included baked garlic and crostini, a salad, clam chowder, the entree, and such desserts as flan, chocolate-carrot cake, and bread pudding with rum-raisin sauce.

2 Seaside

17 miles S of Astoria, 79 miles W of Portland, 7 miles N of Cannon Beach

Seaside is a town with a split personality. On the one hand it's a historic beach resort dating from 1899, filled with quaint cottages and tree-lined streets. On the other hand it is the most densely developed beach town in the state and has all the trappings today's families associate with a beach vacation, including miniature golf courses, bumper boats, video arcades, and lots of souvenir shops.

This is not the sort of place most people imagine when they dream about the Oregon coast, and if you're looking for a quiet, romantic weekend getaway, don't head here. As one of the closest beaches to Portland, crowds and traffic are a way of life in Seaside on summer weekends. The town is also a very popular conference site, and as such, several of the town's largest hotels cater primarily to this market (and have the outrageous rates to prove it). However, the nearby community of Gearhart, which has long been a retreat for wealthy Portlanders, is as quiet as any town as you'll find on this coast.

ESSENTIALS

GETTING THERE   Seaside is on U.S. 101 just north of the junction with U.S. 26, which connects to Portland. **Pacific Pierce Stages** (☎ 503/436-1859 or 503/717-1651) provides bus service from Portland via Astoria and also continues on to Cannon Beach. **Bay Shuttle** (☎ 800/376-6118 or 360/642-4196) also offers service between Portland and Seaside. **Sunset Empire Transit** (☎ 800/776-6406 or 503/325-0563) provides public bus service from Seaside to Astoria and Cannon Beach.

VISITOR INFORMATION   Contact the **Seaside Chamber of Commerce,** 7 N. Roosevelt (P.O. Box 7), Seaside, OR 97138-0007 (☎ 800/444-6740 or 503/738-6391).

FESTIVALS   Each year in the second week of July, the **Miss Oregon Pageant** is held in Seaside. The second week of August is a large **Beach Volleyball Tournament.**

ENJOYING THE BEACH & SEASIDE'S OTHER ATTRACTIONS

Seaside's centerpiece is its 2-mile-long beachfront **Promenade** (or Prom), which was built in 1921. It's divided into the North Prom and the South Prom by the Turnaround, a local landmark at the west end of Broadway. Here at the Turnaround a bronze statue of Meriwether Lewis and William Clark marks the official end of the trail for the Lewis and Clark expedition. South of this statue on Lewis & Clark Way between the Promenade and Beach Drive, 8 blocks south of Broadway, you'll find the **Lewis and Clark Salt Works,** a reconstruction of a fire pit used by members of the famous expedition. During the winter of 1805–06, while the expedition was camped at Fort Clatsop near present-day Astoria, Lewis and Clark sent several men southwest 15 miles to a good spot for making salt from seawater. It took three men nearly 2 months to produce four bushels of salt for the return trip to the east. Five kettles were used for boiling seawater, and the fires were kept stoked 24 hours a day. Ironically, Captain Clark felt no need for salt, though Meriwether Lewis and the rest of the men felt it was necessary for the enjoyment of their meager rations.

However, history is not what attracts most people to Seaside. Miles of **white-sand beach** begin just south of Seaside at the foot of the imposing Tillamook Head and stretch north to the mouth of the Columbia River. Though the waters here are quite cold and only a few people venture in farther than knee-deep, there are lifeguards on duty all summer, which is one reason Seaside is popular with families. At the south end of Seaside beach is one of the best surf breaks on the north coast. If you want to try surfing these waves, you can rent a board and wetsuit at **Cleanline Surf,** 719 First Ave. (☎ 503/738-7888). A complete rental package runs $35 a day for adults. You can also rent body boards here.

However, because the waters here never warm up to comfortable swimming temperatures, kite flying, beach cycling, and other nonaquatic activities prove far more popular than swimming or surfing. All over town there are places that rent in-line skates, four-wheeled bicycles called surreys, and three-wheeled cycles (fun cycles) for pedaling on the beach. These latter are the most popular and the most fun, but can only really be used when the tide is out and the beach is firm enough to pedal on. Skates rent for $6 an hour, while cycles go for between $6 and $20 an hour depending on what sort you want. Try **Seaside Surrey Rental, Iron Coach,** or **Prom Bike & Hobby Shop,** all of which are on Avenue A 1 block south of Broadway near the beach. You can also rent pedal boats, kayaks, and canoes on the Necanicum River from **Paddle Fun** (☎ 503/717-0125), which has its rental dock at Quatat Park on Broadway. They charge $11 to $20 an hour for boat rentals.

If you prefer hiking to cycling, head south of town to the end of Sunset Boulevard where you'll find the start of the **Tillamook Head Trail,** which leads 6 miles over the headland to Indian Beach in **Ecola State Park.** This trail leads through shady forests of firs and red cedars with a few glimpses of the Pacific along the way.

If it's horseback riding that interests you, there are several stables just south of Seaside on U.S. 101 that offer rides. Try **Faraway Farms** (☎ **503/738-6336**), which offers rides both on their own property and on the beach.

Golfers can play a round at the **Seaside Golf Club,** 451 Ave. U (☎ **503/ 738-5261**), **The Highlands at Gearhart,** 1 Highlands Rd. (☎ **503/738-5248**), or the **Gearhart Golf Links,** on North Marion Street in Gearhart (☎ **503/738-3538**). Expect to pay around $25 for 18 holes at these courses.

In addition to the miles of sandy beach, the **Seaside Aquarium,** 200 N. Promenade (☎ **503/738-6211**), where you can feed the seals, is also popular. Admission is $5 for adults and $2.50 for children.

At the **Seaside Museum,** 570 Necanicum Dr. (☎ **503/738-7065**), you can see Native American artifacts dating from A.D. 230 as well as more recent items of historic significance. It's open daily from 10:30am to 4:30pm; admission is $2. The adjacent **Butterfield Cottage** is decorated much as a summer cottage would have looked in 1912.

WHERE TO STAY
IN SEASIDE
Moderate

Ebb Tide. 300 N. Promenade, Seaside, OR 97138. ☎ **800/468-6232** or 503/738-8371. 83 rms. TV TEL. $90–$140 double. AE, DISC, MC, V.

With a wide variety of rooms and a location right on the Promenade, this older hotel is one of the best values in Seaside. The best rooms, however, don't have ocean views, but instead are in a new wing on the inland side of the hotel. Other rooms have been recently redone, and most have fireplaces and kitchenettes. Some rooms also have whirlpool tubs. All the rooms have refrigerators. An indoor swimming pool, whirlpool, sauna, and exercise room are available.

✪ **The Gilbert Inn.** 341 Beach Dr., Seaside, OR 97138. ☎ **800/410-9770** or 503/738-9770. Fax 503/717-1070. Web site: http://www.clatsop.com/gilbertinn. 9 rms, 1 suite. TV TEL. $79–$99 double; $105 suite. Rates include full breakfast. AE, DISC, MC, V.

One block from the beach and 1 block south of Broadway, on the edge of both the shopping district and one of Seaside's old residential neighborhoods, stands the Gilbert Inn, a big yellow Queen Anne–style Victorian house with a pretty little yard. Alexander Gilbert, who had this house built in 1892, was once the mayor of Seaside, and he built a stately home worthy of someone in such a high position. Gilbert made good use of the plentiful fir trees of the area; the interior walls and ceilings are constructed of tongue-and-groove fir planks. The current owners, Dick and Carole Rees, have decorated the house in country French decor that manages to enhance the Victorian ambience.

✪ **Seaside Inn.** 581 S. Promenade, Seaside, OR 97138. ☎ **800/772-PROM** or 503/ 738-6403. Fax 503/738-6403. 14 rms. TV TEL. $90–$199 double. Rates include full breakfast. DISC, MC, V.

This four-story contemporary bed-and-breakfast inn adds a touch of architectural interest to the traditional facades along the Prom, and inside you'll find other nontraditional touches. All the rooms are different and span a wide range of styles to appeal to a wide range of tastes. Our favorite is the rock'n'roll room, which features a bed made from the rear of a 1959 Oldsmobile. Hula hoops and lava lamps further set the scene. Other rooms are far less outrageous and are primarily calculated to put you in a romantic mood (a wicker room, a room with a log bed, a mountain cabin room, a golf room). The clock tower room is the ultimate here and has a round king bed, double whirlpool tub, and loads of windows. Most rooms have ocean views and whirlpool tubs. Breakfast is served in the oceanfront lobby where there's also a bar for guests.

Shilo Inn—Seaside Oceanfront Resort. 30 N. Promenade (at Broadway), Seaside, OR 97138-5823. ☎ **800/222-2244** or 503/738-9571. Fax 503/738-0674. 112 rms. TV TEL. $65–$229 double. AE, DISC, MC, V.

Located right on the Turnaround that marks the end of the trail for the Lewis and Clark expedition, the Shilo Inn is a very comfortable and modern beachfront convention/resort hotel. However, high prices in summer are a bit out of line for what you get. But, if you expect to spend more time in the pool than on the beach, you might want to consider this hotel—the recreation facilities here are the best in town. The indoor swimming pool, whirlpool tub, steam room, sauna, and exercise room all overlook the beach and are separated from the lobby by a wall of glass that lets people in the lobby look out at the ocean as well. Oceanfront guest rooms all have large balconies, fireplaces, and kitchenettes, so you can enjoy your stay no matter what the weather, but these are the most expensive and overpriced rooms here. The hotel's dining room has a splendid view of the beach and serves seafood in the $10 to $15 range. Sunday brunch is especially popular. Expect some form of live entertainment in the lounge on summer nights.

Inexpensive

Hillcrest Inn. 118 N. Columbia St., Seaside, OR 97138. ☎ **800/270-7659** or 503/738-6273. 23 rms, 3 cottages. TV TEL. $32–$95 double. MC, V.

This lodging has a mix of older cottages and newer motel-style units and prices are some of the best in town. All the units cluster around a small lawn and flower-filled gardens beneath a few shady pine trees. Our favorites here are the two-bedroom cottages, which manage to capture a bit of the old Seaside atmosphere. However, some of the newer rooms are more comfortable and include whirlpool tubs, fireplaces, or both. It's only 2 blocks to the beach or Broadway.

Riverside Inn Bed & Breakfast. 430 S. Holladay Dr., Seaside, OR 97138. ☎ **800/826-6151** or 503/738-8254. Fax 503/738-7375. 11 rms. TV. $45–$90 double. Rates include full breakfast. AE, DISC, MC, V.

Though it's located on busy Holladay Drive, the Riverside Inn is an oasis amid the traffic and businesses. Beautiful gardens frame the restored 1907 home and its attached cottages. Through the backyard flows the Necanicum River, and a sprawling multilevel deck lets you enjoy the riverside location. Inside, all the rooms are a bit different, with antique country decor and an emphasis on fishing collectibles. The Captain's Quarters room, way up on the third floor, features a skylight directly over the bathtub and has the feel of a well-appointed artist's garret. Another of our favorite rooms here is the Old Seaside, a two-room unit with its own private deck. If you're planning a long stay, there are some rooms with kitchenettes.

IN GEARHART

Gearhart by the Sea. 1157 N. Marion Ave. (P.O. Box 2700), Gearhart, OR 97138. ☎ **800/547-0115** or 503/738-8331. Fax 503/738-0881. 85 condos. TV TEL. $119–$141, 1-bedroom; $150–$184, 2-bedroom. DISC, MC, V.

Although this four-story condominium hotel isn't the most attractive building on the coast (stark cement exterior), it is an ideal accommodation for golfers. The Gearhart

Golf Links are directly across the street. Condos all have full kitchens, fireplaces, and ocean views, but the best views go to the two-bedroom units, which makes this a good choice for families or pairs of golfing couples. While the golf course is right across the street, the beach is actually a bit farther across the sand dunes. Amenities include an indoor swimming pool, whirlpool, coffee shop, restaurant, and lounge.

⊘ Gearhart Ocean Inn. 67 N. Cottage St. (P.O. Box 2161), Gearhart, OR 97138. ☎ **503/ 738-7373.** 11 rms. TV. $49–$89 double. MC, V.

This old motor court–style motel has been fully renovated with all the care that's usually lavished on Victorian homes. A taupe exterior with white trim gives the two rows of wooden buildings a touch of sophistication, and roses and Adirondack chairs add character to the grounds, though a wide expanse of gravel parking lot does detract somewhat from the effect. The rooms all have lots of character and have been fully renovated. The most expensive rooms are two stories with wood floors, a kitchen, and even a garage. The decor is a combination of country cute and casual contemporary.

WHERE TO DINE

If you're looking for a quick meal, some picnic food, or something to take back and cook in your room, drop by the **Bell Buoy Crab Co.,** 1800 S. Holladay Dr. (☎ 503/738-2722), which sells not only cooked Dungeness crabs, but award-winning shrimp chowder, clam chowder, smoked salmon, fresh seafood, and canned fish, crab, and razor clams. If it's a good latte you need, don't miss **Java Reef,** 2674 U.S. 101 N. (☎ 503/717-0482), which pulls a great espresso and boasts the best view of any espresso shack on the coast (it has a deck overlooking the Necanicum River estuary).

IN SEASIDE

Dooger's Seafood & Grill. 505 Broadway. ☎ **503/738-3773.** Reservations not accepted. Meals $5–$20. AE, DISC, MC, V. Daily 11am–10pm. SEAFOOD.

For no-frills, simple, decent seafood in a family atmosphere, try Dooger's. Prices are reasonable, especially at lunch, when you can order from a list of specials that includes steamers, calamari, or petrale sole accompanied by a salad topped with bay shrimp. Try their tasty clam chowder. In case you've already eaten too much, the dinner menu includes alternative smaller portion servings of all the main dishes.

Vista Sea Café. 150 Broadway. ☎ **503/738-8108.** Pizzas $10–$22; sandwiches $4.50–$5.50. MC, V. Summer Sun–Thurs 11:30am–10pm, Fri–Sat 11:30am–10pm (shorter hours in winter). PIZZA/SANDWICHES.

Whether you're in the mood for pizza or soup and a sandwich, you can't go wrong here. High-backed antique booths and a few tables in a bright and artistically decorated dining room give the cafe a touch of class, and big windows let in plenty of sunshine in the summer. Whatever you do, don't leave without trying the clam chowder, which is served with a delicious homemade beer bread. On the pizza menu you'll find such creations as pesto pizza and a veggie and blue-cheese pizza.

IN GEARHART

⊘ Pacific Way Cafe and Bakery. 601 Pacific Way, in Gearhart. ☎ **503/738-0245.** Sandwiches/salads $5–$10. MC, V. Wed–Sun 9:30am–4:30pm. BAKERY/SANDWICHES.

You'll find this former mom-and-pop grocery store in the center of nearby Gearhart. The present owners are admittedly mentally stuck in the 1930s, as the vintage interior of the restaurant will attest. Bakery items, in this the most authentically European bakery on the coast, are delicious, especially the cinnamon rolls, marionberry scones, and pecan sticky buns, and along with an espresso they make a fine excuse for lounging in the flower-filled courtyard, weather permitting. There are appetizing sandwich concoctions available in the main cafe. The only thing wrong with this place is that it isn't open daily.

3 Cannon Beach

7 miles S of Seaside, 112 miles N of Newport, 79 miles W of Portland

When most people dream of a vacation on the Oregon coast, chances are they're dreaming of a place like Cannon Beach: weathered cedar-shingle buildings, picket fences behind drifts of nasturtiums, quiet gravel lanes, interesting little art galleries, and massive rock islands rising from the surf just off the wide sandy beach. If it weren't for all the other people who think Cannon Beach is a wonderful place, this town would be perfect. However, Cannon Beach is suffering from its own quaintness and the inevitable upscaling that usually ensues when someplace begins to gain national recognition. Once the Oregon coast's most renowned artists' community, Cannon Beach is now going the way of California's Carmel—lots of upscale shopping tucked away in utterly tasteful little plazas along a neatly manicured main street. Oh well, we still love it.

Cannon Beach was named for several cannons that washed ashore after the sloop of war *Shark* wrecked on these rocks in 1846. The most famous of the area's monoliths is **Haystack Rock,** which rises 235 feet above the water at the edge of the beach. Because of their resemblance to piles of hay, such offshore rocks are known generically as haystack rocks or sea stacks, but this is *the* Haystack Rock and is the most photographed rock on the Oregon coast.

One glance up and down the beach at the many offshore sea stacks and it's easy to understand what has attracted artists and vacationers alike to tiny Cannon Beach. Despite the crowds, Cannon Beach still has a village atmosphere, and summer throngs and traffic jams can do nothing to assault the fortresslike beauty of the rocks that lie just offshore.

ESSENTIALS

GETTING THERE   Cannon Beach is on U.S. 101 just south of the junction with U.S. 26. **Pacific Pierce Stages** (☎ **503/436-1859** or 503/717-1651) provides bus service from Portland via Astoria and Seaside. **Bay Shuttle** (☎ **800/376-6118** or 360/642-4196) also offers service between Portland and Cannon Beach. **Sunset Empire Transit** (☎ **800/776-6406** or 503/325-0563) provides public bus service between Cannon Beach and Seaside and Astoria.

VISITOR INFORMATION   Contact the **Cannon Beach Chamber of Commerce,** 207 N. Spruce St. (P.O. Box 64), Cannon Beach, OR 97110 (☎ **503/436-2623**).

GETTING AROUND   The **Cannon Beach Shuttle,** which provides free van service up and down the length of town, operates Friday through Tuesday from 10am to 6pm. Watch for signed shuttle stops. Donations for the ride are accepted.

FESTIVALS   Each year in late April, the **Puffin Kite Festival** fills the skies over Cannon Beach with colorful kites and features stunt kite flying exhibitions. In early June, the **Sand Castle Day** contest turns the beach into one vast canvas for sand sculptors from all over the region, and in early November, the **Stormy Weather Arts Festival** celebrates the arrival of winter storms. On summer Sunday afternoons, the **Concerts in the Park** series stages free concerts in a variety of musical styles at City Park on the corner of Second and Spruce streets.

EXPLORING THE TOWN, THE COAST & NEARBY STATE PARKS

Seven miles of wide sandy **beach** stretch south from Cannon Beach, but it's the off-shore rocks and not the abundance of sand that have made this stretch of coast so popular. Most of the rocks are protected as the nesting grounds of numerous species of sea birds. The most colorful of these is the **tufted puffin,** which you should be able to spot sitting on the rocks. Though Haystack Rock is the area's most famous mono-lith, another offshore rock is the site of the **Tillamook Rock Lighthouse,** which was built in 1879 and decommissioned in 1957. Today it is used as a columbarium, a vault for the interment of the ashes of people who have been cremated.

Kite flying, surf fishing, and beachcombing are all popular Cannon Beach pastimes. If you've always dreamed of riding a horse on the beach, your dream can come true here. Guided rides are offered by **Sea Ranch Stables** (☎ 503/436-2815). The price is $25 per hour and the rides head down Ecola Creek to the beach and then into Ecola State Park.

Ecola State Park, just north of town, offers the most breathtaking vantage point from which to soak up the view of Cannon Beach and Haystack Rock. The park also has several picnic areas perched on bluffs high above the crashing waves and a trail that leads 6 miles over Tillamook Head to Seaside. This was the southernmost point that Lewis and Clark explored on the Oregon coast. Admission is $3 per vehicle on weekends and holidays.

Three miles south of town is **Arcadia Beach Wayside,** one of the prettiest little beaches on the north coast, and another mile farther south you'll find **Hug Point State Park,** which has picnic tables, a sheltered beach, and the remains of an old wagon road that once hugged this point. **Oswald West State Park,** 10 miles south of Cannon Beach, is one of our personal favorites of all the parks on the Oregon coast. A short paved trail leads to a driftwood-strewn cobblestone beach on a small cove. Headlands on either side of the cove can be reached by hiking trails that offer splendid views. The waves here are popular with surfers, and there's a primitive camp-ground into which you must walk, though the walk is only a few hundred yards.

One of the funnest ways to see the beach here is from a funcycle, a three-wheeled beach cycle. These cycles allow you to ride up and down the beach at low tide. Funcycles can be rented from **Manzanita Fun Merchants,** 1160 S. Hemlock St. (☎ **503/436-1880**), and **Mike's Bike Shop,** 284 N. Spruce St. (☎ **503/436-1266**). Street and mountain bikes are also available for rent from these shops. Rental rates for bikes are around $6 to $7 per hour.

For many Cannon Beach visitors, **shopping** is the town's greatest attraction. In the heart of town, along Hemlock Street, you'll find dozens of densely packed small shops and galleries offering original art, fine crafts, unusual gifts, and casual fashions. Galleries worth seeking out include **Jeffrey Hull Gallery,** 178 N. Hemlock St. (☎ **503/436-2600**); **The White Bird Gallery,** 251 N. Hemlock St. (☎ **503/ 436-2681**); **Northwest by Northwest Gallery,** 239 N. Hemlock St. (☎ **503/ 436-0741**); and **Windridge Gallery,** 224 N. Hemlock St. (☎ **503/436-2406**). South of downtown, you'll find **Icefire Glassworks,** 116 E. Gower St. (☎ **503/436-2359**), a glass-blowing studio that features beautiful pieces of art glass. Across the street from this studio is the **Cannon Beach Arts Association Gallery,** 1064 S. Hemlock St. (☎ **503/436-0744**), which mounts shows in a wide variety of styles not usually seen in other Cannon Beach galleries, which tend to be heavy on beach landscapes.

Also in downtown Cannon Beach, you'll find the **Coaster Theater Playhouse,** 108 N. Hemlock St. (☎ **503/436-1242**), one of the best little playhouses in Oregon. In addition to plays, the theater stages performances of classical music and jazz. Tickets range from $12 to $15.

WHERE TO STAY

If you're heading here with the whole family or plan to stay awhile, consider renting a house, cottage, or apartment. Offerings range from studio apartments to luxurious (and large) oceanfront houses and prices span an equally wide range. Contact **Cannon Beach Property Management** (☎ **503/436-2021**) or **Arch Cape Property Services** (☎ **800/632-9526** or 503/436-1607) for more information.

✪ **Cannon Beach Hotel Lodgings.** 1116 S. Hemlock St., Cannon Beach, OR 97110. ☎ **503/436-1392.** Fax 503/436-1396. 26 rms. TV TEL. June–Sept $69–$169 double; Oct–May $39–$149 double. Rates include continental breakfast. AE, CB, DC, DISC, MC, V.

With its white picket fence, green shutters, and cedar-shingle siding, the Cannon Beach Hotel seems to have been on the Cannon Beach scene for ages and fits in perfectly with the town's atmosphere. The rooms vary in size, which means that even those on a budget can afford something here. However, the best rooms are those with fireplaces and whirlpool tubs, and two of these rooms have partial ocean views. Though it's not in the best location in Cannon Beach (there are parking lots all around the hotel), it's one of the best deals and has the ambience of a small European inn. Also available are rooms in the rustic Hearthstone Inn and a few secluded rooms in a third building called the Courtyard.

Hallmark Resort. 1400 S. Hemlock St., Cannon Beach, OR 97110. ☎ **800/345-5676** or 503/436-1566. Fax 503/436-0324. 134 rms and suites. TV TEL. May–Sept $109–$229 double. Oct–May $59–$149 double. AE, CB, DC, DISC, MC, V.

Situated on a bluff at the south end of town and with a head-on view of Haystack Rock, the Hallmark is the most luxurious hotel in Cannon Beach, and the wide range of rates reflects the variety of rooms available. The lowest rates are for nonview standard rooms and the highest rates are for oceanfront two-bedroom suites. In between these extremes are all manner of rooms, studios, and suites. The best values are the limited-view rooms, many of which have fireplaces and comfortable chairs set up to take in what little view there might be. Most rooms have a small refrigerator and a coffeemaker, and some have kitchenettes. There are even a few cottages available through the hotel. Though the grounds aren't spacious, there are several little Japanese gardens tucked in some unlikely spots, so be sure to stroll around.

Services: Concierge.

Facilities: Indoor swimming pool, two whirlpool spas, sauna, meeting rooms.

St. Bernards. 3 E. Ocean Rd., Arch Cape, OR 97102. ☎ **800/436-2848** or 503/436-2800. 7 rms. TV TEL. $129–$189 double. Rates include full breakfast. AE, MC, V.

If you can't find time in your schedule for that trip to France this year, a stay at St. Bernard's will provide a reasonable facsimile. Although the setting, just off U.S. 101 between Cannon Beach and Manzanita, won't convince you that you're in Provence, the building itself is as grand a manor house as any château in the south of France. Newly built and incorporating elements from castles and chateaux, this inn is straight out of a fairy tale. European antiques and original art fill the house, which has tile floors and an abundance of tapestry-cloth furnishings. Each of the rooms is designed to fulfill a different fantasy of the perfect romantic escape. There is the Provence room, of course, but there are also the circular tower room, with its own soaking tub; the Gauguin, filled with paintings by you know who; the Tapestry room, with a stained glass ceiling and an ocean view from the soaking tub. Get the picture? Lavish, multicourse breakfasts are served in the conservatory, and evening social hour is usually held by the fireplace.

The Sea Sprite. 280 Nebesna St. (P.O. Box 933), Cannon Beach, OR 97110. ☎ **503/ 436-2266.** 6 rms. TV. $75–$165 double (lower rates in off season). MC, V.

This small motel is located in the Tolovana Park area south of Cannon Beach, and though it has been around for quite a few years, it still makes a great choice for families. All the rooms have kitchens and most have woodstoves. However, it's the views of Haystack Rock that convince most people that the Sea Sprite is aging gracefully.

○ **Stephanie Inn.** 2740 S. Pacific St., Cannon Beach, OR 97110. ☎ **800/633-3466** or 503/ 436-2221. Fax 503/436-9711. 46 rms, 4 suites. A/C TV TEL. $139–$249 double; $289–$389 suite. Rates include full breakfast. Children 12 and over are welcome. AE, CB, DC, DISC, MC, V.

Simply stated, the Stephanie Inn is the most classically romantic inn on the Oregon coast (the perfect place for an anniversary or other special weekend away). With flower boxes beneath the windows and neatly manicured gardens by the entry, the inn is reminiscent of New England's country inns, but the beach out the back door is definitely of Pacific Northwest origin. Inside, the lobby feels warm and cozy with its river-rock fireplace, huge wood columns, and beamed ceiling. The guest rooms, all individually decorated, are equally cozy. All come with small refrigerators, wet bars, and VCRs, and most also have double whirlpool tubs and fireplaces. The higher you go in the three-story inn, the better the views and the more spacious the outdoor spaces (patios, balconies, and decks). Smoking is not permitted.

Dining/Entertainment: A bounteous buffet breakfast is served each morning in the second-floor dining room, which surprisingly does not have a view of the water. Creative prix-fixe dinners ($30) are also served (reservations are required).

Services: Room service, complimentary afternoon wine, morning newspaper, video library, complimentary shuttle to downtown Cannon Beach, massages.

The Waves/The Argonauta Inn/White Heron Lodge. 188 W. Second St. (P.O. Box 3), Cannon Beach, OR 97110. ☎ **800/822-2468** or 503/436-2205. Fax 503/436-1490. 50 rms and suites. TV TEL. $79–$295 double. DISC, MC, V.

Variety is the name of the game in eclectic Cannon Beach, and The Waves plays the game better than any other accommodation in town. This lodge, only a block from the heart of town, consists of more than four dozen rooms, suites, cottages, and beach houses at The Waves and two other jointly managed lodges, The Argonauta Inn and the White Heron Lodge. If clean and new appeal to you, try one of the rooms in the Garden Court, but our favorites are the cottages of The Argonauta Inn. Surrounded by beautiful flower gardens in the summer, these old cottages overlook the beach and capture the spirit of Cannon Beach. For sybarites and romantics, there are fireplaces in some rooms and a whirlpool spa overlooking the ocean. Plans call for these rooms to be completely renovated by summer 1998. If you want to get away from the crowds, ask for an apartment at the White Heron Lodge.

CAMPGROUNDS

At the north end of town, the **Sea Ranch R.V. Park,** 415 N. Hemlock St. (P.O. Box 214), Cannon Beach, OR 97110 (☎ **503/436-2815**), offers sites for RVs and tents. The campground is green and shady and is right across the street from the road to Ecola State Park. Rates range from $17 to $20 per night. You can also try **Wright's for Camping,** P.O. Box 213, Cannon Beach, OR 97110 (☎ **503/436-2347**), which is set back in the trees on the inland side of the road at the second Cannon Beach exit off U.S. 101 and charges $15 for campsites. At either of these, you'll need to make reservations at least a month in advance for summer weekends.

WHERE TO DINE

If you've got a weakness for good bakeries as we do, check out the **Cannon Beach Bakery,** 144 N. Hemlock St. (☎ **503/436-2592**), or **Hane's Bakerie,** 1064 S. Hemlock St. (☎ **503/436-0120**). For good coffee, stop in at the **Espresso Bean,** 1235 S. Hemlock St. (☎ **503/436-0522**).

Bistro Restaurant. 91 N. Hemlock St. ☎ **503/436-2661.** Reservations recommended. Main courses $13.75–$19.75. MC, V. Daily 5–9:30pm. Closed Wed in winter. NORTHWEST.

The best of Cannon Beach is rarely in plain view. Such is the case with the Bistro Restaurant. You'll see the restaurant's sign toward the north end of the shopping district, but the restaurant itself is set back a bit from the street behind a small garden and down a brick walkway. Step through the door and you'll think you've just stepped into a French country inn. Stucco walls, old prints of flowers, and fresh flowers on the tables are all the decor this tiny place can afford without growing cramped. But the simple decor allows diners to focus their attention on exquisitely prepared dishes such as sautéed oysters in lemon sauce or a seafood stew made with fennel, leeks, tomatoes, curry, and saffron. There is live guitar music on Friday and Saturday evenings, and there is even a tiny bar. If you're searching for atmosphere and good food, this is the place.

Café de la Mer. 1287 S. Hemlock St. ☎ **503/436-1179.** Reservations recommended. Main courses $16.50–$25. AE, MC, V. Tues–Sat 5:30–9:30pm. FRENCH/NORTHWEST.

Almost directly across the street from the Hallmark Resort, down at the south end of Cannon Beach, you'll spot a Williamsburg-blue colonial-style building that houses Cannon Beach's most upscale restaurant. Pink tablecloths and burgundy napkins, slender wine glasses, and art deco wall sconces give the interior a contemporary styling not evident from the outside. The menu focuses almost exclusively on seafood (six out of eight entrees on a recent evening), with the likes of bouillabaisse, salmon with lemon and capers, and a seafood salad. Seafood also fills the appetizer menu, which, when we last visited, included oysters with Pinot Gris and herbs.

Lazy Susan Café. 126 Hemlock St. ☎ **503/436-2816.** Breakfast main courses $3–$7.25; salads/sandwiches $5.50–$9.25. No credit cards. June 15–Sept 14 Wed–Mon 8am–8pm; Sept 15–June 14 Mon and Wed 8am–2:30pm, Thurs–Sun 8am–8pm. BREAKFAST/SALADS/LIGHT DINNER.

Cannon Beach is a great place to be for breakfast. The air is invigorating and you can linger over the delicious waffles or omelets at the Lazy Susan. Tucked into the back of a little brick courtyard shared with the Coaster Theater, the Lazy Susan is a quaint little cottage with unpainted siding, window boxes full of flowers in summer, and white Victorian railings leading up to the front door. If you sleep in, don't worry, breakfast is available all day. Nightly dinner specials include a choice of dessert.

Midtown Café. 1235 S. Hemlock St. ☎ **503/436-1016.** Breakfast $2.75–$8.25; lunch $4.25–$7.25. No credit cards. Wed–Sat 7am–2pm, Sun 8am–2pm. NATURAL/INTERNATIONAL.

Located next door to the Café de la Mer, the Midtown Café is a diner for the health-conscious gourmands of the 1990s. This little place is only open for breakfast and lunch, but packed into those two meals are some of the most innovative dishes on this stretch of the coast. How about a burrito for breakfast, or some eclectic hippie soup? If you need a kick-start in the morning, try the chocolate-espresso smoothie. You can be sure that anything you order will be as fresh as possible. These folks even grind their own flour and make their own jams, marmalades, ketchup, and salsa. One meal and we're sure you'll be hooked.

EN ROUTE TO OR FROM PORTLAND

If you'd like to see a large herd of Roosevelt elk, watch for the Jewell turnoff about 37 miles before reaching Cannon Beach on U.S. 26. From the turnoff, continue 10 miles north following the WILDLIFE VIEWING signs to the **Jewell Meadows Wildlife Area,** where there's a large meadow frequented throughout most of the year by anywhere from 75 to 200 elk. In June, you may see elk calves, and in the September and October rutting season, big bulls can be heard bugling and seen locking antlers.

Twelve miles past the U.S. 26 turnoff for Jewell, you'll find **Saddle Mountain State Park,** which is a favorite day hike in the area. A 2½-mile trail leads to the top of Saddle Mountain, from which there are breathtaking views up and down the coast. In the spring, rare wildflowers are abundant along this trail. The trail is steep and rocky, so wear sturdy shoes or boots and carry water.

WHERE TO DINE

Camp 18 Restaurant. In Elsie 22 miles east of Seaside on U.S. 26. ☎ **503/755-1818.** Main courses $11–$15. AE, DISC, MC, V. Daily 7am–9pm. AMERICAN.

If you're interested in learning about how logging was done in the days before clear cutting, there is no better place than this combination restaurant and logging museum. The restaurant is in a huge log lodge with lots of chain saw art, axes for door handles, and a hollowed out stump for a hostess desk. The 85-foot-long ridge pole in the restaurant is the largest of its kind in the country and weighs 25 tons. There are also a pair of stone fireplaces and lots of old logging photos. After tucking into logger-size meals (don't miss the marionberry cobbler), you can wander the grounds studying old steam logging equipment. A gift shop sells logging-oriented souvenirs.

4 Tillamook County

Tillamook: 75 miles W of Portland, 51 miles S of Seaside, 44 miles N of Lincoln City

Tillamook is a mispronunciation of the word *Killamook,* which was the name of the Native American tribe that once lived in this area. The name is now applied to a county, a town, and a bay. While this is one of the closest stretches of coast to Portland, it is not a major destination due to the fact that there are no large beachfront towns in the area. The town of Tillamook, which lies inland from the Pacific at the south end of Tillamook Bay, is the area's commercial center, but it is the surrounding farmland that has made the biggest name for Tillamook County. Ever since the first settlers arrived in Tillamook in 1851, dairy farming has been the mainstay of the economy, and in the area's fragrant fields graze large herds of contented cows. These cows provide the milk for the Tillamook County Creamery Association's cheese factory, which turns out a substantial share of the cheese consumed in Oregon. With no beaches to attract visitors, the town of Tillamook has managed to turn its dairy industry into a tourist attraction. No, this isn't the cow-watching capital of Oregon, but the town's cheese factory is now one of the most popular stops along the Oregon coast, annually attracting more than 800,000 visitors.

While the town of Tillamook is not exactly a beach town, there are in the area a few beachside hamlets that offer a variety of accommodations, activities, and dining options. Tillamook is also the starting point for the scenic Three Capes Loop, which links three state parks and plenty of great coastal scenery.

ESSENTIALS

GETTING THERE   Tillamook is on U.S. 101 at the junction with Ore. 6, which leads to Portland. **Tillamook County Transportation** (☎ **800/815-8283** or 503/

815-8283) provides bus service between Portland and Manzanita, Nehalem, Wheeler, Rockaway Beach, Garibaldi, Bay City, and Tillamook.

VISITOR INFORMATION   For more information on the area, contact the **Tillamook Chamber of Commerce,** 3705 U.S. 101 N., Tillamook, OR 97141 (☎ **503/842-7525**); **Nehalem Bay Area Chamber of Commerce,** P.O. Box 238, Wheeler, OR 97147 (☎ **503/368-5100**); or the **Garibaldi Chamber of Commerce,** P.O. Box 915, Garibaldi, OR 97118 (☎ **503/322-0301**).

EXPLORING THE COUNTY

MANZANITA   As the crowds have descended on Cannon Beach, people seeking peace and quiet, a slower pace, and smaller crowds have migrated south to the community of Manzanita. Located south of Neahkanie Mountain, Manzanita enjoys a setting similar to Cannon Beach's but without the many haystack rocks. There isn't much to do in Manzanita except walk on the beach and generally do some serious relaxing, which is exactly why most people come here. If you absolutely must do something, try renting a beach bike from **Manzanita Fun Merchants,** 186 Laneda Ave. (☎ **503/368-6606**). The low-slung, three-wheel beach bikes are a great way to explore the beach. You could also play a round of golf on the meandering fairways of the nine-hole **Manzanita Golf Course,** Lake View Drive (☎ **503/368-5744**), which charges $24 for 18 holes. One other great reason to stay in Manzanita is that this little community has a couple of the north coast's best restaurants (see "Where to Dine," below).

The beach at Manzanita stretches for 5 miles from the mouth of the Nehalem River to the base of Neahkanie Mountain. This beach is a favorite of both surfers and sailboarders. The latter have the option of sailing either in the waves or in the quieter waters of Nehalem Bay. Access to both the bay and the beach is provided at **Nehalem Bay State Park** (☎ **503/368-5154**), which is just south of Manzanita and encompasses all of Nehalem Spit. The park, which includes a campground (and an airstrip), has a 2-mile paved bike path, a horse camp, and horse trails. Out at the south end of the spit, more than 50 harbor seals can often be seen lounging on the beach. To reach the seal area requires a 5-mile round-trip hike.

WHEELER   Located on Nehalem Bay, this little wide spot in the road has long been popular for crabbing and fishing. However, in recent years it has also become a favorite north coast sea kayaking locale. The marshes of the bay provide plenty of meandering waterways to explore, and several miles of the Nehalem River can also be easily paddled if the tides are in your favor. There are now two places in town where you can rent a kayak: **Annie's Kayaks,** 487 Hwy. 101 (☎ **503/368-6055**), and **Wheeler on the Bay Lodge & Marina,** 580 Marine (☎ **800/469-3204** or 503/368-5858). Rates are $10 to $18 per hour or $25 to $45 per day. Annie's also offers guided tours.

If you're interested in trying your hand at crabbing, contact **Jetty Fishery** (☎ **503/368-5746**), which is located just south of Wheeler at the mouth of the Nehalem River. They rent boats and crab rings and also offer dock crabbing. The folks here also offer a ferry service across the river to Nehalem Bay State Park, where you can often see lots of harbor seals lying out on the beach.

Although we personally don't care for the wines at **Nehalem Bay Winery,** 34965 Ore. 53 (☎ **503/368-WINE**), many people do, and there is no denying that the fruit wines here are interesting, if a bit overpriced. It's worth a stop just to visit the historic half-timbered building that houses the tasting room. This building was constructed in 1909 as part of the Tillamook Creamery Association (think Tillamook cheese factory).

ROCKAWAY BEACH   Rockaway Beach has little of the picturesque scenery of Cannon Beach or Manzanita, but it does have plenty of wide sandy beach. The town has a rather run-down feel to its narrow strip of aging cottages, but is still quite popular with families who rent beach houses for their summer vacation.

GARIBALDI   Named (by the local postmaster) in 1879 for Italian patriot Giuseppi Garibaldi, this little town is located at the north end of Tillamook Bay and is the region's main sportfishing and crabbing port. Even before the arrival of white settlers in the region, this spot was a fishing and whaling village of the Tillamook Indians. If you've got an urge to do some salmon or bottom fishing, this is the place to book a trip. Try **Troller Charters** (☎ **800/546-3666** or 503/322-3666), **Siggi-G Ocean Charters** (☎ **503/322-3285**), **Kerri Lin Charters** (☎ **503/355-2439**), or **Garibaldi Charters** (☎ **800/900-HOOK** or 503/322-0007). Fishing rates are around $60 to $65 for a full-day of salmon or bottom fishing. Deep-sea halibut fishing will run you $125 to $140 for a full day.

If bay and river fishing for salmon and steelhead is more your speed, contact **No-How Fun Services** (☎ **503/322-3369**), which offers salmon fishing trips on Tillamook and Nehalem bays for $100 per person per day. Spring and fall are salmon season.

These companies also offer **whale-watching** and **bird-watching** trips, and **Troller Charters** (☎ **800/546-3666** or 503/322-3666) offers quick trips (known as ocean ecotours) around Tillamook Bay for $10. At the **Garibaldi Marina,** 300 Mooring Basin Rd. (☎ **503/322-3312**), you can rent boats, tackle, and crab rings, if you want to do some fishing or crabbing on your own.

Garibaldi is also where you'll find the depot for the **Fun Run Express** (☎ **800/685-1719**), an excursion train that runs along some of the most scenic portions of this section of coast. At times the tracks are right beside the water. The 28-mile trip includes a turnaround at the Tillamook Naval Air Station Museum's blimp hangar. Trips are offered on Saturday and Sunday between late June and mid-October, and the round-trip cost is $10 for adults and $5 for children 12 and under.

TILLAMOOK   Tillamook has long been known as one of Oregon's foremost dairy regions, and Tillamook cheese is ubiquitous throughout the state. So it's no surprise that the **Tillamook Cheese Factory,** on U.S. 101 just north of Tillamook (☎ **503/842-4481**), is the most popular tourist attraction in town. Not only can visitors observe the cheese-making process (cheddars are the specialty here), but there's also a large store where all manner of cheeses and other edible gifts are available. The factory is open daily from 8am to 8pm in summer and 8am to 6pm in winter.

If the Tillamook Cheese Factory seems too crowded for you, head back toward town a mile and you'll see the **Blue Heron French Cheese Company,** 2001 Blue Heron Dr. (☎ **503/842-8281**), which is on the same side of U.S. 101 as the Tillamook Cheese Factory. Located in a big old dairy barn with a flagstone floor, this store stocks the same sort of comestibles as the Tillamook Cheese Factory, though the emphasis here is on brie (which, however, is not made locally). Farm animals make this a good stop for kids. Blue Heron is open daily from 8am to 8pm in summer and 8am to 5pm in winter.

If you'd like to find out more about the cows that produce the milk for the cheese factories, the **Tillamook County Creamery Association** (☎ **503/815-1300**) offers tours of local dairy farms. Tours cost $8 for adults, $6 for children 5 to 16 (or $25 for a family of four). Tours, which are led by area farmers, leave from the cheese factory daily at 3pm between mid-June and the end of August.

At the **Tillamook County Pioneer Museum,** 2106 Second St. (☎ **503/ 842-4553**), you'll find the expected hodgepodge of antique cars, old kitchen appliances, blacksmith's tools, and the like, but you'll also find an unusual natural-history display showing examples of different colors and where they're found in nature. The museum is open Monday through Saturday from 8am to 5pm and on Sunday from 11am to 5pm (closed Monday from October 1 to mid-March). Admission is $2 for adults, $1.50 for seniors, 50¢ for students 12 to 17.

A hangar built during World War II for a fleet of navy blimps is 2 miles south of town off U.S. 101 and lays claim to being the largest free-standing wooden building in the world. Statistics bear out the impressiveness of this building: 250 feet wide, 1,100 feet long, and 170 feet high. The blimp hangar now houses the **Tillamook Naval Air Station Museum,** 6030 Hangar Rd. (☎ **503/842-1130**), which contains a respectable collection of old planes including a Stearman biplane, a P-51 Mustang, a B-25 Mitchell, an F4U Corsair, and a PBY-5A Catalina. Of course, there are also exhibits on lighter-than-air flight as well. The museum is open daily from 9am to 6pm. Admission is $6 for adults, $5 seniors, $4 youths ages 13 to 17, and $2.50 for children ages 7 to 12.

Although there are no blimp rides being offered, you can go up in a small plane to see this section of the coast. Contact **Tillamook Air Tours** (☎ **503/842-1942**), which charges $25 per person for a 20-minute flight and $35 for a 30-minute flight. Tours are in a restored 1942 Stinson Reliant V-77 plane. You may even see whales from the plane.

If you're a quilter, be sure to stop in at the **Latimer Quilt and Textile Center,** 2105 Wilson River Loop Rd. (☎ **503/842-8622**), which is housed in an old wooden schoolhouse. This center not only has quilting supplies, but also has a reference library and exhibits. It also offers classes, does quilt restorations, and serves as a repository for important regional textiles.

Golfers can play a round at the 18-hole **Alderbrook Golf Course,** 7300 Alderbrook Rd. (☎ **503/842-6413**), which charges $20 for 18 holes, or the much less challenging nine-hole **Bay Breeze Golf Course,** 2325 Latimer Rd. (☎ **503/ 842-1166**), which is located near the cheese factory.

If you're interested in outdoor activities, you can hike to **Munson Falls,** the tallest waterfall in the Coast Range, at Munson Creek County Park, 7 miles south of Tillamook off U.S. 101. The trail to the falls is only about ¼ mile long and leads through a stand of old-growth forest.

Anglers interested in going after salmon or steelhead in Tillamook Bay or area rivers should contact **Bob Rees' Professional Fishing Guide Service** (☎ **503/ 842-8249**), **Bob Brown's Guided Sport Fishing** (☎ **503/842-9696**), **Oregon Alaska Sportfishing** (☎ **503/842-5171**), or **The Guide Shop** (☎ **800/24-FISH'N**).

THE THREE CAPES SCENIC LOOP   The Three Capes Scenic Loop begins just west of downtown Tillamook and leads past Cape Meares, Cape Lookout, and Cape Kiwanda. Together these three capes offer some of the most spectacular views on the northern Oregon coast. All three capes are state parks and all make great whale-watching spots in the spring or storm-watching spots in the winter. To start the loop, follow Third Street out of town and watch for the right turn for Cape Meares State Park. This road will take you along the shore of Tillamook Bay and around the north side of Cape Meares, where the resort town of Bayocean once stood. Built early in this century by developers with a dream to create the Atlantic City of the West, Bayocean was constructed at the end of a sand spit that often felt the full force of winter storms.

When Bayocean homes began falling into the ocean, folks realized that this wasn't going to be the next Atlantic City. Today there's no sign of the town, but the long sandy beach along the spit is a great place for a walk and a bit of bird watching.

Just around the tip of the cape, you'll come to **Cape Meares State Park,** which is the site of the **Cape Meares Lighthouse.** The lighthouse is open to the public and houses a small museum. The views from atop this rocky headland are superb. Continuing around the cape, you come to the residential community of **Oceanside,** from where you have an excellent view of the **Three Arch Rocks** just offshore. The beach at Oceanside is a popular spot and is often protected from the wind in the summer. Oceanside is a popular lunch stop for people doing the Three Capes Loop.

Three miles south of Oceanside, you'll come to tiny **Netarts Bay,** which is well known for its excellent clamming and crabbing. Continuing south, you come to **Cape Lookout State Park,** which has a campground, picnic areas, beaches, and several miles of hiking trails. The most breathtaking trail leads out $2^1/2$ miles out to the end of Cape Lookout, where, from several hundred feet above the ocean, you can often spot gray whales in the spring and fall.

Cape Kiwanda, which lies just outside the town of Pacific City, is the last of the three capes and is preserved as Cape Kiwanda State Park. At the foot of the cape's sandstone cliffs you'll find sand dunes and tide pools, and it's possible to scramble up to the top of the cape for dramatic views of this rugged piece of shoreline. At the base of the cape is the staging area for Pacific City's beach-launched dory fleet. These flat-bottomed commercial fishing boats are launched from the beach and plow through crashing breakers to get out to calmer waters beyond. When the day's fishing is done, the dories roar into shore at full throttle and come to a grinding stop as high up on the beach as they can. This is Oregon's only such fishing fleet and is celebrated each year during the annual Dory Derby on the third weekend in July.

The beach at the base of Cape Kiwanda is also one of the north coast's best surfing spots, and the high sand dune behind the beach has perfect conditions for hang gliding and paragliding. Schools that offer classes here include **Over the Hill Paragliding** (☎ 503/667-4557) and the **Hang Gliding and Paragliding School of Oregon** (☎ 503/223-7448).

If you'd like to do a bit of horseback riding in the area, contact **Into the Sunset** (☎ 503/965-6326). Pacific City is another good place to stop for a meal or coffee (see "Where to Dine," below). South of Pacific City, the scenic loop rejoins U.S. 101.

NESKOWIN The quaint little community of Neskowin is nestled at the northern foot of Cascade Head, 12 miles north of Lincoln City. The tiny cottages and tree-lined lanes have for decades been the summer retreats of inland families. Quiet vacations are the rule in Neskowin, where you'll find only condominiums and rental houses. Beach access here is provided at **Neskowin Beach State Park,** which faces Proposal Rock, a tree-covered haystack rock bordered by Neskowin Creek.

If you'd like to go for a horseback ride on the beach, contact **Neskowin Stable,** 48490 Hawk Ave. (☎ 503/392-3277), which charges $20 per hour. The stable is open mid-May through September. In Neskowin, you'll also find two nine-hole golf courses. The **Hawk Creek Golf Course,** 48480 U.S. 101 (☎ 503/392-4120), plays up the valley of Hawk Creek with mountains rising on three sides. The greens fee is $20 for 18 holes. Across the highway, in a wide flat area is the **Neskowin Beach Golf Course,** Hawk Avenue (☎ 503/392-3377), which isn't quite as scenic and charges a $12 greens fee for nine holes.

If you're interested in art, check out the **Hawk Creek Gallery,** 48460 U.S. 101 S. (☎ 503/392-3879), which features the paintings of Michael Schlicting, a master watercolorist.

Just to the south of Neskowin is the rugged and unspoiled **Cascade Head.** Rising 1,770 feet from sea level, this is one of the highest headlands on the coast and creates its own weather, which causes rain to fall here more than 180 days a year. Lush forests of Sitka spruce and windswept cliff-top meadows thrive in this rainy climate and are home to such a diversity of flora and fauna that the Nature Conservancy purchased much of the land here. Trails onto Cascade Head start about 2 miles south of Neskowin. Trails through the Nature Conservancy's preserves, which have been set aside to protect the habitat of the rare Oregon silverspot butterfly, are closed from January 1 to July 16 due to the nature of the butterflies life cycle.

On the south side of Cascade Head, you'll find the **Sitka Center for the Arts and Ecology,** Neskowin Coast Foundation, P.O. Box 65, Otis, OR 97368 (☎ **503/ 994-5485**), which, during the summer, offers classes on various subjects from writing to woodcarving to painting to ecology.

WHERE TO STAY
In Manzanita

If you want to rent a vacation house in Manzanita, contact **Ribbon Realty Rentals,** 467 Laneda Ave. (P.O. Box 326), Manzanita, OR 97130 (☎ **503/368-6009**).

✪ **The Inn at Manzanita.** 67 Laneda St. (on Manzanita's main street and just a few blocks from the beach), Manzanita, OR 97130. ☎ **503/368-6754.** 13 rms. TV TEL. $100–$145 double (lower off-season midweek rates available). Minimum 2-night stay on weekends and from July 1 to Labor Day; 3 nights on some holidays. MC, V.

Searching for an unforgettably romantic spot for a weekend getaway? This is it. Right in the heart of Manzanita and within steps of a couple of the best restaurants on the northern Oregon coast, the Inn at Manzanita is a great place to celebrate an anniversary or any other special event. Double whirlpool tubs sit between the fireplace and the bed in every room, and balconies look out through shady pines to the ocean. The weathered cedar-shingle siding blends unobtrusively with the natural vegetation, and the grounds are planted with beautiful flowers for much of the year. A wet bar and small refrigerator let you chill a bottle of wine. If all this has you worrying that you'll forget about the outside world, never fear—a newspaper will be left at your door every morning.

Ocean Inn. Manzanita Rental Company, 32 Laneda Ave. (P.O. Box 162), Manzanita, OR 97130. ☎ **800/579-9801** or 503/368-6797. 10 rms. TV TEL. May–Sept $95–$135 double. Oct–Apr $85–$125 double. MC, V.

With four remodeled apartments right on the beach and six more new apartments set back a bit from the sand, this inn is a good choice if you want the space of a one-bedroom apartment and appreciate modern amenities and comfortable, new furnishings. All but one of the rooms have an ocean view. Of the newer apartments, five are on the second floor and have balconies overlooking the beach. Several rooms have woodstoves, most have kitchens, and one has a whirlpool tub.

In Wheeler
Wheeler on the Bay Lodge. U.S. 101 and 580 Marine (P.O. Box 580), Wheeler, OR 97147. ☎ **503/368-5858.** 10 rms. TV TEL. $75–$105 double. AE, MC, V.

It would be easy to pass off this renovated lodge as just another fisherman's motel, but that would be a big mistake. Located right on the shore of Nehalem Bay, this lodge has one of our favorite rooms on the coast. The Honeymoon room here has walls of glass looking onto the bay, a private deck, a fireplace, and best of all, a whirlpool tub that's situated to grab the best views. Six of the rooms here have spas, and most of these have water views. Other rooms sport distinctive decor: a "Mess

O' Trout" string of lights, bold sunflower patterns everywhere, tropical fish motifs. Although this isn't a bed-and-breakfast, all the rooms are different and have that individualized touch. A great spot for a romantic weekend.

IN GARIBALDI

Hill Top House. 617 Holly Ave. (P.O. Box 145), Garibaldi, OR 97118. ☎ **503/322-3221.** 2 rms. $69.50–$89 double. MC, V.

Located high on a hill above the rest of the town of Garibaldi, this contemporary home commands a fabulous view of town, the marina, Tillamook Bay, and the distant mountains. Of the two guest rooms the Blue Heron Room is the larger and more luxurious, with its own whirlpool tub and private balcony. This room takes up the entire top floor of the inn, though if you insist on privacy, you might want to opt for the smaller Sandpiper Room, since the Blue Heron room has no door but rather heavy curtains both at the top and bottom of the stairs that lead up to the room. Guests can also soak in a hot tub out in the garden (which by the way is beautifully landscaped and tended) and enjoy the same superb views. Hosts Don and Shuzz Hedrick come to innkeeping from careers in education.

IN OCEANSIDE

House on the Hill. 1816 Maxwell Mountain Rd. (P.O. Box 187), Oceanside, OR 97134. ☎ **503/842-6030.** 16 rms. TV TEL. May–Oct $75–$120 double. Nov–Apr $60–$85 double. DISC, MC, V.

Set 250 feet above Oceanside's beach on a promontory jutting into the ocean, the House on the Hill is a collection of pale-blue two-story buildings, several of which look like truncated A-frames. The rooms here are large and the views are stunning, with the Three Arch Rocks directly offshore. In many rooms you can even lie in bed and soak up the views. With too much asphalt around the buildings, the grounds leave a bit to be desired, but, oh those views. You won't find a more spectacular setting; cliffs drop off from the edge of the property. Consequently, this is not a good choice for families with small children.

Ocean Front Cabins. 1610 Pacific Ave. NW (P.O. Box 203), Oceanside, OR 97134. ☎ **503/842-6081.** 7 cabins. $50–$65 cabin for 2. MC, V.

The Ocean Front Cabins is a collection of funky old cabins, but if you don't mind swapping cramped quarters, paneled walls, and low ceilings for being only 100 feet from the beach with an unobstructed view of the waves and the Three Arch Rocks, then you might find these cabins perfect. Be forewarned however, that there's nothing standardized or fancy about these cabins. Young people, especially surfers, will be right at home here. A few have kitchenettes, which is a definite plus in a town with only one restaurant. These cabins are very popular, so call in February for summer reservations.

Oceanside Inn. 1440 Pacific Ave. NW, Oceanside, OR 97134. ☎ **800/347-2972** or 503/842-2961. TV. 9 rms. $50–$95 double. MC, V.

Located right next door to Roseanna's Oceanside Café (see "Where to Dine," below), this restored older inn sits at the top of a steep stairway down to the beach and has five rooms with ocean views. Of these, room 6 is our favorite. It's up on the second floor and has three walls of windows to take in the great views. This room also has a whirlpool tub, and at $80 is a real bargain for the area. If you opt for an economical room without a view, you can still hang out on the large deck that's perched high above the beach. This place isn't fancy, but it is comfortable.

Sea Rose. 1685 Maxwell Mountain Rd. (P.O. Box 122), Oceanside, OR 97134. ☎ **503/842-6126.** 2 rms. $75–$90 double. No credit cards.

Located about halfway up the very steep Maxwell Mountain Road, you'll find one of Oceanside's newest B&Bs. Although this inn isn't very large, it's cozy and has outstanding ocean views. Interesting antiques fill the common areas, while a simple country decor prevails in guest rooms. Both rooms do, however, have claw-foot tubs, and the Antoinette room has a private deck

IN CLOVERDALE

Hudson House Bed & Breakfast Inn. 37700 U.S. 101 S., Cloverdale, OR 97112. ☎ **503/ 392-3533.** 4 rms. $60–$85 double. AE, DISC, MC, V.

Although this historic farmhouse, built in 1906 and set behind a white picket fence, is located right on busy U.S. 101, it is in such a striking setting, overlooking acres and acres of pastureland, that it is well worth considering as a base for exploring the area. If you want space, opt for the Mary Esther Suite, which includes the original parlor as a sitting room and also has a private porch. The next best bet is the Laura Room, which also has its own sitting room, as well as a claw-foot tub. The original owner of this home, Clyde Hudson, was a photographer, and many of his photos of the Cloverdale area are displayed around the inn. A Victorian farmhouse decor predominates.

✪ Sandlake Country Inn. 8505 Galloway Rd., Cloverdale, OR 97112. ☎ **503/965-6745.** 4 rms. $80–$125 double. DISC, MC, V.

Although the Sand Lake area is best known as a playground for noisy all-terrain vehicles and dune buggies, this inn is a quiet and very romantic retreat surrounded by colorful gardens. Needless to say, off-roaders don't usually stay here. The Honeymoon Suite, which takes up the inn's entire second floor, is the most spacious room here and includes both a double whirlpool tub and a claw-foot tub. It also has a fireplace visible both from the bedroom and the sitting room. Downstairs in the Timbers room, which is almost as large, you'll find a fireplace and a double whirlpool as well, but you'll also get a rustic lodge atmosphere complete with exposed 3-by-12 timbers that were salvaged from a shipwreck and used to build this home in 1894. For even greater privacy, there is a separate cottage alongside a little creek.

IN NESKOWIN

In addition to the condominium resort listed here, there are numerous vacation cottages and beach houses for rent in Neskowin. Contact **Sea View Vacation Rentals,** P.O. Box 1049, Pacific City, OR 97135 (☎ **503/965-7888**), or **Grey Fox Vacation Rentals,** P.O. Box 364, Neskowin, OR 97149 (☎ **503/392-4355**). This latter company even rents one house that has an indoor swimming pool. Rates range from $100 to $250 per night. Both of these companies also rent homes in nearby Pacific City.

Neskowin Resort. 48990 U.S. 101 S. (P.O. Box 728), Neskowin, OR 97149. ☎ **503/ 392-3191.** Fax 503/392-4264. 25 condos. TV TEL. July 1–Sept 15 $89–$125 double; $165–$325, 4 to 6 people. Sept 16–June 30 $59–$79 double; $115–$225, 4 to 6 people. No credit cards.

Most units at this condominium resort have views of Proposal Rock; the views, combined with the tranquillity of Neskowin, set this place apart from hotels in nearby Lincoln City. All the units have kitchens, which makes this a popular choice with families. Hawk Creek runs along the back of the resort and just across the parking lot is a good little cafe. The views from the rooms here are among the best on the Oregon coast.

CAMPGROUNDS

Despite the fact that **Oswald West State Park** is a walk-in campground, the sites are closer together than those at most car campgrounds. Don't say I didn't warn you if the guy in the next campsite keeps you up all night with his snoring. Surfers and boardsailors will likely prefer **Nehalem Bay State Park,** where they can keep a closer eye on their equipment. **Roy Creek County Park** is a nearby, though inland, alternative to the area's state parks.

On the Three Capes Loop, west of Tillamook, there are several campgrounds. **Cape Lookout State Park** is the largest and nicest of these. A little farther south are the forest service's **Sand Beach Campground,** which is an off-road vehicle (ORV) staging area and very noisy, and **Whalen Island County Park,** which is right on Sand Lake. **Webb County Park,** just across the road from Cape Kiwanda, and **Woods County Park** are both popular with hang glider and paraglider pilots.

Inland alternatives in this area include **Kilchis River County Park,** north of Tillamook at the end of Kilchis River Road; six Tillamook State Forest campgrounds along the Wilson River; **Trask County Park,** 12 miles east of Tillamook on Trask River Road; **Rocky Bend Campground,** 15¹/₂ miles east of Beaver up Blaine Road; **Hebo Lake Campground,** 5 miles east of Hebo; and **Mount Hebo Campground,** 3 miles past Hebo Lake Campground.

WHERE TO DINE
IN MANZANITA

If you're just looking to grab a quick bite of fresh seafood, try **Manzanita Seafood Market,** 320 Laneda Ave. (☎ **503/368-CRAB**), where you can get clam chowder, crab and shrimp burgers, and fish-and-chips.

✪ **Blue Sky Café.** 154 Laneda Ave. ☎ **503/368-5712.** Reservations highly recommended. Main courses $10–$23. No credit cards. Daily 5:30–9:30pm. NORTHWEST.

On the left as you approach the beach on the main street through town, you'll see a pale-gray beachy building with colorful raised flower beds in front. Inside, the decor is more casual than Jarboe's across the street. We could make a dinner of thick slabs of fresh-baked bread smeared with the Blue Sky's potted Montrachet cheese with fresh herbs, sun-dried tomatoes, roasted garlic and olive oil, but that would mean never making it past the appetizer list. Entrees show influences from around the globe, and are particularly well integrated in the numerous fresh-fish dishes. Salmon might be marinated in mustard seed vinaigrette then baked with garlicky bread crumbs and blue cheese or rock shrimp might be sautéed with black beans, cilantro-pumpkin seed pesto and orange peel. For dessert, who could pass up something known as a thermonuclear chocolate device (a brownie topped with a chocolate truffle and covered with caramel sauce and whipped cream)?

Cassandra's Pizza. 60 Laneda Ave. ☎ **503/368-5593.** Pizzas $8–$22.50. No credit cards. Sun–Thurs 4:30–9:30pm, Fri–Sat 4:30–10pm. PIZZA.

With a surfboard for a counter and others hanging from the walls, there's no question of who likes to grab their pizzas here. Even if you don't surf, though, you'll enjoy the hand-thrown pizzas, of which there are no less than three Hawaiian style (the North Shore, the Waikiki, and the Pipeline), all of which have pineapples and Canadian bacon (go figure).

✪ **Jarboe's in Manzanita.** 137 Laneda Ave. ☎ **503/368-5113.** Reservations highly recommended. Main courses $16.50–$18; fixed-price dinner $29. MC, V. Summer, Thurs and Sun–Mon 5–9pm, Fri–Sat 5–9:30pm (shorter hours other months). NORTHWEST.

Housed in a tiny restored beach cottage, Jarboe's is about as intimate as a restaurant gets. There are only a few tables in the two tiny dining rooms, which makes reservations imperative. The menu changes daily, but is always reliable, and while the prix-fixe dinners are really the way to go here, if you aren't that hungry, you can still order à la carte. On any given day, there will be four appetizers, four entrees, and four desserts available, which helps to reduce decision-making time. On a recent evening, a complete dinner might have consisted of a terrine of mussels with saffron and basil; mesquite grilled sea bass with grilled eggplant, arugula, baby zucchini, and capers; and a lime tart with crème anglaise to finish things off.

IN WHEELER

Heron Rock Waterfront Grill. 380 Marine Dr. ☎ **503/368-7887.** Reservations not accepted. Main dishes $8–$20. AE, DISC, MC, V. Mon and Thurs 5–9pm, Fri–Sat 11:30am–9:30pm, Sun 11:30am–9pm. Closed Tues–Wed. AMERICAN.

Located right on the shore of Nehalem Bay, this modern restaurant has a great deck for summer dining. While Wheeler has traditionally attracted mostly fishermen, this restaurant appeals to a more upscale clientele and is popular with people who come down here to sea kayak or to stay at the very comfortable hotel next door. The menu is surprisingly varied and includes fish-and-chips as well as grilled rib chops with blue cheese butter and warm poblano potato salad. How about halibut with a horseradish-blackberry crust and wild mushrooms and a lemon-scented couscous? Even at lunch you'll find plenty of creative dishes, such as a smoked chicken with brie, red pepper, and onion chutney. Plenty of Oregon wines are also available.

IN ROCKAWAY BEACH

If you like smoked salmon, don't miss **Karla's Smokehouse,** 2010 U.S. 101 N. (☎ **503/355-2362**), which sells the best smoked fish and smoked oysters on the coast and has been doing so for more than 30 years. The smoked tuna belly is particularly succulent, and anything here makes great picnic food. Karla's is open daily in summer and on weekends only in the winter.

IN GARIBALDI

If you've got a sweet tooth, be sure to stop in at **Bayfront Bakery & Deli,** U.S. 101 (☎ **503/322-3787**), where you can indulge in fresh pecan rolls, Danishes, muffins, and pies. Also worth visiting, if you happen to be in the market for some fresh seafood to cook for dinner, are **Miller's Seafood Market,** U.S. 101 (☎ **503/322-0355**), and **Smith's Pacific Shrimp Co.,** Fisherman's Wharf, South Seventh Street (☎ **503/322-3316**).

Pirate's Cove. U.S. 101 N. ☎ **503/322-2092.** Reservations only for 8 or more people. Main courses $10–$18.50. DISC, MC, V. Daily noon–9pm. SEAFOOD.

Set atop a bluff just north of the town of Garibaldi, this restaurant commands an outstanding view across Tillamook Bay, and while the view alone would be enough to recommend this place, the extensive menu is surprisingly varied. Seafood is definitely the order of the day here, and with plenty of oyster farms in the area, you would be remiss if you didn't start your meal with a few oyster shooters or some oyster stew. The seafood pasta dishes are usually flavorful and filling, and the salmon and halibut dishes are also good bets.

IN BAY CITY

If you want to try some Tillamook Bay oysters, stop in at **Pacific Oyster Co.,** which is just off U.S. 101 at the end of the boardwalk. Here you can order up oyster shooters at the oyster bar and watch the oyster shuckers at work.

Artspace. U.S. 101 and Fifth St. ☎ **503/377-2782.** Reservations recommended. Main courses $9–$15. No credit cards. Thurs–Sat noon–8pm; Sun brunch 10am–3pm (summer only). SEAFOOD/SANDWICHES.

You just can't miss this unusual place as you drive through the hamlet of Bay City. Just watch for the building with Matisse-like murals on the outside walls. Located just off U.S. 101 several miles north of Tillamook, Artspace is both an art gallery and a small restaurant with a view of Tillamook Bay. The ambience is laid-back and offerings from the kitchen range from oysters Italia to lemon chicken to seafood fettucine. For lunch we like the oyster burgers and fish burgers. Be sure to ask about dessert before you eat too much to indulge. The art here is mostly by Oregon artists, though the owners also sell artists' estates.

IN & NEAR TILLAMOOK

If you need to stock up your larder for the beach house or are on your way back from a weekend at the beach, don't miss an opportunity to stop in at **Bear Creek Artichokes** (☎ **503/398-5411**), which is located 11 miles south of Tillamook on U.S. 101. This is one of the only commercial artichoke farms in Oregon and usually has fresh artichokes throughout the summer and fall. The farm stand also has lots of other great produce, as well as cut and dried flowers. The display gardens offer a pleasant break from driving.

La Casa Medello. 1160 U.S. 101 N. ☎ **503/842-5768.** Main dishes $7–$10. MC, V. Sun–Fri 11am–9pm, Sat noon–9pm. MEXICAN.

If you're passing through Tillamook and haven't already filled up on cheese samples and ice cream at the cheese factory, La Casa Medello, in an old cedar shingled house on the north side of town, is a good bet for a full meal. With hardwood floors and a college town feel, this casa serves up filling burritos, tacos, and tostadas. Be sure to start off with the guacamole.

IN OCEANSIDE

Roseanna's Oceanside Café. 1490 Pacific Ave. ☎ **503/842-7351.** Reservations highly recommended. Main courses $10–$18. MC, V. Mon–Fri 11am–9pm, Sat 10:30am–10pm, Sun 8am–9pm. SEAFOOD/INTERNATIONAL.

When you're the only restaurant in town, you can't help staying busy, but Roseanna's is such a Scenic Loop legend that people come from miles around to eat here and don't seem to mind long waits to get a table. What brings them are the reliable meals and the view of the beach and offshore rocks. The menu mixes the traditional with international influences without getting overly creative. Lunch prices are reasonable, with such offerings as a full-flavored cioppino soup or oyster sandwich. Angels on horseback (oysters wrapped in bacon and broiled) are one of our favorite appetizers here. Entrees offer a choice of shellfish or fish with a choice of sauces (apricot-ginger glaze, aioli, or sweet pepper-and-tomato coulis, for example). The wait for a table can be long, so make a reservation if possible. If you just want a quick snack, there are barstools at the front counter.

IN PACIFIC CITY

If you find yourself in need of espresso in Pacific City, try the **White Moon Cow Cafe,** 35490 Brooten Rd. (☎ **503/965-5101**), which is a de facto community center for the local countercultural crowd. For tasty baked goods, stop in at **The Grateful Bread Bakery & Restaurant,** 34805 Brooten Rd. (☎ **503/965-7337**), which has tables both inside and out on a deck.

☉ Pelican Pub & Brewery. 33180 Cape Kiwanda Dr. ☎ **503/965-7007.** Reservations not accepted. Main courses $5–$13. AE, DISC, MC, V. Sun–Thurs 11am–10pm, Fri–Sat 11am–midnight. PUB FOOD.

With hands down the best view of any brew pub in Oregon, the Pelican is the only brew pub in all of Tillamook County. The building overlooks Cape Kiwanda and is right on the beach, with its own beach volleyball court in back, lots of windows for taking in the views, and a good selection of ales, including Tsunami Stout and our personal favorite, the Doryman's Dark Ale. Sandwiches, burgers, and pizzas are the menu mainstays here, but of course you can also get fish-and-chips and fried shrimp.

The Riverhouse. Brooten Rd. ☎ **503/965-6722.** Reservations not accepted. Main courses $6–$20. MC, V. Sun–Fri 11am–9pm, Sat 11am–10pm (closes 1 hr. earlier in winter). AMERICAN.

This tiny place is built on the bank of the Nestucca River and has great river views out its many windows. Because there is nothing but forest across the river, the Riverhouse feels as if it's miles out in the country, though it is only a few blocks from Pacific City's main intersection and a couple more from the beach. With a timeless roadside diner feel and a casual, friendly atmosphere, this is the top pick in town for a quiet sit-down dinner. While burgers and sandwiches are the order of the day at lunch, the dinner menu features prawns in a creamy wine sauce, fresh fish amandine, halibut basted with butter, lemon pepper, and dill, as well as filet mignon on crepes Florentine.

5 Lincoln City/Gleneden Beach

88 miles SW of Portland, 44 miles S of Tillamook, 25 miles N of Newport

Lincoln City is not really a city, but a collection of five small towns that stretch for miles along the coast. Over the years these towns all grew together as this became the most popular beach destination for vacationers, especially families, from Portland and Salem. Today there's no specific downtown area, and though there may be more motel rooms here than anywhere else on the Oregon coast, there's little to distinguish most of the thousands of rooms. However, family vacationers looking for a long beach with lots of sand and steady winds for flying kites will find Lincoln City to their liking. Motel rates, though often high for what you get, are generally better than in beach towns that are long on charm, and there are an abundance of vacation homes for rent. Likewise, restaurants catering to large families and small pocketbooks proliferate here. Such restaurants purvey hot meals rather than haute cuisine, and you can eat your fill of seafood without going broke.

Once referred to as "20 miracle miles," Lincoln City is no longer the miracle it once was. Miracle miles have become congested urban sprawl, and a summer weekend in Lincoln City can mean coping with bumper-to-bumper traffic. Not surprisingly many have come to think of this as "20 miserable miles." If at all possible, come during the week or during the off-season to avoid the crowds.

Once you get off U.S. 101, though, Lincoln City has neighborhoods as charming as any on the coast. It is also here, in the Gleneden Beach area just south of Lincoln City, that you'll find the coast's most prestigious resort. Also to be found in this area are some of Oregon's best art galleries and some interesting artists' studios.

ESSENTIALS

GETTING THERE   Ore. 22 from Salem merges with Ore. 18 before reaching the junction with U.S. 101. From Portland, take Ore. 99W to McMinnville and then head west on Ore. 18.

VISITOR INFORMATION   For more information on the area, contact the **Lincoln City Visitor and Convention Bureau,** 801 SW U.S. 101, Suite 1, Lincoln City, OR 97367 (☎ **800/452-2151** or 541/994-8378), or the **Lincoln City Chamber of Commerce,** 4039 NW Logan Rd. (P.O. Box 787), Lincoln City, OR 97367 (☎ **541/994-3070**).

GETTING AROUND   Car rentals are available from **Robben Rent-A-Car** (☎ **800/305-5530** or 541/994-5530). If you need a taxi, contact **Lincoln Cab Co.** (☎ **541/996-2003**). Public bus service between the Rose Lodge on Ore. 18 and Newport, south of Lincoln City, is provided by **Lincoln County Transit** (☎ **541/765-2177,** ext. 4900), but is available on weekdays only.

FESTIVALS   Annual **kite festivals** include the Spring Kite Festival in early May and the Fall International Kite Festival around Columbus Day weekend. In addition, Lincoln City hosts the annual **Cascade Head Music Festival** each June, and in July there's the annual **Sandcastle Building Contest.** On the nearby Siletz Indian Reservation, the **Siletz Pow Wow** takes place in August.

ENJOYING THE BEACH & THE OUTDOORS

Lincoln City's 7^{1}/$_{2}$-mile-long **beach** is its main attraction. However, cold waters and constant breezes conspire to make swimming a pursuit for Polar Bear Club members only. The winds, on the other hand, make this beach the best kite-flying spot on the Oregon coast. If you didn't bring your own kite, you can buy one at **Catch the Wind,** 266 SE U.S. 101 (☎ **541/994-9500**). Among the better beach-access points are the D River State Wayside on the south side of the river and the Road's End State Wayside up at the north end of Lincoln City. Road's End is also a good place to explore some tide pools. You'll find more tide pools on the beach at Northwest 15th Street and Southwest 32nd Street.

Adding to the appeal of Lincoln City's beach is **Devil's Lake,** which drains across the beach by way of the D River, the world's shortest river. Boating, sailing, waterskiing, boardsailing, swimming, fishing, and camping are all popular Devil's Lake activities. Access points on the west side of the lake include **Devil's Lake State Park (West),** Sixth Street (☎ **541/994-2002**), which has a campground, and **Regatta Grounds Park** and **Holmes Road Park,** both of which are off West Devil's Lake Road and have boat ramps and picnic tables. On the east side you'll find **Devil's Lake State Park (East)** 2 miles east on East Devil's Lake Road and **Sand Point Park** on View Point Lane near the north end of East Devil's Lake Road. Both of these parks have picnic tables and swimming areas. If you don't have your own boat, you can rent canoes, kayaks, paddleboats, aquabikes, and various motorboats at **Blue Heron Landing,** 4006 W. Devil's Lake Rd. (☎ **541/994-4708**). Rates range from $9 an hour for a canoe or kayak up to $35 an hour for a runabout or pontoon boat. You'll also find bumper boats here at Blue Heron Landing.

Golfers have two Lincoln City options. The top choice is the Scottish inspired (though solidly Northwestern in character) **Salishan Golf Links,** on U.S. 101 in Gleneden Beach (☎ **541/764-3632**), which charges $60 for 18 holes of golf in the summer months. This resort course is a longtime Oregon coast favorite. Other than this, it's the **Lakeside Golf & Fitness Club,** 3245 Club House Dr. (☎ **541/994-8442**), which charges $30 for 18 holes.

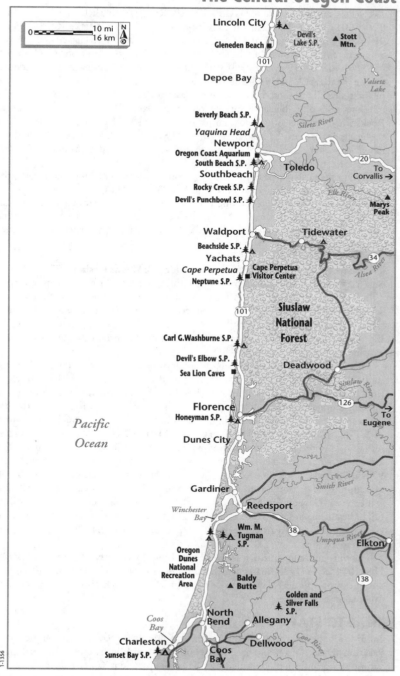

The Central Oregon Coast

0 [scale bar] 10 mi
16 km

N

Lincoln City

Devil's
Lake S.P.

Stott
Mtn.

Gleneden Beach

101

Depoe Bay

Valsetz
Lake

Beverly Beach S.P.

Siletz River

Yaquina Head
Newport
Oregon Coast Aquarium
South Beach S.P.
Southbeach

Toledo

20

To
Corvallis →

Rocky Creek S.P.
Devil's Punchbowl S.P.

Elk River

Marys
Peak

Waldport

Tidewater

Beachside S.P.
Yachats
Cape Perpetua
Neptune S.P.

Cape Perpetua
Visitor Center

34

Alsea River

101

Siuslaw
National
Forest

Carl G. Washburne S.P.

Devil's Elbow S.P.
Sea Lion Caves

Deadwood

Siuslaw River

Florence
Honeyman S.P.

126

To
Eugene

Dunes City

Pacific
Ocean

Gardiner

Smith River

Winchester
Bay

Reedsport

Wm. M.
Tugman
S.P.

38

Umpqua River

Elkton

Oregon
Dunes
National
Recreation
Area

Baldy
Butte

Golden and
Silver Falls
S.P.

138

North
Bend

Allegany

Coos
Bay

Dellwood

Charleston

Coos River

Sunset Bay S.P.

Coos
Bay

T-1356

Cyclists can rent bikes at **David's Bicycle Rental,** 960 SE U.S. 101 (☎ **541/ 996-6001**), or at **Blue Heron Landing,** 4006 W. Devils Lake Rd. (☎ **541/ 994-4708**). Rates range from $15 to $25 per day. If you want to challenge the waves, you can rent a surfboard or body board at the **Oregon Surf Shop,** 4933 SW U.S. 101 (☎ **541/996-3957**). If you'd like to do some horseback riding, contact **Ocean Trails** (☎ **541/994-4849**), which offers rides both on the beach and on inland trails. Hikers should head north to **Cascade Head** where there are several miles of hiking trails on public and Nature Conservancy land. The trailheads are off Three Rocks Road (on the south side) and off Forest Road 1861 on the north side. Both trailheads are reached by heading north on U.S. 101. Anglers in need of a guide to take them where the fish are biting can contact **Jerry's Guide Service** (☎ **503/ 879-5058**).

If you're a gardener or enjoy visiting public gardens, schedule time to visit the **Connie Hansen Garden,** 1931 NW 33rd St. (☎ **541/994-6338**). This cottage garden was created by the late Connie Hansen over a 20-year period and abounds in primroses and rhododendrons, which make it a great place to visit in the spring. The gardens are open on Tuesday and Saturday from 10am to 2pm or by appointment.

INDOOR PURSUITS

These days the hottest thing in town is the **Chinook Winds Casino,** 1777 NW 44th St. (☎ **888/CHINOOK**), a massive gambling palace run by the Confederated Tribes of Siletz Indians and located right on the beach at the north end of town. The casino offers bingo, blackjack, poker, slot machines, and keno. Of course, there's also plenty of cheap food available and a video-games room for the kids. Big-name entertainers help bring in folks who wouldn't otherwise consider visiting a casino.

This area actually has a surprising number of interesting art galleries and artists' studios, several of which are near Salishan. Just off U.S. 101, north of the resort, you'll find **Alder House II,** 611 Immonen Rd. (no phone), which is the oldest glass-blowing studio in Oregon. The shop and studio are open daily from 10am to 5pm between March 15 and November 30. Also on Immonen Road (which is just north of Salishan) is **Mossy Creek Pottery** (☎ **541/996-2415**), with an imaginative selection of porcelain and stoneware by Oregon potters. Right on U.S. 101 in this same area, you'll find the impressive **Freed Gallery,** 6119 SW U.S. 101 (☎ **541/ 994-5600**), which has an excellent selection of art glass and ceramic work, as well as sculptures and paintings in a wide variety of styles. Garden enthusiasts will also want to visit **Garden Art & Gifts,** 3001 SW U.S. 101 (☎ **541/994-2660**), a store full of beautiful garden accessories and garden-oriented art. One other gallery worth checking out is the **Ryan Gallery,** 4270 N. U.S. 101 (☎ **541/994-5391**), at the north end of town.

The only museum in town is the **North Lincoln County Museum,** 4907 SW U.S. 101 (☎ **541/996-6614**), which has rooms decorated with historic artifacts and antiques from pioneer days. It's open Wednesday through Sunday from noon to 4pm; admission is free.

WHERE TO STAY

In addition to the town's many hotels and motels, Lincoln City has plenty of vacation rental houses and apartments offering good deals, especially for family vacations. For information on renting a house or apartment, contact **Beachfront Vacation Rentals** (☎ **800/224-7660** or 503/760-8654), **Horizon Rentals and Property Management** (☎ **800/995-2411** or 503/994-2226), **Pacific Retreats**

(☎ **800/473-4833**), or **Shoreline Properties** (☎ **541/994-7028**). Rates generally range from around $100 up to $250 for houses for anywhere from 4 to 12 people.

EXPENSIVE

Dock of the Bay. 1116 SW 51st St., Lincoln City, OR 97367. ☎ **800/362-5229** or 541/996-3549. Fax 541/996-4759. 21 rms. TV TEL. June–Sept $129–$149 double. Lower rates off-season. MC, V.

The southern end of Lincoln City is bordered by Siletz Bay, and it's here, right on the water, that you'll find these condominiums. The waterfront rooms offer great views of the bay and its rocky islets. The beach here is protected, which makes it a good place for small children. The condos are all quite large and most have kitchens, fireplaces, and balconies. A whirlpool spa keeps guests warm summer and winter alike. Although you don't get a lot of amenities for your money here, you do get plenty of space and a good location right on the sand.

The Inn at Spanish Head. 4009 SW U.S. 101, Lincoln City, OR 97367. ☎ **800/452-8127** or 541/996-2161. Fax 541/996-4089. 120 rms, 35 suites. TV TEL. $125–$155 double; $195–$285 suite. Lower rates in winter. AE, DC, DISC, MC, V. Free valet parking.

Located toward the south end of Lincoln City, this hotel is the only high-rise hotel on the Oregon coast, but you'd never know it from the parking lot. From the entry, the hotel appears to be only two stories tall. What isn't readily apparent is that the lobby is on the ninth floor (there are eight stories below the parking lot level) due to the fact that the hotel is built into a steep cliff that rises up from the beach. This is a condominium resort and all the rooms are individually owned, which means there's a different decor in every room. However, the furnishings are reliably comfortable. Many rooms have kitchens, and there are larger suites for family vacationers. Best of all, all the rooms have an ocean view.

Dining/Entertainment: The Panorama restaurant and lounge, on the 10th floor, provides a dizzying view and fresh seafood with Northwest flavorings and is one of Lincoln City's better restaurants. Sunday brunch ($15.95) is also served here. In the Ocean View Lounge, there are happy-hour specials on weeknights.

Services: Room service.

Facilities: The beachside outdoor pool with glass railings to block the wind is, because of its great location, the best pool in town. There are also a whirlpool, sauna, exercise room, coin laundry, and games room.

✪ **Salishan Lodge.** 7760 U.S. 101, Gleneden Beach, OR 97388. ☎ **888/725-4742** or 541/764-2371. Fax 541/764-3681. 205 rms. MINIBAR TV TEL. Jan 1–Mar 13 $119–$219 double; Mar 14–June 12 $159–$249 double; June 13–Oct 31 $189–$269 double; Nov 1–Dec 31 $129–$229 double. AE, CB, DC, DISC, MC, V.

The largest and most luxurious resort on the coast, the Salishan Lodge is nestled amid towering evergreens on a hillside at the south end of Siletz Bay. Unfortunately, the resort is almost half a mile from the beach and on the inland side of U.S. 101. However, since most guests are here to play golf, few seem to mind this inconvenience. Guest rooms, which are spread out around just a portion of the resort's 750 acres, come in three different sizes. However, whichever size room you opt for, try to get a second-floor room. Most of these have cathedral ceilings and stone fireplaces. For breathtaking views, you'll have to shell out top dollar for a Chieftain or Siletz Bay room. In 1997, the resort underwent a complete renovation that gave both the lobby and guest rooms a fresh, lodge look (think Eddie Bauer).

Dining/Entertainment: See "Where to Dine," below, for details on the Salishan Dining Room. There's also a less expensive restaurant as well as a coffee shop. The Attic Lounge is a quiet upscale spot for a late-night cocktail or a game of pool.

Services: Concierge, room service, valet/laundry service, baby-sitting, in-room massages.

Facilities: 18-hole golf course, driving range, pro shop, indoor pool, indoor and outdoor tennis courts, whirlpool, exercise room, saunas, children's games room, playground, walking trails, beach access.

MODERATE

Cozy Cove. 515 NW Inlet Ave., Lincoln City, OR 97367. ☎ **800/553-COVE** or 541/994-2950. Fax 541/996-4332. 69 rms and suites. TV TEL. $46–$169 double. DC, DISC, MC, V.

Located near the mouth of the D River, the Cozy Cove offers some good deals among its wide range of guest rooms. The hotel is on a long, wide stretch of beach with easy access, and only a short walk away you'll find several good restaurants. Some rooms have fireplaces and balconies, while others have kitchens or whirlpool tubs or some combination of all of these amenities. There's a seasonal outdoor pool and a year-round whirlpool. While the best (and most expensive) rooms are those facing the beach, there are very economical nonview rooms as well. Our favorite rooms are the oceanfront rooms with fireplaces and whirlpool tubs in the windows ($130).

Historic Chandler House Bed & Breakfast. 1205 SW Harbor St., Lincoln City, OR 97367. ☎ **541/994-5010.** 2 rms. $95–$118 double. DISC, MC, V.

Previously owned by a woodworker, this small historic home has lots of beautiful wood details inside. However, it is the inn's perennial gardens, done in a sort of Northwest interpretation of the English cottage garden style, that are the most captivating aspect here. Any avid gardener should make this their first choice in Lincoln City. Neither of the two guest rooms is very large, but one has a separate sitting room, which makes it the preferable of the two rooms. At press time, a new suite was under construction in what was once a backyard workshop. When completed, this should be the inn's most spacious and comfortable room.

Shilo Inn. 1501 NW 40th Place, Lincoln City, OR 97367-4811. ☎ **800/222-2244** or 541/994-3655. 187 rms, 61 suites. TV TEL. $89–$139 double; $169–$219 suite. AE, DC, DISC, MC, V.

Located at the north end of town adjacent to the Chinook Winds Casino, this sprawling resort is a favorite coastal convention hotel, and as such always seems less a place to take a vacation than a place to do business. You'll find the Shilo at the north end of town. The dunes here are quite low, so you can almost step out the door and onto the beach. The first-floor oceanfront rooms have patios, and most other rooms include such amenities as two phones and hair dryers. Some rooms also have microwaves and refrigerators. The newest suites are some of the largest and nicest rooms in town and have three TVs (one in the bathroom) and three phones, as well as fireplaces, microwaves, coffeemakers, refrigerators, and wet bars.

Dining/Entertainment: The dining room has a long wall of glass overlooking the beach, and almost every table has a good view. In the lounge there's nightly dance music.

Services: Room service.

Facilities: Indoor pool, whirlpool, sauna, video-games room.

Spyglass Inn. 2510 SW Dune Ave., Lincoln City, OR 97367. ☎ **541/994-2785.** 3 rms. $85–$105 double. MC, V.

Located at the end of a gravel road high on a wooded bluff overlooking the ocean, this contemporary B&B feels as if it is far out in the country, though it is within the city limits. The views from the house are superb, and all three guest rooms take in much of the grand panorama. The tile-floored living room commands the most expansive view, and it is here that you'll find a telescope and binoculars for bringing the distant shoreline (and occasionally whales) a bit closer. In winter, a fireplace keeps this room warm. In the loft library, there are lots of books and games. Guest rooms all have either a whirlpool tub or a soaking tub for two. The Blue Iris Suite is the largest of the rooms and has a two-person whirlpool tub with an ocean view. However, the views are a bit better from the Berry Room, which also has a soaking tub for two. Both of these rooms have private balconies as well.

CAMPGROUNDS

There's a campground at **Devil's Lake State Park,** just off U.S. 101 north of the D River.

WHERE TO DINE

If you're looking for some good smoked salmon or smoked oysters while you're in town, stop by **Mr. Bill's Village Smokehouse,** 2981 SW U.S. 101 (☎ **888/ MR-BILLS** or 503/994-4566). If you're looking for a good cup of espresso, stop in combination coffeehouse/bookstore **Café Roma,** 1437 NW U.S. 101 (☎ **541/ 994-6616**).

EXPENSIVE

✪ Bay House & Bistro. 5911 SW U.S. 101. ☎ **541/996-3222.** Reservations recommended. Main courses $17–$26. AE, DISC, MC, V. Sun–Fri 5:30–9pm, Sat 5–9pm. Closed Mon–Tues Nov–Apr. NORTHWEST.

With a big wall of glass overlooking the Siletz Bay and Salishan Spit, the Bay House, between Lincoln City and Gleneden Beach, provides fine dining and dramatic sunsets (and good bird watching if you're interested). There are snowy linens on the tables, and service is gracious. For starters, we have a weakness for the bay shrimp wontons with the zesty lime dipping sauce. Entrees include such unusual creations as panfried oysters in a ginger broth. The Bay House also has a wine shop and a bistro lounge area for cocktails and appetizers. If you have time for only one dinner while in the area, make it here.

Chez Jeanette. 7150 Gleneden Beach Loop, Gleneden Beach. ☎ **541/764-3434.** Reservations highly recommended. Main courses $14–$25. AE, DISC, MC, V. Daily 5:30–9pm. FRENCH/ NORTHWEST.

You'll find Chez Jeanette south of Salishan Lodge on a side road that leads to Gleneden Beach. Just watch for the quaint little cottage on your left. Once inside, you'll swear you're in a French country inn, the perfect spot for a romantic dinner. It would be a shame not to start your meal with one or the other (or both) of the two house specialty appetizers: steamed mussels with a saffron sauce flavored with just a touch of Pernod and oysters with a blue-cheese/sauterne sauce. The two sauces are as different as night and day: one soft and subtle, the other bright and brassy. Every night there are different seafood specials as well as a wild game special and a pasta du jour.

The Dining Room at Salishan Lodge. U.S. 101, Gleneden Beach. ☎ **541/764-2371.** Reservations recommended. Main courses $16.25–$26.50. AE, CB, DC, DISC, MC, V. Daily 4–10pm. NORTHWEST.

Salishan Lodge is the Oregon coast's premier full-service resort, and as such also boasts one of the coast's best restaurants. The menu is as creative as any you'll find in the region and can more than hold its own with popular restaurants in Portland. The menu changes regularly to take advantage of the ever-changing offerings of fresh Northwest ingredients. However, expect plenty of seafood-based appetizers the likes of citrus-basted fry bread and pine-cured salmon or oysters on the half-shell with sherry vinegar, pepper, and shallot mignonette. The main courses are more evenly split among meats and seafoods, with a few vegetarian offerings as well. Traditional Native American–style alder-planked salmon here gets a new twist, a Pinot Noir jus. Now that's Northwest cuisine! Lots of windows assure every diner at this ever-popular restaurant a tranquillity-inducing view of the lush forest outside. Service is professional and unobtrusive, and the wine cellar, with more than 15,000 bottles, is positively legendary. If you can put together a party of seven or more people, you can even have dinner in the wine cellar.

MODERATE

✪ **Kyllo's Seafood Grill.** 1110 NW First Court. ☎ **541/994-3179.** Reservations not accepted. Main courses $8–$19; lunch $4.50–$11. AE, DISC, MC, V. Sun–Thurs 7am–9:30pm, Fri–Sat 7am–10:30pm. SEAFOOD.

Providing a touch of urban chic on a family oriented beach, Kyllo's is housed in a very contemporary building that features concrete floors and walls, a big copper fireplace, plenty of deck space, and walls of glass to take in the view of the D River and the ocean. A colorful, narrow mural winds around the dining room, and there are unusual deconstructivist wall lamps. If all this sounds like you're going to be paying for the atmosphere, think again. Prices for such dishes as large and tasty crab cakes, halibut with lemon-caper sauce, or calamari with aioli are quite reasonable. Dinner salads are almost large enough to be meals unto themselves, especially if you opt to add crab or shrimp. You'll almost certainly have to wait for a table if you come here on a summer evening.

INEXPENSIVE

Chameleon Cafe. 2145 NW U.S. 101. ☎ **541/994-8422.** Reservations for 5 or more people only. Main courses $7–$14. MC, V. Mon–Sat 11:30am–9pm (until 8pm in winter). INTERNATIONAL/VEGETARIAN.

The Chameleon lives up to its name by offering completely different cuisines on a single menu. There are Mediterranean dishes and on Friday nights, there's Thai food. Although the food here is primarily vegetarian, you'll also find a few fish dishes, such as fish tacos, on the menu. We ordered the grilled marinated eggplant sandwich with feta cheese, sun-dried and fresh tomatoes, and a thin slice of red onion, and when it arrived we could hardly be distracted enough to try our accompanying Caesar salad.

The Dory Cove Restaurant. 5819 Logan Rd. ☎ **541/994-5180.** Main courses $9–$19; lunch $4.50–$10. DISC, MC, V. Mon–Sat 11:30am–9pm, Sun noon–8pm. Take the road that turns off U.S. 101 at the Lighthouse Pub. BURGERS/SEAFOOD.

Locals swear by this traditional favorite up in the Road's End neighborhood on the north side of Lincoln City, and on any given summer day, you'll have to take your place in line at lunch or dinner. What keeps people flocking to this place are not just the good seafood meals at very reasonable prices (surf and turf with a New York steak and beer-battered crab legs runs less than $19), but the unusual burgers, which include fish burgers, scallops burgers, oyster burgers, and shrimp burgers, none of which have a speck of beef in them. Full meals here are meant for the hungry so bring a hearty appetite. While most of the seafood is fried, you will find some broiled dishes.

Salmon River Cafe. Lincoln City Plaza, 4079-B NW Logan Rd. ☎ **541/996-FOOD.** Main courses $10–$13.50; lunch $5.50–$7.50. No credit cards. Mon–Tues 8:30am–4pm, Wed–Thurs 8:30am–8pm, Fri–Sat 8am–9pm, Sun 8am–8pm. AMERICAN/ITALIAN.

Located in a nondescript shopping plaza at the north end of town, this combination casual restaurant and deli is run by Barbara Lowry, who got her Lincoln City start at the upscale Bay House. The menu is short and simple, but everything is made fresh daily and is available either in the dining room or to go from the deli. While lunches consist mainly of burgers, the dinner menu might include pork tenderloin with roasted sweet bell peppers or rock shrimp in a reduced cream sauce with nutmeg, garlic, and lemon juice. Italian and Northwest wines are available to accompany meals. Families are always welcome at this casual spot. On weekends, there are free wine tastings.

A GOOD PLACE TO EAT EN ROUTE TO OR FROM PORTLAND

✪ **Otis Café.** Ore. 18, Otis. ☎ **541/994-2813.** Reservations not accepted. Breakfast $4–$7; lunch $5–$8; dinner $7–$9. DISC, MC, V. Daily 7am–9pm (June–Sept, Mon–Sat only). AMERICAN.

If you've ever seen the determination with which urbanites head for the beach on summer weekends, you can understand what a feat it is to get cars to stop before they've got sand in the treads of their tires. This tiny roadside diner 5 miles north of Lincoln City and 4 miles shy of the beach manages to do just that with its black bread, cinnamon rolls, and fried red potatoes. The homemade mustard and killer salsa also have their loyal fans. Pies—marionberry, strawberry/rhubarb, walnut— have crusts for the noncholesterol conscious and are memorable even in this land of perfect pies. Expect a line out the screen door (couples and solo diners usually find a seat faster than larger groups). Breakfasts and dinners are usually so large that one order could serve two people.

6 Depoe Bay

13 miles S of Lincoln City, 13 miles N of Newport, 70 miles W of Salem

Depoe Bay calls itself the smallest harbor in the world, and once you've seen the town's tiny harbor you'll have to agree. Though the harbor covers only 6 acres, it's home to more than 100 fishing boats. As fascinating as the harbor itself is the narrow channel, little more than a crack in the coastline's solid rock wall, that leads into Depoe Bay. During stormy seas, it's almost impossible to get in or out of the harbor safely. Storm waves also bring on the impressive fountains of Depoe Bay's famous spouting horns, which are produced when waves break in narrow fissures in the area's rocky coastline.

Shell mounds and kitchen middens around the bay indicate that Native Americans long called this area home. In 1894, the U.S. government deeded the land surrounding the bay to a Siletz Indian known as Old Charlie Depot, who had taken his name from an army depot at which he had worked. Old Charlie later changed his name to DePoe, and when a town was founded here in 1927, it took the name Depoe Bay. Though most of the town is located a bit off the highway, you'll find, right on U.S. 101, a row of garish souvenir shops, which sadly mar the beauty of this rocky section of coast. Among these shops are several family restaurants and charter-fishing and whale-watching companies.

ESSENTIALS

GETTING THERE   From the north, the most direct route is Ore. 99W/18 to Lincoln City and then south on U.S. 101. From the south take U.S. 20 from Corvallis to Newport and then go north on U.S. 101.

VISITOR INFORMATION   Contact the **Depoe Bay Chamber of Commerce,** 630 SE U.S. 101 (P.O. Box 21), Depoe Bay, OR 97341 (☎ **541/765-2889**).

WHAT TO SEE & DO

Aside from watching the boat traffic passing in and out of the world's smallest harbor, the most popular activity here, especially when the seas are high, is watching the spouting horns across U.S. 101 from Depoe Bay's souvenir shops. Spouting horns, which are similar to blowholes, can be seen all along the coast, but nowhere are they more spectacular than here at Depoe Bay. These geyserlike plumes occur in places where water is forced through narrow channels in basalt rock. As the channels become more restricted, the water shoots skyward under great pressure and can spray 60 feet into the air. If the surf is really up, the water can carry quite a ways, and more than a few unwary visitors have been soaked.

   Sportfishing and whale watching draw most visitors to town these days. You can arrange for either at **Tradewinds** (☎ **800/445-8730** or 541/765-2345), at the north nd of the bridge; **Joan-E Charters** (☎ **800/995-FUNN** or 541/765-2222), at the south end of the bridge; **Depoe Bay Ocean Charters** (☎ **800/550-5726** or 541/ 765-FISH); or **Dockside Charters** (☎ **800/733-8915** or 541/765-2545), down by the marina. Whale-watching trips run $10 for 1 hour and $18 for 2 hours, and fishing trips run $50 for 5 hours up to $140 for 12 hours of halibut or tuna fishing.

   North of town, you'll find tide pools among the rocks in the small coves at **Boiler Bay State Park,** although the beach itself is not accessible from the state park pull-off on U.S. 101. To reach the beach, go a half mile north and watch for a trail. Just north of here, you'll find easier beach access at **Fogarty Creek State Park,** a beautiful little cove with basalt cliffs at one end and a creek flowing across the beach. The parking area is on the east side of U.S. 101.

WHERE TO STAY

✪ **Channel House.** 35 Ellingson St., Depoe Bay, OR 97341. ☎ **800/447-2140** or 541/ 765-2140. Fax 541/765-2191. 10 rms, 2 suites. TV TEL. $75–$95 double ocean-view, $150 oceanfront; $195–$225 suite. Rates include full breakfast. AE, DISC, MC, V.

The narrow, cliff-bordered channel into diminutive Depoe Bay is one of the most challenging harbor entrances in Oregon, and perched above it is the Channel House, one of the coast's most luxurious and strikingly situated small inns. A contemporary building with lots of angles and windows, the Channel House offers large rooms, most of which have gas fireplaces and private decks with whirlpool tubs. You can sit and soak as fishing boats navigate their way through the channel below you. There are few lodgings with as dramatic a view anywhere on the Oregon coast.

✪ **Inn at Otter Crest.** Otter Crest Loop Rd. (P.O. Box 50), Otter Rock, OR 97369. ☎ **800/ 452-2101** or 541/765-2111. Fax 541/765-5047. 120 rms and suites. TV TEL. $99–$129 double; $119–$299 suite. DISC, MC, V.

The Inn at Otter Crest is one of the Oregon coast's premier resorts and reflects the region in both architecture and setting. The inn's numerous weathered-cedar buildings are surrounded by 35 acres of forests and beautifully landscaped gardens on a rocky crest above a secluded cove. If you want to get away from it all and enjoy a bit of forest seclusion on the beach, there's no better spot. Most rooms have excellent ocean views through a wall of glass that opens onto a balcony. Our favorite rooms are the loft suites, which have fireplaces, kitchens, and high ceilings. Service here is rather casual, in keeping with Northwest attitudes.

   Dining/Entertainment: The Flying Dutchman is located downhill from the guest rooms near the resort's swimming pool. The menu focuses on local seafood.

   Facilities: Outdoor swimming pool, hot tub, sauna, tennis, hiking trails.

The Surfrider. 3115 NW U.S. 101, Depoe Bay, OR 97341. ☎ **800/662-2378** or 541/764-2311. Fax 541/764-2634. 42 rms. TV TEL. Mid-June–Sept 30 $70–$125 double. Oct 1–mid-June $60–$95 double. AE, DISC, MC, V.

Though it has been around for many years, this low-rise motel just north of Depoe Bay is still a family favorite on the Oregon coast. It's hidden from the highway, which gives it a secluded feel, and there are great views from the open bluff-top setting. You can choose between basic motel rooms and rooms with fireplaces, kitchens, or hot tubs. At the foot of a long staircase is a wide beach on a small cove. The dining room and lounge offer a great view of the tiny cove of Fogarty Creek State Park. The hotel also has an indoor swimming pool and hot tub.

WHERE TO DINE

At the **Siletz Tribal Smokehouse,** on U.S. 101 south of the bridge (☎ **800/828-4269** or 541/765-2286), you can buy smoked salmon and other seafood. The Smokehouse is run by the Confederated Tribes of the Siletz and is a great place to buy picnic fixings as you head out to the beach.

Tidal Raves. 279 NW U.S. 101. ☎ **541/765-2995.** Reservations recommended. Main courses $11–$17; lunch $8–$10. MC, V. Daily 11am–9pm. SEAFOOD.

Up at the north end of Depoe Bay's strip of tourist shops is a place that has had folks raving for years now. With its bright, uncluttered decor and big windows for taking in the view of wave-carved sandstone cliffs, Tidal Raves offers Depoe Bay diners a contemporary restaurant with a view. Keep your eyes on those cliffs outside the windows and you just might see water spouting up through some of the famous blowholes. The menu offers plenty of straightforward seafood, but it also includes some creative preparations such as Cajun sautéed oysters and Thai barbecued prawns.

EN ROUTE SOUTH TO NEWPORT

The road south from Depoe Bay winds its way through grand scenery of rugged splendor as it passes several small, picturesque coves. Just south of town, **Rocky Creek State Park,** with windswept lawns, picnic tables, and great views of buff-colored cliffs and spouting horns, is a good place for a picnic. In a few more miles you'll come to the **Otter Crest Scenic Loop,** which takes in some spectacular vistas and leads to **Cape Foulweather,** which was named by Capt. James Cook in 1778. This was Cook's first glimpse of land after leaving the Sandwich Islands (Hawaii), and the sighting initiated the first English claims to the region. The cape frequently lives up to its name, with winds often gusting to more than 100 miles per hour. Keep an eye out for the sea lions that sun themselves on offshore rocks near Cape Foulweather. At press time, this scenic loop was closed due to a road washout caused by a winter storm. However, a historic building now used as a gift shop provides a protected glimpse of the sea from atop Cape Foulweather.

At the south end of the scenic loop, you'll find the **Devil's Punchbowl** overlook, which provides a glimpse into a collapsed sea cave that during high tides or stormy seas becomes a churning cauldron of foam. Adjacent to Devil's Punchbowl, in a small cove, you'll find the **Marine Gardens,** where, at low tide, numerous tide pools can be explored. From this cove, you can also explore inside the Devil's Punchbowl. South of Devil's Punchbowl State Park, lies **Beverly Beach State Park,** which has a campground and is a popular surfing spot.

7 Newport

23 miles S of Lincoln City, 58 miles W of Corvallis, 24 miles N of Yachats

The air smells of fish and shrimp, and freeloading sea lions doze on the docks while they wait for their next meal from the processing plants along the waterfront. Dockworkers unloading fresh fish mingle with vacationers licking ice-cream cones, and both fishing boats and pleasure craft ply the waters of the bay. As coastal towns go, Newport has a split personality.

Newport got its start in the late 1800s as both an oystering community and one of the earliest Oregon beach resorts, and many of the old cottages and historic buildings can still be seen. While the town's Nye Beach area has the feel of a turn-of-the-century resort, the downtown bay front is, despite its souvenir shops, galleries, and restaurants, still a working port and home port for the largest commercial fishing fleet on the Oregon coast. The site of the Oregon Coast Aquarium and now the home of Keiko, the killer whale that starred in the movie *Free Willy,* Newport is one of the most popular towns on the Oregon coast. Oysters are also still important to the local economy and are raised in oyster beds along Yaquina Bay Road east of town.

Though in recent years it has come close to matching the overdevelopment of Lincoln City, this fishing port on the shore of Yaquina Bay still manages to offer a balance of industry, history, culture, beaches, and family vacation attractions.

ESSENTIALS

GETTING THERE   Newport is on U.S. 101 at the junction with U.S. 20, which leads to Corvallis. **Lincoln County Transit** (☎ 541/265-4900), provides bus service from Lincoln City in the north and Yachats in the south.

VISITOR INFORMATION   Contact the **Greater Newport Chamber of Commerce,** 555 SW Coast Hwy., Newport, OR 97365 (☎ 800/262-7844 or 541/265-8801).

GETTING AROUND   Public bus service is provided by **Lincoln County Transit** (☎ 541/265-4900), which operates north to Lincoln City and south to Yachats. If you need a taxi, call **Yaquina Cab** (☎ 541/265-9552). Currently, between June and September, the passenger-only **Yaquina Bay Ferry** (☎ 541/270-4060) operates between the Newport bay front (from the dock beside Sea Gull Charters) and Newport Marina near the Oregon Coast Aquarium. This ferry allows you to avoid the summer traffic jams that often plague Newport.

FESTIVALS   In late July each year, the music of composer Ernest Bloch, who once lived in this area, is celebrated during the **Ernest Bloch Music Festival** (☎ 541/265-2787). In August, the **Jazz on the Water Festival** (☎ 541/265-4074) brings world-class jazz to the Newport Marina.

SEEING THE SIGHTS

✪ **Oregon Coast Aquarium.** 2820 SE Ferry Slip Rd. ☎ **541/867-3474.** Admission $8.50 adults, $7.50 seniors and children 13–18, $4.25 children 4–12. Memorial Day to Labor Day daily 9am–6pm; Labor Day to Memorial Day daily 10am–5pm. Closed Dec 25.

Even before Keiko, the star of the hit children's movie *Free Willy,* ever moved to the Oregon Coast Aquarium, this was the biggest attraction on these shores. Now, with Keiko in residence and slowly regaining his health, the aquarium is more popular than ever. Keiko, a 7,700-pound killer whale (orca), was airlifted to the aquarium in 1996 from his cramped quarters in a Mexico City amusement park. He now lives in a state-of-the-art computerized pool that's five times as large as his old quarters. If he recovers his health sufficiently, he may be returned to the wild.

Before you even make it through the doors of this modern aquarium, you begin to learn about life along the Oregon coast. Once inside, there are so many fascinating displays that it's easy to spend the better part of a day here. After Keiko, the stars of the aquarium are the playful sea otters, but the clown-faced tufted puffins, which are kept in a walk-through aviary, are big favorites as well. The sea lions sometimes rouse from their naps to put on impromptu shows, and the lucky visitor even gets a glimpse of a giant octopus with an arm span of nearly 20 feet. Artificial waves surge in a tank that reproduces, on a speeded-up scale, life in a rocky intertidal zone. And so far, you haven't even made it to the indoor aquarium displays. In these you'll find various coastal habitats and the life-forms that inhabit them. There are examples of sandy beaches, rocky shores, salt marshes, kelp forests, and even the open ocean, where diaphanous jellyfish drift lazily on the currents.

Because this is the most popular attraction on the Oregon coast, lines to get in can be very long. Arrive early if you're visiting on a summer weekend.

OSU Hatfield Marine Science Center. 2030 Marine Science Dr. ☎ **541/867-0100.** Admission $3 donation. Memorial Day to Labor Day daily 10am–6pm; Labor Day to Memorial Day Thurs–Mon 10am–4pm.

Before the Oregon Coast Aquarium was built, Newport was already known as a center for marine science research. This facility, though primarily a university research center, also contains displays that are open to the public, and reopened in May of 1997 after an extensive remodeling. The new exhibits, though not quite as impressive as those at the Oregon Coast Aquarium, highlight current topics in marine research. Aquarium tanks exhibit examples of Oregon sea life and interpretive exhibits explain life in the sea. Definitely a worthwhile adjunct to a visit to see Keiko and friends.

Yaquina Bay Lighthouse. In Yaquina Bay State Park, 846 SW Government St. ☎ **541/ 265-5679.** Free admission. Memorial Day to mid-Sept daily 11am–5pm (shorter hours other months).

The Newport area has two lighthouses, and of the two, the historic Yaquina Bay Lighthouse, built in 1871, is the oldest building in Newport. This lighthouse is not the classic tower style, but is instead a two-story wood-frame house with the light on the roof. The building served as both home and lighthouse, but only operated until 1874 when the Yaquina Head Lighthouse was constructed. This latter lighthouse, located 3 miles north of here at Yaquina Head Outstanding Natural Area, was supposed to stand on Cape Foulweather, but heavy seas made it impossible to land there. Instead, the light was built on Yaquina Head, and so powerful was the light that it supplanted the one at Yaquina Bay.

OTHER ATTRACTIONS: BEACHES, FISHING, SHOPPING & MORE

Beaches in the Newport area range from tiny rocky coves where you can search for agates to long, wide stretches of sand perfect for kite flying. Right in town you'll find the **Yaquina Bay State Park,** which borders on both the ocean and the bay and is home to the **Yaquina Bay Lighthouse.** North of Newport is **Agate Beach,** which was once known for the beautiful agates that could be found there. However, in recent years sand has covered the formerly rocky beach, hiding the stones from rock hunters. This beach has a stunning view of Yaquina Head, 3 miles north of Newport.

Yaquina Head is an ancient volcano that's now preserved as the **Yaquina Head Outstanding Natural Area** (☎ 541/265-2863). Here you'll also find the **Yaquina Head Lighthouse,** which is open for tours ($2 adults, $1 children, or $5 family) throughout the summer daily between 9 and 11:30am. Yaquina Head is home to thousands of nesting sea birds, and the raucous cries of glaucous-winged and western gulls fill the air. Other birds you'll see here include cormorants and pigeon guillemots. Harbor seals can also be seen lounging on the rocks, and in early winter and spring, gray whales can be spotted migrating along the coast. On the cobblestone beach below the lighthouse, you can explore tide pools at low tide. There is even a wheelchair-accessible tide-pool trail in a cove that once was the site of a rock quarry. For an introduction to the natural and human history of this headland, visit the new **Yaquina Head Interpretive Center** ($2 adults, $1 children, $5 family), which houses displays covering everything from the sea life of tide pools to the life of lighthouse keepers and their families.

Two miles south of Newport, you'll come to **South Beach State Park,** a wide sandy beach with picnic areas and a campground (that also rents yurts). Another 4 miles south is **Ona Beach State Park,** a sandy beach with a picnic area under the trees and Beaver Creek flowing through the park and across the beach to the ocean. Another 2 miles will bring you to **Seal Rock State Park,** where a long wall of rock rises from the waves and sand and creates numerous tide pools and fascinating nooks and crannies to explore.

Fishing for salmon, tuna, halibut, and bottom fish can be quite productive in area waters. You can charter a fishing boat on the bay front at **Newport Sportfishing,** 1000 SE Bay Blvd. (☎ **800/828-8777** or 541/265-7558); **Newport Tradewinds,** 653 SW Bay Blvd. (☎ **800/676-7819** or 541/265-2101); or **Sea Gull Charters,** 343 SW Bay Blvd. (☎ **800/865-7441** or 541/265-7441). Fishing trips run anywhere from $60 to $150 depending on what you're fishing for and how long you stay out. Newport claims to be the Dungeness crab capital of the world, and if you'd like to find out if this claim is true, you can rent crab rings and boats at **Sawyer's Landing,** 4098 Yaquina Bay Rd. (☎ **541/265-3907**), or at the **Embarcadero Marina,** 1000 SE Bay Blvd. (☎ **541/265-5435**). Expect to pay $40 to $50 for a boat and two crab rings for half a day. **Clamming** is also popular, and sometimes productive, in the Newport area. Pick up a tide table at a local business and head out on the flats with your clam shovel and a bucket. Whale-watching tours are offered throughout the year by **Marine Discovery Tours,** 345 SW Bay Blvd. (☎ **800/903-BOAT** or 541/265-6200). Two-hour cruises are around $18. If you'd rather just go for a sail, contact **Newport Daysail Adventures** (☎ **541/265-7441**).

If you'd like to delve into local history, stop by the **Burrows House Museum,** 545 SW Ninth St. (☎ **541/265-7509**), and the affiliated Log Cabin Museum. The Burrows House was built in 1895 as a boardinghouse and now contains exhibits of household furnishings and fashions from the Victorian era. The **Log Cabin Museum** houses Siltetz Indian artifacts from the area, as well as exhibits on logging, farming, and maritime history. Both museums are open Tuesday through Sunday: June to September from 10am to 5pm and October to May from 11am to 4pm. The works of local and regional artists are showcased at the **Newport Visual Arts Center,** 839 NW Beach Dr. (☎ **541/265-6540**), open Tuesday through Sunday: April to September from noon to 4pm and October to March from 11am to 3pm.

As one of the coast's most popular family vacation spots, Newport has all the tourist traps one would expect. Billboards up and down the coast advertise the sorts of places that kids demand to be taken to. Tops on this list are **Ripley's Believe It or Not** and the **Wax Works Museum.** Across the street from these you'll find **Undersea Gardens,** where a scuba diver feeds fish, including a giant octopus, in a large tank beneath a boat moored on the bay front. All three attractions share the same address and phone number: Mariner Square, 250 SW Bay Blvd. (☎ **541/265-2206**). Admission for each is $6 adults, $3.50 children; or $15 adult, $8.50 children for all three attractions.

Golfers can head out to the nine-hole **Agate Beach Golf Course,** 4100 N. Coast Hwy. (☎ **541/265-7331**), north of town.

You'll find Newport's greatest concentration of interesting shops down on the bay front. **Breach the Moon Gallery,** 434 SW Bay Blvd. (☎ **541/265-9698**), features art glass and art with ocean and whale themes. Nearby is **Oceanic Arts,** 444 SW Bay Blvd. (☎ **541/265-5963**), which sells interesting crafts, including wind chimes and lots of ceramics. The **Wood Gallery,** 818 SW Bay Blvd. (☎ **541/265-6843**), specializes in wooden items including boxes and musical instruments. South of Newport, on U.S. 101 in Seal Rock, you'll find **Triad Gallery** (☎ **541/563-5442**), which has an eclectic array of fine arts and crafts and is the most strikingly designed art gallery on the Oregon coast.

The Newport Performing Arts Center, 777 W. Olive St. (☎ **541/265-ARTS**), hosts local and nationally recognized performers throughout the year. Tickets run $5 to $20.

WHERE TO STAY
EXPENSIVE
✪ **Starfish Point.** 140 NW 48th St., Newport, OR 97365. ☎ **541/265-3751.** Fax 541/265-3040. 6 condo apts. $155–$175 apt for 2 to 6. Off-season rates available. 2-night weekend minimum. AE, DISC, MC, V.

Located north of town in a grove of fir trees on the edge of a cliff, the Starfish Point condominiums are our favorite rooms in the area. Each of the six condos has two bedrooms and two baths spaced over two floors. Between the two floors you'll find a cozy sitting area in an octagonal room that's almost all windows. This room is in addition to the spacious living room with its unusual wicker furniture, fireplace, stereo, VCR, and Asian accent pieces. The bathrooms here are extravagant affairs with two-person whirlpool tubs, skylights or big windows, and hanging plants. A path leads down to the beach, and to the north is Yaquina Head, one of the coast's picturesque headlands. You're a ways out of town here, so you might want to cook your own meals and savor the solitude.

MODERATE
Embarcadero. 1000 SE Bay Blvd., Newport, OR 97365. ☎ **800/547-4779** or 541/265-8521. Fax 541/265-7844. 150 rms. TV TEL. Summer, $70–$190 double. Lower rates off-season. AE, CB, DC, DISC, MC, V.

Located on Yaquina Bay, the Embarcadero is a condominium resort that offers Newport's most luxurious accommodations. The resort combines Northwest materials and landscaping and contemporary architecture, and is popular with the boating set, who tie up at the resort's marina. The three-story buildings have unobstructed views of Yaquina Bay, and the guest rooms have their own decks. The larger one- and two-bedroom suites have fireplaces and kitchens.

The Embarcadero dining room has a good view of the bay and serves fairly straightforward American and continental fare. Facilities include an indoor pool, whirlpool, and saunas, and sportfishing charters and boat rentals are available.

Hallmark Resort. 744 SW Elizabeth St., Newport, OR 97365. ☎ **888/448-4449** or 541/265-2600. 152 rms. TV TEL. $69–$239 double. Rates include continental breakfast. AE, DISC, MC, V.

With an interior done up to resemble that of a modern cruise ship, this hotel near the old Yaquina Bay Lighthouse is Newport's best bet if you want to be right on the beach and have lots of modern amenities. A viewing room overlooking the ocean provides a warm, dry vantage point for whale watching if you don't have a waterfront room. The best (and most expensive) rooms have double whirlpool tubs and gas fireplaces. Although you won't find a restaurant on the premises, continental breakfast is served in the Officers' Mess. Facilities include an indoor swimming pool and adjacent large spa, a sauna, an exercise room, a video-games room, and a library with puzzles and a checkers board.

✪ **Nye Beach Hotel & Cafe.** 219 NW Cliff St., Newport, OR 97365. ☎ **541/265-3334.** Fax 541/265-3622. 18 rms. $60–$145 double. AE, DISC, MC, V.

Located on the same block as the literary Sylvia Beach Hotel, the Nye Beach has adopted the visual and performing arts as its theme, and instead of having a resident cat, has resident tropical birds. The wide open combination lobby and dining room has a warehouselike feel, though just outside lie the beach and the roaring ocean waves. A funky urban chic pervades this hotel, appealing most to young urbanites for whom there are very few hip beach retreats on the Oregon coast. While all the guest rooms have balconies and ocean views, room decor diverges wildly from that of most oceanfront hotels in the area. Bent-willow love seats, tubular metal bed frames imported from Holland, old movie and theater posters, and Indonesian masks all add up to a decidedly eclectic style here. The best rooms are the oceanfront spa rooms with gas fireplaces ($105 to $145 a night). The restaurant in the lobby serves three meals a day.

✪ **Sylvia Beach Hotel.** 267 NW Cliff St., Newport, OR 97365. ☎ **541/265-5428.** 20 rms. $66–$146 double. Rates include full breakfast. AE, MC, V.

This eclectic four-story green-shingled hotel pays homage to literature and is probably the Oregon coast's most famous lodging. The rooms are named for different authors, and in each room you'll find memorabilia, books, and decor that reflect these authors' lives, times, and works. The Agatha Christie Room, the hotel's most popular, seems full of clues, while in the Edgar Allan Poe Room, a pendulum hangs over the bed and a stuffed raven sits by the window. Among the writers represented are Tennessee Williams, Colette, Hemingway, Alice Walker, Jane Austen, F. Scott Fitzgerald, Emily Dickinson, and even Dr. Seuss. If you happen to be allergic to cats, you'll want to pass on this inn since there is a resident cat. The Tables of Content restaurant downstairs is a local favorite (see "Where to Dine," below). Hot wine is served in the library at 10pm each evening.

Tyee Lodge. 4925 NW Woody Way, Newport, OR 97365. ☎ **888/553-8933** or 541/265-8953. 5 rms. $95–$115 double. Rates include full breakfast. MC, V.

Located just south of Yaquina Head, this oceanfront bed-and-breakfast sits atop a high bluff surrounded by tall trees. Guest rooms here are large and all have good ocean views, as do the living and dining rooms. Although the first floor of the inn dates back more than 50 years, the upper floor, which houses all the guest rooms was only recently added on. A complete interior renovation has left the entire house looking very fresh and modern. In the breakfast room, you'll find a telescope for whale watching, and on cooler days, a fireplace warms the living room. A stylish Eddie Bauer look predominates.

Vikings Motel. 729 NW Coast St., Newport, OR 97365. ☎ **541/265-2477.** 14 cabins, 22 condo apts. TV. $65–$80, 1-bedroom cabin for 2; $70–$95, 2-bedroom cabin for 2; $85–$225 condo for 2. AE, DC, DISC, MC, V.

Though there are more of the new condominiums here than old cabins, the cabins are still most appealing, especially if you're on a budget. Certainly not for everyone, these rustic old places are rather dark and eclectically furnished but are right on the beach and are comfortable nonetheless. Most cabins come with kitchens, which makes them an even better deal. Built in 1925 and modeled after Cape Cod cottages, the cabins are reminiscent of times gone by when families spent their annual vacation clamming, fishing, and beachcombing. The most popular accommodation here is a room called the Crow's Nest, which has a great view. The condos are clean, modern, and individually decorated and have kitchens.

CAMPGROUNDS

If you're looking for a place to pitch a tent or are interested in renting a yurt, try to get into **South Beach State Park** (☎ 541/867-4715), which is located 2 miles south of Newport at the mouth of Yaquina Bay. With 244 campsites and 10 yurts, this is one of the biggest state park campgrounds on the coast. Make reservations through **Reservations Northwest** (☎ 800/452-5687).

WHERE TO DINE
MODERATE

Canyon Way Restaurant & Bookstore. 1216 SW Canyon Way. ☎ **541/265-8319.** Reservations recommended. Main courses $12.50–$24.50; lunch $5.25–$11. AE, DISC, MC, V. Mon 11am–3pm, Tues–Thurs 11am–3pm and 5–8:30pm, Fri–Sat 11am–3pm and 5–9pm. CONTINENTAL/AMERICAN/NORTHWEST.

Located just up the hill from Bay Boulevard, this big pink building is a combination restaurant, deli, bookstore, and gift shop. A vaguely Southwestern exterior, patios, and attractive flower gardens make this a very relaxing spot for lunch or dinner. Pastas and sauces, which are available to go, are made fresh daily in such flavorful combinations as sun-dried tomato pesto prawns. At dinner you can start things off with Santa Fe baked oysters or duck pâté, and then follow up with cod Provençal, steak au poivre, or New Orleans bouillabaisse. Early dinners ($10.95), available between 5 and 6pm, are a good deal.

Nye Beach Cafe. 219 NW Cliff St. ☎ **541/265-3334.** Reservations recommended on weekends. Main courses $8–$15; lunch $4.25–$7.25. AE, DISC, MC, V. Daily 7:30am–4pm and 5–10pm. INTERNATIONAL.

With a warehouselike dining room and a deck overlooking the beach, this very hip place is a fun spot for an economical meal. For a starter, try the shrimp quesadilla, which is served with an excellent fresh salsa. The thick and flavorful cioppino is another good bet. The menu is as eclectic as the surroundings and includes enchiladas, chicken satay, Indian curries, and several Cajun dishes. Luckily, main courses aren't so filling that you won't have room for the carrot cake, which our waiter described as the best in the world. He just might have been right. Wines are very reasonably priced. For breakfast, try the Nye Beach eggs Benedict, made with chorizo; at lunch, the crab cakes are a good bet.

Tables of Content. Sylvia Beach Hotel, 267 NW Cliff St. ☎ **541/265-5428.** Reservations required. Fixed-price 4-course dinner $17.50. AE, MC, V. Seatings Sun–Thurs 7pm, Fri–Sat 6 and 8:30pm. INTERNATIONAL.

Located downstairs in the Sylvia Beach Hotel, an homage to the literary arts, this cleverly named restaurant serves delicious and very reasonably priced four-course dinners. While on any given night you'll have limited choices, if you enjoy creative cookery and eclectic combinations, you'll likely leave your table perfectly content. Expect the likes of black-bean soup, Greek salad, scallops in saffron sauce, wild rice, fresh vegetables, a chocolate-berry trifle, and coffee or tea.

The Whale's Tale. Bay Blvd. and Fall St. ☎ **541/265-8660.** Reservations not accepted. Main courses $11–$19; lunch $5–$7. AE, DISC, MC, V. Mon–Fri 8am–10pm, Sat–Sun 9am–10pm. SEAFOOD.

Opened in the 1970s and still owned by its founder, the Whale's Tale is a tried-and-true place for locals who seek it out for the clam chowder and such great breakfasts as poppy seed pancakes or huevos rancheros. Lunch and dinner include Greek salads, catch of the day with fruit salsa, veggie lasagna, or grilled oysters. Service is friendly, whether you're a long-time customer or just visiting. On summer days, there is usually a line out the door both at lunch and at dinner.

Yuzen. U.S. 101, Seal Rock. ☎ **541/563-4766.** Reservations recommended on weekends. Main courses $9.50–$25; lunch $5.50–$11.50. MC, V. Tues–Sun 11am–2pm and 4–9pm. JAPANESE.

Located 8 miles south of Newport in Seal Rock, this Japanese restaurant is in an unlikely looking Tudor house. A long menu includes such unusual dishes as octopus salad and smoked eel, but also includes sushi, sashimi, teriyaki salmon steak, and several special dinners.

INEXPENSIVE

Cosmos Cafe & Gallery. 740 W. Olive St. ☎ **541/265-7511.** Reservations not accepted. Main courses $5–$7. DISC, MC, V. Mon–Sat 8am–9pm. INTERNATIONAL.

Located in the historic Nye Beach neighborhood, this combination casual cafe and art gallery is in a modern building and has ocean views both from the main dining room and from a small front porch. Both Cajun and Greek influences show up on the menu, and you'll also find the likes of eggplant sandwiches. The Newport Performing Arts Center is across the street, which makes this a good bet for a simple meal before a show.

Mo's. 622 SW Bay Blvd. ☎ **541/265-2979.** Reservations not accepted. Complete dinner $6–$10. AE, DISC, MC, V. Daily 11am–9pm. SEAFOOD.

Established in 1942, Mo's has become so much of an Oregon coast institution that it has spawned not only an annex across the street but several other restaurants up and down the coast. Clam chowder is what made Mo's famous, and you can get it by the bowl, by the cup, or family style. You can even get frozen clam chowder base to go. Basic seafood dinners are fresh, large, and inexpensive, and the seafood-salad sandwiches are whoppers. There are also such dishes as cioppino, gazpacho with shrimp, and slumgullion (clam chowder with shrimp). There's a good chance you'll have to wait in line whether you're here for lunch or dinner.

Rogue Ales Public House. 748 SW Bay Blvd. ☎ **541/265-3188.** Sandwiches $5–$7; pizzas $7.25–$21. MC, V. PUB GRUB.

This microbrewery's fresh ales, of which there can be as many as a dozen on tap at any given time, are not only delicious to drink, but they also end up in a number of the pub's most popular dishes. The chili is made with amber ale. The pizza dough is made with stout. The English bangers are served with a beer mustard, and the oyster shooters come with an ale sauce. You'll find the pub downtown on the bay.

DRIVING ON TO YACHATS WITH A STOP IN WALDPORT

Located at the mouth of the Alsea River 8 miles north of Yachats, Waldport is a popular **fishing** spot with anglers who head upriver to catch salmon, steelhead, and cutthroat trout. **Crabbing** and **clamming** are also good here in the Alsea Bay. To learn a little more about the area, visit the **Alsea Bay Bridge Interpretive Center,** 620 NW Spring St. (☎ **541/563-2002**).

A Charming Place to Stay

Cliff House Bed & Breakfast. 1450 Adahi Rd. (P.O. Box 436), Yaquina John Point, Waldport, OR 97394. ☎ **541/563-2506.** Fax 541/563-4393. 3 rms, 1 suite. TV. $120–$150 double; $245 suite. 2-night minimum on weekends, 3-night on holidays. Rates include full breakfast. DISC, MC, V.

The setting of this B&B, perched on the edge of a cliff overlooking the mouth of the Alsea River and 8 miles of beach, should be enough to take your breath away. The guest rooms are beautifully decorated, and depending on which room you take, you may find a four-poster bed, a wood stove, huge skylights, a wall of windows overlooking the ocean, or, should you stay in the Bridal Suite, a huge bathroom with mirrored ceiling, double whirlpool tub, and double shower. There's a hot tub and massages are available.

8 Yachats

26 miles S of Newport, 26 miles N of Florence, 138 miles SE of Portland

Located on the north side of 800-foot-high Cape Perpetua, the village of Yachats (pronounced *Yah*-hots) is known as something of an artists' community. When you get your first glimpse of the town's setting, you, too, will likely agree that there's more than enough beauty here to inspire anyone to artistic pursuits. Yachats is an Alsi Indian word meaning "dark waters at the foot of the mountains," and that sums up perfectly the setting of this small community (pop. 700). The tiny Yachats River flows into the surf on the south edge of town, and to the east stand steep, forested mountains. The shoreline on which the town stands is rocky, with little coves here and there where you can find agates among the pebbles paving the beach. Tide pools offer hours of exploring, and in winter, storm waves create a spectacular show. Uncrowded beaches, comfortable motels, and one of the coast's best restaurants all add up to a great spot for a quiet getaway.

ESSENTIALS

GETTING THERE From the north, take Ore. 34 west from Corvallis to Waldport and then head south on U.S. 101. From the south, take Ore. 126 west from Eugene to Florence and then head north on U.S. 101.

VISITOR INFORMATION Contact the **Yachats Area Chamber of Commerce,** 441 U.S. 101 (P.O. Box 728), Yachats, OR 97498 (☎ **541/547-3530**).

EXPLORING THE AREA

Looming over tiny Yachats is the impressive bulk of Cape Perpetua, which, at 800 feet high, is the highest spot on the Oregon coast. Because of the cape's rugged beauty and diversity of natural habitats, it has been designated the **Cape Perpetua Scenic Area.** The **Cape Perpetua Interpretive Center** (☎ **541/547-3289**) is located up a steep road off U.S. 101 and houses displays on the natural history of the cape and the Native Americans who harvested its bountiful seafood for thousands of years. The visitor center is open daily from 9am to 5pm between Memorial Day and Labor Day and on weekends from 10am to 4pm the rest of the year; admission is $3 for adults and $1 for children. Within the scenic area are 18 miles of hiking trails, tide pools, ancient forests, scenic overlooks, and a campground. During the summer, guided hikes are offered twice a day. If you're here on a clear day, be sure to drive to the top of the cape for one of the finest vistas on the coast. Waves and tides are a year-round source of fascination along these rocky shores, and Cape Perpetua's tide pools are some of the best on the coast. However, it is more dramatic interactions of waves and rocks that attract most people to walk the oceanside trail here: At the Devil's Churn, a spouting horn caused by waves crashing into a narrow fissure in the basalt shoreline sends geyserlike plumes of water skyward and waves boil through a narrow opening in the rocks.

If you're looking for wide sandy beach, continue south to the **Stonefield Beach Wayside, Muriel Ponsler Memorial Wayside,** or **Carl G. Washburne State Park.** The last offers 2 miles of beach, hiking trails, and a campground.

Between April and October each year, **fishing** in Yachats takes on an unusual twist. It's during these months that thousands of smelts, a sardinelike fish, spawn in the waves that crash in the sandy coves just north of Yachats. The fish can be caught using a dip net, and so popular are the little fish that the town holds an annual **Smelt Fry** each year on the second weekend in July.

Gray whales also come close to shore near Yachats. You can see them in the spring from Cape Perpetua, and throughout the summer several take up residence at the mouth of the Yachats River. Strawberry Hill Wayside, south of Cape Perpetua, is another good place to spot whales, as well as sea lions, which can be seen lounging on the rocks offshore from this wayside.

A couple of historic buildings in the area are also worth a visit if you're spending any amount of time in Yachats. Built in 1927, the **Little Log Church by the Sea,** on the corner of Third and Pontiac streets, is now a museum housing displays on local history. Nine miles up Yachats River Road you'll find a **covered bridge** that was built in 1938 and is one of the shortest in the state.

The Yachats area has two interesting crafts galleries worth visiting: **Earthworks Gallery,** 2222 U.S. 101 N. (☎ **541/547-4300**), which is located north of town, and the **Back Porch Gallery,** U.S. 101 and Fourth Street (☎ **541/547-4500**), which is attached to the New Morning Cafe right in town.

WHERE TO STAY

In addition to the hotels listed below, there are also plenty of rental homes available in Yachats. Contact **Ocean Odyssey,** P.O. Box 491, Yachats, OR 97498 (☎ **800/ 800-1915** or 541/547-3637) or **Yachats Village Rentals,** 230 Aqua Vista Dr. (P.O. Box 44), Yachats, OR 97498 (☎ **541/547-3501**). Rates range from around $100 to $125 per night.

The Adobe. 1555 U.S. 101 N. (P.O. Box 219), Yachats, OR 97498. ☎ **800/522-3623** or 541/ 547-3141. 92 rms, 12 suites. TV TEL. $58–$95 double; $110–$150 suite. Lower rates off-season. AE, CB, DC, DISC, MC, V.

The Adobe has long been a Yachats favorite. The setting, on a windswept rocky head-land on the edge of town, affords great views up and down the coast. Our favorite rooms are the fireplace rooms, which also have some of the best ocean views. Other rooms have balconies or whirlpool tubs. The least expensive rooms are those facing the hills to the east of town. In front of the hotel at low tide there are tide pools to explore and tiny beaches where you can find agates among the pebbles. There's no pool but there is a whirlpool. The Adobe dining room is a circular room with the best ocean views for miles around. The menu is, of course, primarily seafood. A separate two-floor lounge offers similar views.

Overleaf Lodge. 2055 U.S. 101 N., Yachats, OR 97498. ☎ **800/338-0507** or 541/547-4880. Fax 541/547-4888. 39 rms, 3 suites. TV TEL. $95–$155 double; $195–$225 suite. Rates include continental breakfast. DISC, MC, V.

Situated overlooking the rocky shoreline at the north end of Yachats, this small hotel is the newest lodging in the area and offers some of the most luxurious and tastefully decorated rooms on the central coast. Built in a sort of modern interpretation of the traditional Victorian beach cottage, this lodge caters primarily to couples seeking a romantic escape. Guest rooms all have VCRs, refrigerators, microwaves, and balconies. However, for a truly memorable stay, book one of the Restless Waters rooms, which have whirlpool tubs overlooking the crashing waves below. If you don't want to spring for one of these rooms, you can still curl up in a sunny little window nook beside your balcony and watch the waves in relative comfort. Many rooms also have fireplaces. Throughout the hotel you'll find artwork by Oregon artists. Should you be so inclined, you can even work out in a small exercise room. Massages are available.

✪ **Shamrock Lodgettes.** 105 U.S. 101 S. (P.O. Box 346), Yachats, OR 97498. ☎ **800/ 845-5028** or 541/547-3312. Fax 541/547-3843. 13 rms, 6 cabins. TV. $71–$95 double; $95–$112 cabin for 2. AE, CB, DC, MC, V.

This collection of classic log cabins at the mouth of the Yachats River bewitched us the first time we saw it. Spacious lawns and old fir trees give the rustic cabins a relaxed old-fashioned appeal that just begs you to kick back and forget your cares for the duration. Each log cabin has a tile entry, hardwood floors, a kitchenette, a stone fireplace, and a big picture window that takes in a view of either the beach or the river. Otherwise, however, these cabins are pretty basic. The motel rooms are more up-to-date and also have fireplaces and views. Some rooms also have whirlpool tubs. A health spa features an exercise room, hot tub, and sauna. Massages are also available at very reasonable rates.

PLACES TO STAY SOUTH OF YACHATS

Heceta Head Lightstation. 92072 U.S. 101 S., Yachats, OR 97498. ☎ **541/547-3419** or 541/547-3696. 3 rms (1 with private bath). $95–$125 double. MC, V.

The Heceta Head Lighthouse is the most photographed lighthouse on the Oregon coast due to its spectacular setting on a forested headland. While you can't spend the night in the lighthouse itself, you can stay in the former lighthouse keeper's home, a white clapboard Victorian building high atop an oceanfront bluff and set behind a picket fence. Because the house is a national historic site, it has been preserved much the way it might have looked when it was still active. Breakfasts are elaborate seven-course meals that will take you at least an hour, so leave plenty of time in your day's schedule. This is one of the most popular B&Bs on the coast, so you'll need to book your room 2 to 3 months in advance for a weekday stay and 5to 6 months in advance for a weekend stay. Oh, and by the way, this old house is haunted.

Ocean Haven. 94770 U.S. 101, Florence, OR 97439. ☎ **541/547-3583.** Fax 541/547-3583. 8 rms, 5 with bath. $35–$85 double. MC, V.

Rustic and cozy, the Ocean Haven is a great place to hole up with family or friends. Opt for either the North Up or South Up room and you'll find yourself ensconced in a room with two walls of glass overlooking the ocean. When the weather's good, you're only a short trail away from the beach, and when it's stormy, you can hole up in your room and watch the waves through big windows. Despite its lack of a private bath, the Shag's Nest cottage is the lodge's most popular room. This private elfin cottage is across the grass from the main lodge and perched on the edge of the bluff. You can lie in bed gazing out to sea with a fire crackling in the fireplace, but you'll have to walk back to the main lodge for a bathroom (there are currently plans to add a bathroom to this cottage). If you're looking for a good value and rooms that are a little bit out of the ordinary, this is the place.

Sea Quest Bed and Breakfast. 95354 U.S. 101, Yachats, OR 97498. ☎ **800/341-4878** or 541/547-3782. Fax 541/547-3719. 5 rms. $130–$160 double. MC, V.

Set on a low bluff above the beach, this sprawling contemporary inn is about as luxurious a place as you'll find anywhere on the central Oregon coast. All the rooms have private entrances and whirlpool tubs, so, obviously, privacy and romance are high priorities here. All the rooms also have ocean views. In the second-floor great room, you'll find expansive views and a convivial atmosphere most evenings. There's also a huge deck if you want to take in the salt air. Miles of beach stretch away from the inn in both directions.

✪ **Ziggurat Bed & Breakfast.** 95330 U.S. 101 S., Yachats, OR 97498. ☎ **541/547-3925.** 1 rm, 2 suites. $125–$140 double. No credit cards. Closed Jan and Christmas.

Located 6¹/₂ miles south of Yachats on a wide, flat stretch of beach, the Ziggurat is an architectural gem on this jewel coast. The four-story pyramidal contemporary home rises beside a salmon stream on the edge of the dunes. The interior is every bit as breathtaking, with contemporary art and international artifacts on display. A maze of rooms and stairways leads to the two huge first-floor suites, the larger of which covers more than 700 square feet. In these fascinating spaces you'll find slate floors, walls of windows, spacious bathrooms, private saunas, and contemporary furnishings—in short, they're the most stunning rooms on the coast. Up at the apex of the pyramid is the third room, which has a half bath in the room plus a full bath two flights below. This room has two decks and the best views in the house. If you like contemporary styling, this will be your favorite lodging on the coast.

CAMPGROUNDS

For exploring the rugged Cape Perpetua area, the forest service's **Cape Perpetua Campground,** in a wooded setting set back a little ways from the water, is your best option. Just south of Cape Perpetua, there are a couple more campgrounds within Siuslaw National Forest. **Tillicum Beach Campground** is right on the beach and is popular with RVs. **Rock Creek Campground** is tucked back in the woods along a pretty creek and is a good choice for tenters and anyone who dislikes crowds. The area's state park option is **Carl G. Washburne State Park,** which is the only coastal state park that does not take reservations. Campsites are across the highway from a pretty beach just north of Heceta Head.

WHERE TO DINE

One of Yachats' most popular restaurants is the dining room at **The Adobe** (see "Where to Stay," above, for details). For a quick sandwich, check out **Orca Wholefoods Natural Foods Market & Deli,** 84 Beach St. (☎ 541/547-4065), which also happens to have a nice view.

✪ **La Serre.** Second Ave. and Beach St. ☎ **541/547-3420.** Reservations highly recommended. Main courses $13–$23. AE, MC, V. Mon and Wed–Sat 5–9pm, Sun 9am–noon (seasonally) and 5–9pm. Closed Jan. CONTINENTAL.

For years, La Serre has served up the best food in the area, and although the greenhouse setting is attractive, if you're like us you'll be immediately distracted by the dessert table just inside the front door. Hanging from the ceiling are more plants and lots of old Japanese glass floats, the sort that frequently wash up on the shores of this coast. You could start your dinner with some Manhattan clam chowder, a delicious surprise here on the West Coast. The entree menu includes everything from a simple shrimp sandwich to filet mignon to fisherman's stew, a gentle tomato-flavored cioppino with so much fish, shrimp, clams, crab, and oysters in it that you don't know where to start. The desserts are as good as they look: pear crunch, hazelnut cheesecake with raspberry sauce, and a wickedly rich flourless chocolate cake.

New Morning Cafe and Coffee House. 373 U.S. 101. ☎ **541/547-3848.** Main courses $11.50–$14. No credit cards. Daily 11am–8pm. INTERNATIONAL.

For years this has been *the* place in Yachats for breakfast, pastries, and espresso, and now the New Morning stays open until the evening. The dinner menu is an eclectic melange of flavors ranging from beef Stroganoff to tamale pie to lemon creme salmon Florentine. The little weather-beaten shack of a place has loads of character, with an abundance of wood, a loft dining area, and a deck that connects to a small craft gallery. If you're looking for a casual, inexpensive meal amid laid-back surroundings, this is the place.

DRIVING ON TO FLORENCE

Traveling south from Cape Perpetua, you pass several waysides and parks providing picnic areas, campgrounds, and access to the beach. Of these, **Devils Elbow State Park** offers the most breathtaking setting. Situated on a small sandy cove, the park has a stream that flows across the beach on its route to the ocean. Just offshore stand several haystack rocks, and visible from the beach is **Heceta Head Lighthouse,** the most photographed lighthouse on the Oregon coast. Heceta (pronounced Huh-*see*-tuh) Head is a rugged headland that's named for Spanish explorer Capt. Bruno Heceta. The old lighthouse keeper's home is now a bed-and-breakfast (see above).

A mile farther south you'll come to ✪ **Sea Lion Caves,** 91560 U.S. 101 (☎ **541/ 547-3111**), which, at more than 300 feet long and 120 feet high, is the largest sea cave in the United States. The cave was discovered in 1880, and since 1932 has been one of the most popular stops along the Oregon coast. The cave and a nearby rock ledge are the only year-round mainland homes for Steller's sea lions, hundreds of which reside here throughout the year. This is the larger of the two species of sea lion that frequent this coast, and bulls can weigh almost a ton. The sea lions spend the day lounging and barking up a storm, and the bickering of the adults and antics of the pups never fail to entertain visitors. Although at any time of year, you're likely to find quite a few of the sea lions in the cave, it is during the fall and winter that the majority of the sea lions move into the cave. Today, a combination of stairs, pathways, and an elevator lead down from the bluff-top gift shop to a viewpoint in the cave wall. Admission is $6 for adults, $4 for children 6 to 15. The cave is open daily from 9am until one hour before dark, and the best time to visit is late in the afternoon, when the sun shines directly into the cave and the crowds of people are smaller.

Another 6 miles south is the **Darlingtonia Wayside,** a small botanical preserve protecting a bog full of *Darlingtonia californica* plants, an insectivorous pitcher plant that's also known as the cobra lily. You'll find this interesting preserve on Mercer Lake Road.

9 Florence

50 miles S of Newport, 50 miles N of Coos Bay, 60 miles W of Eugene

Florence and its environs, which lie at the northern end of the Oregon Dunes National Recreation Area (see section 10, below), have long been a popular summer vacation spot for families. Sand dunes, beaches, the Siuslaw River, and 17 freshwater lakes combine to provide an abundance of recreational opportunities. However, with few roads providing access to the ocean's shore, this area is known more for its lakes than for its beaches. Many area lakes are ringed with summer homes, while on others, you'll find state park and national forest campgrounds. Tops among area recreational activities are probably waterskiing, riding off-road vehicles (ORVs) through the sand dunes, and fishing. Consequently this area is not especially popular for romantic weekend getaways.

This said, Florence does have quite a bit of charm. Along the town's Siuslaw River waterfront, many old wooden buildings have been restored. Today, there are interesting shops to explore and waterfront seafood restaurants in which to dine. The charming character of this neighborhood is all the more appealing when compared to the unsightly sprawl along U.S. 101.

Keep in mind, however, that the area's popularity means crowds, and in the summer months campgrounds and hotels around here stay full and traffic can be bumper-to-bumper through town. Luckily, with miles and miles of protected shoreline, sand dunes, and forests within the national recreation area and nearby Honeyman State Park, there are plenty of opportunities for escaping the crowds.

ESSENTIALS

GETTING THERE Florence is on U.S. 101 at the junction with Ore. 126 from Eugene.

VISITOR INFORMATION Contact the **Florence Area Chamber of Commerce,** 270 U.S. 101 (P. O. Box 26000), Florence, OR 97439 (☎ 541/997-3128).

FESTIVALS Each spring, rhododendrons blossom profusely throughout this region and have become so much a symbol of Florence that the town holds a **Rhododendron Festival** each year on the third weekend of May.

SEEING THE SIGHTS & ENJOYING THE OUTDOORS

Florence's **Old Town,** on the north bank of the Siuslaw River, is one of the most charming historic districts on the Oregon coast. The restored wood and brick buildings capture the flavor of a 19th-century fishing village, and many of the buildings now house interesting shops, galleries, and restaurants. Shops worth checking out include **bonjour!,** 1336 Bay St. (☎ 541/997-8194), featuring rayon, linen, and sand-washed silk fashions for women; **Traveler's Cove,** 1362 Bay St. (☎ 541/997-6854), an interesting Asian import shop and cafe; **Mysteries & Motorcars,** 138 Maple St. (☎ 541/902-0215), a bookshop specializing in automotive collectibles; and **Incredible and Edible Oregon,** 1350 Bay St. (☎ 541/997-7018), where you can pick up regional delicacies and wines.

South of town, the **Siuslaw Pioneer Museum,** 85294 U.S. 101 S. (☎ 541/997-7884), designed to resemble a covered wagon, displays pioneer and Native American artifacts from this area. It's open Tuesday through Sunday from 10am to 4pm (closed in December); admission is by donation.

C&M Stables, 90241 U.S. 101 N. (☎ 541/997-7540), located 8 miles north of Florence, offers rides either on the beach or through the dunes. Rides last 1 to 2 hours, and prices range from $20 to $30. A more unusual excursion can be had on the **Seahorse Stagecoach** (☎ 541/999-0319), a horse-drawn wagon that makes trips on the beach.

At the same time that stagecoaches were plying the beaches of Oregon, paddle wheelers were plying its rivers. The *Westward Ho!* (☎ 541/997-9691), a half-scale replica of an 1850s stern-wheeler, revives the days of riverboat travel with its various river cruises. Regular cruises cost $10.35 for adults, $5.35 for children 4 to 12; the dinner cruise is $33.35. The *Westward Ho!* leaves from a dock on the old town waterfront and operates daily between April and October; other months the schedule is more limited.

If you'd like to see the area's sand dunes and lakes from the air, contact **M&M Seaplane Operations,** 83595 U.S. 101 S. (☎ 541/997-6567), or **Florence Aviation,** 2001 Airport Way (☎ 541/997-8069). Fares start around $36. The former company operates floatplanes that fly off of Woahink Lake.

If you want to get on or in the water, you can rent surfboards, body boards, sea kayaks, and scuba diving equipment from **Central Coast Watersports,** 1560 Second St. (☎ **800/789-DIVE** or 541/997-1812), which also offers diving classes and tours. If you want to rent a personal watercraft and roar around on Woahink Lake, check with **M&M Seaplane Operations,** 83595 U.S. 101 S. (☎ **541/997-6567**), which charges $45 an hour for personal watercraft rentals.

If golf is your sport, try the 18-hole **Sandpines Golf Course,** 1201 35th St. (☎ **541/997-1940**), which, in 1994, was voted the best new public golf course in the country by *Golf Digest* magazine. This course, which plays through dunes and pine forest, continues to get rave reviews. You'll pay $45 for a round of golf here. Alternatively, you can try the 18-hole **Ocean Dunes Golf Links,** 3345 Munsel Lake Rd. (☎ **800/468-4833** or 541/997-3232), which also plays through the dunes and charges $28 for 18 holes.

WHERE TO STAY

Driftwood Shores Resort & Conference Center. 88416 First Ave., Florence, OR 97439. ☎ **800/422-5091** or 541/997-8263. Fax 541/997-5857. 136 rms, 20 suites. TV TEL. $84–$126 double; $193–$272 suite for up to 6 people. AE, CB, DC, DISC, MC, V.

Located north of Florence's Old Town district, this is the only oceanfront lodging in the area. As such, it's popular year-round, so be sure to book early. The rooms vary in size and amenities, but all have ocean views and balconies. Most also have kitchens, which makes this a great place for a family vacation (and three-bedroom suites are as large as many vacation homes). There's an indoor pool and whirlpool, and the Surfside Restaurant and Lounge serves reasonably priced seafood and steaks with a view from every table.

The Edwin K Bed & Breakfast. 1155 Bay St. (P.O. Box 2687), Florence, OR 97439 ☎ **800/ 8-EDWIN-K** or 541/997-8360. 6 rms. $90–$125 double. Rates include full breakfast. DISC, MC, V.

Located only 2 blocks from Old Town Florence, this vintage 1914 home is one of the most luxurious B&Bs on the coast. The four upstairs rooms are the most spacious, and two overlook the Siuslaw River, which is just across the street and has a huge sand dune rising up on its far shore. One of these two front rooms has a clawfoot tub on a raised tile platform beside the bed, while the other has a double whirlpool tub in the room. Other rooms are not quite as plushly appointed but are quite comfortable nevertheless. Decor draws on early American styles. In the living room and dining room, you'll find beautiful original paneling. Breakfasts are lavish formal affairs with fine china and crystal. This is definitely a place to feel pampered.

✪ The Johnson House. 216 Maple St. (P.O. Box 1892), Florence, OR 97439. ☎ **800/ 768-9488** or 541/997-8000. 6 rms (3 with private bath). $95–$125 double. Rates include full breakfast. MC, V.

A white house behind a white picket fence conjures up classic images of small-town America, and with Old Town Florence only a block away, it's easy to maintain the image (if you can tune out the summer crowds). The Johnson House is the oldest home in Florence, and has been completely renovated. Today, it's filled with antiques and surrounded by perennial gardens. The guest rooms are bright and cozy, and there's a comfortable parlor where guests can gather to swap stories of their day's outings. Our favorite room is the little cottage at the back of the gardens. The breakfasts are elaborate and filling.

River House Motel. 1202 Bay St., Florence, OR 97439. ☎ **541/997-3933.** 40 rms. Summer $58–$120 double. Off-season $38–$95 double. AE, DISC, MC, V.

Overlooking the Siuslaw River drawbridge and sand dunes on the far side of the river, the River House is only one block from the heart of Florence's Old Town district. This modern motel offers comfortable and attractive rooms, most of which have views and balconies. The largest and most expensive rooms are those with a double whirl-pool tub. There's also an indoor hot tub available to all guests.

CAMPGROUNDS

North of Florence are the first of this region's many campgrounds, **Sutton** and **Alder Dune,** both of which are operated by the forest service. These campgrounds are linked by a hiking trail through the dunes. Just outside Florence at the Siuslaw River's north jetty is **Harbor Vista County Park,** an alternative to ever-crowded Honeyman State Park.

WHERE TO DINE

When you need a good cup of espresso, stop in at **Old Town Coffee Co.,** 1269 Bay St. (☎ **541/902-9336**). For great ice cream, everyone swears by **BJ's Ice Cream,** 1441 Bay St. (☎ **541/997-7286**), which makes 48 of its own flavors, many of which use old family recipes dating from 1917.

Bridgewater Seafood Restaurant. 1297 Bay St. ☎ **541/997-9405.** Reservations recommended. Main courses $5–$18. MC, V. Daily 11:30am–10:30pm (shorter hours in the off-season). AMERICAN/SEAFOOD.

Located in a restored building in Old Town, this eclectic eatery combines a Wild West storefront facade with a tropical interior complete with wicker furniture and potted plants. In the summer there's patio dining, and any time of year the lounge area is a cozy place to wait out the rain. The menu is long and includes everything from jambalaya and scampi Provençal to pasta, burgers, and chowders.

International C-Food Market. 1498 Bay St. ☎ **541/997-7978.** Reservations recommended. Main courses $9–$26. DISC, MC, V. Daily 11am–10pm. SEAFOOD.

Located on a dock on the old waterfront, this restaurant also happens to be a fish processing facility, which means the seafood served here is as fresh as you'll find anywhere on the coast. The warehouselike space has loads of windows providing views of the river, and interesting undersea murals on every wall that doesn't have a window. The same owners of this restaurant also have a clam processing facility, so don't pass up the teamed Manila clams. Order up a pot and be sure to ask for some "tiger's milk," a drink made from the clam broth, lemon juice, Tabasco sauce, and cracked pepper. After this, you can hardly go wrong. The crab cakes are another good bet, and together with the steamed clams, make a great meal.

Lovejoy's of San Francisco. 195 Nopal St. ☎ **541/902-0502.** Reservations recommended. Main dishes $6–$15. DISC, MC, V. Tues–Sun 11am–9pm. BRITISH.

Although Florence seems an unlikely location for a traditional British restaurant and tea room, Lovejoy's was an immediate hit. While the menu consists primarily of fish-and-chips and other classic pub fare, there are nightly three-course dinners for $10 to $15 that have locals flocking to this restaurant. Each night sees only one of these specials, which might be rabbit and onion casserole, stuffed pork chops, or a colonial curry. Of course, tea, with all the traditional sandwiches, crumpets, scones, and double Devon cream is very popular here. The restaurant may be moving across the street, so, if you don't find it at this address, look around.

✪ **Traveler's Cove.** 1362 Bay St. ☎ **541/997-6845.** Main courses $7–$13. AE, DISC, MC, V. Summer daily 10am–9pm; other months Sun–Thurs 10am–5pm, Fri–Sat 10am–7pm. INTERNATIONAL.

This eclectic eatery is at the back of an unusual little import shop right on the waterfront in Old Town Florence. It's the only eatery in town with a riverside deck. Lunch is the main meal here, with lots of good sandwiches, a crab quiche, Thai chicken Caesar salad, and vegetarian chili. The hot apple dumplings are rich and heavy and go well with an espresso in the middle of the afternoon.

Windward Inn. 3757 U.S. 101 N. ☎ **541/997-8243.** Reservations recommended. Main courses $6–$19; lunch $5–$10. AE, DISC, MC, V. Daily 7am–9pm (sometimes later Fri–Sat). AMERICAN/CONTINENTAL.

With all the sophistication of an elegant historic hotel, the Windward is Florence's biggest and most luxurious restaurant, but way back in 1932 it was just a roadside diner and gas station. Today a small dining room and a few decorative antique gas pumps are all that remain of these humble beginnings. Each of the current dining rooms has a slightly different atmosphere. The menu is almost exclusively seafood from start to finish. The blackened Cajun oysters make a good starter and among the entrees, the broiled herbed scallops and salmon fillet poached in Riesling, butter, and dill are good choices. In the high-ceilinged lounge you'll find a marble floor and a long bar, and on Friday and Saturday evenings a pianists plays.

10 Dune Country

Winchester Bay: 91 miles SW of Eugene, 23 miles N of Coos Bay, 25 miles S of Florence

The **Oregon Dunes National Recreation Area,** which is the largest area of sand dunes on the West Coast and includes more than 14,000 acres of dunes, stretches for more than 40 miles along the coast between Florence and Coos Bay. Within this vast area of shifting sands, there are dunes more than 500 feet tall, numerous lakes both large and small, living forests, and skeletal forests of trees that were long ago "drowned" beneath drifting sands. It is also here that you'll find the longest unbroken, publicly owned stretches of coastline on the Oregon coast.

The national recreation area is divided roughly at its midway point by the Umpqua River, on whose banks you'll find the towns of Gardiner, Reedsport, and Winchester Bay, each of which has a very distinct character. **Gardiner** was founded in 1841 when a Boston merchant's fur-trading ship wrecked near here, and is the oldest of the three towns. An important mill town in the 19th century, Gardiner has several stately Victorian homes. It also still has a huge pulp mill that fills the town's air with a disgusting stench that keeps most travelers speeding though town too fast to even notice the many historic homes.

Next comes **Reedsport,** which is the largest of these three communities and is the site of numerous cheap motels as well as the Umpqua Discovery Center, a museum focusing on the history and natural history of this region.

The town of **Winchester Bay** is almost at the mouth of the Umpqua River and is known for its large fleet of charter-fishing boats. The fishing boats are moored at Salmon Harbor marina, where a stroll along the docks is almost certain to turn up a boat willing to take you out fishing for salmon, bottom fish, steelhead, striper, or sturgeon.

ESSENTIALS

GETTING THERE   Gardiner, Reedsport and Winchester Bay are all on U.S. 101 at or near the junction with Ore. 38 from Elkton, which in turn is reached from I-5 by taking either Ore. 99 from Drain or Ore. 138 from Sutherlin.

VISITOR INFORMATION   For more information on the dunes, contact the **Oregon Dunes National Recreation Area,** 855 Highway Ave., Reedsport,

OR 97467 (☎ **541/271-3611**). At this address, you'll find a visitor center where you can pick up a map of the region and learn about various camping and recreational opportunities within the national recreation area. The visitor center is open daily from 9am to 5pm in summer, and in other months is open Monday through Friday from 8am to 4:30pm and Saturday and Sunday from 10am to 4pm.

Housed in this same building is the **Reedsport/Winchester Chamber of Commerce,** 855 Highway Ave. (P.O. Box 11), Reedsport, OR 97467 (☎ **800/247-2155** or 541/271-3495), which can provide you with more area information.

THE OREGON DUNES NATIONAL RECREATION AREA

The first Oregon dunes were formed between 12 and 26 million years ago by the weathering of inland mountain ranges. Though the dunes are in constant flux, they reached their current size and shape about 7,000 years ago after the massive eruption of the Mount Mazama volcano, which emptied out the entire molten-rock contents of the mountain, and in the process created the caldera that would become Crater Lake.

Water currents and winds are the factors responsible for the dunes. Currents move the sand particles north each winter and south each summer, while constant winds off the Pacific Ocean blow the sand eastward, piling it up into dunes that are slowly marching east. Over thousands of years the dunes have swallowed up forests, leaving some groves of trees as remnant tree islands.

Freshwater trapped behind the dunes has formed numerous freshwater lakes, many of which are now ringed by campgrounds and vacation homes. These lakes are popular for fishing, swimming, and boating. The largest of the lakes lie outside the national recreation area and are, from north to south, Woahink Lake, Siltcoos Lake, Tahkenitch Lake, Clear Lake, Eel Lake, North Tenmile Lake, and Tenmile Lake. Smaller lakes that are within the recreation area include Cleawox Lake, Carter Lake, Beale Lake, and Horsfall Lake. Traditionally, these lakes have been in a constant state of change, however, with the construction of homes around the lakeshores, there is now the necessity of maintaining lakes at their current shape and size.

European beach grass is playing an even greater role in changing the natural dynamics of this region. Introduced to anchor sand dunes and prevent them from inundating roads and river channels, this plant has been much more effective than anyone ever imagined. Able to survive even when buried under several feet of sand, European beach grass has covered many acres of land and formed dunes in back of the beach. These dunes effectively block sand from blowing inland off the beach, and as winds blow sand off the dunes into wet, low-lying areas, vegetation takes hold, thus eliminating areas of former dunes. It is predicted that within 50 years, these dunes will all have been covered with vegetation and will no longer be the barren, windswept expanses of sand seen today.

There are numerous options for exploring the dunes. **Jessie M. Honeyman State Park** (☎ **541/997-3641**), 3 miles south of Florence, is a unique spot with a beautiful forest-bordered lake and towering sand dunes. The park offers camping, picnicking, hiking trails, and access to Cleawox and Woahink lakes. On Cleawox Lake, there are a swimming area and boat rental facility. The dunes adjacent to Cleawox Lake are used by off-road vehicles.

The easiest place to get an overview of the dunes is at the **Dunes Overlook,** 10 miles south of Florence. Here you'll find viewing platforms high atop a forested sand dune that overlooks a vast expanse of bare sand. Another easy place from which to view the dunes is the viewing platform on the Taylor Dunes Trail, which begins at the **Carter Lake Campground,** 7^1/$_2$ miles south of Florence. It is an easy ^{1}/$_2$-mile walk to the viewing platform.

If you want to get your shoes full of sand and wander among these Saharan sand dunes, there are several places to try. If you only have time for a quick walk in the sand, head to **Carter Lake Campground,** where you can continue on from the Taylor Dunes viewing platform. The beach is less than a mile beyond the viewing platform, and roughly half this distance is through dunes. From this same campground, you can hike the **Carter Dunes Trail.** The beach is $1^1/2$ miles away through dunes and forest, and meadows known as a deflation plain. A $3^1/2$-mile loop trail leads from the **Dunes Overlook** (see above) out to the beach by way of Tahkenitch Creek, a meandering stream that flows through the dunes and out to the ocean. Another mile south of the Dunes Overlook, you'll find the **Tahkenitch Trailhead,** which accesses an 8-mile network of little-used trials that wander through dunes, forest, marshes, and meadows. Continuing south from here, you'll find several more trails starting from the **Tahkenitch Campground.** Here, the **Dunes Trail** leads 2 miles across the dunes to the beach, while the **Threemile Lake Trail** leads 3 miles through forest to Threemile Lake (and also connects to the beach and eventually makes a loop with the Dunes Trail). However, for truly impressive dunes, the best route is the **Umpqua Dunes Trail,** which has its trailhead $1/2$ mile south of **Eel Creek Campground,** which is $10^1/2$ miles south of Reedsport. This $2^1/2$-mile round-trip trail leads through an area of dunes 2 miles wide by 4 miles long. Don't get lost!

About 30% of the sand dunes are open to **off-road vehicles (ORVs),** and throngs of people flock to this area to roar up and down the dunes. If you'd like to do a little off-roading in the dunes, you can rent a miniature dune buggy for around $30 to $40 an hour from **Sandland Adventures,** 85366 U.S. 101 S. (☎ **541/997-8087**), 1 mile south of town; or **Sand Dunes Frontier & Theme Park** (☎ **541/997-3544**), which has its facilities 4 miles south of Florence. Both of these companies also offer guided tours of the dunes in a variety of vehicles from dune buggies to four-wheel-drive trucks. Both companies also have little amusement parks as well. Down at the southern end of the recreation area, you can rent vehicles or take tours from **Spinreel Dune Buggy Rentals,** 9122 Wildwood Dr. (☎ **541/759-3313**), located just off U.S. 101; or **Pacific Coast Recreation,** 4121 U.S. 101 (☎ **541/756-7183**), located 5 miles north of North Bend. The latter company operates its tours in World War II military surplus transport vehicles. The tours cost $12 for adults and $8 for children. Off-road vehicles rent for $25 to $30 per hour.

If you'd rather avoid the dune buggies and ORVs, stay away from the dunes between the South Jetty area (just south of Florence) and Siltcoos Lake; the area adjacent to Umpqua Lighthouse State Park just south of Winchester Bay; and the area from Spinreel Campground south to the Horsfall Dune & Beach Access Road, which is just north of the town of North Bend.

The area's most interesting annual event is the **Dune Musher's Mail Run,** which takes place each year in March and attracts dogsled teams from all over the United States and Canada. Teams race from Horsfall Beach near Coos Bay all the way to Florence, with miniteams of three or four dogs covering 55 miles in 3 days and full-size teams of 5 to 12 dogs covering 72 miles in 2 days. For this race, dogsleds with fat tires (instead of skids) are used. Racers carry special commemorative envelopes that are canceled at both Horsfall Beach and Florence. For more information, contact Beverly Meyers at ☎ **541/269-1269.**

In 1997, a three-year "Recreation Fee Demonstration Project" was initiated within the recreation area. Currently there is a $3 per car day-use fee, which covers use of all facilities and parking lots. If you just want to stop at the Dunes Overlook, there is a $1 fee.

OTHER AREA ATTRACTIONS & ACTIVITIES

In downtown Reedsport on the Umpqua River waterfront, you can visit the **Umpqua Discovery Center,** 409 Riverfront Way (☎ **541/271-4816**). This modern museum contains displays on the history and ecology of the area. It's open in summer, daily from 9am to 5pm; in winter, Wednesday through Sunday from 10am to 4pm. Admission is $3 for adults, $1.50 for children 5 to 12. Outside the discovery center, you'll find an observation tower that is sometimes a good place to do a little bird watching. Also docked just outside the center is the *Hero,* a 125-foot-long research vessel that was built in 1968 for service in Antarctica. It's open daily from 10am to 4pm; admission is $4 for adults, $2 for children 5 to 12.

If you want to get out on the water, you can take a jet-boat tour with **Umpqua Jet Adventures,** 423 Riverfront Way (☎ **800/353-8386** or 541/271-5694), which offers two-hour trips at $15 for adults and $8 for children ages 4 to 11.

At the **Dean Creek Elk Viewing Area,** 1 mile east of town on Ore. 38, you can spot 120 or more elk grazing on 1,000 acres of meadows that have been set aside as a preserve. During the summer months, the elk tend to stay in the forest where it's cooler.

In Winchester Bay, you can visit the historic **Umpqua River Lighthouse.** The original lighthouse was at the mouth of the Umpqua River and was the first lighthouse on the Oregon coast. It fell into the Umpqua River in 1861 and was replaced in 1894 by the current lighthouse. Adjacent to the lighthouse is the **Visitors Center & Museum,** 1020 Lighthouse Rd. (☎ **541/271-4631**), which is housed in a former coast guard station and contains historical exhibits and an information center. Here at the museum, you can arrange to join a tour of the lighthouse. Tours are offered Wednesday through Saturday between 10am and 5pm and on Sunday between 1 and 5pm.

Across the street from the lighthouse is a **whale-viewing platform** (best viewing months are November to June). Also nearby is the very pretty **Umpqua Lighthouse State Park,** the site of the 500-foot-tall sand dunes that are the tallest in the United States. The park offers picnicking, hiking, and camping amid forests and sand dunes.

WHERE TO STAY

In addition to the bed-and-breakfast listed here, you'll find numerous cheap motels in Reedsport and Winchester Bay that cater primarily to anglers and off-roading enthusiasts.

Riverboat Bed & Breakfast. P.O. Box 1208, Winchester Bay, OR 97467. ☎ **800/348-1922** or 541/271-1137. 6 rms. $125–$145 double. Rates include full breakfast. MC, V.

This 100-foot-long modern stern-wheeler is one of the most unique B&Bs on the Oregon coast and is docked in the Salmon Harbor Marina in Winchester Bay. The guest rooms here are small, as you'd expect on any boat, but they all have big windows and private bathrooms. A parlor on the main deck provides a space for gathering to meet other guests or just enjoy the feel of being aboard an old-fashioned riverboat.

CAMPGROUNDS

You'll find 13 Forest Service campgrounds and three state park campgrounds within the Oregon Dunes National Recreation Area. **Jesse M. Honeyman State Park,** just a few miles south of Florence, is one of the most popular state parks in Oregon and stays full throughout the summer. With two lakes, swimming, canoeing, sand dunes, and shady forests, it's easy to understand its popularity. Just south of this state park you'll find the Siltcoos Recreation Area, where **Lagoon Campground** and **Waxmyrtle Campground** are the better choices (Driftwood II Campground is an ORV staging area). Nearby, **Tyee Campground** is set on the bank of the Siltcoos River and is popular with boaters. **Carter Lake Campground,** on a popular swimming and boating lake, is another quiet choice in this area. The **Tahkenitch Campground,** however, is probably the best choice in the area. It's set in the forest on the edge of the dunes. Nearby is lakefront **Tahkenitch Landing Campground,** which is popular with anglers.

South of Reedsport and Winchester Bay, you'll find **Umpqua Lighthouse State Park,** in the forest just south of Winchester Bay, and **William M. Tugman State Park,** at the south end of Eel Lake. **Eel Creek Campground,** adjacent to the Umpqua Dunes, is a quiet choice down at this end of the national recreation area. The southern end of the Oregon Dunes NRA has been given over to dune buggies and ORVs. Campgrounds catering to off-roaders include **Spinreel, Horsfall, Horsfall Beach, Bluebill,** and Umpqua Lighthouse State Park.

For reservations at the state park campgrounds, contact **Reservations Northwest** (☎ **800/452-5687**). The only national forest campgrounds that except reservations are Driftwood II, Horsfall, and Wild Mare Horse Camp. For reservations, call the **National Forest Reservation Service** (☎ **800/280-2267**).

WHERE TO DINE IN WINCHESTER BAY

If you're craving some smoked salmon or other type of fish, drop by **Sportsmen's Cannery & Smokehouse** (☎ **541/271-3293**), on Bayfront Loop in Winchester Bay.

Bayfront Bistro. 208 Bayfront Loop, Winchester Bay. ☎ **541/271-9463.** Reservations recommended. Main courses $9–$15; lunch $4–$9. MC, V. Daily 11am–9:30pm (shorter hours in winter). AMERICAN.

While the menu is none too French at this cozy little place in the Salmon Harbor Marina area, the Bayfront does a respectable job of conjuring up the atmosphere of a Parisian bistro. Whatever you order, be sure it's oysters, which come from right here in the Umpqua River. You can get them panfried, Cajun-style, on the half shell, as shooters, in burgers, as an appetizer, or as an entree. Friday and Saturday nights are prime rib nights, but you could still start with an oyster appetizer. There's a modest selection of Oregon wines and microbrews. On cool days, you can curl up on the couch by the fireplace before or after a meal. At lunch, simple sandwiches dominate (including those oyster burgers).

Cafe Français. U.S. 101, Winchester Bay. ☎ **541/271-9270.** Reservations recommended. Main courses $17–$20. MC, V. Wed–Sun 5–10pm. FRENCH.

A town known as one of the fishing capitals of Oregon hardly seems the place to find a country French restaurant, but there it is, right on busy U.S. 101. With flower boxes in the windows and fine linens on the tables, this place is a world away from the family restaurants that line the roads in this area (nothing here is deep-fried; amazing!). The menu consists of a handful of daily specials, which might include lingcod cheeks with capers, filet mignon with béarnaise sauce, chateaubriand in cream sherry with soft green peppercorns, or scallops in a white wine reduction with ginger. There is a good selection of wines from Oregon, France, and California. For a starter, you can usually opt for escargot, oysters on the half shell, or stuffed mushrooms.

Crabby Gourmet. 225 Eighth St., Winchester Bay. ☎ **541/271-9294.** Reservations for 8 or more people only. Main courses $15–$19; lunch $4–$15. CB, DC, JCB, MC, V. Mon–Thurs 11am–3pm, Fri–Sat 11am–3pm and 5:30–8:30pm, Sun 10am–3pm (shorter hours and closed on Mon in winter). AMERICAN/INTERNATIONAL.

With barely half a dozen tables inside and a couple more out front, this is another of Winchester Bay's memorable little restaurants. While it's hard to pass up the local oysters on the half shell for a starter, the homemade Italian sausage in puff pastry and smoked salmon pâté are both worth considering. This is crab country and you would be remiss if you didn't order the Dungeness crab lasagna roll, but there are also pork medallions with sautéed Granny Smith apples and, of course, a daily fish special. For lunch, we recommend the crab melt or smoked turkey and brie croissant sandwich. Sunday brunch is one of Crabby's best meals, with Dungeness crab omelets and an oyster scramble.

11 Coos Bay, North Bend & Charleston

85 miles NW of Roseburg, 48 miles S of Florence, 24 miles N of Bandon

Coos Bay, North Bend, and Charleston are together known as Oregon's bay area, and with a combined population of 35,000 people, this bay area is the largest urban center on the Oregon coast. Coos Bay and North Bend are the bay's commercial center and have merged into a single large town, while nearby Charleston maintains its distinct character as a small fishing port.

As the largest natural harbor between San Francisco and Puget Sound, Coos Bay has long been an important port. Logs and wood products are the main export, but with the controversy over raw log shipments to Japan and the continuing battle to save old-growth forests in the Northwest, Coos Bay's days as a timber-shipping port may be numbered. In response to the economic downturn of the port, the bay area is gearing up to attract more tourists. An attractive waterfront boardwalk, complete with historical displays, has been added in downtown Coos Bay, and what was once a huge lumber mill is now the site of the equally large **Mill Resort & Casino.** Even if it isn't the most beautiful town on the Oregon coast, Coos Bay has a lot of character and also has quite a few tourist amenities, including several good restaurants, moderately priced motels, and even a few B&Bs, that together make this a good place to spend a night if you are touring the coast on the cheap. And a closer look turns up, not far away, a trio of state parks that are, in our opinion, the most beautiful on the coast.

ESSENTIALS

GETTING THERE   From the north, take Ore. 99 from just south of Cottage Grove. This road becomes Ore. 38. At Reedsport, head south on U.S. 101. From the south, take Ore. 42 from just south of Roseburg.

The **North Bend–Coos Bay Municipal Airport** is served by Horizon Air (☎ **800/547-9308**).

VISITOR INFORMATION   Contact the **Bay Area Chamber of Commerce & Visitor Bureau,** 50 E. Central Ave. (P.O. Box 210), Coos Bay, OR 97420 (☎ **800/ 824-8486** or 541/269-0215).

GETTING AROUND   If you need a taxi, contact **Coos Yellow Cab** (☎ **541/ 267-3111**). Car rentals are available in Coos Bay from **Hertz** and **Enterprise Rent-a-Car.**

FESTIVALS   Each year during the last 2 weeks of July, the **Oregon Coast Music Festival** (☎ **800/676-7563** or 541/269-2720) brings a wealth of music to the area. Classical, jazz, bluegrass, swing, blues, and pop are all part of the festival, which is held in different locations around the bay area.

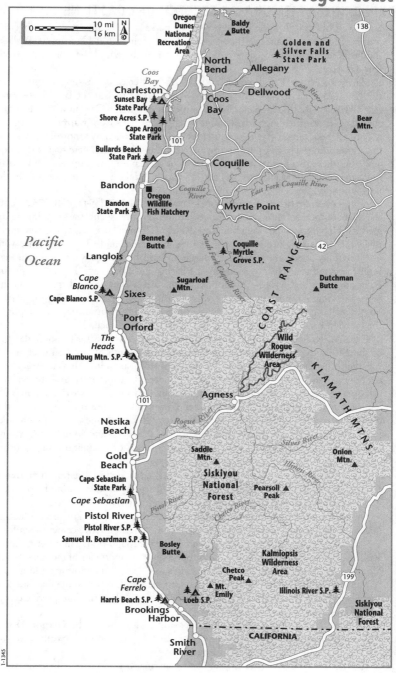

The Southern Oregon Coast

0 10 mi
16 km

N

138

Oregon
Dunes
National
Recreation
Area

Baldy
Butte

Golden and
Silver Falls
State Park

*Coos
Bay*

North
Bend

Allegany

Charleston
Sunset Bay
State Park

Coos
Bay

Dellwood

Coos River

Shore Acres S.P.

Cape Arago
State Park

Bear
Mtn.

101

Bullards Beach
State Park

Coquille

Bandon

Oregon
Wildlife
Fish Hatchery

*Coquille
River*

East Fork Coquille River

Bandon
State Park

Myrtle Point

*Pacific
Ocean*

Bennet
Butte

Coquille
Myrtle
Grove S.P.

42

Langlois

South Fork Coquille River

COAST RANGES

Cape
Blanco

Sugarloaf
Mtn.

Dutchman
Butte

Cape Blanco S.P.

Sixes

Port
Orford

*The
Heads*

Wild
Rogue
Wilderness
Area

KLAMATH MTNS.

Humbug Mtn. S.P.

101

Agness

Rogue River

Nesika
Beach

Silver River

Gold
Beach

Saddle
Mtn.

Onion
Mtn.

Cape Sebastian
State Park

Siskiyou
National
Forest

Illinois River

Cape Sebastian

Pearsoli
Peak

Pistol River

Pistol River S.P.

Pistol River

Chetco River

Samuel H. Boardman S.P.

Bosley
Butte

Kalmiopsis
Wilderness
Area

*Cape
Ferrelo*

Chetco
Peak

199

Harris Beach S.P.

Loeb S.P.

Mt.
Emily

Illinois River S.P.

Siskiyou
National
Forest

Brookings
Harbor

CALIFORNIA

Smith
River

1-1345

EXPLORING A MEMORABLE STRETCH OF COASTLINE

Southwest of Coos Bay you'll find three state parks and a county park that together preserve some of the most breathtaking shoreline anywhere in the Northwest. Walkers should note that the three state parks are connected by a trail that makes an excellent day hike.

Start your exploration of this beautiful stretch of coast by heading southwest on the Cape Arago Highway. In 12 miles you'll come to **Sunset Bay State Park** (☎ 541/888-4902). This park has one of the few beaches in Oregon where the water actually gets warm enough for swimming (although folks from warm-water regions may not agree). Sunset Bay is almost completely surrounded by sandstone cliffs, and the entrance to the bay is quite narrow, which means the waters here stay fairly calm. Together these two factors allow the waters of the bay to warm up a bit more than the waters of other beaches on the coast. Picnicking and camping are available in the park, and there are lots of tide pools to explore.

Another 3 miles brings you to **Shore Acres State Park** (☎ 541/888-3732), once the estate of local shipping tycoon Louis J. Simpson, who spent years developing his gardens. His ships would bring him unusual plants from all over the world, and eventually the gardens grew to include a formal English garden and a Japanese garden with a 100-foot lily pond. The gardens and his home, which long ago was torn down, were built atop sandstone cliffs overlooking the Pacific and a tiny cove. Rock walls rise up from the water and have been sculpted by the waves into unusual shapes. During winter storms, wave watching is a popular pastime here. The water off the park is often a striking shade of blue, and **Simpson Beach,** in the little cove, just might be the prettiest beach in Oregon. A trail leads down to this beach.

Cape Arago State Park (☎ 541/888-4902) is the third of this trio of parks. Just offshore from the rugged cape lie the rocks and small islands of Simpson Reef, which together offer sunbathing spots for hundreds of seals (including elephant seals) and sea lions. Their barking can be heard from hundreds of yards away, and though you can't get very close to the seals, with a pair of binoculars you can see them quite well. The best viewing point is at **Simpson Reef Viewpoint** (at press time the road to this overlook was closed due to a landslide). On either side of the cape are coves with quiet beaches, although the beaches are closed from March 1 to June 30 to protect young seal pups. Tide pools along these beaches offer hours of fascination during other months.

Also in the vicinity of these three state parks you'll find **Bastendorff Beach County Park** (☎ 541/888-5353), north of Sunset Bay at the mouth of Coos Bay, which offers a long, wide beach that's popular with surfers.

Four miles down Seven Devils Road from Charleston you'll find the **South Slough National Estuarine Reserve** (☎ 541/888-5558). An interpretive center (open from 8:30am to 4:30pm, daily in summer and Monday through Friday in other months) set high above the slough provides background on the importance of estuaries. South Slough is in the process of being restored after many years of damming, diking, and reclamation of marshlands by farmers. A hiking trail leads down to the marshes, and there is good canoeing or sea kayaking in the slough. Ask at the interpretive center for information.

Coos Bay and North Bend are also the southern gateway to the **Oregon Dunes National Recreation Area** (see section 10 of this chapter), and from North Bend you can see the dunes on the far side of Coos Bay.

Charleston is the bay area's charter-fishing marina. If you'd like to do some sport-fishing, contact **Bob's Sport Fishing** (☎ 800/628-9633 or 541/888-4241) or **Betty**

Kay Charters (☎ 800/752-6303 or 541/888-9021). Expect to pay around $55 for a 6-hour bottom-fishing trip and $120 for a 12-hour halibut-fishing trip.

Golfers can choose between the 18-hole **Kentuck Golf Club,** 675 Golf Course Lane (☎ 541/756-4464), north of North Bend off East Bay Drive, or the **Sunset Bay Golf Course,** 11001 Cape Arago Hwy. (☎ 541/888-9301), a nine-hole course near Sunset Bay State Park.

In addition to all the outdoor recreational activities around the bay area, there are also a few small museums. The **Coos Art Museum,** 235 Anderson Ave., Coos Bay (☎ 541/267-3901), is a highly regarded little museum that hosts changing exhibits in a wide variety of styles and media. It's open Tuesday through Sunday from 11am to 5pm; admission is by donation. The **Coos County Historical Society Museum,** 1220 Sherman Ave., North Bend (☎ 541/756-6320), contains artifacts pertaining to the history of Coos County and southern coastal Oregon. Here you can also pick up copies of walking-tour brochures that will guide you to the historic buildings of both North Bend and Coos Bay. It's open Tuesday through Saturday from 10am to 4pm; admission is $1 for adults, 25¢ for children 5 to 12. At the **Marshfield Sun Printing Museum,** Front Street and Bayshore Drive, Coos Bay (☎ 541/756-6418), you can see a preserved 19th-century newspaper office and exhibits on printing in the region and around the country. The museum is open Tuesday through Saturday from 1 to 4pm in summer (other times by special arrangement).

At Coos Bay you enter myrtle wood country. The myrtle tree grows only along a short section of coast in southern Oregon and northern California and is prized by woodworkers for its fine grain and durability. A very hard wood, it lends itself to all manner of platters, bowls, goblets, sculptures, and whatever. All along this section of coast you'll see myrtle wood factories and shops where you can see how the raw wood is turned into finished pieces. The **Oregon Connection/House of Myrtlewood,** on U.S. 101 south of Coos Bay (☎ 541/267-7804), is one of the bigger myrtle wood factories. The **Real Oregon Gift,** 3955 U.S. 101 (☎ 541/756-2220), 5 miles north of North Bend, is another large factory and showroom. If you'd like to see some myrtle trees in their natural surroundings, visit **Golden and Silver Falls State Park** (☎ 541/269-0215), which is 25 miles northeast of Coos Bay on Coos River Road (take the Allegany exit off U.S. 101). Here, in addition to seeing myrtle trees, you can hike to two 100-foot-high waterfalls.

Despite its industrial appearance, Coos Bay supports a surprisingly well-developed performing-arts scene. The **Little Theater on the Bay** (☎ 541/756-4336), which has its theater on Sherman Avenue in North Bend, has been around since 1947 and does six productions per year, including musicals and children's theater. **On Broadway Thespians,** On Broadway Theater, 226 S. Broadway, Coos Bay (☎ 541/269-2501), offers 12 productions a year, including classical and contemporary dramas and musicals. Ticket reservations for both theaters can be made through **The Box Office** (☎ 800/676-7563).

Part of the renovation of the Coos Bay waterfront has been the construction of **The Mill Resort & Casino,** 3201 Tremont Ave., North Bend (☎ 800/953-4800 or 541/756-8800). Here you can play slot machines, blackjack, poker, and bingo. There are also several restaurants and a lounge.

WHERE TO STAY

If you're looking for cheap accommodations, you won't do any better than the **Motel 6,** 1445 Bayshore Dr., Coos Bay, OR 97420 (☎ 800/466-8356 or 541/267-7171), charging $40 for a double.

Coos Bay Manor Bed & Breakfast Inn. 955 S. Fifth St., Coos Bay, OR 97420. ☎ **800/ 269-1224** outside Oregon, or 541/269-1224. 5 rms (3 with private bath). $70 double with shared bath, $85 double with private bath. Rates include full breakfast. AE, DISC, MC, V.

Built in the colonial style in 1912, this restored home in a quiet residential neighborhood in downtown Coos Bay is your best bet in the area if you're looking for a bed-and-breakfast. The guest rooms are large and vary from a Victorian room full of ruffles and lace to the masculine Cattle Baron's Room, which has bear and coyote rugs.

Edgewater Inn. 275 E. Johnson Ave., Coos Bay, OR 97420. ☎ **800/233-0423** or 541/ 267-0423. Fax 541/267-4343. 82 rms. A/C TV TEL. $75–$110 double. AE, DISC, MC, V.

This is Coos Bay's only waterfront hotel, and though the water it fronts on is only a narrow stretch of the back bay, you can watch ships in the harbor. Pilings and exposed beams used in the portico reflect the local logging-and-shipping economy. The guest rooms are large and furnished with blond-wood bureaus and headboards. The deluxe rooms are particularly well designed, with a breakfast bar, coffeemaker, minirefrigerator, extralarge TV, two sinks, lots of counter space, and a hair dryer in the bathroom. Other deluxe rooms have in-room spas. Most rooms also have balconies overlooking the water (and industrial areas). Facilities include an indoor pool, a hot tub, an exercise room, a fishing and ship-viewing dock, and a games room.

Red Lion Coos Bay. 1313 N. Bayshore Dr., Coos Bay, OR 97420. ☎ **800/547-8010** or 541/ 267-4141. Fax 541/267-2884. 143 rms. A/C TV TEL. $70–$80 double. AE, CB, DC, DISC, MC, V.

This is the largest and most luxurious hotel in Coos Bay, and even so, it's quite reasonably priced. As the town's only convention lodging, the Red Lion is often full, so if you decide this is the place for you, book early. With its acres of parking and sprawling two-story buildings, the hotel is none too attractive, but if it's big-hotel amenities you want, it's got them. The guest rooms are larger than in most similar hotels, which makes rooms here a good choice for families. There's a dining room serving steaks and seafood, as well as a sports bar with karaoke. Room service and a free airport shuttle are available, as is access to a nearby health club. Facilities include an outdoor pool.

CAMPGROUNDS

About 12 miles outside Coos Bay, you'll find **Sunset Bay State Park,** which has the only beach on this coast where people actually go in the water much and is on one of the prettiest stretches of coastline in the state. However, it doesn't make a very good base for exploring due to its location well off U.S. 101. **Bastendorff Beach County Park** (☎ **541/888-5353**), north of Sunset Bay at the mouth of Coos Bay, is an alternative to the crowded, frequently full Sunset Bay State Park campground.

WHERE TO DINE

In addition to the restaurants listed below, you might want to check out **Kaffe 101,** 134 S. Broadway (☎ **541/267-4894**), which serves espresso, pastries, and ice cream.

Bank Brewing Company. 201 Central Ave., Coos Bay. ☎ **541/267-0963.** Reservations not accepted. Main courses $7–$15. MC, V. Mon–Thurs 11:30am–10pm, Fri 11:30am–midnight, Sat noon–midnight, Sun noon–8pm. AMERICAN.

Housed in a 1923 bank building in downtown Coos Bay, this is the area's only brew pub and is a great place for pizza and a pint. Of the 10 brews produced here, there are usually four or so on tap at any given time. While pizza seems to be the meal of choice here, there are also a variety of sandwiches, as well as such dinners as seafood fettucine, barbecued baby back ribs, and a daily fresh fish special. Occasional live music.

Benetti's. 260 S. Broadway, Coos Bay. ☎ **541/267-6066.** Reservations for 6 or more people only. Main courses $8–$15. MC, V. Sun–Thurs 5–9pm, Fri–Sat 5–10pm. ITALIAN.

Dark, candlelit, and romantic, this is the best Italian restaurant in town and usually has a line out the door at dinnertime. As soon as you step through the door, the aromas of an Italian kitchen wash over you. Straightforward southern Italian fare dominates the menu, and for those who can't decide what to order, there's a combination plate that includes ravioli, lasagna, cannelloni, and spaghetti.

Blue Heron Bistro. 100 Commercial Ave., Coos Bay. ☎ **541/267-3933.** Reservations recommended. Main courses $5–$13.50. DISC, MC, V. Daily 11am–10pm. INTERNATIONAL.

A casual cafe, espresso bar, deli, and international restaurant all rolled up in one—that's what you'll find at the Blue Heron, which is in the heart of downtown Coos Bay and right on U.S. 101. Add to this one of the largest assortments of imported beers on the coast and you have the sort of place that's perfect for lunch, dinner, or just a quick bite to eat over a newspaper or magazine from the restaurant's extensive library. Blue Heron chefs cruise the world in search of tantalizing dishes, from German bratwurst (nitrite free) to Indonesian satay to blackened red snapper. If you've got some friends with you, don't miss the Greek antipasto plate.

Portside. 8001 Kingfisher Dr., Charleston. ☎ **541/888-5544.** Reservations recommended. Main courses $11–$25. AE, DC, MC, V. Daily 11:30am–11pm. SEAFOOD.

Charleston is home to Coos Bay's charter and commercial fishing fleets, and so it should come as no surprise that it's also home to the area's best seafood restaurant. Under different names, this restaurant has been in business for more than 30 years and has developed quite a reputation. Check the daily fresh sheet to see what just came in on the boat. Preparations tend toward traditional continental dishes, of which the house specialty is a bouillabaisse Marseilles that's just swimming with shrimp, lobster, crab legs, butter clams, red snapper, scallops, and prawns—a seafood symphony. The restaurant overlooks the boat basin and is popular with families.

12 Bandon

24 miles S of Coos Bay, 85 miles W of Roseburg

Once known primarily as the cranberry capital of Oregon (you can see the cranberry bogs south of town along U.S. 101), Bandon is now better known as an artists' colony. It's also set on one of the most spectacular pieces of coastline in the state. Just south of town, the beach is littered with boulders, monoliths, and haystack rocks that seem to have been strewn by some giant hand. Sunsets are stunning—it's easy to see why artists have been drawn here. Today, there are several excellent art galleries in downtown Bandon, which makes shopping a favorite activity here.

Just north of town the Coquille River empties into the Pacific, and at the river's mouth stands a picturesque and historic lighthouse. The lighthouse was one of only a handful of Bandon buildings to survive a fire in 1936 that destroyed nearly the entire town.

Despite the fact that most buildings in downtown date only from the 1930s, Bandon has a quaint seaside village atmosphere. The marina on the edge of downtown is always a lively place, and the downtown shops are among the most interesting on the coast.

ESSENTIALS

GETTING THERE   From Roseburg, head west on Ore. 42 to Coquille where you take Ore. 42S to Bandon, which is on U.S. 101.

VISITOR INFORMATION   Contact the **Bandon Chamber of Commerce,** 300 SE Second St. (P.O. Box 1515), Bandon, OR 97411 (☎ **541/347-9616**).

FESTIVALS   Bandon is the cranberry capital of Oregon, and each year in September the impending harvest is celebrated with the **Bandon Cranberry Festival.** Other festivals include the **Seafood and Wine Festival** held over Memorial Day weekend and the **Festival of Lights,** held each year during the Christmas season.

OUTDOOR ACTIVITIES & BANDON ATTRACTIONS

Head out of Bandon on Beach Loop Road and you'll soon see why rock watching is one of the area's most popular pastimes. Wind and waves have sculpted monoliths along the shore into contorted spires and twisted shapes. The first good place to view the rocks is at **Coquille Point,** at the end of 11th Street. From here you can see Table Rock and the Sisters. From the **Face Rock Viewpoint** you can see the area's most famous rock, which resembles a face gazing skyward. Nearby stand a dog, a cat, and kittens. An ancient Chinook tribal legend tells how a young woman, Ewauna, swam into the sea and, while gazing at the moon, was seized by a sea monster. Her dog, cat, and kittens tried to save her but to no avail, and they were all turned into stone. A trail leads down to the beach from the viewpoint, so you can go out and explore some of the rocks that are left high and dry by low tide. South of the rocks, along a flat stretch of beach backed by sand dunes, there are several beach access areas, all of which are within **Bandon State Park.**

Across the river from downtown Bandon, you'll find **Bullards Beach State Park** (☎ **541/347-2209**). Within the park are beaches, a marsh overlook, hiking and horseback riding trails, a picnic area, a campground, and a boat ramp. Fishing, crabbing, and clamming are all very popular in the park. Also within the park, you'll find the historic **Coquille River Lighthouse,** which was built in 1896. This lighthouse is one of the only lighthouses to ever be hit by a ship—in 1903 an abandoned schooner plowed into the light. In December the lighthouse is decorated with Christmas lights. During the summer, tours of the lighthouse are offered Monday and Tuesday between noon and 4pm, and Wednesday through Sunday from 10am to 4pm.

At Bandon, as elsewhere on the Oregon coast, **gray whales** migrating between the Arctic and Baja California, Mexico, pass close to the shore and can often be spotted from land. The whales pass Bandon between December and February on their way south and between March and May on their way north. Early morning, before the wind picks up, is the best time to spot whales. Coquille Point, at the end of 11th Street, and the bluffs along Beach Loop Road are the best vantage points.

More than 300 species of birds have been spotted in the Bandon vicinity, making this one of the best sites in Oregon for **bird watching.** The **Oregon Islands National Wildlife Refuge,** which includes 1,400 rocks and islands off the state's coast, includes the famous monoliths of Bandon. Among the birds that nest on these rocks are rhinoceros auklets, storm petrels, gulls, and tufted puffins. These latter birds, with their large colorful beaks, are the most beloved of local birds, and their images show up on all manner of local souvenirs. The **Bandon Marsh National Wildlife Refuge,** at the mouth of the Coquille River, is another good spot for bird watching. In this area you can expect to see grebes, mergansers, buffleheads, plovers, and several birds of prey.

Anglers can head offshore for bottom fish, salmon, tuna, and halibut with **Port O' Call,** 155 First St. (☎ **541/347-2875**), which charges $50 to $125 for a fishing trip. If you're interested in exploring the Coquille River, you can rent a sea kayak from **Adventure Kayak,** 315 First St. (☎ **541/347-3480**), which also offers kayak

In case you want to be welcomed there.

We're here to see that you're always welcomed at establishments everywhere. That's why millions of people carry the American Express® Card – for peace of mind, confidence, and security, around the world or just around the corner.

do more

Cards

In case you're running low.

We're here to help with more than 118,000 Express Cash locations around the world. In order to enroll, just call American Express before you start your vacation.

do more

Express Cash

And just in case.

We're here with American Express® Travelers Cheques and Cheques *for Two*.® They're the safest way to carry money on your vacation and the surest way to get a refund, practically anywhere, anytime.

Another way we help you...

do more

Travelers Cheques

tours and lessons. Boats rent for $12 to $20 per hour and tour prices range from $35 to $65. This company also rents bicycles for $12 for 1 hour or $16 for 4 hours. If you'd rather ride a horse down the beach, contact **Bandon Beach Riding Stables** (☎ 541/347-3423), on Beach Loop Drive south of Face Rock. A 1-hour ride is $20. The **Bandon Face Rock Golf Course,** 3235 Beach Loop Dr. (☎ 541/347-3818), offers a scenic nine holes not far from the famous Face Rock. The greens fee is $14 to $15 for 18 holes.

If you're interested in local history, stop in at the **Coquille River Museum** (☎ 541/347-2164), which is right on U.S. 101 at the corner of Fillmore Street (1 block from Bandon Cheese). The museum contains Native American artifacts, historic photos (including ones of the fire that burned Bandon to the ground), displays on lifesaving, and other examples of Bandon history. It's open Monday through Saturday from 10am to 4pm; admission is $1. If you're a fan of old architecture, head over to the nearby town of Coquille, which is known for its turn-of-the-century Victorian homes.

The ♦ **West Coast Game Park,** 7 miles south of town on U.S. 101 (☎ 541/347-3106), bills itself as America's largest wild animal petting park and is a must for families. Depending on what young animals they have at the time of your visit, you might be able to play with a leopard or bear cub. It's open daily from 9am to 7pm in summer, with shorter hours other months. Admission is $7 for adults, $6 for seniors, $5.75 for children 7 to 12, $4.25 for children 2 to 6.

Animals of a different sort are also the attraction at **Free Flight Bird and Marine Mammal Rehabilitation Center,** 1185 Portland Ave. (☎ 541/347-3882), which takes in and cares for injured birds and other animals. At any given time, the center might be caring for seals, sea lions, an elk calf, a bear cub, a bald eagle, or tiny songbirds. During the summer, volunteers are on hand daily from 2 to 4pm, other months, call for an appointment.

SHOPPING

Shopping is Bandon's main attraction these days, and in downtown Bandon, just off U.S. 101, you'll find many interesting shops and galleries in restored buildings.

Nearly a dozen galleries sell artworks by regional artists. Among our favorite galleries are the **210 Second Street Gallery,** 210 Second St. (☎ 541/347-4133), which is one of the largest galleries on the Oregon coast and represents nearly 100 artists who work in a variety of media; **Campbell's Glassworks,** 275 E. Second St. (☎ 541/347-9810), which does custom stained-glass designs and also sells a variety of glass gifts; and **Spirit of Oregon,** 112 Second St. (☎ 541/347-4311), offering hand-thrown ceramics, handmade rugs, baskets, and locally designed clothing. South of town, along U.S. 101, watch for **Vitra Blown Glass Studio** (☎ 541/347-4723) and **Laurel Grove Pottery** (☎ 541/347-8078).

At the **Bandon Cheese Factory,** located right on U.S. 101 in the middle of town (☎ 541/347-2456), you can watch cheese being made, try some samples, and maybe pick up some fixings for a picnic on the beach. A few blocks away, **Cranberry Sweets,** on the corner of First Street and Chicago Avenue (☎ 541/347-9475), sells handmade candies. Some of the candies are made from cranberries, but there are also many noncranberry candies among the 200 varieties available.

If you haven't yet visited a myrtle wood factory and showroom, you can visit **Seagull Myrtlewood** (☎ 541/347-2248), 3 miles south of town at the intersection of U.S. 101 and Beach Loop Road, or **Zumwalt's Myrtlewood Factory** (☎ 541/347-3654), 6 miles south of town on U.S. 101.

Stormy Weather

"And the forecast for the weekend at the coast calls for high winds and heavy rain as another storm front moves in off the Pacific Ocean." This sort of weather forecast would keep most folks cozily ensconced at home with a good book and a fire in the fireplace, but in Oregon, where storm watching has become a popular winter activity, it's the equivalent of "Surf's up!"

Throughout the winter, Oregon's rocky shores and haystack rocks feel the effects of storms that originate far to the north in cold polar waters. As these storms slam ashore, sometimes with winds topping 100 mph, their huge waves smash against the rocks with breathtaking force, sending spray flying. The perfect storm-watching days are those rare clear days right after a big storm, when the waves are still big but the sky is clear. After a storm is also the best time to go beachcombing—it's your best chance to find the rare hand-blown Japanese glass fishing floats that sometimes wash ashore on the Oregon coast.

So popular is storm watching that some bed-and-breakfast inns keep lists of people who are interested in storms and will give potential guests a call when the waves reach impressive proportions. There's also a storm-watchers club in Bandon.

Among the best storm-watching spots on the coast are the South Jetty at the mouth of the Columbia River in Fort Stevens State Park, Cannon Beach, Cape Meares, Depoe Bay, Cape Foulweather, Devil's Punchbowl on the Otter Crest Scenic Loop, Seal Rock, Cape Perpetua, Shore Acres State Park, Cape Arago State Park, Face Rock Viewpoint outside Bandon, and Cape Sebastian.

Among the best lodgings for storm watching are the Inn at Otter Crest north of Depoe Bay, the Channel House in Depoe Bay, the Cliff House in Waldport, the Adobe Motel Resort in Yachats, and the Sunset Motel in Bandon. The coast's best restaurants for storm watching are Tidal Raves in Depoe Bay, the dining room of the Adobe Motel Resort in Yachats, and Lord Bennett's at the Sunset in Bandon.

WHERE TO STAY

✪ Bandon Beach House. 2866 Beach Loop Rd., Bandon, OR 97411. ☎ **541/347-1196.** 2 rms. $125 double. No credit cards.

Although this modern, lodgelike oceanfront home is quite large, it has only two rooms for rent, which means that you can expect plenty of space here. The setting, atop a 50-foot-high bluff overlooking the beach, is among the most dramatic in the area, and the inn more than lives up to this sense of drama. Each guest room is huge and has a river-rock fireplace, beautiful maple floor, and walls of windows with ocean views, and one of the rooms has its own deck. Classically elegant furnishings, including leather chairs and oriental carpets, set the tone.

Lighthouse Bed and Breakfast. 650 Jetty Rd. SW (P.O. Box 24), Bandon, OR 97411. ☎ **541/347-9316.** 5 rms. $90–$145 double. MC, V.

Located on the road that leads to the mouth of the Coquille River, this riverfront B&B has a view of the historic Bandon Lighthouse. With its weathered cedar siding, large decks, and small sunroom, this is the quintessential beach house. Guest rooms range from a small room with the private bath across the hall to a spacious room with views of the ocean and lighthouse, a wood-burning stove, and a double whirlpool tub overlooking the river. Both the beach and old town Bandon are within a very short walk.

Sea Star Guesthouse and AYH Hostel. 375 Second St., Bandon, OR 97411. ☎ **541/ 347-9632.** Fax 541/347-9533. 4 rms, 39 hostel beds. TV. $53–$90 double; $13 per night dorm bed for members, $16 for nonmembers. MC, V.

The guest house, a two-story contemporary beach home overlooking Bandon's marina, is your best choice for accommodations in the old town waterfront district. Both downstairs rooms here have views of the harbor, but the upstairs rooms are the better choices. These have skylights and open beams. The larger of the two has a loft sleeping area, while the smaller has a four-poster bed. Dorms in the hostel are small, so if you're traveling with some friends, you might want to get one all to yourself. There are four family rooms as well. Guests can use a small lounge and kitchen.

Sunset Motel. 1755 Beach Loop Rd. (P.O. Box 373), Bandon, OR 97411-0373. ☎ **800/ 842-2407** or 541/347-2453. Fax 541/347-3636. 57 rms, 14 cabins/condos. TV TEL. $45–$105 double; $90–$185 cabin/condo for 2 to 8 people. AE, DISC, MC, V.

Nowhere in Oregon will you find a better ocean view than here at the Sunset Motel, where you'll also find everything from economy motel rooms to contemporary condos, rustic cabins, and classic cottages. Dozens of Bandon's famous rock spires, sea stacks, and monoliths rise from the beach or just offshore in front of the motel, making sunsets from the Sunset truly memorable. If you want modern accommodations, opt for the Vern Brown addition rooms, and if you want something romantic and private, try to get one of the cottages, several of which were built back in the 1930s or 1940s. The adjacent Lord Bennet Restaurant has some of the best food in town, and there's no question about its having *the* view in Bandon. A hot tub, video rentals, and guest laundry round out the motel's amenities.

Windermere. 3250 Beach Loop Rd., Bandon, OR 97411. ☎ **541/347-3710.** 17 rms. TV. $59–$95 double. Lower rates off-season. AE, MC, V.

Turning into the Windermere's driveway on a gray blustery day, you can almost hear a voice calling for "Heathcliff." The *Wuthering Heights* setting is a combination of moorlike surroundings and the English cottage-style architecture of this 60-year-old beach getaway. Set on the edge of a wide sand beach, the Windermere has seen better years, but for families on a budget or anyone who enjoys old-fashioned accommodations, the rooms here are quite adequate. All the rooms have oceanfront decks, and some have sleeping lofts or kitchens.

CAMPGROUNDS

Bullards Beach State Park, across the Coquille River from downtown Bandon, has 190 campsites and two yurts for rent. To make reservations, call **Reservations Northwest** (☎ 800/452-5687). South of Bandon, you'll find more campsites at **Boice-Cope County Park** on Floras Lake in Langlois. There are also campsites up the Sixes River at **Edson Creek Park,** which is 4 miles off U.S. 101. Farther up this same road, you can camp at the **Sixes River Recreation Site.**

WHERE TO DINE

When it's time for espresso, stop in at **Rayjen Coffee Company,** 350 Second St. SE (☎ 541/347-1144), in a tiny cottage on the edge of old town. For a quick meal of incredibly fresh fish-and-chips, you can't beat **Bandon Fish Market,** 249 First St. (☎ 541/347-4282), which is right on the waterfront and has a few picnic tables out front. At press time, **Harp's,** an old standby on the Bandon restaurant scene, was in the process of moving to 480 SW First St., a renovated building on the waterfront near the start of Beach Loop Road.

Andrea's Old Town Café. 160 Baltimore Ave. ☎ **541/347-3022.** Reservations recommended. Main courses $11–$16; lunch $5–$8. MC, V. Daily 9am–3:30pm and 5:30–9pm. Closed Sun–Thurs night in winter. INTERNATIONAL.

Though it looks as if it's just another ducks-and-chicks, country-cute family restaurant from the outside and a well-worn natural-foods college cafe on the inside, Andrea's is neither. This restaurant defies classification. By day it's an ever-popular omelet-and-sandwich place where the Hangtown fry omelet, made with oysters and ham, is a breakfast must and the seafood sandwiches, such as the oyster sandwich, are simply outstanding. At night, a daily changing menu takes over and you might find leg of lamb stuffed with prosciutto, rosemary, and garlic. Friday is pizza night at Andrea's, and the pizzas are the best on the beach.

Bandon Boatworks. 275 Lincoln Ave. SW. ☎ **541/347-2111.** Reservations recommended both lunch and dinner. Main courses $11–$24.50; lunches $5–$9.50. AE, DISC, MC, V. Mon–Sat 11:30am–2:30pm and 5–9pm, Sun noon–8:30pm. SEAFOOD.

Located directly across the Coquille River from the historic Bandon Lighthouse, this large seafood restaurant has the second-best view in town. Through the large picture windows, you can watch the waves crashing on the jetties at the mouth of the river, while you dine on the likes of grilled teriyaki prawns or oysters flambéed with brandy and anisette. Burgers and sandwiches predominate on the lunch menu.

Lord Bennett's at the Sunset. 1695 Beach Loop Dr. ☎ **541/347-3663.** Reservations recommended. Main courses $12–$18; lunch $6–$9. AE, DISC, MC, V. Daily 11am–3pm and 5–10pm (until 9pm in winter). CONTINENTAL.

Lord Bennett's is the only restaurant in Bandon overlooking the bizarre beachscape of contorted rock spires and sea stacks, and this fact alone makes it a must for a meal. However, great continental meals make the restaurant doubly worthwhile. Sunsets are an absolute must at Lord Bennett's, and since sunsets come late in the day in the summer, you might want to eat a late lunch the day you plan to eat here. We suggest starting dinner with some steamed clams before moving on to such main courses as coconut shrimp with pineapple-jalapeño salsa. There's a decent wine list, and the desserts are both beautiful and delicious.

13 The Port Orford Area

27 miles S of Bandon, 79 miles N of Crescent City, 95 miles W of Grants Pass

Port Orford, today little more than a wide spot in the road, actually has a longer history than any other town on the coast other than Astoria. Named by Capt. George Vancouver on April 5, 1792, this natural harbor in the lee of Port Orford Heads, became the first settlement right on the Oregon coast, when, in 1851, settlers and soldiers together constructed Fort Orford. A fort was necessary due to hostilities with the area's native population. Eventually the settlers fled inland, crossing the Siskiyou Mountains. Today, Port Orford's biggest claim to fame is as the westernmost incorporated town in the contiguous 48 states.

While the first settlers made camp here because there was something of a natural harbor, these days, the area's fishing fleet is hauled out of the water nightly by a large crane. The fact is that this really isn't a harbor at all, but just a slightly protected cove on a very wave-swept coastline. Working out of this tiny port is a fishing fleet and sea urchin harvesting industry. The roe (eggs) of sea urchins is considered a delicacy in Japan, but American palates have yet to develop a taste for the slimy, smelly eggs.

Perhaps because of the remote location and perhaps because bad weather keeps the hordes at bay, this area has become something of a magnet for artists. In both Port

Orford and the tiny hamlet of Langlois to the north, you will find art galleries show-casing the works of local artists.

Nearby Cape Blanco, just north of Port Orford and discovered and named by Spanish explorer Martín de Aguilar in 1603, once made an even grander claim than Port Orford when it was heralded as the westernmost point of land in the lower 48. Today, that claim has been laid to rest by Cape Flattery, Washington, and Cape Blanco now only claims to be the westernmost point in Oregon.

ESSENTIALS

GETTING THERE   Port Orford is on U.S. 101 and can be reached from I-5 either by taking a winding, often one-lane road over the Siskiyou Mountains from Grants Pass or by taking Ore. 42 west from Roseburg.

VISITOR INFORMATION   For more information on this area, contact the **Port Orford Chamber of Commerce,** P.O. Box 637, Port Orford, OR 97465 (☎ **541/ 332-8055**).

EXPLORING THE AREA

For a good view of Port Orford and this entire section of coast, drive up to the **Port Orford Heads Wayside,** where you'll find a short trail out to an overlook. This is the site of a former coast guard lifesaving station, and the old buildings are in the pro-cess of being renovated and turned into an interpretive center and history museum. The route to the wayside is well marked. Right in Port Orford, you can visit **Battle Rock Park** and learn the history of the rock refuge that rises out of Port Orford's beach. If you want to walk the beach, this is a good one, as is the beach at the end of Paradise Point Road just north of town.

Cape Blanco now lends its name to **Cape Blanco State Park** (☎ **541/332-6774**), where you'll find miles of beaches and hiking trails through windswept meadows, a campground, picnic areas, and a boat ramp on the Sixes River. This high headland is also the site of the **Cape Blanco Lighthouse,** which was built in 1870 and is the oldest continuously operating lighthouse in Oregon. Not far from the lighthouse is the **Hughes House Museum,** a restored Eastlake Victorian home that was built in 1898 and is furnished with period antiques. It's open May to September only, Thurs-day through Monday from 10am to 4pm and on Sunday from noon to 4pm. In this same area north of Port Orford, you'll find the Elk River and the Sixes River, which are both well known for their fall and winter steelhead and salmon runs.

If you're interested in boardsailing, check out the **Floras Lake Windsurfing School,** at the Floras Lake House Bed & Breakfast, 92870 Boice Cope Rd. (☎ **541/ 348-2573**), which offers rentals and lessons. You'll find Floras Lake west of U.S. 101 south of the community of Langlois. Equipment is also available at **Big Air Windsurfing,** 48435 U.S. 101, Langlois (☎ **541/348-2213**). Surfers will want to check out the break at Hubbard Creek, which is south of town.

Six miles south of Port Orford, you'll find **Humbug Mountain State Park** (☎ **541/332-6774**), where Humbug Mountain rises 1,756 feet from the ocean's waves. A pretty campground is tucked into the forest at the base of the mountain and a trail leads to the summit.

Another 6 miles brings you to a place the kids aren't going to let you pass. The **Prehistoric Gardens,** 36848 U.S. 101 S. (☎ **541/332-4463**), is a lost world of life-size dinosaur replicas. Though they aren't as realistic as those in *Jurassic Park,* they'll make the kids squeal with delight. The gardens are open daily from 8am to dusk; admission is $6 for adults, $5 for seniors and youths 12 to 18, $4 for children 5 to 11.

Art galleries in the Port Orford area include the **Cook Fine Art Gallery,** 705 Oregon St. (☎ **541/332-0045**), which features beautiful wood sculptures and furniture as well as prints and ceramics; **Grantland Mayfield Gallery,** 246 Sixth St. (☎ **541/332-6610**), which features a wide variety of work; and **Port Orford Pottery Studio,** 917 U.S. 101 (☎ **541/332-0313**), which specializes in unusual pottery wall sculptures made from molds of fish. In Langlois, north of Port Orford, you'll find **Raincoast Arts,** 48358 U.S. 101 (☎ **541/348-9992**), which is housed in an old wooden commercial building and features works in a wide variety of styles (wood craft, weaving, pottery, photography) and media by local artists.

WHERE TO STAY

The Castaway. P.O. Box 844, Port Orford, OR 97465. ☎ **541/332-4502.** 13 rms. TV TEL. $45–$75 double. Lower rates in off-season. DISC, MC, V.

Located on a hill high above Port Orford harbor and commanding a sweeping panorama of the southern Oregon coast, this modest motel is far more comfortable than it appears from the outside. All the rooms take in the superlative view, and most have comfy little sunrooms from which to gaze off to sea. The rooms are also quite large and well maintained, and some have kitchenettes. Out back there is a lawn with a few benches overlooking the harbor.

Floras Lake House Bed & Breakfast. 92870 Boice Cope Rd., Langlois, OR 97450. ☎ **541/348-2573.** Fax 541/348-2573. Web site: http://www.harborside.com/home/f/floraslk/lakebnb.htm. 4 rms. $95–$125 double. Rates include full breakfast. DISC, MC, V.

Located north of Port Orford near the community of Langlois, this contemporary B&B is close to the shore of Floras Lake, which is popular for boardsailing (the inn offers sailboard rentals and lessons). The guest rooms all have views of the lake, and the two more expensive rooms have fireplaces. Across the back of the house are several large decks that provide plenty of lounging areas.

Home by the Sea. 444 Jackson St. (P.O. Box 606), Port Orford, OR 97465. ☎ **541/332-2855.** Web site: http://www.homebythesea.com. 2 rms. $85–$95 double. Rates include full breakfast. MC, V.

Set high atop a bluff overlooking the ocean, this contemporary B&B offers large guest rooms with some of the best views on the coast. Pet birds fill the house with their songs, and in the downstairs living room area you'll still get that million-dollar view. The inn is a block off U.S. 101 and is within walking distance of several restaurants.

Sixes River Hotel & Farm. 93316 Sixes River Rd. (P.O. Box 327), Sixes, OR 97476. ☎ **800/828-5161** or 541/332-3900. Fax 541/332-2023. Web site: http://www.harborside.com/sixesriverhotel. 5 rms. $85 double. Rates include full breakfast. MC, V.

About 6 miles north of Port Orford, near the turnoff to Cape Blanco State Park, stands the last remaining building in Sixes, once an active logging-and-mining community. Built in 1895, the fully restored Sixes River Hotel is surrounded by farmland and makes a good base for exploring the coast and nearby state parks. The guest rooms are simply furnished and sport a country decor.

The inn's restaurant is one of the finest on the south coast and serves reservation-only five-course dinners ($22). Much of the produce is organically grown here on the farm.

WHERE TO DINE

In addition the restaurant listed below, you can get simple vegetarian fare at **Sisters Natural Grocery & Cafe,** 832 Oregon St. (☎ **541/332-3640**).

Spaghetti West. 236 Sixth St. ☎ **541/332-9378.** Main courses $8.50–$15.50. AE, MC, V. Thurs–Mon 11am–3pm and 5–9pm. ITALIAN.

Located right across from the beach and Battle Rock, this casual restaurant features not only Italian food, but barbecue. There are also daily seafood specials that aren't always Italian in heritage (grilled tuna with an oriental sauce). A variety of pastas can be matched with an equally wide variety of sauces, such as grilled chicken with Gorgonzola cheese or mushrooms and greens flambéed in a vodka cream sauce. For dessert opt for the blackberry sourdough cake or the tiramisu.

14 Gold Beach

54 miles N of Crescent City, Calif.; 32 miles S of Port Orford

In California, gold prospectors of the mid–19th century had to struggle through rugged mountains in search of pay dirt, but here in Oregon they could just scoop it up off the beach. The black sands at the mouth of the Rogue River were high in gold (as were the river and other nearby streams), and it was this gold that gave the town its name. The white settlers attracted by the gold soon came in conflict with the local Rogue River (or TuTuNi) Indians. Violence erupted in 1856, but within the year the Rogue River Indian Wars had come to an end and the TuTuNis were moved to a reservation.

The TuTuNis had for centuries found the river to be a plentiful source of salmon, and when the gold played out, commercial fishermen moved in to take advantage of the large salmon runs. The efficiency of their nets and traps quickly decimated the local salmon population, and a salmon hatchery was constructed to replenish the runs. In the 20th century, sportfishing on the Rogue River became so famous that it attracted western author Zane Grey. His novel *Rogue River Feud* chronicles the conflict that arose between the sportfishermen and the commercial fishermen.

Today, the area is more peaceful, but it's still the Rogue River that draws visitors to Gold Beach.

ESSENTIALS

GETTING THERE From the north, take Ore. 42 west from Roseburg to Bandon and then head south on U.S. 101. From the south, the only route to Gold Beach is from California via U.S. 101. There is also a narrow, winding road over the mountains to Gold Beach from Galice (near Grants Pass).

VISITOR INFORMATION Contact the **Gold Beach Visitor's Center & Chamber of Commerce,** 1225 S. Ellensburg Ave., Suite 3, Gold Beach, OR 97444 (☎ **800/525-2334** or 541/247-7526).

WHAT TO SEE & DO: FISHING, HIKING & COASTAL SCENERY

While there is of course a beach at Gold Beach, it is surprisingly not the area's main attraction. That distinction goes to the Rogue River, which empties into the Pacific at the town of Gold Beach. This is the most famous fishing and rafting river in the state, and since 1895 mail boats have been traveling up the Rogue River from Gold Beach to deliver mail and other freight to remote homesteads. Back when this route was initiated, it took 4 days to make the 64-mile round-trip run. Today, however, you can cover the same length of river in just 6 hours in powerful hydrojet boats that use water jets instead of propellers and have a very shallow draft, which allows them to cross rapids and riffles only a few inches deep. Along the way you may see deer, black bear, river otters, and bald eagles. A running narration covers the river's colorful history. Three different trips are available ranging in length from 64 to 104 miles. Two companies operate these trips. **Rogue River Mail Boat Trips** (☎ **800/458-3511** or 541/247-7033) leaves from a dock ¼ mile upriver from the north end of the Rogue River Bridge. **Jerry's Rogue River Jet Boats** (☎ **800/451-3645** or 541/247-4571) leaves from the Port of Gold Beach on the south side of the Rogue River Bridge. Fares range from $30 to $75 for adults and $12 to $35 for children.

An alternative to the jet-boat trips is to do a white-water rafting trip down the Rogue. These are offered by **Rogue White Water Rafting** (☎ **541/247-6022** or 541/247-6504). The 4-hour float costs $65 for adults and $30 for children.

Fighting salmon and steelhead are what have made the Rogue River famous, and if you'd like to hire a guide to take you to the best **fishing** holes, you've got plenty of options. Some guides to check out include **Rogue River Outfitters** (Denny Hughson) (☎ **541/247-2684**), and **Steve Beyerlin** (☎ **800/348-4138** or 541/247-4138). A half day of fishing will cost you around $100 and a full day will cost around $125. Clamming and crabbing can also be quite productive around Gold Beach.

Jerry's Rogue River Museum (☎ **541/247-4571**), located at the Port of Gold Beach and affiliated with Jerry's Jet Boat Tours, is actually the more modern and informative of the town's two museums. It focuses on the geology and cultural and natural history of the Rogue River. It's open daily from 7am to 7pm; admission is free. At the diminutive **Curry County Historical Museum,** 920 S. Ellensburg Ave. (☎ **541/247-6113**), you can learn more about the history of the area and see plenty of Native American and pioneer artifacts. The museum is open June to September, Tuesday through Saturday from noon to 4pm; the rest of the year, on Saturday from noon to 4pm. Admission is by donation.

Golfers can play a round at **Cedar Bend Golf Course,** 34391 Squaw Valley Rd. (☎ **541/247-6911**), 12 miles north of Gold Beach off U.S. 101. If you'd like to go horseback riding, contact **Indian Creek Trail Rides,** half a mile up Jerry's Flat Road in Wedderburn (☎ **541/247-7704**), or **Hawk's Rest Ranch** (☎ **541/247-6423**) in Pistol River, 10 miles south of Gold Beach. Expect to pay between $20 and $30 for a 1- to 2-hour ride.

Hikers have an abundance of options in the area. At the **Schrader Old-Growth Trail,** about 8 miles up Jerry's Flat Road near the Lobster Creek Campground, you can hike through an ancient forest and see for yourself the majestic trees that so many people in the Northwest are fighting to save. In spring, the **Lower Illinois River Trail,** 27 miles up South Bank Road and another 3¼ miles up County Road 450, is abloom with wildflowers. Backpackers can hike the **Rogue River Trail,** which is 40 miles long and parallels the river most of the way. If you don't want to carry a heavy pack, lodges along the river provide meals and accommodations. This hike is most often started at the upper end and hiked downstream, however. Mountain bikers can ride a portion of the Lower Rogue River Trail between Agness and a spot near the Lobster Creek Bridge. The **Oregon Coast Trail,** which extends (in short sections) from California to Washington, has several segments both north and south of Gold Beach. The most spectacular sections of this trail are south of town at Cape Sebastian and in **Samuel H. Boardman State Park.** For more information on hiking in the Gold Beach area, contact the Gold Beach Chamber of Commerce (see above) or the **Siskiyou National Forest,** Gold Beach Ranger District, 1225 S. Ellensburg Rd. (P.O. Box 7), Gold Beach, OR 97444 (☎ **541/247-6651**). If you'd like to hike this region with a guide, contact **Rogue Quest** (☎ **541/247-0915**), which offers a variety of guided hikes ranging in price from $55 for a half day to $80 for a full day.

WHERE TO STAY

Inn at Nesika Beach. 33026 Nesika Rd., Gold Beach, OR 97444. ☎ **541/247-6434.** 4 rms. $100–$130 double. Rates include full breakfast. No credit cards.

Located 5¹/₂ miles north of Gold Beach, this modern Victorian-style inn is set on a bluff above the beach and has expansive ocean views from its many windows. All four guest rooms have whirlpool tubs and feather beds, which make this one of the coziest and most romantic lodgings on the south coast. Three of the guest rooms also have gas fireplaces, and two have private decks. Needless to say, every room has a great view. Hardwood floors throughout the three-story inn provide a classic feel. Hostess Ann Aresnault provides guests with sumptuous, large breakfasts each morning.

Ireland's Rustic Lodges. 1120 S. Ellensburg Ave. (P.O. Box 774), Gold Beach, OR 97444. ☎ **541/247-7718.** 28 rms, 9 cottages, 3 houses. TV. $45–$66 double. Lower rates off-season. MC, V.

The name sums it all up—rustic cabins set amid shady grounds that are as green as Ireland (and beautifully landscaped, too). Though there are some modern motel rooms here, they just can't compare to the quaint old cabins, which have stone fireplaces, paneled walls, and unusual door handles made from twisted branches. Built in 1922, the cabins are indeed rustic and are not for those who need modern comforts. The mature gardens surrounding the cabins are beautiful any time of year but particularly in late spring.

Jot's Resort. 94360 Waterfront Loop (P.O. Box J), Gold Beach, OR 97444. ☎ **800/367-5687** or 541/247-6676. Fax 541/247-6716. 140 rms. TV TEL. Summer $85–$95 double; $125–$295 condo. Off-season $50–$75 double; $90–$200 condo apt. AE, CB, DC, DISC, MC, V.

Stretching along the north bank of the Rogue River, Jot's has a definite fishing orientation and is very popular with families. The resort offers a wide variety of room sizes and rates, but every room has a view of the water and the Rogue River Bridge. The deluxe rooms here are the most attractively furnished, while the condos are the most spacious (some have spiral staircases that lead up to loft sleeping areas). The dining room and lounge offer reasonably priced meals. Fishing guides, deep-sea charters, boat and bicycle rentals, and jet-boat trips can all be arranged, and there are indoor and outdoor pools, a whirlpool, a sauna, a games room, and a boat dock and marina.

✪ Tu Tu Tun Lodge. 96550 North Bank Rogue, Gold Beach, OR 97444. ☎ **541/247-6664.** Fax 541/247-0672. 16 rms, 2 suites, 2 houses. TEL. $135–$169 double; $185–$195 suite; $200–$310 house. Lower rates in winter. MC, V.

Tu Tu Tun is the most luxurious lodging on the south coast, and can hold its own against any luxury lodge anywhere in the country. In fact, it has developed something of a national reputation in recent years as much for its sophisticated styling as for its idyllic setting. The main lodge building incorporates enough rock and natural wood to give it that rustic feel without sacrificing any modern comforts, and the immense fireplace in the lounge is the center of activity. On warm days, the patio overlooking the river is a great spot for relaxing and sunning, and on cold nights logs crackle in a fire pit. The guest rooms are large and beautifully furnished with slate-topped tables and tile counters. Each room has a private patio or balcony, and should you get an upstairs room, you'll have a high ceiling and an excellent river view. Some rooms also come with a fireplace or outdoor soaking tub.

Dining/Entertainment: The dining room overlooks the river and serves four-course fixed-price dinners ($33.50) focusing on Northwest cuisine. For those heading out on the river, box lunches are available.

Services: Fishing guides and boat rentals arranged.

Facilities: Outdoor pool, four-hole pitch-and-putt golf course, horseshoe pits, games room with pool table, dock, hiking trails.

NEARBY FISHING LODGES

The Rogue River is one of the most famous fishing rivers in the United States and was also one of the first designated National Wild and Scenic Rivers in the country. Along the river's length are a number of rustic fishing lodges, several of which can only be reached by boat. These lodges are popular with rafting companies and fishing guides heading downstream from the Grants Pass area. Fishing lodges are, in general, rustic riverside retreats with small guest rooms and dining rooms serving fixed menus. However, in the tiny rural community of **Agness,** at the end of a 35-mile winding road from Gold Beach, you'll find several lodges that can be reached by car.

Paradise Bar Lodge. P.O. Box 456, Gold Beach, OR 97444. ☎ **800/525-2161,** 541/247-6022, or 541/247-6504. Fax 541/247-7714. 14 rms. $154–$390 double. Rates include all meals. MC, V.

You can fly in, hike in, raft in, or jet-boat in, but you can't drive in, and as far as we're concerned, that's reason enough for a trip to the Paradise Bar Lodge. Located 52 miles upriver from Gold Beach and 13 miles from the nearest road access, the lodge was built in the early 1960s, but the area was first homesteaded in the early 1900s. The lodge buildings are up above the river on an open hill and command a sweeping view of the river's turbulent waters. Basic rooms and more spacious cabins, some with loft sleeping areas, are available. Though steelhead and salmon fishing and white-water rafting are the main topics of discussion here. Hiking trails lead along the banks of the river and up to the top of nearby Deak's Peak.

Facilities: Airstrip, volleyball court, croquet equipment, horseshoes, driving range and putting green, museum.

Santa Anita Lodge. 36975 Agness-Illahe Rd., Agness, OR 97406. ☎ **541/247-6884.** 8 rms, 3 with bath. $200 double. Rates include all meals. AE, MC, V.

Built in the 1930s, the Santa Anita Lodge captures the essence of the Rogue River experience in its classic fishing-lodge decor. Though the exterior is unremarkable, step through the door and you'll enter a different world—massive timbers, wood stoves and stone fireplaces, and a trophy room filled with the mounted heads of the original owner's big-game hunting expeditions around the world. A huge deck overlooks the river and a meadow where elk and bear are often seen. Deer and wild turkeys are regular visitors to the lodge grounds, and best of all, the fishing is great right in front of the lodge. The three guest rooms with private baths also have walls of glass and wood stoves in the rooms. Even if you aren't into fishing, these rooms would be ideal for a quiet getaway.

CAMPGROUNDS

Up the Rogue River between Gold Beach and Agness, you'll find two campgrounds: **Lobster Creek** and **Quosatana.** A third, **Illahee,** is another 6 miles past Agness, though not on the river. At Foster Bar, above Agness, there is an unofficial campground right on the river.

WHERE TO DINE

The best meals in Gold Beach are served in the dining room at **Tu Tu Tun Lodge** (see "Where to Stay," above, for details). If you're looking for a good cup of espresso, drop by the **One Horse Coffee Co.,** 29964 Ellensburg Ave. (☎ **541/247-2760**), at the north end of town on U.S. 101.

Grant's Pancake & Omelette House. 94682 Jerry's Flat Rd. ☎ **541/247-7208.** Reservations not accepted. Breakfasts $3–$7. MC, V. Daily 5:30am–2pm.

While you can get burgers and sandwiches here at lunch, this is really a breakfast place. In fact, it's the most popular breakfast joint for miles around, and you're likely to find a line out the door on any summer morning. Boysenberry waffles, corned beef hash, and smoked pork chops are the sort of hearty fare that pulls the masses in.

Nor'wester. Port of Gold Beach. ☎ **541/247-2333.** Reservations for 5 or more people only. Main courses $13–$40. AE, MC, V. Daily 5–9pm. SEAFOOD.

Large portions of simply prepared fresh seafood are the mainstay of the menu at this dockside restaurant where you can watch fishing boats in the mouth of the Rogue River. The steak-and-seafood combinations are popular choices for big appetites, but we prefer such dishes as pasta and shrimp tapenade and coquille St. Jacques. Most entrees are around $18.

SOUTH OF GOLD BEACH: THE MOST BREATHTAKING STRETCH OF THE OREGON COAST

Gold Beach itself is a wide sandy beach, but just a few miles to the south, the mountains once again march into the sea, creating what many say is the single most spectacular section of coastline in Oregon. Though it's only 34 miles from Gold Beach to the town of **Brookings,** you can easily spend the whole day making the trip. Along the way are numerous viewpoints, picnic areas, hiking trails, and beaches.

The first place to stop is at **Cape Sebastian,** 5 miles south of Gold Beach. This headland was named by a Spanish explorer in 1603 and towers 700 feet above the ocean. Between December and March, this is a good vantage point for whale watching. A 2-mile trail leads down to the water. In another 2 miles you come to Meyers Creek, which is in **Pistol River State Park.** Here you can get a closer look at some of the rugged rock formations that make this coastline so breathtaking. This is the most popular boardsailing and surfing beach on the south coast and is also a good clamming beach.

About 2 miles farther south, you'll come to the sand dunes at the mouth of Pistol River. This was the site of a battle during the Rogue River Indian Wars of 1856. In another 6 miles, you come to the **Arch Rock Viewpoint,** a picnic area with a stunning view of an offshore monolith that has been carved into an arch by the action of the waves. Two miles beyond this, you come to the **Natural Bridge Viewpoint.** These two arches were formed when a sea cave collapsed. In 2 more miles you cross the **Thomas Creek Bridge,** which at 345 feet high is the highest bridge in Oregon. In a little more than a mile, you come to **Whalehead Beach State Park,** where a pyramidal rock just offshore bears a striking resemblance to a spy-hopping whale. There's a better view of Whalehead Rock half a mile south.

In another 1¹/₂ miles you'll come to **House Rock Viewpoint,** which offers sweeping vistas to the north and south. At **Cape Ferrelo Viewpoint** and **Lone Ranch State Park** just to the south, you'll find a grassy headland. Just south of here, watch for the **Rainbow Rock Viewpoint,** which has a panorama of a stretch of beach strewn with large boulders. Three more miles brings you to **Harris Beach State Park** (☎ **541/469-2021**), the last stop along this coast. Here you'll find picnicking and camping and a good view of **Goat Island,** which is the Oregon coast's largest island.

15 Brookings-Harbor & the Oregon Banana Belt

26 miles N of Crescent City, 35 miles S of Gold Beach

Brookings and Harbor together comprise the southernmost community on the Oregon coast. Because of the warm year-round temperatures, this region is known as the Oregon Banana Belt, and you'll see palm trees and other cold-sensitive plants thriving in gardens around town. Farms south of town specialize in growing Easter lilies, and in fact grow virtually all of the Easter lilies sold in the United States. Other plants that thrive in this climate include coast redwoods, Oregon myrtles, and wild azaleas.

ESSENTIALS

GETTING THERE   From the north, take Ore. 42 west from Roseburg to Bandon and then head south on U.S. 101. From the south, the only route to Brookings is from California via U.S. 101. There is also a narrow, winding road over the mountains to Gold Beach from Galice (near Grants Pass).

VISITOR INFORMATION   For more information on this area, contact the **Brookings-Harbor Chamber of Commerce,** 16330 Lower Harbor Rd. (P.O. Box 940), Brookings, OR 97415 (☎ **800/535-9469** or 541/469-3181).

FESTIVALS   The Brookings area is home to a native azalea that is celebrated each Memorial Day weekend with an **Azalea Festival.**

EXPLORING THE OREGON BANANA BELT

The Chetco River is known throughout Oregon as one of the best salmon and steelhead rivers in the state. It is also one of the prettiest rivers and offers opportunities for swimming, rafting, and canoeing. One interesting way to experience the Chetco River is on a combination backpacking and paddling trip with **Wilderness Canyon Adventures** (☎ **541/247-6924**), which offers several different trips with rates ranging from $60 for a 1-day trip up to $1,080 for a 6-day trip. Another company, **Discover Oregon** (☎ **800/924-9491** or 541/469-7110), offers mountain-biking tours in the Chetco Ranger District for $60 to $65 per person. For information on hiking in the area, which includes the high country of the Kalmiopsis Wilderness, contact the **Chetco Ranger District,** 555 Fifth St., Brookings, OR 97415 (☎ **541/ 469-2196**).

If you want to head out to sea to do your fishing, contact **Tidewind Sportfishing** (☎ **541/469-0337**), which operates out of Harbor and offers both salmon and bottom fishing trips for $55 per person, as well as whale-watching excursions ($25 per person).

The area's botanical attractions are one of the most interesting reasons to pay a visit to the Brookings area. Not far from town, you can see old-growth myrtle trees (from which the ubiquitous myrtle wood souvenirs of the south coast are made) at **Loeb State Park,** which is 8 miles up the Chetco River from Brookings on North Bank Road. Myrtle (*Umbellularia californica*) occurs naturally only along the southern Oregon coast and Northern California coast. Just beyond Loeb State Park you'll come to one of the largest stands of coast redwood trees in Oregon. This is as far north as the redwoods naturally grow. A hiking trail winds through the big trees and connects to Loeb State Park. The region's wild azaleas, celebrated each year over Memorial Day weekend, come into bloom in May. The best place to see them is at **Azalea State Park** near the south end of Brookings.

To learn about the history of the area, drop by the **Chetco Valley Historical Museum,** 15461 U.S. 101 S. (☎ **541/469-6651**), which is located south of town just off the highway. The museum is in the oldest standing house in the area (built 1857), and out front is the nation's largest Monterey cypress tree. The museum is open Wednesday through Sunday from noon to 5pm, and admission is by donation.

One of the more unusual places to visit in the area is the **Brandy Peak Distillery,** Tetley Road (☎ **541/469-0194**), which is located north of Brookings off U.S. 101 (take Carpenterville Road). This microdistillery produces fruit brandies in wood-fired pot stills. The distillery is open for tours and tastings Tuesday through Saturday from 1 to 5pm between March and November and from 10am to 6pm in December. Other times by appointment.

WHERE TO STAY

Best Western Beachfront Inn. 16008 Boat Basin Rd. (P.O. Box 2729), Harbor, OR 97415. ☎ **800/468-4081** or 541/469-7779. Fax 541/469-0283. 78 rms. TV TEL. $64–$110 double. AE, CB, DC, DISC, MC, V.

The Beachfront Inn is the only oceanfront accommodation in this area. Most rooms are fairly large and all have ocean views, balconies, microwaves, and refrigerators. The more expensive rooms also have whirlpool tubs with picture windows over them. There's an outdoor pool and a whirlpool.

✪ **Chetco River Inn.** 21202 High Prairie Rd., Brookings, OR 97415. ☎ **541/670-1645.** $95–$135 double. Rates include full breakfast. MC, V.

Set on 35 very secluded acres on the banks of the Chetco River, this contemporary B&B caters to nature lovers and anglers and makes a great weekend retreat for anyone looking to get away from it all. However, in order to get away, you'll first have to find the lodge, which is 16 miles from town up North Bank Road (the last 3 miles are on gravel). The lodge makes use of alternative energies, yet is filled with antiques, so don't expect rustic surroundings here. The Siskiyou National Forest surrounds the lodge property, and hiking, swimming, and star gazing are popular pastimes here. If you don't feel like leaving the woods, you can arrange to have dinner here at the lodge.

South Coast Inn Bed & Breakfast. 516 Redwood St., Brookings, OR 97415. ☎ **800/525-9273** or 541/469-5557. Fax 541/469-6615. 3 rms, 1 cottage. $79–$89 double. Rates include full breakfast. AE, DISC, MC, V.

Although the guest rooms here are fairly plain, the location of this 1917 craftsman bungalow makes it a good choice for anyone seeking a B&B in the Brookings area. Two of the guest rooms have good views, and the cottage, across the garden from the main house, offers a more private setting. Guests have use of a large living room full of antiques, where a fire often crackles in the stone fireplace. Although the weather here never gets really cold, there are also a sauna and whirlpool.

CAMPGROUNDS

The best base for exploring the scenic wonders of **Samuel H. Boardman State Park** is **Harris Beach State Park,** which is on the beach just a few miles to the south. Unfortunately, very few campsites have ocean views. Also nearby, up the North Bank Chetco River Road out of Brookings, is **Loeb State Park,** which is set amid redwood trees and old-growth myrtle trees along the bank of the beautiful Chetco River. A bit farther up the Chetco is the forest service's **Little Redwood Campground,** which is the site of a very popular swimming hole. South of Brookings up the Winchuck River, you'll find the forest service's **Winchuck Campground.**

WHERE TO DINE

For a good cup of espresso in Brookings, stop in at **Java Java Espresso Bar,** 613 Chetco Ave. (☎ **541/469-3042**). For smoked salmon, head south of town to **The Great American Smokehouse & Seafood Co.,** 15657 U.S. 101 S. (☎ **541/ 469-6903**), which sells a wide variety of smoked and canned seafood and also has a sit-down restaurant. For a quick fish-and-chips meal, locals swear by **Wharfside Seafood Restaurant,** 16362 Lower Harbor Rd. (☎ **541/469-7316**), which gets its fish straight off the boats.

Chive's. 1025 Chetco Ave. ☎ **541/469-4121.** Reservations recommended. Main courses $12–$16. MC, V. Wed–Sat 11am–2pm and 5–9pm, Sun 9:30am–2:30pm (brunch) and 2:30–9pm. NORTHWEST.

If you've just reached Oregon from California and are looking for your first bite of Northwest cuisine, this is a good choice. Leaded glass and coral-pink walls make this place surprisingly formal for Brookings, but you can still show up in jeans and T-shirts to try the likes of a salad with pear, endive, and watercress dressed with goat cheese and walnuts; roast breast of pheasant with soft polenta, creamed demi-glace, and sweet peas; or crisp salmon cakes with lemon-caper beurre blanc. Dishes are all artistically presented, and there are always interesting daily specials. Dessert is a high point of a meal here in more ways than one; such dishes as a sabayon (zabaglione) with marsala wine or a bread pudding with a Jack Daniels sauce shouldn't be served to minors. There's a good selection of reasonably priced wines.

Rubio's. 1136 Chetco Ave. ☎ **541/469-4919.** Complete dinner $8–$14. AE, DISC, MC, V. Tues–Sun 11am–9pm. MEXICAN.

A wild paint job makes Rubio's, up at the north end of town, unmistakable, and if you can stand the traffic noise and the weather is clear, you can eat out on the front patio. Inside this old cottagelike building, the lace curtains, red tablecloths, and Mexican music are reassuring after the rush of traffic on the highway. The fiery salsa is a Brookings legend and is available to go. You can order a fixed-price dinner combination or create your own Mexican banquet by mixing and matching various dishes.

Portland 6

Portland may not be as lively as Seattle, but in its own laid-back way it has a lot to offer. However, to truly appreciate this city you'll have to cultivate an appreciation for Portland's subtle charms. A stroll through the Japanese Gardens on a misty May morning; a latte on the bricks at Pioneer Courthouse Square as the Weather Machine sculpture goes through its motions; an evening spent perusing the acres of volumes at Powell's "City of Books"; shopping for crafts at the Saturday Market; a summer festival on the banks of the Willamette River; a quick trip to the beach or Mount Hood—these are the quintessential Portland experiences. Of course, the city has museums, but, with the exception of the Museum of Science and Industry, they're small compared to those in Seattle. Sure, there are theaters for live stage shows, but not in the overwhelming numbers to be found in Seattle.

However, Portland seems to be a city on the verge. Restaurants and nightclubs are proliferating as never before, and the Trail Blazers, the city's NBA basketball team, have just gotten a new coliseum. In hopes of alleviating traffic congestion, the city is extending its modern light-rail system into the western suburbs, and companies such as Nike and Intel are feeding the local economy. Attracted by the city's quality of life, more and more people are moving to Portland from all over the country.

Consequently, Portland today is growing quickly, though so far with a deliberation that has not compromised the city's values and unique characteristics. Whether this controlled and intelligent growth can continue remains to be seen. However, for now Portland remains a city both cosmopolitan and accessible, with a subtle appeal and a laid-back attitude that's refreshing in this high-speed, high-stress age.

1 Orientation

ARRIVING

BY PLANE   Portland International Airport (☎ 503/335-1234) is located 10 miles northeast of downtown Portland. A taxi from the airport to downtown will cost you around $23.

Getting Downtown from the Airport   All the major **car-rental companies** have locations at the airport, so it's easy to fly in and rent a car. See "Getting Around," later in this chapter, for details.

Many Portland hotels provide courtesy shuttle service to and from the airport, so be sure to check at your hotel when you make a reservation. Another way to get into town if you haven't rented a car at the airport is to take the **Raz Transportation Downtown Shuttle** (☎ **503/246-4676** or 503/246-3301). Because of construction at the airport, a bus labeled "Ground Transportation" located outside the baggage claim area will take you out to where the Raz Shuttle is parked. The shuttle will take you directly to your hotel for $9. Shuttles operate every 30 minutes from about 6am to midnight daily.

Tri-Met public bus no. 12 leaves the airport approximately every 15 minutes from 5:30am to 11:50pm for the trip to downtown Portland. The trip takes about 40 minutes and costs $1.05. The bus between downtown and the airport operates between 5am and 12:30am and leaves from Southwest Sixth Avenue and Main Street.

Driving from the airport to downtown takes about 20 minutes by way of I-205 to I-84, and the route is well signed.

BY CAR   Portland's major interstates and smaller highways are **I-5** (north to south), **I-84** (east), **I-405** (circles around the west and south of downtown Portland), **I-205** (bypasses the city to the east), and **U.S. 26** (west).

BY TRAIN   Amtrak trains use the historic **Union Station** at 800 NW Sixth Ave., in northwest Portland near downtown (☎ **800/872-7245** for Amtrak reservations, or 503/273-4866).

BY BUS   The **Greyhound bus station,** at 550 NW Sixth Ave., is also in northwest Portland near downtown (☎ **800/231-2222** or 503/243-2357).

VISITOR INFORMATION

The walk-in office for the **Portland Oregon Visitors Association Information Center** is at Two World Trade Center, 25 SW Salmon St., in downtown Portland (☎ **800/345-3214** or 503/222-2223). The mailing address is Three World Trade Center, 26 SW Salmon St., Portland, OR 97204-3299. There's also an **information booth** by the baggage-claim area at the Portland airport.

If you happen to see two people walking down a Portland street wearing matching kelly-green hats and jackets, they're probably members of the **Portland Guide Service.** They'll be happy to answer any questions you have about the city.

CITY LAYOUT

Portland is located in northwestern Oregon at the confluence of the Columbia and Willamette rivers. Circling the city to the west are the West Hills, which rise to more than 1,000 feet. Some 90 miles west of the West Hills is the Pacific Ocean and the spectacular Oregon coast. To the east are rolling hills that extend to the Cascade Mountains, about 50 miles away. The most prominent peak in this section of the Cascades is Mount Hood (11,235 feet), a dormant volcanic peak that looms over the city on clear days. From many parts of the city it's also possible to see Mount St. Helens, another volcano, which blew its top in 1980.

MAIN ARTERIES & STREETS   **I-84** (Banfield Freeway or Expressway) comes into Portland from the east. East of the city is I-205, which bypasses downtown Portland but runs past the airport. **I-5** (East Bank Freeway) runs through on a north-south axis, passing along the east bank of the Willamette River directly across from downtown. **I-405** (Stadium Freeway and Foothills Freeway) circles around the west and south sides of downtown. **U.S. 26** (Sunset Highway) leaves downtown heading west toward Beaverton and the coast. **Ore. 217** (Beaverton-Tigard Highway) runs south from U.S. 26 in Beaverton.

The most important street to remember in Portland is **Burnside Street.** This is the dividing line between north and south Portland. Dividing the city from east to west is the **Willamette River,** which is crossed by eight bridges in the downtown area. All these bridges are named: from north to south they are Fremont, Broadway, Steel, Burnside, Morrison, Hawthorne, Marquam, and Ross Island. In addition to these bridges there are others farther from the downtown area.

For the sake of convenience we'll define downtown Portland as the area within the **Fareless Square.** This is the area in which you can ride for free on the city's public buses and MAX light-rail system. Fareless Square is that area bounded by I-405 on the west and south, by Hoyt Street on the north, and by the Willamette River on the east.

FINDING AN ADDRESS   Finding an address in Portland can be easy if you keep a number of things in mind. Every address in Portland, and even extending for miles out from the city, includes a map quadrant—Northeast (NE), Southwest (SW), and so on. The dividing line between east and west is the Willamette River; between north and south it's Burnside Street. Any downtown address will carry a Southwest (SW) or Northwest (NW) prefix. An exception to this rule is the area known as North Portland. Streets here have a "North" designation. This is the area across the Willamette River from downtown going toward Jantzen Beach.

Avenues run north-south and streets run east-west. Street names continue on both sides of the Willamette River. Consequently, there's a Southwest Yamhill Street and a Southeast Yamhill Street. In northwest Portland the street names are alphabetical from Burnside to Wilson. Front Avenue is the road nearest the Willamette River on the west side, and Water Avenue is the nearest on the east side. After these, the numbered avenues begin. On the west side you'll also find Broadway and Park Avenue between Sixth Avenue and Ninth Avenue. With each block, the addresses increase by 100, beginning at the Willamette River for avenues and at Burnside Street for streets. Odd numbers are generally on the west and north sides of the streets and even numbers on the east and south sides.

Here's an example. You want to go to 1327 SW Ninth Ave. Because it's in the 1300 block, you'll find it 13 blocks south of Burnside Street, and because it's an odd number, on the west side of the street.

Getting *to* the address is a different story since streets in downtown Portland are mostly one way. Front Avenue is two way, but then First, Third, Fifth, Broadway, Ninth, and Eleventh are one way southbound. Alternating streets are one way northbound.

STREET MAPS   Stop by the **Portland Oregon Visitors Association,** Two World Trade Center, 25 SW Salmon St., or write to them at Three World Trade Center, 26 SW Salmon St., Portland, OR 97204-3299 (☎ **800/345-3214** or 503/222-2223), for a free map of the city. **Powell's "City of Books,"** 1005 W. Burnside St. (☎ **800/878-7323** or 503/228-4651), has an excellent free map of downtown that also includes a walking-tour route and information on many of the sights you'll pass along the way. Members of the **American Automobile Association** can get a free map of the city at the AAA offices at 600 SW Market St. (☎ **503/222-6734**) and 8555 SW Apple Way in Beaverton (☎ **503/243-6444**).

NEIGHBORHOODS IN BRIEF

Downtown   This term usually refers to the business and shopping district south of Burnside Street and north of Jackson Street between the Willamette River and

13th Avenue. You'll find the major department stores, dozens of restaurants, most of the city's performing-arts venues, and almost all the best hotels in this area.

Chinatown   Portland has had a Chinatown almost since the city's earliest days. It's entered through the colorful Chinatown Gate at West Burnside Street and Fourth Avenue. Although there are a few nightclubs in the area, this is not a good place to wander late at night.

Skidmore District (Old Town)   This is Portland's original commercial core, and centers around Southwest Ankeny Street and Southwest First Avenue. Many of the restored buildings have become retail stores, but despite the presence of the Saturday Market, the neighborhood has never become a popular shopping district, mostly because of its welfare hotels, missions, street people, and drug dealing. Continued attempts to clean up this area are bringing some improvement. There are several nightclubs here.

Nob Hill/Northwest   Centered along Northwest 23rd and Northwest 21st avenues at the foot of the West Hills, this is an old residential neighborhood that has been taken over by upscale shops, espresso bars, and restaurants and is currently Portland's most fashionable neighborhood.

The Pearl District   This neighborhood of galleries, artists' lofts, cafes, breweries, and shops is bounded by the Park blocks, Lovejoy Street, I-405, and Burnside Street. Crowds flock here on the first Thursday of the month, when the galleries and other businesses are open late.

Irvington   Though not as attractive as Northwest, Irvington, which centers around Broadway in northeast Portland, is almost as trendy. For several blocks along this avenue, you'll find unusual boutiques, import stores, and lots of excellent but inexpensive restaurants.

The Rose Quarter   The relatively new Rose Garden arena, home to the Trail Blazers and the Portland Winter Hawks, is the main focal point of this sports and entertainment oriented neighborhood. Although the neighborhood is still more of an idea than a reality, it does also include Memorial Coliseum and several restaurants and bars.

Hollywood District   This section of northeast Portland centers around the busy commercial activities of Sandy Boulevard near 42nd Avenue. The district came into being in the early years of this century; the name comes from a landmark movie theater. Throughout this neighborhood are Craftsman-style houses and vernacular architecture of the period.

Sellwood   This area in southeast Portland is the city's antique district, full of restored Victorian houses.

Hawthorne District   This enclave of southeast Portland is full of eclectic boutiques, moderately priced restaurants, and hip young college students from nearby Reed College.

2 Getting Around

BY PUBLIC TRANSPORTATION

FREE RIDES   Portland is committed to keeping its downtown uncongested, and to this end it has invested a great deal in its public transportation system. The single greatest innovation and best reason to ride the Tri-Met public buses and MAX light-rail system is that they're free within an area known as the **Fareless Square.** That's right, free! There are 300 blocks of downtown included in the Fareless Square, and as long as you stay within the boundaries you don't have to pay a cent. This applies to both the buses and the MAX light-rail trolleys. Fareless Square covers the area between I-405 on the south and west, Hoyt Street on the north, and the Willamette River on the east.

FARES   Outside Fareless Square, fares on both Tri-Met buses and MAX are $1.05 or $1.35, depending on how far you travel. Seniors 65 years and older pay 50¢ with valid proof of age. You can also make free transfers between the bus and the MAX light-rail system.

A **day ticket** costing $3.25 is good for travel to all zones and is valid on both buses and MAX. Day tickets can be purchased from any bus driver.

BY BUS

Tri-Met buses operate daily over an extensive network. You can pick up the *Tri-Met Guide,* which lists all the bus routes with times, or individual route maps and time schedules at the **Tri-Met Customer Assistance Office,** behind and beneath the waterfall fountain at Pioneer Courthouse Square (☎ **503/238-7433**). The office is open Monday through Friday from 9am to 5pm. Nearly all Tri-Met buses pass through the Transit Mall on Southwest Fifth Avenue and Southwest Sixth Avenue.

BY MAX

The **Metropolitan Area Express (MAX)** is Portland's aboveground light-rail system, which now connects downtown Portland with the suburb of Gresham, 15 miles to the east. MAX is basically a modern trolley, and, in fact, there are vintage trolley cars that operate certain times of the day. You can ride the MAX for free if you stay within the boundaries of the Fareless Square, which includes all the downtown area. However, be sure to buy your ticket before you get on the MAX if you're traveling out of the Fareless Square. There are ticket-vending machines at all MAX stops that tell you how much to pay for your destination. These machines also give change. The MAX driver cannot sell tickets. Ticket inspectors randomly check tickets—if you don't have one, you can be fined up to $300.

The MAX light-rail system crosses the Transit Mall on Southwest Morrison Street and Southwest Yamhill Street. Transfers to the bus are free.

BY CAR

Although downtown Portland is so compact that you can easily get around on foot or by hopping a free trolley or bus, to see outlying attractions it's best to have a car.

RENTALS   You'll find all the major car-rental companies represented in Portland, and there are also many independent and smaller car-rental agencies listed in the *Portland Yellow Pages.* At Portland International Airport (where it's necessary to take a shuttle to the car-rental area because of airport construction), you'll find the following companies: **Avis** (☎ **800/831-2847** or 503/249-4950), which also has an office downtown at 330 SW Washington St. (☎ 503/227-0220); **Budget** (☎ **800/ 527-0700** or 503/249-6500), which also has offices downtown at 2033 SW Fourth Ave., on the east side at 2323 NE Columbia Blvd., and in Beaverton at 10835 SW Canyon Rd.; **Dollar** (☎ **800/800-4000** or 503/249-4792), which also has an office downtown at NW Broadway and NW Davis St. (☎ 503/228-3540); **Hertz** (☎ **800/654-3131** or 503/249-8216), which also has an office downtown at 1009 SW Sixth Ave. (☎ 503/249-5727); and **National** (☎ **800/227-7368** or 503/249-4900). Outside the airport is **Thrifty,** at 10800 NE Holman St. (☎ **800/367-2277** or 503/ 254-6563), which also has an office downtown at 632 SW Pine St. (☎ 503/227-6587).

PARKING   Parking downtown can be a problem, especially if you show up week-days after workers have gotten to their offices. When parking on the street, be sure to notice the meter's time limit, which can be as little as 15 minutes. Most common are 30- and 60-minute meters. You don't have to feed the meters after 6pm or on Sunday.

The best parking deal in town is at the **Smart Park** garages, which charge 75¢ per hour or $3 all day on the weekends. You'll find Smart Park garages at First Avenue and Jefferson Street; Fourth Avenue and Yamhill Street; Tenth Avenue and Yamhill Street; Third Avenue and Alder Street; O'Bryant Square; and Front Avenue and Davis Street. If you make a purchase, the merchant will usually validate your parking ticket, so don't forget to take it along with you.

Rates in other public lots range from about $1 up to about $2.75 per hour.

DRIVING RULES   You may turn right on a red light after a full stop, and if you are in the far left lane of a one-way street, you may turn left into the adjacent left lane of a one-way street at a red light after a full stop. Everyone in a moving vehicle is required to wear a seat belt.

BY TAXI

Because Portland is fairly compact, getting around by taxi can be economical. Although there are almost always taxis waiting in line at major hotels, you won't find them cruising the streets—you'll have to phone for one. **Broadway Cab** (☎ **503/227-1234**) and **Radio Cab** (☎ **503/227-1212**) both offer 24-hour radio-dispatched service and accept American Express, Discover, MasterCard, and VISA. Fares are $2.50 for the first mile and $1.50 for each additional mile.

BY BICYCLE

Bicycles are a popular way of getting around Portland. The traffic is not very heavy and drivers are accustomed to sharing the road with bicyclists. For leisurely cycling, try the promenade in Waterfront Park, on the east side of the river between the Hawthorne and Burnside Bridges. The Terwilliger Path runs for 10 miles from Portland State University to Tryon Creek State Park in the West Hills. You can pick up a copy of a bike map of the city at most bike shops. Bicycles can be rented downtown at **Bike Central,** 835 SW Second Ave. and Taylor Street (☎ **503/227-4439**), where rental fees are about $20 to $30 per day, or, in season, at **The Bike Gallery,** 821 SW 11th Ave. (☎ **503/222-3821**), where a bike rents for $40 per day.

ON FOOT

City blocks in Portland are about half the size of most city blocks, and the entire downtown area covers only about 13 blocks by 26 blocks. This makes Portland a very easy city to explore on foot. The city has been very active in encouraging people to get out of their cars and onto the sidewalks downtown. The sidewalks are wide and there are many small parks with benches for resting, fountains for cooling off, and works of art to soothe the soul.

FAST FACTS: Portland

American Express   The **American Express Travel Service Office** is at 1100 SW Sixth Ave. (☎ **503/226-2961**), open Monday through Friday from 9am to 5pm.

Area Code   The area code for the Portland metropolitan area is 503. For the rest of Oregon it's 541.

Baby-sitters   Call **Wee-Ba-Bee Child Care** (☎ **503/786-3837**) if your hotel doesn't offer baby-sitting services.

Camera Repair   Call **Associated Camera Repair,** 3401 NE Sandy Blvd. (☎ **503/232-5625**).

Car Rentals   See "Getting Around," earlier in this chapter.

Dentist   Contact the **Multnomah Dental Society** for a referral at ☎ **503/223-4738** or 503/223-4731.

Doctor   Contact the **Medical Society Doctor Referral Service** at ☎ **503/222-0156.**

Emergencies   In case of medical, police, or fire emergency, phone ☎ **911.**

Eyeglass Repair   See **Binyon's Eyeworld Downtown** at 803 SW Morrison St. (☎ **503/226-6688**).

Hospitals   Three area hospitals are **Legacy Good Samaritan,** 1015 NW 22nd Ave. (☎ **503/229-7711**); **Providence St. Vincent Hospital,** 9205 SW Barnes Rd. (☎ **503/216-1234**), off U.S. 26 (Sunset Highway) before Oregon Hwy. 217; and the **Oregon Health Sciences University Hospital,** 3181 SW Sam Jackson Park Rd. (☎ **503/494-8311**), just southwest of the city center.

Hotlines   You may find the following telephone numbers useful during your stay in Portland: **Alcoholics Anonymous** (☎ **503/223-8569**); **Portland Center for the Performing Arts Information Hotline** (☎ **503/796-9293**); **women's crisis line** (☎ **503/235-5333,** or toll free in Oregon 888/235-5333).

Information   See "Orientation," earlier in this chapter.

Liquor Laws   The legal drinking age in Oregon is 21. Bars can stay open until 2am.

Newspapers/Magazines   Portland's morning daily newspaper is the ***Oregonian.*** For arts and entertainment information and listings, consult the *Arts and Entertainment* section of the Friday *Oregonian* or pick up a free copy of ***Willamette Week*** at Powell's Books and other bookstores, convenience stores, or cafes. Another free weekly tabloid is ***Our Town.*** The ***Portland Guide*** is a weekly tourism available at the Portland Oregon Visitors Association and some hotels.

   6th & Washington News Shop, 617 SW Washington St. (☎ **503/221-1128**), carries a large selection of out-of-town newspapers and magazines. There's also another location at 832 SW Fourth Ave.

Police   To reach the police, call ☎ **911.**

Post Offices   The **main post office,** 715 NW Hoyt St., is open Monday through Friday from 7am to 6:30pm, Saturday from 8:30am to 5pm. There are also convenient post offices at 204 SW Fifth Ave., open Monday through Friday from 8:30am to 5pm, and 1505 SW Sixth Ave., open Monday through Friday from 7am to 6pm, Saturday from 10am to 3pm. The phone number for each of these post offices is ☎ **800/275-8777.**

Radio   KOPB-FM (91.5) is the local National Public Radio station.

Rest Rooms   There are public restrooms underneath the Starbucks coffee shop in Pioneer Courthouse Square and in downtown shopping malls.

Safety   Because of its small size and emphasis on keeping the downtown alive and growing, Portland is still a relatively safe city, and in fact strolling the downtown streets at night is a popular pastime. Take extra precautions, however, if you venture into the entertainment district along West Burnside Street or Chinatown at night. Parts of northeast Portland are controlled by street gangs, so before visiting anyplace in this area, get very detailed directions so that you don't get lost. If you plan to go hiking in Forest Park, don't leave anything valuable in your car. This holds true in the Old Town district as well.

Taxes   Portland is a shopper's paradise: there's no sales tax. However, there is a 9% tax on hotel rooms within the city of Portland. Outside the city, the room tax varies.

Taxis   See "Getting Around," earlier in this chapter.

Time Zone   Portland is in the Pacific standard time (PST) zone, making it 3 hours behind the East Coast.

Weather   Call ☎ **503/243-7575.**

3 Accommodations

The rates listed below do not include the hotel-room tax of 9%. A few of the hotels include breakfast in their rates, and this has been noted in the listing. Others offer complimentary breakfast only on certain deluxe floors. If you're planning to visit during the busy summer months, make your reservations as far in advance as possible and be sure to ask if there are any special rates available. Almost all large hotels offer weekend discounts of as much as 50%. In fact, you might even be able to get a discount simply by asking for one. Who knows—if the hotel isn't busy, you might just be able to negotiate.

For information on B&Bs in Portland, contact **Northwest Bed & Breakfast Reservation Service,** 1067 Hanover Court S., Salem, OR 97302 (☎ **503/243-7616** or 503/370-9033), which represents dozens of B&Bs in Oregon, Washington, British Columbia, and Northern California. Rates for B&Bs average $65 to $125 for double rooms. For information on other B&Bs in the Portland area, call the **Portland Oregon Visitors Association** (☎ **800/345-3214**) for a brochure put out by Metro Innkeepers.

DOWNTOWN
VERY EXPENSIVE

✪ **The Benson.** 309 SW Broadway, Portland, OR 97205. ☎ **800/426-0670** or 503/228-2000. Fax 503/226-4603. 287 rms, 46 junior suites, 9 suites. A/C TV TEL. $205–$215 double ($130–$140 weekends); $245 junior suite ($170 weekends); $350–$700 suite. AE, CB, DC, DISC, EURO, JCB, MC, V. Valet parking $12.

The doorman in a top hat is the first tip-off that this hotel is Portland's most traditional and exclusive hotel. The fact that presidents stay here whenever they're in town is another good clue that these are the poshest accommodations in town. Built in 1912, the Benson exudes old-world sophistication and elegance. The guest rooms vary considerably in size, but all are luxuriously furnished. The deluxe kings are particularly roomy, but the corner junior suites are the hotel's best deal. Not only are these rooms quite large, but the abundance of windows makes them much cheerier than other rooms.

   Dining/Entertainment: In the vaults below the lobby is the London Grill, which is best known for its tableside preparations. Piatto is a much more casual place serving contemporary Italian dishes. The Lobby Court has a bar and also serves buffet lunches. There's live jazz here in the evenings.
   Services: 24-hour room service, concierge, valet parking, valet/laundry service.
   Facilities: Exercise room, gift shop.

Governor Hotel. SW 10th Ave. and Alder St., Portland, OR 97205. ☎ **800/554-3456** or 503/224-3400. Fax 503/241-2122. 100 rms, 28 suites. A/C MINIBAR TV TEL. $185–$195 double ($125–$145 weekends); $200 junior suite; $210–$500 suite. AE, CB, DC, JCB, MC, V. Valet parking $13.

This historic hotel is a homage to the Lewis and Clark Expedition, and throughout the hotel, you'll spot references to the famous explorers. The lobby, though small, has a classically Western feel, with a fireplace and overstuffed leather chairs. Classic styling aside, it is the athletic club in the basement that is the hotel's greatest asset. Guest rooms vary considerably in size, but even the smallest is beautifully decorated. Unfortunately, bathrooms are, in general, quite cramped by today's standards and lack counter space. Suites are spacious, and some even have huge patios overlooking the city.

Dining/Entertainment: Jake's Grill, a large, old-fashioned restaurant with burnished wood columns and slowly turning overhead fans, is just off the lobby. The menu features grilled steak and seafood.

Services: 24-hour room service, concierge, personal computers and fax machines available, complimentary morning newspaper and coffee, overnight shoeshine, valet/laundry service.

Facilities: Business center, hearing-impaired accommodations. The Princeton Athletic Club, down in the lower level of the hotel, includes a lap pool, indoor running track, whirlpool spa, steam rooms, sauna, and exercise room.

○ **The Heathman Hotel.** 1001 SW Broadway at Salmon St., Portland, OR 97205. ☎ **800/551-0011** or 503/241-4100. Fax 503/790-7110. 151 rms, 47 suites. A/C MINIBAR TV TEL. $180–$205 double (from $140 weekends); $220–$225 junior suite; $275–$675 suite. AE, CB, DC, DISC, MC, V. Parking $12.

The Heathman, which abuts the Portland Center for the Performing Arts and has on display an outstanding collection of art ranging from 18th-century oil paintings to Andy Warhol prints, is the address of choice for visiting patrons of the arts. Understated luxury and superb service also help make this one of the finest hotels in the city. While the marble and teak lobby itself is tiny, it opens onto the Tea Court, where the original eucalyptus paneling creates a warm, old-world atmosphere. The basic rooms tend to be quite small, but are nonetheless attractively furnished and set up for business travelers. None of the rooms really have views to speak of, but some rooms on the west side do have views of a mural done just for the hotel.

Dining/Entertainment: The Heathman Restaurant is one of the finest in Portland, and B. Moloch/Heathman Bakery & Pub, the hotel's casual, contemporary pub 2 blocks away, is also popular. Both restaurants have cozy bars. (See "Dining" in this chapter for details on both restaurants.) Afternoon tea is served daily, and there are also evening wine tastings. The hotel also has a Mezzanine Bar.

Services: 24-hour room service, concierge, valet/laundry service, complimentary newspaper.

Facilities: Privileges at nearby athletic club, on-site fitness suite with a few machines (personal trainers also available).

○ **Hotel Vintage Plaza.** 422 SW Broadway, Portland, OR 97205. ☎ **800/243-0555** or 503/228-1212. Fax 503/228-3598. 107 rms, 21 suites. A/C MINIBAR TV TEL. $175–$185 double ($140–$165 weekends); $205–$225 suite. All rates include continental breakfast. AE, CB, DC, DISC, MC, V. Valet parking $13.

If you enjoy a good glass of wine and are interested in learning more about regional wines, the Vintage Plaza should be your choice. Italianate decor and a wine theme are in evidence throughout the hotel. Complimentary evening wine tastings in the lobby feature Oregon and Washington wines. Although the standard rooms

Portland Accommodations

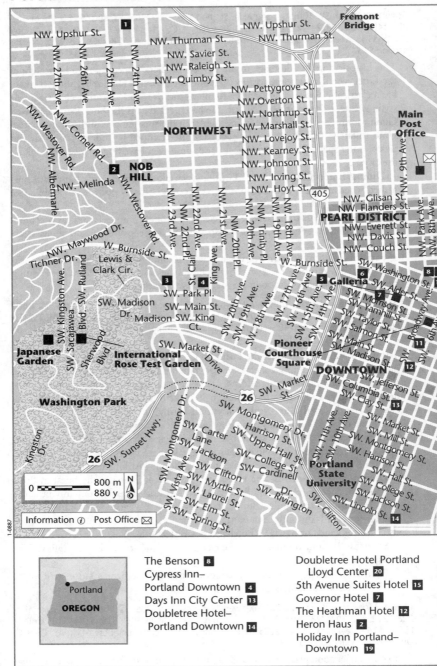

The Benson **8**
Cypress Inn–
Portland Downtown **4**
Days Inn City Center **13**
Doubletree Hotel–
Portland Downtown **14**

Doubletree Hotel Portland
Lloyd Center **20**
5th Avenue Suites Hotel **15**
Governor Hotel **7**
The Heathman Hotel **12**
Heron Haus **2**
Holiday Inn Portland–
Downtown **19**

142

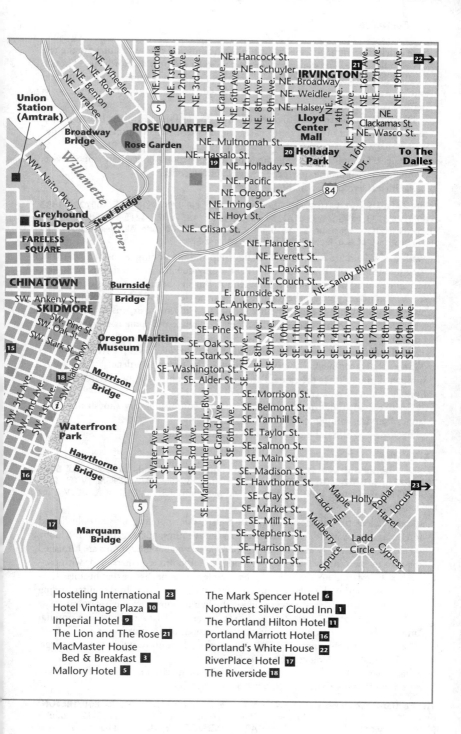

Hosteling International **23**
Hotel Vintage Plaza **10**
Imperial Hotel **9**
The Lion and The Rose **21**
MacMaster House
  Bed & Breakfast **3**
Mallory Hotel **5**

The Mark Spencer Hotel **6**
Northwest Silver Cloud Inn **1**
The Portland Hilton Hotel **11**
Portland Marriott Hotel **16**
Portland's White House **22**
RiverPlace Hotel **17**
The Riverside **18**

have much to recommend them, the starlight rooms and two-level suites are the real scene-stealers here. The starlight rooms in particular are truly extraordinary. Though small, they have greenhouse-style windows that provide very romantic views at night and let in lots of light during the day. The two-level suites, some with Japanese soaking tubs, are equally stunning.

Dining/Entertainment: Pazzo Ristorante, one of Portland's best Italian restaurants, is a dark and intimate trattoria serving northern Italian cuisine (see "Dining" in this chapter for details).

Services: Complimentary evening wine, 24-hour room service, shoeshine service, complimentary morning newspaper, valet/laundry service.

Facilities: Executive gym, business center.

✪ **RiverPlace Hotel.** 1510 SW Harbor Way, Portland, OR 97201-5105. ☎ **800/227-1333** or 503/228-3233. Fax 503/295-6161. 84 rms, 47 suites. A/C TV TEL. $215–$255 double (from $175 weekends except summer); $250 junior suite; $285–$700 suite. All rates include continental breakfast. AE, CB, DC, JCB, MC, V. Valet parking $14.

With the Willamette River at its back doorstep and the sloping lawns of Waterfront Park to one side, the RiverPlace is Portland's only downtown waterfront hotel. This fact alone would be enough to recommend it, but this boutique hotel's quiet atmosphere also makes it an excellent choice. The river-view standard king rooms are the hotel's best deal, but the junior suites are only slightly more expensive and provide a bit more space. More than half the rooms are suites, and some come with woodburning fireplaces and whirlpool baths.

Dining/Entertainment: The Esplanade Restaurant overlooks the river and serves Northwest and continental fare (see "Dining" in this chapter for details). For al fresco summer dining, there's the casual Patio. Just off the lobby is a comfortable bar with live piano music and a crackling fire in cool weather.

Services: 24-hour room service, concierge, complimentary shoeshine, valet/laundry service, complimentary morning paper.

Facilities: Whirlpool, sauna, privileges at athletic club.

EXPENSIVE

✪ **5th Avenue Suites Hotel.** 506 SW Washington St., Portland, OR 97204. ☎ **800/711-2971** or 503/222-0001. Fax 503/222-0004. 82 rms, 139 suites. A/C MINIBAR TV TEL. $165 double ($125 weekends), $180–$240 suite ($140 weekends). AE, DC, DISC, JCB, MC, V. Valet parking $14.

Located a block from Pioneer Courthouse Square, this unpretentious yet sophisticated hotel is in a renovated department store. In the evenings, guests gather in the lobby to enjoy complimentary evening tastings of regional wines. Guest rooms are furnished in a turn-of-the-century country style, and plush upholstered chairs, beds with padded headboards and luxurious comforters, and fax machines assure that business travelers will be comfortable. Bathrooms have lots of counter space. In the suites, sliding French doors with privacy curtains divide the living room from the bedrooms.

Dining/Entertainment: The Red Star Tavern and Roast House is a popular American bistro-style restaurant specializing in foods of the Northwest.

Services: Complimentary evening wine tasting, 24-hour room service, concierge, complimentary morning coffee and newspaper.

Facilities: Fitness center with numerous exercise machines, day spa offering massages and other body treatments, business center.

The Portland Hilton Hotel. 921 SW Sixth Ave., Portland, OR 97204-1296. ☎ **800/HILTONS** or 503/226-1611. Fax 503/220-2565. 455 rms, 16 suites. A/C TV TEL. $135–$225 double ($109–$119 weekends); $200–$850 suite. AE, CB, DC, DISC, JCB, MC, V. Self parking $14, valet parking $17.

While business travelers, conventions, and tour groups comprise the bulk of the business here, the Hilton is very conveniently located for vacationers as well. Within just a couple of blocks are the Portland Center for the Performing Arts and several museums. An indoor swimming pool and extensive health club also make this a good choice for active travelers. Rooms here tend to be fairly small, so opt for a double-double or king room if you want a bit more space. Bathrooms, which lack much counter space, are also a bit small. Be sure to request a floor as high as possible to take advantage of the views. The corner rooms with king-size beds are our favorites.

Dining/Entertainment: From its 23rd-floor aerie, Alexander's offers a striking panorama of Portland, the Willamette River, and snow-covered Mount Hood (see chapter 8). Back down at lobby level is the informal Bistro 921 restaurant and bar, with regional and international cuisine.

Services: Room service, concierge, laundry/valet service, overnight shoeshine service.

Facilities: An athletic club with indoor skylit swimming pool, saunas, steam rooms, and an extensive array of exercise machines, fitness trainers, and aerobics classes; business center.

Portland Marriott Hotel. 1401 SW Front Ave., Portland, OR 97201. ☎ **800/228-9290** or 503/226-7600. Fax 503/221-1789. 503 rms, 6 suites. A/C TV TEL. $145–$205 double ($119–$160 weekends); $300–$450 suite. AE, CB, DC, DISC, EURO, JCB, MC, V. Valet parking $13.

Located just across Waterfront Park and Naito Parkway from the Willamette River, the Portland Marriott is the flashiest of the city's hotels. A massive portico with Japanese-style landscaping leads guests into a high-ceilinged lobby filled with bright lights. Most of the guest rooms have small balconies, and if you ask for a room overlooking the river, you can throw back the glass door to the balcony, and consider that the view used to be of a noisy freeway (it was torn out to build the park). On a clear day Mount Hood looms in the distance. Unfortunately, the furnishing and carpets are in need of replacement, but if you can overlook a bit of wear and tear, you can enjoy the views and the almost-waterfront location.

Dining/Entertainment: Fazzio's Cafe is a family restaurant serving breakfast, lunch, and dinner. Champions is a sports bar with all the requisite sports memorabilia on the walls. The lobby bar attracts a much more sedate crowd.

Services: Room service, concierge floor, valet/laundry service, shoeshine stand, baby-sitting service, massages.

Facilities: Exercise room, indoor pool, whirlpool, saunas, game room, hair salon, gift shop, newsstand, business center.

MODERATE

Days Inn City Center. 1414 SW Sixth Ave., Portland, OR 97201. ☎ **800/899-0248** or 503/221-1611. Fax 503/226-0447. 173 rms. A/C TV TEL. $79–$110 double. AE, CB, DC, MC, V. Free parking.

Although this 1960s vintage hotel lacks much in the way of character or charm, it's the most economical choice if you are looking to stay right in downtown Portland. The hotel has been recently renovated and has new carpets and furniture throughout. In the guest rooms, you'll find a couple of unusual touches: a small shelf of hardcover books (mostly *Reader's Digest* condensed books) as well as framed old photos of Portland. With its brass rails and wood trim, the Portland Bar and Grill is popular with the business set for lunch and happy-hour hors d'oeuvres. Hotel services include valet/laundry service, room service, and complimentary newspaper. There's also a seasonal outdoor swimming pool.

Imperial Hotel. 400 SW Broadway, Portland, OR 97205. ☎ **800/452-2323** or 503/228-7221. Fax 503/223-4551. 136 rms. A/C TV TEL. $85–$100 double. AE, CB, DC, DISC, MC, V. Free parking.

Although it doesn't quite live up to its regal name, this older hotel across the street from the Benson hotel is a fine choice if you're on a budget. While the staff may be young and not as polished as at more expensive hotels, they usually are good about seeing to guests' needs. It would be hard to find such reasonably priced downtown accommodations in any comparable city. The corner king rooms, with large windows, should be your first choice here, and barring this, at least ask for an exterior room. These might get a little street noise, but they're bigger than the interior rooms and get more light. Rooms have in-room safes, refrigerators, and hair dryers. There's also morning newspaper delivery, room service, and valet/laundry service. Local phone calls are free. The hotel's restaurant is rather nondescript and unmemorable, but in the lounge, old movie posters on the walls add a bit of retro character.

☼ The Riverside. 50 SW Morrison Ave., Portland, OR 97204-3390. ☎ **800/899-0247** or 503/221-0711. Fax 503/274-0312. 140 rms. A/C TV TEL. $99–$170 double. AE, CB, DC, DISC, MC, V. Free parking.

Although this 1960s vintage hotel overlooking Waterfront Park looks very nondescript from the outside, the renovated contemporary interior makes it one of the most stylish hotels in town. As the name implies, you are only steps from the Willamette River (although not actually on the water), but you are also close to businesses, restaurants, and shopping. Guest rooms are as boldly contemporary in design as the lobby and restaurant, sort of downscale *Architectural Digest.* If contemporary is your style, make this your Portland choice. With its modern styling and cozy fireside lounge, the Riverside Club offers guests a very stylish place to relax over a drink or enjoy a meal. Large windows look out over the Waterfront Park and the river, and the menu is surprisingly creative. Hotel services include room service, valet/laundry service, complimentary newspaper, and passes to two fitness clubs.

INEXPENSIVE

☼ Mallory Hotel. 729 SW 15th Ave., Portland, OR 97205-1994. ☎ **800/228-8657** or 503/223-6311. Fax 503/223-0522. 136 rms, 26 suites. A/C TV TEL. $70–$110 double; $110 suite. AE, CB, DC, MC, V. Free parking.

The Mallory has long been a favorite of Portland visitors who want the convenience of a downtown lodging but aren't on a bottomless expense account. This is an older hotel, and the lobby, which is done in deep forest green with ornate gilt plaster work trim and crystal chandeliers, has a certain classic (though somewhat faded) grandeur. Time seems to have stood still here (with a doorman in a pith helmet and a lounge straight out of the 1950s). In 1998, the new west-side Max line will begin service right past the hotel, which will make the Mallory more convenient than ever. The rooms are not as luxurious as the lobby might suggest and are smaller than comparable rooms at the Imperial or Days Inn, but they are comfortable and clean. Local calls are free and there is valet/laundry service.

The dining room at the Mallory continues the grand design of the lobby. Heavy drapes hang from the windows, and faux-marble pillars lend just the right air of imperial grandeur.

NOB HILL/NORTHWEST PORTLAND
MODERATE

☼ Northwest Silver Cloud Inn. 2426 NW Vaughn St., Portland, OR 97210-2540. ☎ **800/205-6939** or 503/242-2400. Fax 503/242-1770. 81 rms. A/C TV TEL. $80–$128 double. All rates include continental breakfast. AE, DC, DISC, MC, V. Free parking.

😊 **Family-Friendly Hotels**

Days Inn City Center *(see p. 145)*   For families on a budget, this Days Inn is a reliable choice. It may not be full of charm, but the rooms are up-to-date and there's and outdoor pool.

Doubletree Lloyd Center *(see p. 148)*   Let the kids loose in the huge Lloyd Center Shopping Mall across the street and they'll stay entertained for hours (there's even an ice-skating rink in the mall). There's also a large shady park across from the hotel.

Portland Marriott Hotel *(see p. 145)*   The game room and indoor pool are popular with kids, and just across the street is Tom McCall Waterfront Park, which runs along the Willamette River.

This hotel is located just north of Portland's trendy Nob Hill neighborhood, and though it faces the beginning of the city's industrial area, it is still a very attractive and comfortable place. Reasonable rates are the main draw here, but the hotel is also within a 5-minute drive of half a dozen of the city's best restaurants. The standard rooms have refrigerators, while the minisuites come with refrigerators, wet bars, microwave ovens, and a separate seating area. The most expensive rooms are the king rooms with whirlpool tubs. Local phone calls are free, and facilities include a fitness room and a whirlpool spa. Try to get a room away from Vaughn Street. To find the hotel, take I-405 to Ore. 30 west and get off at the Vaughn Street exit.

BED & BREAKFASTS

✪ **Heron Haus.** 2545 NW Westover Rd., Portland, OR 97210. ☎ **503/274-1846.** Fax 503/243-1075. 6 rms. TV TEL. $125–$250 double. Rates include continental breakfast. MC, V. Free parking.

A short walk from the bustling Nob Hill shopping and dining district of northwest Portland, Heron Haus offers outstanding accommodations, spectacular views, and tranquil surroundings. There's even a small swimming pool with a sundeck. Surprisingly, the house still features some of the original plumbing. In most places this would be a liability but not here, since the plumbing was done by the same man who plumbed Portland's famous Pittock Mansion. One shower has seven shower heads; another has two. In another room there's a modern whirlpool spa that affords excellent views of the city. Several rooms now have fireplaces.

MacMaster House Bed & Breakfast Inn. 1041 SW Vista Ave., Portland, OR 97205. ☎ **800/774-9523** or 503/223-7362. 7 rms (2 with private bath). $75–$90 double with shared bath; $115–$120 double with private bath. Rates include full breakfast. AE, DC, MC, V. Free parking.

Located adjacent to both Washington Park and the trendy shops and restaurants of the Nob Hill neighborhood, this imposing mansion sits high above the street and is furnished with the sort of authentic eclecticism that characterized the Victorian era. Many of the guest rooms have interesting murals on the walls, and there's even a painting on the side of an old tub in the third floor shared bathroom. Three rooms have fireplaces, and one of these has a claw-foot tub. Some of the rooms are on the third floor, and the inn itself is up a flight of stairs from the street, so you need to be in good shape to stay here. Although the inn is not as immaculate as many B&Bs, it makes up for this with loads of character.

JANTZEN BEACH & NORTH PORTLAND

Located on Hayden Island in the middle of the Columbia River, Jantzen Beach, named for the famous swimwear company that got its start here, is a beach in name only. Today this area is a huge shopping mall complex aimed primarily at Washingtonians, who come to Oregon to do their shopping, thus avoiding Washington's sales tax. Jantzen Beach is also home to a pair of large convention hotels that are among the city's only waterfront hotels. Both hotels are, however, in the flight path for the airport, and although the rooms themselves are adequately insulated against noise, the swimming pools and sundecks can be pretty noisy.

EXPENSIVE

Doubletree Hotel Portland Jantzen Beach. 909 N. Hayden Island Dr., Portland, OR 97217. ☎ **800/222-TREE** or 503/283-4466. Fax 503/283-4743. 320 rms, 24 suites. A/C TV TEL. $119–$190 double ($85–$99 weekends); $195–$350 suite. AE, CB, DC, DISC, EURO, JCB, MC, V. Free parking.

With a design calculated to conjure up images of old Columbia River docks, this is the more resortlike of Doubletree's two Jantzen Beach convention hotels. Arranged in wings around two garden courtyards, one of which has a swimming pool and two tennis courts, the rooms are as large as you're likely to find in any Portland hotel. Most have balconies and many have excellent views of the river and sometimes Mount St. Helens. Bathrooms are equally spacious.

Dining/Entertainment: Elegant dining in plush surroundings with great river views can be found at Maxi's Restaurant, which specializes in seafood. For much more casual dining there's the Coffee Garden in the lobby. Tuesday through Saturday nights come alive to the sound of live rock 'n' roll bands at Maxi's Lounge, which has art nouveau decor.

Services: Room service, complimentary airport shuttle, valet/laundry service.
Facilities: Heated outdoor pool, whirlpool, tennis courts, gift shop.

THE ROSE QUARTER & NORTHEAST PORTLAND
EXPENSIVE

Doubletree Hotel Portland Lloyd Center. 1000 NE Multnomah St., Portland, OR 97232. ☎ **800/222-TREE** or 503/281-6111. Fax 503/284-8553. 476 rms, 10 suites. A/C TV TEL. $139–$175 double ($99–$124 weekends); $269–$575 suite. AE, CB, DC, DISC, EURO, JCB, MC, V. Parking $9.

Located across the street from the Lloyd Center shopping mall, a large, shady park, and a light-rail station, this convention hotel is a very convenient choice if you don't want to be right in downtown. There are several dining options here and a very pleasant pool in a Northwest garden setting. Most rooms are quite spacious, and some have balconies. The views from the higher floors are stunning. On a clear day you can see Mount Hood, Mount St. Helens, and even Mount Rainier. Ask for a room in the south tower, these rooms are larger and have been renovated more recently than other rooms. This south tower is also accessed by glass elevators, which are always a lot of fun to ride.

Dining/Entertainment: Maxi's Restaurant, with its etched glass walls and chandeliers, serves seafood and steaks. If you're more in the mood for Mexican, head to Eduardo's Cantina. For family dining there's the Coffee Garden. For those seeking a quiet place for conversation and a drink, there's the Quiet Bar.

Services: Room service, concierge, complimentary airport shuttle, valet/laundry service.
Facilities: Heated outdoor swimming pool, exercise room, gift shop.

INEXPENSIVE

Howard Johnson Express. 3939 NE Hancock St., Portland OR 97212. ☎ **503/288-6891.** Fax 503/288-1995. 48 rms. A/C TV TEL. $50–$58 double. AE, DC, DISC, MC, V. Free parking.

Located in the Hollywood District of Northeast Portland about halfway between the airport and downtown, this economical choice is in a rather unusual spot (tucked away several blocks from the interstate), but is worth searching out if you need a budget accommodation close in. Rooms vary in size, so be sure to ask for one of the larger rooms. The neighborhood takes its name from the mission-revival buildings and Craftsman bungalows that are reminiscent of old Hollywood.

BED & BREAKFASTS

✪ **The Lion and the Rose.** 1810 NE 15th Ave., Portland, OR 97212. ☎ **800/955-1647** or 503/287-9245. Fax 503/287-9247. 6 rms (5 with private bath). TEL. $115–$120 double. AE, MC, V.

This imposing Queen Anne Victorian bed-and-breakfast inn is within 4 blocks of half a dozen excellent restaurants and cafes, as well as eclectic boutiques and a huge shopping mall. The living room and dining room are beautifully decorated with period antiques, and breakfasts are sumptuous affairs that are meant to be lingered over. Guest rooms each have a distinctively different decor and feel ranging from the bright colors and turret sitting area of the Lavonna room to the deep greens of the Starina room, which features an imposing Edwardian bed and armoire.

Portland's White House. 1914 NE 22nd Ave., Portland, OR 97212. ☎ **800/272-7131** or 503/287-7131. Fax 503/249-1641. 9 rms. $88–$139 double. Rates include full breakfast. MC, V. Free parking.

This imposing Greek-revival mansion bears a more than passing resemblance to its namesake in Washington, D.C. Massive columns frame the entrance, and behind the mahogany front doors, a huge entrance hall with original hand-painted wall murals is flanked by a parlor, with French windows and a piano, and the formal dining room, where the large breakfast is served. A double staircase leads past a large stained-glass window to the second-floor accommodations. Canopy and brass queen beds, antique furnishings, and bathrooms with claw-foot tubs further the feelings of classic luxury. Request the balcony room and you can gaze out past the Greek columns and imagine you're the president. There are also three rooms in the restored carriage house. There is free airport pick-up and afternoon tea.

THE AIRPORT AREA

Moderately priced hotels have been proliferating in this area over the past few years, which makes this a good place to look for a room if you arrive with no reservation. Hotels in this area generally provide better value than hotel's in the Rose Quarter (near the Oregon Convention Center and Rose Garden stadium), which is where you'll find comparably priced accommodations.

The **Super 8 Motel,** 11011 NE Homan St. (☎ **503/257-8988**), just off of Airport Way after you go under the I-205 overpass is conveniently located but charges a surprisingly high $61 to $73 a night for a double.

EXPENSIVE

Shilo Inn Suites Hotel Portland Airport. 11707 NE Airport Way, Portland, OR 97220-1075. ☎ **800/222-2244** or 503/252-7500. Fax 503/254-0794. 200 suites. A/C TV TEL. $109–$155 double. Rates include continental breakfast. AE, DC, DISC, MC, V. Free parking.

If you want to stay near the airport and want a spacious room and the facilities of a deluxe hotel, this is one of your best bets. All the rooms here are called suites, and although they don't actually have separate seating and sleeping rooms, they do have plenty of room and lots of other amenities. There is lots of bathroom counter space, and three TVs in the rooms (including one in the bathroom). Other amenities include hair dryers, VCRs, and double sinks.

Dining/Entertainment: The hotel's dining room is in the convention center wing and serves surprisingly creative dishes amid casual surroundings. There's a cigar room and a piano lounge adjacent to the restaurant. The complimentary breakfast is served in a large TV lounge just off the lobby.

Services: Room service, complimentary airport shuttle, valet service.

Facilities: Indoor swimming pool, whirlpool spa, exercise room.

MODERATE

✪ **Silver Cloud Inn Portland Airport.** 11518 NE Glenn Widing Rd., Portland, OR 97220. ☎ **800/205-7892** or 503/252-2222. Fax 503/257-7008. 102 rms, 8 suites. A/C TV TEL. $89–$99 double; $119–$139 suite. Rates include continental breakfast. AE, DC, DISC, MC, V. Free parking.

Conveniently located right outside the airport, this hotel has the best back yard of any hotel in the Portland area. A lake, lawns, trees, and bird feeders all add up to a tranquil setting despite the proximity of both the airport and a busy nearby road. Rooms are designed primarily for business travelers, but even if you aren't here on business, they offer good value, especially the king rooms with whirlpool tubs. There are refrigerators and microwaves in all the rooms, and some suites have gas fireplaces. Best of all, every room has a view of the lake. The hotel also offers complimentary airport shuttle and guest laundry and free local phone calls. There's also an indoor pool, a whirlpool, and an exercise room.

4 Dining

Over the past couple of years the Portland restaurant scene has been hopping. Good new restaurants seem to be opening weekly, and many of these are locating in the Northwest neighborhood, especially along Northwest 21st Avenue. If you want a wide selection of great restaurants to choose from, stroll along this street and see what strikes your fancy.

DOWNTOWN

EXPENSIVE

Atwater's Restaurant and Bar. U.S. Bancorp Tower, 111 SW Fifth Ave. ☎ **503/275-3600.** Reservations highly recommended. Main courses $17–$25. Fixed-price 4-course menu without wine $45, with wine $65. AE, CB, DC, MC, V. Mon–Sat 5:30–9pm, Sun 5:30–8:30pm. NORTHWEST.

Atwater's whispers elegance from the moment you step off the elevator on the 30th floor. A rosy light suffuses the hall at sunset, while richly colored carpets on a blond hardwood floor and large, dramatic flower arrangements add splashes of color throughout the restaurant. In the middle of the dining room is a glass-enclosed wine room that would put many wineshops to shame. But the primary attractions here are the incredible view—far below are the Willamette River and Portland, off in the distance stands Mount Hood—and the Pacific Northwest cuisine. The combinations of regional ingredients are unexpected and delectable in such dishes as beef tenderloin with morel mushrooms, roasted fennel, leeks, and Pinot Noir sauce. The adjoining bar is a casually elegant place to have a cocktail and listen to live jazz.

✪ **Couvron.** 1126 SW 18th Ave. ☎ **503/225-1844.** Reservations recommended. Main courses $23–$36; tasting menu $60. AE, DISC, MC, V. Tues–Thurs 11:30am–2pm and 5:30–9pm, Fri 11:30am–2pm and 5:30–10pm, Sat 5:30–10pm. CONTEMPORARY FRENCH.

Located in the Goose Hollow neighborhood at the foot of the West Hills, this small French restaurant is utterly unremarkable looking from the exterior and thoroughly French and unpretentiously sophisticated on the inside with the feel of a country cottage. The menu is one of the most extraordinary in the city, combining the finest of ingredients in unusual flavor combinations that almost always hit the mark. A recent menu included an exceedingly complex appetizer of pan-roasted Hudson Valley foie gras served with toasted brioche, crawfish stew, and a port wine and lobster sauce. Port wine showed up again in the main courses in a sauce served over a duo of honey-glazed duck breast and confit served with white bean ragout and port-candied turnips. With dishes here being so memorable, it's not surprising that many people opt for the six-course tasting menu so that they can sample a wide range of dishes. Serious about desserts? How about a Napoleon of chocolate creme brûlée and raspberries served with bittersweet chocolate-hazelnut sauce?

✪ **The Heathman Restaurant and Bar.** The Heathman Hotel, SW Broadway at Salmon St. ☎ **503/241-4100.** Reservations highly recommended. Main courses $12–$25. AE, CB, DC, MC, V. Breakfast Mon–Fri 6:30–11am, Sat–Sun 6:30am–2pm; lunch Mon–Fri 11am–2pm; dinner daily 5–11pm. NORTHWEST/FRENCH.

The menu in this elegant hotel dining room changes seasonally, but one thing remains constant: ingredients used are the very freshest of Oregon and Northwest seafoods, meat, wild game, and produce with a French accent. On the walls are Andy Warhol's Endangered Species—rhino, zebra, lion, panda, and others—part of the Heathman's extensive collection of classic and contemporary art. A recent winter menu offered pheasant with wild mushrooms and cabbage; ravioli with smoked salmon cream, leeks, and shiitake mushrooms; and mahimahi with sun-dried tomato and fennel risotto. Local fruit appears in many of the rich desserts. Northwest microbrewery beers are on tap in the bar, while an extensive wine list spotlights Oregon.

MODERATE

Alexis Restaurant. 215 W. Burnside St. ☎ **503/224-8577.** Reservations recommended. Main courses $9–$14. AE, DC, DISC, MC, V. Mon–Fri 11:30am–2pm; Mon–Thurs 5–10pm, Fri and Sat 5–11pm, Sun 4:30–9pm. GREEK.

Alexis is a classic Greek taverna, and the crowds keep it packed as much for the great food as for the fun atmosphere. On weekends there's belly dancing, and the menu has all your Greek favorites. The main dishes are good, but the appetizers are out of this world. The not-to-be-missed list includes saganaki (panfried cheese flamed with ouzo), kalamarakia (perfectly fried squid), octopus, and the tart and creamy avgolemono soup. Accompany these with Alexis's own fresh bread, and wash it all down with a bottle of Demestica wine for a soul-satisfying meal.

✪ **B. Moloch/Heathman Bakery & Pub.** 901 SW Salmon St. ☎ **503/227-5700.** Reservations not accepted. Main courses $7–$13. AE, DC, DISC, MC, V. Mon–Thurs 7am–10pm, Fri 7am–11:30pm, Sat 8am–11:30pm, Sun 8am–10:30pm. NORTHWEST.

At B. Moloch, corporate climbers and bicycle messengers rub shoulders, quaff microbrews, and chow down on creative pizzas. Ostensibly, this is the bakery for the Heathman Hotel dining room a block away, and to that end a cavernous wood-burning brick oven was installed. Nouvelle pizzas from said oven are the mainstay of the menu, but if you're not in the mood for pizza, there are sandwiches, pasta dishes, great soups and salads, and daily specials.

Brasserie Montmartre. 626 SW Park Ave. ☎ **503/224-5552.** Reservations highly recommended. Main courses $10–$18. AE, CB, DC, MC, V. Mon–Thurs 11:30am–2am, Fri 11:30am–3am, Sat 10am–3am, Sun 10am–2am; bistro menu available daily from 2pm–closing. NORTHWEST/FRENCH.

Though the menu lacks the creativity of other Northwest and French restaurants in Portland, and dishes are sometimes disappointing, The Bra (as it's known) is

Portland Dining

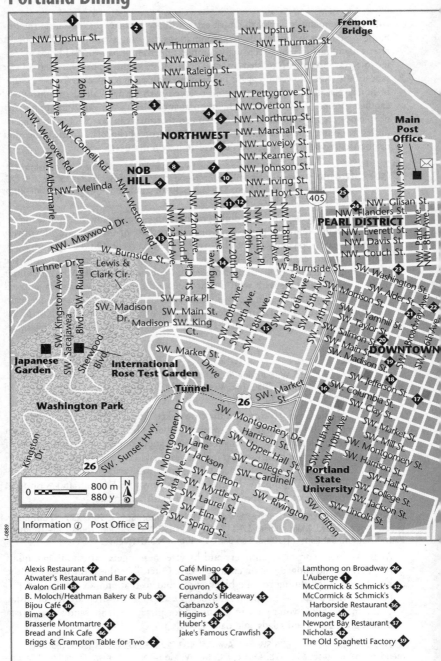

Alexis Restaurant 27
Atwater's Restaurant and Bar 29
Avalon Grill 38
B. Moloch/Heathman Bakery & Pub 20
Bijou Café 30
Bima 25
Brasserie Montmartre 21
Bread and Ink Cafe 46
Briggs & Crampton Table for Two 2

Café Mingo 7
Caswell 41
Couvron 15
Fernando's Hideaway 35
Garbanzo's 6
Higgins 18
Huber's 34
Jake's Famous Crawfish 23

Lamthong on Broadway 26
L'Auberge 1
McCormick & Schmick's 32
McCormick & Schmick's
 Harborside Restaurant 36
Montage 40
Newport Bay Restaurant 37
Nicholas 42
The Old Spaghetti Factory 39

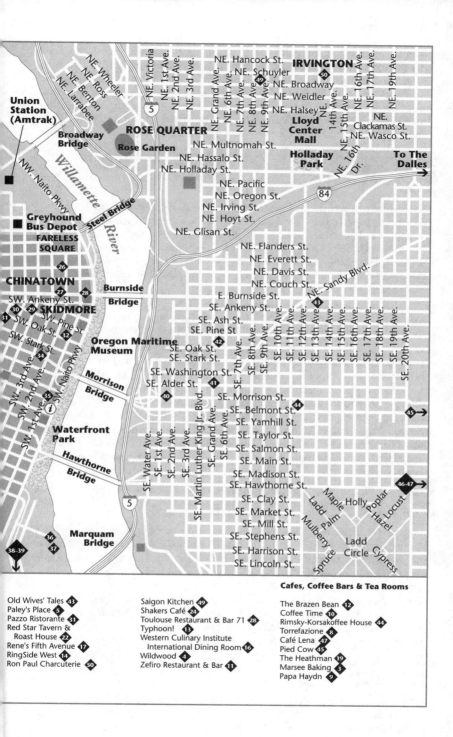

popular for its fun atmosphere. There's live jazz nightly, a magician performs Tuesday through Saturday nights, and on every table you'll find a paper tablecloth and a container of crayons. This playfulness is balanced out by dark, formal dining rooms, with black and white tile floors, velvet banquettes, and silk lamp shades that lend an air of fin de siècle Paris. You might start your meal with a sampling of pâtés, then have a cup of onion soup with three cheeses, move on to salmon with lingonberry-and-ginger butter, and finish off with one of the divinely decadent pastries. The wine list is extensive but not expensive.

✿ Fernando's Hideaway. 824 SW First Ave. ☎ **503/248-4709.** Reservations recommended. Main courses $13–$20. AE, DC, MC, V. Mon–Thurs 5–10pm, Fri–Sat 5–11pm, Sun noon–9pm. SPANISH.

Excellent tapas, such as spicy oysters and stuffed calamari, have made Fernando's enormously popular, but the Spanish entrees are also a delight. A roasted chicken with an apricot and nut sauce arrived beautifully arranged with wedges of potato and dollops of spinach. Salads, such as eggplant or fruit and cheese combinations, are equally delicious. There are good Spanish wines on the menu and service is professional, without the attitude you might expect at such a trendy place. For dessert the flan with mocha sauce is excellent.

✿ Higgins. 1239 SW Broadway. ☎ **503/222-9070.** Reservations highly recommended. Main courses $15–$21, lunch $7–$13. AE, DC, MC, V. Mon–Fri 11:30am–2pm; daily 5–10:30pm; bistro menu served daily 2pm–midnight. NORTHWEST/MEDITERRANEAN.

Higgins, located just up Broadway from the Heathman Hotel, where chef Greg Higgins first made a name for himself in Portland, strikes a balance between contemporary and classic in both its decor and its cuisine. The menu, which changes frequently, explores contemporary culinary horizons, while the decor in the trilevel dining room opts for wood-paneling and elegant place settings. Adding a dash more classic ambience are waiters in long white aprons. Both subtle and earthy flavors abound here. Manila clams steamed in amber ale with ancho chiles and onions was a heavenly way to begin, and garlic-roasted chicken with a sauce of walnuts and Pinot Noir with buttermilk whipped potatoes was inventive enough to be interesting, yet homey and satisfying. Be sure to leave room for dessert.

Huber's. 411 SW Third Ave. ☎ **503/228-5686.** Reservations recommended, but not accepted Friday or Saturday evenings. Main courses $5–$19. AE, DISC, MC, V. Mon–Fri 11:30am–4pm; Mon–Thurs 4–10pm, Fri–Sat 4–11pm. CONTINENTAL.

Portland's oldest restaurant first opened its doors to the public in 1879, though it didn't move to its present location until 1911. You'll find this very traditional establishment tucked inside the Oregon Pioneer Building. Down a quiet hallway you'll come to a surprising little room with a vaulted stained-glass ceiling, Philippine mahogany paneling, and the original brass cash register. The house specialty has been turkey since the day the first Huber's opened, so there really isn't any question of what to order. You can gobble turkey sandwiches, turkey Delmonico, turkey nouvelle, or turkey mushroom pie. The menu even has wine recommendations to accompany the different turkey dishes. Lunch prices are much lower, with the turkey sandwich the star of the hour.

Jake's Famous Crawfish. 401 SW 12th Ave. ☎ **503/226-1419.** Reservations recommended. Main courses $9–$29. AE, DC, DISC, MC, V. Mon–Thurs 11:30am–midnight; Fri 11:30am–1am; Sat 4pm–1am, Sun 4:30–11pm. SEAFOOD.

Jake's has been serving up crawfish (crayfish) since 1909 at an address that has housed a restaurant or bar since 1892. The back bar came all the way around Cape Horn in 1880, and much of the rest of the restaurant's decor looks just as old and well

😊 Family-Friendly Restaurants

Chez José East *(see p. 163)*   Though this place is no Taco Bell, it's definitely family friendly, so don't hesitate to bring the kids.

Old Wives' Tales *(see p. 162)*   This is just about the best place in Portland to eat if you've got small children. There are children's menus at all meals and in the back of the restaurant, there's a playroom that will keep the little ones entertained while you enjoy your meal.

The Old Spaghetti Factory *(see p. 163)*   This chain of inexpensive Italian restaurants got its start in Portland, and the restaurant here just might have the best location of any in the chain—right on the bank of the Willamette River. Kids enjoy the atmosphere and parents enjoy the low prices.

---

worn. The noise level after work, when local businesspeople pack the bar, can be loud, and the wait for a table can be long if you don't make a reservation. However, don't let these obstacles dissuade you from visiting this Portland institution. There's a daily fresh sheet listing 12 to 15 specials, but there's really no question about what to eat at Jake's: crawfish, which are always on the menu and are served several different ways. During happy hour and after 9:30pm, bar appetizers are only $1.95.

☺ **McCormick & Schmick's.** 235 SW First Ave. ☎ **503/224-7522.** Reservations highly recommended. Main courses $13–$20; bar meals $1.95; lunch $6–$12. AE, DC, MC, V. Mon–Fri 11:30am–4:30pm; Sun–Thurs 5–10pm, Fri–Sat 5–11pm; bar meals daily 1:30–6:30pm and 9:30pm–close. SEAFOOD.

Patterned after traditional seafood establishments, this restaurant is noted for the freshness of its ingredients. The daily fresh sheet begins with a listing of what's available that day and might list 25 different types of seafood. Whether it's king salmon or Dungeness crab, seafood is king here, and the oysters go by their first names: Olympia, Royal Miyagi, and Quilcene. If you aren't interested in live oysters as an appetizer, there are plenty of cooked seafoods to start you out. The extensive wine list features excellent Oregon wines, and while you're waiting for a table, you might want to try one of the more than 30 single-malt scotches available. Both the up-and-coming and the already-there keep this place bustling.

McCormick & Schmick's Harborside Restaurant. 0309 SW Montgomery St. ☎ **503/220-1865.** Reservations recommended. Main courses $10–$20, lunch $5–$12. AE, CB, DC, DISC, MC, V. Mon–Sat 11:30am–2pm; Sun–Thurs 5–10pm, Fri–Sat 5–11pm. SEAFOOD.

Anchoring the opposite end of RiverPlace Esplanade from the RiverPlace Hotel, this large and glitzy seafood restaurant offers a view of the Willamette to go with its excellent seafood. Four dining levels assure everyone a view of the river and marina below, and in summer, customers head out to tables on the Esplanade. Because it's so popular, the place tends to be noisy and the help seems a bit harried; however, don't let this detract from the fine food. Although seafood (such as crab-stuffed salmon, razor clams with rémoulade sauce, and grilled sea scallop fettuccine) is the main attraction here, the menu is quite extensive. The clientele is mostly upscale, especially at lunch and in the après-work hours.

Newport Bay Restaurant. 0425 SW Montgomery St. ☎ **503/227-3474.** Reservations recommended. Main courses $11–$19; lunch and light main courses $6–$10. AE, CB, DC, DISC, MC, V. Sun–Thurs 11am–10pm, Fri–Sat 11am–11pm, Sun brunch 10am–3pm. Closes 1 hour later in summer. SEAFOOD.

Though there are Newport Bay restaurants all over Portland, this one has the best location—floating on the Willamette River. Located in the marina at Portland's beautiful RiverPlace shopping-and-dining complex, the Newport Bay provides excellent views of the river and the city skyline, especially from the deck. Popular with young couples, families, and boaters, this place exudes a cheery atmosphere and service is efficient. Nearly everything on the menu has some sort of seafood in it, even the quiche, salads, and pastas. Main courses are mostly straightforward and well prepared—nothing too fancy.

✪ **Pazzo Ristorante.** Hotel Vintage Plaza, 627 SW Washington St. (at Broadway). ☎ **503/228-1515.** Reservations highly recommended. Main courses $13–$18; lunch $7–$15. AE, CB, DC, DISC, MC, V. Breakfast Mon–Fri 7–10:30am, Sat 8–10:30am, Sun 8–11am; lunch Mon–Sat 11:30am–2:30pm; dinner Mon–Thurs 5–10pm, Fri–Sat 5–11pm, Sun noon–10pm. NORTHERN ITALIAN.

The atmosphere in Pazzo is not nearly as rarefied as in the adjacent hotel lobby—rustic decor and red-and-white-checked tablecloths speak of an Italian country ristorante. The food here, on the whole, is creative and tends toward the rich side. We started with *radicchio e pancetta alla griglia,* a wild, highly flavored dish of bitter grilled radicchio and a sauce of creamy goat cheese. *Fritto misto,* fried calamari with rock shrimp, fennel, and sautéed green beans, was enhanced by a sweet red pepper sauce. In fact, we recommend anything with this sauce. Dessert here is a must. I like the tiramisu.

Red Star Tavern & Roast House. 503 SW Alder St. ☎ **503/222-0005.** Reservations recommended. Main courses $10–$18. AE, DISC, MC, V. Mon–Thurs 6:30–10:30am, 11:30am–2:30pm, and 5–10pm; Fri 6:30–10:30am, 11:30am–2:30pm, and 5–11pm; Sat 8–11am, noon–3pm, and 5–11pm; Sun 8am–2pm and 5–10pm. AMERICAN.

Big and always busy, the Roast House was an instant hit when it opened. Obviously this American bistro provides something that Portlanders crave: big portions of well-prepared and upscale down-home comfort food. With a wood oven, rotisseries, and a smoker, roasted meats are the specialty here, with the spit-roasted pork loin a particular favorite. However, you can also get risotto, oak roasted vegetables, and goat cheese and roasted garlic ravioli. Side dishes include buttermilk mashed potatoes, brick-oven baked beans, and sweet potato hash. Decor in the large, open restaurant is a comfortable mix of old and new styling, with interesting murals on the walls.

RingSide West. 2165 W. Burnside St. ☎ **503/223-1513.** Reservations highly recommended. Steaks $14–$22; seafood main courses $17–$38. AE, DC, DISC, MC, V. Mon–Sat 5pm–midnight, Sun 4–11:30pm. STEAK.

RingSide has long been a favorite Portland steakhouse. Though boxing is the main theme of the restaurant, the name delivers a two-fisted pun as well, referring to the incomparable onion rings that should be an integral part of any meal here. Have your rings with a side order of one of their perfectly cooked steaks for a real knockout meal. There is also a RingSide East at 14021 NE Glisan St. (☎ 503/255-0750), on Portland's east side, with basically the same menu but not as much atmosphere. It's open for lunch Monday through Friday from 11:30am to 2:30pm.

✪ **Toulouse Restaurant & Bar 71.** 71 SW Second Ave. ☎ **503/241-4343.** Reservations recommended. Main courses $12–$22. Tues–Thurs 11:30am–9:30pm, Fri–Sat 11:30am–10:30pm. AE, MC, V. MEDITERRANEAN.

Located in one of the prettiest spaces in the Old Town neighborhood, this spacious restaurant has a contemporary, yet comfortable feel. The space is equally divided between the restaurant and the bar, and you'll frequently find as many people dining in the bar (a simpler menu) as in the restaurant. There are also a few tables out on the sidewalk. What attracts the crowds here is mostly the selection of offerings from the wood-fired grill and rotisserie, such dishes as mesquite-grilled beef tenderloin with artichoke ragout and apple cider sauce. However, it would be easy enough to just make a meal of the appetizers, which include an astounding "grand" aioli that comes with mussels, oysters, a pile of Roquefort cheese, wood-roasted vegetables, fried brie, stuffed grape leaves, and an assortment of olives and cornichons.

INEXPENSIVE

Bijou Café. 132 SW Third Ave. ☎ **503/222-3187.** Reservations not accepted. $3–$8. No credit cards. Daily 7am–3pm. NATURAL FOODS.

The folks who run the Bijou take both food and health seriously. They'll let you know that the eggs are from Chris's Egg Farm in Hubbard, Oregon, and they'll serve you a bowl of steamed brown rice for breakfast. However, the real hits here are the hash browns and the muffins. Don't leave without trying these two. At lunch, there are salads made with organic produce whenever possible. Even the meats are natural.

Lamthong on Broadway. 213 SW Broadway. ☎ **503/223-4214.** Reservations recommended for Fri–Sat. Main courses $7–$11. AE, JCB, MC, V. Mon–Fri 11am–2pm; Mon–Thurs 5–9pm; Fri–Sat 5–10pm. THAI.

Lamthong is a dependable Thai restaurant that has been around the Portland area long enough to have branches in the suburbs. The cuisine served here is similar to that at the Saucebox, located across the street, but here you get more for your money. I like to start with the soft spring rolls or spicy calamari salad, and follow up with an entree of sweet basil with chicken, or the rich and spicy *Mussamun* curry with beef, potato, bay leaves, and peanuts.

Rene's Fifth Avenue. 1300 SW Fifth Ave. ☎ **503/241-0712.** Reservations recommended. Lunch $6–$15. MC, V. Mon–Fri 11:30am–2:30pm. CONTINENTAL.

Comfortable and elegant, this 21st-floor lunch spot in the First Interstate Tower is always crowded. Local businesspeople flock here as much for the great view as for the food. The menu, though short, is varied and includes daily specials and plenty of seafood. When I last visited, I had a blackened salmon special with lemon sauce, pasta salad, soup, and a splendid view of the Northwest hills, for $8.95. You won't find a view this good at better prices anywhere else in the city.

Western Culinary Institute International Dining Room. 1316 SW 13th Ave. ☎ **800/ 666-0312** or 503/223-2245. Reservations required. Five-course lunch $7.95; 6-course dinner $10.95; Thursday buffet $15.95. MC, V. Tues–Fri 11am–1pm and 6–8pm. CONTINENTAL.

If you happen to be a frugal gourmet whose palate is more sophisticated than your budget, you'll want to schedule a meal here. The dining room serves five- to six-course gourmet meals prepared by advanced students at prices even a budget traveler can afford. A sample dinner menu might begin with velouté Andalouse followed by pâté of rabbit, a pear sorbet, grilled chicken breast with blackberry-balsamic sauce, Chinese salad with smoked salmon, and divine chocolate-mousse cake. Remember, that's all for less than $11! The four-course lunch for only $7.95 is just as good a deal.

NOB HILL/NORTHWEST PORTLAND
EXPENSIVE

Briggs & Crampton Table for Two. 1902 NW 24th Ave. ☎ **503/223-8690.** Reservations several months in advance. Three- or four-course lunch for 2 people $75. V, MC. Tues–Fri 12:30pm. NORTHWEST.

This personalized dining experience occurs in a screened-off area in the front parlor of an atmospheric old house in Northwest Portland. Lunch starts with an appetizer, followed by a sorbet, breads, the main course with side dishes, dessert, and coffee. Dishes are influenced by what is in season, be it a certain type of fish, morel mushrooms, berries, or what have you. The person that serves the food also prepares it, so attention is concentrated on the special needs and desires of the dining pair. The wine list has some nice selections on it. Reservations are taken quarterly in January, April, July, and October.

L'Auberge. 2601 NW Vaughn St. ☎ **503/223-3302.** Reservations highly recommended. Main courses $16–$22; 4-course, fixed-price dinner $37. AE, CB, DC, DISC, MC, V. Sun–Thurs 5pm–midnight, Fri–Sat 5pm–1am. NORTHWEST/FRENCH.

Located at the edge of the industrial district, this restaurant offers some of the best French and Northwest cuisine in Portland and is a favorite special-occasion restaurant. A formal atmosphere reigns in the main dining room, but on Sunday nights the French flavor is forsaken in favor of succulent ribs and burgers, and a movie is shown in the bar. The fixed-price dinners feature meals with a French origin but translated with a Northwest accent. Before dining, be sure to stop by the bar to have a look at the delectable morsels on the dessert tray. On the prix fixe menu, you get a couple of choices of main dishes, such as rack of lamb with port garlic sauce or seared duck breast with maple-roasted figs and house-made chestnut spätzle. An à la carte international bistro menu is also available.

✪ **Wildwood.** 1221 NW 21st Ave. ☎ **503/248-WOOD.** Reservations highly recommended. Main courses $16–$24. AE, MC, V. Mon–Sat 11:30am–2:30pm; Mon–Thurs 5:30–10pm, Fri–Sat 5:30–10:30pm, Sun 5–8:30pm; Sun brunch 10am–2pm. AMERICAN REGIONAL.

With an elegant and spare interior decor straight out of *Architectural Digest* and a menu that changes daily, it isn't surprising that Wildwood is a hit with urban sophisticates. With booths, a meal counter, a bar area, and a patio, the restaurant appeals to celebratory groups, couples, and solo diners. And if you can't get a reservation, it's a great place to just have a couple of the delicious appetizers at the bar or counter. The menu relies primarily on the subtle flavors of the Mediterranean. Recently, the appetizers list included an unusual prosciutto and mango salad with goat cheese, toasted almonds, and curry citrus vinaigrette. Main courses included mesquite roasted lamb with eggplant and sweet pepper ragout with a rosemary-infused potato cake.

MODERATE

Bima. 1338 NW Hoyt St. ☎ **503/241-3465.** Reservations recommended. Main courses $12–$16. AE, MC, V. Mon–Thurs 11:30am–10pm, Fri–Sat 11:30am–11pm. GULF COAST.

A barely noticeable entryway leads into a cavernous converted warehouse, where the space is softened and romanticized with lighting and oversized booths. Food here is an unusual combination of Southern and Caribbean styles, a refreshing contrast to other Portland restaurants. We shared an appetizer of tiny kumomoto oysters and followed that up with corn bread—large, thick moist slices with a hint of crunchy corn. Catfish fillets covered in crushed pecans were served with chipotle flavored polenta cakes. Jicama avocado salad with a mango vinaigrette was good, but the jambalaya was too fiery for our tastes.

✪ **Café Mingo.** 807 NW 21st Ave. ☎ **503/226-4646.** Reservations not accepted. Main courses $7–$10. AE, DISC, MC, V. Mon–Wed 5–10pm; Thurs–Sat 5–11pm. ITALIAN.

The only problem with this intimate, immensely popular little cafe is that it doesn't take reservations. You almost always have to wait (on the sidewalk) for a table. The solution? Try getting here as early as possible. The interior is as attractive as that of any other upscale restaurant here on Restaurant Row, but the prices are inexpensive in comparison. The short menu focuses on simple Italian comfort food, painstakingly prepared, such as *inslata caprese* (a salad with tomato, house-made fresh mozzarella, basil, and extravirgin olive oil) and polenta with mushrooms and Italian sausage.

Paley's Place. 1204 NW 21st Ave. ☎ **503/243-2403.** Reservations highly recommended. Main courses $14–$18. AE, MC, V. Tues–Thurs 5:30–10pm, Fri–Sat 5:30–10:30pm. NORTHWEST/ FRENCH.

Paley's is located in a turn-of-the-century Victorian house, and in good weather, the front porch is the preferred place to dine. This porch also doubles as an open-air storage area for some of the restaurant's fresh produce, which lends a traditional European flavor to the surroundings. Inside, comforting soft pastel colors and tables placed close together give the small dining room a homey and casual feel. Chef Vitaly Paley combines the best of Northwest produce with other ingredients to make such vibrantly flavorful dishes as a salad of roasted beets with pears, blue cheese, organic greens, and toasted hazelnuts. Main courses might include pasta with roasted garlic, pecorino cheese, and chanterelle mushrooms from the porch display, or sautéed sweetbreads with leek-potato gratin and pomegranate sauce. The wine list includes both Northwest and French selections, and for dessert, we can't pass up the crème brûlée and the pear-walnut tart with honey.

✪ **Zefiro Restaurant & Bar.** 500 NW 21st Ave. ☎ **503/226-3394.** Reservations highly recommended. Main courses $14–$18. AE, DC, MC, V. Mon–Fri 11:30am–2:30pm; Mon–Thurs 5:30–10pm, Fri–Sat 5:30–10:30pm. MEDITERRANEAN.

Zefiro, which initiated the explosion of upscale restaurants on Northwest 21st Avenue, has for many years now been considered the best restaurant in Portland. While old-style French and Italian dishes predominate on the menu, Moroccan, Greek, Spanish, and even Asian influences creep in. For a starter, be sure to try the fragrant bowl of mussels steamed with leeks, white wine, saffron, cream, and thyme if it happens to be on the menu. Roasted mahimahi with an herb salsa verde made from tarragon, parsley, thyme, oregano, capers, garlic, lemon, and olive oil was a recent entree that captured all the fragrance of a Mediterranean herb garden in one dish. For dessert, order anything lemony, such as a lemon tartlet, lemon sorbet, or lemon ice cream, and you won't go wrong. The chic minimalist decor allows the outstanding creativity of the kitchen to take the fore, and service is always outstanding.

INEXPENSIVE

Garbanzo's. NW 21st Ave. and NW Lovejoy St. ☎ **503/227-4196.** Reservations not accepted. Salads $3–$5; sandwiches $4–$5; dinners $7–$9. AE, DISC, MC, V. Sun–Thurs 11:30am–1:30am, Fri–Sat 11:30am–3am (closes 1 hour earlier in winter). MIDDLE EASTERN.

Calling itself a falafel bar, this casual little place has become very popular, especially late at night. The menu includes all the usual Middle Eastern offerings, most of which also happen to be approved by the American Heart Association. You can eat at one of the tiny cafe tables or get your order to go. They even serve beer and wine. Another Garbanzo's is at 3433 SE Hawthorne Blvd. (☎ 503/239-6087).

Shakers Café. 1212 NW Glisan St. ☎ **503/221-0011.** Breakfast $3–$7, lunch $5–$7. No credit cards. Mon–Fri 7am–3:30pm, Sat 7:30am–3:30pm, Sun 7:30am–2pm. AMERICAN.

I seem to have a penchant for lunch counters—they're casual, fast, and these days, the food you find there is pretty good. Take Shakers Café in the Pearl District, for example, which takes its name from the 250 to 300 salt and pepper shakers on display. For breakfast, there's homemade scones and blue corn cakes. Lunch includes typical and not-so typical diner fare such as marinated chicken breast sandwiches, veggie or turkey burgers, grilled tuna fish sandwiches, homemade soups, and root beer floats. Service at the tables can be slow, but it's quicker at the counter.

Typhoon! 2310 NW Everett St. ☎ **503/243-7557.** Reservations recommended. Main courses $8–$14. AE, DC, DISC, MC, V. Mon–Thurs 11:30am–2:30pm and 5–9pm, Fri–Sat 11:30am–2:30pm and 5–10pm, Sun 5–9pm. THAI.

Located just off Northwest 23rd Avenue, this trendy Thai restaurant is a bit pricey (for Thai food), but the unusual menu offerings generally aren't available at other Portland Thai restaurants. Be sure to start a meal with the *miang kum,* which consists of dried shrimp, tiny chiles, ginger, lime, peanuts, shallots, and toasted coconut drizzled with a sweet-and-sour sauce and wrapped up in a spinach leaf. The eruption of flavors that takes place on your taste buds is absolutely astounding. (We first had this in Thailand and waited years to get it here in the United States.) Also not to be missed is the *hor mok,* a sort of shrimp and coconut pudding appetizer. The whole front wall of the restaurant slides away for Thai-style open-air dining in the summer.

SOUTHEAST PORTLAND
EXPENSIVE

✪ **Genoa.** 2832 SE Belmont St. ☎ **503/238-1464.** Reservations required. Fixed-price 4-course dinner $40; 7-course dinner $50. AE, CB, DC, DISC, MC, V. Mon–Sat 5:30–11:30pm; (4-course on Fri–Sat limited to 5:30 and 6pm only). ITALIAN.

This is one of the best Italian restaurants in Portland. Everything is made fresh in the kitchen, from the breads to the luscious desserts that are temptingly displayed just inside the front door. This is an ideal setting for a romantic dinner, and service is personal. The fixed-price menu changes every couple of weeks, but a typical dinner might start with small and spicy pimientos stuffed with salt cod and baked with puréed vegetables and garlic, followed by a creamy wild mushroom soup. There is always a choice of main courses, such as fresh sturgeon braised in red wine with bacon and shallots or Oregon quail stuffed with wild and cultivated mushrooms and served with creamy polenta and watercress. Desserts, such as a mouth-puckering lemon tart tempered by raspberry sauce and the mellow crème fraîche, are standouts.

MODERATE

✪ **Assaggio.** 7742 SE 13th Ave. ☎ **503/232-6151.** Reservations accepted only for parties of 6 or more. Main courses $9–$14. MC, V. Tues–Thurs 5–10pm, Fri–Sat 5–10:30pm. ITALIAN.

This neighborhood trattoria in Sellwood focuses its attentions on pastas and wines, and to that end the menu lists 15 pastas and the wine list includes more than 100 wines, almost all of which are from Italy. The atmosphere of this tiny place is extremely theatrical, with indirect lighting, dark walls, and Mario Lanza playing in the background. While pastas are the main attraction, this does not mean the flavors are not robust. Don't be surprised if after taking your first bite, you suddenly here a Verdi aria. *Assaggio* means a sampling, and that is exactly what you get if you order salad, bruschetta, or pasta Assaggio style—a sampling of several dishes all served family style. This is especially fun if you're here with a group.

Bread and Ink Cafe. 3610 SE Hawthorne Blvd. ☎ **503/239-4756.** Reservations recommended. Main courses $12.50–$18.50; Sun brunch $11.50. AE, DISC, MC, V. Mon–Thurs 7am–9pm, Fri 7am–10pm, Sat 8am–10pm, Sun 9am–2pm; and 5–9pm. NORTHWEST.

This funky restaurant is Hawthorne Boulevard's most upscale restaurant, yet it is still more of a casual neighborhood cafe. Every meal here is carefully and imaginatively prepared using fresh Northwest ingredients, and consequently, flavors change considerably with the seasons. A recent spring menu included fennel-roasted pork loin with rhubarb chutney and cold-smoked steelhead in a ginger-infused broth with buckwheat noodles. Desserts are a mainstay of Bread & Ink's loyal patrons, so don't pass them by. The Yiddish Sunday brunch is one of the most filling in the city.

❂ **Caprial's Bistro and Wine.** 7015 SE Milwaukee Ave. ☎ **503/236-6457.** Reservations highly recommended. Main courses $14–$19. MC, V. Tues–Fri 11am–3:30pm, Sat 11:30am–3:30pm; Wed–Thurs 5–9pm, Fri–Sat 5–9:30pm. NORTHWEST.

Caprial Pence, who helped put the Northwest on the national restaurant map, is the chef here, and even though this is a strong contender for best restaurant in Portland, it is a very casual place with only about 12 tables. There's no need to dress up, but you do need to make reservations well in advance (at least a week ahead for Friday or Saturday night). About half the restaurant is given over to a superb selection of wine and a wine bar; you may buy a bottle from the wine shop and open it at your table for a small additional charge. Main courses combine perfectly cooked meats and fishes, such as roast pork loin or lightly breaded oysters, with vibrant sauces, such as cranberry-shallot compote or sweet red-pepper pesto. Desserts, such as chocolate-almond-ricotta cake, are rich without being overly sweet. You'll get a large piece of whatever you order, so save room.

❂ **Fiddleheads.** 6716 SE Milwaukee Ave. ☎ **503/233-1547.** Reservations recommended. Main courses $14–$19.75. AE, DISC, MC, V. Mon–Fri 11:30am–10pm, Sat 10am–11pm, Sun 10am–9pm. NATIVE AMERICAN DERIVATIVE.

The setting is handsome: open, yet with cozy tones inspired by Native American designs. The menu, likewise, draws on traditional Native American fare. The Calapooya salad makes a good starter, but the crispy fried oyster tacos, accented with savory guacamole, are just too good to pass up. The hunter's style pasta is tossed with firm dark pheasant meat, boar bacon, and wild mushrooms in a smooth and flavorful Madeira sauce, while the *tatonka* is an Oregon buffalo stew with corn dumplings, vegetables, and roasted chiles. Chocolate Marquis, one of several house-made desserts, is a delicious flourless chocolate cake garnished with blackberry sauce, cookies, and mint. The full wine list includes many moderately priced bottles. Half a dozen vegetarian dishes appear on the menu, and brunch is served on Saturday and Sunday. Service is some of the best in town.

Montage. 301 SE Morrison St. ☎ **503/234-1324.** Reservations not accepted. Main courses $5–$16. No credit cards. Sun–Thurs 6pm–2am, Fri–Sat 6pm–4am. CAJUN.

A cacophony of voices and throbbing music punctuated by waiters bellowing out orders for oyster shooters slams you in the face as you step through the door of this in spot *under* the Morrison Bridge. They've definitely got the right idea here—Cajun dishes, such as blackened catfish, crawfish étouffée, jambalaya, frog legs, and alligator salad, all at surprisingly low prices. A lengthy wine menu promises you'll find something to your liking. If you don't like noisy places, don't even think of eating here—otherwise, it's great fun.

INEXPENSIVE

Caswell. 533 SE Grand St. (at Washington St.) ☎ **503/232-6512.** Reservations not usually accepted. Main courses $5–$9.50. MC, V. Mon–Sat 5pm–midnight. PIZZA/PASTA.

Located in a former Starbucks space Caswell is proof that a good plate of pasta doesn't have to be expensive. The pasta carbonara, with sautèed pancetta and a smoky prosciutto in garlic cream sauce, was flavorful and appealing, as was the ravioli, a complexly flavored pillow stuffed with cheeses and wood oven–baked vegetables. For an appetizer, we loved the crostini accompanied by a casserole of creamy spinach and artichoke hearts. Pizzas and salads round out the menu. The bar serves single malt Scotch and microbrews.

El Palenque. 8324 SE 17th Ave. ☎ **503/231-5140.** Main courses $5–$12. MC, V. Daily 11am–9:30pm. MEXICAN/SALVADORAN.

Though El Palenque bills itself as a Mexican restaurant, the Salvadoran dishes are the real reason for a visit. If you've never had a *pupusa,* this is your opportunity. A pupusa is basically an extrathick corn tortilla with a meat or cheese filling inside, accompanied by spicy shredded cabbage. Instead of adding the filling after the tortilla is cooked, the filling goes in beforehand. What you end up with is a sort of griddle-cooked turnover. Accompany your pupusa with some fried plantains and a glass of *horchata* (a sweet and spicy rice drink) for a typically Salvadoran meal.

✪ **Nicholas.** 318 SE Grand St. (between Pine and Oak sts.). ☎ **503/235-5123.** Reservations not accepted. Main courses $2–$8. No credit cards. Mon–Sat 10am–9pm. LEBANESE.

Delicious food and cheap prices keep this little hole-in-the-wall crowded. In spite of the heat from the pizza oven and the crowded conditions, the customers and wait staff still manage to be friendly. Our favorite dish is the *Manakishe,* Mediterranean pizza with thyme, oregano, sesame seeds, olive oil, and lemony-flavored sumac. Also available are a creamy humus, baba ghanoush, kabobs, falafel and gyros.

Old Wives' Tales. 1300 E. Burnside St. ☎ **503/238-0470.** Reservations recommended for dinner. Main courses $5–$15, breakfast $4–$8. AE, DISC, MC, V. Sun–Thurs 8am–9pm, Fri–Sat 8am–10pm. INTERNATIONAL/VEGETARIAN.

Old Wives' Tales is a sort of Portland countercultural institution. The menu is mostly vegetarian, with multiethnic dishes, such as spanakopita and burritos, and a smattering of chicken and seafood dishes. Breakfast here is popular and is served until 2pm daily. Old Wives' Tales's other claim to fame these days is as the city's best place to eat out with kids if you aren't into the fast food scene. The restaurant has a children's menu and a play room.

Saburo's Sushi House. 1667 SE Bybee Blvd. ☎ **503/236-4237.** Reservations not accepted. Sushi $3–$5, combination dinners $6–$8. MC, V. Tues–Sun 4:30–9:30pm. SUSHI.

Located in Sellwood, as is El Palenque, above, this sushi restaurant is so popular you'll most likely have to wait for a table. But when your sushi finally arrives, you'll know it was worth it. Our favorite is the *sabu* roll with lots of fish, and the *maguro* tuna sushi with generous slabs of tuna. Most Westerners don't care for the sea urchin, but you can try it if you're brave.

NORTHEAST PORTLAND
EXPENSIVE

Salty's on the Columbia. 3839 NE Marine Dr. ☎ **503/288-4444.** Reservations highly recommended. Main courses $9.50–$32. AE, CB, DC, DISC, MC, V. Mon–Sat 11:15am–3pm, Sun brunch 9:30am–2pm; Mon–Thurs 5–9:30pm, Fri–Sat 5–10pm, Sun 5–9pm. SEAFOOD.

While it's a ways out from downtown, Salty's is one of Portland's best waterfront restaurants. Located out on the Columbia River near the airport, this sprawling restaurant offers views that take in the river, mountains, and forests. Preparations here are creative, especially on the daily specials menu, and portions are large. Salmon is particularly popular. Try it smoked over alder wood, a traditional Northwest preparation. If seafood is not your thing, there are a few steak and chicken dishes. A warning: Though the decks look appealing, the noise from the airport can be distracting.

MODERATE

✪ **Ron Paul Charcuterie.** 1441 NE Broadway. ☎ **503/284-5347.** Reservations not accepted. Sandwiches $6–$8; main courses $10–$14. AE, MC, V. Mon–Thurs 8am–10:30pm, Fri 8am–midnight, Sat 9am–midnight, Sun 9am–4pm. Beaverton location closed on Sun. MEDITERRANEAN/DELI.

Chef Ron Paul has become a Portland institution over the years. This is a casual deli-style place in an upwardly mobile neighborhood in northeast Portland. Light streams through the walls of glass illuminating long cases full of tempting pasta-and-vegetable salads, cheeses, quiches, pizzas, sandwich fixings, and, most tempting of all, decadent desserts. On our most recent foray here, we had a basil pesto stuffed chicken breast, overflowing with portobello mushrooms, that came with a chickpea salad accented with rosemary and sage—delicious combinations. There are also locations at 6141 SW Macadam Ave. (☎ 503/977-0313) and 8838 SW Hall Blvd., Beaverton (☎ 503/646-3869). The Beaverton location is closed Sunday. All have extensive selections of Northwest wines.

INEXPENSIVE

✪ **Chez José East.** 2200 NE Broadway. ☎ **503/280-9888.** Reservations not accepted. Main courses $5–$10. MC, V. Mon–Thurs 11:30am–10pm, Fri–Sat 11:30am–11pm, Sun 4–9pm (the bar serves food until 1 hour later each night). MEXICAN.

It's immediately obvious upon perusing the menu here that this isn't the same sort of Mexican food you get at Taco Bell. While a squash enchilada with peanut sauce (spicy and sweet with mushrooms, apples, jicama, and sunflower seeds) sounds weird, it actually tastes great. But don't worry, there's plenty of traditional fare on the menu too (and at traditional cheap prices, too). Because the restaurant doesn't take reservations, it's a good idea to get here as early as possible, before the line starts snaking out the door. There's also a Chez José West, 8502 SW Terwilliger Blvd. (☎ 503/244-0007).

Saigon Kitchen. 835 NE Broadway. ☎ **503/281-3669.** Reservations required Fri–Sat only. Main courses $6–$16. AE, MC, V. Mon–Sat 11am–10pm, Sun noon–10pm. VIETNAMESE/THAI.

Vietnamese restaurants have begun opening around Portland's east side. These generally inexpensive places offer amazing variety and provide some of the most interesting flavor combinations this side of Thailand. Saigon Kitchen is among the best of the crop. If the menu proves too bewildering, try a combination dinner and let the kitchen make the decisions. The spring rolls (chazio rolls on the menu) shouldn't be missed, however, nor should the curried chicken. The salads, such as shrimp and barbecued pork, are tangy and spicy. Another Saigon Kitchen is at 3829 SE Division St. (☎ 503/236-2312).

SOUTHWEST PORTLAND
MODERATE

Avalon Grill. 4630 SW Macadam Ave. ☎ **503/227-4630.** Reservations recommended for weekend evenings. Main courses $15–$22; light meals $8–$16; Sun brunch $15.95. AE, MC, V. Mon–Sat 11:30am–1am, Sun 10am–midnight; lower-level restaurant closes at 9pm Sun–Thurs and 10pm Fri–Sat. NORTHWEST.

This is a great place to come for a drink, a light meal and outstanding views of the Willamette River. A mushroom-and-spinach lasagna constructed of very thin layers of sweet potato was a tasty assortment of flavors, and the goat cheese ravioli with Dungeness crab had a spicy tomato sauce reminiscent of *bouillabaisse,* but main courses are a little pricey for what you get. What you're paying for here is the ambience and the riverside setting. Monday through Friday from 3:30 to 6:30pm, there's an inexpensive happy hour menu, and in the evenings there is frequently live jazz.

INEXPENSIVE

The Old Spaghetti Factory. 0715 SW Bancroft St. ☎ **503/222-5375.** Reservations not accepted. Main courses $4.60–$8.40. CB, DC, DISC, MC, V. Mon–Thurs 11:30am–2pm and 5–10pm, Fri 11:30am–2pm and 5–11pm, Sat 1–11pm, Sun noon–10pm. ITALIAN.

Sure this is a chain restaurant, but incredibly low prices, great decor, a fabulous waterfront location on the bank of the Willamette River, and the fact that the chain had its start right here in Portland are reason enough to give this place a chance. This is the best waterfront restaurant in town for kids, and is a lot of fun for adults, too. Sort of a cross between a church, a trolley depot, and a Victorian brothel, this restaurant will keep you entertained and won't cost much more than McDonald's. To find it, watch for the big building with the blue tile roof.

CAFES & COFFEE BARS

The Brazen Bean, 2075 NW Glisan St. (☎ **503/294-0636**), is open evenings until late, which suits its opulent Victorian theme. There are board games to play, and a smoking room. **Café Lena,** 2239 SE Hawthorne Blvd. (☎ **503/238-7087**), located in the funky Southeast Hawthorne neighborhood, has live music and tasty food but is best known for its poetry nights. **Coffee Time,** 710 NW 21st Ave. (☎ **503/497-1090**), is a favorite Northwest neighborhood hangout with tables outside, and a variety of atmospheres inside. **Pied Cow,** 3244 SE Belmont St. (☎ **503/230-4866**), is in a Victorian house decorated in Bohemian chic, where there are couches on which to lounge and an outdoor garden.

Rimsky-Korsakoffee House, 707 SE 12th Ave. (☎ **503/232-2640**), is legendary for the rudeness of its wait staff, but live classical music, great desserts, and a skewed sense of humor keep patrons loyal. Oh, there's no sign on the old house to let you know this is the place, but you'll know once you open the door; open after 7pm. **Torrefazione Italia,** 838 NW 23rd Ave. (☎ **503/228-2528**), serves its classic brew in hand-painted Italian crockery, and has a good selection of pastries to go with your drink.

BAKERIES & DESSERT PLACES

Marsee Baking. 1323 NW 23rd Ave. ☎ **503/295-4000.** Sweets $1–$5; sandwiches $5. Mon–Thurs 7:30am–9pm, Fri–Sat 7:30am–10pm, Sun 8am–8pm. BAKERY.

When you've just got to have something gooey and rich, there's no better place to get it than at this bakery on trendy 23rd Avenue. The cases overflow with cakes, pies, and tarts as well as bagels, focaccia, and panini (Italian sandwiches) with various fillings. Also at 845 SW Fourth Ave., near Pioneer Place shopping center (☎ 503/226-9000), and at the Portland International Airport shopping mall.

Papa Haydn. 701 NW 23rd Ave. ☎ **503/228-7317.** Reservations not accepted except for Sun brunch. Main courses $16–$24; desserts $4–$6. AE, MC, V. Tues–Thurs 11:30am–11pm, Fri–Sat 11:30am–midnight, Sun brunch 10am–3pm. ITALIAN.

Say the words *Papa Haydn* to a Portlander and you'll see eyes glaze over and a wispy, blissful smile appear. What is it about this little bistro that sends locals into accolades of superlatives? Just desserts. That's right, Papa Haydn is legendary for dessert. Lemon chiffon torte, raspberry gâteau, black velvet, Georgian peanut butter mousse torte, tiramisu, and boccone dolce are just some of the names that stimulate a Pavlovian response in locals. Expect a line at the door. Also at 5829 SE Milwaukee Ave. (☎ 503/232-9440).

QUICK BITES

If you're just looking for something quick, cheap, and good to eat, there are lots of great options around the city. Downtown, at **Good Dog/Bad Dog,** 708 SW Alder St. (☎ 503/222-3410), you'll find handmade sausages. The kosher frank with kraut and onions is a good deal. For more upscale meals, duck into the **Ron Paul Express,**

507 SW Broadway (☎ **503/221-0052**), which is an outpost of a local chain of excellent and reasonably priced restaurants. Salads and sandwiches are good, but the cakes and pastries here are to die for.

Designer pizzas topped with anything from artichoke hearts to bacon to peanut sauce and teriyaki chicken can be had at **Pizzicato Gourmet Pizza**. Find them downtown at 705 SW Alder St. (☎ **503/226-1007**); in Northwest at 505 NW 23rd Ave. (☎ **503/242-0023**); and in Southeast at 2811 E. Burnside (☎ **503/236-6045**).

Over in southeast Portland, you can't miss the **Kitchen Table Café** (400 SE 12th Ave.; ☎ **503/230-6977**) in the yellow and purple building on the corner of Southeast Oak and Southeast 12th streets. This is a great place for homemade pies and soups, salads, and breads. If you're in the mood for a great burger, head to **Dots,** 2521 SE Clinton St. (☎ **503/235-0203**), which serves big, fat, juicy burgers in a setting that abounds in 1950s kitsch.

5 Attractions

THE TOP ATTRACTIONS

International Rose Test Garden. 400 SW Kingston Ave., Washington Park. ☎ **503/ 823-3636.** Free admission. Daily dawn to dusk. Bus: 63.

Covering 4¹/₂ acres of hillside in the West Hills above downtown Portland, these are the largest and oldest rose test gardens in the United States. They were established in 1917 by the American Rose Society, itself founded in Portland. Though you will likely see some familiar roses in the Gold Medal Garden, most of the 400 varieties on display here are new hybrids being tested before marketing. Among the roses in bloom from late spring to early winter, you'll find a separate garden of miniature roses. After seeing these acres of roses, you will certainly understand why Portland is known as the City of Roses and why the Rose Festival in June is the city's biggest annual celebration.

✪ Japanese Garden Society of Oregon. Off Kingston Ave. in Washington Park. ☎ **503/ 223-1321.** Admission $5 adults, $2.50 students and seniors, free for children 6 and under. Apr 1–May 31 and Sept 1–Sept 30, daily 10am–6pm; June 1–Aug 31, daily 9am–8pm; Oct 1– Mar 31, daily 10am–4pm. Closed Thanksgiving, Christmas, and New Year's Day. Bus: 63.

I have always loved Japanese gardens and have visited them all over the world. Outside of those in Japan, this is still my favorite. What makes it so special is not only the design, plantings, and tranquillity, but the view. From the Japanese-style wooden house in the center of the garden, you have a view over Portland to Mount Hood on a clear day. This perfectly shaped volcanic peak is so reminiscent of Mount Fuji that it seems almost as if it were placed there just for the sake of this garden.

Portland Saturday Market. Underneath Burnside Bridge (between SW First Ave. and SW Ankeny St.). ☎ **503/222-6072.** Free admission. First weekend in Mar to Christmas Eve, Sat 10am–5pm and Sun 11am–4:30pm. Bus: 12, 19, 20. MAX: Skidmore Fountain Station.

The Saturday Market (held on both Saturday and Sunday) is arguably Portland's single most important and best-loved event. Every Saturday and Sunday nearly 300 artists and craftspeople sell their crafts and creations here. You'll also find flowers, fresh produce, ethnic and unusual foods, and lots of free entertainment. This is the single best place in Portland to shop for one-of-a-kind gifts. On Sunday, on-street parking is free.

Pioneer Courthouse Square. Bounded by Broadway, Sixth Ave., Yamhill St., and Morrison St. Any downtown bus. MAX: Pioneer Courthouse Sq. Station.

Portland Attractions

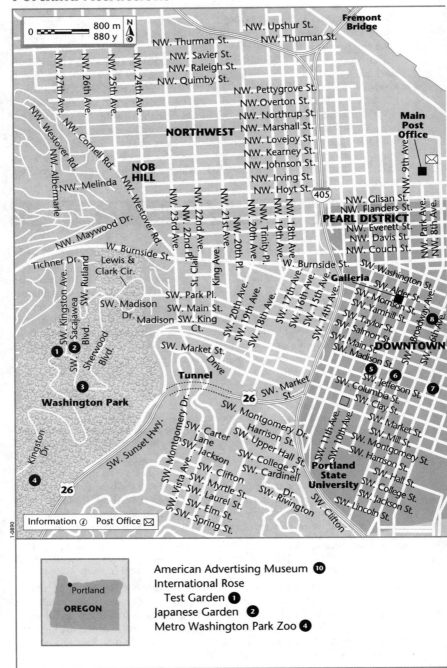

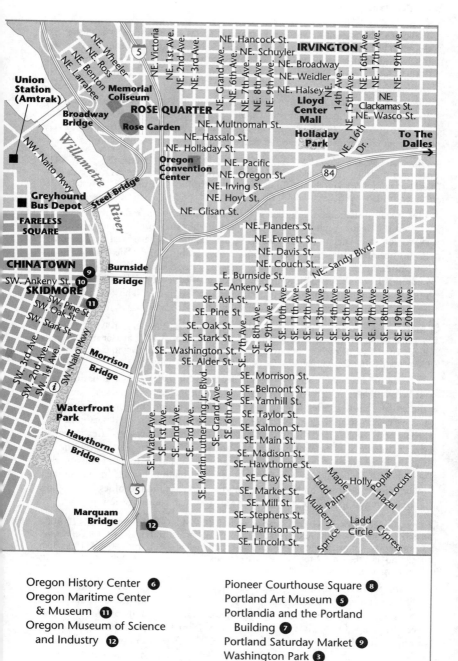

Oregon History Center **6**
Oregon Maritime Center
  & Museum **11**
Oregon Museum of Science
  and Industry **12**

Pioneer Courthouse Square **8**
Portland Art Museum **5**
Portlandia and the Portland
  Building **7**
Portland Saturday Market **9**
Washington Park **3**

Today it's the heart of downtown Portland and acts as an outdoor stage for everything from flower displays to concerts to protest rallies, but not too many years ago this beautiful brick-paved square was nothing but a parking lot. The parking lot itself had been created by the controversial razing in 1951 of the Portland Hotel, an architectural gem of a Queen Anne–style château. Today the square, with its tumbling waterfall fountain and free-standing columns, is Portland's favorite gathering spot, especially at noon, when the Weather Machine, a mechanical sculpture, forecasts the upcoming 24 hours. Keep your eyes on the square's brick pavement. Every brick contains a name (or names) or statement, and some are rather curious.

Portland Art Museum. 1219 SW Park Ave. ☎ **503/226-2811.** Admission $6 adults, $4.50 seniors and students, $2.50 children 6–15, free for children under 5; seniors half price every Thurs. Half price 4–9pm on the first Thurs of each month. Tues–Sun 10am–5pm; first Thurs of each month 10am–9pm. Bus: 6. MAX: Library Station.

This small museum has a respectable collection of European, Asian, and American art, but the major emphasis is on visiting exhibitions that feature a range of artistic expression from ancient to avant-garde. Recent exhibitions have been a collection of Rodin's bronze sculptures, the Ancient Tombs of China, and Dale Chihuly's glass sculptures, all of which attracted large crowds. The smaller galleries often feature photography exhibits and video installations. On Wednesday nights (except in summer), the Museum After Hours program presents live music. The adjacent Northwest Film Center shows an eclectic mix of films.

◊ Metro Washington Park Zoo. 4001 SW Canyon Rd., Washington Park. ☎ **503/226-1561.** Admission $5.50 adults, $4 seniors, $3.50 children ages 3–11, free for children under 2; free second Tues of each month from 3pm to closing. Memorial Day to Labor Day daily 9:30am–6pm; Labor Day to Memorial Day daily 9:30am–4pm. Bus: 63.

This zoo has been successfully breeding elephants for many years and has the largest breeding herd in captivity. The African exhibit includes a simulated rain forest and zebras, rhinos, giraffes, hippos, and other animals in one of the most lifelike habitats we've ever seen in a zoo. Equally impressive is the Alaskan-tundra exhibit, with grizzly bears, wolves, and musk oxen. For the younger set there's a petting zoo filled with farm animals. The Washington Park and Zoo Railway travels between the zoo and the International Rose Test and Japanese gardens. Tickets for the miniature railway are $2.75 for adults, $2 for senior citizens and children 3 to 11. In the summer, there are jazz concerts on Wednesday nights and rhythm and blues concerts on Thursday nights from 7 to 9pm. Concerts are free with zoo admission.

◊ Oregon Museum of Science and Industry (OMSI). 1945 SE Water Ave. ☎ **800/955-6674** or 503/797-4000. Admission $6 adults, $4.50 seniors and children 4–13, OMNIMAX and light shows cost extra, although discounted combination tickets are available. Thurs 3pm until closing all tickets are 2-for-1. Tues–Sat 9:30am–5:30pm (until 7pm in summer), Thurs 9:30am–8pm. Closed Christmas. Bus: 63.

The impressive OMSI building on the east bank of the Willamette River has six huge halls full of fun and fascinating exhibits. Two of the most exciting exhibits allow visitors to touch a tornado or ride an earthquake. This is a hands-on museum, and everyone is urged to get involved with displays, from a discovery space for toddlers to physics and chemistry labs for older children. There's plenty of pure entertainment at an OMNIMAX theater and the Murdock Sky Theater, which features laser-light shows and astronomy presentations. The USS *Blueback* submarine (used in the film *The Hunt for Red October*) is docked here and tours are given daily. An open-air train departs from OMSI to Oaks Amusement Park May through October; call ☎ **503/659-5452** for schedule.

✪ **American Advertising Museum.** 50 SW Second Ave. ☎ **503/226-0000.** Admission $3 adults, $1.50 seniors and children 12 and under. Wed–Sat 11am–5pm, Sun noon–5pm. Bus: 12, 19, 20. MAX: Skidmore Fountain Stop.

I long ago gave up watching television and listening to commercial radio because I have no tolerance for advertising. That this is my favorite Portland museum should tell you something about the exhibits. You'll learn (and perhaps reminisce) about historic advertisements, celebrities, and jingles from the 1700s to now. Special shows in the past have included a retrospective of Portland's Homer Groening (father of Matt Groening, creator of *The Simpsons*), including his cartoons, films, and advertising.

MORE ATTRACTIONS
ARCHITECTURAL HIGHLIGHTS
✪ **Portlandia and the Portland Building.** 1120 SW Fifth Ave. Any downtown bus.

Portlandia is the symbol of the city, and this hammered bronze statue of her is the second-largest such statue in the country. The largest, of course, is New York City's Statue of Liberty. The massive kneeling figure holds a trident in one hand and with the other reaches toward the street. Strangely enough, this classically designed figure reminiscent of a Greek goddess perches above the entrance to Portland's most controversial building: The Portland Building, considered the first postmodern structure in the country. Today anyone familiar with the bizarre constructions of Los Angeles architect Frank Gearhy would find it difficult to understand how such an innocuous and attractive building could have ever raised such a fuss, but it did.

Pittock Mansion. 3229 NW Pittock Dr. ☎ **503/823-3624.** Admission $4.25 adults, $3.75 seniors, $2 children 6–18. Daily noon–4pm. Closed 3 days in late Nov, most major holidays, and the first 3 weeks of Jan. Bus: 20 to Burnside and Barnes, then a $1/2$-mile walk.

At nearly the highest point in the West Hills, 1,000 feet above sea level, stands the most impressive mansion in Portland. Once slated to be torn down to make way for new housing, this grand château built by the founder of Portland's *Oregonian* newspaper has been fully restored and is open to the public. Built in 1914 in a French Renaissance style, the mansion featured many innovations, including a built-in vacuum system and amazing multiple showerheads in the baths. Today it is furnished with 18th- and 19th-century antiques, much as it might have been at the time the Pittocks occupied the building. Lunch and afternoon tea are available in the **Gate Lodge,** the former caretaker's cottage (☎ **503/823-3627**), and reservations are recommended.

MUSEUMS
Oregon History Center. 1200 SW Park Ave. ☎ **503/222-1741.** Admission $6 adults and seniors, $3 students, $1.50 children 6–12; free Thurs for seniors. Tues–Sat 10am–5pm, Sun noon–5pm. Bus: 6 or any downtown bus. MAX: Library Station.

The Oregon Territory was a land of promise and plenty. Thousands of hardy individuals set out along the Oregon Trail to cross a vast and rugged country to reach the fertile valleys of Oregon's rivers. Today the state of Oregon is still luring immigrants with its bountiful natural resources, and those who wish to learn about the people who discovered Oregon before them should visit this well-designed museum. Oregon history, from before the first white men arrived to well into this century, is chronicled in fascinating educational exhibits, incorporating parts of old buildings, old snow skis, dolls, bicycles, fashions, Native American artifacts, nautical and surveying instruments, even a covered wagon. Museum docents, with roots stretching from the days of the Oregon Trail, are often on hand to answer questions. There is also a research library that includes many journals from early pioneers. You can't miss this complex—stretching across the front is an eight-story-high trompe l'oeil mural.

World Forestry Center. 4033 SW Canyon Rd. ☎ **503/228-1367.** Admission $3 adults, $2 seniors and children 6–18, free for children under 6. Daily 9am–5pm (10am–5pm in winter). Closed Christmas. Bus: 63.

This center serves as an educational facility teaching visitors about the importance of our forest resources. Here you'll find exhibits on forests of the world and old-growth trees.

Oregon Maritime Center & Museum. 113 SW Front Ave. ☎ **503/224-7724.** Admission $4 adults, $3 seniors, $2 students, free for children under 8. Summer Wed–Sun 11am–4pm; winter Fri–Sun 11am–4pm. Bus: 12, 19, 20. MAX: Skidmore Fountain Station.

On display here, you'll find models of ships that once plied the Columbia and Willamette rivers, early navigation instruments, and maritime memorabilia. The historic stern-wheeler *Portland,* moored across Waterfront Park from the museum, is also open to the public.

OFFBEAT ATTRACTIONS

The Candy Basket. 1924 NE 181st Ave. (1 block south of I-84 at exit 13). ☎ **800/ 864-1924** or 503/666-2000. Free admission. Mon–Fri 9am–6pm, Sat 10am–5pm.

It's not exactly Willy Wonka's Chocolate Factory, but here at The Candy Basket you'll find an art deco–style 20-foot chocolate waterfall, and it smells great. If you really like chocolate, it's worth the jaunt out here. Tours that explain the ins and outs of this family-owned chocolate business are given on Tuesday, Wednesday, and Thursday at 9:30am, and, of course, chocolate samples are included. At the small store you can buy the likes of cashew beaver paws and marionberry creams.

Where's the Art!!/Church of Elvis. 720 SW Ankeny St. ☎ **503/226-3671.** Donation. Guided tours of World Headquarters are usually available daily from noon–5pm and Fri and Sat 8pm–midnight. Bus: Any downtown bus.

One of Portland's most bizarre attractions, this upstairs "museum" is full of kitschy contraptions such as the Vend-O-Matic Mystery Machine with whirling dolls heads. What is it? Well, celebrity-spokesmodel/minister S.G. Pierce will give you a tour of the World Headquarters here to explain it all because, as she says "the tour *is* the art form." Cheap, not legal, weddings are offered. Great fun if you are a fan of Elvis, tabloids, or the unusual. If you've seen Elvis anytime in the past decade, a visit is absolutely mandatory.

6 Especially for Kids

The **Oregon Museum of Science and Industry** is primarily geared for kids, with lots of hands-on exhibits, including a NASA training room, a full computer lab, a chicken hatchery, and laser shows in its planetarium (see "The Top Attractions," above). The **Metro Washington Park Zoo** is particularly known for its elephant-breeding program. From inside the zoo, it's possible to take a small train through Washington Park to the Rose Gardens (see "The Top Attractions," above).

In addition to these, there are a couple of other attractions in Portland geared toward kids.

Portland Children's Museum. 3037 SW Second Ave. ☎ **503/823-2227.** Admission $3.50 adults and children, free for children under 1. Daily 9am–5pm. Closed some national holidays. Bus: 1, 5, 12, 40, 43, or 45.

Visitors can shop in a kid-size grocery store, play waiter or diner in a restaurant, or pretend to be a doctor in a medical center. In H2 Oh! kids can blow giant bubbles and pump water. The Children's Cultural Center presents a child's view of such environments as an African or Native American village complete with artifacts and hands-on activities. There's plenty to entertain kids at this big little museum.

Oaks Park. East end of the Sellwood Bridge. ☎ **503/233-5777.** Free admission; all activities are on individual tickets. May–Oct Mon–Fri noon–5pm, Sat noon–10pm, Sun noon–9pm; longer hours during the summer. Bus: 40.

What would summer be like without the screams of happy thrill-seekers risking their lives on a roller coaster? Beneath the shady oaks for which this amusement park is named, you'll find plenty of wild rides, waterfront picnic sites, miniature golf, music, and the largest roller-skating rink in the Northwest. The Samtrak Excursion train runs along the Willamette River from Oaks Park to OMSI (Oregon Museum of Science and Industry) May through October; call ☎ **503/659-5452** for schedule.

7 Parks & Gardens

With 4,800 acres of wilderness, **Forest Park** (☎ **503/823-4492**), bounded by West Burnside Street, Newberry Road, St. Helens Road, and Skyline Road, is the largest forested city park in the United States. There are 50 miles of trails and old fire roads for hiking, jogging, and mountain biking. More than 100 species of birds call these forests home, making this park a bird-watcher's paradise. Along the forest trails, you can see huge old trees and quiet picnic spots tucked away in the woods.

Adjacent to this park, you'll also find the **Portland Audubon Society,** 5151 NW Cornell Rd. (☎ **503/292-6855**), which has 4 miles of hiking trails on its forested property. In keeping with its mission to promote enjoyment, understanding, and protection of the natural world, these nature trails are open to the public. You can also visit the nature center or wildlife care center here.

Right in downtown, **Tom McCall Waterfront Park** serves as the city's festival locale and premier Willamette River access point. There are acres of lawns, shade trees, sculptures, and fountains. The paved path through the park is popular with in-line skaters and joggers. Also in this park are the Waterfront Story Garden, dedicated to storytellers, and the Japanese-American Historical Plaza, which is dedicated to Japanese-Americans who were sent to internment camps during World War II.

South of downtown, you'll find **Tryon Creek State Park** on Terwilliger Road. This park is similar to Forest Park and is best known for its displays of trillium flowers in the spring. A bike path to downtown Portland starts here and there are also several miles of walking trails within the park.

The Berry Botanic Garden. 11505 SW Summerville Ave. ☎ **503/636-4112.** Adults $5. Open daylight hours by appointment. Bus: 35 or 36.

Originally founded as a private garden, the Berry Botanic Garden now is working to save endangered plants of the Pacific Northwest. There is a large collection of rhododendron shrubs here, so many in fact that they create a forest. A native plant trail, a fern garden, and rock gardens with unusual plants are all here to enjoy, but you must call ahead to make a reservation before arriving.

Leach Botanical Garden. 6704 SE 122nd Ave. ☎ **503/761-9503.** Free admission. Tues–Sat 10am–4pm, Sun 1–4pm. Bus: 71.

In the 1920s and '30s, Lilla Leach was a noted Northwest botanist. She and her husband John Leach lovingly built this garden together, and in the late 1970s they donated it to the city of Portland. Diverse types of garden displays include a bog garden, rock gardens, a Northwest woodland, and a Southeastern azalea garden. The visitor center is in the Manor House, which features beautiful woodwork.

Crystal Springs Rhododendron Garden. SE 28th Ave. ☎ **503/777-1734** or 503/771-8386. Admission charged Mar 1–Labor Day, Thurs–Mon from 10am–6pm, $2. Daily dawn to dusk. Bus: 19.

Eight months out of the year this is a tranquil garden, with a waterfall and ducks to feed. But when the rhododendrons and azaleas bloom from March to June, it becomes a spectacular mass of blazing color. The Rhododendron Show and Plant Sale is held here on Mother's Day weekend.

Hoyt Arboretum. 4033 SW Canyon Rd. ☎ **503/823-3654.** Free admission. Open daily 6am–10pm. Bus: 63.

Only about 10 minutes from downtown Portland, this 175-acre arboretum has 850 species of trees from temperate regions around the world and 10 miles of hiking trails. At the south end of the arboretum is the Vietnam Veterans Living Memorial. To reach the Arboretum, take West Burnside Street $1^1/2$ miles west of the Northwest shopping district and look for the sign; or take the zoo exit from Hwy. 26.

The Grotto—National Sanctuary of Our Sorrowful Mother. NE 85th Ave. and Sandy Blvd. ☎ **503/254-7371.** Free admission; elevator $1.50. Open daily summer 9am–8pm, winter 9am–5:30pm. Closed Christmas and Thanksgiving. Bus: 12.

One of the main features at this forested 62-acre sanctuary is a shallow rock cave carved into the foot of a cliff that contains a marble replica of Michelangelo's *Pietà*. Although the Grotto is Catholic, it is open to visitors of all faiths. An elevator ride to the top of the bluff offers panoramic views of the Cascade Mountains, the Columbia River Valley, and Mount St. Helens. This retreat is at its best in the summertime and during the Christmas season when the grounds are decorated with thousands of lights and a choral festival is held. There are also a couple of chapels on the grounds, a nice gift shop, and a coffee shop.

8 Organized Tours

BUS TOURS   Gray Line (☎ **800/422-7042** or 503/285-9845) offers several half-day and full-day city sightseeing tours. But the trip we most recommend is the full-day Mount Hood loop—if you aren't doing the driving, you can enjoy the scenery more. Other tours offered are an excursion to the Columbia Gorge that includes a ride on a stern-wheeler, and a northern Oregon coast tour. Tour prices range from $22 to $42 for adults, and from $11 to $21 for children.

BOAT TOURS   If you're interested in seeing Portland from the water, you've got lots of options. Traditionalists will want to book a tour with **Cascade Stern-Wheelers** (☎ **503/223-3928**), which offers stern-wheeler cruises on the Columbia River in the Columbia Gorge (summer only) and the Willamette River through downtown Portland (year-round). A trip up the Columbia River, with its towering cliffs, is a spectacular and memorable excursion. Two-hour cruises are $12.95 for adults and $7.95 for children. Call for information on brunch, dinner, and dance cruises.

If a modern yacht is more your speed, try the ***Portland Spirit*** (☎ **800/224-3901** or 503/224-3900). This 75-foot custom-built yacht seats more than 300 people on two decks, and offers views of downtown Portland on lunch, brunch, and dinner cruises featuring Northwest cuisine. Saturday night it becomes a floating nightclub with live bands or a DJ. Call for reservations and schedule. Prices range from $10 to $46 for adults and $14 to $18 for children.

Rose City Riverboat Cruises (☎ **503/234-6665**) offers another alternative—a modern catamaran power yacht that cruises the Willamette River between mid-April and October. Dinner, moonlight, Sunday brunch, Portland harbor, and historical river tours are offered. Prices range from $9 to $30, with lower fares for children and seniors.

For high-speed tours up the Willamette River, there are the **Willamette Falls Jetboats** (☎ **888/JETBOAT** or 503/231-1532). The high-powered open-air boats blast their way up river from downtown Portland to the impressive Willamette Falls at Oregon City. The two-hour tours, which start at OMSI, are $22 for adults and $14 for children.

WALKING TOURS   If you'd like to learn more about downtown Portland, contact **Apple Tours** (☎ **800/939-6326** or 503/638-4076) for a walking tour of the area. You'll learn about Portland's architecture and colorful history. Tours cost $15 for adults, $13 for seniors, and $5 for children.

Peter's Downtown Tour (☎ **503/665-2558** or 503/816-1060), led by university instructor Peter Chausse, is a 2-hour walking tour of downtown that includes visits to the fountains, parks, historic places, art, and architecture that make Portland the energetic city that it is. Tours are in the afternoon (call for reservations) and cost $10 for adults and $5 for children.

WINERY & BREWERY TOURS   If you're interested in learning more about Oregon wines and want to tour the nearby wine country, contact **Grape Escape** (☎ **503/282-4262**), which offers an in-depth winery tour of the Willamette Valley. An all-day tour includes stops at several wineries, an elegant picnic lunch, and pick-up and drop-off at your hotel. Tours are $65.

If craft beers and ales are more to your tastes, consider the **Portland Brew Bus** (☎ **888/BIG-BREW**). The Brew Bus, a Gray Line motorcoach, takes you on a 4-hour tour of three breweries and brew pubs, where you'll get two- to three-ounce samples of about 20 brews—and, you don't have to be concerned about driving yourself around. This isn't a pub crawl, but a way to learn a lot about the process of craft brewing. Tours are $39.95.

NATURE TOURS   **Ecotours of Oregon** (☎ **503/245-1428**) offers a variety of tours and hikes. They travel to the Columbia River Gorge, Mount Hood, Mount St. Helens, the Oregon coast, ancient forests, and places to whale-watch or experience Native American culture. Visits to wineries, microbreweries, and custom tours can also be arranged. Tour prices range from $38 to $60.

A CARRIAGE TOUR   The **John Palmer House** (☎ **503/284-5893**), a restored Victorian bed-and-breakfast, offers tours of the city by horse-drawn carriage on Friday, Saturday, and Sunday throughout the year. Tours cost $75 for a carriage that can carry four people.

A TROLLEY TOUR   The **Willamette Shore Trolley** (☎ **503/222-2226**), a fully restored trolley dating from the early part of this century, is an excursion trolley that operates on a 7-mile line connecting Portland with the prestigious suburb of Lake Oswego. The trip takes 45 minutes each way and round-trip fares are $5 adults, $3 children age 3 to 12. The Portland trolley station is just south of the RiverPlace Athletic Club on Harbor Way (off Naito Parkway at the south end of Tom McCall Waterfront Park). The Lake Oswego station is on State Street, between "A" Avenue and Foothills Road.

9 Outdoor Activities

If you're planning ahead for a visit to Portland, contact **Metro Regional Parks and Greenspaces,** 600 NE Grand Ave., Portland, OR 97232-2736 (☎ **503/797-1850;** Web site: www.multnomah.lib.or.us/metro), for their *Metro Green Scene* publication which lists tours, hikes, classes, and other outdoor activities and events in the Portland metro area.

BEACHES The nearest ocean beach to Portland is **Cannon Beach,** about 90 miles to the west. See chapter 5 for more information.

There are a couple of freshwater beaches on the Columbia River within 45 minutes of Portland. **Rooster Rock State Park,** just off I-84 east of Portland, includes several miles of sandy beach, as does **Sauvie Island,** off Ore. 30 northwest of Portland. You'll need to obtain a parking permit for Sauvie Island; it's available at the convenience store located just after you cross the bridge onto the island. Both beaches include sections that are clothing optional.

BIKING You'll notice many bicyclists on Portland streets. If you want to get rolling with everyone else, head over to **Fat Tire Farm,** 2714 NW Thurman St. (☎ **503/222-3276**), to rent a mountain bike for $30 a day. In nearby Forest Park, the **Leif Erikson Trail** is a car-less stretch of dirt road that goes on for miles and is popular with bicyclists and runners. You can rent a bike downtown at **Bike Central,** 835 SW Second Ave. and Taylor Street (☎ **503/227-4439**), where rental fees are about $20 to $30 per day. Once you have your bike, you can head for **Waterfront Park,** where there's a 2-mile bike path. The **Terwilliger Path** starts at the south end of Portland State University and travels for 10 miles up into the hills to Tryon Creek State Park. The views from the top are breathtaking. Stop by a bike shop to pick up a bicycling map for the Portland metro area.

BOARDSAILING Serious enthusiasts already know about the boardsailing mecca at the town of **Hood River** on the Columbia River. The winds come howling down the gorge with enough force to send sailboards airborne. Several shops in Hood River rent boardsailing equipment. Right in Portland, you can rent boards at **Gorge Performance Windsurfing,** 7400 SW Macadam Blvd. (☎ **503/246-6646**), which is conveniently close to **Willamette Park,** which is on the Willamette River and is the city's best boardsailing spot. You'll find this park at the corner of Southwest Macadam Boulevard and Southwest Nebraska Street. Another good spot for experienced sailors is on **Sauvie Island,** where you'll find many miles of sandy beaches. The easiest spot for beginners is across the Columbia River in Vancouver, Washington, at **Vancouver Lake State Park.**

FISHING The Portland area is salmon, steelhead, sturgeon, and trout country. You can find out about licenses and seasons from the **Oregon Department of Fish and Wildlife,** P.O. Box 59, Portland, OR 97207 (☎ **503/229-5403**). If you prefer to have a guide take you where the big ones are biting, contact the **Oregon Outdoor Association,** P.O. Box 9486, Bend, OR 97708 (☎ **541/683-9552**), for a copy of their annual directory. A day of fishing will cost you between $100 and $170 per person. **Page's Northwest Guide Service** (☎ **503/760-3373**) will take you out fishing for salmon, steelhead, walleye, and sturgeon on the Columbia or Willamette rivers, Portland area streams, or Tillamook Bay (all gear is included). **Reel Adventures** (☎ **503/622-5372** or 503/789-6860), located in Sandy, Oregon, offers a similar fishing guide service.

GOLF There are plenty of public courses around the area, and greens fees at municipal courses are as low as $18 for 18 holes on a weekday and $20 on weekends and holidays. Municipal golf courses operated by the Portland Bureau of Parks and Recreation include **Eastmoreland Golf Course,** 2425 SE Bybee Blvd. (☎ **503/ 775-2900**); **Heron Lakes Golf Course,** 3500 N. Victory Blvd. (☎ **503/289-1818**); and **Rose City Golf Course,** 2200 NE 71st Ave. (☎ **503/253-4744**). However, if you want to play where the pros play, head west from Portland 20 miles to **Pumpkin Ridge Golf Club,** 12930 NW Old Pumpkin Ridge Rd. (☎ **503/ 647-4747**), which has hosted the U.S. Women's Open and Tiger Wood's last amateur tournament.

ICE SKATING   The **Lloyd Center Ice Chalet** at the Lloyd Center mall (☎ **503/ 288-6073**) has skate rentals and a fairly good skating surface.

IN-LINE SKATING   **Waterfront Park** is a popular and fairly level place for skating. In-line skates can be rented at the nearby **Sports Works,** 421 SW Second Ave. (☎ **503/227-5323**), for $20 a day, which includes all safety gear.

SEA KAYAKING   You can rent a sea kayak at **Ebb & Flow Paddlesports,** 0604 SW Nebraska St. (☎ **503/245-1756**), and cart it a couple of blocks to where you can paddle on the Willamette River. Rental rates for a double start at $26 for half a day.

TENNIS   Portland Parks and Recreation operates more than 120 tennis courts, both indoor and out, all over the city. Outdoor courts are generally free and available on a first-come, first-served basis. My personal favorites are those in Washington Park just behind the International Rose Test Garden. Some of these courts can be reserved by contacting the **Portland Tennis Center,** 324 NE 12th Ave. (☎ **503/ 823-3189**). If the weather isn't cooperating, head for the Portland Tennis Center itself. They have indoor courts and charge $6 to $6.75 per hour per person for singles matches and $3.75 to $4.25 per hour per person for doubles. The hours here are 6:30am to 10pm during the week, closing later on the weekend.

10 Day Spas

If you'd rather opt for a massage than a hike in the woods, consider spending a few hours at a day spa. These facilities offer such treatments as massages, facials, seaweed wraps, and the like. Portland day spas include **Aveda Lifestyle Store & Spa,** 5th Avenue Suites Hotel, 500 Washington St. (☎ **503/248-0615**); **Boutique Alternáre,** 1444 NE Broadway (☎ **503/282-8200**); and **A New Dawn Salon & Spa,** 5512 SW Kelly St. (☎ **503/244-3437**). Expect to pay $45 to $65 for a 1-hour massage and $155 to $285 for a full day of pampering.

11 Cheering for the Home Team & Other Spectator Sports

In addition to the phone numbers listed below, **TicketMaster** (☎ **503/224-4400**) is an alternative source of tickets for the Trail Blazers, the Portland Winter Hawks, Portland Power, the Portland Rockies Baseball Club, and certain other sporting events.

The **Rose Garden** arena (☎ **503/797-9617** for tickets; 503/321-3211 event information hotline) is home to the Trail Blazers and the Portland Winter Hawks, and also hosts a variety of other athletic events and concerts. This relatively new arena is the main focal point of what has become known as the **Rose Quarter**. This sports- and entertainment-oriented neighborhood is still more an idea than a reality, but it does include the Rose Garden, Memorial Coliseum, and several restaurants and bars. To reach the Rose Garden or Memorial Coliseum, take the Rose Quarter exit off

I-5. Parking is expensive, so you might want to consider taking the MAX light-rail line from downtown Portland.

AUTO RACING   Portland International Raceway, 1940 N. Victory Blvd. (☎ **503/285-6635**), operated by the Portland Bureau of Parks and Recreation, is home to road races, drag races, motocross and other motorcycle races, go-cart races, and even vintage-car races. February to October are the busiest months here. Admission is $6 to $75.

BASEBALL   The Portland Rockies Baseball Club (☎ **503/223-2837**) plays class A minor-league ball at the Civic Stadium, SW 20th Avenue and Morrison Street. The box office is open Monday through Friday from 9am to 5pm and from 9am the day of the game. Tickets are $2.50 to $6.50 for adults, $1 to $4.50 for children 14 and under.

BASKETBALL   The NBA's Portland Trail Blazers (☎ **503/231-8000**) pound the boards at the Rose Garden. Call for current schedule and ticket information. Tickets are $15 to $73. Depending on the teams record, tickets can be hard to come by.

Portland Power (☎ **503/236-HOOP**), of the newly formed American Basketball League, plays professional women's basketball at Memorial Coliseum. Tickets are $11 to $43.

GREYHOUND RACING   The race season at the Multnomah Greyhound Track, NE 223rd Avenue, Wood Village (☎ **503/667-7700**), runs from May to September. Post time is 7pm Wednesday through Saturday, with Sunday matinees at 1pm. To reach the track, take I-84 east to the 181st Street exit south and then turn left on Glisan Street. It's also easy to reach the park by public transit. Take the MAX light-rail system to the Gresham City Hall or Central Station and transfer to bus no. 81, which goes directly to the racetrack. Admission is $1.25 to $3.50.

HORSE RACING   Portland Meadows, 1001 N. Schmeer Rd. (☎ **503/285-9144**), is the place to go if you want a little horse-racing action. The race season runs from October to April, with post time at 6:30pm on Friday and 12:30pm on Saturday and Sunday. By car, take I-5 north to the Delta Park exit. Admission is $2 to $3.

ICE HOCKEY   The Portland Winter Hawks (☎ **503/238-6366**), a junior-league hockey team, carve up the ice at Memorial Coliseum and the Rose Garden from October to March. Call for schedule and ticket information. Tickets are $10 to $14.

MARATHON   The Oregon Road Runners Club Portland Marathon is held sometime in late September to early October. The 26.2-mile run is supplemented by shorter runs such as the mayor's walk and the kid's run. For further information, call ☎ **503/226-1111.**

12 Shopping

Perhaps the single most important fact about shopping in Portland, and all of Oregon for that matter, is that there's **no sales tax.** The price on the tag is the price you pay. If you come from a state with a high sales tax, you might want to save your shopping for your visit to Portland.

THE SHOPPING SCENE

Over the past few years Portland has managed to preserve and restore a good deal of its historic architecture, and many of these late 19th-century and early 20th-century buildings have been turned into unusual and very attractive shopping centers. **New Market Village** (120 SW Ankeny St.), **Morgan's Alley** (515 SW Broadway), and **Skidmore Fountain Building** (28 SW First Ave.) are all outstanding examples of how Portland has preserved its historic buildings and kept its downtown area filled with happy shoppers.

However, it is the blocks around **Pioneer Courthouse Square** that are the heartland of upscale shopping in Portland. It is here that you will find Nordstrom, Niketown, Saks Fifth Avenue, Pioneer Place shopping mall, and numerous other upscale boutiques and shops.

Portland's most "happening" area for shopping is the **Nob Hill neighborhood** along Northwest 23rd Avenue beginning at West Burnside Street. Here you'll find block after block of unusual boutiques that are, unfortunately, rapidly being replaced by such chains as the Gap, Urban Outfitters, and Pottery Barn. For shops with a more downbeat and funky flavor, head out to the **Hawthorne District,** which is the city's counterculture shopping area (lots of tie-dye and imports). In the **Pearl District,** of which Northwest Glisan Street and Northwest 10th Avenue is the center, you'll find the city's greatest concentration of art galleries. Northeast Broadway around Northeast 15th Avenue is home to several interesting interior design and home decor shops.

SHOPPING FROM A TO Z
ANTIQUES

Old Sellwood Antique Row, at the east end of Sellwood Bridge on Southeast 13th Street, with its old Victorian homes and turn-of-the-century architecture, is Portland's main antique district. You'll find 13 blocks with more than 30 antique dealers and restaurants.

ART GALLERIES

If you're in the market for art, try to arrange your visit to coincide with the **first Thursday of the month.** On these days galleries in downtown Portland schedule coordinated openings in the evening. Stroll from one gallery to the next, meeting artists and perhaps buying an original work of art. As an added bonus, the **Portland Art Museum,** 1219 SW Park Ave. (☎ **503/226-2811**), offers half-price admission from 4 to 9pm on these nights.

An art gallery guide listing almost 60 Portland galleries is available at the **Portland Oregon Visitors Association Information Center,** Two World Trade Center, 25 SW Salmon St. (☎ **800/345-3214** or 503/222-2223), or at galleries around Portland.

✪ **Art of the People.** 818 SW First Ave. ☎ **503/221-0569.**

Art of the People features contemporary paintings and sculpture, and folk and religious art by artists of Latin American descent. Monthly shows sometimes focus on historical and cultural aspects of Latin American art and traditions.

Augen Gallery. 817 SW Second Ave. ☎ **503/224-8182.**

When it opened 16 years ago, the Augen Gallery focused on internationally recognized artists such as Dine, Warhol, and Hockney, and now has expanded its repertoire to regional contemporary painters and printmakers.

Blackfish Gallery. 420 NW Ninth Ave. ☎ **503/224-2634.**

Artist-owned since 1979, the Blackfish is a large and relaxing space in which to contemplate the cutting-edge and sometimes thought-provoking images.

The City of Books

Though Seattle claims the largest library system in the country, Portland has **Powell's "City of Books,"** the bookstore to end all bookstores (1005 W. Burnside St.; ☎ **800/878-7323** or 503/228-4651; Web site: www.powells.com). Covering an entire city block three floors deep, Powell's sells more than three million volumes each year. Though there are arguments over whether the City of Books is the biggest bookstore in the country, most people agree that Powell's has more titles on its shelves than any other bookstore in the United States. In any case, there's no denying Powell's is a contender for the claim to biggest bookstore in the country.

Powell's has its origins in two used-bookstores, one in Chicago and one in Portland, both of which opened in the early 1970s. The Chicago store was opened by current store owner Michael Powell, while the Portland store was opened by Walter Powell, Michael's father. In 1979, Michael joined his father in Portland, and together they began building the store into what it is today.

The City of Books is different from many other bookstores in that it shelves all its books, new and used, hardback or paperback, together, and with roughly three-quarters of a million new and used books on the shelves at any given time, the store had to give up trying to keep a computer inventory of what's in stock. This can be extremely frustrating if you're looking for an old or out-of-print title, but employees are good about searching the shelves for you, and if they don't have what you're looking for, they can try tracking a copy down. The up side of not being able to go straight to the book you're looking for is that you end up browsing.

Browsing is what Powell's is really all about. Once inside you can pick up a store map that will direct you to color-coded rooms containing different collections of books. In the Gold Room, you'll find science fiction and children's books; in the Rose Room, you'll find books on ornithology, civil aviation, Christian theology, and metaphysics among other subjects; in the Orange Room, there are books on art history, antiques, film, drama, and music. Serious book collectors won't want to miss a visit to the Rare Book Room, where you can buy a copy of a copy of the writing's of Cicero published by the Aldine Press in 1570. Of course, you'd need to read Latin. The most expensive book ever sold here was a Fourth Folio Shakespeare with archival repairs for $6,000.

It's so easy to forget the time while browsing at Powell's, that many customers miss meals and end up in the store's in-house cafe. The Anne Hughes Coffee Room serves espresso and pastries and is always packed with folks perusing books they've pulled from the shelves. This is also where Powell's keeps its extensive magazine rack. So, don't fret if you forgot to pack a lunch for your Powell's outing.

But wait, I forgot to mention that the City of Books outgrew this space and had to open a few satellite stores. There's Powell's Technical Bookstore, 33 NW Park St. (☎ 503/228-3906); Powell's Books for Cooks and Gardeners, 3739 SE Hawthorne Blvd. (☎ 503/235-3802); Powell's Travel Store, Pioneer Courthouse Square, SW Sixth Avenue and Yamhill Street (☎ 503/228-1108); Powell's Books at Cascade Plaza, 8775 SW Cascade Ave., Beaverton (☎ 503/643-3131); Powell's Books For Health, Legacy Emanuel Hospital, 501 N. Graham St. (☎ 503/413-2988); Powell's at PDX, Portland International Airport (☎ 503/249-1950); and several others.

Warning: Before stepping through Powell's door, check your watch. If you haven't got an hour of free time, you enter at your own risk. Getting lost in the miles of aisles has caused many a bibliophile to miss an appointment. Be prepared.

✪ **The Laura Russo Gallery.** 805 NW 21st Ave. ☎ **503/226-2754.**

The focus here is on Northwest contemporary artists. Talented emerging artists as well as the estates of well-known artists are showcased. Laura Russo has been on the Portland art scene for a long time and is highly respected.

Margo Jacobsen Gallery. 1039 NW Glisan St. ☎ **503/224-7287.**

In the heart of the Pearl District, this gallery is where you'll find most of the crowds milling about on First Thursdays. Margo Jacobsen promotes contemporary painters, with a focus on ceramics and glass.

Pulliam Deffenbaugh Gallery. 522 NW 12th Ave. ☎ **503/228-6665.**

Located next to the Quartersaw Gallery (see below), this gallery represents a long list of both talented newcomers and masters from the Northwest.

Quartersaw Gallery. 528 NW 12th Ave. ☎ **503/223-2264.**

With an emphasis on figurative and expressionistic landscape, Quartersaw is a showcase for progressive Northwest art. Located in the Pearl District.

✪ **Quintana Galleries.** 501 SW Broadway. ☎ **503/223-1729.**

This large bright space is virtually a small museum of Native American art, selling everything from Northwest Indian masks to contemporary painting and sculpture by various American Indian artists. The jewelry selection is outstanding. Prices, however, are not cheap.

AN ART GLASS GALLERY

✪ **The Bullseye Connection.** 1308 NW Everett St. ☎ **503/227-2797.**

Located in the Pearl District, the Bullseye Connection is a large open exhibition and sales space for glass artists, whose pieces include sculpture and delightful glass jewelry, paperweights, and marbles. My favorite piece here is the Dale Chihuly chandelier of pink erbium glass, a mass of glowing fruitlike objects. Workshops and lectures related to glass-making are given here.

CRAFTS

For the largest selection of local crafts, visit **Portland Saturday Market** (see "The Top Attractions" under "Attractions," earlier in this chapter, and "A Market," below). This entertaining outdoor market is a showcase for local crafts.

✪ **Contemporary Crafts Gallery.** 3934 SW Corbett Ave. ☎ **503/223-2654.**

In business since 1937, this is the nation's oldest nonprofit art gallery showing exclusively artwork in clay, glass, fiber, metal, and wood. It's located in a residential neighborhood between downtown and the John's Landing neighborhood, and has a spectacular tree-shaded porch overlooking the Willamette River. The bulk of the gallery is taken up by glass and ceramic pieces, with several cabinets of designer jewelry.

Graystone Gallery. 3279 SE Hawthorne Blvd. ☎ **503/238-0651.**

This gallery in the Southeast Hawthorne neighborhood is full of fun and whimsical artwork and home furnishings, including paintings, jewelry, furniture, and greeting cards.

Hoffman Gallery. 8245 SW Barnes Rd. ☎ **503/297-5544.**

The Hoffman Gallery is located on the campus of Oregon College of Art and Craft, which has been one of the nation's foremost crafts education centers since 1906. The gallery offers installations and group shows by local, national, and international artists. The adjacent gift shop has an outstanding selection of hand-crafted items. The grounds here are serene and relaxing, and there is also a cafe on the premises open to the public.

○ **The Real Mother Goose.** 901 SW Yamhill St. ☎ **503/223-9510.**

This is Portland's premier crafts shop. They showcase only the very finest contemporary American crafts, including imaginative ceramics, colorful art glass, intricate jewelry, exquisite wooden furniture, and sculptural works. Hundreds of craftspeople and artists from all over the United States are represented here. Other locations include Washington Square, Tigard (☎ 503/620-2243); and Portland International Airport, Main Terminal (☎ 503/284-9929).

DEPARTMENT STORES

Meier & Frank. 621 SW Fifth Ave. ☎ **503/223-0512.**

Meier & Frank is a Portland institution, doing business here for more than 100 years. Their flagship store on Pioneer Courthouse Square was built in 1898 and, with 10 stories, was at one time the tallest store in the Northwest. Today those 10 stories of consumer goods still attract crowds of shoppers. The store is open daily, with Friday usually the late night. Other locations include 1100 Lloyd Center (☎ **503/281-4797**) and 9300 SW Washington Square Rd. in Tigard (☎ **503/620-3311**).

Nordstrom. 701 SW Broadway. ☎ **503/224-6666.**

Directly across the street from Pioneer Courthouse Square and a block away from Meier & Frank, Nordstrom is a top-of-the-line department store that originated in the Northwest and takes great pride in its personal service and friendliness. There is even a pianist playing a baby grand to accompany shoppers on their rounds. Other Nordstoms in the area are at 1001 Lloyd Center (☎ **503/287-2444**) and 9700 SW Washington Square Rd. in Tigard (☎ **503/620-0555**).

FASHION

In addition to the Columbia and Nike outlet stores listed below, Adidas is planning to open a shoe and apparel outlet store at the corner of Northeast Martin Luther King Jr. Boulevard and Alberta Street.

Norm Thompson. 1805 NW Thurman St. ☎ **503/221-0764.**

Known throughout the rest of the country from its mail-order catalogs, Norm Thompson is a mainstay of the well-to-do in Portland. Classic styling for men and women is the name of the game here. A second store is at Portland International Airport (☎ **503/249-0170**).

The Portland Pendleton Shop. 900 SW Fifth Ave. (entrance is actually on Fourth Ave. between Salmon and Taylor). ☎ **503/242-0037.**

Pendleton wool is as much a part of life in the Northwest as forests and salmon. This company's fine wool fashions for men and women define the country-club look in the Northwest and in many other parts of the country. Pleated skirts and tweed jackets are de rigueur here, as are the colorful blankets that have helped keep generations of Northwesterners warm through long chilly winters.

Athletic & Outdoor Wear

Columbia Sportswear Company. 911 SW Broadway and Taylor St. ☎ **503/226-6800.**

This new flagship store is surprisingly low key, given that the nearby Nike flagship store and the new REI in Seattle are designed to knock your socks off. Displays showing the Columbia line of outdoor clothing are rustic, with lots of natural wood. The most dramatic architectural feature of the store is the entryway, in which a very wide tree trunk seemingly supports the roof, and a mini-video light show plays upon the floor.

Columbia Sportswear Company Outlet Store. 8128 SE 13th Ave. ☎ **503/238-0118.**

This outlet store in Sellwood (go over the Sellwood Bridge) sells well-made outdoor and sports clothing from one of the Northwest's premiere outdoor clothing manufacturer. Prices here are a lot less than in other retail stores.

Nike Factory Outlet. 3044 NE Martin Luther King Jr. Blvd. (³/₄ mile north of Broadway) ☎ **503/281-5901.**

The Nike outlet is one season behind the current season at Niketown, selling swoosh brand running, aerobic, tennis, golf, basketball, kids, and you-name-it sports clothing and accessories at discounted prices.

⭐ **Niketown.** 930 SW Sixth Ave. ☎ **503/221-6453.**

This superglitzy, ultracontempo showcase for Nike products blasted onto the Portland shopping scene with all the subtlety of a Super Bowl celebration. Matte black decor, George Segal–style plaster statues of athletes, and videos everywhere give Niketown the feel of a sports museum or disco. A true shopping experience.

Children's Clothing

Hanna Andersson. 327 NW Tenth Ave. (Pearl District). ☎ **800/222-0544** or 503/321-5275.

Based on Swedish designs with comfort and warmth in mind, Hanna's carries 100% cotton clothing in babies, kids, women, and unisex sizes. Striped Swedish long johns, snuggly baby suits, and girl's dresses are some of the things you'll see here.

Men's Clothing

Mario's. 921 SW Morrison St. ☎ **503/227-3477.**

Located inside the Galleria, Mario's sells self-consciously stylish European men's fashions straight off the pages of *GQ* and *M.* Prices are as high as you would expect. If you long to be European, but your birth certificate says otherwise, here you can at least adopt the look.

Women's Clothing

Changes. 927 SW Yamhill St. ☎ **503/223-3737.**

Located next door to The Real Mother Goose gallery, this shop specializes in handmade clothing, including hand-woven scarves, jackets, and shawls, hand-painted silks, and other wearable art.

⭐ **The Eye of Ra.** 5331 SW Macadam Ave. ☎ **503/224-4292.**

Women with sophisticated tastes in ethnic fashions will want to visit this pricey shop in The Water Tower at John's Landing shopping center. Silk and rayon predominate, and there is plenty of ethnic jewelry by creative designers to accompany any ensemble. Ethnic furniture and home decor are also for sale.

Mercantile. 735 SW Park St. (across the street from Nordstom). ☎ **503/223-6649.**

This specialty store for women carries modern classic clothing from blue jeans to black tie. Both European and American designers are represented, from Zannela Italian separates to the whimsical fashions of Nicole Miller. You'll find stylish purses, exquisite formal wear, and cashmere sweaters. The occasional sale yields some good selections at marked-down prices.

M. Sellin Ltd. 3556 SE Hawthorne Blvd. ☎ **503/239-4605.**

Located in the relaxed and low-key Hawthorne district, this shop carries women's clothes that feature natural fabrics, comfortable styling, and ethnic designs. There's also a good selection of jewelry at reasonable prices.

GIFTS/SOUVENIRS

For unique locally made souvenirs, your best bet is Portland Saturday Market (see "A Market," below, for details).

Made in Oregon. 921 SW Morrison St. (in the Galleria). ☎ **800/828-9673** or 503/241-3630.

This is your one-stop shop for all manner of made-in-Oregon gifts, food products, and clothing. Every product they sell is either grown, caught, or made in Oregon. This is the place to visit for salmon, filberts, jams and jellies, Pendleton woolens, and Oregon wines.

Other Portland area branches can be found in Portland International Airport's Main Terminal (☎ **503/282-7827**); in Lloyd Center, SE Multnomah St. and SE Broadway (☎ **503/282-7636**); and in Old Town at 10 NW First Ave. (☎ **503/ 273-8354**). All branches are open daily, but hours vary from store to store.

JEWELRY

❂ **Twist.** 30 NW 23rd Place. ☎ **503/224-0334.**

Twist showcases handmade jewelry from artists around the United States, from Thomas Mann techno-romantic jewelry to imaginative charm bracelets to hand-sculpted earrings. Surely you'll find a piece you'll want to wear every day. They also carry furniture, housewares, and pottery. Another store is located in Pioneer Place mall (☎ **503/222-3137**).

MALLS/SHOPPING CENTERS

The Galleria. 921 SW Morrison St. ☎ **503/228-2748.**

Located in the heart of downtown Portland, The Galleria is a three-story atrium shopping mall with more than 50 specialty shops and restaurants, including a Made in Oregon store. Before being restored and turned into its present incarnation, this building was one of Portland's earliest department stores. Parking validation available at adjacent parking garage.

Jantzen Beach Center. 1405 Jantzen Beach Center. ☎ **503/289-5555.**

This large shopping mall is located on the site of a former amusement park, and the old carousel still operates. There are four major department stores and more than 80 other shops. You'll also find the REI co-op recreational-equipment store here.

Lloyd Center. Bounded by SE Multnomah St., NE Broadway, NE 16th Ave., and NE Ninth Ave. ☎ **503/282-2511.**

Lloyd Center was the largest shopping mall on the West Coast when it opened in 1960. In 1991 an extensive renovation was completed to bring it up to current standards. There are 5 anchor stores and more than 200 specialty shops here, including a Nordstrom and a Meier & Frank. A food court, ice-skating rink, and eight-screen cinema complete the mall's facilities.

❂ **New Market Village.** 120 SW Ankeny St. ☎ **503/228-2392.**

Housed in a brick building built in 1872, this small shopping center is listed in the National Register of Historic Places. You'll find it directly across the street from the Skidmore Fountain and the Portland Saturday Market. A long row of freestanding archways salvaged from a demolished building creates a courtyard on one side of the New Market Village building.

✪ **Pioneer Place.** 700 SW Fifth Ave. ☎ **503/228-5800.**

Located only a block from Pioneer Courthouse Square, Portland's newest downtown shopping center is also its most upscale. Anchored by a Saks Fifth Avenue, Pioneer Place is where the elite shop when looking for high fashions and expensive gifts. You'll also find Portland's branch of the Nature Company and the city's only Godiva chocolatier here.

The Water Tower at John's Landing. 5331 SW Macadam Ave. ☎ **503/228-9431.**

As you're driving south from downtown Portland on Macadam Avenue, you can't miss the old wooden water tower for which this unusual shopping mall is named. Standing high above the roof of the mall, it was once used as a storage tank for fire-fighting water. Hardwood floors, huge overhead beams, and a tree-shaded courtyard paved with Belgian cobblestones from Portland's first paved streets give this place plenty of character. There are about 40 specialty shops and restaurants here.

A MARKET

✪ **Portland Saturday Market.** Underneath Burnside Bridge (between SW First Ave. and SW Ankeny St.). ☎ **503/222-6072.**

Portland Saturday Market (held on both Saturday and Sunday) is arguably the city's single most important and best-loved event. Every Saturday and Sunday nearly 300 craftspeople can be found selling their creations here. In addition to the dozens of crafts stalls, you'll find flowers, ethnic and unusual foods, and lots of free entertainment. This is the single best place to shop for one-of-a-kind gifts in Portland. At the heart of the Skidmore District, Portland Saturday Market makes an excellent starting or finishing point for a walk around Portland's most historic neighborhood. On Sunday, on-street parking is free. Open first weekend in March through Christmas Eve, Saturday 10am to 5pm, Sunday 11am to 4:30pm; closed January and February.

RECREATIONAL GEAR

Oregon Mountain Community (OMC). 60 NW Davis St. ☎ **503/227-1038.**

Located on the second floor in back of Import Plaza at the corner of Northeast First Avenue, OMC carries a large selection of Patagonia and other high-quality apparel, and everything from books about outdoor sports to backpacks, camping equipment, tents, and backcountry and telemarking ski equipment.

REI (Recreational Equipment Inc.). 1798 Jantzen Beach Center (☎ **503/283-1300**) and 7410 SW Bridgeport Rd., Tigard (☎ **503/624-8600**).

REI first began in the Northwest, and now has stores all over the country. They carry their own line of outdoor clothing, and other brands as well. You'll find just about anything you need here for mountaineering, hiking, camping, bicycling, and kayaking.

TOYS

✪ **Finnegan's Toys & Gifts.** 922 SW Yamhill St. ☎ **503/221-0306.**

Your inner child will be kicking and screaming in the aisles if you don't buy that silly little toy you never got when you were young. Kids love this place, too. It's the largest toy store in downtown Portland.

WINE

Harris Wine Cellars Ltd. 2300 NW Thurman St. ☎ **503/223-2222.**

Located at the northern and less fashionable end of Northwest 23rd Avenue, Harris Wine Cellars caters to serious wine connoisseurs, and has been doing so for many years. It isn't glamorous, but the folks here know their wine. Hearty lunches are also available. Open Monday through Saturday from 10am to 6pm.

Oregon Wines on Broadway. 515 SW Broadway (in Morgan's Alley). ☎ **503/228-4655.**

This cozy wine bar/shop is located diagonally across from the Hotel Vintage Plaza. Here you can taste Oregon's Pinot Noir, Chardonnay, Gewürztraminer, or other wines, and then buy a bottle or two.

13 Portland After Dark

Portland has become the Northwest's second cultural center. Its symphony orchestra, ballet, and opera are all well regarded, and the many theater companies offer classic and contemporary plays. If you are a jazz fan, you'll feel right at home—there's always a lot of live jazz being played around town. In summer, festivals move the city's cultural activities outdoors.

To find out what's going on during your visit, pick up a copy of *Willamette Week,* Portland's weekly arts-and-entertainment newspaper. You can also check the Friday A&E section and Sunday editions of the *Oregonian,* the city's daily newspaper.

Many theaters and performance halls in Portland offer discounts to students and senior citizens. You can often save money by buying your ticket on the day of a performance or within a half hour of curtain time.

Tickets for many of the venues listed below can be purchased through **GI Joe's/ TicketMaster** (☎ **503/790-2787** or 503/224-4400) or **Fastixx** at Fred Meyer (☎ **503/224-TIXX**).

THE PERFORMING ARTS

For the most part, the Portland performing arts scene revolves around the **Portland Center for the Performing Arts,** 1111 SW Broadway (☎ **503/248-4335**), which is comprised of four theaters in three different buildings. The **Arlene Schnitzer Concert Hall,** Southwest Broadway and Southwest Main Street, known locally as the Schnitz, is an immaculately restored 1920s movie palace that still displays the original Portland theater sign and marquee out front and is home to the Oregon Symphony. This hall also hosts popular music bands, lecturers, a travel-film series, and many other special performances. Free tours of the Schnitz are held Wednesday at 11am and Saturday at 11am, noon, and 1pm. Directly across Main Street from the Schnitz, at 1111 SW Broadway, is the sparkling glass jewel box known as the **New Theater Building.** This building houses both the **Intermediate** and **Winningstad** theaters. The Intermediate Theatre is home to Portland Center Stage, while the two theaters together host stage productions by local and visiting companies. Free tours of this building are offered Wednesday at 11am and Saturday at 11am, noon, and 1pm. A few blocks away from this concentration of venues is the 3,000-seat **Portland Civic Auditorium,** Southwest Third Avenue and Southwest Clay Street, the largest of the four halls and the home of the Portland Opera and the Oregon Ballet Theatre. In addition to resident companies mentioned above, these halls together host numerous visiting companies each year, including touring Broadway shows.

OPERA & CLASSICAL MUSIC

Founded in 1896, the **Oregon Symphony** (☎ **800/228-7343** or 503/228-1353), which performs at the Arlene Schnitzer Concert Hall, 1111 SW Broadway, is the oldest symphony orchestra on the West Coast, and under the expert baton of conductor James de Preist, it has achieved national recognition. Several series, including classical, pops, Sunday matinees, and children's concerts, are held during the September-to-June season. Ticket prices range from $10 to $50 (seniors and students may purchase half-price tickets one hour before a classical concert).

Each season, the **Portland Opera** (☎ **503/241-1802**), which performs at Portland Civic Auditorium at the corner of SW Third Avenue and SW Clay Street, offers five different productions of grand opera and musical theater. The season runs from September to May. Ticket prices range from $21 to $100 (students may attend dress rehearsals for a nominal charge).

Other classical music ensembles of note in Portland include the **Portland Baroque Orchestra** (☎ **503/222-6000**), which performs on period instruments at a couple of different Portland venues, and the **Portland Youth Philharmonic** (☎ **503/223-5939**), which is the oldest youth orchestra in the country and which showcases very talented musicians ages 10 to 23.

Summer is the time for Portland's annual chamber music binge. **Chamber Music Northwest** (☎ **503/223-3202**) is a 5-week-long series that starts in late June and attracts the world's finest chamber musicians. Performances are held at Reed College and Catlin Gable School.

THEATER

Portland Center Stage (☎ **503/274-6588**), which stages performances at the Portland Center for the Performing Arts, 1111 SW Broadway, is Portland's largest professional theater company. They stage a combination of five classic and contemporary plays during their October-to-April season. Ticket prices range from $11 to $35.

Portland's oldest Equity theater, the **Portland Repertory Theater,** World Trade Center, 25 SW Salmon St. (☎ **503/224-4491**), offers consistently excellent productions, and is acclaimed for its presentations ranging from off-Broadway hit comedies to world-premiere dramas by contemporary American and British playwrights. Ticket prices range from $25 to $27 ($20 previews).

The play's the thing at **Tygres Heart Shakespeare Co.** (☎ **503/222-9220**), which performs at the Dolores Winningstad Theatre, 1111 SW Broadway, and old Will would be proud. Tygres Heart remains true to its name and stages only works by the bard himself. Ticket prices range from $8 to $25.

If its musicals you want, you've got plenty of options in Portland. At Civic Auditorium, you can catch the latest touring Broadway show thanks to the **Portland's Broadway Theater Season** (☎ **503/241-1407**). Also at the Civic, you can catch older, more tried and true shows courtesy of the **U.S. Bank Broadway Series** (☎ **503/228-9571**). For other classics from Broadway's past, check the schedule of the **Musical Theatre Company** (☎ **503/224-8730**), a semiprofessional company that performs at the Intermediate Theatre.

For more daring theater productions, see what's on tap at the **Artists Repertory Theater,** 1111 SW Tenth Ave. (☎ **503/294-7373**); the **Main Street Playhouse,** 904 SW Main St. (☎ **503/282-9303**); the **Stark Raving Theater,** 4319 SE Hawthorne Blvd. (☎ **503/232-7072**); or the **Miracle Theater,** 525 SE Stark St. (☎ **503/236-7253**).

DANCE

Although the **Oregon Ballet Theatre** (☎ 503/222-5538), which performs at the Portland Civic Auditorium, is best loved for its sold-out performances each December of *The Nutcracker,* this company also stages the annual American Choreographers Showcase. This latter performance often features world premieres. Rounding out the season are performances of classic and contemporary ballets. Ticket prices range from $10 to $65.

Imago, 17 SE Eighth Ave. (☎ 503/231-9581), uses a variety of unusual masks and outlandish costumes to produce strange and whimsical performance pieces. Each number they do is a cross between vaudeville, carnival, theater, and dance. A national reputation keeps the company on the road much of the year, but devoted fans here at home never miss one of the outrageous performances. Tickets are $15 for adults, $12 for students and seniors, and $8 for children.

PERFORMANCE ART

When funding for performance art disappeared in Portland, the **Portland Institute for Contemporary Art,** also known as PICA (☎ 503/242-1419), was created as a resource for exploring and supporting experimental art and new music in the city. Using various venues around the city, PICA presents innovative performances by well-known artists such as Philip Glass, Karen Finley, Spalding Gray, as well as by less established performance artists and musicians. PICA also presents visual exhibitions focusing on contemporary trends in the regional, national, and international art scene. Call for current schedule. Ticket prices range from $12 to $20.

SUMMER CONCERT SERIES

When summer hits, Portlanders like to head outdoors to hear music. Most of this music is popular rock, reggae, jazz, blues, and folk, and most of these series schedule enough variety over the summer that they'll eventually appeal to almost every music listener in the city.

Outdoor music series to check on in the summer include the **Washington Park Rose Garden Concerts** (David Byrne, Soul Coughing, Shawn Colvin, Calobo, and Taj Mahal in 1997) over Labor Day weekend; **Music by Blue Lake** at Blue Lake Park east of downtown Portland near the airport (local acts; ☎ 503/797-1850); and **Rhythm & Zoo Concerts** at Washington Park Zoo Amphitheater (Richard Thompson, The Bobs, Karla Bonoff, Booker T. Jones, Michele Schocked in 1997; ☎ 503/226-1561).

THE CLUB & MUSIC SCENE
FOLK & ROCK

Aladdin Theater. 3017 SE Milwaukee Ave. ☎ 503/233-1994. Tickets $10–$20.

This former movie theater now serves as one of Portland's main venues for touring performers from a very diverse musical spectrum that includes blues, rock, ethnic, country, folk, and jazz.

Berbati's Pan. 231 SW Ankeny St. ☎ 503/248-4579. Cover $2–$7.

Located in Old Town and affiliated with a popular Greek restaurant, this is currently one of Portland's most popular rock clubs. A wide variety of acts, often those on the verge of breaking into the national limelight, play here.

✪ Crystal Ballroom. 1332 West Burnside St. ☎ 503/225-0047. Cover free to $10.

The Crystal Ballroom has a long and not-so-illustrious history. It first opened before 1920, and since then has seen performers from the early jazz scene to The Grateful

Dead. The McMenamin Brothers (of local brewing fame) have now renovated the Crystal Ballroom and refurbished its dance floor, which due to its mechanics actually floats. The ballroom is now host to a variety of performances and special events nearly every night of the week. A brewery and Ringlers Pub round out the complex.

Key Largo. 31 NW First Ave. ☎ **503/223-9919.** Cover $3–$9 (sometimes higher for national acts).

One of Portland's most popular nightclubs, Key Largo has been packing in music fans for more than a decade. A tropical atmosphere prevails at this spacious club and basic American food is served. Rock, reggae, blues, and jazz performers all find their way to the stage here, with local R&B bands a mainstay. A nationally known act occasionally shows up here. Open nightly.

La Luna. 215 SE Ninth Ave. ☎ **503/241-5862.** Cover $6.50–$18.

The stage at La Luna is in a cavernous room with a ceiling so high that the cigarette smoke doesn't get too bad. Here you can catch a wide range of lesser-known national acts for a reasonable price. The club also includes a small cafe where you can get a snack between the acts, and a lounge with a pool table upstairs.

Laurelthirst. 2958 NE Glisan St. ☎ **503/232-1504.** Cover $2–$3.

Basically just a neighborhood pub, the Laurelthirst is well known in Portland as the city's best place to hear live bluegrass and folk music. With the recent resurgence of interest in bluegrass, this place is more popular than ever. There's free live music at happy hour and then more music later in the evening.

JAZZ & BLUES

Brasserie Montmartre. 626 SW Park Ave. ☎ **503/224-5552.** No cover.

There's live jazz nightly from 8:30pm at this French restaurant. Both food and music are popular with a primarily middle-aged clientele that likes to dress up when it goes out on the town.

Jazz De Opus. 33 NW Second Ave. ☎ **503/222-6077.** $5 cover on weekends; 50¢ surcharge on drinks other nights.

This restaurant/bar has long been one of Portland's bastions of jazz, with a cozy room and smooth jazz on the stereo. You can also catch live jazz performances nightly.

The Green Room. 2280 NW Thurman St. ☎ **503/228-6178.** No cover.

Located just around the corner from Northwest 23rd Avenue, this is a classic backstreets blues bar. Little more than a local bar, this nondescript place books the best of the local blues brothers and sisters.

Parchman Farm. 1204 SE Clay St. ☎ **503/235-7831.** Cover $2 Fri–Sat.

If you're into blues, Parchman Farm is a good place to hang out. There's live music nightly Monday through Saturday starting about 9pm, and if you're hungry you can order a gourmet pizza or prime rib from the menu.

COMEDY & CABARET

ComedySportz Arena. 1963 NW Kearney St. ☎ **503/236-8888.** Cover $7.

This is the home of the ever-popular ComedySportz improv comedy troupe. Shows are Friday and Saturday nights and the nature of the beast is that you never know what to expect. Have fun.

Darcelle's XV. 208 NW Third Ave. ☎ **503/222-5338.** Cover $8. Reservations recommended Fri–Sat.

This is a campy Portland institution with a female-impersonator show that has been a huge hit for years. Shows are Wednesday and Thursday at 8:30pm and Friday and Saturday at 8:30 and 10:30pm.

DANCE CLUBS

In addition to the clubs listed here, there is dancing several nights a week at **Bar 71.** See below for details.

Red Sea. 318 SW Third Ave. ☎ **503/241-5450.** Cover $4.

By day this is an Ethiopian restaurant, but by night it's the busiest Afro-Caribbean dance club in Portland. The dance floor is small and the place gets hot, but the music, a mix of Afro-pop, reggae, and calypso is imminently danceable. There's live reggae on Thursday nights.

✪ **Rock 'n' Rodeo.** 220 SE Spokane St. ☎ **503/235-2417.** Cover $5 after 8:30pm.

If you're a fan of Western line dancing, West Coast swing, or the two-step (or you just want to learn), join the fun at Rock 'n' Rodeo where a 1-hour lesson will cost only a buck. Lessons start at 7pm nightly. Afterward, this place becomes a swirl of cowboy boots, skirts, and tight jeans.

GAY DANCE CLUBS

Embers. 110 NW Broadway. ☎ **503/222-3082.** Cover Thurs $2, Fri–Sat $3.

Though this is still primarily a gay disco, straights have discovered its great dance music and have started making the scene as well. Lots of flashing lights and sweaty bodies until the early morning. There are drag shows 7 nights a week.

Panorama. 341 SW Tenth Ave. ☎ **503/221-7262.** Cover Fri-Sat $4 before 2am, $6 after 2am.

Open only on Friday and Saturday, Panorama is a large dance club playing currently popular dance music. It's connected to The Brig, a smaller dance club, and Boxes, a video club. The admission allows you into all three. With several different environments and a mixed crowd, an evening here can be quite entertaining. The crowd is mostly gay.

THE BAR & BREW PUB SCENE
BARS

✪ **Atwater's Restaurant and Bar.** 111 SW Fifth Ave. ☎ **503/275-3600.**

Up on the 30th floor of the pale-pink U.S. Bancorp Tower is one of Portland's most expensive restaurants and certainly the one with the best view. However, if you'd just like to sit back and sip a martini while gazing out at the city lights below, you can do so at the splendid bar. Perfect for a romantic nightcap. Thursday through Saturday evenings there is live jazz. The lounge menu here is one of the most creative in Portland.

✪ **Bar 71.** 71 SW Second Ave. ☎ **503/241-0938.** Cover $1–$5 for dance club.

Hands down the most romantic bar in town, this is the perfect place to sip a blue martini while snuggled up on the maroon velvet sofa with the one you love. Attached to a French restaurant, Bar 71 has great bar food, and Thursday through Sunday, there's an open-air dance patio out back.

Gypsy. 625 NW 21st Ave. ☎ **503/796-1859.**

This is Portland's premier lounge scene with a classic Sputnik-era decor and martinis to match. This is retro, not the real thing, and has been somewhat upgraded for

Portland's Brewing Up a Microstorm

Though espresso is the drink that drives Portland, it is to the city's dozens of brew pubs that educated beer drinkers head when they want to relax over a flavorful pint of ale. No other city in America has as great a concentration of brew pubs, and it was here that the craft brewing business got its start in the mid-1980s. Today, brew pubs continue to proliferate with cozy neighborhood pubs vying for business with big, polished establishments.

To fully appreciate what the city's craft brewers are concocting, it helps to have a little beer background. There are four basic ingredients in beer: malt, hops, yeast, and water. The first of these, malt, is made from grains, primarily barley and wheat, which are roasted to convert their carbohydrates into the sugar needed to grow yeast. The amount of roasting the grains receive during the malting process will determine the color and flavor of the final product. The darker the malt, the darker and more flavorful the beer or ale. There is a wide variety of malts, each providing its own characteristic flavor. Yeast in turn converts the malt's sugar into alcohol. There are many different strains of yeast that all lend different characters to beers. The hops are added to give beer its characteristic bitterness. The more "hoppy" the beer or ale, the more bitter it becomes. The Northwest happens to be the nation's only commercial hop-growing region with 75% being grown in Washington and 25% being grown in Oregon and Idaho.

Pilsners are the most common beers in America and are made from pale malt with a lot of hops added to give them their characteristic bitter flavor. Lagers are made in much the same way as pilsners but are cold-fermented, which gives them a distinctive flavor. Ales, which are the most common brews served at microbreweries, are made using a warm fermentation process and usually more and darker malt than is used in lagers and pilsners. Porters and stouts get their characteristic dark coloring and flavor from the use of dark, even charred, malt.

To these basics, you can then add a few variables. Fruit-flavored beers, which some disparage as soda-pop beer, are actually an old European tradition and when considering the preponderance of fresh fruits in the Northwest, are a natural. If you see a sign for nitro beer in a pub, it doesn't mean they've got explosive brews, it means they've got a keg charged with nitrogen instead of carbon dioxide for an extracreamy head. A nitro charge is why Guinness Stout is so distinctive. Cask-conditioned ales, served almost room temperature and with only their own carbon dioxide to create the head, are also gaining in popularity. While some people think these brews are flat, others appreciate them for their unadulterated character. What this all adds up to is a lot of variety in Portland pubs. Cheers!

the '90s. The small bar through the velvet-covered door from the restaurant is generally livelier than the main bar.

The Lobby Court. The Benson, 309 SW Broadway. ☎ **503/228-2000.**

If you never knew cigars or martinis ever went out of fashion, this is the bar for you. The Circassian walnut paneling and crystal chandeliers make this the classiest bar in town. Several nights a week there's live jazz.

Jake's Famous Crawfish. 401 SW 12th Ave. ☎ **503/226-1419.**

Although Jake's is best known for its crawfish, the bar is one of the busiest in town when the downtown offices let out. In business since 1892, Jake's has the most historic feel of any bar in town. Definitely not to be missed.

McCormick & Schmick's Pilsner Room. 0309 SW Montgomery St. ☎ **503/220-1865.**

Located at the south end of Tom McCall Waterfront Park overlooking the Willamette River and RiverPlace Marina, the Pilsner Room keeps more than 20 local microbrews on tap, but it also does a brisk cocktail business. The crowd is upscale and the view is one of the best in town.

BREW PUBS

If you're a beer connoisseur, you'll probably find yourself with little time out from your brew tasting to see any other of Portland's sights. This is the heart of the North-west craft brewing explosion and has more microbreweries and craft breweries (microbreweries are smaller) than any other city in the United States. They're brewing beers up here the likes of which you won't taste anywhere else this side of the Atlantic.

✪ Bridgeport Brewery & Brew Pub. 1313 NW Marshall St. ☎ **503/241-7179.**

Portland's oldest microbrewery was founded in 1984, and is housed in the city's old-est industrial building (where workers once produced rope for sailing ships). The brewery has four to seven of its brews on tap on any given night (including several cask-conditioned ales), and live music on the first Thursday of the month. They make great pizza here, too—the crust is made with wort, a byproduct of the brewing process.

Lucky Labrador Pub. 915 SE Hawthorne Blvd. ☎ **503/236-3555.**

With a warehouse-size room, industrial feel, and picnic tables on the loading dock out back, this brew pub is classic southeast Portland. The crowd is young and dogs (not just Labradors) are welcome.

✪ Ringlers Pub. 1332 West Burnside St. ☎ **503/225-0543.**

Located almost across the street from the huge Weinhard Brewery, this cavernous pub is filled with big old signs and Indonesian antiques. Mosaic pillars frame the bar and there are big booths as well as cozy cafe tables. A block away are two other associ-ated pubs, one below street level that has a beer cellar feel and the other in a flat-iron building. Together these three pubs offer the most atmospheric ale houses in town. This is one of the newest McMenamin brothers' microbrewery outposts, which now includes more than 30 pubs in the greater Portland metropolitan area and beyond. The McMenamins pride themselves in crafting flavorful and unusual ales with bizarre names like Terminator Stout and Purple Haze. Some of their other area pubs include the **Blue Moon Tavern,** 432 NW 21st St. (☎ 503/223-3184), on a fashionable street in northwest Portland; **The Ram's Head,** 2282 NW Hoyt St. (☎ **503/221-0098**), between 21st and 22nd avenues; and ✪ **Cornelius Pass Roadhouse,** Sunset Highway and Cornelius Pass Road, Hillsboro (☎ **503/640-6174**), in an old farmhouse.

Widmer Brewing and Gasthaus. 955 N. Russell St. ☎ **503/281-3333.**

Located in an industrial area just north of the Rose Garden arena, this place has the feel of a classic workingman's pub. This is the brewery for Portland's largest craft brewing company, which is best known for its hefeweizen. German food is served.

GAY BARS

The area around the intersection of Southwest Stark Street and West Burnside Street has the largest concentration of gay bars in Portland. These include **C.C. Slaughter's,** 1014 SW Stark St. (☎ **503/248-9135**); **Eagle Tavern,** 1300 W. Burnside St. (☎ **503/241-0105**); **Scandal's Tavern,** 1038 SW Stark St. (☎ **503/227-5887**);

and **Silverado,** 1217 SW Stark St. (☎ **503/244-4493**). Also in this same area, at the corner of Stark Street and 10th Avenue is **Panorama** (☎ **503/221-RAMA**), a dance club popular with both gays and straights.

MOVIES

Portland brew pub magnates the McMenamin brothers have hit upon a novel way to sell their craft ales, in movie pubs. Although it's often hard to concentrate on the movies being screened, it's always a lot of fun to attend a show. The **Bagdad Theater & Pub,** 3702 SE Hawthorne Blvd. (☎ **503/230-0895**), a restored classic Arabian Nights movie palace shows second-run films and pours more than 20 microbrews at the bar. There's good pizza by the slice to go with your brew and a separate nontheater pub.

The **Mission Theater & Pub,** 1624 NW Glisan St. (☎ **503/223-4031**), was the McMenamin brothers' first theater pub. Movies are recent releases that have played the main theaters already but not yet made it onto video.

Located in the heart of downtown, the **Koin Center**, Third Avenue and Clay Street (☎ **503/243-3516**), a six-plex, is Portland's main theater for first-run, foreign, _____ _____ndent films. Buy tickets early, screening rooms here are small and often ____ **Northwest Film Center,** 1219 SW Park Ave. (☎ **503/221-1156**), ____ith the Portland Art Museum, is a repertory cinema that schedules an ____nd of classics, foreign films, daring avant-garde films, documentaries, ____ic series.

___de Trip to Oregon City & the End ___he Oregon Trail

____irst white settlers began crossing the Oregon Trail in the early 1840s, their ___ was Oregon City and the fertile Willamette Valley. At the time Portland ___be founded and Oregon City, set beside powerful Willamette Falls, was ___town in Oregon. However, with the development of Portland and the ___he capital to Salem, Oregon City began to lose its importance. Today this ___an industrial town, though one steeped in Oregon history and well worth

___o Oregon City from Portland, you can take I-5 south to I-205 east or you ___outh from downtown Portland on Southwest Riverside Drive and drive ___e wealthy suburbs of Lake Oswego and West Linn. Once in Oregon City, ___op should be just south of town at the **Willamette Falls overlook** on Ore. ___gh the falls have been much changed by industry over the years, they are ___ressive sight.

___City is divided into upper and lower sections by a steep bluff. A **free mu-** ___**vator** connects the two halves of the city and affords a great view from its ___ area at the top of the bluff. You'll find the 100-foot-tall elevator at the ___eventh Street and Railroad Avenue. Service is available from 6am to 8pm ___n the upper section of town that you will find the town's many **historic**

___City's most famous citizen was retired Hudson's Bay Company chief factor John McLoughlin, who helped found Oregon City in 1829. By the 1840s, immigrants were pouring into Oregon, and McLoughlin provided food, seeds, and tools to many. Upon retirement in 1846, McLoughlin moved to Oregon City, where he built what was at that time the most luxurious home in Oregon. Today the **McLoughlin House,** 713 Center St. (☎ **503/656-5146**), is a National Historic Site

"MERE CHRISTIANITY" by C.S. LEWIS shows which belief system is the most logical. "TO HELL AND BACK" by Dr. M. RAWLINGS – Half of his flatliners had very negative after-life experiences.

and is open to the public. The house is furnished as it would have been in McLoughlin's days and includes many original pieces. The house is open Tuesday through Saturday from 10am to 5pm (4pm in winter) and on Sunday from 1 to 4pm. Admission is $3 for adults, $2.50 for senior citizens, and $1 for children.

Several other Oregon City historical homes are also open to the public. The **Clackamas County Historical Museum,** 211 Tumwater Dr. (☎ 503/655-5574), houses collections of historic memorabilia and old photos from this area. The museum is open Monday through Friday from 10am to 4pm and Saturday and Sunday from 1 to 5pm. Admission is $3.50 for adults, $2.50 for senior citizens and $1.50 for children ages 6 to 12. The **Stevens Crawford House,** 603 Sixth St. (☎ 503/655-2866), is a foursquare-style home and is furnished with late 19th-century antiques. The house is open Tuesday through Sunday from 10am to 4pm (plus Monday from 1 to 4pm in summer). Admission is $3 adults, $2 seniors, and $1.50 children 6 to 12. The **Ermatinger House,** on the corner of Sixth and John Adams streets (☎ 503/557-9199), is the town's oldest home. The hours are Saturday and Sunday from noon to 4pm. Admission is $2 for adults.

The story of the settlers who traveled the Oregon Trail is told at the **End of the Oregon Trail Interpretive Center,** 1726 Washington St. (☎ 503/657-9336), which is designed to resemble three giant covered wagons. The center is open Monday through Saturday from 9am to 5pm and Sunday from 11am to 5pm; admission is $4.50 for adults, $2.50 for seniors and children 5 to 12. There are guided tours. During the summer of 1998 and thereafter, the history of the Oregon Trail will come alive at the interpretive center with the staging of the *Oregon Trail Pageant.* Performances are in July and early August.

Another interesting chapter in Oregon pioneer history is preserved 13 miles south of Oregon City in the town of **Aurora,** which was founded in 1855 as a Christian communal society. Similar in many ways to more famous communal experiments such as the Amana Colony and the Shaker communities, the Aurora Colony lasted slightly more than 20 years. Today Aurora is a National Historic District and the large old homes of the community's founders have been restored. Many of the old commercial buildings now house **antique stores,** which are the main reason most people visit the town. You can learn about the history of Aurora at the **Old Aurora Colony Museum,** on the corner of Second and Liberty streets (☎ 503/678-5754). Between March and December, the museum is open Tuesday through Saturday from 10am to 4pm and on Sunday from noon to 4pm. Admission is $3.50 for adults, $3 for seniors, and $1.50 for children under 18.

On your way back to Portland, consider taking the **Canby ferry,** which is one of the last remaining ferries on the Willamette River. To take the ferry head 4 miles north on Oreg. 99E to Canby and watch for ferry signs.

7

The Willamette Valley: The Bread & Wine Basket of Oregon

For more than 150 miles, from south of Eugene to the Columbia River at Portland, the Willamette River (pronounced Wih-*lam*-it) flows between Oregon's two major mountain ranges. Protected from winter winds by the Cascade Range to the east and tempered by cool moist air flowing off the Pacific Ocean, which lies to the west on the far side of the Coast Range, the Willamette Valley enjoys a mild climate that belies its northerly latitudes. It was along the banks of the Willamette that Oregon's first towns sprang up, and today the valley is home to Oregon's largest cities, its most productive farmlands, the state capital, and the state's two major universities.

The Willamette Valley was the Eden at the end of the Oregon Trail, a fabled land of rich soils, mild winters, and plentiful rains. Families were willing to walk 2,000 miles across the continent for a chance at starting a new life. The valley became the breadbasket of the Oregon country, and today, despite the urban sprawl of Portland, Salem, and Eugene, the Willamette Valley still produces an agricultural bounty unequaled in its diversity. Although the region offers history and culture, its idyllic rural scenery and prolific farms are what enchant most visitors. Throughout the year, you can sample the produce of this region at farms, fruit stands, and wineries. In spring, commercial fields of tulips and irises paint the landscape with bold swaths of color. In summer, there are farm stands near almost every town, and many farms will let you pick your own strawberries, raspberries, blackberries, peaches, apples, cherries, and plums. In the autumn, you can sample the filbert and walnut harvest, and at any time of year, you can do a bit of wine tasting at dozens of wineries.

1 The Wine Country

McMinnville: 38 miles SW of Portland, 26 miles NW of Salem

If it hadn't been for Prohibition, wine connoisseurs might be comparing California wines to those of Oregon rather than vice versa. Oregon wines had already gained a national reputation when the state voted in Prohibition. It would be a few years before more liberal California would outlaw alcohol, and in the interim, the Golden State got the upper hand. Oregon wines didn't begin to make themselves known again until the 1970s, but by then Napa Valley was well established. Perhaps someday Willamette Valley wineries will be as well known—in fact, they're already winning awards. Oregon

Pinot Noirs have gained such international attention that even some French wineries have planted vineyards here and begun producing their own Oregon wines.

The Willamette Valley is on the same latitude as the great wine regions of France and the weather is quite similar—plenty of spring rains, then long, hot summer days and cool nights. Unfortunately, wineries here must contend with the potential specter of dark clouds and early autumn rains. These rains can sometimes wreak havoc on Willamette Valley wines, but most years, the grapes get harvested before the rains begin to fall.

The Yamhill County wine country begins in the town of Newberg, home to George Fox College, a Quaker school. However, the heart of the region is really the town of Dundee, above which are the Red Hills that produce some of the area's best wines. This is also where you'll find some of the best area restaurants. McMinnville, which is home to Linfield College, a small liberal arts college with an attractive campus, is the largest town in wine country and anchors the western end of the region. You'll find more good restaurants here.

ESSENTIALS

GETTING THERE   You'll find the heart of wine country between Newberg and McMinnville along Ore. 99W, which heads southwest out of Portland.

VISITOR INFORMATION   Contact the **Greater McMinnville Chamber of Commerce,** 417 N. Adams St., McMinnville, OR 97128 (☎ **503/472-6196**), or the **Newberg Area Chamber of Commerce,** 115 N. Washington St., Newberg, OR 97132 (☎ **503/538-2014**).

FESTIVALS   The most prestigious festival of the year is the **International Pinot Noir Celebration** (☎ **800/775-4762**), held each year on the last weekend in July or first weekend in August. The 3-day event, which is usually sold out months in advance, includes tastings, food, music, and seminars. Registration forms are mailed out in February each year. At the **Vintage Festival** in Newberg each September, vintage cars, airplanes, motorcycles, bicycles, and boats are on display. Admission is $6 each day.

TOURING THE WINERIES

Heading southwest from Portland on Ore. 99W, you soon leave the urban sprawl behind and enter the rolling farm country of Yamhill County. These hills, on the north side of the Willamette Valley, provide almost ideal conditions for growing wine grapes, and a patchwork quilt of vineyards, interspersed with orchards and woodlands, now blankets the slopes. The views from these hills take in the Willamette Valley's fertile farmlands as well as the snowcapped peaks of the Cascades. Between Newberg and McMinnville, you'll find more than 20 wineries and tasting rooms, and if you wander off the main highway, you'll find still more wineries and vineyards to the north near Hillsboro and Forest Grove and to the south around Salem. Wines produced at these vineyards include Pinot Noir, Pinot Gris, Chardonnay, Gewürztraminer, Riesling, Muller-Thurgau, and several sparkling wines.

Most, but not all, wineries maintain tasting rooms that are open to the public, usually between 11am or noon and 5pm. During the summer, most tasting rooms are open daily, but in other months they may be open only on weekends or by appointment. However, many of the best wineries are only open a couple of weekends a year, usually Memorial Day weekend and Thanksgiving weekend. If you're serious about your wine, the best thing to do is contact several of the smaller wineries that are only open by appointment and set up a tour of some of the region's lesser known

The Willamette Valley

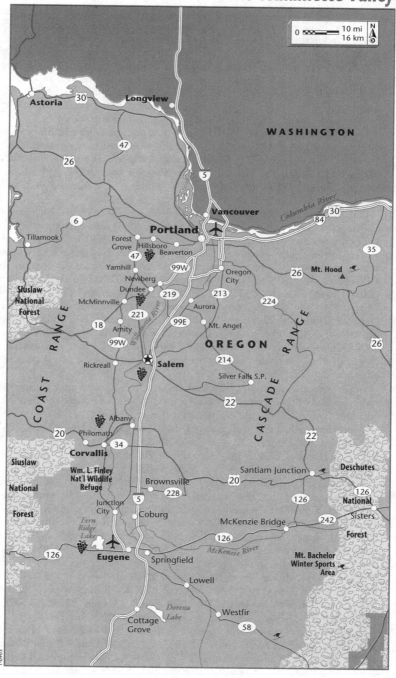

0 — 10 mi
16 km

N

WASHINGTON

OREGON

COAST RANGE

CASCADE RANGE

Astoria

Longview

30

47

26

6

Tillamook

Forest Grove

Hillsboro

Beaverton

Yamhill

Newberg

Dundee

McMinnville

Amity

Rickreall

Salem

Albany

Philomath

Corvallis

Wm. L. Finley Nat'l Wildlife Refuge

Junction City

Coburg

Brownsville

Eugene

Springfield

Lowell

Cottage Grove

Westfir

Vancouver

Portland

Oregon City

Aurora

Mt. Angel

Silver Falls S.P.

Santiam Junction

McKenzie Bridge

Sisters

Mt. Hood

Mt. Bachelor Winter Sports Area

Siuslaw National Forest

Siuslaw National Forest

Deschutes National Forest

Columbia River

Willamette River

McKenzie River

Fern Ridge Lake

Dorena Lake

5

84

30

35

26

26

99W

219

213

224

221

18

99W

99E

214

22

22

20

34

20

228

126

126

126

126

242

58

1-0903

wineries. For the dilettante, an afternoon of wine tasting can be a very educational experience, while for the oenophile, it provides a chance to uncover some rare gems. If you're interested, you're almost always welcome to tour the facilities.

Many wineries also have a few picnic tables, so if you bring some goodies with you and then pick up a bottle of wine, you'll be set for a great picnic. At some wineries, you'll be asked to pay a tasting fee, and at others the selections of the day can be sampled free while other vintages can be sampled for a few dollars. Still other wineries charge for sampling any premium reserve wines. Many wineries have celebrations, festivals, music performances, and picnics throughout the summer.

For more information about the Oregon wine scene, including a calendar of winery events, pick up a copy of *Oregon Wine,* a monthly newspaper, in any local wine shop, or contact the **Oregon Wine Press,** 644 SE 20th Ave., Portland, OR 97214 (☎ **503/232-7607**). The **Yamhill County Wineries Association,** P.O. Box 871, McMinnville, OR 97218 (☎ **503/434-5814**), publishes a free map and guide to the local wineries. You can pick up copies at any winery.

Ore. 99W as it passes through the towns of Newberg, Dundee, and McMinnville has become something of a wine alley and is slowly taking on the trappings of Napa Valley: big wineries with big parking lots, big crowds, and often (but not always) mediocre wines. These wineries specialize in snagging beach-bound traffic. Wineries with tasting rooms right on or just off the highway include, from east to west: **Rex Hill Vineyards,** 30835 N. Ore. 99W, Newberg (☎ 503/538-0666); **Duck Pond Cellars,** 23145 Ore. 99W, Dundee (☎ 503/538-3199); **Argyle,** 691 Ore. 99W, Dundee (☎ 503/538-8520); **Sokol Blosser Winery,** 5000 Sokol Blosser Lane, Dundee (☎ 503/864-2282); and **Yamhill Valley Vineyards,** 16250 Oldsville Rd., McMinnville (☎ 800/825-4845). One other winery, **Champoeg Wine Cellars,** 10375 Champoeg Rd. NE, Aurora (☎ 503/678-2144), is located southeast of Newberg several miles, and while not right on the highway, is best visited along with other wineries along Ore. 99W.

North and south of the Ore. 99W corridor, you'll find several more groupings of wineries. Each of these groupings makes a good day's tasting route and have been organized here so that you can easily link them together as such.

Wineries in the Red Hills just north of Dundee include **Torii Mor Winery,** 18325 NE Fairview Dr., Dundee (☎ 503/434-1439); **Lange Winery,** 18380 NE Buena Vista Rd., Dundee (☎ 503/538-6476); **Erath Vineyards,** 9009 NE Worden Hill Road, Dundee (☎ 800/539-9463 or 503/538-3318); and **Wine Country Farm Cellars,** 6855 Breyman Orchards Rd., Dayton (☎ 800/261-3446 or 503/864-3446).

Wineries south of Ore. 99W that make a good assortment for an afternoon's tasting include **Kristin Hill Winery,** 3330 SE Amity-Dayton Hwy., Amity (☎ 503/835-0850); **Amity Vineyards,** 18150 Amity Vineyards Rd. SE, Amity (☎ 503/835-2362); **Cuneo Cellars,** 9360 SE Eola Hills Rd., Amity (☎ 503/835-2782); and **Stangeland Winery,** 8500 Hopewell Rd. NW, Salem (☎ 503/581-0355).

Between McMinnville and Forest Grove, off of Ore. 47, you'll find **Château Benoit,** 6580 NE Mineral Springs Rd., Carlton (☎ 800/248-4835 or 503/864-2991); **Autumn Wind Vineyard,** 15225 NE North Valley Rd., Newberg (☎ 503/538-6931); **Elk Cove Vineyards,** 27751 NW Olson Rd., Gaston (☎ 503/985-7760); and **Kramer Vineyards,** 26830 NW Olson Rd. Gaston (☎ 503/662-4545).

In the vicinity of the town of Forest Grove, you'll find **Montinore Vineyards,** 3663 SW Dilley Rd., Forest Grove (☎ 503/359-5012); **Laurel Ridge Winery,** 46350 David Hill Rd., Forest Grove (☎ 503/359-5436); **Shafer Vineyard Cellars,** 6200 NW Gales Creek Rd., Forest Grove (☎ 503/357-6604); and **Tualatin Vineyards,** NW 10850 Seavey Rd., Forest Grove (☎ 503/357-5005). Also in this area, you'll find the **Momokawa Sake Brewery,** 820 Elm St. (☎ 503/357-7056), which produces sake rice wine here and also sells premium sakes imported from Japan.

Just outside the town of Hillsboro, you'll find **Oak Knoll Winery,** 29700 SW Burkhalter Rd., Hillsboro (☎ 503/648-8198); **Ponzi Vineyards,** 14665 SW Winery Lane, Beaverton (☎ 503/628-1227); and **Cooper Mountain Vineyards,** 9480 SW Grabhorn Rd., Beaverton (☎ 503/649-0027).

Area wineries that are open on Memorial Day and/or Thanksgiving weekends only or by appointment include **Adelsheim Vineyard,** 22150 NE Quarter Mile Lane, Newberg (☎ 503/538-3652); **Archery Summit,** 18599 NE Archery Summit Rd., Dundee (☎ 503/864-4300); **Cameron Winery,** 8200 Worden Hill Rd., Dundee (☎ 503/538-0336); **Chehalem,** 31190 NE Veritas Lane, Newberg (☎ 503/538-1470); **The Eyrie Vineyards,** P.O. Box 697, Dundee (☎ 503/472-6315); **Panther Creek Cellars,** 455 N Irvine Rd., McMinnville (☎ 503/472-5667); **Ken Wright Cellars,** 338 W. Main St., Carlton (☎ 503/852-7070); **Willakenzie Estate,** 19143 NE Laughlin Rd., Yamhill (☎ 503/662-3280); and **Tempest Vineyards,** 600 Karla's Rd., Amity (☎ 503/252-1383).

There are also several good wine shops in the area. For a selection of area wines (several of which can be tasted on any given day), you can visit **Old Noah's Wine Cellar,** 511 E. Third St., McMinnville (☎ 503/434-2787), which is designed to look just like an old wine cellar, or the **Oregon Wine Tasting Room,** 19702 SW Ore. 18, Sheridan (☎ 503/843-3787), which is adjacent to the Lawrence Gallery. In the town of Carlton, you'll find **The Tasting Room,** 105 W. Main St. (☎ 503/852-6733), which specializes in wines from wineries that are not usually open to the public, which makes this an absolute must of a stop if you can't be around on Memorial Day or Thanksgiving weekend.

So as not to get pulled over by the local police, you might want to limit the number of wineries you visit to between three and five in an afternoon. This will also allow you time to stop and enjoy the countryside. You might even consider having a designated driver.

ALTERNATIVE WINE COUNTRY TOURING

If you'd rather do your wine tasting on a guided tour, contact **Grape Escape** (☎ **503/282-4262**), which offers in-depth winery tours of the Willamette Valley. An all-day tour includes stops at several wineries, an elegant picnic lunch, and pickup and drop-off at your hotel. Tours are $65.

You can also see the wine country from the air on a hot-air balloon ride with **Vista Balloon Adventures** (☎ 800/622-2309 or 503/625-7385), which charges $175 per person for a 1-hour flight, or through **Rex Hill Vineyards** (☎ **503/538-0666**), which charges $180 per person or $350 per couple for a 1-hour flight followed by brunch at the vineyard. Alternatively, you can opt for a flight over the region in a glider. Contact **Cascade Soaring,** McMinnville Airport (☎ **503/472-8805**), which offers a variety of flights ranging in duration from 15 to 55 minutes and in price from $35 to $150. Gliders carrying one or two passengers are used.

OTHER THINGS TO SEE & DO

Seven miles south of Newberg off Ore. 219, on the banks of the Willamette River, is **Champoeg State Park** (pronounced Sham-*poo*-ee) (☎ 503/633-8170). It was here, in the area known as French Prairie (home to several families of French Canadian settlers), that the region's first pioneers voted in 1843 for the formation of a provisional American government. This occurred at a time when the British, in the form of the Hudson's Bay Company, exercised a strong control over the Northwest.

The park includes a campground, a bike path, a picnic area, a historic home, a log cabin, and a visitor center that traces Champoeg's history from its days as an Native American village up through its pioneer farming days. During the summer, the park's amphitheater hosts several popular-music concerts by nationally known performers. Park admission is $3.

Near downtown Newberg, the **Hoover-Minthorn House Museum,** 115 S. River St. (☎ **503/538-6629**), preserves the childhood home of Herbert Hoover, the 31st president of the United States. It's open March to November, Wednesday through Sunday from 1 to 4pm; December and February, Saturday and Sunday from 1 to 4pm (closed January). Admission is $2 for adults, $1.50 for seniors and students, 50¢ for children 5 to 11.

Between Dundee and McMinnville, you'll find the town of Lafayette, which is home to the **Yamhill County Historical Museum and Barn,** on the corner of Sixth and Market streets (☎ **503/864-2589**). The museum, which houses a collection of pioneer memorabilia, is open on Saturday and Sunday from 1 to 4pm (Wednesday through Sunday in summer).

It has been several years since Howard Hughes's famous **"Spruce Goose"** flying boat left Long Beach, California, to take up residence in McMinnville, but as of yet, the plane's new home has still not been completed. Currently, it looks like the new museum may open in 1999 or 2000. Check with the McMinnville Chamber of Commerce.

SHOPPING IN THE AREA

If you're interested in picking up some local art or crafts, there are several places worth visiting in the area. At **Red Hills Pottery,** 9545 NE Red Hills Rd. (☎ **503/538-5918**), Donna Gettel produces beautiful wood-fired porcelain ware. To reach this pottery studio, take Ninth Street north, then turn right on Fairview Drive and right again on Red Hills Road. West of Dundee, watch for the **Water Wall Gallery,** 18825 N. Ore. 99W (☎ **503/864-3220**), which features artistic waterfalls and fountains, bonsai trees, and Asian-influenced art. West of McMinnville near Sheridan, you'll find the **Lawrence Gallery** (☎ **503/843-3633**). This large art gallery has a sculpture garden, water garden, and several rooms full of artworks by regional artists; it's open daily. Not far past this gallery, you'll find the display gardens of **George Stastny Stone Pots,** 20901 Caleb Payne Rd. (☎ **503/843-7654**). Don't expect to take home one of the sculpted cement planters for sale here (they weigh hundreds of pounds), but maybe you could have one shipped home.

If you enjoy shopping for antiques and collectibles, there are several places in the area that you may want to visit. If your tastes run to vintage furniture from the 1940s and 1950s, check out **Viva Gallery** (☎ **503/538-4349**) on Ore. 99W on the east side of Dundee. In Lafayette, there is the **Lafayette Schoolhouse Antique Mall,** Ore. 99W (☎ **503/864-2720**), which is located in a 1910 schoolhouse and is filled with more than 100 dealers. Up in Carlton, you'll find interesting English wardrobes and other European antiques at **RD Steeves Imports,** 209 N. Yamhill St. (☎ **503/852-6519**).

Fans of outlet shopping won't want to miss the **Tanger Factory Outlet Center,** on Ore. 18 at Norton Lane in McMinnville (☎ **503/472-5387**).

To stock up on local jams, wines, and other gourmet food items, visit the **Laube Orchards Fruit Stand,** 18400 N. Ore. 99W (☎ **503/864-2672**), which sells a wide selection of produce and gourmet foods from around the area. If you like chocolate, you might want to head down to Amity and stop in at the **Brigittine Monastery,** 23300 Walker Lane (☎ **503/835-8080**), which is known for making a heavenly fudge. The fudge and truffles are on sale at the guest reception area, which is open daily but closes for lunch.

WHERE TO STAY
IN THE NEWBERG AREA

Partridge Farm Bed & Breakfast. 4300 E. Portland Rd., Newberg, OR 97132. ☎ **503/ 538-2050.** 3 rms. May 1–Oct 31 $80–$110 double. Nov 1–Apr 30 $70–$100 double. Rates include full breakfast. MC, V.

Under the same ownership as the nearby Rex Hill Winery, this old yellow farmhouse feels secluded even though it's right on busy Ore. 99W (and gets a bit of traffic noise). Shade trees, beautiful gardens full of perennials, berry hedges, and fruit trees give Partridge Farm a relaxing country atmosphere that, on a sunny summer afternoon, positively begs to be enjoyed with a glass of wine and a good book. Inside, there's a hint of French country sophistication. All the rooms are large and are furnished with period antiques that complement the mood of this turn-of-the-century home.

✪ **Springbrook Hazelnut Farm.** 30295 N. Ore. 99W, Newberg, OR 97132. ☎ **800/ 793-8528** or 503/538-4606. 2 rms, 1 suite, 1 cottage, 1 carriage house. $95 double; $195 suite; $150 cottage; $135 carriage house. Rates include full breakfast. No credit cards.

Only 20 miles from Portland, this 70-acre working farm is a convenient rural get-away for anyone who craves a vacation with a slower pace. The four craftsman-style buildings here are all listed on the National Register of Historic Places and include the main house with its two rooms and a suite, a carriage house, and a cottage. Original artwork abounds in the boldly decorated and decidedly colorful main house. Both of the main buildings overlook the farm's pond and lovely back garden. In addition, you'll have access to a swimming pool and tennis courts, and through the hazelnut orchard you'll find Rex Hill Vineyards. The little white cottage has been beautifully restored with an antique fireplace mantle, fir floors, and a tiled bathroom, and offers spacious accommodations complete with a kitchen, washer, and dryer. The cottage overlooks the farm's pond and a meadow that's filled with daffodils in the spring

IN THE DUNDEE AREA

Wine Country Farm. 6855 Breyman Orchards Rd., Dayton, OR 97114. ☎ **800/261-3446** or 503/864-3446. 6 rms, 1 suite. $75–$115 double; $125 suite. Rates include full breakfast. MC, V.

This bed-and-breakfast inn has one of the best views in the area, and with its 5 acres of grape vines, should satisfy all those wishing to steep themselves in the atmosphere of wine country. When this 1910 farmhouse was renovated and converted into a B&B, the owners even gave the facade the look of a French farmhouse. Two of the rooms have good views, as do the breakfast room and the deck that runs the entire length of the house. A croquet lawn and horseshoe pit provide traditional rural recreational activities when guests aren't out wine tasting. The farm also raises Arabian horses and buggy rides are available. There's also a wine-tasting room here.

IN THE MCMINNVILLE AREA

Best Western—The Vineyard Inn. 2035 S. Ore. 99W, McMinnville, OR 97128. ☎ **800/ 528-1234** or 503/472-4900. Fax 503/434-9157. 65 rms. A/C TV TEL. $67–$88 double. Rates include continental breakfast. AE, CB, DC, DISC, MC, V.

This modern hotel is one of the first in the area to actively cater to the growing numbers of oenophiles who are touring Oregon's wine country. Purple and lavender are the predominant colors here, and there are wine posters throughout the hotel. The guest rooms are very comfortable and most are quite spacious. You'll find a microwave and a refrigerator in every room. An indoor pool, exercise room, and whirlpool provide a bit of exercise and relaxation in the evening. You'll find the Vineyard Inn at the west end of McMinnville.

Mattey House. 10221 NE Mattey Lane, McMinnville, OR 97128. ☎ **503/434-5058.** 4 rms. $85–$95 double. MC, V.

Located between Lafayette and McMinnville, this restored 1892 Queen Anne Victorian farmhouse sits on 10 acres of farmland behind 1 ¹/₂ acres of Muller-Thurgau grape vines. This is a grand old house, and up on the second floor, you'll find a tiny balcony overlooking the vineyard. It's the perfect spot for a glass of wine in the afternoon. Guest rooms are decorated in county Victorian style, with antique beds. The Riesling Room, with its claw-foot bathtub, is our favorite. Innkeepers Jack and Denise Seed are British and keep copies of magazines from their homeland scattered about the inn.

Steiger Haus. 360 Wilson St., McMinnville, OR 97128. ☎ **503/472-0821** or 503/472-0238. 5 rms. $70–$100 double. Rates include full breakfast. DISC, MC, V.

Set on tree-shaded grounds just a few blocks from downtown McMinnville, this inn makes a good base for exploring the surrounding wine country. The contemporary three-story building sports lots of windows and decks, and has a multilevel, parklike yard. Depending on which room you choose, you may enjoy a superb view of the garden through a bay window or perhaps have a nice deck for afternoon lounging. The most expensive room has its own fireplace. We like the treetop room the best. This inn is within walking distance of several good restaurants.

✪ **Youngberg Hill Vineyard B&B.** 10660 SW Youngberg Hill Rd., McMinnville, OR 97128. ☎ **503/472-2727.** Fax 541/472-1313. Web site: www.youngberghill.com. 5 rms. A/C. $130–$150 double. Rates include full breakfast. MC, V.

Set on a 50-acre farm that includes 12 acres of vineyards, this is the quintessential wine country inn. Set atop a hill at the end of a long gravel driveway, the modern inn commands a view of the rolling hills of the Willamette Valley, snow-capped Cascades peaks, and the Coast Range. After pulling up a chair on one of the inn's porches, pouring a glass of Pinot Noir, and gazing out over the rolling hills, you'll likely be entertaining notions of cashing in the mutual funds to start a vineyard of your own. Two of the guest rooms have their own fireplaces and large decks wrap around both floors of the inn. Appropriately, the inn has an extensive wine cellar emphasizing Oregon wines, and wine tastings are available. Big farm breakfasts, often using produce from the farm, get visitors off to a good start each morning as they head out to explore the surrounding wine country.

IN THE YAMHILL AREA

Flying M Ranch. 23029 NW Flying M Rd., Yamhill, OR 97148. ☎ **503/662-3222.** Fax 503/662-3202. 28 rms, 7 cabins. $50–$70 double; $75–$200 cabin for 2 to 10; $10 campsite. Picnicking $3. AE, DC, DISC, MC, V.

If you feel like mixing a bit of wine-country touring with the Wild West, the Flying M Ranch is the place for you. Located 4 miles down a gravel road at the foot of the Coast Range, this ranch on the North Yamhill River caters to folks who want to do a bit of horseback riding and play at being cowboys. The center of ranch activity is the big log lodge where every inch of wall space seems to display hunting trophies, from musk-ox and buffalo heads to bearskins and even a stuffed cougar. Overnight trail rides ($175 per person) are also available.

Dining/Entertainment: Inside the lodge, there's a large dining room overlooking the Yamhill River. The menu features plenty of cowboy standards as well as a few dishes you'd only expect from a big-city restaurant. In the lounge, you can marvel at the bar, which is made from a 6-ton log. There's usually live country music on Friday and Saturday nights. Steak-fry horseback rides are also offered.

Services: Horseback riding ($17 per hour or special rates for day-long rides), hayrides.

Facilities: Airstrip, swimming pond, tennis courts, basketball court, volleyball courts, horseshoe pits.

WHERE TO DINE
IN DUNDEE

Red Hills Provincial Dining. 276 Ore. 99W. ☎ **503/538-8224.** Reservations recommended. Main courses $14.50–$18.50; lunch $6.50–$8. MC, V. Tues–Fri 11:30am–2pm and 5–9pm, Sat–Sun 5–9pm. PROVINCIAL EUROPEAN.

Located in a 1920s craftsman bungalow on the east side of town, this restaurant serves food that's well paired with the wines of the region. The dinner menu changes daily and is limited to five or six appetizers and an equal number of main courses. Local wines and produce make frequent appearances in such dishes as venison pâté with hazelnuts, dark rum, and mushrooms or salmon with a wild-ginger/Pinot Gris sauce. Lunches display a welcome creativity too, with focaccia sandwiches a mainstay. There's a very good selection of wines available (also sold retail).

✪ **Tina's.** Ore. 99W, Dundee. ☎ **503/538-8880.** Reservations recommended. Dinner $16.50–$25; lunch $7–$10. AE, MC, V. Mon 5–9pm, Tues–Fri 11:30am–2pm and 5–9pm, Sat–Sun 5–9pm. CONTINENTAL/NORTHWEST.

Tina's, long a favorite wine-country dining stop, was scheduled to move into a larger space at press time, which should make it easier to get weekend reservations. However, the menu, which is constantly changing but always has a good selection of seafood, should still be as short as always, with an emphasis on serving a few well-prepared dishes. There are usually almost as many desserts available as there are entrees, and the wine selection, of course, emphasizes local wines.

IN MCMINNVILLE

✪ **Nick's Italian Café.** 521 E. Third St. ☎ **503/434-4471.** Reservations recommended. 5-course fixed-price dinner $29. No credit cards. Tues–Thurs 5:30–9pm, Fri–Sat 5:30–10pm, Sun 5–8pm. NORTHERN ITALIAN.

There's nothing in Nick's narrow storefront windows to indicate that this is one of the best restaurants around. However, when you step through the door and are immediately confronted by the rich tones of carved and polished wood, you'll know that this is someplace special. Each evening, there's a fixed-price five-course dinner, although à la carte meals are also available if you aren't hungry enough for five courses. Dinner might start with an artichoke served with tarragon mayonnaise, followed by minestrone soup. A fresh-fennel salad served with tomatoes and kalamata olives is followed by a pesto, chanterelle mushroom, and hazelnut lasagna. For the entree, there's always a choice between three dishes—say, grilled halibut, veal piccata, or peppercorn steak.

Third Street Grill. 729 E. Third St. ☎ **503/435-1745.** Reservations recommended. Main courses $14–$19. DISC, MC, V. Mon–Sat 5pm–9pm. NORTHWEST.

Down at the east end of Third Street, in an old Victorian home surrounded by a white picket fence, you'll find an elegant little restaurant serving some of the most creative meals in the region. Expect appetizers the likes of crab and salmon cakes with a spicy chipotle-pepper aioli and lemon rémoulade, and entrees including hazelnut-crusted halibut on roasted jalapeño-jicama slaw with a mango sauce. Salads also get the creative treatment here, so don't overlook the greens when contemplating a starter. The restaurant also has its own little wine shop.

IN CARLTON

Caffè Bisbo. 214 Main St. ☎ **503/852-RAGU.** Reservations recommended. Main courses $9–$11; Sun brunch $8. MC, V. Wed–Sat 5–9pm, Sun 9am–1pm. ITALIAN.

This family-run restaurant is small and features a short menu, but each dish is lovingly prepared by chef Claudio Bisbocci, while his wife, Joanne, works the front. If you're lucky, you just might find Claudio's pesto lasagna on the day's menu, but even if you don't, the lasagna, with homemade noodles, is always excellent. The chicken cacciatore, bathed in olives and olive oil, is also excellent. However, the very best is held out for last. Caffè Bisbo's tiramisu is absolutely heavenly. In the summer, there is dining on a deck overlooking a small park.

NEAR SHERIDAN

The Fresh Palate Cafe. 19706 SW Ore. 18 (between McMinnville and Sheridan). ☎ **503/843-4400.** Reservations recommended on weekends. Main courses $5–$10. MC, V. Daily 11am–5pm. SANDWICHES/PASTA.

This bright little lunch spot is located upstairs from the Lawrence Gallery and is popular both with people touring the wine country and with families headed to or from the beach. The menu is simple and straightforward. Because this is the best place for miles around, there is usually a wait for a table on summer weekends.

EN ROUTE TO THE BEACH

It used to be almost impossible to get beach-bound traffic on Ore. 18 west of McMinnville to stop for anything, but that was before the **Spirit Mountain Casino** (☎ 800/760-7977 or 503/879-2350) opened in the town of Grand Ronde. These days a lot of the traffic on this highway isn't even going to the beach, it's headed to this large, glitzy temple of luck. Locals swear that the food here is the best around, and the prices can't be beat. Also in Grand Ronde is the unusual **Jim's Trading Post,** 29335 Salmon River Hwy. (☎ **503/879-5411**), which bills itself as "Oregon's Unique Bookstore" and is a sort of miniature version of the famous Powell's City of Books in Portland.

2 Salem

47 miles S of Portland, 40 miles N of Corvallis, 131 miles W of Bend, 57 miles E of Lincoln City

As the state capital, Salem has become the third-largest city in Oregon (pop. 100,000), and running the state has become the city's main occupation. True to its origins (it was founded by a Methodist missionary), the city still wears its air of conservatism like a minister's collar. No one has ever accused Salem of being too raucous or rowdy. Though it's the seat of state government, the city, home to Willamette University, feels more like a small Midwestern college town than a Pacific Rim capital. Even when both the school and the legislature are in session, the city hardly seems charged with energy. The quiet conservatism does, however, give the city a certain charm that's not found in the other cities of the Willamette Valley.

Salem's roots date from 1834, when Methodist missionary Jason Lee, who had traveled west to convert the local Indians, founded Salem, making it the first American settlement in the Willamette Valley. In 1842, one year before the first settlers crossed the continent on the Oregon Trail, Lee founded the Oregon Institute, the first school of higher learning west of the Rockies. In 1857, the first textile mill west of the Mississippi opened here, giving Salem a firm industrial base. However, despite all these historic firsts, Oregon City and Portland grew much faster and quickly became the region's population centers. Salem seemed doomed to backwater status until the year 1859 when Oregon became a state and Salem was chosen to become the state capital.

ESSENTIALS

GETTING THERE   Salem is on I-5 at the junction of Ore. 22, which heads west to connect with Ore. 18 from Lincoln City and southeast to connect with U.S. 20 from Bend.

Amtrak has passenger rail service to Salem. The station is at 13th and Oak streets.

VISITOR INFORMATION   Contact the **Salem Convention & Visitors Association,** 1313 Mill St. SE, Salem, OR 97301 (☎ **800/874-7012** or 503/581-4325; fax 503/581-4540; Web site: http://www.oregonlink.com/~salem/scva/).

GETTING AROUND   Car rentals are available from **Hertz, Budget,** and **National.** If you need a taxi, contact **Salem Keizer Yellow Cab** (☎ **503/362-2411**). Public bus service throughout the Salem area is provided by **Salem Area Transit** (☎ **503/588-BUSS**), which goes by the name of Cherriots.

FESTIVALS   Two of the biggest events of the year in Salem are the **Oregon State Fair,** which is held from late August to early September, and the **Salem Arts Festival,** the largest juried art fair in Oregon.

WHAT TO SEE & DO
HISTORIC BUILDINGS & NEIGHBORHOODS

If you're interested in touring Salem's historic neighborhoods, stop by the **Salem Visitors Center** at Mission Mill Village and pick up copies of the **walking-tour** brochures for the Gaiety Hill/Bush's Pasture Park Historic District and the Court-Chemeketa Residential Historic District. There are also several restored homes in Riverfront Park on Water Street, and on the tree-shaded campus of Willamette University just across State Street from the Capitol Mall.

Mission Mill Village. 1313 Mill St. SE. ☎ **800/874-7012** or 503/585-7012. Admission $4 adults, $3 seniors, $1.50 children. Tues–Sat 10am–4:30pm. Closed major holidays.

The sprawling red **Thomas Kay Woolen Mill,** a water-powered mill built in 1889, has become one of the most fascinating attractions in Salem. The restored buildings house exhibits on every stage of the wool-making process, and in the main mill building, the water-driven turbine is still in operation, producing electricity for these buildings. Also on these neatly manicured grounds are several other old structures (including the **Jason Lee House,** which was built by Salem's founder in 1841 and is the oldest frame house in the Northwest), a cafe, and a collection of interesting shops. The **Marion Museum of History,** also on the grounds, houses exhibits on the history of the area with a particularly interesting exhibit on the local Kalapuyan Indians. Because this complex also houses the **Salem Visitors Information Center,** it should be your first stop in town.

Oregon State Capitol. 900 Court St. (Visitor Services Center). ☎ **503/986-1388.** Free admission. Building open year-round, tours offered early June to Labor Day Mon–Fri 7:30am–5:30pm, Sat 9am–4pm, Sun noon–4pm. Tours by appointment other months. Closed national holidays.

Stark and boxy, the Oregon State Capitol was built in 1938 in a modernistic Greek revival style of white Italian marble and is topped by *The Oregon Pioneer,* a 23-foot-tall gilded statue. Inside the building, which is open to the public, there are murals of historic Oregon scenes. Tours of the capitol are available during the summer, with separate tours up into the buildings tower.

Bush House and Bush Barn Art Center. 600 Mission St. SE. ☎ **503/363-4714** (Bush House) and 503/581-2228 (Bush Barn Art Center). Bush House, $2.50 adults, $2 students and seniors, $1 children; Bush Barn Art Center, free. Bush House, June–Sept Tues–Sun noon–5pm; Oct–May Tues–Sun 2–5pm. Bush Barn Art Center, Tues–Fri 10am–5pm, Sat–Sun 1–5pm. Closed major holidays.

Sitting at the top of a shady hill, this imposing Italianate Victorian home was built between 1877 and 1888. Inside the Bush House, you can see the original furnishings, including 10 fireplaces and even the original wallpaper. The house is surrounded by 100 acres of parkland known as Bush's Pasture Park. Also on the grounds are the oldest greenhouse conservatory in Oregon and the Bush Barn Art Center. The latter includes a sales gallery as well as exhibition spaces that feature changing art exhibits. Each year on the third weekend in July, Bush's Pasture Park is the site of the Salem Art Fair and Festival, one of the most popular art festivals in the Northwest.

Historic Deepwood Estate. 1116 Mission St. SE. ☎ **503/363-1825.** Admission $3 adults, $2.50 seniors, $1 children. May–Sept Sun–Fri noon–4:30pm. Oct–Apr Sun–Mon, Wed, and Fri 1–4pm.

While the Bush House is huge and imposing, the Deepwood Estate home, a Queen Anne–style Victorian is light and airy, a delicate jewel box of a house. Numerous lightning rod–topped peaked roofs and gables create the complex lines that give this house its elegance. Built in 1894 and set amid nearly 6 acres of shady gardens and forest, this historic home is renowned for its wealth of stained-glass windows and golden oak moldings.

OTHER AREA MUSEUMS

Antique Powerland Museum. 3995 Brooklake Rd. NE, Brooks. ☎ **503/393-2424.** Admission $1. Apr–Oct daily 10am–6pm. Nov–Mar daily 10am–4pm.

Dedicated to the preservation of old farm equipment and related items, this museum is best known as the site of the annual Great Oregon Steamup, which is held each year on the last weekend in July and the first weekend in August. Steam engines and old tractors make up the bulk of the equipment here. Also on the grounds is the **Pacific Northwest Truck Museum** (☎ **503/463-8701**), which is open on weekends throughout the summer.

Jensen Arctic Museum. 590 W. Church St., Monmouth. ☎ **503/838-8468.** Admission $2 adults, $1 children. Wed–Sat 10am–4pm.

While Monmouth may seem an unlikely location for a museum dedicated to the natural and cultural history of the Arctic, it is here that the museum's founder lived while working with Alaskan Eskimo peoples. The core of the museum's exhibits is Dr. Jensen's personal collection, but over the years, the museum has become a repository for more than 60 other collections.

PARKS, GARDENS & FLOWER FIELDS

Salem's new **Riverfront Park,** on the waterfront in downtown, has brought the city's focus back on the Willamette River, which for long has been almost completely ignored. This new park features a state-of-the-art playground, amphitheater, and meandering pathways. It is also home to the **Gilbert House Children's Museum** (see below).

Each year between mid-May and early June, the countryside around Salem bursts into color as commercial iris fields come into bloom. The two biggest growers open their farms during bloom time. **Cooley's Gardens,** 11553 Silverton Rd. NE (☎ **503/873-5463**), with 250 acres and more than three million irises, is the world's largest bearded iris grower. To reach the gardens, take the Market Street exit and drive east to Lancaster Road; at Lancaster, turn left and drive north to Silverton Road where you make a right turn. It's less than 10 miles on Silverton Road. **Schreiner's Iris Gardens,** 3625 Quinaby Rd. NE, Brooks (☎ **503/393-3232**), also has 250 acres of irises, and is an equally impressive sight. To reach Schreiner's, take the Brooks exit off I-5 north of Salem. From late March to late April, you can see fields of tulips in bloom at **Wooden Shoe Bulb Company,** 33814 S. Meridian Rd., Woodburn (☎ **800/711-2006** or 503/634-2243).

North of Salem 8 miles you'll find **Willamette Mission State Park** (☎ **503/393-1172**), which preserves the site of the first settlement in the Willamette Valley. It was here that Methodist missionary Jason Lee and four assistants established their first mission in 1834. Today, there are many miles of walking, biking, and horseback riding paths through the park, which is also home to the largest black cottonwood tree in the country.

WINE TOURING

Some people claim that the best Pinot Noirs in Oregon come from Salem area wineries. If you'd like to do some wine tasting and decide for yourself, there are quite a few wineries in the area that have tasting rooms. An area wine tour could start south of Salem at **Willamette Valley Vineyards,** 8800 Enchanted Way SE, Turner (☎ **503/588-9463**), and then return to near downtown Salem and **Honeywood Winery,** 1350 Hines St. SE, Salem (☎ **800/726-4101** or 503/362-4111). From downtown, head west of Salem to the town of Rickreall where you'll find **Flynn Winery,** 2200 Pacific Hwy. W., Rickreall (☎ **503/623-8683**), and **Eola Hills Wine Cellars,** 501 S. Pacific Hwy., Rickreall (☎ **503/623-2405**). From here, continue west on Ore. 22 to **Chateau Bianca,** 17485 Ore. 22, Dallas (☎ **503/623-6181**).

Northwest of Salem is one of the region's best wine-touring neighborhoods. To reach the wineries in this area, head west out of town on Ore. 22, turn north on Ore. 221, and then left onto Orchard Heights Road, where you'll find **Orchard Heights Winery,** 6057 Orchard Heights NW, Salem (☎ **503/363-0375**). From here, continue west, then turn right onto Oak Grove Road and right again onto Crowley Road where you'll find **Oak Grove Orchards,** 6090 Crowley Rd., Rickreall (☎ **503/364-7052**). After this, continue north on Oak Grove Road, turn right on Zena Road, and then left on Bethel Heights Road, where you'll find **Bethel Heights Vineyards,** 6060 Bethel Heights Rd. NW, Salem (☎ **503/581-2262**). To find two more wineries, continue up Bethel Heights Road and turn right on Spring Valley Road where you'll soon come to both **Witness Tree Vineyards,** 7111 Spring Valley Rd. NW, Salem (☎ **503/585-7874**), and **Cristom Vineyards,** 6905 Spring Valley Rd. NW, Salem (☎ **503/375-3068**). On the way back to Salem on Ore. 221, you can stop in at **Redhawk Vineyard,** 2995 Michigan City Rd. NW, Salem (☎ **503/362-1596**), which is best known for its "Grateful Red" wine.

Area wineries that are open only on a few weekends of the year (usually Memorial Day and Thanksgiving weekends, but sometimes other weekends) include **Evesham Wood Vineyard,** 4035 Wallace Rd. NW (☎ **503/371-8478**), and **St. Innocent Winery,** 2701 22nd St. SE, Salem (☎ **503/378-1526**).

ESPECIALLY FOR KIDS

The Gilbert House Children's Museum. 116 Marion St. NE. ☎ **503/371-3631.** Admission $4. Tues–Sat 10am–5pm, Sun noon–4pm (also open Mon Mar–June).

A.C. Gilbert was the inventor of the Erector Set, the perennially popular children's toy that has inspired generations of budding engineers, and here in the restored Gilbert house, kids can learn all about engineering, art, music, drama, science, and nature through fun hands-on exhibits. At press time, there were plans to open an outdoor science center.

Enchanted Forest. 8462 Enchanted Way SE. ☎ **503/363-3060.** Admission $6.95 adults, $5.95 seniors, $6.25 children 3–12. Mar 15 to Labor Day daily 9:30am–6pm; Sept Sat–Sun 9:30am–6pm. Closed Oct–Mar 14. Take I-5 7 miles south of Salem to Exit 248.

Classic children's stories come to life at this amusement park for kids. In addition to Storybook Land, English Village, and a mining town, there's a haunted house, a bobsled run, a log-flume ride, and a comedy theater. Rides cost extra. Adjacent to Enchanted Village is **Thrill-Ville USA** (☎ **503/363-4095**), a small amusement park with a roller coaster, water slides, and other rides and activities.

OUTDOOR ACTIVITIES

Public golf courses in the Salem area include the **McNary Golf Course,** 6255 River Rd. N., Keizer (☎ **503/390-5057**), and the **Salem Golf Club,** 2025 Golf Course Rd. S., Salem (☎ **503/363-6652**).

If it's bird watching that interests you, there are two national wildlife refuges in the area that are excellent places to observe ducks, geese, swans, and raptors. **Ankeny National Wildlife Refuge** is 12 miles south of Salem off I-5 at exit 243. **Basket Slough National Wildlife Refuge** is northwest of the town of Rickreall on Ore. 22. Fall through spring are the best times of year for birding here.

EXCURSIONS FROM SALEM

Located 26 miles east of Salem on Ore. 214, **Silver Falls State Park** (☎ **503/873-8681**) is the largest state park in Oregon and is also one of the most popular. Hidden in the lush canyons and dark old-growth forests of this park are 10 silvery waterfalls. You can walk behind a couple of them, and all are connected by various loop trails. You can spend an afternoon or several days exploring the park. Camping, swimming, picnicking, bicycling, and horseback riding are all popular activities. Guided horseback rides are available Memorial Day through Labor Day ($25 for a 1-hour ride, $44 for 2 hours, $60 for 3 to 4 hours). For reservations, call ☎ **503/873-3890**). If you'd rather lead a llama through the woods, contact **Wiley Woods Ranch** (☎ **503/362-0873**), which offers 1- to 3-hour guided llama treks through the state park. Rates range from $10 to $25. Just don't expect to ride the llamas, they carry gear not people.

Not far from the state park is the town of Mt. Angel, which is best known as the site of a huge **Mt. Angel Oktoberfest** (☎ **503/845-9440**), which is held on the second weekend of September each year. With polka bands from around the world, beer and wine gardens, loads of great German food, and dancing in the streets, this is just about the biggest party in the state.

Other times of year you can visit the **Mount Angel Abbey** (☎ **503/845-3030**), which stands atop a 300-foot bluff on the edge of town and has peaceful gardens, an architecturally interesting library, and a collection of rare books. The abbey, which was established by Benedictine monks in 1882, also has a gift shop and offers tours by appointment. It is also sometimes possible to stay here on religious retreats. The abbey is also the site of the annual Abbey Bach Festival, which takes place each year on the last Wednesday, Thursday, and Friday in July and sells out months in advance.

Any time of year, you can get microbrew ales and anything from German sausages to a Tex-Mex burger at the **Mt. Angel Brewing Company,** 210 Monroe St. (☎ **503/845-9624**).

WHERE TO STAY

Bethel Heights Farm Bed & Breakfast. 6055 Bethel Heights Rd. NW, Salem, OR 97304. ☎ **503/364-7688.** 2 rms. $70–$80 double. MC, V.

If you're in the area specifically to do a bit of wine touring, there is no better location than this contemporary inn in the middle of the Eola Hills wine region. Set high on a hill overlooking the Willamette Valley and the distant Cascades (including Mount Jefferson), the inn is on a 20-acre farm. When not out wine tasting, you can visit the farms four-horned Jacob sheep or sit by the large pond. The gourmet breakfasts include homemade jams and syrups and even flour stone ground right here at the farm.

✪ **Marquee House.** 333 Wyatt Ct. NE, Salem, OR 97301. ☎ **800/949-0837** or 503/391-0837. Web site: http://www.oregonlink.com/marquee/. 5 rms, 3 with bath. $55–$60 double without bath, $75–$90 double with bath. Rates include full breakfast. MC, V.

Fans of old movies will want to make this their address in Salem. All the rooms are named for well-known movies and are furnished to reflect the movie theme. We like the Topper Room with its black-tie theme and the Blazing Saddles Room with its Wild West decor. This B&B is located on a narrow lane in a quiet residential neighborhood and has Mill Creek running through the back yard. The gardens are impressive, and in winter there are murder-mystery weekends.

Phoenix Inn. 4370 Commercial St. SE, Salem, OR. ☎ **800/445-4498** or 503/588-9220. Fax 503/585-3616. 88 rms. A/C TV TEL. $70–$115 double. Rates include continental breakfast. AE, CB, DC, DISC, MC, V.

This is the best hotel in Salem these days and is popular with legislators and business travelers. The rooms (called "minisuites" here) are in fact quite large and well designed for both business and relaxation. There are two phones (free local calls), hair dryers, microwave ovens, refrigerators, and wet bars in all the rooms. The top-end rooms also have whirlpool tubs. Facilities include an indoor pool, whirlpool, and exercise room.

WHERE TO DINE

If you have a sweet tooth, you won't want to miss **Gerry Frank's Konditorei,** 310 Kearney St. SE (☎ **503/585-7070**), which sells an amazing selection of extravagant cakes and pastries. For a good cup of espresso, head to **The Beanery,** 545 Court St. (☎ **503/399-7220**). If you're just looking for a good place to spend the evening with friends, check out **The Ram Border Cafe & Big Horn Brewery,** 515 12th St. SE (☎ **503/363-1904**). For Sunday brunch, consider **Eola Hills Wine Cellars,** 501 S. Ore. 99W, Rickreall (☎ **503/623-2405**), which serves gourmet omelets, panfried oysters, pasta, Belgian waffles, sparkling wine, and more for $17.95. Reservations are required.

Alessandro's Park Plaza Restaurant. 325 High St. SE. ☎ **503/370-9951.** Reservations recommended. Main courses $9.50–$22.50; lunch $6.25–$9.50. AE, DISC, MC, V. Mon–Thurs 11:30am–2pm and 5:30–9pm, Fri 11:30am–2pm and 5:30–10pm, Sat 5:30–10pm. ITALIAN.

Located on a pretty little park just south of Salem's shopping district, the Park Plaza is Salem's best Italian restaurant. The building housing the restaurant looks like little more than a parking garage, but inside you'll find a half-timbered Tudor-look dining room where classical music plays softly on the stereo. Service is very professional even though the atmosphere is fairly casual. Chef Alessandro Fasani's sauces are made fresh daily from the finest of ingredients, including fresh herbs and the best of Northwest seafood. The wine list features moderately priced Italian and Oregon wines.

Court Street Dairy Lunch. 347 Court St. ☎ **503/363-6433.** Meals $4–$7. AE, MC, V. Mon–Fri 7am–2pm. BURGERS.

In business since the 1920s, the Court Street Dairy Lunch is the quintessential burger place and a Salem institution. Burgers and sandwiches "just like Mom used to make" are the attraction. The specialties of the house are the ranch burger and ranch dog, marionberry pie, and chocolate malts.

DaVinci Italiano Ristorante. 180 High St. SE. ☎ **503/399-1413.** Reservations recommended. Main courses $14–$19. AE, DISC, MC, V. Mon–Thurs 11:30am–1:30pm and 5–9pm, Fri 11:30am–1:30pm and 5–10pm, Sat–Sun 5–9pm. ITALIAN.

Wonderful aromas greet you as you step through the door of this casual yet elegant restaurant in a restored downtown building. The ambience is early 20th century, with a pressed-tin ceiling and lots of oak and exposed brick. Those aromas are soon followed, after you take a seat at your table, by a delicious bread and olive oil in which to dip it. Menu offerings run the gamut from traditional fare to designer pizzas and more unusual dishes such as grilled ahi with cranberry ravioli.

Karma's Café. 1313 Mill St. SE. ☎ **503/370-8855.** Meals $4.50–$6.50. DISC, MC, V. Mon–Fri 9am–4:30pm, Sat 10am–4:30pm. DELI.

We can't imagine a more pleasant place to lunch on a sunny summer afternoon in Salem. The deck in front of Karma's sandwich shop is right in the middle of Mission Mill Village and overlooks the big red mill. You can hear water flowing through the stream and are almost completely surrounded by history. Soups, salads, and sandwiches are the fare here, and a wide selection of Oregon wines are available both with meals and for tasting (taste 6 wines for $2.50 or 10 wines for $3.25).

✪ **Morton's Bistro Northwest.** 1128 Edgewater St. W. ☎ **503/585-1113.** Reservations recommended. Main courses $14.50–$20. MC, V. Tues–Sat 5–10pm. AMERICAN REGIONAL.

This romantic little bistro on the west side of the Willamette River serves up the most imaginative meals in Salem. The menu changes regularly depending on the whim of the chef, the availability of ingredients, the season, and even the weather. On a recent summer evening, flavors ranged from the subtle scents of saffron- and fennel-steamed mussels to the fiery flavors of penne diablo made with crab and andouille sausage. Other summer standouts included chicken in a brandy-cream sauce and a mixed grill of smoked pork loin and chicken sausage with grilled polenta and apple chutney.

SALEM AFTER DARK

The Oregon Symphony performs in Salem between September and May, with concerts held at Smith Auditorium on the campus of Willamette University. For more information, contact the **Oregon Symphony Association** (☎ **503/364-0149**). There are also regularly scheduled performances by touring companies at the historic **Elsinore Theater,** 170 High St. SE (☎ **800/992-8499** or 503/370-7469).

3 Corvallis & Albany

40 miles S of Salem, 45 miles N of Eugene, 55 miles E of Newport

Corvallis, whose name is Latin for "heart of the valley," is set amid flat farmlands in the center of the Willamette Valley and is home to Oregon State University, a noted center for agricultural research. The fields around Corvallis produce much of the nation's grass-seed crop, and in late summer, after the seed has been harvested, the remaining stubble has traditionally been burned. The field burnings, which have been scaled back in recent years, still can blanket the valley with dense black smoke, making driving quite difficult along certain roads.

Nearby Albany, 13 miles northeast, was a prosperous town in territorial days. Located on the banks of the Willamette River, the town made its fortune as a shipping point in the days when the river was the main transportation route for the region. More than 500 historic homes make Albany the best-preserved town in the state.

ESSENTIALS

GETTING THERE   Albany is on I-5 at the junction with U.S. 20, which heads east to Bend and west to Newport. Corvallis is 12 miles west of I-5 at the junction of U.S. 20, Ore. 99W, and Ore. 34.

VISITOR INFORMATION   Contact the **Corvallis Convention & Visitors Bureau,** 420 NW Second St., Corvallis, OR 97330 (☎ **800/334-8118** or 541/ 757-1544), or the **Albany Visitors Association,** 300 SW Second Ave. (P.O. Box 965), Albany, OR 97321 (☎ **800/526-2256** or 541/928-0911).

GETTING AROUND   Public bus service around the Corvallis area is provided by the **Corvallis Transit System** (☎ **541/757-6998**).

FESTIVALS   **Da Vinci Days** (☎ **800/334-8118**), held each year in mid-July, is Corvallis's most fascinating festival. The highlight of this celebration of art, science, and technology is the **Kinetic Sculpture Race** in which competitors race homemade, people-powered vehicles along city streets, through mud, and down the Willamette River. Prizes are given for engineering and artistry. Though Albany celebrates its Victorian heritage with a July **Victorian Days** and an **Old Fashioned Christmas Celebration,** the **World Championship Timber Carnival,** held each year on the Fourth of July, is the town's biggest celebration. This festival is the largest of its kind and attracts logging contestants from around the world.

EXPLORING CORVALLIS

The **Corvallis Arts Center,** 700 SW Madison Ave. (☎ **541/754-1551**), housed in an old church, schedules changing exhibits of works by regional artists, and its gift shop has a good selection of fine crafts. The center is open Tuesday through Sunday from noon to 5pm; admission is free.

To learn more of the history of the area, take U.S. 20 6 miles west to **Philomath,** which is the county seat of Benton County. Here, you'll find the historic Benton County Courthouse, a stately 1888 building still in use today. Nearby is the **Benton County Historical Museum,** 1101 Main St. (☎ **541/929-6230**). The museum building itself was built in 1867 as part of Philomath College. The museum contains primarily exhibits on early pioneer life, but also includes a collection of Native American artifacts. This museum is open Tuesday through Saturday from 10am to 4:30pm and admission is free.

SEEING THE HISTORIC SIGHTS IN ALBANY

Albany is a hidden jewel that lies right on I-5 but is overlooked by most motorists because the only thing visible from the Interstate is a smoke-belching wood-pulp mill. Behind the industrial screen lies a quiet town that evokes days of starched crinolines and straw boaters. Throughout the mid- to late 19th century, Albany experienced prosperity as it shipped agricultural and wood products downriver to Oregon City and Portland. Though every style of architecture popular during that period is represented in the buildings of downtown Albany's historic districts, it is the town's many elegant Victorian homes that capture the attention of visitors. Stop by the

Albany Visitors Association or the **information gazebo** at the corner of Eighth and Ellsworth streets and pick up a guide to the town's historic buildings. Each year, on the last Saturday of July, many of the historic homes are opened to the public for a **Summer Historic Homes Tour,** and on the third Sunday in December, they are opened for a **Christmas Parlour Tour.** For information on these homes' tours, contact the Albany Visitors Association.

Two sparkling white 1890s churches—the **Whitespires Church** and **St. Mary's Church**—were built in the Gothic revival style and are quite striking. The **Monteith House,** 518 Second Ave. SW (☎ **541/928-0911**), built in 1849, is the town's oldest frame building; it's open June to September only, Wednesday through Saturday from 1 to 4pm; admission is free. It was here that the Oregon Republican party was formed.

To learn more about Albany's past, stop in at the **Albany Regional Museum,** 302 Ferry St. SW (☎ **541/967-6540**), which is in the basement of the Albany library. It's open June to September, Wednesday through Sunday from noon to 4pm; September to May, on Wednesday and Saturday from noon to 4pm. Admission is free. The **Albany Fire Museum,** 120 34th St. SE (☎ **541/967-4389**), houses historical fire-fighting equipment and is open by appointment only.

The most unusual way to delve into Albany's past is by attending one of the living history dramas presented by **Flinn's Living History Theater,** 222 First Ave. W. (☎ **800/636-5008** or 541/928-5008). Tales of women's lives in pioneer days, a murder mystery from the turn of the century, and another murder mystery from Prohibition days are currently in the repertoire of this dinner theater, which also doubles as a tea room. There are several special programs at Christmas.

While touring the historic districts, you can stop in at more than a dozen antique stores, most of which are on First and Second streets downtown.

WINE TOURING

If you'd like to do a bit of wine tasting while you're in the Corvallis area, you can stop in at any of the following wineries and vineyards: North of Corvallis, near the town of Monmouth, you'll find **Airlie Winery,** 15305 Dunn Forest Rd., Monmouth (☎ **503/838-6013**); **Serendipity Cellars Winery,** 15275 Dunn Forest Rd., Monmouth (☎ **503/838-4284**), both of which are off Ore. 99W. Just outside Albany, you'll find **Springhill Cellars,** 2920 NW Scenic Dr., Albany (☎ **541/928-1009**). South of Corvallis off Ore. 99W are **Tyee Wine Cellars,** 26335 Greenberry Rd., Corvallis (☎ **541/753-8754**), and **Bellfountain Cellars,** 25041 Llewellyn Rd., Corvallis (☎ **541/929-3162**).

OUTDOOR ACTIVITIES

If you're a bird watcher, the **William L. Finley National Wildlife Refuge,** 12 miles south of Corvallis on Ore. 99W, is a good place to add a few more birds to your life list. Head west 16 miles from Corvallis on Ore. 34 and you'll come to **Mary's Peak,** the highest peak in the Coast Range. A road leads to the top of the mountain, but there is also a trail that leads from the campground up through a forest of old-growth noble firs to the meadows at the summit.

WHERE TO STAY

IN CORVALLIS

✪ **Hanson Country Inn.** 795 SW Hanson St., Corvallis, OR 97333. ☎ **541/752-2919.** 3 rms. TV TEL. $65–$75 double. Rates include full breakfast. AE, DC, DISC, MC, V. Take Western Blvd. to West Hills Rd.; Hanson St. is on the right just past the fork onto West Hills Rd.

Situated atop a knoll on the edge of town and surrounded by 5 acres of fields and forests, this B&B feels as if it's out in the country yet is within walking distance of the university. The Dutch colonial–style farmhouse was built in 1928 and features loads of built-in cabinets, interesting woodwork, and lots of windows. The decor is in a pastel country motif, and one of the rooms also has its own sitting room.

Super 8 Motel. 407 NW Second St., Corvallis, OR 97330. ☎ **800/800-8000** or 541/758-8088. Fax 541/758-8267. 101 rms. AC TV TEL. $57–$65 double. AE, CB, DC, DISC, MC, V.

It may seem hard to believe that a Super 8 Motel could be one of the best accommodations in town, but Corvallis just doesn't have too many places to stay. This budget motel has a great location on the bank of the Willamette River only a few blocks from downtown. There's an indoor pool and a whirlpool spa, and local calls are free.

IN ALBANY

Brier Rose Inn. 206 Seventh Ave. SW, Albany, OR 97321. ☎ **541/926-0345.** 5 rms (4 with private bath). $49–$59 double without bath; $69–$89 double with bath. Rates include full breakfast. AE, MC, V.

This turreted Queen Anne–style Victorian B&B is on a busy corner in the heart of Albany's historic district. With its balconies, bay windows, curving porches, stained glass, and numerous styles of siding, it's a classic example of Victorian excess. Common areas are filled with period antiques, though the guest rooms are more simply furnished.

WHERE TO DINE
IN CORVALLIS

The Gables. 1121 NW Ninth St. ☎ **541/752-3364.** Reservations recommended. Main courses $13–$26. AE, DISC, MC, V. Daily 5–9pm. CONTINENTAL.

Since 1958, this somewhat formal restaurant has been where college students take their visiting parents. The cuisine is reliable if none too creative. Steaks and prime rib are the pillars of the Gables, though seafood is also available. Both the pâté maison and the smoked salmon are good starter choices. If you can get here between 5 and 6pm Monday through Thursday, or Friday from 5 to 5:30pm, smaller dinners are served at lower prices.

Nearly Normal's. 109 NW 15th St. ☎ **541/753-0791.** Reservations not accepted. Main courses $4–$8.50. No credit cards. Mon–Fri 8am–9pm, Sat 9am–9pm. VEGETARIAN/INTERNATIONAL.

Housed in an old bungalow half a block from campus, Nearly Normal's is your basic college town standby, an international and natural-foods eatery. Nearly Normal's serves up filling portions of food that spans the globe from barbecued tempeh to scarlet pesto to falafel to Grandma Nina's spaghetti. If it's sunny out, try to get a seat out back in the patio area planted with apple trees and kiwi vines. As often as possible, ingredients are organically grown.

The Wine Cellar. In The Cannery Mall, 777 NW Ninth St. ☎ **541/754-0100.** Reservations recommended. Main courses $10–$13. MC, V. Mon–Tues 11am–5pm, Wed–Sat 11am–5pm and 5:30–9pm, Sun 11am–5pm. NEW AMERICAN.

Located in the basement at the back of an unusual shopping mall on the north side of Corvallis, this combination wine shop and restaurant serves up some of the best food in town. Salmon in parchment is the house specialty, but a recent menu also included wild chicken breast stuffed with wild rice and currants, as well as pork loin with a fennel-root sauce. Of course, plenty of good wines are available to go with your meal, and there is also a tasting bar.

IN ALBANY

If you need a good cup of coffee, try **Boccherini's Coffee & Tea House,** 208 SW First Ave. (☎ 541/926-6703), in a downtown historic building with exposed brick walls. For quick deli meals accompanied by Oregon wine, try the **Wine Depot & Deli,** Two Rivers Market, 300 Second Ave. (☎ 541/967-9499). If it's a good pint of ale that you crave, there's **Wyatt's Eatery & Brewhouse,** 211 NW First Ave. (☎ 541/917-3727).

Capriccio Ristorante. 442 First Ave. W. ☎ **541/924-9932.** Reservations recommended. Main courses $10–$18.75. AE, DC, DISC, MC, V. Tues–Thurs 5–9pm, Fri–Sat 5–10pm. ITALIAN.

Located in historic downtown Albany, this restaurant is cavernous, but with its sparkling halogen lights high overhead, it still manages to feel romantic. The menu here is surprisingly sophisticated for Albany. For an antipasto, you can opt for clams steamed in white wine and herbs or perhaps the house-made chicken pâté stuffed with ham and pistachios. For an entree, it's hard to pass up the baby shrimp and pesto lasagna.

○ **Novak's Hungarian Restaurant.** 2835 Santiam Hwy. SE. ☎ **541/967-9488.** Reservations recommended. Main courses $8–$15. DISC, MC, V. Sun–Fri 11am–9pm, Sat 4–9pm. HUNGARIAN.

From the outside, Novak's looks as if it could be a car-repair garage, especially when considering the surrounding neighborhood. However, as soon as you walk through the door you'll be hit with Hungarian hospitality. The tongue-twisting dishes on the menu challenge the long-held belief that Eastern European cuisine means meat and potatoes. More often than not, Hungarian pearl noodles or fresh bread accompany dishes here. The homemade pork sausage is very good, though the chicken paprika, in its creamy red sauce, is probably the restaurant's most popular dish.

4 Eugene & Springfield

40 miles S of Salem, 71 miles N of Roseburg, 61 miles E of Florence

Though Eugene is the second-largest city in Oregon (pop. 110,000), you're more likely to spot tie-dyed T-shirts than silk ties on its downtown streets. This lively laid-back character is due in large part to the presence of the University of Oregon, the state's liberal arts college. The U of O, as it's known here in Oregon, has helped the city develop a very well rounded cultural scene at the heart of which is the grandiose, glass-gabled **Hult Center for the Performing Arts.** On the university's tree-shaded 250-acre campus you'll also find an art museum, a natural-history museum, and a science museum. Eugene has been known for years as a home to liberal-minded folks who have adopted alternative lifestyles. Though 1960s nostalgia has produced a new wave of hippies all over the country in the past few years, many flower children here in Eugene never grew up. At the **Saturday Market,** a weekly outdoor craft market, you can see the works of many of these colorful and creative spirits.

ESSENTIALS

GETTING THERE   Eugene is located just off I-5 at the junction with I-105, which connects Eugene and Springfield, and Ore. 126, which leads east to Bend and west to Florence. Ore. 58 leads southeast to connect with U.S. 97 between Klamath Falls and Bend. Ore. 99W is an alternative to I-5.

The **Eugene airport** is located 9 miles northwest of downtown off Ore. 99W. It's served by Horizon and United.

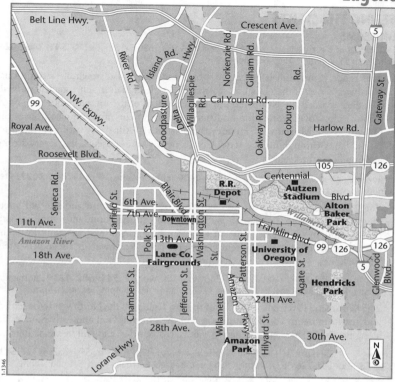

Amtrak passenger trains stop in Eugene. The station is at East Fourth Avenue and Willamette Street.

VISITOR INFORMATION   Contact the **Convention & Visitors Association of Lane County, Oregon,** 115 W. Eighth Ave., Suite 190 (P.O. Box 10286), Eugene, OR 97440 (☎ **800/547-5445** or 541/484-5307).

GETTING AROUND   Car rentals are available at the Eugene airport from **Hertz, Budget, Avis,** and **National.** If you need a taxi, contact **Eugene Yellow Cab** (☎ **541/343-7711**). **Lane Transit District (LTD)** (☎ **541/687-5555**) provides public transit throughout the metropolitan area and out to a number of nearby towns including McKenzie Bridge, which is up the scenic McKenzie River; some routes do not run on Sunday. You can pick up bus-route maps and other information at the **LTD Customer Service Center** at the corner of Tenth Avenue and Willamette Street. LTD fares are 80¢ for adults, 40¢ for seniors and children 5 to 11.

FESTIVALS   The **Eugene Celebration** (☎ **541/687-5215**), held the third weekend in September, is a 3-day celebration that includes a wacky parade and the crowning of the annual Slug Queen. In mid-July, all the region's hippies, both young and old, show up in nearby Veneta for the **Oregon Country Fair** (☎ **541/343-4298**), a showcase for music and crafts. Also of note is **Junction City's Scandinavian Festival** (☎ **541/998-9372**), which celebrates the region's Scandinavian heritage and is held each year on the second weekend in August. Junction City is 14 miles northwest of Eugene.

SEEING THE SIGHTS

MUSEUMS

University of Oregon Museum of Natural History. 1680 E. 15th Ave. ☎ **541/346-3024.** Admission $1 donation. Wed–Sun noon–5pm.

This modern museum is housed in a building designed to resemble a traditional Northwest Coast Indian longhouse. Ancient peoples and even more ancient animals that once roamed the Northwest are the main focus of the museum, but temporary exhibits also cover worldwide traditional cultures. The museum also houses the **Oregon State Museum of History,** which is a repository for artifacts found on public lands throughout the state. Consequently, the museum has a very strong anthropological collection.

University of Oregon Museum of Art. 1430 Johnson Lane. ☎ **541/346-3027.** Free admission. Wed–Sun noon–5pm.

You'll find the university's art museum just east of 14th Avenue and Kincaid Street on the U of O campus. Asian art is the museum's strong point, and primitive African art, Indian sculptures, Russian icons, and Persian miniatures round out the international collections. Contemporary art of the Northwest is also represented. Throughout the year, there are changing exhibits.

Lane County Historical Museum. 740 W. 13th Ave. ☎ **541/682-4239.** Admission $2 adults, $1 senior citizens, 75¢ children 3–17. Wed–Fri 10am–4pm, Sat noon–4pm.

The Willamette River valley was one of the first regions of the Northwest to be settled, and at this museum you'll find displays on the Oregon Trail and early pioneer life along the river. There are also period rooms, old vehicles, and children's exhibits.

Springfield Museum/Historic Springfield Interpretive Center. 590 Main St. ☎ **541/726-2300** or 541/726-3677. Admission $1 adults. Wed–Fri 10am–4pm, Sat noon–4pm.

More area historical artifacts, here focusing on the region's industrial, logging, and agricultural heritage, are on display in this renovated 1908 Pacific Power & Light building. The collection of old photos is very evocative.

Maude Kerns Art Center. 1910 E. 15th Ave. ☎ **541/345-1571.** Admission by donation. Mon–Tues and Thurs–Fri 9am–5pm, Wed 9am–6pm, Sat noon–5pm.

The works of contemporary local, regional, and national craftspeople are the subjects of changing exhibits at this small gallery. You'll find this art center just up the street from the Museum of Natural History.

Oregon Air and Space Museum. 90377 Boeing Dr. ☎ **541/461-1101.** Admission $3 adults, $1 children 6–11. Thurs–Sun noon–4pm.

Located near the Eugene airport, the museum focuses on the history of aviation in Oregon. Numerous aircraft, including an F-4 Phantom, an F-86F, and an L-19, are on display.

Willamette Science & Technology Center (WISTEC). 2300 Leo Harris Pkwy. ☎ **541/687-3619.** Admission $3 adults, $2 seniors and children 3–17. Wed–Fri noon–5pm, Sat–Sun 11am–5pm.

With loads of cool hands-on exhibits, this is the place to bring the kids to teach them about science. You might even learn something yourself. This building also houses a planetarium that offers changing features throughout the year.

PARKS & GARDENS

Alton Baker Park, on the north bank of the Willamette River, is Eugene's most popular park and offers jogging and biking trails. Across the river, **Skinner Butte Park** on the north side of downtown Eugene includes a 12-mile bike path. Nearby

The Bridges of Lane County

In Robert James Waller's runaway hit novel *The Bridges of Madison County,* photographer Robert Kincaid hales from the Puget Sound area, but *National Geographic* sends him all the way to Madison County, Iowa, to photograph covered bridges. Kincaid could have saved himself a lot of miles on that beat-up old pickup truck if he had just headed south into Oregon, where he would have found the largest concentration of covered bridges west of the Mississippi.

Today, there are 53 covered bridges still standing in Oregon, down from more than 300 as recently as the 1930s. The oldest covered bridge is the Upper Drift Creek Bridge near Lincoln City, which dates from 1914, but there are also bridges built as recently as 1988. Built of wood and covered to protect them from the rain and extend their life, the covered bridges of Oregon are found primarily in the Willamette Valley, where early farmers needed safe river and stream crossings to get their crops to market. The highest concentration of covered bridges is found in Lane County, which stretches from the crest of the Cascade Range all the way to the Pacific Ocean and is home to 20 covered bridges.

You can get a map and guide to Lane County's covered bridges from the **Convention & Visitors Association of Lane County, Oregon,** 115 W. Eighth Ave., Suite 190, Eugene, OR 97440 (☎ **800/547-5445** or 541/484-5307).

To do a bit of covered bridge touring, head southeast from Eugene on Ore. 58. for 5 miles, turn left on Parkway Road, and go 3 miles north. Turn southeast on Jasper-Lowell Road and in 4 miles turn onto Place Road where you'll find the Pengra Bridge, which was restored in 1994. Another 4 1/2 miles on the Jasper-Lowell Road will bring you to the Unity Bridge. Continuing into the town of Lowell, you can visit the Cannon Street Bridge, a tiny pedestrian bridge built in 1988. South of Lowell on the Jasper-Lowell Road, you'll find the Lowell Bridge. When the Jasper-Lowell Road reaches Ore. 58, turn east and continue 21 miles to Westfir, where you'll find the Office Bridge, which at 180 feet in length is the longest covered bridge in Oregon. Heading back toward Eugene on Ore. 58, watch for Lost Creek Road, 11 miles east of I-5. After 1.8 miles on Lost Creek Road, turn onto Rattlesnake Road. In half a mile, turn south on Lost Valley Lane to Parvin Road and the Parvin Bridge.

Another good bridge route begins in Cottage Grove. Here in town, you can see the Centennial Bridge, a pedestrian bridge on Main Street. This bridge was built in 1987 from timbers salvaged from a dismantled covered bridge. From here, cross the river and drive 3/4 mile south on South River Road to the Chambers Bridge. This is the only remaining covered railroad bridge in Oregon. Head back into Cottage Grove and take Row River Road 2 1/2 miles to Layng Road. In 1.4 miles, you'll come to the Currin Bridge. Continuing another 1.2 miles south on Layng Road will bring you to the Mosby Creek Bridge. Continue south and turn left on Mosby Creek Road. You'll soon come to Garoutte Road, where you'll see the Stewart Bridge. Drive 2 1/2 miles north on Garoutte Road and turn right onto Shoreview Drive. Follow this road 6.7 miles to the Dorena Bridge.

Another easy covered bridge tour begins in Albany, which is in Linn County (north of Lane County). Contact the **Albany Visitors Association,** 300 Second Ave. SW, Albany, OR 97321 (☎ **800/526-2256** or 541/928-0911), for a map and guide to this tour, which visits 10 covered bridges. If you still haven't had enough covered bridges, there are seven more near Roseburg, south of Eugene. Brochures available from the **City of Roseburg Visitors & Convention Center,** 410 SE Spruce St. (P.O. Box 1262), Roseburg, OR 97470 (☎ **800/444-9584** or 541/672-9731), will guide you to the area's covered bridges.

are the **Owen Memorial Rose Gardens.** At the **Mount Pisgah Arboretum,** Frank Parish Road, south of town off Seavey Loop Road, you can hike 5 miles of trails through meadows and forests. Set beneath towering fir trees high on a hill overlooking the city, **Hendricks Park and Rhododendron Garden** is one of the prettiest parks in the city, especially in the spring when the rhododendrons bloom. You'll find this park in southeast Eugene off Franklin Boulevard (U.S. 99). Take Walnut Street to Fairmount Boulevard and then turn east on Summit Avenue.

WINE TOURING

Eugene is at the southern limit of the Willamette Valley wine region, and there are more than half a dozen wineries and vineyards within 30 miles of the city. To do a bit of wine touring, head west out of Eugene on Ore. 126 to the Elmira and Veneta area where you'll find the following wineries, all of which have tasting rooms that are open on a regular basis (usually noon to 5 daily in summer and weekends only other months): **Hinman Vineyards,** 27012 Briggs Hill Rd., Eugene (☎ **541/345-1945**); **Chateau Lorane,** 27415 Siuslaw River Rd., Lorane (☎ **541/942-8028**); **LaVelle Vineyards,** 89697 Sheffler Rd., Elmira (☎ **541/935-9406**); and **Secret House Vineyards Winery,** 88324 Vineyard Lane, Veneta (☎ **541/935-3774**).

Another concentration of wineries can be found about midway between Eugene and Corvallis. These include **Rainsong Vineyards,** 92989 Templeton Rd., Cheshire (☎ **541/998-1786**); **High Pass Winery,** 24757 Lavell Rd., Junction City (☎ **541/998-1447**), which are only open Memorial Day weekend and Thanksgiving weekend; and **Alpine Vineyards,** downtown Alpine (☎ **541/424-5851**).

OUTDOOR ACTIVITIES

With two rivers, the McKenzie and the Willamette, flowing through the Eugene/Springfield area, it isn't surprising that this city has quite a bit of water-oriented activities. You can rent canoes, kayaks, rafts, and pedal boats at **River Runner Supply,** 2222 Centennial Blvd. (☎ **800/223-4326** or 541/343-6883), which is in Alton Baker Park. Rates range from $4 to $6 per hour. For more exciting river running, contact **The Oregon Paddler** (☎ **800/267-6848** or 541/741-8661), which offers a quick and easy Willamette River float trip right through Eugene ($24.50). This company also does longer and more exciting rafting trips on both the Willamette and McKenzie rivers ($49.50 to $200). See the "Up the McKenzie River" section of chapter 9, "The Cascades," for more information on rafting the upper reaches of the McKenzie River.

The calmer waters of **Fern Ridge Reservoir,** 12 miles west of Eugene on Ore. 126, attract boardsailing enthusiasts. Sailing, powerboating, waterskiing, and swimming are also popular.

Eugene is Oregon's best bicycling city, and if you'd like to see why, you can rent a bike at **Pedal Power Bicycles,** 535 High St. (☎ **541/687-1775**). This store has road bikes, mountain bikes, and tandems. Rates start at $5 per hour or $20 per day.

Golfers have plenty of Eugene options, including the **Fiddler's Green Golf Club,** 91292 Ore. 99N (☎ **541/689-8464**); the **Oakway Golf Course,** 2000 Cal Young Rd. (☎ **541/484-1927**); the **Riveridge Golf Course,** 3800 N. Delta Hwy. (☎ **541/345-9160**).

SHOPPING

You can shop for one-of-a-kind crafts at Eugene's **Saturday Market** (☎ **541/686-8885**), which covers more than two downtown blocks beginning at the corner of Eighth Avenue and Oak Street. The bustling outdoor arts-and-crafts market was founded in 1970. Good, inexpensive food, fresh produce, and live music round out the offerings of this colorful event. The market is held every Saturday from 10am to 5pm between April and December.

Other days of the week, you can explore the **Market District,** a 6-block area of restored buildings that now house unusual shops, galleries, restaurants, and night-clubs. The **Fifth Street Public Market,** 296 E. Fifth St. at the corner of Fifth Avenue and High Street, is the centerpiece of the area, and has a courtyard that almost always features some sort of free entertainment. Among the interesting shops here, you'll find **Twist,** selling fine crafts and wildly artistic jewelry; **French Quarter,** selling fine linens; **Watches by Gosh,** with an amazing variety of watches and sunglasses; and **The Nike Store,** selling you know what. Directly across Fifth Avenue is the **5th & Pearl building,** which houses the city's best restaurant (Chanterelle), a couple of music stores, and an antique shop, among others. **Station Square,** a block west on Fifth Avenue, is a modern upscale mall designed to look like an old train station. Also nearby is **Down to Earth,** 532 Olive St. (☎ **541/342-6820**), a fascinating garden and housewares shop housed in an old granary building. If you're interested in Asian art, stop by the **White Lotus Gallery,** 760 Willamette St. (☎ **541/345-3276**), which specializes in the contemporary art of Asia.

WHERE TO STAY

Best Western New Oregon Motel. 1655 Franklin Blvd., Eugene, OR 97403. ☎ **800/528-1234** or 541/683-3669. Fax 541/484-5556. 128 rms. A/C TV TEL. $58–$80 double. AE, CB, DC, DISC, EURO, MC, V.

Located across the street from the university campus, this Best Western is a convenient and economical choice. Although the motel looks a bit old from the outside, guest rooms are in good shape and come with refrigerators and hair dryers. If you're in need of a bit of exercise or relaxing, you'll find racquetball courts, an indoor swimming pool, a whirlpool tub, saunas, an exercise room, and a sundeck.

✪ **The Campbell House.** 252 Pearl St., Eugene, OR 97401. ☎ **800/264-2519** or 541/343-1119. Fax 541/343-2258. 12 rms. TV TEL. $75–$275 double. AE, MC, V. Rates include full breakfast.

Located only 2 blocks from the Market District and set on Skinner's Butte overlooking the city, this large Victorian home was built in 1892 and now offers convenience and comfort. The guest rooms here vary considerably in size and price so there's something to fit all tastes and budgets. Breakfasts are served in a sunny room with a curving wall of glass, and there's also a parlor with a similar glass wall. Several of the guest rooms on the first floor have high ceilings, and down in the basement is a pine-paneled room with a fishing theme and another with a golf theme. The upstairs rooms have plenty of windows, and in the largest room you'll find wood floors and a double whirlpool tub.

Eugene Hilton Hotel. 66 E. Sixth Ave., Eugene, OR 97401. ☎ **800/445-8667** or 541/342-2000. Fax 503/342-6661. 271 rms, 12 suites. A/C TV TEL. $95–$150 double; $185–$275 suite. AE, CB, DC, DISC, MC, V.

If you're looking for the amenities of a high-rise, business hotel right in downtown Eugene, the Hilton is your only choice. The Hult Center for the Performing Arts is right next door and dozens of restaurants and cafes are within a few blocks. Try to get a room on an upper floor so you can enjoy the views. If you need plenty of room, there are minisuites that have sleeping alcoves.

Dining/Entertainment: The hotel's coffee shop is just off the lobby, while the more formal dining room is up on the 12th floor and offers great views. The Lobby Bar is a convenient place for an after-work drink, and up on the top floor is a more lively nightclub.

Services: Room service, free airport shuttle, complimentary health-club membership.
Facilities: Indoor pool, exercise room, whirlpool, saunas.

✪ **The Secret Garden.** 1910 University St., Eugene, OR 97403. ☎ **888/484-6755** or 541/
484-6755. 10 rms. $95–$240 double. Rates include full breakfast. MC, V.

This newly opened B&B is housed in what was once a sorority house, though
before that it was the home of Eugene pioneer Alton Baker, for whom the city's
waterfront park is named. Today, the large inn is run by the granddaughter of Portland shipping and steel magnate Henry Kaiser and is filled with family heirlooms and
other European and Asian art and antiques. Guest rooms are beautifully and very
tastefully decorated with interesting touches here and there to add visual interest. One
of our favorite rooms is the Scented Garden, which has floor lamps made from
Tibetan horns and a gorgeous sitar on display. On every guest room door, you'll find
painted some memorable quotation, and in the upstairs sitting room, there is a
fascinating mural of Daphne turned into a tree. Yes, there is a secret garden as well
as a not so secret one. The former is a unique outdoor room with living walls that
hide a whirlpool tub.

✪ **Valley River Inn.** 1000 Valley River Way (P.O. Box 10088), Eugene, OR 97440. ☎ **800/
543-8266** or 541/687-0123. Fax 541/683-5121. Web site: http://www.valleyriverinn.com.
257 rms, 15 suites. A/C TV TEL. $155–$200 double; $215–$300 suite. AE, CB, DC, DISC,
MC, V. Valet parking $5.

Though it's a few minutes' drive from downtown and the university, the Valley River
Inn claims an envious location on the bank of the Willamette River. The low-rise
hotel is lushly landscaped to evoke the green forests of the Northwest, and though
all the rooms are large and have a balcony or patio, the riverside rooms have the best
views. Eugene's largest shopping mall is adjacent, and an extensive network of paved
riverside walking/jogging/bicycling paths pass the hotel.

Dining/Entertainment: Sweetwater's Restaurant, with its long wall of glass overlooking the river, is one of the city's best restaurants and serves primarily moderately
priced Northwest cuisine. In the same large room is a more casual bar and grill with
live contemporary music most evenings.

Services: Concierge, room service, free airport shuttle, access to nearby health club,
bicycle rentals.

Facilities: Outdoor pool, whirlpool, saunas, exercise room.

WHERE TO DINE
EXPENSIVE

Adam's Place. 30 E. Broadway. ☎ **541/344-6948.** Reservations recommended. Main courses
$15–$22. AE, MC, V. Tues–Thurs 11:30am–2pm and 5–9pm, Fri 11:30am–2pm and 5–10pm,
Sat 5–10pm. NORTHWEST.

Located downtown on the pedestrian mall, this restaurant conjures up the atmosphere
of an old English inn and is now one of the most elegant dining establishments in
the city. The menu is short and changes frequently, but on a recent summer evening
the appetizer menu included fragrant salmon-and-dill potato pancakes as well as fresh
oysters with a mignonette of cranberries, shallots, and rice wine. Entree flavors tend
to the simpler end of creative cookery, with emphasis on subtle flavors and perfect
preparation. Salmon might be finished with a spicy orange glaze and then topped
with toasted black and white sesame seeds, or rack of lamb might be crusted in herbs
and garlic and served with a morel-and-brandy demi-glace. In the summer, you can
also dine under the stars out on the patio. Several nights each week there is live music,
either jazz or classical.

Ambrosia. 174 E. Broadway. ☎ **541/342-4141.** Reservations recommended for parties of 6 or more. Main courses $10–$14. MC, V. Sun–Thurs 11:30am–10pm, Fri–Sat 11:30am–11pm. REGIONAL ITALIAN.

The white-tiled entry, exposed brick walls, pressed-tin ceiling, and ornately carved wooden back bar all combine to give Ambrosia a genuine historical appeal. The menu offers quite a few tempting dishes. Pasta fans will enjoy the creamy farfalle (bow ties) with prosciutto, sun-dried tomatoes, red-pepper flakes, and Parmesan. Many of the entrees are familiar, such as lemon chicken or scampi, but the chicken with fontina cheese, fresh basil, and a roasted-pepper sauce is a delicious and unusual dish.

Chanterelle. 207 E. Fifth St. ☎ **541/484-4065.** Reservations highly recommended. Main courses $14–$24. AE, CB, DISC, MC, V. Tues–Thurs 5–10pm, Fri–Sat 5–11pm. CONTINENTAL.

This small continental restaurant is located in one of downtown Eugene's many restored old industrial buildings that have been turned into chic shopping centers. There are few surprises on the menu, just tried-and-true recipes prepared with reliable expertise and served with gracious attentiveness. Escargots bourguignonne, oysters Rockefeller, tournedos of beef, and steak Diane are just some of the familiar dishes on the Chanterelle menu. You'll also sometimes find emu, moose, and buffalo on the menu. A long wine list offers plenty of choices for the perfect accompaniment to your meal.

MODERATE

✪ **Zenon Café.** 898 Pearl St. ☎ **541/343-3005.** Reservations not accepted. Main courses $6.75–$16.25. MC, V. Mon–Thurs 8am–11pm, Fri–Sat 8am–midnight, Sun 9:30am–11pm. INTERNATIONAL.

Urbanites visiting Eugene will be glad to know that they can find sophistication even in such a small city. The interior of this trendy (and noisy) cafe is black on black, with just a hint of bare wood for accent. The menu, which changes daily, is long and emphasizes whatever flavor combinations are currently in vogue. The globe-trotting menu assures all adventurous eaters of finding something they've never tried before. Before you ever reach your table, though, you'll have to run the gamut of the dessert case, which usually flaunts about 20 irresistible cakes, pies, tortes, and other pastries.

INEXPENSIVE

Mekala's. 296 E. Fifth Ave. ☎ **541/342-4872.** Reservations recommended. Main courses $7.50–$15. AE, MC, V. Mon–Thurs 11am–9pm, Fri 11am–10pm, Sat noon–10pm, Sun noon–9pm. THAI.

Located on the second floor of the Fifth Street Public Market, Mekala's has a bit of Thai decor. Separated from the main dining room by several French doors is a patio dining area with a few tables. Brick floors give the restaurant a feel of age. The menu is quite long and includes a substantial vegetarian section. On a cool evening nothing warms better than a big bowl of thom yom kung, a sour-and-spicy shrimp soup. The homoke soufflé, made with coconut milk and various seafoods, is an unusual and delicious dish that rarely turns up on Thai menus in this country.

Mona Lizza. 830 Olive St. ☎ **541/345-1072.** Main courses $9–$15. AE, DC, MC, V. Daily 11:30am–11:30pm. ITALIAN.

Affiliated with the Eugene City Brewery and the West Bros. BBQ next door, this restaurant offers wood-oven pizzas, pasta, and microbrew ales brewed on the premises. The dark brick-and-wood interior has a classic publike feel. Pool tables keep customers entertained. The dessert case just inside the front door may have you thinking about a salad instead of a big plate of pasta. There's a great collection of Mona Lisa paintings hanging on the walls.

Poppi's Anatolia. 992 Willamette St. ☎ **541/343-9661.** Reservations accepted for 6 or more people only. Main course $6.50–$11.25. MC, V. Mon–Thurs 11:30am–9:30pm, Fri 11:30am–10pm, Sat 11:30am–3pm and 5–10pm, Sun 5–9:30pm. GREEK/INDIAN.

This cozy little cafe just off the downtown pedestrian mall serves an unusual combination of cuisines, and with its funky atmosphere and low prices represents everything a good college-town restaurant should be. Plates are piled high with the flavors of the East, and it's hard to say whether the Greek or the Indian dishes are the more flavorful. However, one thing is for sure, the fresh chutneys that accompany the Indian dishes are outstanding.

EUGENE AFTER DARK

With its two theaters and nonstop schedule, the **Hult Center for the Performing Arts,** Seventh Avenue and Willamette Street (☎ **541/682-5000**), is the heart and soul of this city's performing arts scene. The center's huge glass gables are an unmistakable landmark of downtown Eugene, and each year this sparkling temple of the arts manages to put together a first-rate schedule of performances by the Eugene Symphony, the Eugene Ballet Company, the Eugene Opera, and other local and regional companies, as well as visiting companies and performers. Tickets run $6 to $40. During the summer, the center hosts the Oregon Bach Festival, the Oregon Festival of American Music, and the Eugene Festival of Musical Theatre. Summer concerts are also held at the **Cuthbert Amphitheater** in Alton Baker Park. October through May, there are free Thursday lunchtime concerts.

To find out what's happening in town, pick up a copy of the free *Eugene Weekly,* which is available at restaurants and shops around town.

NIGHTCLUBS, BARS, COFFEEHOUSES & BREW PUBS

In addition to the places listed below, you'll find plenty of microbreweries in Eugene. These include the **High Street Brewery & Cafe,** 1243 High St. (☎ **541/345-4905**); the **East 19th Street Cafe,** 1485 E. 19th St. (☎ **541/342-4025**); ○ **Eugene City Brewery,** 844 Olive St. (☎ **541/345-8489**); **Steelhead Brewery & Cafe,** 199 E. Fifth Ave. (☎ **541/686-2739**); **Fields Restaurant & Brewpub,** 1290 Oak St. (☎ **541/341-6599**); and the **Wild Duck Restaurant & Brewery,** 169 W. Sixth St. (☎ **541/485-DUCK**).

Cafe Paradiso. 115 W. Broadway. ☎ **541/484-9933.**

This is one of Eugene's most popular coffeehouses and has an eclectic schedule of live music, including open-mike nights. Good coffee and voluptuous scones.

○ **Jo Federigo's Café & Bar.** 259 E. Fifth Ave. ☎ **541/343-8488.**

Housed in a historic granary building, Jo Federigo's is both a popular restaurant and Eugene's favorite jazz club. There's live music nightly.

Oregon Electric Station. 27 E. Fifth Ave. ☎ **541/485-4444.**

This building dates from 1914, and with a wine cellar in an old railroad car, lots of oak, and a back bar that requires a ladder to access all the various bottles of premium spirits, it's the poshest bar in town.

WOW Hall. 291 W. Eighth Ave. ☎ **541/687-2746.**

The historic Woodmen of the World Hall now serves as a sort of community center for the performing arts and hosts an eclectic array of concerts and performances by alternative bands.

The Columbia Gorge 8

The Columbia Gorge, which begins a few miles east of Portland and extends for nearly 70 miles to The Dalles, is a giant bridge that cuts through the Cascade Range and connects the rain-soaked west-side forests with the desert-dry sagebrush scrublands of central Oregon. This change in climate is caused by moist air condensing into snow and rain as it passes over the crest of the Cascades. Most of the air's moisture falls on the western slopes, so that the eastern slopes and the land stretching for hundreds of miles beyond lie in what's called a rain shadow. Perhaps nowhere else on earth can you so easily witness this rain-shadow effect. It's so pronounced that as you come around a bend on I-84 just east of Hood River, you can see dry grasslands to the east and dense forests of moisture-loving Douglas fir over your shoulder to the west. In between the two extremes lies a community of plants that's unique to the Columbia Gorge. Springtime in the gorge sees colorful displays of wildflowers, many of which exist only here.

The Columbia River is second only to the Mississippi in the volume of water it carries to the sea, but more than just water flows through the Columbia Gorge. As the only break over the entire length of the Cascade Range the gorge acts as a massive natural wind tunnel. During the summer the sun bakes the lands east of the Cascades, causing the air over these lands to rise. Cool air from the west side then rushes up the river, whipping through Hood River with near gale force at times. These winds, blowing against the downriver flow of water, set up ideal conditions for boardsailing. The reliability of these winds, and the waves they kick up, has turned Hood River, once an ailing lumber town, into the Aspen of boardsailing.

The Columbia River is older than the hills. It's older than the mountains, too. And it's the river's great age that accounts for why the waters cut a gorge through the Cascades. The mountains have actually risen up around the river. Though the river's geologic history dates back 40 million years or so, it was a series of recent events, geologically speaking, that gave the Columbia Gorge its very distinctive appearance. About 15,000 years ago, toward the end of the last Ice Age, huge dams of ice far upstream burst and sent floodwaters racing down the Columbia. As the floodwaters swept through the Columbia Gorge, they were as much as 1,200 feet high. Ice and rock carried by the floodwaters helped the river to scour out the sides of the once gently sloping gorge, leaving behind the steep-walled gorge that we know today. The waterfalls that attract so many oohs and aahs are the most dramatic evidence of these great floods. As early as 1915, a scenic highway was built through the gorge, and in 1986 much of the area was designated the Columbia Gorge National Scenic Area to preserve its spectacular and unique natural beauty.

For centuries the Columbia River has been an important route between the maritime Northwest and the dry interior. Lewis and Clark canoed down the river in 1805, and pioneers followed the Oregon Trail to its shores at The Dalles. It was here at The Dalles that many pioneers transferred their wagons to boats for the dangerous journey downriver to Oregon City. The set of rapids known as The Dalles and the waterfalls of the Cascades were the two most dangerous sections of the Columbia Gorge, so towns arose at these two points to transport goods and people around the treacherous waters. Locks and a canal helped circumvent these two sections of white water, but today the rapids of the Columbia lie flooded beneath the waters behind the Bonneville and The Dalles dams. Though the ease of navigating the river today has dimmed the importance of the Cascade Locks and The Dalles, these two river towns are still steeped in the history of the Columbia River Gorge.

1 The Columbia Gorge National Scenic Area

Columbia Gorge: begins 18 miles E of Portland

Stretching from the Sandy River in the west to the Deschutes River in the east, the Columbia Gorge National Scenic Area is one of the most breathtakingly dramatic pieces of scenery in the United States. Carved by floods of unimaginable proportions and power, this miles-wide canyon is flanked on the north by Mount Adams and on the south by Mount Hood, both of which rise more than 11,000 feet high. With its basalt cliffs painted with colorful lichens, diaphanous waterfalls, and dark forests of Douglas firs rising above the Columbia River, the Gorge is a year-round recreational area where hiking trails lead to hidden waterfalls and mountain-top panoramas, mountain bike trails meander through the forest, and boardsailors race across wind-whipped waters.

The Columbia Gorge National Scenic Area is also as controversial as it is beautiful. Over the years since this area received this federal designation, the fights over the use of private land within the Gorge have been constant. The pressure to develop this scenic marvel of the Northwest has been unrelenting and land owners throughout the Gorge have fought against restrictions on how they can develop their lands. To find out more about protecting the Gorge, contact the **Friends of the Columbia Gorge** (☎ **503/241-3762**), which, each spring, offers numerous guided wildflower hikes.

ESSENTIALS

GETTING THERE   I-84 and the Historic Columbia River Highway both pass through the gorge on the Oregon side of the Columbia.

VISITOR INFORMATION   Contact the **Columbia River Gorge National Scenic Area,** Wacoma Center, 902 Wasco Ave., Hood River, OR 97031 (☎ **541/386-2333**).

LEARNING ABOUT THE GORGE & ITS HISTORY

✪ **Columbia Gorge Interpretive Center.** 990 SW Rock Creek Dr., Stevenson. ☎ **509/427-8211.** Admission $6 adults, $5 seniors and students, $4 children 6–12, free for children 5 and under. Daily 10am–5pm. Closed Easter, Thanksgiving, Christmas, and New Year's.

This museum on the Washington side of the Gorge is your best introduction to the Gorge and focuses on early Native American inhabitants and the development of the

The Columbia Gorge

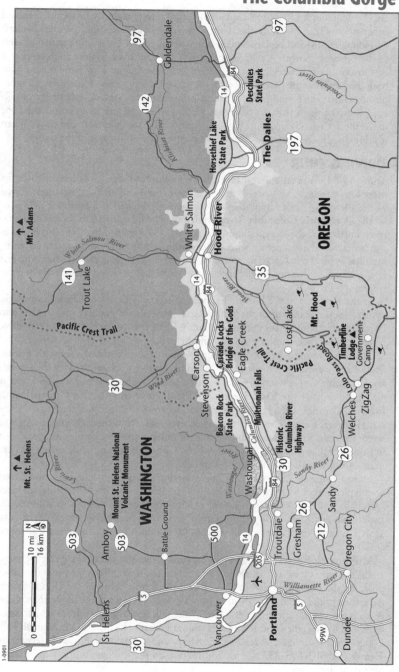

area by white settlers. Exhibits contain historical photographs by Edward Curtis and other photos that illustrate the story of portage companies and paddlewheelers. Period quotations and explanations of gorge history put the museum's many artifacts in their proper context. A relic here that you can't miss is a 37-foot-high replica of a 19th-century fish wheel, which gives an understanding of how salmon runs have been threatened in the past as well as in the present. Displays also frankly discuss other problems that the coming of civilization brought to this area. A slide program tells the history of the formation of the gorge, and when the volcanoes erupt, the floor in the theater actually shakes from the intensity of the low-volume sound track. When it's not cloudy, the center has an awesome view of the south side of the Gorge.

A DRIVING TOUR

Though I-84 is the fastest road through the Columbia Gorge, it is certainly not the most scenic route. The Gorge, with its many natural and artificial wonders, is well worth a leisurely day's explorations and is best appreciated at a more leisurely pace on the ✪ **Historic Columbia River Highway,** which begins 16 miles east of downtown Portland at the second Troutdale exit off I-84. Opened in 1915, this highway was a marvel of engineering when it was built and, by providing access by automobiles, opened the Gorge up to casual visits. However, this manufactured marvel was, and still is, dwarfed by the spectacular vistas that present themselves along the route.

At the very start of the historic highway, you'll find **Lewis & Clark State Park,** which is near the mouth of the Sandy River. This park is popular with anglers and Portlanders looking to cool off in the Sandy River during the hot summer months. There is also a rock-climbing area within the park.

The first astounding view of the Gorge comes at the **Portland Women's Forum State Park** viewpoint. This is also likely to be your first encounter with the legendary Columbia Gorge winds. To learn more about the historic highway and how it was built, stop at the **Vista House,** 733 feet above the river on **Crown Point.** Inside this historic 1916 building, there are informative displays, including old photos. However, most visitors can't tear their eyes away from the view long enough to concentrate on any of the exhibits. Some 30 miles of breathtaking views spread out in front of you as you gaze up and down the Columbia River. A side road near here leads 14 miles to the top of Larch Mountain.

From Crown Point, the historic highway drops down into the gorge and passes several picturesque **waterfalls**—Latourelle Falls, Shepherd's Dell Falls, Bridalveil Falls, Mist Falls, and Wahkeena Falls—that are either right beside the road or a short walk away. If you're interested in a longer hike, there are trails linking several of the falls, as well as other trails that lead to viewpoints and deep into the adjacent wilderness area.

Multnomah Falls is the largest and the most famous waterfall along this highway, and is the state's most visited natural attraction. At 620 feet from the lip to the lower pool, it's the tallest waterfall in Oregon and the fourth tallest in the United States. An arched bridge stands directly in front of the falls and is a favorite of photographers. A steep paved trail leads from the foot of the falls up to the top, from which other trails lead off into the **Mount Hood National Forest.** The historic Multnomah Falls Lodge has a restaurant, snack bar, gift shop, and a **National Forest Interpretive Center** (☎ **503/695-2372**) with information on the geology, history, and natural history of the Gorge.

East of Multnomah Falls, the scenic highway passes by **Oneonta Gorge,** a narrow rift in the cliffs. Through this tiny gorge flows a stream that serves as a pathway for anyone interested in exploring upstream to **Oneonta Falls.** There are also a couple of trails here that head upstream through the forest to Triple Falls and Pony Tail Falls (the trail passes behind this latter waterfall).

Continuing east on the highway, you'll pass **Benson State Park,** which offers picnicking and swimming, and **Horsetail Falls,** which is shortly before the historic highway merges with I-84. Just after the two highways merge, you come to the exit for **Bonneville Lock and Dam** (☎ 541/374-8820). The **Bradford Island Visitors Center** has exhibits on the history of this dam, which was built in 1927. One of the most important features of the dam is its fish ladder, which allows adult salmon to return upriver to spawn. Underwater windows let visitors see fish as they pass through the ladder. Visit the adjacent fish hatchery to see how trout, salmon, and sturgeon are raised before being released into the river. At this same exit off I-84, you'll find access to a newly restored 1½-mile-long section of the Historic Columbia River Highway that is now open to hikers and bikers.

Beyond the dam is Eagle Creek, probably the single best area in the gorge for a hike. The ☼ **Eagle Creek Trail** leads past several waterfalls and, if you have time for only one hike in the Gorge, it should be this one. You'll also find a campground and picnic area here.

Not far beyond Eagle Creek is the **Bridge of the Gods,** which connects Oregon and Washington at the site where, according to a Native American legend, a natural bridge used by the gods once stood. Geologists believe that the legend may have some basis in fact. There is evidence that a massive rock slide may have once blocked the river at this point.

Just beyond the Bridge of the Gods is **Cascade Locks.** It was at this site that cascades once turned the otherwise placid Columbia River into a raging torrent that required boats to be portaged around the cascades. In 1896 the Cascade Locks were built, allowing steamships to pass the cascades unhindered. When the locks were opened, they made traveling between The Dalles and Portland much easier. However, the completion of the Columbia River Scenic Highway in 1915 made the trip even easier by land. With the construction of the Bonneville Lock and Dam, the cascades were flooded and the locks became superfluous.

There are two small museums here at the locks. The **Cascade Locks Historical Museum,** Marine Park (☎ 541/374-8535), which is housed in the old lock-tender's house, includes displays of Native American artifacts and pioneer memorabilia, as well as the Northwest's first steam engine. It's open daily May through September, from noon to 5pm.

The **Port of Cascade Locks Visitors Center,** which has displays on river travel in the past, is also the ticket office for the stern-wheeler *Columbia Gorge* (☎ 541/374-8427 or 503/223-3928), which makes regular trips on the river all summer. These cruises provide a great perspective on the Gorge. Fares for the 2-hour scenic cruises are $12.95 for adults and $7.95 for children; dinner, lunch, breakfast, brunch, and other special cruises run $25.95 to $35.95 for adults and $16.95 to $30.95 for children.

Should you decide not to take the historic highway and stay on I-84, you may want to stop at **Rooster Rock State Park,** especially if it's a hot summer day. This park has a long sandy beach, and in a remote section of the park there's even a clothing-optional beach. From I-84 there's also easy access to Multnomah Falls, which is the main attraction of the Historic Columbia River Highway.

Another driving option is to cross to the Washington side of the Columbia River and take Wash. 14 east from Vancouver. This latter highway actually provides the most spectacular views of both the Columbia Gorge and Mount Hood. If you should decide to take this route, be sure to stop at **Beacon Rock,** an 800-foot-tall monolith that has a trail leading to its summit. At one time there was talk of blasting the rock apart to build jetties at the mouth of the river. Luckily, another source of rock was used and this amazing landmark continues to guard the Columbia. If you want to make better time, you can cross back to Oregon on the Bridge of the Gods. Continuing on the Washington side of the river, you'll come to Stevenson, site of the above-mentioned Columbia Gorge Interpretive Center.

Beyond Stevenson, you come to the town of Carson, where you can avail yourself of the therapeutic waters of the **Carson Hot Springs Resort** (☎ **509/427-8292**), located just north of town. It's open daily from 8:30am to 7pm; charges are $10 for a soak that includes a postsoak wrap and $32 for an hour's massage. The resort has been in business since 1897 and looks every bit of its age. However, it's just this old-fashioned appeal that keeps people coming back year after year to soak in the hot mineral springs (separate men's and women's soaking tubs) and get massaged. There are also some very basic hotel rooms ($30 to $35) and cabins ($40 to $50) available. If you're looking for natural hot springs, the folks here can give you directions to some that are nearby.

BOARDSAILING, FISHING & HORSEBACK RIDING

If you're looking for someplace to launch your sailboard along this stretch of the Gorge, try **Rooster Rock State Park,** near the west end of the Gorge, or **Viento State Park,** just west of Hood River.

To hire a guide to take you fishing for salmon or steelhead, contact Mike Claggett of **Mike's Guide Service** (☎ **541/374-2228**) in Cascade Locks. Fishing trips run $60 for a half day and $110 for a full day.

If you'd like to play cowboy in the Gorge, you can go horseback riding at **Mountain Shadow Ranch** (☎ **541/374-8592**), which is also located in Cascade Locks. Expect to pay around $20 for a 1-hour ride and $35 for a 2-hour ride.

WHERE TO STAY

Best Western Columbia River Inn. 735 WaNaPa St. (P.O. Box 580), Cascade Locks, OR 97014. ☎ **800/595-7108** or 541/374-8777. Fax 541/374-2279. 63 rms. A/C TV TEL. $79–$124 double. Rates include continental breakfast. AE, CB, DC, DISC, MC, V.

Located at the foot of the Bridge of the Gods and ideally located for exploring the Gorge, this modern motel has splendid views from its river-view rooms. Many of the rooms also have small balconies, although nearby railroad tracks can make it a bit noisy for sitting out. Luckily, rooms are well insulated against train noises. For a splurge, you can opt for a spa room. Facilities include an indoor pool and whirlpool and exercise room.

✪ **McMenamins Edgefield Bed & Breakfast Resort.** 2126 SW Halsey St., Troutdale, OR 97060. ☎ **800/669-8610** or 503/669-8610. 103 rms (3 with bath), 24 hostel beds. $75–115 double; $18 hostel bed. Rates include full breakfast. AE, DISC, MC, V.

B&Bs don't usually have 100 rooms, but this is no ordinary inn. Located 30 minutes east of downtown Portland and ideally situated for exploring the Columbia Gorge and Mount Hood, this flagship of the McMenamin microbrewery empire is the former county poor farm. Today, after extensive remodeling, the property includes not only tastefully decorated guest rooms with antique furnishings, but a brewery, a pub, a beer garden, a restaurant, a movie theater, a winery, a wine-tasting room, meeting facilities, extensive gardens, and a hostel. With so much in one spot, this makes a great base for exploring the area. The beautiful grounds give this inn the feel of a remote retreat, though you are still within a short drive of everything Portland has to offer.

Skamania Lodge. P.O. Box 189, Stevenson, WA 98648. ☎ **800/221-7117** or 509/427-7700. 195 rms, 6 suites. A/C TV TEL. $135–$210 double; $240 suites. Lower rates in winter. AE, CB, DC, DISC, MC, V.

Located on the Washington side of the Columbia Gorge, Skamania Lodge has the most spectacular vistas of any area hotel. It's also the only golf resort in the Gorge, but is also well situated whether you brought your sailboard, hiking boots, or mountain bike. The interior decor is classically rustic with lots of rock and natural wood and Northwest Indian artworks and artifacts on display. In the cathedral-ceilinged lobby, where big wicker chairs are set by the stone fireplace, huge windows take in the Gorge panorama. If you should opt for a fireplace room, you won't have to leave your bed to enjoy a fire. The river-view guest rooms are only slightly more expensive than the forest-view rooms (which also happen to look out over the huge parking lot).

Dining/Entertainment: The casual Northwest cuisine in the lodge's dining room is excellent (and the view of the Gorge is amazing). Adjacent to the dining room is a lounge with a large, freestanding stone fireplace.

Services: Room service, concierge.

Facilities: 18-hole golf course, tennis courts, swimming pool, whirlpool, exercise facility, nature trails, volleyball court.

CAMPGROUNDS

Camping in the Gorge isn't at all the wonderful experience you might at first think. With an interstate highway and a very active railway line paralleling the river, the Gorge tends to be quite noisy. However, there are a few camping options between Portland and Hood River, and these campgrounds do what they can to minimize the traffic noises. **Ainsworth State Park,** 3¹/₂ miles east of Multnomah Falls is most recommendable for the fact that it has showers, although the RV sites are also quite nice. The **Port of Cascade Locks** also operates a campground (nothing more than a lawn with some picnic tables) beside the dock for the stern-wheeler *Columbia Gorge.* Farther east, at exit 41 off I-84, there is **Eagle Creek Campground,** which is the oldest campground in the National Forest system and is popular for its access to the Eagle Creek Trail. At exit 51 off of I-84, there is **Wyeth Campground,** a U.S. Forest Service campground on the bank of Gordon Creek.

WHERE TO DINE

The area's best spot for a meal is the dining room of the **Skamania Lodge** (see above).

Multnomah Falls Lodge. I-84, exit 31. ☎ **503/695-2376.** Main courses $15–$18. AE, MC, V. Mon–Sat 8am–9pm, Sun 8am–2pm and 2:30–9pm. NORTHWEST/AMERICAN.

Built in 1925 at the foot of Multnomah Falls, the historic Multmomah Falls Lodge may be the most touristy place to eat in the entire Gorge, but the setting is excellent and the food isn't half bad. Breakfast, when the crowds haven't yet arrived, is actually the best meal to have here. Try the grilled salmon or trout and eggs. At dinner try the chicken Oneonta, which is stuffed with salmon and mushrooms, or the baked salmon Multnomah, which is served with a brown sugar sauce. For a peek-a-boo view of the falls, try to get a table in the conservatory room. Otherwise you'll have to be content with stone walls and a large fireplace for atmosphere.

Royal Chinook Inn. 2605 NE Corbett Hill Rd., Corbett. ☎ **503/695-3237.** Main courses $14–$18. AE, MC, V. Wed–Sun 4–9:30pm. Take Exit 22 off I-84. SEAFOOD.

The sign out front says "Famous for Smoked Salmon" and with good reason. Don't even think about ordering anything here other than that smoked salmon, which is served as a dinner with a baked potato and smoked-salmon chowder. One of the secrets here is that they try to only use wild Alaskan King salmon, not farm-raised fish, which tend to lack much flavor.

2 Hood River: The Boardsailing Capital of the Northwest

62 miles E of Portland, 20 miles W of The Dalles, 32 miles N of Government Camp

They used to curse the winds in Hood River. Each summer, hot air rising over the desert to the east sucks cool air up the Columbia River Gorge from the Pacific and the winds howl through what is basically a natural wind tunnel. The winds are incessant and gusts can whip the river into a tumult of whitecaps.

But things change, and ever since someone first pulled into town with a sailboard, Hood River has taken to praying for wind. Hood River, you see, is the boardsailing capital of America, and boardsailing has given Hood River, once an ailing lumber town, a new lease on life. People come from all over the world to catch the "nuclear" winds that howl up the Gorge. In early summer the board-heads roll into town in their "Gorge-mobiles," the 1990s equivalent of surfers' woodies, and start listening to the wind reports. They flock to riverside parks on both the Oregon and Washington sides of the Columbia, unfurl their sails, zip up their wetsuits, and launch themselves into the melee of thousands of other like-minded souls shooting back and forth across a mile of windswept water. High waves whipped up by gale-force winds provide perfect launching pads for rocketing skyward. Aerial acrobatics such as flips and 360° turns are common sights. Even if you're not into this fast-paced sport, you'll certainly get a vicarious thrill from watching the board-heads going for air time.

Until recently, Hood River was pretty much a one-trick town, but sometimes the winds just aren't accommodating and even board-heads can get bored sitting on shore waiting for conditions to improve. The town has now become something of an outdoor sports mecca, with a rapidly developing reputation for excellent mountain biking, white-water kayaking and rafting, paragliding, rock climbing, hiking, skiing, and snowboarding. In other, words, Hood River is full of active people.

This town does not exist on sports alone, however, and outside town, in the Hood River Valley, are apple and pear orchards, wineries, and even a brandy distillery. Hood River also claims one of the best hotels in the state, numerous bed-and-breakfast inns, and several good restaurants. Most of the town's old Victorian and Craftsmen houses have been restored, giving Hood River a historic atmosphere to complement its lively boardsailing scene.

ESSENTIALS

GETTING THERE   Hood River is on I-84 at the junction with Ore. 35, which leads south to connect with U.S. 26 near the town of Government Camp.

Amtrak offers passenger rail service to Hood River. The station is at Cascade Avenue and First Street.

VISITOR INFORMATION   Contact the **Hood River County Chamber of Commerce,** 405 Portway Ave., Hood River, OR 97031 (☎ **800/366-3530** or 541/386-2000).

GETTING AROUND   If you happen to be out this way without a car, you can get around town on **Columbia Area Transit** (☎ **541/386-4202**) buses. For a taxi, call **Hood River Taxi & Transportation** (☎ **541/386-2255**).

FESTIVALS   The **Hood River Valley Blossom Festival** is held in mid-April and celebrates the flowering of the valley's pear and apple trees. August brings the **Hood**

River Apple Jam music festival and **Gravenstein Apple Fair,** and mid-October is time for the **Hood River Valley Harvest Fest.** Sports-oriented festivals include the **USA Pear High Wind Classic** windsurfing competition in late June, the **Timberland Gorge Games** in July, and the **Cross Channel Swim** in early September.

BOARDSAILING & OTHER OUTDOOR ACTIVITIES

If you're here to ride the wind or just want to watch others as they race back and forth across the river, head to the **Columbia Gorge Sailpark** at Hood River Marina or the nearby **Event Site** or **The Hook,** both of which are accessed from exit 63 off I-84. Across the river in Washington, try the **fish hatchery,** west of the mouth of the White Salmon River, and **Swell City,** a park about 3 miles west of the bridge. Downtown Hood River is packed with boardsailing related shops. Classes are available through **Gorge Wind Guide Service,** P.O. Box 1594, Hood River, OR 97031 (☎ 541/490-4401); **Front Street Sailboards,** 207 Front St., Hood River, OR 97031 (☎ 541/386-4044); or **Big Winds,** 505 Cascade St., Hood River, OR 97031 (☎ 541/386-6086). These latter two places also rent equipment, while Gorge Wind has demo equipment available for experienced sailors.

When there isn't enough wind for sailing, there's still the option to go **rafting** on the White Salmon River just across the bridge from Hood River. Companies offering raft trips on this river include **Phil's White Water Adventure** (☎ 800/366-2004 or 509/493-3121), **AAA Rafting** (☎ 800/866-RAFT or 509/493-2511), and **Renegade River Rafters** (☎ 509/427-RAFT). The river-rafting season runs from March to October and a half-day trip will cost around $45 per person. White-water kayaking is also popular on the White Salmon River, and if you'd like to take some lessons or rent a kayak, contact **Cascade Whitewater,** 13 Oak St. (☎ 541/386-4286), which also rents sit-on-top kayaks and offers tours on the Columbia and Klickitat Rivers.

Mountain biking has become very popular in this area over the past few years, and Hood River bike shops can direct you to some fun area rides. Check at **Discover Bicycles,** 1020 Wasco St. (☎ 541/386-4820), or **Mountain View Cycles,** 411 Oak St. (☎ 541/386-2453), both of which also rent bikes.

If **fly-fishing** is your passion, drop by the **Gorge Fly Shop,** 201 Oak St. (☎ 800/685-7309 or 541/386-6977), which can not only fill all your angling needs and point you to where the fish are biting, but can also offer guided fly-fishing trips in the area.

If you're interested in **horseback riding,** contact **Fir Mountain Ranch,** 4051 Fir Mountain Rd. (☎ 541/354-2753), which is located about 9 miles south of Hood River and charges around $20 for an hour's horseback ride.

Hikers have their choice of trails in Mount Hood National Forest (try up at **Timberline Lodge** or at **Cooper Spur**), the Columbia Gorge (try **Eagle Creek** or at any of the waterfalls along the Historic Columbia River Highway), or across the river (head up Wash. 141 to **Mount Adams**). At 12,276 feet in elevation, Mount Adams is the second-highest peak in Washington. For more information on hiking on Mount Adams, contact the **Gifford Pinchot National Forest,** Mt. Adams Ranger District, 2455 Wash. 141, Trout Lake, WA 98650 (☎ 509/395-2501).

For guided multisport adventures, there are a couple of area **tour companies** that can arrange an area visit that includes windsurfing, skiing or snowboarding, mountain biking, rafting, hiking, rock climbing, and horseback riding. Contact **Hood River Trails** (☎ 800/979-HIKE) or **Odyssey** (☎ 800/789-2770) for details. Week-long tours cost between $1,000 and $1,300.

Golfers can play nine holes at the **Hood River Golf & Country Club,** 1850 Country Club Rd. (☎ 541/386-3009), or 18 holes at Indian Creek Golf, 3605 Brookside Dr. (☎ 541/386-7770).

THE FRUIT LOOP (EXPLORING THE HOOD RIVER VALLEY)

Before windsurfing took center stage, the Hood River Valley was known as one of Oregon's top fruit-growing regions, and today the valley is still Oregon's top apple- and pear-growing region. From blossom time (April) to harvest season (September and October), the valley offers quiet country roads to explore. Along the way you'll find numerous farm stands, wineries, museums, and interesting shops that reflect the rural heritage of the valley. Pick up a copy of the "Hood River County's Fruit Loop" brochure at the Hood River County Chamber of Commerce visitors center (see "Visitor Information," above).

Be sure to start your tour of the Hood River Valley by stopping at **Panorama Point,** which is off of Ore. 35 just south of town (follow the signs). This hilltop park provides a splendid panorama of the valley's orchards with Mount Hood looming in the distance.

In the fall, fruit stands pop up along the roads around the valley. **Smiley's Red Barn,** 3401 Dethman Ridge Dr. (☎ 541/386-9121), and **Rasmussen Fruit & Flower Farm,** 3020 Thomson Rd. (☎ 541/386-4622)—two of the biggest and best farm stands in the valley—are located adjacent to one another off Ore. 35 about 6 miles south of Hood River. Also not to be missed is the nearby **River Bend Country Store,** 2363 Tucker Rd. (☎ 800/755-7568 or 541/386-8766), where you can stock up on seasonal and organic produce and other homemade specialties. You'll find the store west of Smiley's and Rasmussen's on the opposite side of the valley. Also in the valley, you'll find numerous orchards and farms where you can pick your own fruit. Just keep an eye out for U-PICK signs.

In addition to pears and apples, the Hood River valley also grows quite a few acres of wine grapes. You can visit several wineries here and taste the local fruit of the vine. Area wineries include **Flerchinger Vineyards and Winery,** 4200 Post Canyon Dr. (☎ 800/516-8710 or 541/386-2882), which offers a good Riesling and some experimental wines; and **Hood River Vineyards,** 4693 Westwood Dr. (☎ 541/386-3772), which makes excellent fruit wines. Also in the area, you can sample brandies and traditional eaux-de-vie (fruit brandies) at the **Eve Atkins Distilling Company,** 4420 Summit Dr. (☎ 541/354-2550). Across the Columbia River in Washington, you can visit the **Charles Hooper Family Winery,** Spring Creek Road North Fork (☎ 509/493-2324), in Husum, and the **Mont Elise Vineyards,** 315 W. Steuben Rd. (☎ 509/493-3001), in Bingen.

The little hamlet of Parkdale, at the south end of the Fruit Loop is home to the fascinating little **Hutson Museum** (☎ 541/352-6808), which houses lapidary, archaeology, and anthropology collections, of which the rock collection and exhibits or Native American artifacts are a highlight. On the grounds there are also several historic buildings and the **Ries-Thompson Tea House,** where you can get lunch or afternoon tea (closed Mondays). The museum is open mid-April through October (call for specific hours) and admission is $1 for adults and 50 cents for children. Also in Parkdale, you'll find the **Elliot Glacier Public House,** 4945 Baseline Rd. (☎ 541/352-1022), a brew pub with a great view of Mount Hood. Not far from Parkdale, at the corner of Cooper Spur Road and Ore. 35, you'll find the **Mt. Hood Country Store** (☎ 541/352-6024), which has been in business since 1932 and has a deli with good sandwiches, pizzas, and cinnamon rolls.

Any time of year, but especially during fruit-blossom time, the **Mount Hood Railroad** (☎ 800/TRAIN-61 or 541/386-3556) offers a great way to see the Hood River Valley and its acres of orchards. The diesel locomotives operated by this scenic railroad company depart from the historic 1911 Hood River depot and pull restored

Pullman coaches on 4-hour excursions. The train winds its way up the valley to Parkdale, where you can have tea at the Ries-Thompson Tea House and visit the Hutson Museum. Fares are $21.95 for adults, $18.95 for seniors, $13.95 for children 2 to 11. Dinner and brunch excursions are also offered ($67.50 dinner, $55 brunch).

If you'd like to see the Hood River Valley from the air, contact **Flightline Services,** 3608 Airport Dr. (☎ **541/386-1133**), which offers scenic flights as well as glider rides. Rates range from $18 to $150 per person.

OTHER ATTRACTIONS IN HOOD RIVER

Adjacent to the visitors center is the **Hood River County Museum,** Port Marina Park (☎ **541/386-6772**), which has exhibits of Native American artifacts from this area. There are also plenty of displays on pioneer life. The museum is open mid-April through August, Wednesday through Saturday from 10am to 4pm and on Sunday from noon to 4pm; and in September and October, daily from noon to 4pm. Admission is free.

In downtown Hood River, drop in the **Columbia Art Gallery,** 207 Second St. (☎ **541/386-4512**), to take a look at what area artists are up to. This is a community-sponsored, nonprofit gallery.

WHERE TO STAY

If you're looking for a bed-and-breakfast in the area and the ones listed below are full, you can try calling **Roomfinder** (☎ **541/386-6767**), a free service provided by the Hood River Bed & Breakfast Association.

Best Western Hood River Inn. 1108 E. Marina Way, Hood River, OR 97031. ☎ **800/ 828-7873** or 541/386-2200. Fax 503/386-8905. 149 rms. A/C TV TEL. June–Sept $79.50–$115 double; $155–$175 suite. Oct–May $59.50–$99.50 double; $105–$135 suite. AE, CB, DC, DISC, MC, V.

If you prefer comfort and predictability, this convention hotel is a good bet in Hood River, with amenities such as room service, and an outdoor swimming pool, an exercise room, and a private dock and beach. It's the only area hotel right on the water. The Riverside Grill serves dependable meals with a bit of Northwest imagination and a great view across the river. A diner-style coffee shop provides casual meals.

✪ **Columbia Gorge Hotel.** 4000 Westcliff Dr., Hood River, OR 97031. ☎ **800/345-1921** or 541/386-5566. Fax 503/387-5414. 40 rms. A/C TV TEL. $150–$365 double. Rates include 5-course breakfast. AE, CB, DC, DISC, MC, V.

Located just west of Hood River off I-84, the Columbia Gorge Hotel, built in 1921, is one of Oregon's premier historic hotels. Its distinctive yellow-stucco walls and red-tile roofs may conjure up images of the California coast, while the hotel gardens could hold their own in Victoria, British Columbia. However, the dramatic setting plants this hotel solidly in the Columbia Gorge. Perched more than 200 feet above the Columbia River on a steep cliff, the hotel is almost as impressive as the views. The guest rooms are all a little different, with a mixture of antique and classic furnishings including canopy and brass beds. Unfortunately, many of the rooms are rather cramped, as are the bathrooms, most of which have older fixtures and some exposed pipes. A recent refurbishing has left the guest rooms and public areas looking fresher than they have in years. Windows also don't do justice to the vistas.

Dining/Entertainment: The Columbia River Court Dining Room is best known for its five-course farm breakfast. If you aren't staying at the hotel, breakfast will run you a whopping $22.95. Evening meals feature imaginative Northwest cuisine, with entrees ranging from $18.50 to $29.50.

Services: Limited room service, complimentary newspaper, baby-sitting, turndown service with rose and chocolate, access to nearby health club.

✪ **Hood River Hotel.** 102 Oak Ave., Hood River, OR 97031. ☎ **800/386-1859** or 541/386-1900. Fax 503/386-6090. 32 rms, 9 suites. TV TEL. $69–$99 double; $85–$145 suite. AE, CB, DC, DISC, MC, V.

Located in downtown Hood River, this hotel is an economical alternative to the pricey Columbia Gorge Hotel. Built in 1913, the Hood River Hotel boasts the casual elegance of a vintage hotel; you'll find historic character and rooms decorated with traditional styling. A sidewalk patio, brass rails, and beveled-glass French doors set the tone before you even set foot inside the hotel, and, inside, huge paned windows flood the high-ceilinged lobby with light. On winter nights a fire crackles in the fireplace. Guest rooms are all different and are furnished almost identically to the those at the Columbia Gorge Hotel. Canopy beds, ceiling fans, and oval floor mirrors capture a mood of elegance. Most third-floor rooms have skylit bathrooms, which makes them our favorites. The suites have full kitchens, and of course, river-view rooms are the most expensive. The hotel's casual dining room serves good Italian meals, and room service is also available. You'll find a whirlpool, sauna, and exercise room on the premises.

Inn at the Gorge. 1113 Eugene St., Hood River, OR 97031. ☎ **541/386-4429.** 1 rm (with shared bath); 3 suites. $60 double without bath; $78 suite. Rates include full breakfast. MC, V (add 5% surcharge). Closed early Oct to early May.

Though this bed-and-breakfast is housed in a 1908 Victorian home, it's still a casual sort of place catering primarily to boardsailing enthusiasts. Each of the three suites here has a kitchenette so you can save money on your meals while you're in town. There's a storage area for boardsailing and skiing gear, and mountain bikes are available for guests. The innkeepers are avid board-heads themselves and can steer you to the best spots for your skill level.

✪ **Lakecliff Estate Bed and Breakfast.** 3820 Westcliff Dr. (P.O. box 1220), Hood River, OR 97031. ☎ **541/386-7000.** 4 rms (2 with private bath). $85 double with shared bath, $100 double with private bath. No credit cards.

Situated high atop a cliff in a secluded forest setting on the outskirts of town, this inn was built in 1908 as a summer home and was designed by the architect of Portland's Benson Hotel and the Gorge's Multnomah Falls Lodge. The cedar-shingled main house, which is surrounded by its own 12-acre forested estate, could just as easily be in the Maine woods if not for the Gorge view out the back windows and deck. Guest rooms all have great views, and are decorated in an upscale country style. One room has the bed directly under the window so you can lay under the covers and gaze out at the river far below. Three rooms also have their own fireplaces.

Vagabond Lodge. 4070 Westcliff Dr., Hood River, OR 97031. ☎ **541/386-2992.** Fax 541/386-3317. 39 rms, 5 suites. A/C TV TEL. $49–$69 double; $79 suite. Lower rates in winter. AE, DC, MC, V.

If you've got a banker's tastes but a teller's vacation budget, you can take advantage of the Vagabond Lodge's proximity to the Columbia Gorge Hotel and enjoy the latter's gardens and restaurant without breaking the bank. Actually, the back rooms at the Vagabond are some of the best in Hood River simply for their views (some have balconies). However, this motel's grounds are also quite attractive. There are lots of big old oaks and evergreens, and natural rock outcroppings have been incorporated into the motel's landscaping.

CAMPGROUNDS

Area campgrounds include **Toll Bridge Park,** on Ore. 35, 17 miles south of town, and **Tucker Park,** on Tucker Road (Ore. 281) just a few miles south of town. These two county parks are both on the banks of the Hood River. Farther south, you'll find the **Robinhood Campground** and the **Sherwood Campground,** two national forest campgrounds also on the banks of the Hood River favored by mountain bikers. Eight miles west of Hood River off I-84 is **Viento State Park,** which gets quite a bit of traffic noise both from the interstate and from the adjacent railroad tracks. Eleven miles east of town, you'll find **Memaloose State Park,** which has the same noise problems. These two state parks are popular with boardsailors.

WHERE TO DINE

When you just have to have a bagel, the **Hood River Bagel Co.,** 13 Oak St. (☎ **541/386-2123**), is the best place in town. For espresso and a pastry or a slice of pizza, try **Andrew's Pizza & Bakery,** 107 Oak St. (☎ **541/386-1448**). The best restaurant in town is the dining room at the **Columbia Gorge Hotel** (see "Where to Stay," above, for details).

The Mesquitery. 1219 12th St. ☎ **541/386-2002.** Main courses $9–$16. AE, MC, V. Wed–Fri 11:30am–2pm and 4:30–9:30 or 10pm, Sat–Tues 4:30–9:30 or 10pm. STEAK/SEAFOOD.

Located in the uptown district of Hood River, the Mesquitery is a small and cozy grill with a rustic interior. As the name implies, mesquite grilling is the specialty of the house. Chicken and ribs are most popular, but you can also get a sirloin steak or grilled fish. At lunch there are sandwiches made with grilled meats. If you aren't that hungry, this is a good place to put together a light meal from such à la carte dishes as shrimp burritos, fish tacos, and fettuccine pesto.

Purple Rocks Art Bar & Café. 606 Oak St. ☎ **541/386-6061.** Main courses $5–$7.50. MC, V. Wed–Mon 7am–3:30pm. INTERNATIONAL.

Java, jazz, and fine food are the basis for this self-proclaimed art bar and cafe, which does a brisk breakfast and lunch business (creative sandwiches and large salads). There are plenty of cafe tables and jazz tunes on the stereo, and there's a patio out front (a bit noisy from traffic) and a deck out back with a great view of the river.

Santacroce's. 4780 Ore. 35. ☎ **541/354-2511.** Main courses $7–$18. DISC, MC, V. Wed–Sat 4–11pm, Sun 2–10pm. ITALIAN.

Located adjacent to a large lumber mill south of Hood River up the Hood River Valley, this casual little place is part tavern and part great little Italian place. The sails standing up out front leave no doubt that sailboarders are welcome. Stick to the Italian offerings on the menu, and you can't go wrong. The bracciola (rolled flank steak filled with cheeses) is excellent as is the ricotta and spinach ravioli. Of course, the pizzas are probably the most popular items on the menu.

✪ **Sixth Street Bistro.** 509 Cascade St. ☎ **541/386-5737.** Reservations recommended. Main courses $8–$13. MC, V. Daily 11:30am–10:30pm. AMERICAN/INTERNATIONAL.

Just a block off Oak Street toward the river, the Sixth Street Bistro has an intimate little dining room and patio on the lower floor and a lounge with a balcony on the second floor. Each has its own entrance, but they share the same menu so there's a choice of ambience. There are numerous international touches, such as chicken satay appetizers and a grilled-chicken salad with sesame-ginger dressing, and plenty of interesting pasta dishes, such as Cajun fettuccine and phad Thai. You'll also find seasonal specials and a good list of burgers.

Stonehedge Inn. 3405 Cascade Dr. ☎ **541/386-3940.** Reservations recommended. Main courses $13.50–$18.50. AE, CB, DC, DISC, MC, V. Wed–Sun 5–9pm (sometimes open Mon–Tues in summer). NORTHWEST/CONTINENTAL.

Built as a summer vacation home just after the turn of the century, the Stonehedge Inn is just west of downtown Hood River off Cascade Drive, but it feels as if it were deep in the wilderness. Inside the old home, there's a small lounge with a bar taken from an old tavern, and several dining rooms, each of which has a slightly different feel. The menu sticks to traditional continental dishes (duck à l'orange, steak Diane, rack of lamb), though there are occasional ventures into more creative territory with daily specials.

HOOD RIVER AFTER DARK

Big Horse Brew Pub. 115 State St. ☎ **541/386-4411.**

Located in a vertiginous old house above downtown, this brew pub has a limited selection of brews, but the views from the third floor can't be beat. The pub also does some respectable pub food.

Full Sail Pub & Tasting Room. 506 Columbia St. ☎ **541/386-2281.**

Full Sail brews some of the most consistently flavorful and well rounded beers and ales in the Northwest and has developed a loyal following. This is their main brewery and you have to walk past the brewery itself to get to the pub at the back of this old industrial building a block off Hood River's main drag. Big windows look out over the river. Brewery tours are available.

EAST OF HOOD RIVER: WILDFLOWERS & VIEWS

East of Hood River, you'll find two more sections of the Historic Columbia River Highway (Ore. 30), one of which will be open to hikers and bikers when restored and the other of which is open to automobiles. The former section, between Hood River and Mosier, had been abandoned when I-84 was built and a tunnel on this section of the old highway was filled in, but for the past couple of years the state has been excavating the tunnel with the intention of opening the old highway as a bike path. Check with the Hood River County Chamber of Commerce or an area bike shop to see if this route is open yet.

The second stretch of the old highway, between the towns of Mosier and The Dalles, climbs up onto the Rowena Plateau, which has sweeping vistas that take in the Columbia River, Mount Hood, and Mount Adams. In the springtime (between March and May), the wildflower displays here are some of the best in the state. The best place to observe the flowers is at the Nature Conservancy's **Governor Tom McCall Preserve.** On spring weekends there are usually volunteers on hand guiding wildflower walks through the preserve.

3 The Dalles

128 miles W of Pendleton, 85 miles E of Portland, 133 miles N of Bend

The Dalles, a French word meaning "flagstone," was the name given to this area by early 19th-century French trappers. These early explorers may have been reminded of stepping stones when they first gazed upon the flat basalt rocks that forced the Columbia River through a long stretch of rapids and cascades here. These rapids, which were a barrier to river navigation, formed a natural gateway to western Oregon.

For more than 10,000 years, Native Americans inhabited this site because of the ease with which salmon could be taken from the river as it flowed through the tumultuous rapids. The annual fishing season at nearby Celilo Falls was a meeting point for tribes from all over the West, who would come to fish, trade, and stock-pile supplies for the coming winter.

White settlers, the first of whom came to The Dalles as missionaries in 1838, were latecomers to this area. However, by the 1840s, a steady flow of pioneers was passing through this area, which was effectively the end of the overland segment of the Oregon Trail. Pioneers that were headed for the mild climate and fertile soils of the Willamette Valley would load their wagons onto rafts at this point and float downriver to the mouth of the Willamette and then up that river to Oregon City.

By the 1850s, The Dalles was the site of an important military fort and had become a busy river port. Steamships shuttled from here to Cascade Locks on the run to Portland. The coming of the railroad in 1880, and later the flooding of the river's rapids, reduced the importance of The Dalles as a port town. Today, the city is linking itself to the Columbia Gorge and to that end has opened a new Columbia Gorge Discovery Center and is attracting almost as many boardsailors as nearby Hood River.

ESSENTIALS

GETTING THERE   The Dalles is on I-84 at the junction of U.S. 197, which leads south to Antelope where it connects with U.S. 97.

Amtrak passenger trains stop in The Dalles at First and Federal streets.

VISITOR INFORMATION   Contact **The Dalles Area Chamber of Commerce,** 404 W. Second St., The Dalles, OR 97058 (☎ **800/255-3385** or 541/296-6616).

LEARNING ABOUT THE GORGE

Columbia Gorge Discovery Center/Wasco County Historical Museum. 5000 Discovery Dr. ☎ **541/296-8600.** $6.50 adults, $5.50 seniors, $3 children ages 6–16. Daily 10am–6pm. Closed Thanksgiving, Christmas, and New Year's Day.

These two museums, which are housed in one building and opened in 1997 on the outskirts of The Dalles, serve as the eastern gateway to the Columbia Gorge. In a building constructed to resemble a Northwest Native American longhouse, you'll find exhibits on the geology and history of the Gorge. Among the most fascinating exhibits is a film of Native Americans fishing at Celilo Falls before the falls were flooded by the rising waters behind The Dalles Dam. The museum's star attraction, however, is a 33-foot-long river model with flowing water. On the surrounding museum grounds, there is a **Living History Park,** where interpreters are on hand on summer weekends to discuss the Native American traditions and pioneer experiences. There is also a short nature trail that leads past a small pond.

EXPLORING THE DALLES

Some of The Dalles's most important historic buildings can be seen at the **Fort Dalles Museum,** 15th and Garrison streets (☎ **541/296-4547**). Established in 1850, Fort Dalles was the only military post between Fort Laramie and Fort Vancouver. By 1867 the fort had become unnecessary, and after several buildings were destroyed in a fire, it was abandoned. Today, several of the original buildings are still standing. April through October, the museum is open daily from 10am to 5pm; other months, the museum is open Thursday through Monday from 10am to 4pm (closed in January). Admission is $3, free for children 17 and under.

Within a decade of the establishment of the fort, The Dalles became the county seat of what was the largest county ever created in the United States. Wasco County covered 130,000 square miles between the Rocky Mountains and the Cascade Range. The old **Wasco County Courthouse,** 410 W. Second St. (☎ **541/296-4798**), a two-story wooden structure built in 1859, now houses a historical museum. June through August it's open Monday, Tuesday, Friday, and Saturday from 10am to

4pm; April, May, September, and October, it's open 11am to 3pm (closed other months). Admission is free.

Long before settlers arrived in The Dalles, Lewis and Clark's expedition stopped here. The site of their camp is called **Rock Fort** and is one of the expedition's only documented campsites. You'll find the historic site west of downtown near The Dalles's industrial area. Take West Second Street west, turn right on Webber Street West, and then turn right again on Bargeway Road.

The Dalles's other historic landmark is a much more impressive structure. **St. Peter's Landmark Church,** at the corner of West Third and Lincoln streets, is no longer an active church, but its tall spire is still a local landmark. The church was built in the gothic revival style in 1898, and its spire is topped by a 6-foot-tall rooster that is the symbol of The Dalles.

If you're interested in learning more about the history and the historic buildings of The Dalles, pick up a copy of the historic walking tours brochure at the chamber of commerce. There is also a brochure on the town's many historical murals.

Just east of town rises **The Dalles Lock and Dam** (☎ **541/296-9778**), which provides both irrigation water and electricity. The dam, which was completed in 1957, stretches for 1¹/₂ miles from the Oregon shore to the Washington shore. One of the main reasons this dam was built was to flood the rapids that made this section of the Columbia River impossible to navigate. Among the numerous rapids flooded by the dam were Celilo Falls, which, for thousands of years before the dam was built, comprised the most important salmon-fishing area in the Northwest. Each year thousands of Native Americans would gather here to catch and smoke salmon, putting the dried fish away for the coming winter. The traditional method of catching the salmon was to use a spear or net with a long pole. Men would build precarious wooden platforms out over the river and catch the salmon as they tried to leap up the falls. You can still see traditional Native American fishing platforms near the Shilo Inn here in The Dalles. The dam's **visitor center** has displays on both the history of the river and the construction of the dam, and a small train takes visitors on the guided tours of the dam. It's open mid-April to September (Wednesday through Sunday from 9am to 6pm in April, May, and September; daily from 9am to 6pm between June and August); admission is free. To reach the visitor center, take Exit 87 off I-84 and turn right on Northeast Frontage Road.

For a good view of The Dalles and the Columbia River, head up to **Sorosis Park,** on Scenic Drive, which forms the southern edge of town. East of town 17 miles, you'll find the **Deschutes River State Recreation Area** (☎ **541/739-2322**), which is at the mouth of the Deschutes River and is the eastern boundary of the Columbia Gorge National Scenic Area. The park has several miles of hiking trails, and an old railway right of way that parallels the Deschutes River for 25 miles has been turned into a gravel mountain biking and horseback riding trail. This trail is fairly flat and passes through some spectacular canyon scenery. There is also a campground in the park.

If you're interested in hiring a guide to take you **fishing** for sturgeon, steelhead, or salmon in the area, contact **Young's Fishing Service** (☎ **541/296-5371**). Expect to pay around $125 for a day of fishing.

WHERE TO STAY

Capt. Gray's Guest House. 210 W. Fourth St., The Dalles, OR 97058. ☎ **800/448-4729** or 541/298-8222. 3 rms. A/C TEL. $50–$80 double. Rates include full breakfast. MC, V.

Located just 2 blocks from the downtown business district, Capt. Gray's bed-and-breakfast, in a restored Victorian house, is popular in the summer with visiting windsurfers. The guest rooms are large and filled with Victorian antiques, and one room even has a separate sitting room. The living room is a casual gathering place full of magazines and information on the region. This is a very laid-back sort of place.

The Columbia House Bed & Breakfast. 525 E. Seventh St., The Dalles, OR 97058. ☎ **800/807-2668** or 541/298-4686. 4 rms (3 with private bathrooms). A/C. $60–$85 double. DISC, MC, V.

With movie theme rooms (Humphrey Bogart, Marilyn Monroe, *Gone With the Wind*) and lots of art deco styling throughout, this is one of the most interesting inns in The Dalles. The inn is set at the back of a long driveway and perches atop a bluff overlooking the city and the Columbia River. Out back there are four large decks where guests can soak up the sunshine and views. There's also a fun basement recreation room.

Shilo Inn. 3223 Frontage Rd., The Dalles, OR 97058. ☎ **800/222-2244** or 541/298-5502. Fax 541/298-4673. 112 rms. A/C TV TEL. $65–$99 double. Rates include continental breakfast. AE, DC, DISC, ER, JCB, MC, V.

The Shilo Inn is a couple of miles from downtown and has the most spectacular setting of any lodging in the area. The motel is set on the banks of the Columbia River at the foot of The Dalles Dam, and is adjacent to the Native American ghost town of Lone Pine. The rooms are typical motel units, so it's definitely worth spending a little extra for a river-view room. The dining room and lounge offer moderately priced meals and views of the river. Room service is available and an outdoor pool, whirlpool tub, and sauna provide places to relax.

CAMPGROUNDS

If you're looking for someplace to pitch a tent or park an RV, try **Deschutes River State Recreation Area,** 17 miles east of The Dalles off I-84, or **Horsethief Lake State Park,** across the river near Dallesport, Washington.

WHERE TO DINE

✪ **Baldwin Saloon Historic Restaurant & Bar.** First and Court sts. ☎ **541/296-5666.** Reservations accepted only for parties of 6 or more. Main courses $5.75–$16. MC, V. Sun–Thurs 11am–10pm, Fri–Sat 11am–11pm. Closed 1 hour earlier in winter. AMERICAN/CONTINENTAL.

Built in 1876, the Baldwin Saloon has one of the few remaining cast-iron facades in town. Brick walls, wooden booths, and a high ceiling (high enough to fit a loft with a piano) add to the old-time feel, as does the collection of turn-of-the-century landscape paintings and large bar nudes. Whether your tastes run to burgers or chèvre-stuffed dates, you'll find something to please your palate. One last macabre note: This building once served as a warehouse storing coffins.

Ole's Supper Club. 2620 W. Second St. ☎ **541/296-6708.** Reservations recommended. Main courses $8–$20. AE, DISC, MC, V. Tues–Thurs 4:30–9pm, Fri–Sat 4:30–10pm. PRIME RIB/CONTINENTAL.

Though it's located on a rather industrial stretch of road on the west side of town, this unassuming restaurant is The Dalles's best. The decor certainly won't distract you from your meal, and neither will the views out the windows. But, never mind—the food's great. Prime rib au jus is what has made this restaurant a local legend, and it comes in sizes for hearty appetites (10 ounces) and heartier appetites (16 ounces). The kitchen also does a respectable job on the steaks and seafood, but if you're only here for the day, go with the prime rib. An excellent selection of very reasonably priced wines is available.

9 The Cascades

From the schussing of January and the kayaking of April to the wild-flowers of August and the splashes of fall foliage in October, Oregon's Cascade Range is a year-round recreational magnet. Stretching from the Columbia Gorge in the north to California in the south, the Cascades are a relatively young volcanic mountain range where picture-perfect, snow-capped volcanic peaks rise above lush green forests of evergreens. The Cascade's volcanic heritage is what sets this mountain range apart from others in the West, and throughout these mountains, signs of past volcanic activity are evident. The most dramatic evidence of the Cascades' fiery past is the vast caldera that now is filled by Crater Lake. However, in the volcanic cones of Mount Hood, Mount Jefferson, and the Three Sisters and the lava fields of McKenzie Pass, further evidence of volcanic activity can be seen.

As dramatic as this volcanic geology is, however, it is not what draws most people to these mountains. The main attraction is, of course, the multitude of outdoor sports that can be pursued here. Crystal-clear rivers, churned into white water as they cascade down from high in the mountains, provide numerous opportunities for rafting, kayaking, canoeing, and fishing. High mountain lakes hold hungry trout, and throughout the summer, lakeside campgrounds stay filled with anglers. The Pacific Crest Trail winds the entire length of the Cascades, but it is the many wilderness areas scattered throughout these mountains that are the biggest draw for day hikers and backpackers. At lower elevations, mountain bikers find miles of national forest trails to enjoy. In winter, skiers and snowboarders flock to more than half a dozen ski areas and countless miles of cross-country ski trails, and because winter lingers late in the high Cascades, the ski seasons here are some of the longest in the country. Skiing often begins in mid-November and continues on into April and even May and June at Mount Bachelor. In fact, on Mount Hood, high elevation snowfields atop glacial ice allow a year-round ski season that attracts Olympic ski teams for summer training.

The Cascades also serve as a dividing line between the lush evergreen forests of western Oregon and the dry, high desert landscapes of eastern Oregon. On the western slopes, Douglas firs and western red cedars dominate, while on the east side, the cinnamon-barked ponderosa pine is most common. These trees have been the lifeblood of the Oregon economy for much of this century, and with few

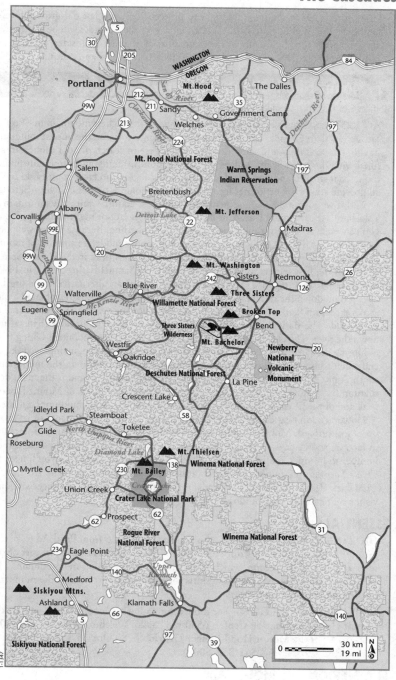

virgin forests left in the state, the fight to protect the state's last old-growth forests has been a long and litigious battle. Today, visitors to the Cascades will be confronted at nearly every turn by the site of clear cuts scarring the mountainsides, yet it is still possible to find groves of ancient trees beneath which to hike and camp.

1 Mount Hood: Skiing, Hiking & Scenic Drives

60 miles E of Portland, 46 miles S of Hood River

At 11,235 feet, Mount Hood, a dormant volcano, is the highest mountain in Oregon. Sitting less than 60 miles east of downtown Portland, it is also the busiest mountain in the state. Summer and winter, people flock here in search of cool mountain air filled with the scent of firs and pines. Campgrounds, hiking and mountain biking trails, trout streams and canoeing lakes, downhill ski areas and cross-country ski trails, all provide ample opportunities for outdoor recreational activities on Mount Hood.

With five downhill areas and many miles of cross-country trails, the mountain is a ski bum's dream come true. You have the country's largest night-skiing area, and you can even ski right through the summer at Timberline. Because its snowcapped summit can be reached fairly easily by those with only a moderate amount of mountain-climbing experience, it's also the most climbed major peak in the United States.

One of the first settlers to visit Mount Hood was Samuel Barlow, who, in 1845, had traveled the Oregon Trail and was searching for an alternative to taking his wagon train down the treacherous waters of the Columbia River. Barlow blazed a trail across the south flank of Mount Hood, and the following year he opened his trail as a toll road. The Barlow Trail, though difficult, was cheaper and safer than rafting down the river. The old trail still exists and is now a hiking and mountain-biking trail.

During the Great Depression, the Works Progress Administration employed skilled craftsmen to build the rustic **Timberline Lodge** at the tree line on the mountain's south slope. Today, the lodge is a National Historic Landmark and is the main destination for visitors to the mountain. The views from here, both of Mount Hood's peak and of the Oregon Cascades to the south, are superb and should not be missed.

However, don't expect to have this mountain all to yourself. Because of its proximity to Portland, Mount Hood sees a lot of visitors both summer and winter, and in fact, on snowy days, the road back down the mountain from the ski areas can be bumper to bumper and backed up for hours. Also keep in mind that you'll need to have a Sno-Park Permit in the winter (available at ski shops around the area) and a Trail Park Permit to park at trailheads in the summer (available at ranger stations, visitor centers, and a few outdoors-oriented shops).

ESSENTIALS

GETTING THERE   Mount Hood is reached by U.S. 26 from Portland (take exit 16A off I-84) and Ore. 35 from Hood River. These highways meet just east of the town of Government Camp, which is the main tourist town on the mountain. The Lolo Pass Road is a gravel road that skirts the north and west sides of the mountain connecting these two highways.

VISITOR INFORMATION   For more information on Mount Hood, contact the **Mount Hood Information Center**, 6500 E. U.S. 26, Welches, OR 97067 (☎ **503/ 622-7674**); or the **Mount Hood Ranger District,** 6780 Ore. 35 S., Mount Hood–Parkdale, OR 97041 (☎ **541/352-6002**).

SUMMER ON THE MOUNTAIN

The historic **Timberline Lodge** (see "Where to Stay," below, for details) is the main destination of most visitors to the mountain in the snow-free months. The lodge,

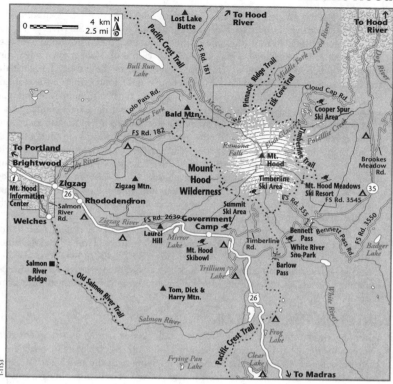

besides having a fabulous view of Mount Hood, is surrounded by meadows that burst into bloom in July and August. Here, in addition to the lodge, you'll find the ✪ **Timberline Trail,** a 41-mile-long trail that circles the mountain. If you just have time for a short hike, head west from the lodge on this trail. The route east passes through dusty ash fields and then drops down into the hot, barren White River Valley. You'll also find snow here any time of year, and there's even summer skiing at the **Timberline Ski Area.** The lift-accessed ski slopes are high above the lodge on the Palmer Glacier and are only open in the morning. It is also possible to ride the lift even if you aren't skiing.

In summer, you can also ride the lift at **Mt. Hood SkiBowl** (☎ 503/222-BOWL), where there are mountain biking trails, hiking trails, and an alpine slide (sort of a summertime bobsled run). You'll also find numerous other rides and activities here, as well as horseback riding stables.

One of the most popular hikes on Mount Hood is the trail to **Mirror Lake,** which, as its name implies, reflects the summit of Mount Hood in its waters. The trail is fairly easy and thus is very popular with families. To add a bit more challenge to the hike, you can continue on to the summit of Tom, Dick & Harry Mountain, the back side of which serves as the Mt. Hood SkiBowl in winter. The view from the summit is superb, and in late summer there are huckleberries along the trail. You'll find the trailhead right on U.S. 26 just before you reach Government Camp.

The east side of the mountain, which is accessed by Ore. 35 from Hood River, is much drier and less visited than the west side. You'll find good hiking trails in the vicinity of **Mount Hood Meadows,** where the wildflower displays in late July and

August are some of the best on the mountain. The loop trail past Umbrella and Sahalie Falls is particularly enjoyable. At Mount Hood Meadows Ski Area, you'll also find summer skiing. Also on this side of the mountain, you'll find the highest segment of the Timberline Trail. This section of trail climbs up Cooper Spur ridge from the historic Cloud Cap Inn, which is no longer open to the public. To reach the trailhead, follow signs off Ore. 35 for Cooper Spur and Cloud Cap. On the east side of Ore. 35, off Forest Service Road 44, you'll also find the best mountain-biking trails in the area. Among these are the Surveyor's Ridge Trail and the Dog Mountain Trail.

If you're looking for a shortcut between the west side of the mountain and Hood River, or you simply want to escape the crowds, try exploring along the **Lolo Pass Road.** Branching off from this road are several smaller roads that lead to some of the best hiking trails on Mount Hood. Also off the Lolo Pass Road, you'll find **Lost Lake,** one of the most beautiful (and most photographed) lakes in the Oregon Cascades. When the water is still, the view of the mountain and its reflection in the lake is positively sublime. Here you'll find campgrounds, cabins, picnic areas, good fishing, and hiking trails that lead both around the lake and up a nearby butte.

If you're interested in a more strenuous mountain experience, Mount Hood offers plenty of mountain- and rock-climbing opportunities. **Timberline Mountain Guides,** P.O. Box 340, Gov't Camp, OR 97028 (☎ **800/464-7704;** fax 503/272-3677), leads summit climbs on Mount Hood and offers snow-, ice-, and rock-climbing courses. A 2-day Mount Hood mountaineering course with summit climb costs $245.

WINTER ON THE MOUNTAIN

Although snowpacks that can be slow to reach skiable depths and frequent midwinter rains make the ski season on Mount Hood unpredictable, in an average year the regular ski season runs from around Thanksgiving right through March or April. Add to this the summer skiing on the Palmer Glacier at Timberline Ski Area and you have the longest ski season in the United States. There are five ski areas on Mount Hood, though two of these are tiny operations that attract primarily beginners and families looking for an economical way to all go schussing together. For cross-country skiers, there are many miles of marked ski trails, some of which are groomed.

The single most important thing to know about skiing on Mount Hood, and almost anywhere in Oregon for that matter, is that you'll have to have a **Sno-Park Permit.** These permits, which sell for $3 a day or $10 for the season, allow you to park in plowed parking areas on the mountain. You can get permits at ski shops in Sandy and Hood River and at a few convenience stores along the road to the slopes.

Mt. Hood SkiBowl (☎ **503/272-3206,** or 503/222-2695 for snow report), located in Government Camp on U.S. 26, is the closest ski area to Portland, and with 1,500 vertical feet, has more expert slopes than any other ski area on the mountain. SkiBowl also claims to be the largest lighted ski area in the United States. Adult lift ticket prices range from $14 for midweek night skiing to $25 for a weekend all-day pass. Call for hours of operation.

Also in Government Camp is the tiny **Summit Ski Area** (☎ **503/272-0256**), which has a single chair lift and a rope tow and only a handful of runs. However, the economical rates make this a good choice for beginners. This is also the site of a very popular snowplay hill where families come to go sledding. Lift tickets are $12 for a full day.

Timberline Ski Area (☎ **503/231-7979** in Portland, 503/272-3311 outside Portland, or 503/222-2211 for snow report) is the highest ski area on Mount Hood and has one slope that is open right through summer. This is the site of the historic

Timberline Lodge. Adult lift ticket prices range from $11 for night skiing to $32 for a weekend all-day pass. Call for hours of operation.

Mount Hood Meadows Ski Resort (☎ **503/337-2222,** or 503/227-7669 for snow report), located 12 miles northeast of Government Camp on Ore. 35, is the largest ski resort on Mount Hood, with more than 2,000 skiable acres, 2,777 vertical feet, and a wide variety of terrain. This is the closest Mount Hood comes to having a ski resort of national standing, and it is here that you'll find the most out-of-state skiers. Snowcat skiing is sometimes available, as is summer skiing. Lift ticket prices range from $17 for night skiing to $35 for a weekend all-day pass. Call for hours of operation.

Continuing on around the mountain from Mount Hood Meadows, you'll find the small **Cooper Spur Ski Area** (☎ **503/230-2084** or 503/352-7803), which is the oldest ski area on the mountain and has a T-bar and a rope tow and 10 short runs. Lift tickets are only $10 a day.

If you're trying to get to the mountain from Portland, but don't want the hassle of driving yourself, consider **Bus/Lift** (☎ **503/287-5438**), which departs from downtown Portland and goes to Mount Hood Meadows and back for about $49. Purchase tickets at **G.I. Joe Ticketmaster** outlets (☎ **503/790-2787**). Also keep in mind that hotels in Hood River usually offer special ski packages that can make a ski vacation on Mount Hood much cheaper than you would think.

If it's **cross-country skiing** that interests you, there are plenty of trails on Mount Hood. For scenic views, head to the **White River Sno-Park,** east of Government Camp. The trails at **Glacier View Sno-Park,** across U.S. 26 from Mount Hood SkiBowl, are good for beginner and intermediate skiers, as are those at **Bennett Pass Sno-Park** on Ore. 35. If you're looking for groomed trails, you'll find them at Trillium Lake (after an often icy ungroomed start), at the **Mount Hood Meadows Nordic Center** ($9 trail pass) on Ore. 35, and at **Teacup Lake** ($3 trail pass), which is located across the highway from the turnoff for Mount Hood Meadows. Teacup Lake is maintained by a local ski club and is the best system of groomed trails on the mountain. In the town of Sandy and at Government Camp, you'll find numerous ski shops that rent cross-country skis.

WHERE TO STAY
MODERATE

Falcon's Crest Inn. P.O. Box 185, Government Camp, OR 97028. ☎ **800/624-7384** or 503/272-3403. Fax 503/272-3454. 3 rms, 2 suites. $95–$99.50 double; $169–$179 suite. AE, DISC, MC, V.

If you're looking for a B&B within walking distance of the ski slopes, this is your best bet on Mount Hood. Tucked into the trees on the edge of Government Camp, Falcon's Crest is a sprawling chalet-style lodge. Both suites, one of which is done up in a Mexican theme, have whirlpool tubs (one outside on a deck), and though a bit incongruous in this mountain setting, the Safari Room, with its deck and view of the ski slopes is a great choice. The inn also serves elegant six-course dinners (Cornish game hen, saltimbocca, beef Wellington) by reservation, and throughout the year there are many special events staged here, including murder mystery dinners.

Mt. Hood Bed & Breakfast. 8885 Cooper Spur Rd., Parkdale, OR 97041. ☎ **800/557-8885** or 541/352-6885. 3 rms, 1 cabin, 1 house. $85–$105 double with or without bath; $105 cabin; $225 house. Rates include full breakfast. No credit cards.

Located on a 42-acre working farm on the northeast side of Mount Hood, this B&B offers a quiet place to get away from it all. As an added bonus, you're only minutes away from a small ski area, and the mountain's major ski areas are less than 30 minutes away. We recommend either the Mount Hood Room or the Mount Adams Room, both of which have views of the respective mountains. An old log cabin on the property has also been renovated and makes for a very private accommodation. Guests can spend time in a barn that has a tennis court, basketball court, and sauna.

Mt. Hood Inn. 87450 E. Government Camp Loop (P.O. Box 400), Government Camp, OR 97028. ☎ **800/443-7777** or 503/272-3205. 56 rms. TV TEL. $105–$145 double. Rates include continental breakfast. AE, DC, DISC, MC, V.

You'll spot this motel at the west end of town beside the Mt. Hood Brew Pub. With their pine furnishings, the guest rooms have a contemporary rustic feel. The king spa rooms, with two-person whirlpool tubs beside the king-size beds, are definitely the best rooms here, but they're somewhat overpriced. Other rooms have refrigerators and microwaves. There's an indoor whirlpool, VCR and video rentals, and ski lockers.

✪ **The Resort at the Mountain.** 68010 E. Fairway, Welches, OR 97067. ☎ **800/669-7666** or 503/622-3101. Fax 503/622-2222. 160 rms, 73 suites. TV TEL. Mid-June to end of Sept $99–$165 double; $175–$225 suite. Oct to mid-June $90–$130 double; $155–$195 suite. AE, DC, DISC, MC, V.

Calling the surrounding area "the Highlands of Oregon," the Resort at the Mountain has adopted a Scottish theme that emphasizes the resort's 27-hole golf course. Beautifully landscaped grounds that incorporate concepts from Japanese garden design hide the resort's many low-rise buildings and make this a tranquil woodsy retreat. The guest rooms are large and all have either a balcony or a patio. Coffeemakers and special closets for ski gear are available in some rooms.

Dining/Entertainment: A casual dining room decked out in plenty of tartan overlooks the golf course. A more formal dining room serves a combination of Northwest, Scottish, and continental dishes at fairly reasonable prices.

Services: Room service (seasonal), laundry/valet service, mountain-bike rentals.

Facilities: 27-hole golf course, four tennis courts, outdoor swimming pool, whirlpool tub, fitness center, horseshoes, hiking and nature trails, volleyball, badminton, croquet, basketball, lawn bowling, pro shop.

✪ **Timberline Lodge.** Timberline, OR 97028. ☎ **800/547-1406** or 503/231-7979. Fax 503/272-3710. 60 rms, 50 with bath. $65 double without bath, $95–$170 double with bath. AE, DISC, MC, V. Sno-park permit required to park in winter.

Constructed during the Great Depression as a WPA project, this classic mountain lodge overflows with craftsmanship, and the grand stone fireplace, huge exposed beams, and wide plank floors of the lobby never fail to impress first-time visitors. Woodcarvings, imaginative wrought-iron fixtures, hand-hooked rugs, and handmade furniture complete the rustic picture. An exhibit in the lower lobby presents the history of the hotel, and tours of the hotel are also offered. The rooms vary in size considerably, with the smallest rooms lacking private bathrooms. The Timberline rooms are huge, while the fireplace rooms are the most expensive. Ask for a north side room on the third floor for the best views. No matter which room you stay in, you'll be surrounded by the same rustic furnishings.

Dining/Entertainment: The rustic Cascade Dining Room is short on mountain views, but the food is excellent (see "Where to Dine," below, for details). The Blue Ox Bar is a dark dungeon of a place, while the Ram's Head Lounge on the mezzanine is a more open and airy spot for a drink.

Facilities: Ski lifts, ski school and rentals, outdoor pool, sauna, whirlpool, hiking trails.

INEXPENSIVE

The Inn at Cooper Spur. 10755 Cooper Spur Rd., Mount Hood, OR 97041. ☎ **541/ 352-6692.** Fax 541/352-7551. 6 rms, 5 cabins, 3 suites. TV TEL. $65–$75 double; $119–$129 cabin or suite. AE, DISC, MC, V.

If you're looking to get away from it all, try an off-season stay at this surprisingly remote lodge. During ski season, though, you might find it difficult to get a reservation (and even in summer, ski teams from around the country stay here while they train on Mount Hood's summer ski slopes). The inn consists of a main building and a handful of modern log cabins that are certainly the more enjoyable rooms. These cabins have two bedrooms and a loft area reached by a spiral staircase. There are full kitchens for those wishing to do their own cooking. The inn's restaurant serves decent meals at reasonable prices. Facilities include whirlpools, a tennis court, a croquet lawn, and a basketball court.

WHERE TO DINE

In addition to the restaurants listed below, the **Mt. Hood Brew Pub,** 87304 E. Government Camp Loop (☎ **503/272-3724**), offers good microbrews and pub food. With at least six beers on tap, and a large selection of Northwest wines, you'll certainly find something to your liking.

Calamity Jane's. 42015 U.S. 26, Sandy. ☎ **503/668-7817.** Burgers $3.50–$11.50. AE, DISC, MC, V. Sun–Fri 11am–10pm, Sat 11am–11pm. BURGERS.

What, you ask, is an $11.50 hamburger? Well, at Calamity Jane's, it's a 1-pound pastrami-and-mushroom cheeseburger. That's right: 1 pound! If you think that's outrageous, wait until you see the other burgers listed on the menu. There's the peanut-butter burger, the George Washington burger (with sour cream and sweet pie cherries), the hot-fudge-and-marshmallow burger—even an unbelievably priced inflation burger. Not all the burgers at this entertaining and rustic eatery are calculated to turn your stomach: Some are just plain delicious. There are even pizza burgers. This place is just east of Sandy on U.S. 26.

✪ **Cascade Dining Room.** In Timberline Lodge, Timberline. ☎ **503/272-3700.** Reservations highly recommended on weekends. Main courses $16–$25. AE, DC, MC, V. Daily 8–10:30am, noon–2:30pm, and 5:30–8:30pm. NORTHWEST.

It may appear a bit casual from the lobby, and there are no stunning views of Mount Hood even though it's right outside the window, but the Cascade Dining Room is by far the best restaurant on Mount Hood. The menu changes regularly, but you'll likely find the likes of sun-dried tomato mousse or smoked salmon cheesecake on the appetizer list. Main courses might include cedar-planked salmon, apple-braised steelhead, or grilled vegetarian anasazi bean cakes. There's a good wine selection, and desserts showcase the variety of local seasonal ingredients such as raspberries, pears, and apples.

Chalet Swiss. 24371 E. Welches Rd., Welches. ☎ **503/622-3600.** Reservations recommended. Main courses $11–$19; lunch $5–$10. AE, DISC, MC, V. Tues–Sat 11:30am–2pm and 5–9pm. SWISS/CONTINENTAL.

The interior of this restaurant looks more like a Swiss barn than a Swiss chalet, with old wagon wheels, huge cowbells, and copper pots decorating the open-beamed dining room; however, there's definitely plenty of Swiss food on the menu. Start with either the raclette, a delicious melted cheese, or the Buendnerfleisch, which is a sort of Swiss prosciutto that's made from beef. If you opt for the latter, then by all means order the cheese fondue Neufchâteloise for a main course. There's nothing quite as satisfying after a cold day on the slopes. There's an extensive wine list.

The Rendezvous Grill. 67149 E. U.S. 26, Welches. ☎ **503/622-6837.** Reservations recommended. Main courses $12–$19; lunch $7–$8.50. AE, DISC, MC, V. Daily 11:30am–9pm. MEDITERRANEAN.

Located right on U.S. 26 in Welches, this casual, upscale restaurant is a great choice for dinner on your way back to Portland after a day on the mountain. While the emphasis here is on the flavors of the Mediterranean, other flavors also show up in the guise of sake-glazed salmon and crab and shrimp cakes with chipotle aioli. The grilled steak with Whidbey's port and blue cheese sauce is a must for steak fans.

2 The Santiam Pass, McKenzie Pass & McKenzie River

Santiam Pass: 82 miles SE of Salem, 40 miles NW of Bend; McKenzie Pass: 77 miles NE of Eugene, 36 miles NW of Bend.

As the nearest recreational areas to both Salem and Eugene, the Santiam Pass, McKenzie Pass, and McKenzie River routes are some of the most popular in the state. Ore. 22, which leads over Santiam Pass, is also one of the busiest routes to the Sisters and Bend areas in central Oregon. Along these highways are to be found some of the state's best white-water rafting and fishing, some of the most popular and most beautiful backpacking areas, and good downhill and cross-country skiing. In the summer, the Detroit Lake recreation area is the main attraction along Ore. 22 and is a favorite of water-skiers and lake anglers. In winter, it is downhill and cross-country skiing at Santiam Pass that brings people up this way.

Ore. 126, on the other hand, follows the scenic McKenzie River, and is favored by white-water rafters and drift-boat anglers fishing for salmon and steelhead. Several state parks provide access to the river. During the summer, Ore. 126 connects to Ore. 242, a narrow road that climbs up and over McKenzie Pass, the most breathtaking pass in the Oregon Cascades.

ESSENTIALS

GETTING THERE   Santiam Pass is a year-round pass and is reached by Ore. 22 from Salem, U.S. 20 from Albany, and Ore. 126 from Eugene. McKenzie Pass is on Ore. 242 and lies to the south of Santiam Pass. It can be reached by all of the same roads that lead to Santiam Pass, but it is closed during the winter months.

VISITOR INFORMATION   For more information on outdoor recreation in this area, contact the **Detroit Ranger Station,** HC60, Box 320, Mill City, OR 97360 (☎ 541/854-3366); the **McKenzie Ranger Station,** McKenzie Bridge, OR 97413 (☎ 541/822-3381); or the **Blue River Ranger Station,** Blue river, OR 97413 (☎ 541/822-3317). For more general information, contact the **McKenzie River Chamber of Commerce,** P.O. Box 1117, Leaburg, OR 97489 (☎ 541/896-3330), which operates a visitor center at the old Leaburg fish hatchery on Leaburg Lake east of Springfield.

ALONG THE SANTIAM PASS HIGHWAY

Detroit Lake is the summertime center of activity on this route, with fishing and waterskiing the most popular activities. North of the lake, you'll find the **Breitenbush Hot Springs Retreat and Conference Center** (☎ 503/854-3314), which allows day use of its hot springs by reservation only. The day use fee is $15 per person and vegetarian meals are available for $6.

At Santiam Pass, you'll find **Hoodoo Ski Area** (☎ 800/949-LIFT for snow report, or 541/822-3799), which has three chair lifts and a rope tow, and 22 runs for all levels of experience. Lift tickets are $22 for adults and $16 for children. Night skiing is available. Here you'll also find the **Hoodoo Nordic Center,** which has more than 16 kilometers of groomed cross-country ski trails and charges $5 to $8 for a trail pass. Also in the Santiam Pass area, you'll find several Sno-Parks. The Maxwell, Big Springs, and Lava Lake East Sno-Parks access the best trails in the area.

UP THE McKENZIE RIVER

The McKenzie River is one of Oregon's most popular white-water rafting rivers, and the cold blue waters offer thrills for rafters from a wide range of experience levels. **The Oregon Paddler** (☎ **800/267-6848** or 541/741-8661), **Oregon Whitewater Adventures** (☎ **800/820-RAFT** or 541/746-5422), **McKenzie River Adventures** (☎ **800/832-5858** or 541/822-3806), and **Jim's Oregon Whitewater** (☎ **800/ 254-JIMS** or 541/822-6003) all offer a variety of trips of varying lengths on the McKenzie. Expect to pay around $50 for a half day of rafting and $65 to $75 for a full day. Overnight trips can also be arranged. A slightly tamer white-water experience can be had on the pontoon platform boats of **McKenzie Pontoon Trips** (☎ **541/741-1905**).

Surprisingly, the McKenzie River town of Blue River is home to one of the best golf courses in Oregon. **Tokatee Golf Club,** 54947 McKenzie Hwy., Blue River (☎ **800/452-6376**), consistently gets high ratings and has a spectacular setting with views of snow-capped Cascade Peaks and lush forests.

Off Ore. 126, between the towns of Blue River and McKenzie Bridge, you'll find the turnoff for the **Aufderheide National Scenic Byway** (Forest Service Road 19). This road meanders for 54 miles through the foothills of the Cascades first following the South Fork McKenzie River (and Cougar Reservoir) and then the North Fork of the Middle Fork Willamette River, which offers excellent fly fishing and numerous swimming holes. At the south end of Cougar Reservoir, you'll find a trail that leads to the very popular **Terwilliger Hot Springs.** The southernmost stretch of this road is the most scenic portion and passes through a deep narrow gorge formed by the North Fork of the Middle Fork Willamette River. Along the route, you'll find several hiking trails, including the trail up **French Pete Creek,** which was one of the first lowland old-growth forests to be protected from logging. At the southern end of the scenic byway is the community of Westfir, which is the site of the longest covered bridge in Oregon.

Between the turnoff for McKenzie Pass and the junction of Ore. 126 and U.S. 20, you'll find some of the Cascades' most enchanting water features. Southernmost of these is **Belknap Lodge & Hot Springs** (☎ **541/822-3512**), where, for $3 an hour or $7 a day, you can soak in a hot mineral swimming pool. Just north of Trail Bridge Reservoir, on a side road off the highway, a 2-mile hike on a section of the McKenzie River Trail will bring you to the startlingly blue waters of the ✪ **Tamolitch Pool.** This pool is formed when the McKenzie River wells up out of the ground after flowing underground for 3 miles. Five miles south of the junction with Ore. 20, you'll come to two picturesque waterfalls—**Sahalie Falls** and **Koosah Falls.** Across the highway from these falls is **Clear Lake,** the source of the McKenzie River. This spring-fed lake truly lives up to its name, and a rustic lakeside resort rents rowboats so you can get out on the water and see for yourself. Be sure to hike the trail on the east side of the lake; it leads to the turquoise waters of **Great Springs,** which is connected to the lake by a 100-yard stream.

One of the most breathtaking sections of road in the state begins just east of **Belknap Hot Springs.** Ore. 242, which is only open in the summer, is a narrow winding road that climbs up through forests and lava fields to **McKenzie Pass,** from which there's a sweeping panorama of the Cascades and blackened, ragged hillsides of lava. These lava fields are some of the youngest in Oregon. An observation building made of lava rock provides sighting tubes so you can identify all the visible peaks, and there are a couple of trails that will lead you out into this otherworldly wasteland. In autumn, this road has some of the best fall color in the state. On the west side of the pass, the short **Proxy Falls** trail leads through old lava flows to a waterfall that has no outlet stream in late summer. The water simply disappears into the porous lava.

WHERE TO STAY

✪ **Belknap Lodge & Hot Springs.** N. Belknap Springs Rd., Belknap Springs, OR 97413. ☎ **541/822-3512.** Fax 541/822-3327. 10 rms, 5 cabins. $60–$90 double, $35–$90 cabin. Rates include continental breakfast. MC, V.

Located on the bank of the McKenzie River, this lodge has recently undergone an extensive remodeling and renovation that has turned it into one of the most enjoyable mountain retreats in the state. As part of the remodeling, extensive lawns and perennial gardens have been planted turning this clearing in the forest into a burst of color in the summer. Guest rooms vary in size, but all have comfortable modern furnishings. Some also have whirlpool tubs or decks overlooking the roaring river. The hot springs, which are actually on the far side of the river and are reached by a foot bridge, are pumped into a small pool between the lodge and the river. There is a library/breakfast room as well as a small exercise room. The cabins are more rustic than the lodge rooms. The lodge also has campsites for tents and RVs ($12 to $18). There are plans to add a restaurant.

Breitenbush Hot Springs Retreat and Conference Center. P.O. Box 578, Detroit, OR 97342. ☎ **503/854-3314.** 43 cabins. $55–$90 per person cabin; $40–$45 per person platform tents; $35–$40 per person campsites. Rates include all meals, use of hot springs, and daily well-being programs. MC, V.

This New Age retreat center deep in the Cascade forests offers a wide range of programs (from drum-making workshops to essene and Taoist retreats to soul retrieval training), but is also open to anyone simply wishing to come for a personal retreat without participating in any specific program. The cabins are very simple, and not all have private bathrooms, but it is this very simplicity that accounts for much of the mellow atmosphere. There are also large tents on platforms, as well as sites where you can pitch your own tent. Both natural hot pools and more formal hot tubs are available and massages are also available.

Holiday Farm. 54455 McKenzie River Dr., Blue River, OR 97413. ☎ **800/823-3715** or 541/822-3715. 16 cottages. $110–$155 cottage. AE, MC, V.

Forget about log cabins, this place is a collection of white cottages reminiscent of those found on Cape Cod. It started out as a stagecoach stop and has been around long enough to have hosted Pres. Herbert Hoover. The best cottages are those that are perched right over the river. The setting, under the big trees and beside the rushing McKenzie River, is as idyllic as you'll find in Oregon. Guests have 90 acres to roam, with 750 feet of riverfront and two private lakes for fishing and swimming. The dining room, a throwback to the early 1960s, serves three meals a day and has a small lounge and game room.

Log Cabin Inn. 56483 McKenzie Hwy., McKenzie Bridge, OR 97413. ☎ **800/355-3432** or 541/822-3432. 8 cabins. $75–$85 cabin for 2 to 4 people. 2-night minimum stay on weekends from Apr to Oct. DISC, MC, V.

Situated on 6^1/$_2$ acres in the community of McKenzie Bridge, this log lodge was built in 1906 after the original 1886 lodge burned to the ground. In the lodge's heyday, its guests included President Hoover, Clark Gable, and the duke of Windsor. Today, you can stay in rustic cabins, all but one of which have their own fireplaces. The one cabin without a fireplace does, however, have a kitchen, which the others do not. Although the one duplex log cabin has cramped rooms, it has a lot of woodsy character. There are also large teepees ($45 per night) that sleep up to six people for anyone interested in camping. The lodge's restaurant is renowned for its high-quality meals, which include such game as wild boar, venison, and buffalo. At under $10, Sunday brunch is a great deal.

CAMPGROUNDS

There are several campgrounds along the McKenzie River on Ore. 126. Of these the **Delta Campground,** set under huge old-growth trees between Blue River and McKenzie Bridge, is one of the finest. Rafters and kayakers tend to gravitate to **Olallie Campground** and **Paradise Campground,** which are east of McKenzie Bridge. Between Paradise and Delta, you'll also find **McKenzie Bridge Campground.**

If you are up this way to hike, mountain bike, or do some flat-water canoeing, there is no better choice than Clear Lake's **Coldwater Cove Campground** on Ore. 126 just south of Santiam Pass junction. South of here on Ore. 126, the **Trail Bridge Campground** makes a good alternative to Coldwater Cove.

Along the popular McKenzie Pass Highway (Ore. 242), you'll find **Scott Lake Campground, Alder Springs Campground,** and **Lava Lake Campground.**

Along the Aufderheide National Scenic Byway, you'll find campgrounds at **Frissell Crossing, Twin Springs, Homestead,** and **French Pete,** all of which are on the banks of the South Fork of the McKenzie River. Toward the south end of this road is **Kiahanie Campground,** which is on the North Fork of the Middle Fork of the Willamette River and is popular with fly anglers.

WHERE TO DINE

The dining room at the Log Cabin Inn is the best place to eat along the McKenzie River. Other than this, there are few casual roadhouses strung out along Ore. 126. For burgers, try the **Vida Cafe,** milepost 26 (☎ **541/896-3289**), or **Finn Rock General Store,** milepost 38 (☎ **541/822-3299**), which has a deck beside the river.

3 The Willamette Pass Route

Oakridge: 41 miles SE of Eugene; Willamette Pass: 68 miles SE of Eugene

Ore. 58, which connects Eugene with U.S. 97 north of Crater Lake, is the state's fastest and straightest route over the Cascades. However, this is not to imply that there isn't anything along this highway worth slowing down for. Flanked by two wilderness areas—Waldo Lake and Diamond Peak—and three major lakes—Waldo, Odell, and Crescent—Ore. 58 provides access to a wide range of recreational activities, chief among which are mountain biking, fishing, and boating in summer and both downhill and cross-country skiing in winter.

The sister towns of Oakridge and Westfir are the only real towns on this entire route and are the only places where you'll find much in the way of services. Westfir is also the southern terminus of the Aufderheide National Scenic Byway, which winds through the Cascade foothills to just outside the town of McKenzie Bridge on Ore. 126. For information on this scenic drive, see above.

ESSENTIALS

GETTING THERE   Ore. 58 begins just south of Eugene off I-5 and stretches for 92 miles to U.S. 97.

VISITOR INFORMATION   For more information on recreational activities in this area, contact the **Oakridge Ranger Station,** 46375 Ore. 58, Westfir, OR 97492 (☎ 541/782-2291), or the **Rigdon Ranger Station,** 49098 Salmon Creek Rd., Oakridge, OR 97463 (☎ 541/782-2283).

FESTIVALS   Each year in mid-July, Oakridge hosts the **Fat Tire Festival,** one of the biggest mountain bike races in the Northwest. At Odell Lake at this same time of year, the **Pioneer Cup Canoe Races** sends paddlers racing across the waters of this mountain lake.

WHAT TO SEE & DO: FROM HOT SPRINGS TO SNOW SKIING

In the Willamette National Forest outside the logging town of Oakridge are miles and miles of great mountain biking trails that have turned the Oakridge area into one of Oregon's top mountain biking regions. Stop by the ranger stations in Westfir and Oakridge to get maps and information on riding these trails. One of the most scenic rides is the 22-mile trail around Waldo Lake. You'll also find mountain biking trails at Willamette Pass Ski Area, where the cross-country ski trails make great bike trails.

If you're keen to soak your weary muscles in some natural hot springs, you'll find some right beside Ore. 58 about 10 miles east of Oakridge. **McCredie Hot Springs** are neither the hottest nor most picturesque hot springs in the state, and what with traffic noise and crowds, they aren't the most pleasant either. However, if you want a quick soak without having to go wandering down gravel roads, they do the trick.

Just before reaching Willamette Pass, you'll see signs for **Salt Creek Falls,** which are well worth a stroll down the short trail to the falls overlook. At 286 feet high, these are the second highest falls in the state. Longer hiking trails also lead out from the falls parking area.

Also just before Willamette Pass is the turnoff for Forest Service Road 5897, which leads 10 miles north to **Waldo Lake,** one of the purest lakes in the world. The lake, which is just over a mile high, covers 10 square miles and is 420 feet deep. When the waters are still, it is possible to see more than 100 feet down into the lake. Because this is such a large lake, and because there are reliable afternoon winds, it is popular for sailboating and boardsailing. Powerboaters and canoeists also frequent the lake. There are several campgrounds along the east shore of the lake, while the west shore abuts the Waldo Lake Wilderness Area. The 22-mile loop trail around the lake is popular with mountain bikers and backpackers, but shorter day hikes, particularly at the south end, are rewarding. The mosquitoes here are some of the worst in the state, so before planning a trip up here, be sure to get a bug report from the Oakridge Ranger Station.

Just over Willamette Pass lie two more large lakes. **Odell Lake** is best known by anglers who come to troll for kokanee salmon and Mackinaw trout. However, it's also a good windsurfing lake. Although the waters never exactly get warm, **Crescent Lake** is the area's best swimming lake, and Symax Beach, in the northeast corner of the lake, is the best swimming area.

At **Willamette Pass Ski Area** (☎ 800/444-5030 for information, 541/484-5030, or 541/345-SNOW for skiing conditions), 69 miles southeast of Eugene on Ore. 58, you'll find 30 downhill runs and 12½ miles (20km) of groomed cross-country trails. The ski area is open daily from mid-November to mid-April. Night skiing is available on Friday and Saturday nights from late December to March. Adult lift tickets $25 per day or $5 per hour (with a 2-hour minimum).

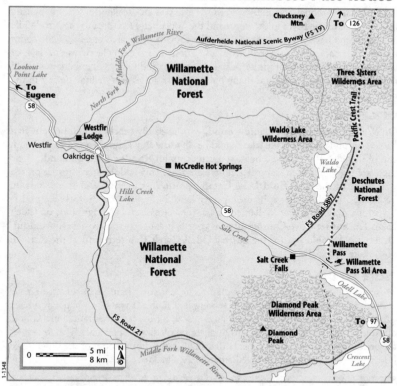

The Willamette Pass Route

WHERE TO STAY

Odell Lake Lodge. P.O. Box 72, Crescent Lake, OR 97425. ☎ **541/433-2540.** 7 rms, 12 cabins. $36–$52 double, $60–$210 cabin. DISC, MC, V.

Located at the east end of Odell Lake just off Ore. 58, this rustic cabin resort is set beneath tall trees beside the lake. Most popular in the summer, when fishing is the sport of choice, the lodge also stays open through the winter and has its own network of groomed cross-country ski trails. The lodge rooms are generally rather small, but the economical prices keep them filled. The cabins vary in size from tiny one-bedroom buildings to one with four bedrooms. All the cabins have woodstoves, and about half overlook the water. The lodge has a dining room serving three meals a day. In summer, the lodge's marina rents fishing boats (and tackle), canoes, row boats, and sailboats. The lodge also rents mountain bikes and cross-country skis. This place is pretty basic, but the location is great.

Westfir Lodge. 48365 First St., Westfir, OR 97492. ☎ **541/782-3103.** 8 rms. A/C. $70–$85 double. Rates include full breakfast. No credit cards.

Housed in what was once the company headquarters for a long-gone lumber mill, this bed-and-breakfast has a very Victorian feel inside and beautiful flower gardens outside. Directly across the street is the longest covered bridge in Oregon, which once connected the offices to the lumber mill itself. Set at the southern end of the

Aufderheide National Scenic Byway, this inn makes an excellent base for exploring both the McKenzie River to the north and the Willamette Pass area to the east. While all the rooms have private bathrooms, only four of these are actually in the room itself; others are across the hall from the guest room. An eclectic assemblage of antiques and artifacts from innkeepers' Ken Symons and Gerry Chamberlain's world travels fill the guest rooms and many public rooms. Rates also include dessert in the evening.

CAMPGROUNDS

On Waldo Lake, the **Islet Campground,** with its sandy beach, should be your first choice. Second choice on the lake should be **Shadow Bay Campground** at the south end of the lake. If you have a boat, you can camp on **Rhododendron Island,** where there are two designated campsites. There are also many paddle-up campsites on the west shore of the lake. **Gold Lake Campground,** just west of Willamette Pass on FS Road 500, is a quiet spot on a pretty lake that allows no motorboats and is fly-fishing only. Just over Willamette Pass, there are several campgrounds on Odell Lake. The **Sunset Cove Campground** is your best choice if you are here to windsurf. Otherwise, I would opt for the quieter **Odell Creek Campground** at the east end of the lake.

WHERE TO DINE

Most people heading up this way plan to be self sufficient when mealtime rolls around, whether they're camping or staying in a cabin. If you don't happen to have a full ice chest, you'll find a couple of pizza places, a Mexican restaurant, and a couple of espresso places in Oakridge. Although none of these is particularly memorable, they're the only places to get a meal other than in the dining room of the Odell Lake Lodge or the pizza place at the Willamette Pass Ski Area.

4 The North Umpqua–Upper Rogue River Scenic Byway

Diamond Lake: 76 miles E of Roseburg, 80 miles NE of Medford

Ore. 138, which heads east out of Roseburg, leads to Diamond Lake and the north entrance to Crater Lake National Park, but it's also one of the state's most scenic highways. Along much of its length, the highway follows the North Umpqua River, which is famed among fly anglers for its fighting steelhead and salmon. However, as far as we're concerned, this deep aquamarine stream is the most beautiful river in Oregon and is well worth a visit even if you don't know a wooly bugger from a muddler minnow. Between Idleyld Park and Toketee Reservoir, you'll find numerous picnic areas, boat launches, swimming holes, and campgrounds.

As Ore. 138 approaches the crest of the Cascades, it skirts the shores of Diamond Lake, which though not even remotely as beautiful as nearby Crater Lake, is still a major recreational destination. The lake, which is almost a mile in elevation, is set at the foot of jagged Mount Thielsen, a spire-topped pinnacle that is known as the "lightning rod of the Cascades." The lake offers swimming, boating, fishing, camping, hiking, biking, and snowmobiling and skiing in winter. Just beyond Diamond Lake is the north entrance to Crater Lake National Park.

The 24-mile long Ore. 230 connects the Diamond Lake area with the valley of the upper Rogue River at the community of Union Creek. While this stretch of the Rogue is neither as dramatic as the North Umpqua or the lower Rogue River, it has its charms, including a natural bridge, a narrow gorge, and some grand old trees.

ESSENTIALS

GETTING THERE   The North Umpqua River is paralleled by Ore. 138, which connects Roseburg, on I-5, with U.S. 97, which parallels the Cascades on the east side of the mountains. This highway leads to the north entrance of Crater Lake National Park.

VISITOR INFORMATION   For information on recreational activities in this area, contact the **North Umpqua Ranger District,** 18782 N. Umpqua Hwy., Glide, OR 97443 (☎ **541/496-3532**); or the **Diamond Lake Ranger District,** HC 60, Box 101, Idleyld Park, OR 97447 (☎ **541/498-2531**).

WHAT TO SEE & DO: FLY FISHING, RAFTING & A WATERFALL

Oregon abounds in waterfalls and white-water rivers, but in the town of Glide, 12 miles east of Roseburg, you'll find the only place in the state where rivers collide. At the interesting **Colliding Rivers Viewpoint,** the North Umpqua River rushing in from the north slams into the white water of the Little River, which flows from the south, and the two rivers create a churning stew.

The most celebrated portion of the river is the 31-mile stretch from Deadline Falls, in Swiftwater Park, to Soda Springs Dam. This stretch of river is open to fly angling only. Between June and October, you can often see salmon and steelhead leaping up Deadline Falls, which has a designated salmon-viewing area down a short trail on the south bank of the river. For fly-fishing needs and advice, stop in at the **Blue Heron Fly Shop** (☎ **541/496-0448**) just off Ore. 138 in Idleyld Park, or **Steamboat Inn** (☎ **541/498-2411**) in Steamboat. If you want to hire a guide to take you out fishing on the North Umpqua River, try **Larry Levine's River Wolf Guide Service** (☎ **541/496-0326**), **North River Guide Service** (☎ **541/496-0309**), **Jerry Q. Phelps** (☎ **541/672-8324**), or **Summer Run Guide Service** (☎ **541/496-3037**). Rates are generally between $100 to $200 per day.

If you'd rather just paddle the river in a kayak or raft, contact **Noah's World of Water** (☎ **800/858-2811** or 541/488-2811), **North Umpqua Outfitters** (☎ **541/673-4599**), **Orange Torpedo Trips** (☎ **800/635-2925** or 541/479-5061), and **Oregon Ridge and River Excursions** (☎ **541/496-3333**), which all offer trips of varying lengths. Rates are around $50 for a half-day trip.

At the turnoff for Toketee Reservoir, you'll find the trailhead for the ¹⁄₂-mile hike to **Toketee Falls.** This double cascade plummets 120 feet over a wall of columnar basalt and is one of the most photographed waterfalls in the state. Also in this same area, past the Toketee Lake Campground, you'll find the **Umpqua Hot Springs** down a short trail. These natural hot springs perch high above the North Umpqua River on a hillside covered with mineral deposits. For longer hikes, consider the many segments of the 79-mile **North Umpqua Trail,** which parallels the river from just east of Glide all the way to the Pacific Crest Trail. The lower segments of this trail are also popular mountain biking routes.

At **Diamond Lake,** just a few miles north of Crater Lake National Park, you'll find one of the most popular mountain recreation spots in the state. In summer, the popular and somewhat run-down **Diamond Lake Resort** is the center of area activities. Here you can rent boats and horses, swim at a small beach, and access the 10¹⁄₂-mile paved hiking/biking trail that circles Diamond Lake.

Near the community of Union Creek, west of the Crater Lake National Park on Ore. 62, are the Rogue River Gorge and a small natural bridge. The gorge, though only a few feet wide in places, is quite dramatic and has an easy trail running alongside. The natural bridge is formed by a lava tube through which flows the Rogue River.

In winter, Diamond Lake Resort serves as the region's main snowmobiling destination, but also serves as a base camp for downhill skiers heading out with **Mount Bailey Snowcats,** which provides access to untracked snow on the slopes of nearby Mount Bailey. A day of snowcat skiing runs around $200. Cross-country skiers will find rentals and groomed trails at the **Diamond Lake Resort Cross Country Ski Center.** There are also many more miles of marked, but not groomed, cross-country ski trails in the area, with the more interesting trails to be found at the south end of the lake. Snowmobile rentals and tours are also available here. For more information on these activities, contact **Diamond Lake Resort** (☎ **800/733-7593**).

WHERE TO STAY & DINE

Diamond Lake Resort. Diamond Lake, OR 97731. ☎ **800/733-7593** or 541/793-3333. Fax 541/793-3309. 40 rms, 10 studios, 42 cabins. TV. $70 double; $75 studio for two; $100–$155 cabin. MC, V.

Located on the shores of Diamond Lake near the north entrance to the national park, this resort has long been a popular family vacation spot, and with Mounts Thielsen and Bailey flanking the lake, this is one of the most picturesque settings in the Oregon Cascades. The variety of accommodations provides plenty of choices, but our favorites are the lakefront cabins, which are large enough for a family or two couples. These have great views of the lake and mountains. If you want to do your own cooking, you'll find kitchenettes in both the cabins and studios. Unfortunately, this resort has gotten fairly run down in recent years. The lodge also offers several dining options, though most visitors opt to cook their own meals. Boat, mountain bike, and horse rentals are available, and there's a small sandy beach and a bumper-boat area. In winter, the resort is most popular with snowmobilers but also attracts a few cross-country skiers, as well as downhillers here to snowcat ski on Mount Bailey.

Prospect Historical Hotel and Motel. 391 Mill Creek Dr., Prospect, OR 97536. ☎ **800/944-6490** or 541/560-3664. Fax 503/560-3825. 23 rms. $60–$80 double. DISC, MC, V.

This hotel, located in the tiny hamlet of Prospect, 30 miles from Crater Lake's Rim Village, is a combination of an 1889 vintage hotel and a modern motel. The old hotel is a big white building with a wraparound porch on which are set several bent-willow couches. The small rooms in the historic hotel have few furnishings, but they do have a country styling that gives them a bit of charm. If you stay in one of these rooms, a continental breakfast is included. The motel rooms are much larger and have televisions and telephones, and some of these rooms also have kitchenettes. The elegant dining room is well known for its excellent meals, with main courses such as rack of lamb, and shrimp scampi ranging in price from $10 to $16. Sunday brunch is particularly popular.

✪ Steamboat Inn. 42705 N. Umpqua Hwy., Steamboat, OR 97447-9703. ☎ **800/840-8825** or 541/498-2230. Fax 541/498-2411. 8 rms, 2 suites, 5 cottages, 4 houses. $125 double; $160 cottages and houses; $235 suites. MC, V.

Located roughly midway between Roseburg and Crater Lake, this inn on the bank of the North Umpqua River is by far the finest lodging on the North Umpqua. While the lodge appeals primarily to anglers, the beautiful gardens, luxurious guest rooms, and gourmet meals also attract a fair number of people looking for a quiet getaway in the forest and a base for hiking and biking. If you aren't springing for one of the suites, which have their own soaking tubs overlooking the river, your best bet will be a stream-side rooms, which are referred to as cabins but really aren't. These have all been recently renovated, have gas fireplaces, and open onto a long deck that overlooks the river. The hideaway cottages are more spacious but don't have river views and are half a mile from the lodge (and the dining room). Dinners are multicourse affairs served in a cozy dining room, and breakfast is available all day. There's also a fly-fishing shop on the premises.

Union Creek Resort. 56484 Ore. 62, Prospect, OR 97536. ☎ **541/560-3565.** 9 rms, 14 cabins. $38–$48 double; $50–$85 cabin for 2 to 6 people. MC, V.

Located almost across the road from the Rogue River Gorge, this cabin resort has been catering to Crater Lake visitors since the early 1900s and is listed on the National Register of Historic Places. Tall trees shade the grounds of the rustic resort, which is right on Ore. 62 about 23 miles from Rim Village. Accommodations include both lodge rooms and very basic cabins (many of which have kitchenettes), and most have been updated in recent years. Across the road from the cabins and lodge building is Beckie's Café, which serves home-style meals and is best known for its pies. This is your best and closest option outside the Crater Lake National Park on the west side.

CAMPGROUNDS

Along the North Umpqua River between Idleyld Park and Diamond Lake, you'll find the Bureau of Land Management's **Susan Creek Campground,** the most upscale public campground along the North Umpqua (it even has hot showers). Up Forest Service Road 38 (between mileposts 38–39), you'll find **Canton Creek Campground,** which is just off Steamboat Creek and **Steamboat Falls Campground.** Nearby on Ore. 138 is **Island Campground.** The larger **Horseshoe Bend Campground,** near Steamboat, is popular with rafters and kayakers on weekends and has well-separated campsites, big views of surrounding cliffs, and access to the North Umpqua Trail. Continuing east, **Eagle Rock Campground** is in deep woods. **Boulder Flat Campground,** right on the highway east of Eagle Rock, is the uppermost campground on the wild-and-scenic section of the river. **Toketee Lake Campground,** at Toketee Reservoir, is situated back from the lake, but there are a few sites on the river.

Diamond Lake has three U.S. Forest Service campgrounds—Diamond Lake, Broken Arrow, and Thielsen View—with a total of 450 campsites. Here you'll also find the **Diamond Lake RV Park** (☎ **541/793-3318**).

Southwest of the Crater Lake National Park on Ore. 62, you'll find **Huckleberry Mountain Campground.** However, this campground is set amid spindly young trees and is devoid of atmosphere. Farther west is **Farewell Bend Campground,** which is set amid big trees on the Rogue River. The next campgrounds are **Union Creek** and **Natural Bridge,** both of which are also along the Rogue River. North of Ore. 62 on Ore. 230, you'll find the **Hamaker Campground,** on a pretty bend in the Rogue River with big trees and meadows across the river.

5 Crater Lake National Park

71 miles NE of Medford, 83 miles E of Roseburg, 57 miles N of Klamath Falls

At 1,932 feet, Crater Lake is the deepest lake in the United States (and is the seventh deepest in the world). But depth alone is not what has made this one of the most visited spots in the Northwest. What truly bewitches visitors to this mountain-filling lake is the startling sapphire-blue waters. They've mesmerized visitors ever since a prospector searching for gold stumbled on the high mountain lake in 1853. In 1902, the lake and its surroundings became a national park, and to this day it's still the only national park in Oregon.

The **caldera** (crater) that today holds the serene lake was born in an explosive volcanic eruption 7,700 years ago. When the volcano, now known as Mount Mazama, erupted, its summit (thought to have been around 12,000 feet high)

collapsed, leaving a crater 4,000 feet deep. It has taken thousands of years of rain and melting snow to create the cold, clear lake we now know as Crater Lake, which today is surrounded by crater walls nearly 2,000 feet high.

The drive into the park winds through forests that hold not a hint of the spectacular sight that lies hidden among these mountains. With no warning except the signs leading to Rim Village, you suddenly find yourself gazing down into a vast bowl full of blue water. Toward one end of the lake, the cone of Wizard Island rises from the lake. This island is the tip of a volcano that has been slowly building since the last eruption of Mount Mazama.

ESSENTIALS

GETTING THERE   If you're coming from the south on I-5, take Exit 62 in Medford and follow Ore. 62 for 75 miles. If you're coming from the north, take Exit 124 in Roseburg and follow Ore. 138. From Klamath Falls, take U.S. 97 north to Ore. 62. In winter, only the south entrance is open. Due to deep snowpack, the north entrance usually doesn't open until sometime in late July.

VISITOR INFORMATION   For more information, contact **Crater Lake National Park,** P.O. Box 7, Crater Lake, OR 97604 (☎ **541/594-2211**).

ADMISSION   Park admission is $10 per vehicle and $5 per person for pedestrians and cyclists.

SEEING THE HIGHLIGHTS

After your first breathtaking view of the lake, you may want to stop by one of the park's two visitor centers. The **Steel Information Center** is located between the south park entrance and the Rim Village, which is where you'll find the smaller and less thorough **Rim Village Visitor Center.** Though the park is open year-round, in winter, when deep snows blanket the region, only the road to Rim Village is kept clear. During the summer (roughly beginning in late June), the Rim Drive provides many viewpoints as it makes a 39-mile-long circuit of the lake.

Narrated boat trips around the lake are the park's most popular activity. These tours last 1³/₄ hours and begin at Cleetwood Cove, which is at the bottom of a very steep 1-mile trail that descends 700 feet from the rim to the lakeshore. Before deciding to take a boat tour, be sure you're in good enough physical condition to make the steep climb back up to the rim. Also, be sure to bring warm clothes, as it can be quite a bit cooler on the lake than it is on the rim. A naturalist on each boat provides a narrative on the ecology and history of the lake, and all tours include a stop on Wizard Island. Tours are offered from late June to mid-September and cost $12.50 for adults and $7 for children.

Of the many miles of **hiking trails** within the park, the mile-long Cleetwood Trail is the only trail that leads down to the lake shore. It's a steep and tiring hike back up from the lake. The trail to the top of Mount Scott, although it's a rigorous 2¹/₂-mile hike, is the park's most rewarding hike. Shorter trails with good views include the 0.8-mile trail to the top of The Watchman, which overlooks Wizard Island, and the 1.7-mile trail up Garfield Peak. The short Castle Crest Wildflower Trail is best hiked in late July and early August. Backpackers can hike the length of the park on the Pacific Crest Trail (PCT) or head out on a few other trails that lead into more remote, though less scenic, corners of the park.

Other summertime park activities include children's programs, campfire ranger talks, history talks, and guided walks. To find out about these, check in *Crater Lake Reflections,* a free park newspaper that is given to all visitors when they enter the park.

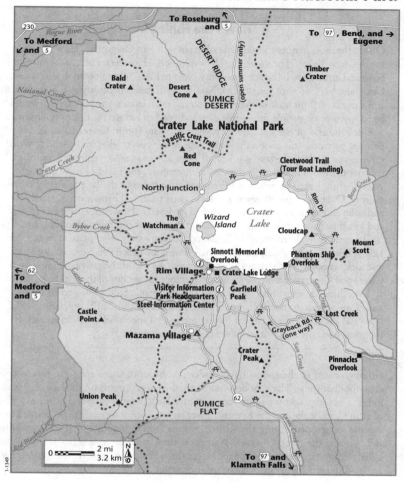

In winter, **cross-country skiing** is popular on the park's snow-covered Rim Drive and in the backcountry. At Rim Village, you'll find several miles of well-marked ski trails, and, weather permitting, the views are the best in the state. Skiers in good condition can usually make the entire circuit of the lake in 2 days, but must be prepared to camp in the snow. Spring, when the weather is warmer and there are fewer severe storms, is actually the best time to ski around the lake.

WHERE TO STAY & DINE

✪ **Crater Lake Lodge.** Mailing address: 1211 Ave. C, White City, OR 97503. ☎ **541/ 830-8700.** Fax 541/830-8514. 71 rms. $99–$129 double. MC, V. Closed mid-Oct to mid-May.

Perched on the edge of the rim overlooking Crater Lake, this lodge was completely rebuilt in 1995 and has since become the finest national park lodge in the Northwest. Not only are the views breathtaking, but the amenities are modern without sacrificing the rustic atmosphere that visitors expect in a mountain lodge. Among the lodge's few original features are the stone fireplace and ponderosa pine-bark walls in the Great Hall. Slightly more than half the guest rooms overlook the lake, and

How's the Fishing?

One of the most frequently asked questions in southern Oregon is, "How's the fishing in Crater Lake?" The answer is, "Not too good." However, there are some rainbows and kokanee to be caught if you're willing to hike 700 feet down to Cleetwood Cove (and back up with your catch). No fishing license is necessary to fish the lake, and there is no limit on how many fish you can take. In fact, the park service would be happy if more people fished this lake and tried to reduce the fish population.

Until the end of the 19th century, there were no fish in Crater Lake, and it is perhaps partly for this reason that this is one of the purest lakes in the world. With no inlets or outlets, the lake was cut off from any chance of naturally acquiring a fish population. However, in the late 19th century, the hand of man intervened where nature feared to tread, and fish were introduced to the lake to attract more visitors. Over the next 50 years, rainbow, cutthroat, and brown trout, steelhead, and coho and kokanee salmon were stocked in the lake. However, only the rainbows and kokanee have survived since the discontinuation of this misguided program.

Other than the shores around Cleetwood Cove, the only other place to fish Crater Lake is from Wizard Island, where you may have good luck if you are stealthy enough and lucky enough. To fish from Wizard Island, take one of the early boat tours from Cleetwood Cove, get off on the island, and arrange to take one of the later boats back.

Two things to remember are that no live or organic bait is allowed in the lake and cleaning fish in the lake is prohibited. In addition to lake fishing, Crater Lake National Park also offers stream fishing for several species of trout. However, for the most part, the park's streams are fairly inaccessible.

---

although most of the rooms have modern bathrooms, there are eight rooms with claw-foot bathtubs. The very best rooms are the corner rooms on the lake side of the lodge. The lodge's dining room serves creative Northwest cuisine and provides a view of both Crater Lake and the Klamath River basin. There continues to be talk of keeping the lodge open during the winter months (when there is superb cross-country skiing along the rim), however, as of press time, no winter opening had yet been scheduled. As at other national park lodges throughout the country, reservations here are hard to come by. Plan as far in advance as you can.

Mazama Village Motor Inn. Mailing address: 1211 Ave. C, White City, OR 97503. ☎ **541/ 830-8700.** Fax 541/830-8514. 40 rms. $78.25 double. MC, V. Closed Nov–May.

Though the Mazama Village Motor Inn isn't on the rim of the crater, it's just a short drive away. The modern motel-style guest rooms are housed in 10 steep-roofed buildings that look much like traditional mountain cabins. A laundry, gas station, and general store make Mazama Village a busy spot in the summer.

CAMPGROUNDS

Tent camping and RV spaces are available on the south side of the park at the **Mazama Village Campground,** where there are 198 sites ($13 to $14 per night). There are also 16 tent sites available at **Lost Creek Campground** ($10 per night) on the park's east side. These campgrounds are open from June to October. Reservations are not accepted at either campground. If you're a backpacker, there's camping in the park's backcountry; be sure to get a backcountry permit at one of the park's two visitors centers. For information on campgrounds outside the park, see "Campgrounds" in "The North Umpqua–Upper Rogue River Scenic Byway" section above.

Southern Oregon

Roughly defined as the region from the California border to just north of Roseburg and lying between the Coast Range and the Cascades, southern Oregon is a mountainous area that seems more akin to Northern California than to the rest of Oregon. Here the Cascade Range, Coast Range, and Siskiyou Mountains converge in a jumble of peaks.

It was gold that first brought white settlers to this area, and it was timber that kept them here. The gold is all played out now, but the legacy of the gold-rush days, when stagecoaches traveled the rough road between Sacramento and Portland, remains in picturesque towns such as Jacksonville and Oakland.

Southern Oregon is quite a hike from the nearest metropolitan areas. From Ashland, the southernmost city in the region, it's a 6-hour trip to either Portland or San Francisco. Despite this distance from major cities, Ashland is renowned for its **Oregon Shakespeare Festival,** which annually attracts tens of thousands of theatergoers. The festival, which now stretches through most of the year, has turned a sleepy mill town into a facsimile of Tudor England. Not to be outdone, the nearby historic town of Jacksonville offers performances by internationally recognized musicians and dance companies throughout the summer.

However, it is rugged beauty and the outdoors that draw most people to the region. Crater Lake National Park, Oregon's only national park, hides within its boundaries a sapphire jewel formed by the massive eruption of Mount Mazama less than 7,000 years ago. In this same area rise two of the most fabled **fly-fishing** rivers in the country. Ever since Zane Grey wrote of the fighting steelhead trout and salmon of the Rogue and Umpqua Rivers, fly fishers have been casting their lines in hopes of hooking a few of these wily denizens of the Cascade Range's cold waters.

In addition to the sources of information listed below in each individual city section, you can get information on all of southern Oregon by contacting the following regional tourism associations: **Southern Oregon Visitors Association,** P.O. Box 1645, Medford, OR 97501-0731 (☎ **541/779-4691**), or the **Southern Oregon Reservation Center,** P.O. Box 477, Ashland, OR 97520 (☎ **800/ 547-8052** or 541/488-1011).

Southern Oregon

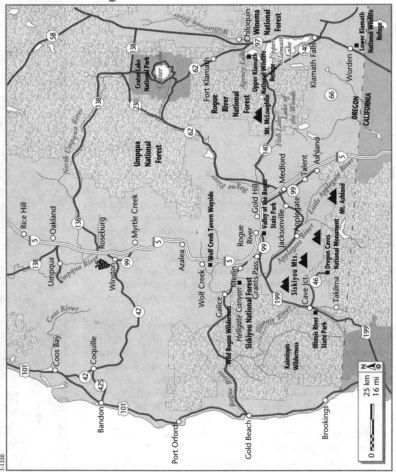

1 Ashland & the Oregon Shakespeare Festival

285 miles S of Portland, 50 miles W of Klamath Falls, 350 miles N of San Francisco

It was the Fourth of July 1935. In a small Ashland theater built by the chautauqua movement, Angus Bowmer, an English professor at Southern Oregon State College, was staging a performance of Shakespeare's *As You Like It*. The Depression had dashed any hopes local businessman Jesse Winburne had of turning Ashland, a quiet mill town in the rugged Siskiyou Mountains, into a mineral-springs resort. However, before the Depression struck, Winburne had managed to construct beautiful Lithia Park. Neither man's love's labor was lost, and today their legacies have turned the town into one of the Northwest's most popular destinations.

Each year more than 300,000 people attend performances of the Oregon Shakespeare Festival, a 9-month-long repertory festival that was born of Bowmer's love of the Bard. Though Ashland never became a mineral-springs resort, Lithia Park, through which still flow the clear waters of Winburne's dreams, is the town's centerpiece. Over the years the festival has attracted all manner of artists to settle in Ashland, giving the town a cosmopolitan air. With the growing popularity of the festival, fine restaurants and bed-and-breakfasts opened to cater to the theatergoers. It seems amazing that a small town roughly 300 miles from San Francisco or Portland could become a cultural mecca, but that's the power of the Bard.

ESSENTIALS

GETTING THERE   Ashland is located on I-5. From the east, Ore. 66 connects Ashland with Klamath Falls.

The nearest airport is the **Rogue Valley International Airport–Medford** in Medford, which is served by Horizon Air and United Airlines. A taxi from the airport to Ashland will cost around $13.

VISITOR INFORMATION   Contact the **Ashland Chamber of Commerce,** 110 E. Main St. (P.O. Box 1360), Ashland, OR 97520 (☎ **541/482-3486**).

GETTING AROUND   If you need a taxi, call **Yellow Cab** (☎ 541/482-3065). Car-rental companies with offices at the Rogue Valley International Airport include Avis and Budget. Public bus service in the Ashland area is provided by the **Rogue Valley Transportation District** (☎ **541/779-2877**).

FESTIVALS   The month-long yuletide **Holiday Festival of Lights** held each year in December is Ashland's other big annual festival.

THE OREGON SHAKESPEARE FESTIVAL

The raison d'être of Ashland, the Oregon Shakespeare Festival is an internationally acclaimed theater festival with a season that stretches from February to October. The season typically includes four works by Shakespeare plus eight other classic or contemporary plays. These plays are performed in repertory, with as many as four being staged on any given day.

The festival complex, often referred to as "the bricks" because of its brick courtyard, is in the center of town and contains three theaters. The visually impressive outdoor **Elizabethan Theatre,** which is modeled after England's 17th-century Fortune Theatre, is used only in the summer and early fall. The **Angus Bowmer Theatre** is the festival's largest indoor theater. The **Black Swan** is the smallest theater and stages contemporary and experimental works.

In addition to the plays, there are **backstage tours** (tickets are $9.50 for adults and $7.10 for children) and a **Shakespeare Exhibit Center** (admission is $2 for adults and $1.50 for children) that houses a collection of props and costumes that were used in past productions. Throughout the festival season there are also talks and special performances. The opening of the Elizabethan Theatre is celebrated each June in Lithia Park with the elaborate Feast of Will.

For more information and upcoming schedules, contact the **Oregon Shakespeare Festival,** 15 S. Pioneer St. (P.O. Box 158), Ashland, OR 97520 (☎ **541/482-4331**). Ticket prices range from $25 to $34, with box seats at the Elizabethan going for $45; children's and preview tickets are less expensive.

EXPLORING THE TOWN

If you'd like to learn a bit more about Ashland's history, take a tour with **Old Ashland Walking Tours,** which offers 1-hour walking tours at 10am Monday through Saturday, June 1 to September 30; assemble at the Plaza Information booth across from Lithia Park. Tickets are $5 for adults and $2 for children.

At the **Schneider Museum of Art,** on the campus of the Southern Oregon State College, 1250 Siskiyou Blvd. (☎ **541/552-6245**), art exhibits change every month or two. The museum is open Tuesday through Saturday from 11am to 5pm.

Ashland's first fame came from its healing mineral waters, and today you can still relax and be pampered at one of the city's day spas. **The Phoenix,** 2425 Siskiyou Blvd. (☎ **541/488-1281**), and the **Beach House,** 625 Beach St. (☎ **541/482-0196**), both offer various body treatments, skin care, and massages.

If you'd like to taste some local wines, stop by the **Ashland Vineyards,** 2775 E. Main St. (☎ **541/488-0088**), just east of town on the far side of I-5, or **Weisinger's,** 3150 Siskiyou Blvd. (☎ **800/551-WINE** or 541/488-5989), just south of town, which has a great view from the tasting room.

The Pacific Northwest Museum of Natural History. 1500 E. Main St. ☎ **541/488-1084.** Admission $6.50 adults, $5.50 seniors, $4.50 children 3–15. Apr–Oct daily 10am–5pm; Nov–Mar daily 10am–4pm. Closed Thanksgiving and Christmas.

Closed at press time due to lack of funds, this museum may again be open when you visit. The museum uses interactive exhibits, computer programs, sights, sounds, and even smells, to introduce the natural history of the Pacific Northwest.

ENJOYING THE GREAT OUTDOORS

A memorable part of your visit will be a long, leisurely stroll through beautiful **Lithia Park.** This 100-acre park follows the banks of Ashland Creek starting at the Plaza. Shade trees, lawns, flowers, ponds, fountains, and, of course, the babbling brook are reminiscent of an English garden. There's no more romantic way to explore the park than by horse-drawn carriage; rides are available from **Devon Carriage Company** (☎ **541/488-7836**).

Summertime thrill-seekers shouldn't pass up the chance to do some **white-water rafting** on the Rogue or Klamath River while in southern Oregon. Trips are offered between April and October by several companies. Try **Noah's World of Water,** 53 N. Main St. (☎ **800/858-2811** or 541/488-2811), or **The Adventure Center,** 40 N. Main St. (☎ **800/444-2819** or 541/488-2819), both of which offer trips lasting from half a day to 3 days. Prices range from $59 to about $450 per person, depending on the length and type of the trip. The former company also offers salmon and steelhead fishing trips, and the latter offers downhill bike rides from the top of Mount Ashland.

Mountain bikes can be rented at **Ashland Mountain Supply,** 31 N. Main St. (☎ **541/488-2749**), and the folks at this shop can point you in the direction of good rides.

Miles of **hiking trails,** including the Pacific Crest Trail, can be found up on Mount Ashland in the Siskiyou Rogue River National Forest.

Horseback riding is available at **Mountain Gate Stables,** 4399 Ore. 66 (☎ **541/482-8873**). Rides start at $20 for 1 hour (two-person minimum).

In the winter there's good downhill and cross-country **skiing** at **Mt. Ashland Ski Area,** 15 miles south of Ashland (☎ **541/482-2897** for information, or **541/482-2754** for snow report). Lift tickets range from $12 to $25. You can rent cross-country skis and pick up ski-trail maps at **Ashland Mountain Supply,** 31 N. Main St. (☎ **541/488-2749**).

SHOPPING

Ashland has the best shopping in southern Oregon. Interesting and unusual shops line East Main Street, so when the curtains are down on the stages, check the windows of downtown.

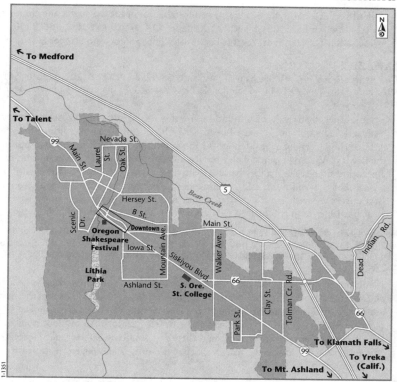

Art galleries abound in Ashland. One of our favorites for contemporary art is the **Hanson Howard Gallery,** 82 N. Main St. (☎ **541/488-2562**). And for a gallery of wearable art, stop by **The Web-sters,** 11 N. Main St. (☎ **541/482-9801**), a knitting and weaving store carrying beautiful sweaters. At **Footlights Theatre Gallery,** 240 E. Main St. (☎ **541/488-5538**), you'll find a wall of posters available for purchase, from *Amadeus* to *West Side Story.*

Johnny Kiwiseed's Fruit Safari, 253 E. Main St. (☎ **800/219-9071** or 541/ 482-5389), has daily samplings of both popular and exotic fruit products that are available for purchase. For a well-rounded selection of wines and other gourmet treats, you can't beat the **Chateaulin Wine Shoppe,** next to the restaurant Chateaulin at 52 E. Main St. (☎ **541/488-9463**).

WHERE TO STAY

Ashland, because of its Shakespearean theme, has become a very popular spot to open a bed-and-breakfast inn. At last count, there were more than 50 bed-and-breakfasts in town, many of which are only open during the festival season. If your reason for coming to Ashland is to attend the Shakespeare Festival, you'll find it most convenient to choose an inn within walking distance of the theaters. By doing so, you'll also be within walking distance of the town's best restaurants and shopping and won't have to deal with finding a parking space before the show. For a comprehensive list of Ashland inns, contact the **Ashland B&B Reservation Network,** P.O. Box 1051, Ashland, OR 97520-0048 (☎ **800/944-0329** or 541/858-1670).

If all you're looking for is a clean, comfortable room for the night, the **Super 8 Motel—Ashland,** 2350 Ashland St., Ashland, OR 97520 (☎ **800/800-8000** or 541/482-8887), is the most reliable bet in town, charging $46 to $62 for a double.

EXPENSIVE

☉ Antique Rose Inn. 91 Gresham St., Ashland, OR 97520. ☎ **888/282-6285** or 541/482-6285. 4 rms. June–Oct $114–$159 double. Nov–May $84–$119 double. Rates include full breakfast. AE, MC, V.

Set in a quiet, shady yard on a hillside above downtown and only 3 blocks from the festival theaters, this inn is housed in an 1888 Queen Anne Victorian home that was ordered from a catalog. Throughout the inn you'll find period antiques that capture the flavor of Victorian times. The Rose Room is the best room in the house and has a beautiful fireplace and a tiny balcony with a view across the valley. However, if its a claw-foot tub you need, ask for either the Lace Room or the Mahogany Room. Breakfasts are lavish, gourmet affairs, and in the evening complimentary wine is available. One room is actually a separate cottage next door to the main house.

Best Western Bard's Inn. 132 N. Main St., Ashland, OR 97520. ☎ **800/528-1234** or 541/482-0049. Fax 503/488-3259. 79 rms. A/C TV TEL. Mid-May to mid-Oct $98–$125 double. Mid-Oct to mid-May $68–$78 double. Rates include continental breakfast. AE, CB, DC, DISC, MC, V.

If you prefer motels to bed-and-breakfast inns, the Bard's Inn should be your first choice in Ashland. The rooms are large and comfortable, and those in the new annex have patios or balconies, though these rooms can get a bit of traffic noise. The older rooms have all been refurbished and have refrigerators. An outdoor pool and hot tub provide a bit of relaxation, and there's a restaurant here as well. However, this motel's most attractive feature is that it's only 2 blocks from the festival theaters.

Chanticleer Bed & Breakfast Inn. 120 Gresham St., Ashland, OR 97520. ☎ **800/898-1950** or 541/482-1919. Fax 541/482-1919. 6 rms. A/C TEL. June–Oct $125–$160 double. Nov–Feb $69–$85 double. Mar–May $95–$125 double. Rates include full breakfast. AE, MC, V.

As one of the oldest bed-and-breakfast inns in Ashland, the Chanticleer has long been a favorite of theatergoers. The 1920s craftsman bungalow is only 3 blocks from "the bricks," and equally close to all the downtown shops and restaurants. European country styling gives the inn an old-world charm that allows you to immerse yourself in the Shakespeare experience. The guest rooms are decorated with antiques, Persian carpets, and down comforters, and look out on either the garden or the valley. Breakfasts are a lavish affair and can be served either in bed or in the dining room overlooking the mountains. Throughout the day there are always treats on hand as well.

Coolidge House. 137 N. Main St., Ashland, OR 97520. ☎ **800/655-5522** or 541/482-4721. 5 suites, 1 cottage. A/C. Apr–Oct $120–$145 suite; $160 cottage. Nov–Mar $85–$105 suite; $125 cottage. Rates include full breakfast. MC, V.

Located right on busy North Main Street only 3 blocks from the theaters, this inn sits high above the street on a hill with commanding views across the valley. The Victorian home was built in 1875 and is one of the oldest homes in Ashland. However, inside you'll find some decidedly modern amenities, as well as interesting antiques. Guest suites all have sitting rooms and large, luxurious bathrooms (unusual in a Victorian B&B), most of which have either a whirlpool tub or a claw-foot tub. The Parlor Suite, with its draped window seat, is the inn's most romantic room. However, if it's views and space you seek, opt for the Sun Suite or the Grape Arbor.

There is a pleasant patio in the back garden. Surprisingly, despite the historic nature of the inn, it manages to be a casual place that appeals to younger travelers.

Country Willows. 1313 Clay St., Ashland, OR 97520. ☎ **800/WILLOWS** or 541/488-1590. Fax 541/488-1611. Web site: www.willowsinn.com. 9 rms, 4 suites. A/C TEL. $90–$125 double; $135–$185 suite. Rates include full breakfast. Lower rates Nov–Mar. AE, DISC, MC, V.

Just outside town and surrounded by 5 acres of rolling hills and pastures, the Country Willows bed-and-breakfast inn offers the tranquillity of a farm only minutes from excellent restaurants and the theaters. If you're looking for a very special room, consider the Sunrise Suite, in a renovated barn behind the main house; it has pine paneling, a high ceiling, a king-size bed, a gas fireplace, and best of all, an old-fashioned tub for two with its very own picture window and skylight. Rooms in the restored farmhouse are smaller, but some offer excellent views across the valley. Ducks, geese, goats, and sometimes horses call the farm home, and there's a 2-mile hiking trail that starts at the back door. You'll also find a pool and whirlpool on the grounds.

Fox House Inn. 269 B St., Ashland, OR 97520. ☎ **541/488-1055.** 2 rms. A/C TV TEL. $135–$145 double. Rates include full breakfast. Lower rates off-season. No credit cards.

The Fox House has the air of a Victorian dollhouse. Compared to other houses of this vintage it's a mere cottage, but the inn more than makes up for its size with elegant Victorian furnishings, unusual touches such as working antique telephones, and private hot tubs. There are also claw-foot bathtubs in both bathrooms. Unlike many Victorian B&Bs, this inn has avoided the Laura Ashley look and instead opted for the dark colors and fabrics (burgundy velvet curtains) that were popular 100 years ago. The "bricks" is only 3 blocks away.

☉ Mt. Ashland Inn. 550 Mt. Ashland Rd., Ashland, OR 97520. ☎ **800/830-8707** or 541/482-8707. Web site: www.mtashland.com. 2 rms, 3 suites. $99–$110 double; $120–$190 suite. Rates include full breakfast. Discounts available Nov–Apr during midweek. MC, V.

Located on 160 acres on the side of Mount Ashland, this massive log home commands distant panoramas from its forest setting, and though the inn is only 15 minutes from downtown Ashland, you're in a different world up here. The Pacific Crest Trail, which stretches from Canada to Mexico, passes through the front yard, and just a few miles up the road is the Ski Ashland ski area. Whether you're in the area for an active vacation or a few nights of theater, this lodge makes a very special base of operations. The decor is straight out of an Eddie Bauer catalog and, in one guest bathroom, there's a stone wall with a built-in waterfall. The Sky Lakes Suite is the best room in the house.

☉ Peerless Hotel. 243 Fourth St., Ashland, OR 97520. ☎ **541/488-1082.** 4 rms, 2 suites. A/C MINIBAR. May–Oct $98–$135 double; $175 suite. Nov–Apr $65–$89 double; $125–$140 suite. Rates include expanded continental breakfast. AE, MC, V.

Located in the historic Railroad District 7 blocks from the festival theaters, this restored brick boarding house from 1900 is now one of Ashland's most interesting lodgings. With the feel of a small historic hotel rather than that of a B&B, the Peerless is filled with antiques and an eclectic array of individually decorated guest rooms. Of these, the West Indies suite, with its balcony, double whirlpool tub, and view of Ashland is by far the most luxurious. However, in other rooms you'll find lush fabrics, unusual murals, stenciling, and tile work that all add up to unexpected luxury. Most rooms have either a whirlpool tub or a claw-foot tub (one even has his-and-hers claw-foot tubs). Adjacent to the hotel are a cafe that provides room service and an affiliated garden gallery.

✪ **The Winchester Country Inn.** 35 S. Second St., Ashland, OR 97520. ☎ **800/972-4991** or 541/488-1113. Fax 541/488-4604. 12 rms, 6 suites. A/C TEL. $95–$140 double; $125–$200 suite. Rates include full breakfast. AE, DISC, MC, V.

Though it calls itself a country inn, the Winchester is right in the heart of downtown Ashland, within a few blocks of the theaters. However, with its massive old shade trees, gazebo, and English cottage garden, you'd never guess you were in town. The rooms are very comfortably furnished with antiques and modern bath fixtures, including sinks built into old bureaus in some rooms. We prefer the upstairs rooms, which get quite a bit more light than the basement rooms. There are also rooms in the building next door, and these are as well designed as those in the main house. A decanter of sherry in each room is a welcome touch upon returning from the theater. For fine dining, you need go no further than the inn's first-floor dining room, which is one of the best restaurants in town (see below for details).

Windmill Inn–Ashland Hills Inn & Suites. 2525 Ashland St., Ashland, OR 97520-1478. ☎ **800/547-4747** or 541/482-8310. Fax 541/488-1783. 158 rms, 72 suites. A/C TV TEL. Early June to early Oct $88–$140 double; $132.50–$250 suite. Early Oct–early June $39–$75 double; $79.50–$225 suite. AE, CB, DC, DISC, MC, V.

Set on the outskirts of Ashland a few miles from downtown, this hotel is the area's premier lodging and the only local hotel offering resort-style amenities. Set on sprawling, attractively landscaped grounds, the inn combines a Northwest aesthetic with urban sophistication and glitz. This translates into large rooms, most with balconies or patios, bathrooms with two sinks, and great views of the surrounding countryside. The dining room serves Northwest regional dishes, and in the adjacent lounge you can watch the big game on TV. Services include room service, complimentary morning coffee and newspaper, free airport shuttle, and valet/laundry service. An indoor swimming pool, hot tub, exercise room, tennis courts, guest bicycles, and jogging trail provide plenty of recreational options.

WHERE TO DINE

If you're headed to the theater after dinner let your wait person know. They will usually do whatever they can to make sure you aren't late!

EXPENSIVE

✪ **Chateaulin.** 50 E. Main St. ☎ **541/482-2264.** Reservations recommended. Main courses $16.75–$25.75. AE, DISC, MC, V. Daily 5–9pm (bar stays open until midnight). FRENCH.

Exposed brick walls and old champagne bottles give this restaurant a casually elegant appearance that's accented by lace curtains and dark-wood furnishings. The menu is almost as traditional as the decor, so you can start your meal with escargots or house paté and then move on to filet mignon with a sauce of red wine, garlic, shallots, thyme, demi-glace, and blue cheese croutons. A separate bar menu caters to smaller appetites. The restaurant's wine list features 100 selections from Oregon, California, and France. This is the best restaurant in town and is located around the corner from the theaters. There is also an attached wine and gourmet foods store if you're interested in classy picnic fare.

Firefly. 15 N. Water St. ☎ **541/488-3212.** Reservations recommended. Main courses $17–$25. MC, V. Summer Wed–Thurs 11:30am–2pm and 5–8pm, Fri–Sat 11:30am–2pm and 5–8:30pm, Sun–Tues 5–8pm; winter Wed–Fri 11:30am–2pm and 5–8pm, Sat–Sun 5–8pm. INTERNATIONAL.

Complex, beautifully presented dishes are the chef's forte at this small bistro. Such selections as mahimahi tamales with chayote salad and cheese and cactus empandas with dark-roasted cumin sauce and lime crema; or mint swordfish, with papadom-fried jasmine rice and lemongrass-coconut prawns are examples of some of the culinary artistry that comes out of the kitchen here. But also available are less elaborate items such as grilled New York steak.

Monet. 36 S. Second St. ☎ **541/482-1339.** Reservations recommended. Main courses $14.50–$22. MC, V. Mid-June to Sept Sun–Mon 5:30–8:30pm, Tues–Sat 11:45am–1:45pm and 5:30–8:30pm; Oct to mid-June Tues–Wed 5:30–8:30pm, Thurs–Sat 11:45am–1:45pm and 5:30–8:30pm. Closed Jan. FRENCH.

Though the big white house across the street from the Winchester Inn looks rather plain from the outside, when you step through the door you'll find a somewhat formal and impeccably set dining room. On warm days, you may want to dine in the garden surrounded by many of the same flowers that appear in Monet's famous garden. The cuisine is modern French. You might find smoked salmon wrapped around avocado mousse and served with a lemon vinaigrette as a starter, and baked pork tenderloin in a kiwi-cream sauce as an entree. For lighter appetites, there's usually an omelet and selection of salads.

○ New Sammy's Cowboy Bistro. 2210 S. Pacific Hwy., Talent. ☎ **541/535-2779.** Reservations highly recommended. Main courses $18–$25, 4-course menu $30. No credit cards. Thurs–Sun 5–9pm. NORTHWEST.

Unmarked yet unmistakable, New Sammy's is a tiny shack of a place in nearby Talent. If it weren't for the fact that the building looks as if the owners got their paint at a Sherwin Williams going-out-of-business sale, you'd drive right past. Be bold. Open the door. Things look different inside.

The menu is as imaginative as the exterior paint job, and everything is as fresh as it gets, with lots of organic produce from local growers and delicious rustic breads. This is a mom-and-pop operation (Mom cooks and Pop serves), and tables are frequently reserved several weeks in advance, so be sure to call ahead for a reservation.

Primavera Restaurant & Gardens. 241A Hargadine St. ☎ **541/488-1994.** Reservations recommended in summer. Main courses $18–$29. AE, MC, V. Wed, Thurs, Sun 5–8:30pm, Fri–Sat 5–9pm. FRENCH/ITALIAN.

In keeping with Ashland's theatrical theme, this restaurant has adopted a very dramatic decor, with rich colors, soft lighting, and theatrically lit paintings inspired by old Ballet Russe posters. In keeping with the atmosphere, you might want to dress up to dine here. A handsome garden at the back makes a fine place to dine before attending a performance. The menu changes regularly and is limited to a few choice treatments of beef, chicken, or fish (salmon especially), and a vegetarian dish. The produce used here is largely organic, and they also make their own breads and ice cream. Don't forget to leave room for a finale such as orange-lavender sorbet with biscotti.

The Winchester Inn. 35 S. Second St. ☎ **541/488-1115.** Reservations highly recommended. Main courses $16–$23; Sun brunch $9–$11. AE, DISC, MC, V. Tues–Sat 5:30–8:30pm, Sun 9:30am–1pm (brunch) and 5:30–8:30pm. INTERNATIONAL.

The dining rooms here, in traditional Victorian decor, take up half the first floor of Ashland's favorite in-town country bed-and-breakfast and overlook an English cottage garden. In summer there is dining on the porch and deck. For a starter, try the warm forest mushroom salad, which features a selection of seasonal mushrooms. Any time of year the teng dah beef, the inn's signature dish, offers an unusual treatment of filet mignon (marinated in soy sauce and flavored with lemon, horseradish, and anise). Sunday brunch is the perfect way to finish a weekend of theater before heading home. During the Christmas season, there are special Dickens's feasts here.

MODERATE

⊙ **Cucina Biazzi.** 568 E. Main St. ☎ **541/488-3739.** Reservations recommended in summer. Four-course fixed-price dinner $17–$28. MC, V. Daily 5:30–8:30pm; hours may be shorter in winter. TUSCAN.

The owners have transformed this Ashland bungalow on the outskirts of town into a cozy Italian cottage, with romantic touches such as lace curtains and candlelight. The menu here, inspired by available seasonal ingredients, changes every week or two, but you might find that the antipasto course is a salad of Tuscan white beans, mushrooms, marinated artichokes, Asiago cheese, and other tempting ingredients. The pasta course might include ravioli tossed with browned butter and crisped sage or spaghetti with clams, Tuscan-style. For al fresco dining, there's an intimate low-walled patio in the back.

Plaza Cafe. 47 N. Main St. ☎ **541/488-2233.** Reservations recommended. Main courses $8.25–$18. DISC, MC, V. Mon–Thurs 11am–9pm, Fri 11am–10pm, Sat 10am–10pm, Sun 10am–9pm. REGIONAL AMERICAN.

Located just opposite the plaza in downtown Ashland, this cafe has an upscale urban atmosphere with a high ceiling and art on the brick walls. Stop in here for the likes of a perfectly grilled Cajun-lime turkey sandwich or a delicious red pepper stuffed with artichoke hearts and feta cheese. Wine prices are good and local organic produce is featured; brunch is served on the weekend.

Quinz. 29 N. Main St. ☎ **541/488-5937.** Reservations recommended. Small plates $4–$10, large plates $11.25–$14. DISC, MC, V. Sun–Thurs 11:30am–2:30pm and 5–9pm, Fri–Sat 11:30am–2:30pm and 5–9:30pm. MEDITERRANEAN.

Also located just opposite the plaza (see above), Quinz is a good place to stop for light and tasty Mediterranean-influenced dishes such as Portuguese-style mussels steamed with chorizo sausage in a very flavorful broth, or a mesclun salad topped with mint-flavored grilled chicken and a lemon-pepper aioli. Service by the youthful staff is very prompt. We like the colorful interior and the more intimate table in back, just behind the wall.

INEXPENSIVE

In addition to the restaurants listed below, **The Paper Moon Espresso Cafe,** 11 N. First St. (☎ **541/488-4883**), serves big portions of vegetarian-friendly food.

Ashland Bakery Cafe. 38 E. Main St. ☎ **541/482-2117.** Breakfast, sandwiches, and main courses $5–$10. MC, V. Daily 7am–8:30pm. INTERNATIONAL.

You'll find this cafe right in the hub of downtown Ashland. It's usually mobbed at breakfast with people reading newspapers and sipping coffee while patiently waiting for their huevos rancheros, tofu scrambles, and avocado-and-cheese omelets. At lunch or dinner it's a good place for a quick sandwich, pizza, or pasta dish. Top it off with a giant cookie from the bakery case.

ASHLAND AFTER DARK

The Oregon Shakespeare Festival may be the main draw, but Ashland is overflowing with talent begging to express itself. From experimental theater to Broadway musicals, the town sees an amazing range of theater productions. To find out what's going on while you're in town, pick up a free copy of either the *Ashland Gazette,* a monthly, or *Sneak Preview,* a biweekly.

Theaters and theater companies in the area include the **Actor's Theatre,** Miracle Playhouse, 101 Talent Ave., Talent (☎ **541/535-5250**); the **Oregon Cabaret Theatre,** First and Hargadine streets (☎ **541/488-2902**), a professional dinner theater; the **Theatre Arts Department of Southern Oregon State College,** 1250 Siskiyou

Blvd. (☎ **541/552-6346**), which stages well-regarded student productions; and the **Ashland Community Theatre,** 125 E. Main St. (☎ **541/482-7532**), which stages new and old popular plays.

Nontheater performing-arts companies include the **Rogue Valley Symphony** (☎ **541/770-6012**) and the **Rogue Valley Opera** (☎ **541/552-6400**).

Throughout the summer there are numerous outdoor events, some free and some not, at the **Lithia Park band shell.** You can pick up a schedule of events at the Ashland Chamber of Commerce, 110 E. Main St. (☎ **541/482-3486**).

2 Jacksonville & Medford: A Slice of Oregon History

16 miles N of Ashland, 24 miles E of Grants Pass

Jacksonville is quite literally a snapshot of southern Oregon history. Because it became a forgotten backwater after the Great Depression, more than 80 buildings from its glory years as a gold-boom town in the mid-1800s stood untouched. The entire town has been restored, thanks to the photos of pioneer photographer Peter Britt, who moved to Jacksonville in 1852 and operated the first photographic studio west of the Rockies. His photos of 19th-century Jacksonville have provided preservationists with invaluable 100-year-old glimpses of many of the town's historic buildings. Britt's name has also been attached to the **Britt Festivals,** another southern Oregon cultural binge that rivals the Oregon Shakespeare Festival in its ability to stage first-rate entertainment.

Though thousands of eager gold-seekers were lured into California's Sierra Nevada by the gold rush of 1849, few struck it rich. Many of those who were smitten with gold fever and were unwilling to give up the search for the mother lode headed out across the West in search of golder pastures. At least two prospectors hit pay dirt in the Siskiyou Mountains of southern Oregon in 1851, at a spot that would soon be known as Rich Gulch. Within a year Rich Gulch had become the site of booming Jacksonville, and within another year the town had become the county seat and commercial heart of southern Oregon. Over the next half century, Jacksonville developed into a wealthy town with brick commercial buildings and elegant Victorian homes. However, in the 1880s, the railroad running between Portland and San Francisco bypassed Jacksonville in favor of an easier route 5 miles to the east. It was at this spot that the trading town of Medford began to develop.

Despite a short rail line into Jacksonville, over the years more and more business migrated to the main railway in Medford. Jacksonville's fortunes began to decline and, by the time of the Depression, residents were reduced to digging up the streets of town for the gold that lay there. In 1927 the county seat was moved to Medford, and Jacksonville was left with its faded grandeur and memories of better times.

Off the beaten path, forgotten by developers and modernization, Jacksonville inadvertently preserved its past in its buildings. In 1966 the entire town was listed on the National Register of Historic Places, and Jacksonville, with the aid of Britt's photos, began a renaissance that today makes it a historical showcase. Together the Britt Festivals and Jacksonville's history combine to make this one of the most fascinating towns anywhere in the Northwest.

ESSENTIALS

GETTING THERE   Medford is right on I-5, 30 miles north of the California state line, and Jacksonville is 5 miles west on Ore. 238.

The **Rogue Valley International–Medford** Airport, at 3650 Biddle Rd., Medford, is served by Horizon Air and United Airlines.

VISITOR INFORMATION   Contact the **Jacksonville Chamber of Commerce,** 185 N. Main St. (P.O. Box 33), Jacksonville, OR 97530 (☎ **541/899-8118**), or the **Medford Visitors & Convention Bureau,** 101 E. Eighth St., Medford OR 97501 (☎ **800/469-6307** or 541/779-4847).

THE BRITT FESTIVALS

Each summer between mid-June and early September, people gather several nights a week for folk, pop, country, jazz, and classical music concerts and modern dance performances. The Britt Festivals are a celebration of music and the performing arts featuring internationally renowned performers. The setting for the performances is an amphitheater on the grounds of Britt's estate. Located only a block from historic California Street, the ponderosa pine–shaded amphitheater provides not only a great setting for the performances, but a view that takes in distant hills and the valley far below.

Both reserved and general-admission tickets are available for most shows. If you opt for a general-admission ticket, arrive early to claim a prime spot on the lawns behind the reserved seats—and be sure to bring a picnic. For information, contact the festival at P.O. Box 1124, Medford, OR 97501 (☎ **800/88-BRITT** or 541/ 773-6077). Tickets range from $8 to $35.

MUSEUMS & HISTORIC HOMES

With more than 80 buildings listed on the National Register of Historic Places, Jacksonville boasts that it's the most completely preserved historic town in the nation. Whether or not this claim is true, there certainly are enough restored old buildings to make the town a genuine step back in time. Along California Street you'll find restored brick commercial buildings that now house dozens of interesting shops, art galleries, and boutiques. On the side streets you'll see the town's many Victorian homes.

If you're interested in visiting several of the sites mentioned below, multiple site tickets may be purchased at the following museums, for the following museums: the Jacksonville Museum of Southern Oregon History, the Children's Museum next door, and the Southern Oregon History Center in Medford. In summer, the Beekman House is also included in this package.

Jacksonville Museum of Southern Oregon History. 206 N. Fifth St. ☎ **541/773-6536.** Admission $3 adults, $2 children 6–12 and seniors 55 and older. Memorial Day to Labor Day daily 10am–5pm; Labor Day to Memorial Day Sun noon–5pm, Wed–Sat 10am–5pm.

In order to get some background on Jacksonville, make this museum your first stop in town. Housed in the old county courthouse, which was built in 1883, the museum has displays on the history of Jacksonville, including 19th-century photos by Peter Britt. A multiple site ticket (see above) also gets you into the adjacent Children's Museum, which is housed in the former jail.

Beekman House. 470 E. California St. ☎ **541/773-6536.** Beekman House, $3 adults, $2 children 6–12 and seniors 55 and older; Beekman Bank, free. Beekman House, Memorial Day to Labor Day daily 1–5pm. Beekman Bank, any time.

At the 1876 Beekman House, history comes alive as actors in period costume portray the family of an early Jacksonville banker. The turn-of-the-century Beekman Bank, 101 W. California St., is also open to the public.

Southern Oregon History Center. 106 N. Central Ave. ☎ **541/773-6536.** $3 adults, $2 children 6–12 and seniors 55 and older. Mon–Fri 9am–5pm, Sat noon–5pm.

Located in downtown Medford, this large museum is a repository for thousands of artifacts pertaining to the history of this region.

✪ **Butte Creek Mill.** 402 N. Royal Ave., Eagle Point. ☎ **541/826-3531.** Free admission. Mon–Sat 9am–5pm.

In nearby Eagle Point, you can visit Oregon's only operating water-powered flour mill. The Butte Creek Mill was built in 1873 and its millstones are still grinding out flour. After looking around at the workings of the mill, you can stop in at the mill store and buy a bag of flour or cornmeal. Next door, the **Oregon General Store Museum,** open 11am to 4pm on Saturday, has a fascinating collection of antique items representing a turn-of-the-century grocery store.

OTHER ATTRACTIONS

Pears and roses both grow well in the Jacksonville and Medford area, and these crops have given rise to two of the country's best known mail-order businesses. **Harry and David's Original Country Village,** 1314 Center Dr. (☎ 541/776-2277), is the retail outlet of a specialty fruit company specializing in mail-order Fruit-of-the-Month Club gift packs. You'll find the store just 1 mile south of Medford at Exit 27 off I-5. You can tour the Harry and David's packing house and then wander through the store in search of bargains. Associated with this store is the **Jackson and Perkins rose test garden** and mail-order rose nursery.

For an overview of Jacksonville's historic buildings, consider a **trolley tour** of town. These leave daily in summer between 10am and 4pm from the corner of Third and California streets; tickets are $4 for adults and $2 for children.

Each year in early autumn, the Jacksonville Boosters Club sponsors a **homes tour** that allows glimpses into many of Jacksonville's most lovingly restored old homes. Contact the Jacksonville Chamber of Commerce for details.

When the Britt Festivals have closed up shop for the year, you can still catch Dixieland jazz at the annual **Medford Jazz Jubilee,** which is held in early October. For information, call ☎ **800/599-0039** or 541/770-6972.

OUTDOOR ACTIVITIES

Rafting and **fishing** on the numerous fast-flowing, clear-water rivers of southern Oregon are two of the most popular sports in this region, and Medford makes a good base for doing a bit of either, or both. **Arrowhead River Adventures** (☎ 800/227-7741 or 541/830-3388) and **River Trips Unlimited** (☎ 800/460-3865 or 541/779-3798)) offer both rafting and fishing; **Rogue Excursions Unlimited** (☎ 541/826-6222) offers fishing. A day of rafting will cost around $50 to $60, and fishing trips cost about $125 per person per day.

If you're here in the spring, you can catch the colorful **wildflower displays** at Table Rocks. These mesas are just a few miles northeast of Medford, and because of their great age and unique structure, create a variety of habitats that allow the area to support an unusual diversity of plants. For more information, contact the **Bureau of Land Management,** Medford District Office (☎ **541/770-2200**).

Information on **hiking** and **backpacking** in the area can be obtained from the **Rogue River National Forest,** 333 W. Eighth St. (P. O. Box 520), Medford, OR 97501 (☎ **541/858-2200**).

For a different perspective on this region, try a **hot-air balloon ride** with **Sunrise Balloon Adventures** (☎ 541/776-2284) or **Oregon Adventures Aloft** (☎ 800/238-0700 or 541/582-1574).

SHOPPING IN JACKSONVILLE

If you're a wine connoisseur, don't miss a chance to peruse the wine racks at the **Jacksonville Inn Wine Shop,** 175 E. California St. (☎ **541/899-1900**), where you might find a bottle of 1811 Tokay Essencia for $5,500 or a bottle of Chateau Lafite-Rothschild for $1,500. To taste some local wines, visit the **Valley View Vineyard,** 100 Upper Applegate Rd. (☎ **800/781-WINE** or 541/899-8468), or the **Gary R. West Tasting Room,** located just outside of Jacksonville at 690 N. Fifth St. (☎ **541/ 899-1829**). The **GeBzz Gallery,** 150 S. Oregon St. (☎ **541/899-7535**) carries a diverse selection of art works, with a Southwestern slant.

WHERE TO STAY
IN JACKSONVILLE

Jacksonville Inn. 175 E. California St., Jacksonville, OR 97530. ☎ **800/321-9344** or 541/ 899-1900. 8 rms, 3 cottages. A/C. $100–$145 double; $200–$235 cottage. Rates include continental breakfast. AE, DC, DISC, MC, V.

Located in the heart of the town's restored business district in a two-story brick building part of which was built in 1861, the Jacksonville Inn is best known for its gourmet restaurant, but upstairs there are eight antique-filled rooms that offer traditional elegance mixed with some modern amenities. Room 1, with its queen-size canopy bed and whirlpool tub for two, is the house favorite. Many rooms have exposed brick walls. Modern bathrooms complement the antique furnishings. If you're looking for more privacy and greater luxury, consider the cottages, which have whirlpool tubs, steam showers, and entertainment centers.

✪ **The McCully House.** 240 E. California St. (P.O. Box 13), Jacksonville, OR 97530. ☎ **800/ 367-1942** or 541/899-1942. Web site: www.wave.net/upg/mccully. 3 rms. A/C. May–Sept $105 double. Oct–Apr $95 double. AE, MC, V.

Built in 1861, the McCully House is one of the oldest buildings currently being used as an inn in the state of Oregon, and with its classic, symmetrical lines and simple pre-Victorian styling, it looks as if it could easily be an 18th-century New England inn. If you like being steeped in local history, this is Jacksonville's best choice. In the McCully Room, you'll even find the original black walnut master bedroom furnishings. Surrounding the inn, and enclosed by a white picket fence, is a formal rose garden with an amazing variety of roses. The inn is also one of Jacksonville's finest restaurants, and the downstairs parlors now serve as dining rooms. However, in summer, most people prefer to eat outside in the garden. Breakfasts are served in a cheery sun room that overlooks the less formal back garden and patio.

The Stage Lodge. 830 N. Fifth St. (P.O. Box 1316), Jacksonville, OR 97530. ☎ **800/ 253-8254** or 541/899-3953. 27 rms, 2 suites. A/C TV TEL. $73–$78 double; $135 suite. Lower rates Oct–Apr. AE, DISC, MC, V.

Jacksonville has several bed-and-breakfast inns, but it's short on moderately priced motels. Filling the bill for the latter category is a motel designed to resemble a 19th-century stage stop, with gables, clapboard siding, and turned-wood railings along two floors of verandas. These details allow the lodge to fit right in with all the original buildings in town. The rooms are spacious and comfortable, and have a few nice touches such as ceiling fans, TV armoires, and country decor.

The Teddy Bear Inn (Jacksonville's Historic Orth House). 105 W. Main St. (P.O. Box 1437), Jacksonville, OR 97530. ☎ **541/899-8665.** Fax 503/899-9146. Web site: www.medford.net/orthbnb. 2 rms, 1 suite. A/C. May–Oct $120–$135 double; $190 suite. Nov–Apr $85–$100 double; $125 suite. Rates include full breakfast. MC, V.

This brick house, built in 1880, stands behind majestic old shade trees on a corner one block off busy California Street. The picket fence, old buggy on the lawn, and inviting front porch cry out small-town Americana. Inside, you'll find an eclectic mix of modern and antique (there's a TV inside the woodstove). However, it is the inn's extensive collection of teddy bears and antique toys that are the main attraction here. With its in-room claw-foot tub and romantic character, Josie's Room is a favorite.

Touvelle House Bed & Breakfast. 455 N. Oregon St. (P.O. Box 1891), Jacksonville, OR 97530. ☎ **800/846-8422** or 541/899-8938. Fax 541/899-3992. Web site: www.wave.net/ upg/touvelle. 6 rms. May–Sept $85–$105 double. Oct–Apr $75–$85 double. AE, DISC, MC, V.

Situated on the edge of town yet still within walking distance of downtown and the Britt Festivals amphitheater, this inn is less formal than others in town, though no less historic in character. Set back from the road in a huge yard, this grand old home was built in the early 1900s in a vaguely Craftsman style. The guest rooms are on three floors, and our favorite is the Western-themed Prairie West Room up on the third floor. Other rooms feature art deco accents, Americana, wicker furniture, and other individual touches. While historic in character, with a wood-paneled great room and a large stone fireplace, the inn also has a hot tub and an outdoor swimming pool.

IN MEDFORD

In addition to the B&B listed below, you'll find dozens of inexpensive chain motels clustered along I-5.

Under the Greenwood Tree. 3045 Bellinger Lane, Medford, OR 97501. ☎ **541/776-0000.** Web site: www.greenwoodtree.com. 5 rms. A/C TEL. $95–$125 double. Rates include full breakfast. V.

Located just west of Medford and taking its name from the 300-year-old oaks that shade the front yard, this bed-and-breakfast offers a step back in time to the days of iced tea on the veranda, croquet on the lawn, and stolen kisses behind the barn. Romance and Americana are the themes here, and you'll find plenty of both. The guest rooms are filled with antiques, and two have separate sitting rooms. Throughout the house you'll find antique quilts and Oriental carpets, which give the inn a touch of country class. Out back is a huge deck overlooking the gazebo, garden, and barns. On the inn's surrounding 10 acres of land, you can explore gardens, old barns, and granaries. A three-course breakfast and afternoon tea are served.

IN THE APPLEGATE VALLEY

Applegate Lodge. 15100 Ore. 238 (P.O. Box 3282), Applegate, OR 97530 ☎ **541/ 846-6690.** A/C. 7 rms. $125–$160 double. MC, V.

This modern lodge, which opened in 1997, is a masterpiece of woodworking, with burnished woods (including fiddleback redwood paneling) and unique wooden details throughout. Situated on the bank of the Applegate River 16 miles outside Jacksonville, the lodge boasts one of the prettiest settings in southern Oregon. The high-ceilinged great room with a river-rock fireplace features a wall of glass looking out on the river, and across the length of the lodge is a deck where you can sit and listen to the music of the water. The guest rooms are all very large, and several of them have loft sleeping areas. All but one of the rooms draws on local themes for its decor. Lots of peeled log furniture give the inn a solidly western feel. Right next door and under the same ownership is the ever-popular Applegate River Ranch House (see "Where to Dine," below, for details). The river here is great for swimming.

WHERE TO DINE
IN JACKSONVILLE

In addition to the establishments mentioned below, **Good Bean Coffee,** 165 S. Oregon St. (☎ **541/899-8740**), is *the* place for a cup of espresso.

Bella Union. 170 W. California St. ☎ **541/899-1770.** Main courses $9.50–$16. AE, MC, V. Mon–Fri 11:30am–10pm, Sat 11am–10pm, Sun 10am–10pm, lounge until midnight daily. ITALIAN/AMERICAN.

For casual dining or someplace to just toss back a cold beer or sip an Italian soda, the Bella Union is Jacksonville's top choice. The lounge hearkens back to the days when the Bella Union was one of Jacksonville's busiest saloons, and in the back of the building is a garden patio. However, it's the main dining room up front that's most popular. Old wood floors, storefront windows, and exposed brick walls conjure up images of gold miners out on the town. Meals range from pizzas to a delicious house chicken that's marinated in Gorgonzola and walnut pesto.

Jacksonville Inn. 175 E. California St. ☎ **541/899-1900.** Reservations recommended. Main courses $13–$40, lunch $7–$14. DISC, MC, V. Dining room, Sun 10am–2pm and 5–9pm, Mon 5–10pm, Tues–Sat 11:30am–2pm and 5–10pm. Bistro, Mon 5–9pm, Tues–Sun 2–10pm. CONTINENTAL.

Old-world atmosphere, either in the basement rathskeller or in the more elegant upstairs dining room, sets the mood for reliable continental fare. Together the cuisine and the decor attract a well-heeled clientele that prefers familiar dishes perfectly prepared, such as surf and turf, veal scaloppini, or rack of lamb. Nightly dinner specials are more adventurous. Pears are a mainstay of the local economy and show up frequently in both entrees and desserts. The inn's wineshop gives diners access to a cellar boasting more than 700 wines.

McCully House Inn. 240 E. California St. ☎ **541/899-1942.** Main courses $12–$24. AE, MC, V. Daily 5–8:30pm. REGIONAL AMERICAN.

The McCully House is one of the oldest homes in Jacksonville. You can't miss it—it's got a beautiful rose-filled garden in front, a fine place to dine on a summer evening. We started out with a dish of blackened calamari, followed by herb and Dijon seared salmon and a seafood grill. Fresh fish is a strong point here, flown in from Seattle's Pike Place Market and innovatively prepared. Next door, McCully Mercantile supplies deli sandwiches for enjoying in the garden or perhaps as a picnic for the Britt Festivals.

IN MEDFORD

Samovar Restaurant. 101 E. Main St., Medford. ☎ **541/779-4967.** Reservations recommended on weekends. Main courses $13–$17, lunch $5–$7.50. MC, V. Mon 9am–3pm, Tues–Sat 9am–3pm and 5–9pm. RUSSIAN/MIDDLE EASTERN.

At this restaurant run by a Russian couple, you'll find soft lights, tablecloths, and classical music—an unexpected scene in downtown Medford. Bakery products made with whole grains, fresh produce, and low-fat poultry and meats are the mainstay ingredients for dishes such as a bracing and delicious borscht with cabbage, tomatoes, and beets (and topped with sour cream, of course). Other Russian and Middle Eastern favorites are blintzes, piroshki (flaky dough pies stuffed with cheese or meat), stuffed cabbage, and skewered kabobs of lamb or chicken. To top off your meal, baklava and Russian and Napoleon tortes are available from the bakery to eat in or take out.

IN THE APPLEGATE VALLEY

Applegate River Ranch House. 15100 Hwy. 238, Applegate. ☎ **541/846-6042.** Reservations recommended in summer and on weekends. Main courses $10–$20. MC, V. Sun–Thurs 4–9pm, Fri–Sat 4–10pm. STEAK/SEAFOOD.

With a deck overlooking the beautiful Applegate River, the location here just can't be beat. We like to enjoy the view with a plate of succulent oak-wood-broiled mushrooms and a glass of crisp Chardonnay. Anything broiled over the local red oak wood is delicious, from chicken to various cuts of steaks. We like to top it all off with a piece of the "hula" pie.

3 The Klamath Falls Area: Bird Watching & Native American Artifacts

65 miles E of Ashland, 60 miles S of Crater Lake

Klamath Falls, which has a history that stretches back more than 14,000 years, is set in a wide, windswept expanse of lakes and high desert just north of the California line. The presence of water (in the form of large lakes) in this dry region has long attracted a wide variety of wildlife (especially waterfowl), which in turn fed the area's Native American population. Native Americans lived on the banks of the Klamath Basin's lakes from which they harvested fish, birds, and various marsh plants. Today, two local museums exhibit extensive collections of Native American artifacts that have been found in this area over the years.

Upper Klamath Lake and adjacent Agency Lake have shrunk considerably over the years as shallow, marshy areas were drained to create pastures and farmland. Today, however, as the lake's native fish populations have become threatened and migratory bird populations in the region have plummeted, there is a growing movement to restore some of the region's drained marshes to more natural conditions. Though large portions of the area are now designated as national wildlife areas, farming and ranching are still considered the primary use of these wildlife lands. However, the many birdwatchers who flock to the region are quick to point out that the Klamath Falls area still has some of the best birding in the state.

The region's shallow lakes warm quickly in the hot summers here, and due in part to the excess nutrients in the waters from agricultural runoff, support large blooms of blue-green algae. While the algae blooms deprive the lake's fish of oxygen, they also provide the area with its most unusual agricultural activity. The harvesting and marketing of Upper Klamath Lake's blue-green algae as a dietary supplement has become big business throughout the country as people have claimed all manner of health benefits from the consumption of this chlorophyll-rich dried algae.

ESSENTIALS

GETTING THERE   Klamath Falls is on U.S. 97, which leads north to Bend and south to the I-5 near Mount Shasta in California. The city is also connected to Ashland by the winding Ore. 66 and to Medford by Ore. 140, which continues east to Lakeview in eastern Oregon. The **Klamath Falls Airport** is served by Horizon Air and United Express. Amtrak's *Coast Starlight* trains stop here en route between San Francisco and Portland.

VISITOR INFORMATION   For more information on the region, contact the **Klamath County Department of Tourism,** 1451 Main St. (P.O. Box 1867), Klamath Falls, OR 97601 (☎ **800/445-6728** or 541/884-0666).

GETTING AROUND   Rental cars are available at Klamath Falls Airport from Avis, Budget, and Hertz.

DELVING INTO LOCAL HISTORY

✪ **Favell Museum of Western Art and Indian Artifacts.** 125 W. Main St. ☎ **541/ 882-9996.** Admission $4 adults, $3 seniors, $2 children 6–16. Mon–Sat 9:30am–5:30pm.

Anyone with an interest in Native American artifacts or Western art will be fascinated by a visit to this unusual museum. On display are thousands of arrowheads, including one made from fire opal, obsidian knives, spear points, stone tools of every description, baskets, pottery, even ancient shoes and pieces of matting and fabric. Though the main focus is on the Native Americans of the Klamath Basin and Columbia River, there are artifacts from Alaska, Canada, other regions of the United States, and Mexico. Few museums anywhere in the country have such an extensive collection and the cases of artifacts can be overwhelming, so take your time. The other half of the museum's collection is Western art by more than 300 artists, including 13 members of the famous Cowboy Artists of America. Paintings, bronzes, photographs, dioramas, and woodcarvings capture the Wild West in realistic, romantic, and even humorous styles.

Klamath County Museum. 1451 Main St. ☎ **541/883-4208.** Free admission. Summer Mon–Sat 10am–4:30pm; winter 8am–4:30pm.

More Native American artifacts, this time exclusively from the Klamath Lakes area, are on display in this museum. A history of the Modoc Indian Wars chronicles the most expensive campaign of the American West. Also of particular interest here are the early–20th-century photos by local photographer Maud Baldwin.

BIRD WATCHING & OTHER OUTDOOR ACTIVITIES

In this dry region between the Cascades and the Rocky Mountains there are few large bodies of water, so the lakes and marshes of the Klamath Basin are a magnet for birds. In the winter the region hosts the largest concentration of bald eagles in the Lower 48. More than 300 eagles can be seen at the **Bear Valley National Wildlife Refuge** near the town of Worden, 11 miles south of Klamath Falls. Other avian visitors and residents include white pelicans, great blue herons, sandhill cranes, egrets, geese, ducks, grebes, bitterns, and osprey. For more information on bird watching in the area, contact the Klamath County Department of Tourism (see above).

If you want to get out and paddle around one of the local lakes, check out the **Upper Klamath Canoe Trail,** which begins near the junction of Ore. 140 and West Side Road northwest of Klamath Falls. The canoe trail wanders through marshlands on the edge of Upper Klamath Lake. For more information, contact the **Winema National Forest,** Klamath Ranger District, 1936 California Ave., Klamath Falls, OR 97601 (☎ **541/885-3400**). Canoes and kayaks can be rented at the adjacent **Rocky Point Resort,** 28121 Rocky Point Rd. (☎ **541/356-2287**). Rates are $6 an hour or $20 for half a day. If you'd like to do a guided canoe trip around the lake, contact **Klamath Lake Touring Company** (☎ **800/718-9690** or 541/883-4622).

If you're more in the mood for white-water thrills, **Cascade River Runners** (☎ **800/884-2113** or 541/883-6340) offers 1-day **white-water rafting** trips on the Class IV-plus Upper Klamath River. This 18-mile run includes 40 major rapids and is not for novices.

If you're truly serious about **trout fishing,** there is no better place in Oregon to get your line wet. Upper Klamath and Agency Lakes and the Wood and Williamson Rivers produce the largest rainbow trout in the West. The unofficial record is 25 pounds, while the official record is 19 pounds. If you want to hire a guide, contact **Kim's Fishing Charters & Lake Tours** (☎ **541/882-4857**), **Miranda's Guide Service** (☎ **541/356-2141**), **John's Guide Service** (☎ **800/233-8223** or 541/ 356-2111), or **Williamson River Anglers** (☎ **541/783-2677**). At Rocky Point Resort (see above) and **Harriman Springs Resort & Marina,** 26661 Rocky Point Rd. (☎ **541/356-2232**), you can rent fishing boats and tackle.

For world-class **fly-fishing** on 6 miles of private Wood River water, consider spending time at **Horseshoe Ranch,** 52909 Ore. 62, Fort Klamath (☎ **541/ 381-2297**). On the Williamson River, you can fish a mile of private waters. For fly-fishing supplies, try the **Fly Shack,** 15430 Ore. 66, Keno (☎ **541/884-4767**).

Horseback rides are available through the **Running Y Stables,** 5115 Running Y Rd. (☎ **541/850-5691**), which charges $21 for a 1-hour ride and $60 for a half-day ride. Pony rides are also available.

The **Running Y Ranch Resort** (☎ **541/850-5580**) is also the place to head for a round of **golf.** Other area courses include the **Shield Crest Golf Course,** 3151 Shield Crest Dr. (☎ **541/884-1493**), and **Harbor Links,** 601 Harbor Isles Blvd. (☎ **541/882-0609**).

Northwest of Klamath Falls about 35 miles on Ore. 140, you'll find the region's main mountain recreation area. Here, in the vicinity of **Lake of the Woods** and **Fish Lake,** you'll find, in summer, the fun High Lakes mountain-bike trail, which leads through a rugged lava field. Also in the area is the hiking trail to the summit of Mount McLoughlin. In winter, this same area has cross-country ski trails. There are rustic cabin resorts and campgrounds on both Lake of the Woods and Fish Lake.

If you'd like to head out on the waters of Upper Klamath Lake, **Meridian Sail Center,** Pelican Marina, 928 Front St. (☎ **541/884-5869**), offers sailboat charters starting at $40 for 2 hours. They also rent sailboats here.

WHERE TO STAY

By the summer of 1998, Klamath Falls should have launched itself into the Oregon resort scene with the opening of the **Running Y Ranch Resort,** 5391 Running Y Rd., Klamath Falls, OR 97601 (☎ **800/244-6015** or 888/797-2624), northwest of town off Ore. 140. This golf resort and time-share condominium community sits on the bank of Upper Klamath Lake amid the ponderosa pines. Although remote, it looks as if it will be as luxurious as any of the central Oregon resorts in the Bend and Sisters areas.

Rocky Point Resort. 28121 Rocky Point Rd., Klamath Falls, OR 97601. ☎ **541/356-2287.** Fax 541/356-2222. 6 rms, 3 cabins. $53 double; $69 cabin. MC, V.

This rustic resort on the west shore of Upper Klamath Lake is the sort of place that conjures up childhood memories of summer vacations by the lake. Neither the rooms nor the cabins are anything special, but the setting is bewitching. Shaded by huge old ponderosa pine trees and partly built atop the rocks for which this point is named, the resort has a great view across the waters and marshes of the Upper Klamath National Wildlife Refuge. Green lawns set with Adirondack chairs go right down to the water, where there is a small boat-rental dock. The rustic restaurant and lounge, complete with moose antlers over the fireplace, boast the best views on the property. Meals are the basic American fare you would expect at such a place. The Upper Klamath Lake canoe trails originate here, and the bird watching is excellent, but fishing is still the favorite pastime here. The resort also has tent and RV sites.

CAMPGROUNDS

Along Ore. 140 between Klamath Falls and Medford, there are several national forest campgrounds. On Fish Lake, **Fish Lake Campground** and **Doe Point Campground** are in nice locations, but they both get a lot of traffic noise. Just west of Fish Lake on F.S. 37, the **North Fork Campground** provides a quieter setting on a trout stream and a scenic mountain-bike trail. **Sunset Campground** and **Aspen Point Campground** at Lake of the Woods are popular in summer with the boat fishing and water skiing crowd. The latter campground is near Great Meadow Recreation Area, has a swimming beach, and is right on the High Lakes mountain-bike trail.

WHERE TO DINE

For dinner with the best view in the area, make a reservation at the **Rocky Point Resort** (see above), which is 30 minutes outside Klamath Falls and is open nightly in summer. Sunday brunch is also served.

Chez Nous. 3927 S. Sixth St. ☎ **541/883-8719.** Reservations recommended. Main courses $15–$31. AE, CB, DC, MC, V. Tues–Sat 5–10pm. FRENCH/AMERICAN.

Sixth Street is one of Klamath Falls's main roads, and here you'll find Chez Nous in a little house tucked in among motels, gas stations, and strip malls. Inside, the old-fashioned elegance of the house is a contrast to its environment and a fitting setting for the primarily traditional fare, such as escargots de Bourgogne and French onion soup for starters and salmon with béarnaise sauce and veal Oscar for entrees.

Saddle Rock Cafe. 1012 Main St. ☎ **541/883-3970.** Main courses $6–$11. AE, MC, V. Mon–Sat 11am–9pm. AMERICAN.

This casual dining spot is in downtown Klamath Falls in an old brick building with green awnings. Exposed brick walls give the restaurant a bit of urban sophistication. Though there are several pasta dishes and sandwiches on the menu, we prefer the rotisseried lemon-rosemary chicken or the barbecued tri-tip.

4 Grants Pass & the Rogue River Valley

63 miles S of Roseburg, 40 miles NW of Ashland, 82 miles NE of Crescent City

"It's the climate," proclaims a sign at the entrance to Grants Pass, and with weather almost as reliably pleasant as California's, the town has become a popular base for outdoor activities of all kinds. With the Rogue River running through the center of town, it's not surprising that most local recreational activities focus around the waters of this famous river. Located at the junction of I-5 and U.S. 199, Grants Pass is also the last large town in Oregon if you're heading over to the redwoods, which are about 90 miles southwest on the northern California coast. A similar distance to the northeast, you'll find Crater Lake National Park, so Grants Pass makes a good base if you're trying to see a lot of this region in a short time.

ESSENTIALS

GETTING THERE Grants Pass is at the junction of I-5 and U.S. 199. The **Rogue Valley International–Medford** Airport, at 3650 Biddle Rd., Medford, is served by Horizon Air and United Airlines.

VISITOR INFORMATION Contact the **Grants Pass–Josephine County Chamber of Commerce,** 1995 NW Vine St. (P.O. Box 970), Grants Pass, OR 97526 (☎ **800/547-5927** or 541/476-7717).

FESTIVALS **Boatnik,** held Memorial Day weekend, is Grants Pass's biggest annual festival and includes jet boat and hydroplane races on the Rogue River as well as lots of festivities at Riverside Park.

OUTDOOR ACTIVITIES: RAFTING, FISHING, HIKING & MORE

Grants Pass is located midway between the source and the mouth of the Rogue River and is an ideal base for river-oriented activities. The Rogue, first made famous by Western novelist and avid fly-fisherman Zane Grey and recently the location for scenes in the film *The River Wild,* is now preserved for much of its length as a National Wild and Scenic River. Originating in Crater Lake National Park, the river twists and tumbles through narrow gorges and steep mountains as it winds its way to the coast at Gold Beach. The most famous section of the river is 250-foot-deep **Hellgate Canyon,** where the river narrows and rushes through a cleft in the rock. The canyon can be seen from an overlook on Merlin-Galice Road, which begins at exit 61 off I-5. From the interstate it's about 10 miles to the canyon overlook.

Several companies offer **river trips** of varying length and in various watercraft. You can even spend several days rafting the river with stops each night at riverside lodges. If you have only enough time for a short trip on the river, we'd recommend a jet-boat trip up to Hellgate Canyon, the most scenic spot on this section of the river. **Hellgate Excursions,** 953 SE Seventh St., Grants Pass (☎ **800/648-4874** or 541/479-7204), operates four different jet-boat trips, with prices ranging from $23 to $39.

Local **white-water rafting** companies offer half-day, full-day, and multiday trips, with the latter stopping either at rustic river lodges or at campsites along the river banks. Rafting companies include **Rogue Wilderness,** 325 Galice Rd., Merlin (☎ **800/336-1647** or 541/479-9554); **Galice Resort,** 11744 Galice Rd., Merlin (☎ **541/476-3818**); **Orange Torpedo Trips,** 210 Merlin Rd., Merlin (☎ **800/635-2925** or 541/479-5061); and **Rogue River Raft Trips,** Morrison's Lodge, 8500 Galice Rd., Merlin (☎ **800/826-1963** or 541/476-3825). Rates are around $45 for a half day and $60 for a full day. Two-day lodge trips start around $225 per person, 3-day camp/lodge trips are about $500, and 4-day camping trips are $525.

At several places near Merlin, you can rent rafts and kayaks of different types and paddle yourself downriver. Try **White Water Cowboys,** 209 Merlin Rd., Merlin (☎ **541/479-0132**); **Galice Resort Store,** 11744 Galice Rd., Merlin (☎ **541/476-3818**); or **Ferron's Fun Trips,** 585 Rogue Rim Dr., Merlin (☎ **800/404-2201** or 541/474-2201). Rental rates are between $20 and $80 per day.

If **fishing** is your passion, the steelhead and salmon of the Rogue River already haunt your dreams. To make those dreams a reality, you'll want to hire a guide to take you where the fish are sure to bite. Rogue Wilderness and Rogue River Raft Trips, both mentioned above, and **Geoff's Guide Service,** 2578 Midway, Grants Pass (☎ **541/474-0602**), offer guided fishing trips of 1 to 4 days. Expect to pay between $100 and $125 per person for a day of fishing.

Golfers can play a round at the **Red Mountain Golf Course,** 324 N. Schoolhouse Creek Rd. (☎ **541/479-2297**), which is 15 minutes north of Grants Pass, or at the **Dutcher Creek Golf Course,** 4611 Upper River Rd. (☎ **541/474-2188**).

Fans of **horse racing** can bet on the ponies at **Grants Pass Downs** at the Josephine County Fairgrounds (☎ **541/476-3215**) on U.S. 199 west of town. The season runs from Memorial Day to the Fourth of July.

OTHER THINGS TO SEE & DO

Though most people visiting Grants Pass are here to enjoy the mountains and rivers surrounding the town, history buffs can pick up a free map of the town's historic buildings at the Tourist Information Center. Two small art museums—the **Grants Pass Museum of Art,** 304 SE Park St. (☎ **541/479-3290**), in Riverside Park, and the **Wiseman Gallery,** 3345 Redwood Hwy., at Rogue Community College (☎ **541/471-3500,** ext. 224)—offer changing exhibits of classic and contemporary art by local and national artists.

Wildlife Images Rehabilitation and Education Center, 11845 Lower River Rd. (☎ **541/476-0222**), is dedicated to nurturing injured birds of prey and other wild animals back to health. The center is located 13 miles south of Grants Pass and is open for tours Tuesday through Sunday at 11am and 1pm by reservation only. Admission is by donation.

Riverside Park, in the center of town, is a popular place to play, especially in the warmer months when people come to cool off in the river.

About midway between Medford and Grants Pass and just 4 miles off I-5 you'll find one of Oregon's most curious attractions: the **Oregon Vortex and House of Mystery,** 4303 Sardine Creek Rd., Gold Hill (☎ **541/855-1543**). This classic tourist trap is guaranteed to have the kids, and some adults, oohing and aahing in bug-eyed amazement at the numerous phenomena that defy the laws of physics. People grow taller as they recede. You, and the trees surrounding the House of Mystery, lean toward magnetic north rather than stand upright. Seeing is believing—or is it? Open March to May and in September and October, daily from 9am to 5pm; June to August, daily from 9am to 6pm (closed November through January). Admission is $6.50 for adults, $4.50 for children 5 to 11.

WHERE TO STAY

✪ **Morrison's Rogue River Lodge.** 8500 Galice Rd., Merlin, OR 97532. ☎ **800/826-1963** or 541/476-3825. Fax 541/476-4953. 4 rms, 9 cabins. $160–$260 double. Rates include all meals. DISC, MC, V. Closed Dec–Apr.

If you're in the area to do a bit of fishing or rafting, we can think of no better place to stay than at Morrison's. Perched on the banks of the Rogue, this fishing lodge epitomizes the Rogue River experience. The main lodge is a massive log building that's rustic yet comfortable; it has a wall of glass that looks across wide lawns to the river. There are B&B–style accommodations in this building, but the spacious cabins seem more appropriate in this setting. The cabins stand beneath grand old trees and all have good views of the river. Fireplaces will keep you warm and cozy in the cooler months. The dining room serves surprisingly creative four-course dinners. Fishing and rafting trips are the specialty here, but there are also tennis courts, an outdoor pool, a putting green, and a private beach.

Paradise Ranch Inn. 7000 Monument Dr., Grants Pass, OR 97526. ☎ **541/479-4333.** Fax 541/479-0218. 15 rms, 1 cottage. A/C. $70–$90 double; $90–$125 cottage. Lower rates Oct–Apr. Rates include continental breakfast. MC, V.

Rolling green hills, white wooden fences, a big barn converted into a lounge—the Paradise Ranch Inn has all the trappings of a classic guest ranch, yet the lush lawns say golf resort. This place is really neither, although it does have a three-hole pitch-and-putt area as well as a gourmet restaurant overlooking a lake, several other lakes and ponds, tennis courts, and a swimming pool, all of which combine to make this a very pleasant place for a getaway. The guest rooms are furnished in a very traditional style, and though nothing fancy, are comfortable. The French and continental cuisine served in the restaurant is some of the best in southern Oregon, and entree prices are in the $10 to $18 range. Other recreational facilities include a jogging path, a whirlpool, a volleyball court, and bicycles.

Pine Meadow Inn. 1000 Crow Rd., Merlin, OR 97532. ☎ **800/554-0806** or 541/471-6277. Web site: www.cpros.com/~pmi. 4 rms. A/C. $80–$110 double. Rates include full breakfast. No credit cards.

Situated between a meadow and a pine forest on 9 acres of land near the Rogue River, this modern farmhouse B&B is secluded yet close to town. The tranquil setting, with a hot tub and koi pond in the back yard, makes it impossible not to slow down and relax here. The guest rooms are all furnished with antiques and have fresh flowers on the guests' arrival. Two rooms have mountain views, while the other two overlook the gardens and forest. The inn is located close to the Wild and Scenic stretch of the Rogue River and makes a good base if you are planning on doing some rafting or fishing.

Riverside Inn Resort & Conference Center. 971 SE Sixth St., Grants Pass, OR 97526. ☎ **800/334-4567** or 541/476-6873. Fax 541/474-9848. Web site: www.riverside inn.com. 174 rms. A/C TV TEL. $60–$275 double. AE, DC, DISC, MC, V.

Located in downtown Grants Pass, the Riverside Inn is, as the name implies, right on the bank of the Rogue River. A weathered wood exterior and cedar-shingle roof give the two-story inn a bit of Northwest flavor, though the setting between two busy bridges is not exactly idyllic. Luckily, a park across the river means the views from most rooms are quite pleasant. The inn sprawls across 3 blocks, and rooms vary in age and quality. Our favorites are the fireplace rooms in the west section and the new whirlpool river-view suites. Avoid the rooms near the road, which can be quite noisy. Though the river-view rooms are a bit more expensive than nonview rooms, they're certainly worth the price.

Dining/Entertainment: The inn's restaurant and lounge offer a great view of the river and some of the best meals in town.

Services: Room service, valet/laundry service, access to nearby health club.

Facilities: Two outdoor swimming pools, whirlpool.

☉ **Weasku Inn.** 5560 Rogue River Hwy., Grants Pass, OR 97527. ☎ **800/4-WEASKU** or 541/471-8000. Fax 541/471-7038. 5 rms, 2 cabins. $85–$250 double; $295 cabin. Rates include continental breakfast. AE, DC, DISC, MC, V.

Set on the bank of the Rogue River just below the Savage Rapids Dam, this log lodge was built in 1924 and was once *the* area fishing lodge. That was back in the days when Clark Gable, Carole Lombard, Walt Disney, Zane Grey, Bing Crosby, and Herbert Hoover used to stay here. Today, after a total renovation, the lodge is once again the sort of place where such luminaries would feel comfortable. Guest rooms, on the second floor of the old log lodge, are spacious and modern and have such interesting details as bent-willow furnishings, coiled-rope lamps, and tiled showers. The riverside cabins have whirlpool tubs, fireplaces, and private decks. Set beneath towering trees a few miles out of Grants Pass, this inn is now one of the most memorable lodgings in southern Oregon.

☉ **Wolf Creek Tavern.** P.O. Box 97, Wolf Creek, OR 97497. ☎ **541/866-2474.** 8 rms. $69–$85 double. Rates include full breakfast. DISC, MC, V.

Originally opened in the 1883 on the old stagecoach road between Sacramento and Portland, the Wolf Creek Tavern is a two-story clapboard building with wide front verandas along both floors. Today the inn, which is 18 miles north of Grants Pass and just off I-5, is the oldest hotel in Oregon and is owned by the Oregon State Parks and Recreation Division. The interior is furnished in period antiques dating from the 1870s to the 1930s. The ladies' parlor downstairs features 1870s vintage antiques, a piano, and old photos. On a winter's night there's no cozier spot than by the fireplace here. The guest rooms are small and simply furnished, much as they may have been in the early 1900s. Simple fare is available in the inn's dining room.

CAMPGROUNDS

Along the Rogue River east of Grants Pass, you'll find the very busy **Valley of the Rogue State Park** just off I-5 near the town of Rogue River. West of Grants Pass, there are several county-operated campgrounds: **Indian Mary Park,** near Galice on Merlin-Galice Road (this is the nicest of these campgrounds and is in the Hellgate Canyon area); **Schroeder Park,** off Ore. 199 (the Redwood Highway) only a mile or so out of town; and **Whitehorse Park,** on Lower River Road about 2¹/₂ miles out of town. Near Indian Mary Park, you'll also find the **Almeda Park,** which is close to the Grave Creek trailhead of the Rogue River Trail.

WHERE TO DINE

If all you need is a pizza and a microbrew, try **Wild River Brewing & Pizza Company,** 595 NE E. St. (☎ **541/471-7487**). For espresso and light meals, **Java House,** 412 NW Sixth St. (☎ **541/471-1922**) is dependable. **The Cake Shop,** 215 Galice Rd.,

Merlin (☎ **541/479-0188**), is only open Friday through Sunday, but if you happen to be there during that time, it's worth a stop for the giant cinnamon rolls. **Morrison's Rogue River Lodge,** 8500 Galice Rd., Merlin (☎ **541/476-3825**), serves the best meals on the river. For nonguests, dinners are $20 to $29. Reservations are required. See above for details.

The Brewery. 509 SW G St. ☎ **541/479-9850.** Main courses $8–$30. MC, V. Tues–Thurs 11:30am–2pm and 4:30–8pm, Fri 11:30am–2pm and 4:30–9pm, Sat 4:30–9pm, Sun 9:30am–1:30pm and 4:30–8pm. AMERICAN/PUB.

Just down the street from the Laughing Clam (see below) is this more traditional restaurant housed in a historic building with a colorful past that includes stints as a brewery. Outside, there's a covered bridge over a stream, and inside a collection of old shot glasses and beer bottles underscores the historic theme. Fare here includes prime rib, chicken cordon bleu, and shrimp scampi. Brunch is served on Sundays.

Hamilton House. 130 NE Terry Lane. ☎ **541/479-3938.** Reservations recommended. Main courses $10–$15. AE, DISC, MC, V. Daily 5–9pm. AMERICAN.

You'll find this attractive old house tucked in between the Wal-Mart and the Fred Meyer just off E Street. The Hamilton House does a respectable job, and there's no denying that the garden views through most of the windows add to a meal. In summer there's also patio dining. The menu includes a torte of creamed cheeses layered with pesto and dried tomatoes that makes a great start to a meal. We prefer the chicken and seafood dishes here. Main courses include pasta jambalaya with chicken, Cajun sausage, and shrimp; scampi sautéed with garlic and herb butter; lime-basil chicken; and marinated prime rib, a house specialty.

The Laughing Clam. 121 SW G St. ☎ **541/479-1110.** Main courses $6–$15. DISC, MC, V. Mon–Sat 11am–11pm. AMERICAN/PUB.

Located in the hip G Street neighborhood, this microbrewery sports a bar that came around Cape Horn by ship a long time ago, and serves up tasty salads, sandwiches and pastas. There are plenty of meatless and seafood selections to accompany a microbrew. We really like the curried coconut prawns and Dungeness crab cakes with spicy chili mayonnaise.

✪ **Meadowview Country Cottage Cafe & Tea Room.** 2315 Upper River Rd. Loop. ☎ **541/476-6882.** Salads and sandwiches $4–$7. DISC, MC, V. Tues–Sat 11am–4pm. Drive west on G St. and look for the sign; it's 1 1/2 miles from downtown Grants Pass. SALADS/SANDWICHES.

Located out in the country and surrounded by flower and vegetable gardens, this casual restaurant provides a glimpse of the good life, Grants Pass style. If you like gardens, you'll especially enjoy a meal here in high summer when the gardens are bursting with life. Lunch (often busy and popular with groups) and afternoon tea are served inside or outside on the lawn. The cafe uses organically grown produce.

Pongsri's. 1571 NE Sixth Ave. ☎ **541/479-1345.** Main courses $6.50–$8. MC, V. Tues–Sun 11am–3pm and 4:30–9pm. THAI/CHINESE.

Located in a nondescript old shopping center near the Grants Pass Visitor Information Center, Pongsri's is a tiny and basic Thai restaurant serving good Thai food. The long menu includes plenty of choices, including lots of seafood. If you like shrimp as much as we do, you'll opt for the tom yum gung, a sour-and-spicy soup that's guaranteed to clear your sinuses. Vegetarians have lots of options here, too, and the lunch special for $3.75 just can't be beat.

North of Grants Pass: Sweet Rolls as Big as Your Head

If you've got a sweet tooth, then you won't want to miss one of the most important stops in Oregon, exit 86 off I-5 in the community of Azalea. Fans of gooey cinnamon rolls and berry pies will find Heaven on Earth, literally. **Heaven on Earth,** 703 Quines Creek Rd. (☎ **541/837-3700**), serves legendary cinnamon rolls that are as big as your head, equally hefty blackberry pies, and turnovers that will have you turning to a new diet when you're done.

5 Oregon Caves National Monument & the Illinois Valley

Cave Junction: 30 miles SW of Grants Pass, 56 miles NE of Crescent City

For many people, U.S. 199 is simply the road to the redwoods from southern Oregon. However, this remote stretch of highway passes through the Illinois Valley and skirts the Siskiyou Mountains. Together the valley and mountains offer quite a bit in the way of recreational activities. The Illinois River, which flows into the Rogue River, is an even wilder river than the Rogue, and its Class V waters are often run by experienced paddlers looking for real white-water adventure. Because the Siskiyou Mountains are among the oldest in Oregon, they support a unique plant community. These mountains are also known for their rugged, rocky peaks, which though not very high, can be very impressive.

ESSENTIALS

GETTING THERE   Cave Junction is on U.S. 199 between Grants Pass and the California state line. Oregon Caves National Monument is 20 miles outside Cave Junction on Ore. 46.

VISITOR INFORMATION   For more information on this area, contact the **Illinois Valley Chamber of Commerce,** 201 Caves Hwy. (P.O. Box 312), Cave Junction, OR 97523 (☎ **541/592-3326**).

EXPLORING THE CAVES

Oregon Caves National Monument. 19000 Caves Hwy. ☎ **541/592-2100.** Admission $6.25 adults, $4 children 6–11. Cave tours May and Tues after Labor Day to Sept 30 daily 8:30am–5pm; June to Labor Day daily 8am–7pm; Oct 1–Apr 30 daily 9:30am–4pm.

High in the rugged Siskiyou Mountains a clear mountain stream cascades through a narrow canyon, and here stands one of southern Oregon's oldest attractions. Known as the marble halls of Oregon and first discovered in 1874, the caves, which stretch for 3 miles under the mountain, were formed by water seeping through marble bedrock. The slight acidity of the water dissolves the marble, which is later redeposited as beautiful stalactites, stalagmites, draperies, soda straws, columns, and flowstone. Guided tours of the caves take about $1^1/_2$ hours, and back up above ground there are several miles of hiking trails that start near the cave entrance. To reach the monument, take Ore. 46 out of Cave Junction and follow the signs.

OTHER THINGS TO SEE & DO IN THE ILLINOIS VALLEY

The Illinois River, when it isn't raging through rock-choked canyons, provides some of the best **swimming holes** in the state. Try the waters at Illinois River State Park, just outside Cave Junction, or ask at the **Illinois Valley Ranger District,** 26568 Redwood Hwy., Cave Junction, OR 97532 (☎ **541/592-2166**), for directions to other good swimming holes in the area. At this ranger station, you can also pick up information and directions for **hiking trails** in the Siskiyous, where the 180,000-acre Kalmiopsis Wilderness is a destination of backpackers.

It seems you're never far from a winery in the Northwest, and Cave Junction is no exception. Area wineries include **Foris,** 654 Kendall Rd. (☎ **800/843-6747** or 541/592-3752), and **Bridgeview,** 4210 Holland Loop Rd. (☎ **541/592-4688**). Cabernet Sauvignon, Merlot, Chardonnay, Riesling, and Muller-Thurgau are the most common varietals produced in this region. You'll see signs for these wineries along U.S. 199 and Ore. 46.

WHERE TO STAY

The most unique accommodation in the area is a tree house complex in the community of Takilma. **Out 'n' About Treehouse Treesort,** 300 Page Creek Rd., Cave Junction, OR 97523 (☎ **800/200-5484** or 541/592-2208), has repeatedly made national news over the past few years due to an ongoing battle between owner Michael Garnier and Josephine County bureaucrats who claim the tree houses are unsafe and illegal (because they don't have concrete foundations). Perhaps the tree houses will still be open to the public when you pass through the area.

Oregon Caves Lodge. 20000 Caves Hwy. (P.O. Box 128), Cave Junction, OR 97523. ☎ **541/592-3400.** Fax 541/592-6654. 22 rms, 4 suites. $69–$89 double; $109 suite. MC, V.

A narrow road winds for 20 miles south into the Siskiyou National Forest climbing through deep forests before finally coming to an end in a narrow, steep-walled canyon. At the very head of this canyon stands the Oregon Caves Lodge, a rustic six-story lodge built in 1934. Huge fir beams support the lobby ceiling and two marble fireplaces beckon (it can be cool here any time of year). About the only thing that's missing from this alpine setting is a view (because the lodge is in a wooded canyon, there are no sweeping vistas). The guest rooms, unfortunately, do not live up to the promise of the rest of the building. They have rather unattractive furnishings, but if you spend your time exploring the caves, hiking the hills, or lounging in the lobby, you'll hardly notice. A 1930s-style soda fountain serves burgers, shakes, and other simple meals, while in the main dining room steak and seafood dinners are available.

CAMPGROUNDS

Although there are no campgrounds in Oregon Caves National Monument, there are a couple of national forest campgrounds nearby. On the road to the national monument, you'll find **Grayback Campground** and **Cave Creek Campground,** both of which are in forest settings on creek banks.

WHERE TO DINE

✪ **Wild River Brewing & Pizza Company.** 249 N. Redwood Hwy. ☎ **541/592-3556.** Sandwiches $2.50–$4.25; pizzas $2.90–$17. DISC, MC, V. Mon–Sat 10am–10pm, Sun 11am–9:30pm. PIZZA/DELI.

If you're a fan of microbrewery ales, a pleasant surprise awaits you in the crossroads community of Cave Junction. This very casual combination pizza parlor and deli also happens to be a respectable little brewery specializing in British ales. The rich and flavorful ales go great with the pizzas, several of which are made with locally made sausage. And for fans of the unusual, there's a pizza with smoked sausage and sauerkraut and another with avocado and sprouts.

6 The Roseburg Area: Lions & Tigers & Wineries, Oh My!

68 miles N of Grants Pass, 68 miles S of Eugene, 83 miles W of Crater Lake National Park

Although primarily a logging mill town, Roseburg is set at the mouth of the North Umpqua River and, consequently, is well situated for exploring one of the prettiest valleys in Oregon. The surrounding countryside bears a striking resemblance to parts of northern California, so it should come as no surprise that there are a half dozen wineries in the area. The hills south of town also look a bit like Africa, which may be why the Wildlife Safari park chose to locate here. Today this drive-through wildlife park is one of the biggest attractions in southern Oregon. In downtown Roseburg, you'll find numerous old Victorian homes, and a drive through these old neighborhoods will be interesting for fans of late–19th-century architecture.

WHAT TO SEE & DO: A WILDLIFE PARK & LOCAL HISTORY

✪ **Wildlife Safari.** Off Ore. 42, just outside Winston (south of Roseburg). ☎ **541/679-6761.** Admission $11.95 adults, $9.95 seniors, $6.95 children 4–12, free for children 3 and under. Summer daily 9am–7pm; winter daily 9am–4pm.

This 600-acre drive-through nature park is home to wild animals from around the world. You'll come face to face with curious bears, grazing gazelles and zebras, shy ostriches, and even lumbering elephants and rhinos. In addition to the drive through the park, you can ride an elephant, visit the educational center, or attend an animal show. Signs as you approach let you know that convertibles are not allowed in the lion or bear enclosures (but rental cars are available).

Douglas County Museum of History & Natural History. Douglas County Fairgrounds. ☎ **541/440-4507.** $3.50 adults, $1 children 3–17. Daily 9am–5pm.

South of town at the Douglas County Fairgrounds you'll find this surprisingly well-designed museum. The unusual, large building that houses it resembles an old mining structure or mill. Inside are displays on the history and natural history of the region. Pioneer farming and mining displays interpret the settlement of the region, but it's the saber-toothed tiger skeleton that really grabs people's attention.

THE NEARBY HISTORIC TOWN OF OAKLAND

About 15 miles north of Roseburg is the historic town of Oakland, which is listed on the National Register of Historic Places. Though the town was founded in the 1850s, most of the buildings here date from the 1890s. A stroll through town soaking up the atmosphere is a pleasant way to spend a morning or an afternoon. You can pick up a self-guided walking-tour map at the **Oakland Museum,** 130 Locust St. (☎ **541/459-4531**), which is housed in an 1893 brick building and contains collections of historic photos, old farm tools, household furnishings, and clothing from Oakland's past. Admission is by donation, and the museum is open daily from 1 to 4pm.

WINE TOURING

The Roseburg area is home to half a dozen wineries, all of which are located within a few miles of I-5. Off exit 119, you can visit **La Garza Cellars,** 491 Winery Lane (☎ **541/679-9654**), and **Girardet Wine Cellars,** 895 Reston Rd. (☎ **541/679-7252**). From exit 125, you can visit **Callahan Ridge Winery,** 340 Busenbark Lane

(☎ **541/673-7901**); **HillCrest Vineyards,** 240 Vineyard Lane (☎ **541/673-3709**); and **DeNino Umpqua River Vineyards,** 451 Hess Rd. (☎ **541/673-1975**). From exit 136, you can visit **Henry Estate Winery,** Ore. 9 west of Umpqua (☎ **541/459-5120**).

WHERE TO STAY

The Beckley House Bed & Breakfast. 338 SE Second St., Oakland, OR 97462. ☎ **541/459-9320.** 2 suites. $65–$85 double. Rates include full breakfast. AE, MC, V.

If you enjoy the atmosphere in Oakland and want to stick around for the night, the Beckley House B&B is the place to stay. This Queen Anne–style Victorian home dates from the late 1800s and is furnished with period antiques. An old Victrola and lots of 1930s magazines provide vintage entertainment. The suites are fairly large and can be joined to a third room with two twin beds if you need space for four people.

Windmill Inn. 1450 NW Mulholland Dr., Roseburg, OR 97470-1986. ☎ **800/547-4747** or 541/673-0901. 128 rms. A/C TV TEL. $65–$79 double. Rates include continental breakfast. AE, DISC, MC, V.

Although this is little more than an off-ramp motel, it offers a few unexpected extras that make it your best choice in Roseburg. There's an outdoor swimming pool plus a hot tub and a sauna. Then there are bicycles for the use of guests, a lending library of best-sellers, breakfast and the newspaper delivered to your door, apples and coffee in the lobby throughout the day, and free local phone calls.

WHERE TO DINE

Shazzam's. 509 SE Jackson St., Roseburg. ☎ **541/672-6978.** Main courses $5–$10. DISC, MC, V. Tues–Sat 11am–8pm. AMERICAN.

Located in downtown Roseburg, this 1950s-style restaurant is loads of fun. All over the walls and stuck into every nook and cranny, there are old bicycles, pedal-cars, toy trucks, even an old Vespa scooter. The food is good, too, with house-made barbecue sauces and dry rubs.

✪ **Tolly's.** 115 Locust St., Oakland. ☎ **541/459-3796.** Main courses $7–$19. AE, DC, MC, V. Mon–Tues 9am–5pm, Wed–Fri 9am–9:30pm, Sat–Sun 8am–9:30pm. AMERICAN.

Since 1964 folks from all over the region have been dropping in on Oakland to have dinner or just a root-beer float or sundae here at Tolly's. Housed in a storefront on Locust Street, Tolly's is both an elegant restaurant and an old-fashioned soda fountain. You can hop onto a stool at the counter and linger over a cold malted-milk shake in a tall glass, or have a dinner of steak or perfectly prepared salmon. Attached to the restaurant are both an antique shop and an art gallery. Service here can be glacially slow.

NORTH OF ROSEBURG: A SERIOUS ICE-CREAM STOP

Consider yourself very lucky if you happen to be driving north from Roseburg on I-5 on a hot summer day. Respite from the heat lies just off the interstate at the Rice Hill exit ramp, where you'll find the legendary **K-R Drive Inn** (☎ **541/849-2570**), where every scoop of ice cream you order is actually a double scoop! Consider this before you order a double scoop of rocky road. The K-R is open daily from 10am to 9pm.

Central Oreon 11

On the west side of the Cascade Range, rain is as certain as death and taxes. But cross the invisible dividing line formed by the mountains and you leave the deluge behind. Central Oregon basks under blue skies nearly 300 days of the year—in fact, it gets so little rain that parts of the region are considered high desert. Such a natural attraction is a constant enticement to Oregonians living west of the Cascades. In summer, they head to central Oregon for hiking, fishing, rafting, and camping, and in winter they descend on the ski slopes of Mount Bachelor, Oregon's best ski resort.

Central Oregon is not so much a geographical area as it is a recreational region, and it doesn't actually lie in the central part of the state. However, because the Cascade Range creates such a distinct and visible dividing line between the wet west side and the dry east side, it is immediately evident that this region is different. A lack of precipitation, due to the rain-shadow effect of the mountains, is responsible for the immediately recognizable character of central Oregon. Ponderosa pines rather than Douglas firs and western red cedars dominate the eastern foothills forests of this region. Farther east, where there is even less annual rainfall, juniper and sagebrush country takes over. It is this classically Western environment that has in part led to the adoption of a Wild West theme in the town of Sisters, which is filled with false-fronted buildings and covered wooden sidewalks.

On closer inspection, however, it becomes evident that it is more than just a lack of rainfall that sets this region apart. Central Oregon's unique volcanic geography provides the scenic backdrop to all the region's many recreational activities. Obsidian flows, lava caves, cinder cones, pumice deserts—these are the sort of features that make the central Oregon landscape unique.

Despite the dryness of the landscape here, water is the region's primary recreational draw. The Deschutes River is the state's most popular rafting river and is fabled among fly anglers for its wild redside rainbow trout and its steelheads. West of Bend, a scenic highway loops past a dozen or so lakes, each with its own unique character and appeal. Closer to Bend, the Deschutes River cascades over ancient lava flows forming impressive waterfalls that are favorite destinations of area hikers.

However, for solitude and scenic grandeur, most hikers and backpackers head out from Bend and Sisters into the Three Sisters

Wilderness, which encompasses its snow-clad namesake peaks. Outside the wilderness, there are also many miles of mountain-biking trails that have made the Bend and Sisters areas the best mountain-biking destination in the state.

While it is the open slopes of Mount Bachelor ski area that attract most visitors in the winter, the area also has many miles of cross-country ski trails, including the state's finest Nordic center (at Mount Bachelor, of course). Snowmobiling is also very popular.

1 North Central Oregon & the Lower Deschutes River

Maupin: 95 miles N of Bend, 100 miles E of Portland, 40 miles S of The Dalles

Dominated by two rivers—the Deschutes and the John Day—north central Oregon is the driest, most desertlike part of this region. It is also the closest sunny destination for rain-soaked Portlanders.

Hot springs, canyonlands, and some of the best rafting and fishing in the state are the main draws in this part of central Oregon. For many visitors, the high desert landscape is a fascinating change from the lushness of the west side of the Cascades. For others it is just too bleak and barren. But there is no denying that the Deschutes River is the busiest river in the state, with rafters and anglers descending en masse throughout the year but especially in summer to challenge the rapids and the red sides under sunny skies.

However, even if the Deschutes is not your destination, this region has several unusual attractions that make it worthwhile for a weekend's exploration. First and foremost of these is the Kah-Nee-Ta Resort, which, with its proximity to Portland and its warm-spring swimming pool, is a powerful enticement after several months of gray skies and constant drizzle west of the Cascades.

Not far from the resort, in the town of Warm Springs, is a fascinating modern museum dedicated to the cultures of Northwest Native Americans. A forgotten page of pioneer days can be found at nearby Shaniko, a ghost town that once made it big as a wool shipping town. Much older history, up to 40-million years of it, is laid bare in the three units of the John Day Fossil Beds National Monument. If the stark hills of the national monument don't give you enough sense of being in the desert, then be sure to visit The Cove Palisades State Park, where three steep-walled canyons have been flooded by the waters of Lake Billy Chinook.

ESSENTIALS

GETTING THERE   Maupin, which is the staging site for most rafting and fishing trips on the lower Deschutes River, is at the junction of U.S. 197, the main route from The Dalles south to Bend, and Ore. 216, which connects to U.S. 26 east of Mount Hood.

VISITOR INFORMATION   For more information on this area, contact the **Greater Maupin Area Chamber of Commerce,** P.O. Box 220, Maupin, OR 97037 (☎ **541/395-2599**).

EXPLORING THE REGION
RAFTING, FISHING & OTHER AQUATIC ACTIVITIES

Flowing through a dry sagebrush canyon lined with basalt cliffs, the lower Deschutes River, from the U.S. 26 bridge outside Warm Springs down to the Columbia River, is one of the most popular stretches of water in Oregon. This section of the river provides lots of Class III rapids. While 1-day rafting trips keep the masses content,

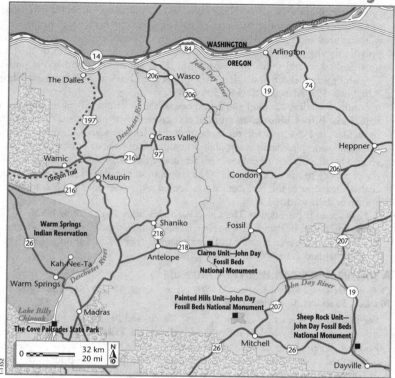

at almost 100 miles in length, the lower Deschutes also provides several options for multiday rafting trips.

Popular 1-day splash-and-giggle trips are offered by dozens of rafting companies and usually start just upstream from Maupin and end just above the impressive Sherar's Falls. Most companies also offer 2- and 3-day trips as well. Rafting companies operating on the lower Deschutes River include **All Star Rafting** (☎ **800/ 909-7238,** 503/235-3663, or 541/395-2201), which also rents rafts and offers kayaking classes; **C&J Lodge** (☎ **800/395-3903** or 541/395-2404), which also operates a bed-and-breakfast inn for rafters in Maupin; **Deschutes River Adventures** (☎ **800/723-8464**), which also rents rafts; **Deschutes Whitewater Services** (☎ 541/395-2232 or 541/395-2647), which also offers raft rentals and car shuttles; **Ewings' Whitewater** (☎ **800/538-RAFT**), which also offers a combination rafting and mountain-biking trip; and **Rapid River Rafters** (☎ **800/962-3327** or 541/ 382-1514). Expect to pay around $75 for a day trip up to around $350 or $400 for a 3-day trip.

If you're just passing through the region but would like to catch a glimpse of some of the lower Deschutes River's more dramatic sections, you can visit **Sherar's Falls,** which are at the Sherar Bridge on Ore. 216 between Tygh Valley and Grass Valley. Native Americans can sometimes be seen dip-netting salmon from the waters of these falls, which can also be reached by following the river road north from Maupin for 8 miles. Just west of Sherar Bridge, you'll also find **White River Falls State Park,** where more waterfalls can be seen.

The stretch of the Deschutes River from Pelton Dam to the Columbia River is one of Oregon's most legendary stretches of **fishing** water and is managed primarily for wild steelhead and the famed red-side rainbow trout. Together these two types of fish provide fly anglers with nearly year-round action. From the mouth of the river upstream to several miles above Maupin, there are several good access points. Fly-fishing supplies are available in Maupin at the **Deschutes Canyon Fly Shop,** 7 N. Hwy. 197, Maupin (☎ **541/395-2565**).

South of Madras 12 miles you'll find one of the most unlikely of settings in the state. **Lake Billy Chinook,** an artificial lake created by the construction of Round Butte Dam in 1964, now fills the canyons of the Metolius, Crooked, and Deschutes rivers and seems lifted straight out of the canyonlands of Arizona or Utah. Here nearly vertical basalt cliffs rise several hundred feet above the lake waters and sagebrush and junipers cling to the rocky hillsides. The lake is most popular with water-skiers and anglers who come to fish for kokanee (landlocked sockeye salmon) and bull trout (also known as dolly vardens).

Lake access is provided at **The Cove Palisades State Park** (☎ **541/546-3412**), where you'll find boat ramps, a marina, campgrounds, picnic areas, and swimming beaches. There are even houseboats for rent here (see below), and at the marina, you'll find a restaurant atop a hill overlooking the lake.

A NATIVE AMERICAN HERITAGE MUSEUM

○ **The Museum at Warm Springs.** U.S. 26, Warm Springs. ☎ **541/553-3331.** Admission $6 adults, $5 seniors, $3 children. Daily 10am–5pm.

For thousands of years the Warm Springs, Wasco, and Paiute tribes have inhabited this region, part of which is today the Confederated Tribes of the Warm Springs Reservation, and adapted to its environment. It is the history of these peoples that is presented in this impressive modern museum. Over the decades prior to the opening of the museum, the tribes amassed an outstanding collection of regional Native American artifacts, which now form the core of the museum's collection. To better display these artifacts, various styles of traditional houses have been reconstructed at the museum and serve as backdrops for displays on everything from basketry and beadwork to fishing and root gathering. Exhibits on traditional drumming, singing, and dancing are of particular interest, and there are new temporary exhibits every 3 months.

A GHOST TOWN & A FOSSIL EXCURSION

Between 1900 and 1911 **Shaniko** was the largest wool-shipping center in the country, and claims to have been the site of the last range war between cattle ranchers and sheep herders. However, when the railroad line from the Columbia River down to Bend bypassed Shaniko, the town fell on hard times. Eventually, when a flood washed out the railroad into town, Shaniko nearly ceased to exist. Today the false-fronted buildings and wooden sidewalks make this Oregon's favorite and liveliest ghost town. Antique shops, a wedding chapel, and a historic hotel make for a fun excursion or overnight getaway. Each year on the first weekend of August, the **Shaniko Days** celebration brings life to the town with stagecoach rides, shoot-outs, and plenty of crafts vendors.

Eight miles south of Shaniko is the town of **Antelope,** which gained infamy back in the early 1980s as the home of Rajneeshpuram, the U.S. commune founded by followers of Indian mystic Bagwhan Shree Rajneesh.

The **John Day Fossil Beds National Monument,** consisting of three separate units separated by as much as 85 miles, preserves a 40-million-year fossil record that indicates this region was once a tropical or subtropical forest. From tiny seeds to extinct relatives of the rhinoceros and elephant, an amazing array of plants and animals have been preserved in this region in one of the world's most extensive and unbroken fossil records.

To see fossil leaves, twigs, branches, and nuts in their natural state, visit the **Clarno Unit,** 23 miles southeast of Shaniko and U.S. 97. Here ancient mudflows inundated a forest, and today these ancient mudflows appear as eroding cliffs, at the base of which a 1/4-mile trail leads past numerous fossils. From here it is an 85-mile drive on Ore. 218 and Ore. 19 to the national monument's **Sheep Rock Unit,** which is the site of the monument **Visitor Center.** Here you can get a close-up look at numerous fossils and sometimes watch a paleontologist at work. The visitor center is open daily in summer from 8:30am to 6pm (hours vary in other months). Just north of the visitors center you'll pass **Blue Basin,** where there's an interpretive trail.

From the Sheep Rock Unit, the monument's **Painted Hills Unit,** along the John Day River near Mitchell, is another 30 miles west on U.S. 26. Here you won't see any fossils, but you will see strikingly colored rounded hills that are favorites of photographers. The bands of color on these hills were caused by the weathering of volcanic ash under different climatic conditions.

For more information, contact the **John Day Fossil Beds National Monument,** HCR 82, Box 126, Kimberly, OR 97848 (☎ **541/987-2333**).

While you can't collect fossils on the national monument, you can dig them up behind the Wheeler High School in the small town of **Fossil,** 20 miles east of the Clarno Unit. You can also dig for agates, jasper, and thundereggs at **Richardson's Recreational Ranch** (☎ **541/475-2680**), 17 miles southwest of Madras off U.S. 97.

WHERE TO STAY & DINE

In addition to the resort and the historic hotel listed below, you'll also find three modern log cabins for rent on the shore of Lake Billy Chinook at **The Cove Palisades State Park.** These cabins rent for $45 to $65 per night for up to five people and are right beside the water. For reservations, call **Reservations Northwest** (☎ **800/452-5687**). Houseboats are also available for rent at Lake Billy Chinook through The Cove Palisades State Park for $1,050 to $1,590 per week (reserve through Reservations Northwest) and through **Chinook Water Chalets,** P.O. Box 40, Culver, OR 97734 (☎ **541/546-2939**), for $1,100 to $1,950 per week.

✪ **Kah-Nee-Ta Resort.** P.O. Box K, Warm Springs, OR 97761. ☎ **800/554-4SUN** or 541/553-1112. 169 rms, 5 suites, 20 teepees. A/C TV TEL. $95–$155 double; $140–$215 suite; $45–$65 tepee. AE, CB, DC, DISC, MC, V.

Although the rooms here are not nearly as nice as those at Bend area resorts, Kah-Nee-Ta, operated by the Confederated Tribes of the Warm Springs Reservation, remains a popular getaway for the simple reason that, being only 120 miles from Portland, it is the closest sunny-side resort for the rain-soaked citizens of the Willamette Valley. The setting, in a remote section of the Warm Springs River valley, gives the resort a unique, isolated atmosphere. Kah-Nee-Ta offers a wide range of activities and accommodations. The main lodge sits atop a bluff that commands a brilliant vista of the high desert, while down by the river you'll find motel units as well as teepees and RV sites. Beside the river you'll also find the resort's famous warm-water swimming pool, which is fed by the spring for which the Warm Springs Indians and the reservation are named.

Dining/Entertainment: Two dining rooms serve a mix of American dishes and Northwest specialties. Over in the camping area by the pool are a snack bar and a more casual restaurant. During the summer months a traditional salmon bake is held on Saturday evening and is followed by traditional Native American dancing.

If you'd like to do your own dancing, check out the Appaloosa Lounge in the main lodge.

Services: Resort shuttle, bicycle rentals, kayak rentals, horseback riding, massage, fishing-rod rentals, white-water rafting trips.

Facilities: Casino, golf course, naturally heated outdoor pool plus a second pool at the main lodge, mineral baths and various spa treatments, fitness center, games room, tennis courts.

✪ **Shaniko Historic Hotel.** Fourth and E sts., Shaniko, OR 97057. ☎ **800/483-3441** or 541/ 489-3441. 18 rms. $66–$96 double. Rates include full breakfast. DISC, MC, V.

This restored two-story brick hotel is a surprisingly solid little place in a ghost town full of glorified shacks. However, don't start thinking that this is a fancy B&B; it's not. Most rooms are fairly small and simply furnished and carpets are getting old, but guests don't seem to mind. No one comes out here to be pampered; they come for a bit of rustic Wild West atmosphere, and that's exactly what they get. The faded elegance hints at the wealth that once made the fortunes of area sheep ranchers, and the covered wooden sidewalk out front conjures up images of the Wild West. The bridal suite is the hotel's largest room.

CAMPGROUNDS

Beavertail Campground, 17 miles southeast of Maupin on the Deschutes River Road, is one of the only established campgrounds in this area. Downriver from Sherar's Falls, there are many undeveloped campsites along the river. At Lake Billy Chinook, west of U.S. 97 between Madras and Redmond, there are several campgrounds. The most developed are the two at **The Cove Palisades State Park.** Farther west, up the Metolius arm of the reservoir on F.S. Road 64, you'll find the forest service's primitive **Perry South Campground.** A little bit farther west is the **Monty Campround,** which is the lowermost campground on the Metolius River's free-flowing waters.

2 The Sisters Area

108 miles SE of Salem, 92 miles NE of Eugene, 21 miles NW of Bend

Lying at the eastern foot of the Cascades, the small Western-theme town of Sisters takes its name from the nearby Three Sisters mountains, which loom majestically over the town. Ponderosa pine forests, aspen groves, and wide meadows surround Sisters, giving it a classic Western setting that the town has cashed in on in recent years. Modern buildings sport false fronts and covered sidewalks, though the predominantly pastel color schemes are more 1990s than 1890s.

Once just someplace to stop for gas on the way to Bend, Sisters is now a destination in itself. A few miles outside of town is the Black Butte Resort, one of the state's finest golf resorts, and also nearby is the tiny community of Camp Sherman, which has been a vacation destination for most of this century. Sisters has also become Oregon's llama capital, with numerous large llama ranches around the area. One of these ranches, just west of town on Ore. 242, also raises elk, which can often be seen from the roadside.

ESSENTIALS

GETTING THERE   The **Redmond Municipal Airport,** 20 miles east of Sisters, is served by Horizon Airlines and United Airlines. **CAC Transportation** (☎ **800/ 955-8267** or 541/382-1687) operates the **Redmond Airport Shuttle** between the airport, Sisters, and Bend. There are also taxis operating from the airport.

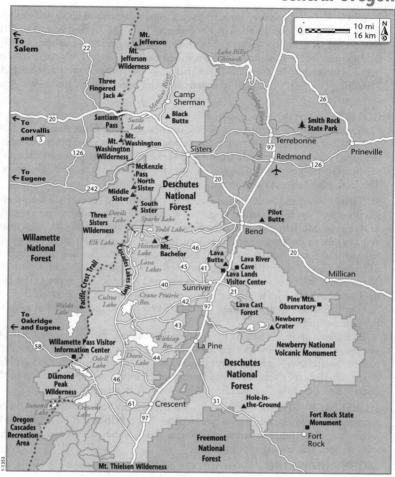

VISITOR INFORMATION   Contact the **Sisters Area Chamber of Commerce,** 352 W. Hood Ave. (P.O. Box 430), Sisters, OR 97759 (☎ **541/549-0251**).

FESTIVALS   During the annual **Sisters Outdoor Quilt Show** on the second Saturday in July, buildings all over town are hung with quilts. The **Sisters Rodeo,** held the second weekend of June, also attracts large crowds.

ENJOYING THE OUTDOORS

While shopping may be the number one recreational activity right in Sisters, the surrounding lands are the town's real main attraction. Any month of the year, you'll find an amazing variety of possible activities within a few miles of town. One of the area's top outdoors attractions lies to the west of Sisters in the community of Camp Sherman. It is here that you'll find the springs that form the **headwaters of the Metolius River.** Cold, crystal-clear waters bubble up out of the ground here and within only a few hundred yards, produce a full-blown river.

FLY-FISHING   If you need some fly-fishing supplies or want to hire a guide to take you out fishing the local waters, **The Fly Fisher's Place,** 151 W. Main Ave. (☎ 541/549-3474), is the place to visit. The folks here can guide you to the best **fly-fishing** spots on the Deschutes, McKenzie, and Crooked rivers. If it's the nearly impossible waters of the Metolius River that you want to try, contact **John Judy Flyfishing** (☎ 541/595-2073) in Camp Sherman, which can set you up with gear and a guide.

GOLFING   The two area resorts, Black Butte Ranch, west of Sisters, and Eagle Crest, east of town, both have two 18-hole courses. At **Black Butte Ranch** (☎ 800/399-2322 or 541/595-1500) you'll play surrounded by ponderosa pines and aspens ($55 greens fee), while at **Eagle Crest** (☎ 541/923-4653), you get a more desertlike experience with junipers and sagebrush surrounding the fairways ($40 greens fee). There are great views at either resort.

HIKING   West and south of Sisters, several excellent and scenic trails lend themselves both to day hikes and overnight trips. Many of these trails lead into the Mt. Washington, Mt. Jefferson, and Three Sisters wilderness areas. Near Camp Sherman, you can hike to the summit of Black Butte for 360° views or hike along the spring-fed Metolius River. Farther west off U.S. 20, you'll find trails leading up to the base of craggy Three Fingered Jack. South of town there are trailheads leading into the Three Sisters Wilderness (the Chambers Lakes area is particularly scenic). The hike up Tam McArthur Rim is another good one if you're looking for spectacular views. Stop by the **Sisters Ranger Station** (☎ 541/549-2111) at the west end of town for information and trail maps.

   To the east of Sisters outside the town of Terrebonne, there are several miles of very scenic hiking trails within **Smith Rock State Park.** The park's 400-foot crags and the meandering Crooked River provide the backdrops for hikes through high desert scrublands. Hiking trails lead through the canyon and up to the top of the rocks. The view of the Cascades framed by Smith Rock is superb.

HORSEBACK RIDING   If Sisters has put you in a cowboy state of mind, you can saddle up a palomino and go for a ride at **Black Butte Stables** (☎ 541/595-2061), which is at Black Butte Ranch west of Sisters. These stables offer a variety of rides, with an hour ride costing about $22.

MOUNTAIN BIKING   Sisters makes an excellent base for mountain bikers, who will find dozens of miles of trails of all skill levels within a few miles of town. In fact, one easy ride starts only a few blocks from downtown's many shops. Other fun rides include the Butte Loops Trail around Black Butte and the strenuous Green Ridge Trail. Stop by the **Sisters Ranger Station** (☎ 541/549-2111) at the west end of town for information and trail maps. During the summer, you can rent bikes in town at **Mountain Supply,** 143 Hood St. (☎ 541/549-3251), for about $7 per day.

ROCK CLIMBING   East of Terrebonne, **Smith Rock State Park** is one of central Oregon's many geological wonders. Jagged rock formations tower above the Crooked River here and attract rock climbers from around the world. Before heading out here to climb, you should pick up a copy of the Alan Watts' *Climber's Guide to Smith Rock* (Chockstone Press, 1992), which describes hundreds of routes among these rocks. You can pick up this book and other climbing supplies at **Redpoint Climbers' Supply,** 975 Smith Rock Way (☎ 800/923-6207 or 541/923-6207), at the corner of U.S. 97 in Terrebonne, and **Rockhard Climbing and Clothing Gear,** 9297 NE Crooked River Dr. (☎ 541/548-4786), right outside the park entrance. This latter shop is also famous for its huckleberry ice cream. If you want to learn how to climb, contact **First Ascent Climbing School & Guide Service** (☎ **800/ 325-5462** or 541/548-5137), which offers group ($75 per day), semiprivate ($90 per day), and private ($165 per day) climbing lessons. **Vertical Ventures** (☎ **541/ 389-7937**) also offers rock-climbing classes at similar prices.

FOLK ART, REINDEERS & OTHER THINGS TO SEE & DO

Fans of folk art should be sure to stop by the **Petersen Rock Gardens,** 7930 SW 77th St., Redmond (☎ **541/382-5574**), 9 miles north of Bend just off U.S. 97. This 4-acre folk-art creation consists of buildings, miniature bridges, terraces, and tiny towers all constructed from rocks. The gardens, built between 1935 and 1952 by a Danish immigrant farmer, are open daily from 9am to dusk; admission is $2 adults, $1 ages 12 to 17, and 50¢ ages 6 to 11.

Rail travel fans might consider an excursion on the **Crooked River Railroad Company Dinner Train,** 525 SW Sixth St. (☎ **541/548-8630**). The 38-mile, $2^1/_2$-hour rail excursion travels from Redmond to Prineville and back. Restored dining cars are the elegant setting for the four-course dinners. Fares are $69 for adults and $32 for children 12 and under. Reservations are required.

A couple of local attractions will likely appeal to kids. **Reindeer Ranch at Operation Santa Claus** (☎ **541/548-8910**), located 2 miles west of Redmond on Ore. 126, is the largest reindeer ranch in the United States and is home to more than 100 reindeer. It's open daily and admission is free.

WHERE TO STAY

In addition to the accommodations listed below, you'll find two very nice rooms available upstairs from the **Kokanee Café** in Camp Sherman (see "Where to Dine," below). They go for $60 double.

❂ **Black Butte Ranch.** P.O. Box 8000, Black Butte Ranch, OR 97759. ☎ **800/452-7455** or 541/595-6211. Fax 541/595-2077. 19 rms, 16 condos, 70 homes. TV TEL. $85–$137 double; $163–$295 condo or home. AE, DISC, MC, V.

This resort 8 miles west of Sisters is built on a former ranch and offers stunning views of the Cascade peaks across the meadows of a wide valley. With its two golf courses and wide range of scheduled activities and recreational opportunities, Black Butte appeals primarily to families. The condos and homes are set amid open lawns between the forest and the meadows, and most have fireplaces and kitchens. Large decks and sliding glass doors let you enjoy the views no matter what the weather. If you're planning to bring the whole family, one of the vacation homes may be the best bet.

Dining/Entertainment: The Lodge restaurant is built around a huge old ponderosa, and large windows provide nearly every table with a view of the mountains or the lake. The menu focuses on steaks and seafood. A cozy lounge is upstairs from the dining room. A poolside cafe provides casual family dining.

Services: Canoe rentals, bicycle rentals, horseback riding, white-water rafting, nature walks, children's programs.

Facilities: Two 18-hole golf courses, outdoor pool, tennis courts, recreation center, sports field, 16 miles of bike and jogging trails, pro shop, sports shop.

Conklin's Guest House. 69013 Camp Polk Rd., Sisters, OR 97759. ☎ **800/549-4262** or 541/549-0123. Fax 541/549-4481. Web site: www.informat.com/bz/conklins. 5 rms. $90–$110 double. Rates include full breakfast. No credit cards.

Surrounded by meadows and with an unobstructed view of the mountains, Conklin's bed-and-breakfast is an excellent choice for anyone who has become enamored of Sisters's Western charm. The inn's country decor fits right in with the town, and a duck pond and a trout pond provide a bit of a farm feel. There's even a swimming pool, and breakfast is served in a tile-floored sunroom. Our favorite room has a big old claw-foot tub surrounded by windows that look out to the Cascades. This room also has its own little balcony. One of the rooms here actually is sort of a dormitory with six beds ($25 to $30 per person per night), which makes it great for families.

✪ **Eagle Crest Resort.** P.O. Box 1215, Redmond, OR 97756. ☎ **800/682-4786** or 541/ 923-2453. 54 rms, 46 suites, 200 two- to three-bedroom townhouses. A/C TV TEL. $61–$97 double; $84–$123 suite; $119–$239 townhouse. AE, DISC, MC, V.

Less than 20 miles east of Sister is another sprawling resort that attracts sun worshipers and golfers. The landscape is much drier here than around Sisters and is dominated by scrubby junipers that give Eagle Crest the feel of a desert resort. The rooms overlook the golf course rather than the mountains, which should give you an idea of most guests' priorities. Facilities here are, unfortunately, geared primarily toward owners of homes and condos.

Dining/Entertainment: The restaurant is located on the opposite side of the golf course from the main building, so you'll have to walk or drive. The decor here is very traditional, and the menu sticks to traditional continental dishes.

Services: Tennis clinics, horseback riding, massage and other spa treatments, aerobics classes, bicycle rentals, complimentary airport shuttle, baby-sitting, teen club.

Facilities: Two golf courses, outdoor pool, hot tub, indoor and outdoor tennis courts, playing field, jogging trails, beauty salon.

✪ **Metolius River Resort.** 25551 SW F.S. Rd. 1419, Camp Sherman, OR 97730. ☎ **800/ 81-TROUT.** 11 cabins. $120–$160 double. Two-night minimum. Lower rates in off-season. MC, V.

These contemporary shake-sided two-story cabins 14 miles west of Sisters are exceptional, offering modern amenities and styling with a bit of a rustic feel. Peeled log beds, wood paneling, river-stone fireplaces, and green roofs give the cabins a quintessential Western appearance. Set on the banks of the spring-fed Metolius River not far from the river's source, the cabins are particularly popular with trout anglers. Despite the name, this is hardly a resort—it's a secluded getaway that will be appreciated by anyone looking for peace and quiet. Great for romantic getaways, too.

CAMPGROUNDS

There are eight forest service campgrounds strung out along F.S. Road 14 north of Camp Sherman. All of these campgrounds are on the banks of the river and are most popular with anglers. The first of these, the **Camp Sherman Campground** is only ¹/₂ mile north of Camp Sherman, while the most remote, the **Lower Bridge Campground,** is 9 miles north (the last ¹/₂ mile of which is on a rough dirt road). South of Sisters, at the end of F.S. Road 16, there are three campgrounds at or near Three Creek Lake.

WHERE TO DINE

No visit to Sisters is complete without a stop at the **Sisters Bakery,** 251 E. Cascade St. (☎ **541/549-0361**), for marionberry pastries and bear claws.

Hotel Sisters and Bronco Billy's Saloon. 190 E. Cascade St. ☎ **541/549-7427.** Reservations recommended. Meals $6–$20. MC, V. Daily 11am–10pm. AMERICAN.

Though it's no longer a hotel, the Hotel Sisters does serve up some Wild West grub in the form of belt-loosening platters of barbecued ribs, chicken breasts, and hot links. The decor, with its Victorian wallpaper and lace curtains, is a bit too fussy for a rib house, but step through the swinging saloon doors into the bar and you'll find genuine Western atmosphere, including a buffalo head on the wall.

✪ **Kokanee Café.** Camp Sherman. ☎ **541/595-6420.** Reservations recommended. Main courses $10–$21. MC, V. Daily 5–9pm. Closed Nov–Mar. NORTHWEST.

The Kokanee Café is located adjacent to the Metolius River Resort in Camp Sherman, about 15 miles west of Sisters. This out-of-the-way place is one of the best restaurants in the region and serves Northwest cuisine with an Oregon slant. The interior of the log building is contemporary rustic with an open-beamed ceiling and wrought-iron chandelier. Out back there's a deck under the ponderosa pines. The menu is short and includes daily chalkboard specials such as king salmon with tarragon cream sauce and fresh-grilled ahi with Szechuan vinaigrette. The always-interesting dessert menu might include Oregon hazelnut cheesecake or berry pie.

3 Bend: Skiing, Hiking, Fishing, Mountain Scenery & More

160 miles SE of Portland, 241 miles SW of Pendleton

Situated on the banks of the Deschutes River, this town was originally named Farewell Bend but said good-bye to its Farewell in 1905 at the insistence of postal authorities. Lumber mills supported the local economy for much of Bend's history, but today retirees, skiers, and lovers of the outdoors are fueling the town's growth.

Today, with only about 33,000 residents, Bend is still the largest city east of the Oregon Cascades, and the surrounding area has more resorts than any other location in the state. To understand why a small town on the edge of a vast high desert could attract so many vacationers, just look to the sky. It's blue. And the sun is shining. For the webfoots who spend months under gray skies west of the Cascades, that's enough of an attraction.

However, Bend doesn't end with sunny skies; it also offers the biggest and best ski area in the Northwest: Mount Bachelor. Several other mountains—the Three Sisters and Broken Top among them—provide a breathtaking backdrop for the city, and their pine-covered slopes, many lakes, and trout streams attract hikers, mountain bikers, sailors, and anglers. A lively downtown area filled with interesting shops, excellent restaurants, and attractive Drake Park (which is named for the city's founder, A.M. Drake, and not for the ducks that are the park's major attraction) complement the outdoor offerings of the area, and it's sometimes difficult to tell which is more popular.

ESSENTIALS

GETTING THERE   Bend is at the junction of U.S. 97, which runs north and south, and U.S. 20, which runs east to west across the state. From the Portland area, the most direct route is by way of U.S. 26 to Madras and then south on U.S. 97.

The **Redmond Municipal Airport,** 16 miles north of Bend, is served by Horizon Airlines and United Airlines. **CAC Transportation** (☎ **800/955-8267** or 541/382-1687) operates the **Redmond Airport Shuttle** between the airport, Sisters, and Bend. In addition, they operate a shuttle bus between the Portland International Airport, Portland's Union Station (Amtrak) and Bend. There are also taxis operating from the airport.

VISITOR INFORMATION   Contact the **Bend Chamber of Commerce,** 63085 N. U.S. 97, Bend, OR 97701-5765 (☎ **541/382-3221**).

GETTING AROUND Car rentals are available from **Avis** (☎ **800/831-2847**), **Budget** (☎ **800/527-0700**), and **Hertz** (☎ **800/654-3131**). If you need a taxi, call **Owl Taxi Service** (☎ **541/382-3311**).

FESTIVALS The **Cascade Festival of Music** (☎ **541/383-2202**), held each August in Drake Park is Bend's biggest festival.

EXPLORING THE BEND AREA

If you'd like to have a guide show you around the area, contact **Wanderlust Tours** (☎ **800/962-2862** or 541/389-8359), which offers trips to many of the region's attractions. Full-day tour rates range from $26 to $52.

✪ **The High Desert Museum.** 59800 S. U.S. 97. ☎ **541/382-4754.** Admission $6.25 adults, $5.75 students and seniors, $3 children 5–12. Daily 9am–5pm. Closed Jan 1, Thanksgiving, and Dec 25. Take U.S. 97 3^1/2 miles south of Bend.

Bend lies on the westernmost edge of the Great Basin, a region that stretches from the Cascade Range to the Rocky Mountains and is often called the high desert. Through the use of historical exhibits, live animal displays, and reconstructions of pioneer buildings, this museum, one of the finest in the Northwest, brings the cultural and natural history of the region into focus. In the main building is a walk-through timeline of Western history. The natural history of the region comes alive in the Desertarium, where live animals of the region can be observed in very natural settings—the frolicking river otters and slow-moving porcupines are the star attractions. A pioneer homestead and a forestry exhibit with a steam-driven sawmill round out the outdoor exhibits. Informative talks are scheduled throughout the day, and throughout the year, the museum holds classes, workshops, and lectures. A discovery center provides a play and learning area for small children, and in 1999, a new birds of prey center is scheduled to open. The museum also has a good little cafe.

Des Chutes Historical Center. 129 NW Idaho Ave. ☎ **541/389-1813.** Admission $2 adults, $1 children 6–12. Tues–Sat 10am–4:30pm.

To learn more about the history of central Oregon, stop by this museum, which is housed in a 1914 stone school building at the south end of downtown.

Pine Mountain Observatory. 35 miles east of Bend off U.S. 20. ☎ **541/382-8331.** Admission $2. May–Sept Fri–Sat from 8:30pm.

The same clear skies that attract vacationers to central Oregon have also attracted astronomers. At this small observatory, you, too, can gaze at the stars and planets through a 15-inch telescope.

EXPLORING CENTRAL OREGON'S VOLCANIC LANDSCAPE

From snow-covered peaks to lava caves, past volcanic activity and geologic history are everywhere visible around Bend. For a sweeping panoramic view of the Cascade Range, head up to the top of **Pilot Butte** at the east end of Greenwood Avenue. From the top of this cinder cone, you can see Mount Hood (11,235 feet), Mount Jefferson (10,495 feet), Three-Fingered Jack (7,848 feet), Mount Washington (7,802 feet), North Sister (10,094 feet), Middle Sister (10,053 feet), South Sister (10,354 feet), Broken Top (9,165 feet), and Mount Bachelor (9,075 feet). All these peaks are volcanic in origin, even Mount Bachelor, which is the site of the Northwest's largest ski resort.

To the south of Bend lies a region of relatively recent volcanic activity that has been preserved as the **Newberry National Volcanic Monument.** The best place to start an exploration of the national monument is at the **Lava Lands Visitor Center,**

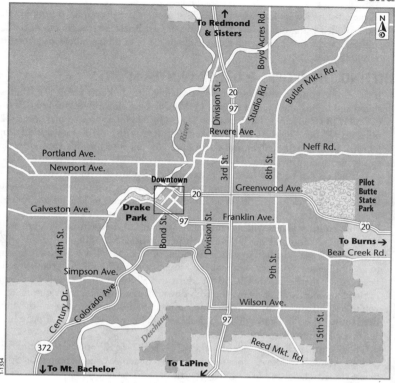

To Redmond & Sisters

Boyd Acres Rd.

Butler Mkt. Rd.

Division St.

20
97

Studio Rd.

River

Revere Ave.

Neff Rd.

Portland Ave.

Newport Ave.

3rd St.

8th St.

Downtown

20

Greenwood Ave.

Pilot Butte State Park

Galveston Ave.

Drake Park

Bond St.

97

Division St.

Franklin Ave.

20

To Burns →
Bear Creek Rd.

14th St.

Simpson Ave.

9th St.

Century Dr.

Colorado Ave.

Wilson Ave.

15th St.

Deschutes

372

97

Reed Mkt. Rd.

↓ To Mt. Bachelor

To LaPine

N

1-1354

58201 S. U.S. 97 (☎ **541/593-2421**), 11 miles south of Bend and open from about April through October. Here you can learn about the titanic forces that sculpted this region. An interpretive trail outside the center wanders through a lava flow at the base of 500-foot-tall **Lava Butte,** an ominous black cinder cone. In summer, a shuttle bus ($2 for adults, $1.50 for children and seniors) will take you to the summit of the cone. From here you have another outstanding view of the Cascades, and can explore the crater on another trail.

A mile to the south, you'll find the **Lava River Cave,** which is actually a long tube formed by lava flows. The cave is more than a mile long and takes about an hour to explore. Admission is $2.50 for adults, $2 for children 13 to 17 and seniors, plus $1.50 for lantern rentals. When lava flowed across this landscape, it often inundated pine forests, leaving in its wake only molds of the trees. At **Lava Cast Forest,** 9 miles down a very rough road off U.S. 97 south of Lava River Cave, a paved trail leads past such molds. Continuing farther south on U.S. 97 will bring you to the turnoff for the **Newberry Crater** area, the centerpiece of the monument. Covering 500 square miles, the crater contains Paulina and East Lakes, both of which are popular with boaters and anglers, and numerous volcanic features, including an astounding flow of obsidian. Today there are rental cabins and campgrounds within the national monument, and 150 miles of hiking trails.

If, after thoroughly exploring all the local volcanic features, you still want to see more geologic wonders, head south 75 miles or so to **Fort Rock State Park** and the nearby **Hole-in-the-Ground,** both of which are off Ore. 31. These unusual volcanic features were formed when lakes of molten lava encountered groundwater and exploded with great violence. The walls of Fort Rock rise straight out of the flat landscape and form almost a full circle. Hole-in-the-Ground is a mile-wide crater 200 to 300 feet deep.

HITTING THE SLOPES & OTHER WINTER SPORTS

If downhill skiing is your passion, you probably already know about the fabulous skiing conditions and myriad runs of ○ **Mount Bachelor Ski & Summer Resort** (☎ **541/382-2442** for information, or 541/382-7888 for a snow report), located 22 miles west of Bend on the Cascades Lakes Highway. With a 3,100-foot vertical drop, 60 runs, 11 lifts, 6 day lodges, and skiing from November to July, it's no wonder that this is the training area for the U.S. Ski Team.

Lift tickets can be purchased for the day or on a point system that allows you to make a few runs and come back another day or share the rest of your points with a friend. Day lift tickets are $39 for adults, $20 for children 7 to 12, and free for children 6 and under.

Cross-country skiers will also find plenty of trails to choose from. Just be sure to stop by a ski shop and buy a **Sno-Park** permit before heading up to the cross-country trailheads, the best of which are along the Cascades Lakes Highway leading to Mount Bachelor ski area. At the ski area itself, there are 90 miles of groomed trails. Passes to use these trails are $10.50 for adults and $5 for children. Ski shops abound in Bend and nearly all of them rent both downhill and cross-country equipment. If you're heading to Mount Bachelor, you can rent equipment there, or try the **Powder House,** 311 SW Century Dr. (☎ **541/389-6234**), on the way out of Bend heading toward Mount Bachelor.

The **Mount Bachelor Super Shuttle** (☎ **541/382-2442**) operates between Bend and the ski resort and leaves from the corner of Colorado Avenue and Simpson Street, where there's a large parking lot. The shuttle costs $1 each way.

If you've had enough skiing, how about a **dogsled ride?** At **Oregon Trail of Dreams** (☎ **800/829-2442** or 541/382-2442) you can take a 1-hour dogsled ride and then learn about the care of sled dogs. Rates are $60 for adults and $10 for children 3 and under. All-day and overnight trips are also available.

Easy 1-mile **snowshoe nature walks** are led by ranger-naturalists on Saturday and Sunday at 10am and 1:30pm starting from the **West Village Ski & Sport Building** on Mt. Bachelor. Meet half an hour before the walk; snowshoes are provided. For more information call ☎ **541/388-5664.**

SUMMER ACTIVITIES

Both hiking and mountain biking are available at Mount Bachelor in the summer, when a chair lift operates to the 9,065-foot top of the mountain; the fare is $10 for adults, $9 for seniors, $5 for children 7 to 12, and free for children 6 and under. From here you may either ride the chair or hike down. Bike rentals are available for biking around the mountain.

FISHING   If fishing is your passion, you've come to the right place. The Deschutes River flows right through downtown Bend and some good trout waters can be found both upstream and downstream of town. The lakes of the Cascade Lakes Highway west of Bend are, however, the most popular fishing destinations in the area. Of these, Hosmer Lake, with its catch-and-release, fly-fishing only, is perhaps the most fabled fishing spot. If you're not familiar with these rivers and lakes, you may want to hire a guide to show you where to hook into a big one. Try contacting **John Garrison** (☎ **541/593-8394**) or **Fishing on the Fly** (☎ **800/952-0707** or 541/389-3252).

Expect to pay between $150 and $165 for a day of fishing. Fly-fishing supplies are available at **The Fly Box,** 1293 NE Third St. (☎ **541/388-3330**).

GOLF   For many of central Oregon's visitors, Bend's abundance of sunshine means only one thing—plenty of rounds of golf at more than 20 area golf courses. Of the resort courses in the area, the three courses at **Sunriver** (☎ **800/962-1769** or 541/ 593-1000) are the most highly regarded, and the recently opened Crosswater course was voted "Best New Resort Course" by *Golf Digest.* This outstanding and scenic course is also one of the most expensive in the area at $115 for 18 holes. Sunriver's two older courses, Meadows and Woodlands, are more reasonably priced at $50 and $65 respectively.

Right in Bend, you'll find more reasonable prices at the Riverhouse resort's **River's Edge Golf Course,** 3075 N. U.S. 97 (☎ **541/389-2828**), where 18 holes will cost you only $36. **Awbrey Glen Golf Club,** Mt. Washington Drive (☎ **800/697-0052** or 541/388-8526), and **Widgi Creek,** Century Drive (☎ **541/382-4449**), are the two most highly regarded semiprivate clubs in the area. Greens fees are $62 and $75, respectively. **Mountain High Golf Course,** China Hat Road (☎ **541/382-1111**), is yet another area 18-hole course open to the public. The greens fee is $40.

HIKING   Hiking is one of the most popular summer activities here, but keep in mind that high-country trails may be closed by snow until late June or early July.

Just to limber up or for a quick breath of fresh air, head up to the north end of Northwest First Street where you'll find a 3-mile-long trail along the Deschutes River. However, our favorite trail is the ✪ **Deschutes River Trail,** which parallels the Deschutes for several miles. To reach this trail, head 10 miles west on the Cascade Lakes Highway (Century Drive) and, after the Inn of the Seventh Mountain, turn left on F.S. 41 and follow the signs to Lava River Falls.

The **Three Sisters Wilderness,** which begins just over 20 miles from Bend or Sisters, offers secluded hiking among rugged volcanic peaks. Permits are required for overnight trips in the wilderness area and are currently available at trailheads. Currently, you'll also need a permit (available in Bend or Sisters at the ranger stations) to park at area trailheads. Contact the **Bend/Fort Rock Ranger Station,** 1230 NE Third St. (☎ **541/388-5664**), or the **Sisters Ranger Station** (☎ **541/549-2111**) in Sisters for trail maps and other information.

HORSEBACK RIDING   Down in Sunriver, you can get saddled up and ride the meadows and ponderosa pine forests at **Saddleback Stables** (☎ **541/593-1221,** ext. 4420), which offers a variety of rides with an hour ride costing about $22.

✪ **MOUNTAIN BIKING**   Mountain biking is fast becoming one of the most popular activities in central Oregon. When the snow melts, the cross-country ski trails become mountain-bike trails. Contact the **Bend/Fort Rock Ranger Station,** 1230 NE Third St. (☎ **541/388-5664**), to find out about trails open to mountain bikes. The most scenic trail open to mountain bikes is the Deschutes River Trail mentioned above.

Guided mountain-bike rides in Newberry National Volcanic Monument are offered by **High Cascade Descent Guide Service** (☎ **800/296-0562** or 541/ 389-0562). An easy downhill ride includes stops at waterfalls and a natural water slide; the cost is $37. Guided rides are also offered by **Pacific Crest Mountain Bike Tours** (☎ **800/849-6589** or 541/383-5058), with rates ranging from $40 to $75.

WHITE-WATER RAFTING   The Deschutes River, which passes through Bend, is the most popular river in Oregon for white-water rafting, although the best sections of river are 100 miles north of here (see the "North Central Oregon & the

Lower Deschutes River" section, above, for details). However, numerous local companies offer trips both on the lower section of the Deschutes and also on the stretch of the upper Deschutes between Sunriver and Bend. This latter stretch of the river is known as the Big Eddy run, and though it is short and really only has one major rapid, it is a quick introduction to rafting. Both **Cascade River Adventures** (☎ **800/770-2161** or 541/389-8370) and **Rapid River Rafters** (☎ **800/962-3327** or 541/382-1514) offer full-day trips on the lower Deschutes for $75 to $85. At the **Inn of the Seventh Mountain** (☎ **541/382-8711,** ext. 601), you can arrange to do the Big Eddy run for only $33.

A SCENIC DRIVE ALONG THE CASCADE LAKES HIGHWAY

During the summer the Cascade Lakes Highway is the most popular excursion out of Bend. Formerly known as Century Drive because it was a loop road of approximately 100 miles, this National Forest Scenic Byway is an 87-mile loop that packs in some of the finest scenery in the Oregon Cascades. Along the way are a dozen lakes and frequent views of the jagged Three Sisters peaks and the rounded Mount Bachelor. The lakes provide ample opportunities for boating, boardsailing, fishing, swimming, and picnicking.

At the **Central Oregon Welcome Center,** 63085 N. U.S. 97 in Bend (☎ **541/ 382-3221**), you can pick up a guide to the Cascade Lakes Highway. From mid-November to late May this road is closed west of Mount Bachelor because of snow.

The first area of interest along the highway is **Dutchman Flat,** just west of Mount Bachelor. This minidesert is caused by a thick layer of pumice that can support only a few species of plants. A little farther and you come to **Todd Lake,** a pretty little lake that is off the highway a bit and can only be reached by a short trail. Swimming, picnicking, and camping are all popular here.

The next lake along this route is **Sparks Lake,** a shallow marshy lake that has lava fields at its southern end. A trail meanders through these forested lava fields with frequent glimpses of the lake. The lake is a popular canoeing spot, though you'll need to bring your own boat. At the north end of the lake, you'll find the trailhead for a popular mountain-biking trail that heads south to Lava Lake. Across the highway from the marshes at the north end of the lake is the **trailhead for Green Lakes,** which are in the Three Sisters Wilderness at the foot of Broken Top Mountain. This is one of the most popular backpacking routes in the region and offers spectacular scenery. The hike to Green Lakes can also be done as a day hike. West of the Green Lakes trailhead is an area known as **Devils Garden,** where several springs surface on the edge of a lava flow. On a boulder here you can still see a few **Native American pictographs.** Apollo astronauts trained here before landing on the moon.

With its wide open waters and reliable winds, **Elk Lake** is popular for sailing and boardsailing. There are cabins, a lodge, and campsites around the lake. **Hosmer and Lava lakes** are both well known as good fishing lakes, while spring-fed **Little Lava Lake** is the source of the Deschutes River. **Cultus Lake,** with its sandy beaches, is a popular swimming lake. At the **Crane Prairie Reservoir** you can observe osprey between May and October. The **Twin Lakes** are examples of volcanic maars (craters) that have been filled by springs. These lakes have no inlets or outlets.

WHERE TO STAY

In addition to the accommodations listed below, you'll find hundreds of condos, cabins, and vacation homes in a wide range of prices available through **Sunset Realty** (☎ **800/541-1756** or 541/593-5018) and **Sunray** (☎ **800/531-1130**).

River Twister

Moving river waters are categorized on a scale of I to VI with Class I waters being swift but lacking any real rapids and Class VI being those waterfalls that not even crazy people paid to advertise beer and other questionable sports products would attempt. So, how do you categorize a tornado? That's a question that Ed Wheeler, river guide for Cascade River Adventures, is probably still pondering.

On July 26, 1996, Wheeler was leading a boatload of six clients through the Deschutes River's popular Big Eddy run just upstream from Bend when a giant dust devil (or miniature tornado depending on who you listen to) dropped onto the river. The twister sucked up water to a height of somewhere between 150 and 200 feet and barreled down the river straight for Wheeler's 1,000-pound raft. Everyone in the boat was more fascinated than fearful of this strange phenomenon, and no one thought to try to get out of its way. When the twister slammed into the raft, it lifted the boat 10 feet into the air, spun it around twice, and threw rafters and equipment into the river before depositing the raft back in the water, upside down. So powerful was the twister that it even sucked people's shoes right off their feet. Luckily no one was hurt, and everyone agreed it was the raft trip of a lifetime.

EXPENSIVE

✪ **Pine Ridge Inn.** 1200 SW Century Dr., Bend, OR 97702. ☎ **800/600-4095** or 541/389-6137. Fax 541/385-5669. 13 rms, 7 suites. A/C TV TEL. $95–$145 double; $140–$225 suite. Rates include full breakfast. AE, CB, DC, DISC, MC, V.

This small luxury inn on the outskirts of town provides an alternative accommodation for anyone who wants first-class surroundings but doesn't need all the facilities (and crowds) of the area's family oriented resorts. This is an ideal choice for romantic vacations and honeymoons, but is also a favorite of business travelers who need to be close to town. The inn is set on a bluff high above the Deschutes River, and though this particular stretch of river is not too attractive, you still get a river view (and pay extra for it, too). Whether you get a regular room or a suite, you'll have tons of space, including such features as sunken living rooms and fireplaces. Lots of antiques and artworks by regional artists give the inn a very distinctive style. Guests also receive complimentary afternoon Northwest wines and microbrews and access to a nearby athletic club.

MODERATE

Best Western/Entrada Lodge. 19221 Century Dr., Bend, OR 97702. ☎ **800/528-1234** or 541/382-4080. 79 rms. A/C TV TEL. $55–$89 double. Rates include continental breakfast. AE, CB, DC, DISC, MC, V.

Located a few miles west of Bend on the road to the Mount Bachelor ski area, this motel charges a little more for the peace and quiet that you won't find in in-town choices. Tall pine trees shade the grounds, and the Deschutes National Forest borders the property. The popular Deschutes River Trail is only a mile away. Facilities include an outdoor pool and a whirlpool.

Inn of the Seventh Mountain. 18575 SW Century Dr., Bend, OR 97702. ☎ **888/INN-7MTN,** 800/452-6810, or 541/382-8711. 260 rms, 159 suites. A/C TV TEL. $59–$115 double; $129–$269 suite. AE, CB, DC, DISC, MC, V.

This resort is the closest accommodation to Mount Bachelor and is especially popular with skiers in the winter. In summer an abundance of recreational activities turns the resort into a sort of summer camp for families. The guest rooms are done in a country decor and come in a wide range of sizes. Many have balconies and/or kitchens. Our favorites are the rooms perched on the edge of the wooded Deschutes River canyon.

Dining/Entertainment: Two restaurants, one serving creative meat-and-potato meals and the other a more casual sort of place, provide options at mealtimes. The fireside lounge is popular for après-ski gatherings.

Services: Tennis clinics, massage, children's summer camp, teen program, arts-and-crafts classes, white-water rafting, float trips, canoe trips, horseback riding, hayrides, mountain-bike rentals.

Facilities: Indoor and outdoor pools, whirlpools, indoor and outdoor tennis courts, pickle-ball courts, roller-skating rink, ice-skating rink, hiking/jogging trails, miniature golf course, playing fields, volleyball, basketball, horseshoes, playgrounds, horse stables.

Lara House Bed & Breakfast. 640 NW Congress St., Bend, OR 97701. ☎ **800/766-4064** or 541/388-4064. 6 rms. $60–$95 double. Rates include full breakfast. DISC, MC, V.

This large 1910 vintage home sits on a big lot diagonally across the street from downtown Bend's Drake Park and Mirror Pond. It is also only 2 blocks to the downtown commercial district, where you'll find lots of good restaurants. Guest rooms are all very spacious and are complemented by a comfortable living room with a fireplace and a sunroom that overlooks the large yard.

✪ Mount Bachelor Village Resort. 19717 Mount Bachelor Dr., Bend, OR 97702. ☎ **800/452-9846** or 541/389-5900. 60 rms, 60 suites. A/C TV TEL. $75–$94 double; $97–$229 suite. Minimum stay 2 nights; discounts for 3 nights or longer. AE, MC, V.

Most of Bend's resorts cater to families in the summer months and consequently can be very noisy and crowded. If you'd rather be able to hear the wind in the trees, this condominium resort is the place to check out. Most of the rooms have separate bedrooms, and many have fireplaces and kitchens. Views aren't too great unless you get one of the condos on the edge of the bluff, but there are balconies. The River Ridge condos are newer, have the better views, and are quite simply some of the nicest rooms in the area, with private outdoor hot tubs on the view decks and whirlpool tubs in the bathrooms.

Dining/Entertainment: The restaurant in the athletic club just down the hill from the condos features a brick oven and offers innovative meals. There's also a fireside lounge up by the swimming pool.

Facilities: Outdoor pool, two whirlpools, a nature trail, and an athletic club that includes indoor tennis courts, a climbing wall, an indoor track, weight room, spa facilities, and a wellness clinic.

✪ Sunriver Lodge & Resort. P.O. Box 3609, Sunriver, OR 97707. ☎ **800/547-3922** or 541/593-1000. Fax 541/593-5458. 130 rms, 81 suites, 262 condos. A/C TV TEL. $89–$149 double; $155–$215 suite; $135–$495 two- to four-bedroom condo. Lower rates off-season. AE, CB, DC, DISC, MC, V.

This sprawling resort is not so much a hotel as it is an entire town, and with a wealth of activities available for active vacationers it is the first choice of families vacationing in the area. Most of the accommodations overlook both the golf course and the mountains. Our favorite rooms are the loft suites, which have stone fireplaces, high ceilings, and rustic log furniture. Lots of pine trees shade the grounds and there are 30 miles of paved bicycle paths connecting the resort's many buildings (two bicycles come with every room). However, no matter how impressive the other facilities here are, it is the three golf courses here that attract the most business.

Dining/Entertainment: Meadow's, the resort's main dining room, displays Northwest creativity, with entree prices in the $10 to $20 range. The adjacent lounge offers a cozy fireplace. A casual cafe downstairs from the Meadow's offers the same view, and a separate lounge features live country and Top 40 music and a great deck. Golfers have two choices for quick meals or a drink. Guests can also dine at The Grille at Crosswater, the resort's newest upscale restaurant.

Services: Concierge, room service, aerobics classes, tennis clinics, horseback riding, bicycle, fishing-gear and canoe rentals, massage, children's programs, white-water rafting, shopping service.

Facilities: Three golf courses (including The Crosswater, which was voted "America's Best New Resort Course" by *Golf Digest,* two pools, 28 tennis courts, indoor miniature golf, ice-skating rink, pro shop.

INEXPENSIVE

Bend Riverside Motel. 1565 NW Hill St., Bend, OR 97701. ☎ **800/284-2363** or 541/389-2363. Fax 541/388-4000. 194 rms. A/C TV TEL. $52–$110 double. AE, CB, DC, DISC, MC, V.

You won't find a better-placed budget lodging in Bend, and if you don't mind rooms that are just a little out of the ordinary for a motel, you'll probably be happy here. Located on the banks of the Deschutes and bounded by Pioneer Park, this renovated older motel is only a few blocks from most of Bend's best restaurants. The cheapest rooms lack views and are rather cramped, however, for less than $25 more you can get a waterfront room with a great view of the Deschutes River. The slightly more expensive studio units also have fireplaces and kitchens. Facilities include an indoor pool, whirlpool, sauna, and tennis court.

✪ **The Riverhouse.** 3075 N. U.S. 97, Bend, OR 97701. ☎ **800/547-3928** or 541/389-3111. 220 rms, 30 suites. A/C TV TEL. $65–$74 double; $74–$175 suite. AE, CB, DC, DISC, MC, V.

Located at the north end of town on the banks of a narrow stretch of the Deschutes River, the Riverhouse is one of the best hotel deals we know of in the state. With its golf course and other resort facilities, it's an economical choice for anyone who wants resort amenities without the high prices. We like the ground-floor rooms that allow you to step off your patio and almost jump in the river. However, the rooms on the upper floor have a better view of this rocky stretch of river. All in all, we'd say that this is the best deal in Bend. Book early.

The hotel's main dining room is a steakhouse with a view of the river, and quick meals and drinks are also available poolside. The lounge features a variety of live entertainment. Facilities include an 18-hole golf course, indoor and outdoor pools, whirlpools, a sauna, an exercise room, and a pro shop.

CAMPGROUNDS

The closest campground to Bend is **Tumalo State Park,** 5 miles northwest of Bend off U.S. 20. **Dillon Falls Campground,** off the Cascade Lakes Highway 6.5 miles west of Bend, is the next closest and is set beside some of the most impressive falls on the river. The biggest campground in the area is **La Pine State Park,** which is accessible from U.S. 97 between Sunriver and La Pine.

Of the many campgrounds along the Cascade Lakes Highway, **Todd Lake Campground,** 25 miles west of Bend, is our favorite because it is enough of a walk from the parking lot to the campsites to discourage most car campers. **Devil's Lake Campground,** also a walk-in campground, is another favorite of ours. Farther south, there are lots of campgrounds on the many lakes along this road. Two of our favorites are the **Mallard Marsh** and **South** campgrounds, both of which are on beautiful Hosmer

Lake. The campgrounds at **Lava Lake** and **Little Lava Lake** are also fairly quiet, and the view from Lava Lake is the finest at any campground on this stretch of road.

WHERE TO DINE

Coffee addicts will want to spend time at the **Café Paradiso,** 945 NW Bond St. (☎ **541/385-5931**), a popular hangout that combines elegance and funkiness, or **Desert High Espresso,** 2205 NE Division St. (☎ **541/330-5987**), located in an unusual stone building that is something of a fold-art construction. The facade of the building is sort of a public rock collection exhibit. For good handcrafted ales and pub food, stop by the ✪ **Deschutes Brewery and Public House,** 1044 NW Bond St. (☎ **541/382-9242**), or the **Bend Brewing Co.,** 1019 Brooks St. (☎ **541/ 383-1599**). For dessert, **Hans,** 915 NW Wall St., (☎ **541/389-9700**), with a decadent selection of cakes and tortes, might catch your fancy.

EXPENSIVE

Broken Top Club Restaurant and Lounge. 61999 Broken Top Dr. ☎ **541/383-8210.** Reservations recommended. Main courses $17–$24, lunch $7–$8. MC, V. Tues–Sat 11:30am–2pm and 6–10pm. NORTHWEST/CONTINENTAL.

The very best reason to come to this restaurant, aside from its posh, rustic ambience, is to view the sun as it sets over Broken Top Mountain. Make sure your reservation coincides with sunset! Located at the private Broken Top Club on the Cascade Lakes Highway, this very upscale restaurant has a wall of glass that looks out on the golf course and a small lake as well as the mountain. The menu here emphasizes both Northwest regional flavors and continental dishes, and includes the likes of baked salmon with a lemon-lime crust and Beef Wellington. If you're in the mood for something lighter, there's also a separate appetizer menu. However, gourmet cuisine aside, the restaurant's best offering is still the fabulous view.

MODERATE

Pine Tavern Restaurant. 967 NW Brooks St. ☎ **541/382-5581.** Reservations highly recommended. Main courses $10.50–$18.95. AE, DISC, MC, V. Mon–Sat 11:30am–2:30pm and 5:30–9:30pm, Sun 5:30–9:30pm. AMERICAN.

Opened in 1936, the Pine Tavern Restaurant has been a local favorite for generations, and neither the decor nor the view has changed much over the years. Knotty pine and cozy booths give the restaurant an old-fashioned feel, while the 200-year-old ponderosa pines growing up through the center of one dining room provide a bit of grandeur. Most people ask for a table in the back room, which overlooks Mirror Pond. The menu is designed to appeal to a wide range of tastes and includes such dishes as sesame-ginger chicken, meat loaf, and fresh salmon. Many of the dishes meet American Heart Association guidelines. The restaurant is popular with families.

✪ **Rosette.** 150 NW Oregon St. ☎ **541/383-2780.** Reservations recommended. Main courses $15–$24, lunch $6–$8. MC, V. Mon 5–9pm, Tues–Thurs 11:30am–1:30pm and 5–9pm, Fri 11:30am–1:30pm and 5–9:30pm, Sat 5–9:30pm. NORTHWEST/CONTINENTAL.

Offering downtown's most innovative cuisine, Rosette is a rather spartan, albeit sophisticated, place. The lack of distractions allows you to focus on the artful creations that come from the kitchen. The menu changes regularly, and on a recent night included a seared duck breast with marionberry sauce. We like the appetizers so much that we're willing to forgo an entree in favor of two or three different starters, such as Dungeness crab cakes with a red pepper and garlic aioli or grilled portobello mushrooms marinated in a rosemary-garlic sauce.

INEXPENSIVE

Baja Norte. 801 NW Wall St. ☎ **541/385-0611.** Main courses $2.25–$6. MC, V. Daily 11am–9pm. MEXICAN.

This colorful Mexican fast-food spot makes its own tortillas and fills them with tasty fillings. You can get chunky fish tacos or thick quesadillas covered with various toppings (we like the artichoke quesadilla). The icy margaritas are a big hit in summer. The meals are big, so bring a good appetite. The crowd here is generally young and athletic.

Bend Woolen Mill. 1854 NE Division St. ☎ **541/317-1061.** Main courses $6–$13. AE, MC, V. Daily 11am–11pm. PUB.

Located a bit north of downtown Bend, this brew pub is housed in a historic woolen mill and attracts a lively crowd of all ages. Daily specials feature chicken and pasta dishes; the day we visited they were serving a delicious zucchini-curry soup. Other tasty items include panfried oysters and a sage-sausage sandwich. Many dishes come with huge servings of barley bread, made with the same barley with which they make their beer, although the beers served here are currently brewed in Hawaii and Boise, Idaho.

Café Santé. 718 NW Franklin St. ☎ **541/383-3530.** Meals $4–$6.50. MC, V. Daily 7am–3pm. VEGETARIAN.

The Santé is a bright and airy little natural-foods cafe that stays packed all through breakfast and lunch. On weekends there's sometimes a line out the door. Organically grown foods are used as often as possible, the juices are fresh squeezed, the cheese is low-fat, the tuna is dolphin-safe. For breakfast, we like the thick slabs of French toast and tofu scrambles, while at lunch the tempeh fajitas are a good bet.

12 Eastern Oregon

So different is eastern Oregon from the wet west side of the Cascades that it is often difficult to remember that it is still the same state. Indeed, the dry eastern ranchlands, deserts, canyons, and mountain ranges of this region have more in common with the landscapes of neighboring Idaho and Nevada. Yet, Oregon it is and though it is remote, the fascinating geography makes it an interesting region to explore when you've had enough of the verdant landscapes west of the Cascades.

With huge cattle ranches sprawling across the countryside (cattle greatly outnumber people in these parts) and the Pendleton Round-Up attracting cowboys and cowgirls from around the country, this region is Oregon's Wild West out east. This part of the state is also steeped in the history of the Oregon Trail, and while it was to the Willamette Valley that most wagon trains were heading, it is here that signs of their passing 150 years ago still abound. All across this region, wagon ruts left by those stalwart overlanders can still be seen, and at several regional museums, the history of the Oregon Trail immigrants is chronicled. While the first pioneers never thought to stop and put down roots in this region, when gold was discovered in the Blue Mountains in the 1860s, fortune seekers flocked to the area. Boom towns flourished and as quickly disappeared, leaving the land to the cattle ranchers and wheat farmers who still call this area home.

Today, however, the region also attracts a handful of outdoors enthusiasts. They come to hike and horseback ride in the Eagle Cap Wilderness of the Wallowa Mountains, to bird watch in the Malheur National Wildlife Refuge, to snow ski in the Blue Mountains, to explore the deepest canyon in the United States, and to raft and fish the Snake, Owyhee, and Grande Ronde Rivers. On the north side of the Wallowa Mountains, the small town of Joseph has even become a center for Western art, with several bronze foundries casting sculptures sold all over the country.

Because this region is so far from the state's population centers, it is little visited by west-siders, who rarely venture farther east than the resorts of central Oregon. Because eastern Oregon is so vast and road distances so great, it does not lend itself to quick weekend trips. At the very least, it takes a 3-day weekend to get out to Joseph and the Wallowa Mountains or the Malheur National Wildlife Refuge. Consequently, should you make it out to this part of the state, leave yourself plenty of time for getting from point A to point B.

Eastern Oregon

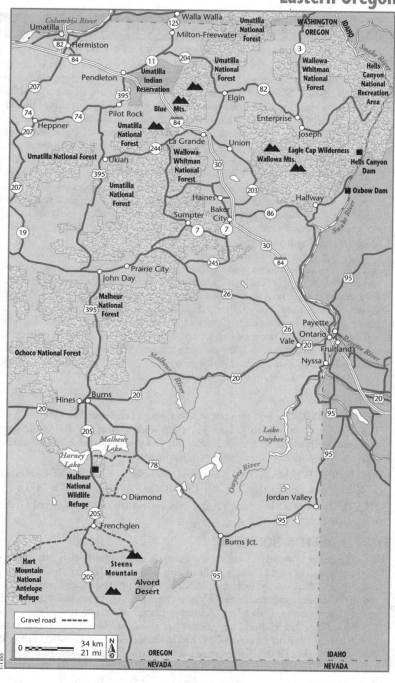

1 Pendleton

125 miles E of The Dalles, 52 miles NW of La Grande, 40 miles S of Walla Walla, Washington

If not for its famous woolen mills, few people outside the region would be familiar with the Pendleton name, but because the blankets and clothing long manufactured by the **Pendleton Woolen Mills** (here and at other mills around the region) have gained such a reputation, the Pendleton name has become as much a part of the West as Winchester, Colt, and Wells Fargo. Today, Pendleton blankets and clothing are as popular as ever, and the town's mill is one of Pendleton's biggest attractions. However, what brings more visitors to town than the mill is a single annual event, the Pendleton Round-Up.

Pendleton, located at the western foot of the Blue Mountains in northeastern Oregon, prides itself on being a real Western town, and as the site of one of the largest and oldest rodeos in the West, it has a legitimate claim. Each year in mid-September, the **Pendleton Round-Up** fills the town with cowboys and cowgirls, both real and urban. For the rest of the year, Pendleton sinks back into its quiet small-town character and begins preparing for the next year's Round-Up.

Once the homeland of the Cayuse, Umatilla, Walla Walla, and Nez Perce Indians, the Pendleton area began attracting settlers in the 1840s, as pioneers who had traveled the Oregon Trail started farming along the Umatilla River. In the 1850s, gold strikes created boom towns in the nearby mountains, and Pendleton gained greater regional significance. Sheep ranching and wheat farming later became the mainstays of the local economy, and by the turn of the century, Pendleton was a rowdy town boasting dozens of saloons and legal bordellos. Today Pendleton is a much quieter place, one that few people notice as they rush by on the interstate. But those who do pull off find a quiet town with a downtown historic district with attractive brick buildings and some stately old Victorian homes.

ESSENTIALS

GETTING THERE   I-84 runs east to west through Pendleton. From the south take U.S. 395, and from the north Ore. 11, which leads to Walla Walla, Washington. **Horizon Airlines** has service to the **Eastern Oregon Regional Airport,** which is located about 4 miles west of downtown Pendleton.

VISITOR INFORMATION   Contact the **Pendleton Chamber of Commerce,** 25 S. Main St., Pendleton, OR 97801 (☎ **800/547-8911** or 541/276-7411).

GETTING AROUND   Hertz rental cars are available at the Eastern Oregon Regional Airport.

THE PENDLETON ROUND-UP

The Pendleton Round-Up, held the second week of September each year, is one of the biggest rodeos in the country and has been held since 1910. In addition to daily rodeo events, there's a nightly pageant that presents a history of Native American and pioneer relations in the area. After the pageant, there's live country-and-western music in the Happy Canyon Dance Hall. A country-music concert and a parade round out the Round-Up. The Hall of Fame, under the south grandstand, holds a collection of cowboy and Indian memorabilia. The city is packed to overflowing during the Round-Up week, so if you plan to attend, reserve early. Tickets sell for $6 to $16 and should be ordered as far in advance as possible (some types of tickets sell out a year in advance). For more information, contact the **Pendleton Round-Up Association,** P.O. Box 609, Pendleton, OR 97801 (☎ **800/457-6336** or 541/276-2553).

OTHER THINGS TO SEE & DO

If you happen to be in town any other week of the year, there are still a few things worth doing. This is the home town of **Pendleton Woolen Mills,** the famed manufacturer of Native American–inspired blankets and classic wool sportswear. At this mill, the raw wool is turned into yarn and then woven into fabric before being shipped off to other factories to be made into clothing. Tours are offered Monday through Friday at 9am, 11am, 1:30pm, and 3pm. Also at the mill is a salesroom that's open Monday through Saturday from 8am to 5pm.

On **Pendleton Underground Tours,** 37 SW Emigrant Ave. (☎ **800/226-6398** or 541/276-0730), the shady underside of old Pendleton is laid bare. You'll go under the streets of the city to see where gamblers, drinkers, Chinese laborers, and prostitutes caroused in the days when Pendleton was the entertainment capital of the Northwest. Tours are offered daily from 9am to 5pm; tickets are $10 for adults and $5 for children 12 and under.

At the **Umatilla County Historical Museum,** 108 SW Frazer Ave. (☎ **541/ 276-0012**), you can learn about the region's more respectable history. The museum is housed in the city's 1909 vintage railway depot and contains exhibits on the Oregon Trail and Pendleton Woolen Mills as well as a display of beautiful Native American beadwork. The museum is open Tuesday through Saturday from 10am to 4pm; admission is $2 for adults and $1 for seniors and children. The museum also is the starting point of a self-guided, historical walking tour of downtown Pendleton's oldest buildings. Pick up a copy of the **self-guided walking tour** brochure at the chamber of commerce and wander around the historic blocks of downtown. Many buildings now also have informational historic plaques. If you're looking for glimpses of the **Oregon Trail,** head 20 miles west of Pendleton to the town of Echo, where you can see wagon ruts left by early pioneers.

Rapidly becoming the biggest year-round attraction in the area is the nearby **Wildhorse Gaming Resort,** 72777 Ore. 331 (☎ **800/654-WILD**), a gambling casino run by the Confederated Tribes of the Umatilla Indian Reservation. You'll find the casino, and its associated motel, RV park, and golf course, east of Pendleton at exit 216 off I-84. Also scheduled to open here in 1998 is the **Tamustalik Cultural Institute,** a museum that will explore the impact pioneer settlement had on the indigenous Cayuse, Walla Walla, and Umatilla Indians who were living in the region when the first settlers arrived. Check with the chamber of commerce for more information.

WHERE TO STAY

In addition to the B&B and hotel below, there's a **Motel 6,** 325 SE Nye Ave., Pendleton, OR 97801 (☎ **800/466-8356** or 541/276-3160), charging $36 to $42 double; and the **Best Western Pendleton Inn,** 400 SE Nye Ave., Pendleton, OR 97801 (☎ **800/528-1234** or 541/276-2135), charging $60 to $74 double. Both are located at Ore. 11 off I-84.

The Parker House Bed and Breakfast. 311 N. Main St., Pendleton, OR 97801. ☎ **800/ 700-8581** or 541/276-8581. 5 rms. TEL. $75–$85 double. Rates include full breakfast. AE, MC, V.

Looking very out of place in this Northwest cow town, this Italianate villa seems lifted from the southern California coast. Built in 1917, this home is only 2 blocks from downtown Pendleton and is surrounded by colorful perennial gardens. As befits the villalike surroundings, a formal atmosphere reigns. The Gwendolyn Room, with its fireplace and semiprivate balcony, is the best room in the house, and in the

Mandarin Room, you'll find the original Chinese wallpaper and Asian styling. In all the guest rooms you'll find plenty of antiques. Breakfasts are elaborate and filling, with fresh-baked breads and unusual entrees.

Pendleton Doubletree Hotel. 304 SE Nye Ave., Pendleton, OR 97801. ☎ **800/222-TREE** or 541/276-6111. Fax 541/278-2413. 170 rms. A/C TV TEL. $76–$99 double. AE, CB, DC, DISC, MC, V.

This is the largest and most luxurious lodging in Pendleton and is located south of town along I-84. As the city's only convention hotel, it's frequently booked up, especially during the Pendleton Round-Up. The rooms are large and many have balconies overlooking spacious lawns and a lake. You'll find a formal dining room, a coffee shop, and a lounge featuring live entertainment, as well as a swimming pool and hot tub. There's also a free airport van.

Working Girls Hotel. 17 SW Emigrant Ave., Pendleton, OR 97801. ☎ **541/276-8181.** 6 rms. $69–$79 double. MC, V.

Pendleton likes to play up its Wild West heritage, and there was a time when brothels were legal here. The historic building that now holds the Working Girls Hotel was just such an establishment, and while female companionship doesn't come with the rooms here anymore, you will find comfortable accommodations. Although the rooms all have private bathrooms, only one of these is actually in the room, all others have their bathrooms directly across the hall. The hotel is operated in conjunction with Pendleton Underground Tours, and hotel guests get a discount on the tour.

WHERE TO DINE

Crabby's Underground Steakhouse and Saloon. 220 SW First St. ☎ **541/276-8118.** Reservations not accepted. Main courses $6–$15. DC, DISC, MC, V. Mon–Sat 4pm–2am. STEAK.

Down a flight of stairs and behind a heavy wooden door that used to lead to a walk-in freezer is a dark and friendly saloon with stone walls that look as if they were blasted from the bedrock. Back during Prohibition a lot of saloons went underground, but today this is the only one in town that evokes Pendleton's wilder days. Crabby's is known as much for its prime rib and steak dinners as for the cold drinks it serves. In the evenings, there is sometimes live music (mostly country).

The Great Pacific Wine and Coffee Company. 403 S. Main St. ☎ **541/276-1350.** Sandwiches $2.50–$5. AE, MC, V. Mon–Thurs 8:30am–6pm, Fri 8:30–7pm, Sat 8:30am–6pm. DELI.

If you happen to be in town at lunch or need an espresso to get you the rest of the way across the hot Oregon plains, this is the place. Sandwiches come on croissants or bagels, and there are also daily soups. Cookies, muffins, truffles, and other sweets round out the menu.

Raphael's Restaurant & Lounge. 233 SE Fourth St. ☎ **541/276-8500.** Reservations recommended. Main courses $9–$22.50. AE, MC, V. Tues–Sat 5–9pm (Tues–Thurs 5–8pm Sept 1–May 31). AMERICAN/CONTINENTAL.

Housed in one of Pendleton's most elegant old homes and right across the street from City Hall, Raphael's is the city's only upscale restaurant. The house's original oak and mahogany trim can be seen throughout the restaurant, but aside from this bit of elegance, the decor is far plainer than the exterior would suggest. A regular menu that includes such dishes as Cajun salmon salad, venison marsala, smoked quail with browned huckleberry sauce, and hickory-roasted prime rib, is complemented by monthly chef's specials.

2 La Grande, Baker City & the Blue Mountains

La Grande: 260 miles E of Portland, 52 miles SE of Pendleton
Baker City: 41 miles SE of La Grande, 75 miles NW of Ontario

Though pioneers traveling the Oregon Trail in the 1840s found good resting places in the Powder River and Grande Ronde valleys, where Baker City and La Grande now stand, few stayed to put down roots in this remote region. It would not be until the 1860s that pioneers actually looked on these valleys as a place to live and make a living. However, those first pioneers who just passed through the region left signs of their passing that persist to this day. Wagon ruts of the Oregon Trail can still be seen in this region, and outside of Baker City stands the most interesting and evocative of the state's museums dedicated to the Oregon Trail experience.

By 1861, however, the Blue Mountains, which had been a major impediment to wagon trains, were crawling with people—gold prospectors. A gold strike in these mountains started a small gold rush that year, and soon prospectors were flocking to the area. The gold didn't last long, and when mining was no longer financially feasible, the miners left the region. In their wake, they left several ghost towns, but the prosperity of those boom times also left the region's larger towns with an enduring legacy of stately homes and opulent commercial buildings, many built of stone that was quarried in the region. Today, the historic commercial buildings of Baker City, the ornate Victorian homes of Union, and the Elgin Opera House are reminders of past prosperity. Although the gold has run out, signs of those raucous days, from gold nuggets to ghost towns, are now among the region's chief attractions.

One of the most arduous and dangerous sections of the Oregon Trail—the crossing of the Blue Mountains—lies just west of present-day La Grande. Today, however, the Blues are no longer the formidable obstacle they once were, but they are still among the least visited mountains in Oregon. The Blues, as they are known locally, offer a wide variety of recreational activities, including skiing and soaking in hot springs, hiking and mountain biking, fishing and camping. With their numerous hotels and restaurants, both La Grande and Baker City make good bases for exploring this relatively undiscovered region.

ESSENTIALS

GETTING THERE Both La Grande and Baker City are on I-84. La Grande is at the junction of Ore. 82, which heads northeast to Joseph and Wallowa Lake. Baker City is at the junction of Ore. 7, which runs southwest to John Day, and Ore. 86, which runs east to the Hells Canyon National Recreation Area.

VISITOR INFORMATION Contact the **Baker County Visitor and Convention Bureau,** 490 Campbell St., Baker City, OR 97814 (☎ **800/523-1235** or 541/523-3356), or the **La Grande/Union County Chamber of Commerce,** 1912 Fourth St., Suite 200, La Grande, OR 97850 (☎ **800/848-9969** or 541/963-8588).

EXPLORING THE LA GRANDE AREA

Oregon Trail history is on view west of La Grande at the ✪ **Oregon Trail Interpretive Center at Blue Mountain Crossing,** which is located at exit 248 off I-84. Here you'll find a 1/2-mile-long trail that leads past wagon ruts through the forest. Informational panels explain the difficulties pioneers encountered crossing these rugged mountains. On most weekends between Memorial Day and Labor Day, there are living history programs as well.

If you have an interest in Victorian architecture, be sure to visit the town of **Union,** 11 miles southeast of La Grande on Ore. 203. Union was the first settlement in the Grande Ronde Valley and flourished as a trading center and county seat of Union County. Today, the small town has numerous large Victorian homes in various states of restoration. Stop by the **Union County Museum,** 333 S. Main St. (☎ **541/ 562-6003**), to learn more about the town's historic buildings and to view the "Cowboys Then and Now" exhibit and also the natural history exhibits. It's open May to October only, Monday through Saturday from 10am to 4:30pm and Sunday from 1 to 4pm; admission is free.

In the town of **Elgin,** 18 miles north of La Grande on Ore. 82, you can take in a film, play, or concert at the restored **Elgin Opera House,** 104 N. Eighth St. (☎ **541/437-3456**), which was built in 1912. The opera house is in the same building that houses the Elgin City Hall.

West of Elgin on Ore. 204, you'll find the **Spout Springs** ski area (☎ **541/ 566-2164**), which offers downhill and cross-country **skiing.** Daily lift tickets are $19.50. In the vicinity of Spout Springs, there are also several sno-parks with marked cross-country ski trails. In summer, there is good mountain biking here.

If you're interested in **bird watching,** head out to the **Ladd Marsh Wildlife Area,** 6 miles south of La Grande off I-84 at the Foothill Road exit. This wetland is home to Oregon's only breeding population of sandhill cranes.

The **hot springs** of this region have been attracting people since long before the first white settlers arrived, and you can still soak your sore muscles in thermal waters at **Lehman Hot Springs,** in Ukiah, 38 miles west of La Grande on Ore. 244 (☎ **541/427-3015**), which is in a remote forest setting. Here you'll find a large, hot swimming pool perfect for an afternoon of lounging around. There are also two smaller and hotter soaking pools (the first of these is too hot to actually get into) as well as an unheated swimming pool (which sees very little use). Also on the premises are campsites and two cabins ($75 to $85 per night), and nearby are hiking, mountain biking, cross-country skiing, and snowmobiling trails. The springs are open daily in summer from 10am to 9pm; in other months there are shorter hours; admission is $5.

In summer, there are plenty of nearby trails to hike or mountain bike. Contact the **Wallowa-Whitman National Forest,** La Grande Ranger District, 3502 Ore. 30, La Grande, OR 97850 (☎ **541/963-7186**) for details.

EXPLORING THE BAKER CITY AREA
OREGON TRAIL HISTORY

✪ **Oregon Trail Interpretive Center.** Ore. 86, Baker City. ☎ **800/523-1235** or 541/ 523-1843. $10 per vehicle or $5 adults, $3.50 seniors and youths 6–18, children under 6 free. Apr–Oct daily 9am–6pm; Nov–Mar daily 9am–4pm. Closed Jan 1 and Dec 25.

Today, atop sagebrush-covered Flagstaff Hill just north of Baker City, stands a monument to what became the largest overland migration in North American history. Between 1842 and 1860 an estimated 300,000 people loaded all their worldly belongings onto wagons and set out to cross the continent to the promised land of western Oregon. Their route took them through some of the most rugged landscapes on this continent, and many perished along the way.

This museum commemorates the journeys of these hardy souls, who endured drought, dysentery, and starvation in the hopes of a better life at the end of the Oregon Trail. Through the use of interactive exhibits that challenge your ability to make the trip, diary quotes, a life-size wagon-train scene, and lots of artifacts from the trail, the center takes you through every aspect of life on the trail. Outside, a trail through the sagebrush leads to ruts left by the wagons on their journey west.

OTHER BAKER CITY ATTRACTIONS

If the Oregon Trail Interpretive Center leaves you fired up to learn more about pioneer days, then stop by the **Oregon Trail Regional Museum,** 2480 Grove St. (☎ **541/523-9308**), which has a large collection of stagecoaches and an extensive mineral collection. It's open late April to late October, daily from 9am to 5pm; admission is $2. At the **U.S. Bank** on Main Street in Baker City, you can see a collection of gold that includes a nugget that weighs in at 80.4 ounces. At the Baker City Visitors & Convention Bureau, you can pick up a brochure that outlines a **walking tour** of the town's most important historic buildings. However, an even better way to learn about this town's colorful past is on a **horse-drawn trolley** tour with **Oregon Trail Trolley** (☎ **541/856-3356**), which operates on Fridays, Saturdays, and holidays throughout the summer. Tours depart from the Oregon Trail Regional Museum. In winter, tours out to a nearby elk feeding station are offered.

THE ELKHORN MOUNTAIN SCENIC LOOP

Rising up on the outskirts of Baker City are the Elkhorn Range of the Blue Mountains. A paved loop road winds up and around the south side of these mountains, providing scenic vistas, access to the outdoors throughout the year, and even a couple of sparsely inhabited ghost towns. Start this loop by heading south out of Baker City on Ore. 245 and then take Ore. 7 west to **Sumpter,** which is 30 miles from Baker City.

Gold-mining history is on display in this rustic mountain town, which, though it has a few too many people to be called a ghost town, is hardly the town it once was. In the boom days of the late 19th and early 20th century, this town boasted several brick buildings, hotels, saloons, and a main street crowded with large buildings. However, when a fire destroyed the town in 1917, it was never rebuilt. Today, only one brick building and a few original wooden structures remain. At the **Gold Post Groceries & Museum** (☎ **541/894-2362**), you can see old photos of Sumpter as well as various artifacts from the town's gold-mining heyday.

Gold kept this community alive for many decades, and between 1935 and 1954, the ominous-looking Sumpter Dredge laid waste to the valley floor as it sat in its own little pond sifting through old streambed gravel for gold. Today, the dredge is preserved as the **Sumpter Dredge State Park** and is currently undergoing restoration.

In its wake, the dredge left 6 miles of tailings that formed hummocks of rock and gouged out areas that have now become small ponds. Although such a mining-scarred landscape isn't usually considered scenic, the Sumpter Valley is today surprisingly alive with bird life that is attracted to the many small ponds. The most popular way to see the valley is on an excursion aboard the **Sumpter Valley Railroad** (☎ **541/894-2268**), which operates a classic steam train on a 5-mile run from west of Phillips Reservoir to the Sumpter Dredge. This railway first began operation in 1890 and was known as the stump dodger. Excursions are operated on Saturdays, Sundays, and holidays from Memorial Day weekend to late September; round-trip fares are $9 for adults and $6.50 for children 6 to 16.

Continuing west on a winding county road for another 14 miles will bring you to ✪ **Granite,** another ghost town that also has a few flesh-and-blood residents. The weather-beaten old buildings on a grassy hillside are the epitome of a western ghost town, and most buildings are marked. You'll see the old school, general store, saloon, bordello, and other important town buildings.

Beyond Granite, the road winds down to the North Fork of the John Day River and then heads back across the mountains by way of the Anthony Lakes area. In winter, there is **downhill skiing** in excellent powder snow at **Anthony Lakes**

Mountain Resort (☎ **541/963-4599** or 541/856-3277), 40 minutes west of Baker City. Although this ski area is small, it has a good variety of terrain. Daily lift tickets are $22. You'll also find good, groomed cross-country ski trails here. The Anthony Lakes area is also very popular with snowmobilers. In summer, there are hiking trails and fishing in the area's small lakes. The vistas in this area are the best on this entire loop drive, with rugged, rocky peaks rising above the forest. Also in this same area, you'll catch glimpses of the irrigated pastures of the Powder River Valley far below.

Coming down onto the valley floor, you reach the tiny farming community of Haines, which is the site of the **Eastern Oregon Museum,** Third Street (☎ **541/856-3233**), a small museum cluttered with all manner of artifacts of regional historic significance. It's open April to October only, daily from 9am to 5pm; admission is by donation. Here in Haines you'll also find the Haines Steak House (see below), one of the best steakhouses in Oregon.

WHERE TO STAY
IN LA GRANDE

In addition to the B&B listed below, there are several inexpensive chain motels in La Grande, including the **Best Western Pony Soldier Inn,** 2612 Island Ave., La Grande, OR 97850 (☎ **541/963-7195**), charging $67 to $85 double; and the **Super 8 Motel,** 2407 E. R Ave., La Grande, OR 97850 (☎ **541/963-8080**), charging $46 to $55 double.

Stang Manor Bed & Breakfast. 1612 Walnut St., La Grande, OR 97850. ☎ **800/286-9463** or 541/963-2400. Fax 541/963-2400. 3 rms, 1 suite. $75–$80 double; $90 suite. Rates include full breakfast. MC, V.

This Georgian colonial mansion, built in the 1920s, looks a bit like the White House and is filled with beautiful woodwork and comfortable guest rooms, a couple of which have the original bathroom fixtures, including a footed bathtub. The best deal here is the three-room suite, which has a fireplace and a sun porch that has been converted into a sleeping room. Breakfasts are elegant affairs served in the formal dining room.

IN BAKER CITY

In addition to the hotel and B&B listed below, you'll find several inexpensive chain motels in Baker City. These include the **Best Western Sunridge Inn,** 1 Sunridge Lane, Baker City, OR 97814 (☎ **541/523-6444**), charging $63 to $79 double; the **Quality Inn,** 810 Campbell St., Baker City, OR 97814 (☎ **541/523-2242**), charging $49 to $59 double; and the **Super 8 Motel,** 250 Campbell St., Baker City, OR 97814 (☎ **541/523-8282**), charging $46 to $55 double.

A'Demain Bed & Breakfast. 1790 Fourth St., Baker City, OR 97814. ☎ **541/523-2509.** 2 rms. $55–$65 double. Rates include full breakfast. No credit cards.

Set on a tree-lined street and built of brick, this is Baker City's most appealing bed-and-breakfast inn. An octagonal turret anchors one corner of the house, and heavy stone columns support the porch. If the turret captures your attention as much as it did ours, you'll want to spend a bit extra to stay in the suitelike room that includes the second-floor turret room as well as a small private balcony. The downstairs room is smaller.

✪ **Geiser Grand Hotel.** 1996 Main St., Baker City, OR 97814. ☎ **888/GEISERG** or 541/523-1889. Fax 541/523-1800. 17 rms, 13 suites. A/C TV TEL. $85–$109 double; $109–$159 suite. AE, DISC, MC, V.

Built in 1889 at the height of the region's gold rush, the Geiser Grand is the grandest hotel in eastern Oregon. With its corner turret and clock tower, the hotel is a classic 19th-century Western luxury hotel. The hotel shut down in 1968 after the cast of the movie *Paint Your Wagon* stayed here, but after a 3-year renovation, the hotel reopened in 1997. In the center of the hotel is the Palm Court dining room, above which is suspended the largest stained-glass ceiling in the Northwest. Throughout the hotel, including in all the guest rooms, ornate crystal chandeliers add crowning touches to this historic hotel. Guest rooms also feature 10-foot windows, most of which look out to the Blue Mountains. Although the Oriental suite is the most opulent in the hotel, it is the two cupola suites that are the most luxurious and evocative of the past. These two suites also are the only rooms with whirlpool tubs. Breakfast is served in a separate and sunny dining room. Prices for meals are very reasonable, and the fare includes fresh fish flown in from Seattle and sourdough bread from San Francisco. Room service is available and there is a saloonlike lounge as well.

IN SUMPTER

Sumpter Bed & Breakfast. 344 NE Columbia St., Sumpter, OR 97877. ☎ **800/640-3184** (in Oregon), or 541/894-0048. 4 rms. $60 double. Rates include full breakfast. MC, V.

Big and drafty and authentically old-fashioned, this B&B was once used as a hospital when this was a booming mining town. New owners Jay and Barbara Phillips have been busy renovating the old building, and there are now additional bathrooms for guests, plus an upstairs sitting room. This is a pretty laid-back and informal place, and makes an ideal base for exploring this remote and historic corner of the state.

CAMPGROUNDS

You'll find several national forest campgrounds along the Elkhorn National Scenic Byway, including **Union Creek Campground,** which is on the shore of Phillips Reservoir southeast of Baker City. Others can be found near Anthony Lakes.

WHERE TO DINE
IN LA GRANDE

If you're in need of a good cup of espresso, drop by **One Smart Cookie,** 1119 Adams Ave. (☎ **541/963-3172**), which, as you might guess, also specializes in cookies. Great breads and pastries, such as orange scones and marionberry cheese tarts, can be had at **Kneads,** 109 Depot St. (☎ **541/963-5413**). Coffee, cookies, soups, and sandwiches are the fare at the **Lifeline Cafe,** 111 Depot St. (☎ **541/962-9568**), a very literate college hangout located next door to Kneads. For a pint of locally brewed beer, drop in at **Blue Mountain Brewing & Public House,** 1502 S Ave. (☎ **541/ 963-5426**), which also serves simple pub fare.

Foley Station. 1011 Adams Ave. ☎ **541/963-7473.** Main dishes $4–$9. MC, V. Tues–Sat 6am–2pm. AMERICAN/NORTHWEST.

With a former chef from Portland's Jake's restaurant chain at the helm, this restaurant is bringing more contemporary cooking styles to La Grande. Not too many restaurants in this corner of the state offer a pecan waffle with maple mascarpone and pralines or an apple puff pancake with vanilla yogurt mousse. Lunch dishes include crab cake sandwiches, white gazpacho with bay shrimp, and build-your-own burgers. There are tentative plans to offer dinners in the future.

Mamacita's. 110 Depot St. ☎ **541/963-6223.** Main courses $6.25–$11. No credit cards. Tues–Fri 11am–2pm and 5–9pm, Sat–Sun 5–9pm. MEXICAN.

With its colorful downtown setting, this small, low-key Mexican place is more college hangout than local Mexican joint. The menu is short but varied. Fire-eaters should try the hot salsa verde.

Ten Depot Street. 10 Depot St. ☎ **541/963-8766.** Reservations recommended. Main courses $9–$25; lunch $6–$11. AE, MC, V. Mon–Fri 11:30am–2:30pm and 5:30–10pm, Sat 5:30–10pm. STEAK/SEAFOOD.

Housed in a historic brick commercial building, this restaurant has a classic turn-of-the-century feel, complete with a saloon on one side. Although the steaks are what most people crave, the salads are large and flavorful, and there are even some vegetarian dishes.

IN THE BAKER CITY AREA

By far the most elegant restaurant in town is the **Palm Court** of the historic Geiser Grand Hotel. All three meals are available here at the hotel, with breakfasts served in a separate dining room. Prices are moderate and seafood is a specialty. See above for details.

Baker City Cafe/Pizza à Fetta. 1915 Washington Ave. ☎ **541/523-6099.** Pizzas $13–$21. MC, V. Mon–Fri 9am–8pm. PIZZA.

When you've just got to have a pizza and you want more than pepperoni or sausage, this is the place. You can dress your pie with the likes of blue cheese, feta, Montrachet, sun-dried tomatoes, kalamata olives, chorizo, and pancetta. Pasta and sandwiches are also available.

Front Street Café & Coffee Company. 1840 Main St. ☎ **541/523-0223.** Reservations not accepted. Meals $5.50–$11. MC, V. Mon–Wed and Sat 7am–4pm, Thurs–Fri 7am–8pm. SANDWICHES/MEXICAN.

Urban coffee shop meets old-fashioned country diner in this antique-filled cafe with exposed brick walls and a big black-and-white tile floor. Gourmet sandwiches, large-and-filling salads, hearty breakfasts, Mexican dishes, and espresso are the lunch and breakfast staples, while the dinner menu includes steaks, burgers, pasta, and salads.

Haines Steakhouse. 910 Front St., Haines. ☎ **541/856-3639.** Reservations recommended. Main courses $10–$20. AE, DC, DISC, MC, V. Mon and Wed–Fri 5–10pm, Sat 4–10pm, Sun 1–9pm. STEAK.

Thick, juicy steaks are the specialty of the house here, but it's the decor as much as the food that attracts people. Log walls and booths, a chuck-wagon salad bar, buffalo and elk heads mounted on the walls, even a totem pole and an old buggy keep diners amused as they eat.

WEST OF BAKER CITY: THE JOHN DAY AREA

In the town of John Day, the fascinating little ✪ **Kam Wah Chung & Co. Museum** (☎ 541/575-0028), on Northwest Canton Street adjacent to City Park, is well worth a visit. It preserves the home and shop of a Chinese doctor who, for much of the first half of this century, administered to his fellow countrymen who were laboring here in John Day. The building looks much as it might have at the time of the doctor's death and contains an office, pharmacy, general store, and living quarters. It's open May to October only, Monday through Thursday from 9am to noon and 1 to 5pm, and on Saturday and Sunday from 1 to 5pm. Admission is $2 for adults, $1.50 for seniors, and $1 for youths 13 to 18, and 50¢ for children 12 and under.

3 Joseph, Enterprise & the Wallowa Mountains

Joseph: 355 miles E of Portland, 80 miles E of La Grande, 125 miles N of Baker City

The Wallowa Mountains, which stand just south of the town of Joseph, are a glacier-carved range of rugged beauty that has been called the Alps of Oregon and the Little Switzerland of America. Though the range is small enough in area to drive around in a day, it's big on scenery and contains the largest designated wilderness area in the state: the **Eagle Cap Wilderness.**

In the northeast corner of the mountains lies Wallowa Lake, which was formed when glacial moraines blocked a valley that had been carved by the glaciers. With blue waters reflecting the rocky peaks, the lake has long attracted visitors. In the fall, the lake also attracts bald eagles that come to feed on spawning kokanee salmon, which turn a bright red in the spawning season.

In recent years, the town of Joseph, just north of Wallowa Lake, has become a center for the casting of **bronze sculptures** with Western themes, and there are now several art galleries in the area. With its natural beauty, recreational opportunities, and artistic bent, this corner of the state today has more to offer than any other area in eastern Oregon.

ESSENTIALS

GETTING THERE   Ore. 82 connects Joseph to La Grande in the west, and Ore. 3 heads north from nearby Enterprise to Lewiston, Idaho, by way of Wash. 129. Bus service from La Grande to Enterprise and Joseph is provided by **Wallowa Valley Stage Lines** (☎ **541/569-2284**).

VISITOR INFORMATION   For more information, contact the **Wallowa County Chamber of Commerce,** 107 SW First St. (P.O. Box 427), Enterprise, OR 97828 (☎ **800/585-4121** or 541/426-4622).

FESTIVALS   The rowdy **Chief Joseph Days** over the last full weekend in July, **Jazz on the Lake** in mid-July, and the **Alpenfest** on the third weekend after Labor Day are the biggest annual events in the area.

THE WALLOWA MOUNTAINS & WALLOWA LAKE

Down at the south end of Wallowa Lake, you'll find **Wallowa Lake State Park** (☎ **541/432-4185**), where there's a swimming beach, picnic area, and campground. Adjacent to the park is the **Wallowa Lake Marina** (☎ **541/432-9115**), where you can rent a canoe, rowboat, paddleboat, or motorboat. This end of the lake has an old-fashioned mountain resort feel, with pony and kiddie rides, go-cart tracks, and the like. However, it is also the trailhead for several trails into the Eagle Cap Wilderness.

For a different perspective on the lake, ride the **Wallowa Lake Tramway** (☎ **541/432-5331**) to the top of 8,200-foot Mount Howard. It operates from mid-May through late September, daily from 10am to 4pm (also operating between Christmas and New Years); the fare is $13.50 for adults, $12 for seniors, and $8 for children 10 and under. The views from the top are excellent and take in Wallowa Lake and the surrounding jagged peaks. There are 2 miles of walking trails on the summit, and food is available at the **Summit Deli & Alpine Patio.**

Because most hikes on the north side of the Cascades start out in valleys and can take up to a dozen miles or so to reach the alpine meadows of the higher elevations, there aren't a lot of great day hikes here. The **backpacking,** however, is excellent. If, however, you're looking for **day hikes,** try taking the tramway to the top of Mount

"I Will Fight No More Forever"

The Wallowa Mountains and Hells Canyon areas were once the homeland of the Nez Perce people. The Nez Perce land, which encompassed rolling hills covered with lush grasses, was perfect for raising horses, and sometime in the early 1700s the tribe came to own horses that were descended from Spanish stock and had been traded northward from the American Southwest. They began selectively breeding this strange new animal, emphasizing traits of speed and endurance. Their horses were far superior to those used by other tribes and became known as Appaloosas. The area where these horses were first bred is now the Palouse Hills country of eastern Washington.

The Nez Perce had befriended explorers Lewis and Clark in 1805 and had remained friendly to white settlers when other Indian tribes were waging wars. However, the Nez Perce's neutrality was rewarded with treaties that twice cut the size of their reservation in half. When one band refused to sign a new treaty and relinquish its land, the stage was set for one of the great tragedies of Northwest history.

En route to a reservation in Idaho, several Nez Perce braves ignored orders from the tribal elders and attacked and killed four white settlers to exact revenge for the earlier murder by whites of a father of one of the braves. This attack brought the ire of settlers, and the cavalry was called in to hunt down the Nez Perce. Tribal elders decided to flee to Canada, and, led by Chief Joseph (also known as Young Joseph), 700 Nez Perce, including 400 women and children, began a 2,000-mile march across Idaho and Montana on a retreat that lasted four months.

Along the way several skirmishes were fought, and the cavalry finally succeeded in defeating the Nez Perce only 40 miles from Canada. At their surrender, Chief Joseph spoke the words for which he has long been remembered: "Hear me my Chiefs, I am tired; my heart is sick and sad. From where the sun now stands, I will fight no more, forever."

The town of Joseph is named after Chief Joseph, and on the outskirts of town you'll find the grave of his father, Old Joseph. Young Joseph is buried on the Colville Indian Reservation in central Washington. Not far from Joseph, near Lewiston, Idaho, you can learn more about the Nez Perce at **Nez Perce National Historical Park.**

Howard, where there are easy trails with great views. If you'd like to head into the **Eagle Cap Wilderness** to the popular **Lake Basin** or anywhere else in the Wallowas, you'll find the trailhead less than a mile past the south end of the lake. For more information on hiking in the Wallowas, contact the **Wallowa Mountains Visitor Center**, 88401 Ore. 82, Enterprise, OR 97828 (☎ 541/426-4978).

Horse packing into the Wallowas is a popular activity, and rides of a day or longer can be arranged through **Eagle Cap Wilderness Pack Station,** 59761 Wallowa Lake Hwy., Joseph, OR 97846 (☎ 800/681-6222 or 541/432-4145). **Millar Pack Station,** 69498 Sherrod Rd., Wallowa, OR 97885 (☎ 541/886-4035), and **Outback Ranch Outfitters,** P.O. Box 269, Joseph, OR 97846 (☎ 541/432-9101), also offer guided pack trips and drop camps in both the Eagle Cap Wilderness and in Hells Canyon. Expect to pay around $150 per person per day for a guided trip. If you'd like to try **llama trekking** and let these South American beasts of burden carry your pack, contact **Hurricane Creek Llama Treks,** 63366 Pine Tree Rd.,

Enterprise, OR 97828 (☎ **800/528-9609** or 541/432-4455). Trips range from $160 to $770.

This region also offers some of the best **trout fishing** in Oregon, and if you'd like a guide take you to the best holes, contact **Eagle Cap Fishing Guides,** 110 S. River St., Enterprise, OR 97828 (☎ **800/676-5379** or 541/426-3493), or **The Joseph Fly Shoppe,** 203 N. Main St., Joseph, OR 97846 (☎ **541/432-4343**). Expect to pay around $175 for a day of fishing.

The Grande Ronde River also provides some good **white-water rafting.** Three- to four-day adventures are offered by **Renegade River Rafters** (☎ **888/ RNE-GADE** or 503/622-5699), which charges $295 to $345.

In winter, the Wallowas are popular with cross-country and backcountry **skiers.** Check at the ranger station in Enterprise for directions to trails. You'll also find a small downhill ski area and groomed cross-country trails at **Ferguson Ridge,** which is 9 miles southeast of Joseph on Tucker Down Road. **Wing Ridge Ski Tours,** P.O. Box 714, Joseph, OR 97846 (☎ **800/646-9050** or 541/426-4322), leads experienced skiers on hut-to-hut ski tours for around $100 per person per day.

JOSEPH, THE TOWN THAT BRONZE BUILT

Though the lake and mountains are the main attraction of this area, the presence of several bronze foundries in the area has made this a sort of Western art community. Along Main Street in Joseph, you'll find several art galleries that specialize in bronze statues. If you'd like to see how all these intricate bronze statues are made you can take a tour through **Valley Bronze of Oregon,** 018 Main St. (☎ **541/432-7445**), which has its foundry at 307 W. Adler St. (☎ **541/432-7551**). Foundry tours are also offered by **Joseph Bronze,** 203 N. Main St. (☎ **541/432-2278**), which has its foundry on the northern outskirts of Joseph on Ore. 82. Other bronze galleries include the **Bronze Gallery of Joseph,** 603 N. Main St. (☎ **541/432-3106**), and the **Wildhorse Gallery,** 508 N. Main St. (☎ **541/432-4242**).

Of particular interest to fans of bronze and Western art is the impressive **Manuel Museum,** 400 N. Main St. (☎ **541/432-7235**), at the west end of town. In addition to housing bronzes by artist David Manuel, the museum includes an outstanding collection of Native American artifacts, John Wayne memorabilia, and a large collection of old wagons. Admission is $5 for adults, $4.50 for seniors, and $1 for children. At the **Wallowa County Museum,** at the south end of Main Street (☎ **541/426-3811**), you can see pioneer artifacts, displays on the Nez Perce Indians, and other items donated to the museum by local families. This old-fashioned community museum is open daily from 10am to 5pm from Memorial Day to late September. On Wednesday afternoons in summer, this museum is the site of reenactments of an 1896 bank robbery (the museum used to be a bank).

WHERE TO STAY

Chandlers' Bed, Bread, and Trail Inn. 700 S. Main St. (P.O. Box 639), Joseph, OR 97846. ☎ **800/452-3781** or 541/432-9765. 5 rms (3 with private bath). $80 double. Rates include full breakfast. MC, V.

Located right in Joseph, Chandler's is a contemporary home with cedar-shingle walls and a boardwalk that leads through a rock garden to the front door. Inside you'll find a high-ceilinged living room with open-beam construction, folk art, quilts, and an "early attic" decor. Three of the rooms have mountain views, and there are also three sitting areas for guest use. In warm weather, breakfast is served in a gazebo in the garden. The inn provides free shuttle service to area trailheads.

Eagle Cap Chalets. 59879 Wallowa Lake Hwy., Joseph, OR 97846. ☎ **541/432-4704.**
23 rms, 9 cabins, 5 condos. TV. $48–$70 double. AE, DC, DISC, MC, V.

With its indoor pool and whirlpool spa, very basic miniature golf course, and wide
range of room types, Eagle Cap Chalets are very popular with families and groups.
Set under tall pines just a short walk from hiking trails and the lake, the rooms here
vary from motel style to rustic-though-renovated cabins. Siding on all the buildings
makes them appear to be built of logs. The cabins and condos have kitchens.

George Hyatt House. 200 E. Greenwood St., Enterprise, OR 97828. ☎ **800/95-HYATT** or
541/426-0241. Web site: www.moriah.com/hyatt/. 4 rms. $95 double. Rates include full break-
fast. MC, V.

Located on the courthouse square in downtown Enterprise, this elegant 1898
Victorian home is surrounded by colorful gardens that make it a veritable oasis in this
often brown landscape. The two porches are ideal spots from which to enjoy the
gardens and tranquil setting. The four guest rooms are furnished with a variety of
antiques that conjure up Victorian times. Two of the rooms have claw-foot tubs, but
the best room is the Queen Anne Room, which is housed in the house's tower, which
was removed in the 1970s and then rebuilt in 1994.

Ramshead Cottage at Wallowa Lake. 84591 Pine Ridge Rd. (P.O. Box 874), Joseph, OR
97846. ☎ **541/432-2002** or 541/426-0107. One 2-bedroom cottage. $115–$160 double.
No credit cards.

Located in the shady pine forest at the south end of Wallowa Lake, this modern
cedar-shingled cottage is operated by Lynn and Doris Steiger who for years ran
a B&B in the wine country outside Portland. The interior decor is rustic yet very
comfortable, and the cottage shows the thoughtful touches you expect from a B&B—
antique furnishings, an excellent library, quality linens. Light fir floors and pine
paneling are found throughout (as opposed to the dark paneling usually found in
older mountain cabins), and an abundance of windows keeps the rooms bright. The
upstairs suite has a living room with a small kitchen, while the downstairs room has
a Murphy bed and a private deck. From the cottage, it's just a short walk either to
the lake or the start of the trails that lead into the Eagle Cap Wilderness.

۞ Wallowa Lake Lodge. 60060 Wallowa Lake Hwy., Joseph, OR 97846. ☎ **541/432-9821.**
Fax 541/432-4885. 22 rms, 8 cabins. May to early Oct $75–$110 double; $85–$145 cabin.
Early Oct to Apr $60–$105 double; $60–$80 cabin. DISC, MC, V.

This rustic two-story lodge at the south end of Wallowa Lake was built in 1923 and
is surrounded by big pines and a wide expanse of lawn. Big comfortable chairs fill
the lobby, where folks often sit by the stone fireplace in the evening. The guest rooms
are divided between those with carpeting and modern bathrooms and those with
hardwood floors, original bathroom fixtures, and antique furnishings (our favorites).
All but two of the latter type have two bedrooms each, and two rooms have
balconies overlooking the lake. The cabins are rustic but comfortable and have full
kitchens. The dining room serves a limited menu of well-prepared dishes that make
use of local produce and meats (don't miss the hazelnut pancakes at breakfast).

A GUEST RANCH IN THE WILDERNESS

Minam Lodge. Eagle Cap Wilderness Pack Station, High Country Outfitters, 59761 Wallowa
Lake Hwy., Joseph, OR 97846. ☎ **800/681-6222** or 541/432-9171. 6 rms. $230–$290 per
person for 2 days and 1 night. Rates include all meals and transportation to and from the ranch.
MC, V.

Located on the Minam River in the Eagle Cap Wilderness, and only accessible on
foot, on horseback, or by small plane, Minam Lodge is a rustic, remote getaway for

lovers of the great outdoors who enjoy horseback riding, hiking, fishing, and hunting. The rustic log cabins are set atop a low hill and have wood stoves for warmth and good-sized windows to let in the sunshine and the views.

A CAMPGROUND

At the south end of Wallowa Lake, you'll find a campground under the trees at **Wallowa Lake State Park.** In addition to campsites, the park has two yurts for rent for $25 a night. For campsite reservations, call **Reservations Northwest** (☎ **800/ 452-5687**).

SOME GOOD PLACES TO EAT IN JOSEPH/WALLOWA LAKE

In addition to the restaurants listed below, you'll find good meat-and-potatoes meals at the **Wallowa Lake Lodge** (see "Where to Stay," above, for details).

Old Town Cafe. 8 S. Main St. ☎ **541/432-9898.** Main dishes $5–$10. No credit cards. Wed–Thurs and Sun–Mon 7am–2pm, Fri–Sat 7am–2pm and 6–9pm. INTERNATIONAL.

This tiny cafe, mostly a breakfast and lunch place, sits right in the middle of Joseph and serves up satisfying portions of excellent food. The menu is very limited, which seems to give the owners plenty of opportunity to perfect their offerings. For breakfast don't miss the breakfast burrito, especially if you are heading out for a day of hiking. These burritos are huge! On Fridays and Saturdays the cafe is open for dinner, and a single entree is offered (chicken marsala and enchiladas were the night's offerings one recent week). Marionberry pie and giant cookies round out the offerings.

Vali's Alpine Restaurant and Delicatessen. 59811 Wallowa Lake Hwy. ☎ **541/432-5691.** Reservations required. Main courses $7.50–$12. No credit cards. Tues–Sun 9:30am–11am and 5:30–7:30pm. Closed weekdays from Labor Day to Memorial Day. EASTERN EUROPEAN.

Just past the Wallowa Lake Lodge you'll find this little restaurant, which specializes in the hearty fare of Eastern Europe. Only one dish is served each evening, so if you like to have options you won't want to eat here. Stuffed cabbage (Tuesday), Hungarian goulash (Wednesday), chicken paprikash (Thursday), schnitzel (Sunday), and apple strudel (every night) should help you stay warm on cold mountain evenings. Hungarian gypsy music plays on the stereo, and at breakfast there are fresh homemade doughnuts.

✪ **Wildflower Bakery/Blue Willow Sausage Kitchen/Terminal Gravity Brewing.** 803 School St. ☎ **541/426-2086.** Main courses $5–$8. No credit cards. Mon–Wed 7am–2pm, Thurs–Sat 7am–2pm and 5–11pm, Sun 5–11pm. INTERNATIONAL.

This area is still sort of in its pioneering stages when it comes to restaurants, and this place is a good example. For years locals knew this as the place to get good, fresh sausage, but now with a bakery/restaurant and a brewery all crammed into one old house, its much more than that. There are only two tables and a few barstools, but the food is still the best in this whole corner of the state. Count yourself very lucky if the night's menu includes traditional Puerto Rican fare from the chef/co-owner's family recipes. The chili is also the best we've ever had and owes its uniqueness to a liberal dose of cocoa. Currently the brewery produces only one brew at a time, but plans to increase output are afoot.

4 Hells Canyon & the Southern Wallowas

South access: 70 miles NE of Baker City; North access: 20 to 30 miles E of Joseph

Sure, the Grand Canyon is an impressive sight, but few people ever realize that it isn't the deepest canyon in the United States. That distinction goes to Hells Canyon, which forms the border between Oregon and Idaho. Carved by the Snake River and bounded on the east by the Seven Devils Mountains and on the west by the Wallowa Mountains, Hells Canyon is as much as 8,000 feet deep. While Hells Canyon isn't quite as spectacular a sight as the Grand Canyon, neither is it as crowded. Because there is so little road access to Hells Canyon, it is one of the least visited national recreation areas in the West.

The Hells Canyon area boasts a range of outdoor activities, but because of blazing hot temperatures in summer, when this rugged gorge lives up to its name, spring and fall are the best times to visit. However, despite the heat, boating, swimming, and fishing are all popular in the summer.

ESSENTIALS

GETTING THERE   The south access to Hells Canyon National Recreation Area is reached off of Ore. 86 between 9 and 48 miles northeast of the town of Halfway depending on which route you follow. Northern sections of the national recreation area, including the Hat Point Overlook, are reached from Joseph on Ore. 82, which begins in La Grande.

VISITOR INFORMATION   For more information, contact the **Hells Canyon National Recreation Area,** 88401 Ore. 82, Enterprise, OR 97828 (☎ **541/ 426-4978**).

EXPLORING THE REGION

Much of Hells Canyon is wilderness and is accessible only by boat, on horseback, or on foot. Few roads lead into the canyon, and most of these are only recommended for **four-wheel-drive vehicles.** If you are driving a car without high clearance, you'll have to limit your exploration of this region to the road to Hells Canyon Dam and the scenic byway that skirts the eastern flanks of the Wallowa Mountains. If you don't mind driving miles on gravel, you can also head out to the **Hat Point Overlook** east of Joseph.

Southern river-level access begins in the community of Oxbow, but the portion of the Snake River that has been designated a National Wild and Scenic River starts 27 miles farther north, below Hells Canyon Dam. Below the dam, the Snake River is turbulent with white water and provides thrills for jet boats and rafts. To get this bottom-up view of the canyon, take Ore. 86 to Oxbow and continue across the river into Idaho to the Hells Canyon Dam. Stop at the **Hells Canyon Creek Information Station** at Hells Canyon Dam in Oxbow to learn more about the canyon.

To get a top-down overview of the canyon, drive to the **Hells Canyon Overlook,** 30 miles northeast of Halfway on Forest Road 39. From here you can gaze down into the canyon, but you won't be able to see the river. This road was scheduled for reconstruction through late 1998 due to damage from landslides, so be sure to find out if the road is open before heading out. An alternate route is open to high-clearance vehicles.

You'll find many miles of **hiking trails** within the national recreation area, but summer heat, rattlesnakes, and poison oak keep all but the most dedicated hikers at bay. For information on trails here, contact the information center for the recreation area (see above).

The best way to see Hells Canyon is by **white-water raft** or in a **jet boat.** Both sorts of trips can be arranged through **Hells Canyon Adventures,** 4200 Hells Canyon Dam Rd., Oxbow, OR 97840 (☎ **800/422-3568** or 541/785-3352). Jet boat tours range from $30 for a 2-hour tour to $95 for a 6-hour tour. A day of white-water rafting runs $125. Jet boat trips are also offered by **Snake River Adventures** (☎ 800/262-8874 or 208/746-6276), which operates out of Lewiston, Idaho. Multiday white-water rafting trips are also offered by **Freewater Expeditions** (☎ 800/818-7423). A 3-day trip will run you $650, while a 6-day trip runs $1,015.

If you'd like to try pedaling a **mountain bike** in Hells Canyon, contact **Hells Canyon Bicycle Tours,** P.O. Box 483, Joseph, OR 97846 (☎ 541/432-2453), which charges $65 to $75 for a day-long ride. **Horseback trips** into the southern Wallowas are offered by **Cornucopia Wilderness Pack Station,** Route 1, Box 50, Richland, OR 97870 (☎ 541/893-6400, or in summer 541/742-5400), with rates around $200 per person per day for fully catered and guided trips. Horses can also be rented here on an hourly or daily basis. You can also opt to explore the southern Wallowas with a llama carrying your gear. Contact **Wallowa Llamas** (☎ 541/742-2961 or 541/742-4930) for more information.

While in this area, you can learn about bison at **Clear Creek Gardens and Game** (☎ 800/742-4992 or 541/742-2238). This ranch outside the town of Halfway offers tours during which you get to see their bison up close, learn more about bison and their cultural significance to the Plains native peoples, and then have a buffalo dinner. Tour and dinner runs $25 for adults, $15 for youths, and $10 for children. Tours alone are $12 for adults, $10 for youths, and $5 for children.

WHERE TO STAY

The Birch Leaf Lodge. Rte. 1, Box 91, Halfway, OR 97834. ☎ **541/742-2990.** 5 rms (1 with private bath). $45–$75 double. MC, V.

Located on a 42-acre farm on the outskirts of Halfway, the Birch Leaf Farm is a tranquil spot in a valley surrounded by the peaks of the Wallowa Mountains. Orchards, pastures, and even several ponds and marshes make the farm a great place to explore, and the bird watching is great. The guest rooms are small and simply furnished, but comfortable. The big country breakfast includes local jams and honey from the farm. In winter, there's excellent cross-country skiing here.

✪ **Pine Valley Lodge.** N. Main St. (P.O. Box 712), Halfway, OR 97834. ☎ **541/742-2027.** 6 rms (all with shared bath), 1 bunkhouse (sleeps 6 to 10 people). $65–$140 double. No credit cards.

This amazing little lodge and restaurant, comprised of four old buildings in downtown Halfway, is a Wild West fantasy created by two very creative artists. With handmade furniture and Western collectibles scattered all about, the main lodge is a fascinating place to just wander around. Two small guest rooms that combine rustic furnishings with the artistic endeavors of the owners are on the second floor. Next door is the Blue Dog, with more rustic Western furnishings and four rooms (which can also be combined to form two suites). Outdoorsy types will like the bunkhouse, aka the Love Shack, which truly is a shack, though with a lot of charm. All in all, this place is unique. The lodge's Halfway Supper Club is located across the street in an old church that was built in 1891 (see below for details).

A GOOD PLACE TO EAT IN HALFWAY

✪ **The Halfway Supper Club.** N. Main St. ☎ **541/742-2027.** Reservations recommended. Main courses $12–$22. No credit cards. Wed–Sun 6–8pm. CONTINENTAL.

Located both in an old church that was built in 1891 and, in summer, on the front porch of the house across the street, this restaurant is part of the wonderfully eclectic and rustic Pine Valley Lodge (see above) and serves the most creative cuisine in this corner of the state. The meals, which include the likes of lamb chops with rosemary and lemon and coq au vin (here known as hunter's chicken), are served amid handmade furniture and painted pillows and wall coverings by the owners. This place is well worth a drive if you're staying anywhere in the vicinity.

5 Ontario & the Owyhee River Region

Ontario: 72 miles SE of Baker City, 63 miles NW of Boise; 130 miles NE of Burns

Ontario, the easternmost town in Oregon, lies in the Four Rivers region, at the confluence of the Owyhee, Snake, Malheur, and Payette Rivers. Irrigated by waters from the massive Owyhee Reservoir, these wide, flat valleys are prime agricultural lands that produce primarily onions, sugar beets, and, as in Idaho, plenty of potatoes. However, this region is also where much of the world's zinnia seeds are grown. During the summer, zinnia fields color the landscape in bold swaths. If you're curious to see the flower fields, head out of Ontario on Oreg. 201.

The biggest attraction in the region is the new **Four Rivers Cultural Center,** which focuses on the various cultures that have made the region what it is today. However, nearby, there is also some Oregon Trail history to be seen. South of Ontario, however, lies one of Oregon's most rugged and remote regions. This corner of the state is rugged high desert, and along the banks of the Owyhee River and Succor Creek, you can see canyons and cliffs that seem far more suited to a Southwestern landscape.

Note: Ontario is on rocky mountain time, not Pacific time.

ESSENTIALS

GETTING THERE   Ontario is on the Idaho line at the junction of I-84 and U.S. 20/26, all of which link the town to western Oregon.

VISITOR INFORMATION   For more information on the Ontario area, contact the **Ontario Visitors & Convention Bureau,** 88 SW Third Ave., Ontario, OR 97914 (☎ **541/889-8012**).

A CULTURAL MUSEUM

Four Rivers Cultural Center. 676 SW Fifth Ave. ☎ **888/211-1222** or 541/889-8191. Admission $4 adults, $3 seniors and children 3–12. Daily 10am–6pm. Closed Thanksgiving, Christmas, and New Year's Day.

While this remote corner of Oregon may seem an unlikely place for a multicultural museum, that is exactly what you'll find at this center, which opened in 1997. The museum focuses on four very distinct cultures that have, and still do, call this region home. The Paiutes were the original inhabitants of the area, and an exploration of their hunting-and-gathering culture is the first exhibit. In the mid–19th century, the first pioneers began arriving in the area and quickly displaced the Paiutes. By the late 19th century, many Mexican cowboys, known as vaqueros or buckaroos, had come north to this region to work the large cattle ranches. Likewise, Basque shepherds settled in the area at this same time and tended large herds of sheep in the more remote corners of the region. The fourth culture focused on is that of the Japanese, who were forced to live in internment camps in the area during World War II. After the war, however, many stayed on in the area.

EXPLORING THE REGION

For more Oregon Trail history, head 18 miles west of Ontario to the small farming community of **Vale.** Here you'll find the **Rinehart Stone House,** 283 S. Main St. (☎ **541/473-2070**), which was built in 1872 and was a stage stop and an important wayside along the route of the Oregon Trail. Today it houses a small historical museum. Large historic murals cover numerous walls around Vale, and a good way to see them is by horse-drawn buggy operated by **Wilcox Horse & Buggy** (☎ **888/ TRY-VALE** or 541/473-2329). The tours also include dinner and old-fashioned music and cost $39.95. Six miles south of Vale, at Keeney Pass, you can see **wagon ruts** left by pioneers traveling the Oregon Trail.

South of Ontario 15 miles, you'll find **Nyssa,** the "Thunderegg Capital of Oregon." **Rockhounding** is the area's most popular pastime, and thundereggs (also known as geodes) are the prime find. These round rocks look quite plain until they are cut open to reveal the agate or crystals within. You'll find plenty of cut-and-polished thundereggs in the rock shops around town. If you'd like to do a bit of rockhounding yourself, you can head south to **Succor Creek State Park,** a rugged canyon where you'll find a campground, picnic tables, and thundereggs waiting to be unearthed.

If you have a four-wheel-drive or high-clearance vehicle, you can continue another 30 minutes to **Leslie Gulch,** an even more spectacular canyon with walls of naturally sculpted sandstone. If you're lucky, you might even see bighorn sheep here. Few places in Oregon have more of the feel of the desert than these two canyons, and just as in the desert Southwest, here, too, rivers have been dammed to provide irrigation waters and aquatic playgrounds. **Lake Owyhee,** 45 miles south of Ontario off Ore. 201, is the longest lake in Oregon and offers boating, fishing, and camping. The Owyhee River above the lake is a designated State Scenic Waterway and is popular for **white-water rafting.** If you're interested in running this remote stretch of river, contact **Renegade River Rafters** (☎ **888/RNE-GADE** or 503/622-5699). A 4-day trip costs $365 per person. Below the Owyhee Dam, 12 miles southwest of the town of Adrian, you'll find a signed **"Watchable Wildlife" area** offering excellent bird watching. You might also spot beavers, porcupines, mule deer, and coyotes.

WHERE TO STAY

For the most part, Ontario is a wayside for people traveling along I-84, and as such, the city's accommodations are strictly off-ramp budget motels. Motel options include a **Best Western Inn,** 251 Goodfellow St., Ontario, OR 97914 (☎ **541/889-2600**), charging $49 to $76 double; a **Super 8 Motel,** 266 Goodfellow St., Ontario, OR 97914 (☎ **541/889-8282**), charging $47 to $55 double; and a **Motel 6,** 275 NE 12th St., Ontario, OR 97914 (☎ 541/889-6617), charging $33 to $36 double.

At nearby **Farewell Bend State Park,** 25 miles northwest of Ontario on I-84, you'll find not only campsites but also covered wagons that can be rented for overnight stays ($25 per night). Don't look for horses to hitch up, though, these wagons stay put. For campsite and covered wagon reservations, call **Reservations Northwest** (☎ 800/452-5687).

WHERE TO DINE IN ONTARIO

When you just have to have a latte or a mocha, head to **Coyote Coffee Company,** 146 SW Fourth Ave. (☎ **541/889-HOWL**), in a tiny cottage a block off Oregon Street, which is downtown Ontario's main street.

Alexander's on the River. 1930 SE Fifth St. ☎ **541/889-8070.** Reservations recommended. Main courses $10–$22. AE, DISC, MC, V. Mon–Thurs 11am–9pm, Fri–Sat 11am–10pm, Sun noon–8pm. AMERICAN.

In the unlikeliest of locations (behind a gravel quarry and the sewage treatment plant), you'll find Ontario's finest restaurant. Despite the neighbors, this restaurant is actually in a very scenic riverfront locale, with large old cottonwood trees shading the deck. Some people even arrive here by boat. This is onion-growing country, so you would be remiss if you didn't order the onion rings or blossoming onion appetizer. In summer, the deck is the place to be.

6 Southeastern Oregon: Land of Marshes, Mountains & Desert

Burns: 130 miles SE of Bend, 130 miles SE of Ontario, 70 miles S of John Day

Southeastern Oregon, the most remote and least populated corner of Oregon, is a region of extremes. Vast marshlands, the most inhospitable desert in the state, and a mountain topped with aspen groves and glacial valleys are among the most prominent features of this landscape. While cattle outnumber human inhabitants and the deer and the antelope play, it's bird life that's the region's number-one attraction. At **Malheur National Wildlife Refuge,** birds abound almost any month of the year attracting flocks of bird watchers, binoculars and bird books in hand.

Because this is such an isolated region (Burns and Lakeview are the only towns of consequence), it is not an area to be visited by the unprepared. Always keep your gas tank topped off and carry water for both you and your car. Two of the region's main attractions, **Steens Mountain** and the **Hart Mountain National Antelope Refuge** are only accessible by way of gravel roads more than 50 miles long. Likewise, a visit to the Alvord Desert will also require spending 60 or more miles on a gravel road.

ESSENTIALS

GETTING THERE   The town of Burns is midway between Bend and Ontario on U.S. 20. Malheur National Wildlife Refuge, Steens Mountain, and Hart Mountain National Antelope Refuge are all located south of Burns off Ore. 205.

VISITOR INFORMATION   For more information on this area, contact the **Harney County Chamber of Commerce,** 18 W. D St., Burns, OR 97720 (☎ 541/573-2636).

EXPLORING THE REGION

Because water is scarce here in the high desert, it becomes a magnet for wildlife wherever it appears. Three marshy lakes—Malheur, Harney, and Mud—south of Burns cover such a vast area and provide such an ideal habitat for bird life that they have been designated the **Malheur National Wildlife Refuge.** The shallow lakes, surrounded by thousands of acres of marshlands, form an oasis that annually attracts more than **300 species of birds,** including waterfowl, shorebirds, songbirds, and raptors. Some of the more noteworthy birds that are either resident or migratory at Malheur are trumpeter swans, sandhill cranes, white pelicans, great blue herons, and great horned owls. Of the more than 58 mammals that live in the refuge, the most visible are mule deer, antelope, and coyotes.

The refuge headquarters is 32 miles south of Burns on Ore. 205, but the refuge stretches for another 30 miles south to the crossroads of Frenchglen. The **visitor center,** where you can find out about recent sightings and current birding hot spots, is open weekdays only, while a **museum** housing a collection of nearly 200 stuffed-and-mounted birds is open daily. Camping is available at two campgrounds near Frenchglen. For more information on the refuge, contact **Malheur National Wildlife Refuge,** HC-72, Box 245, Princeton, OR 97721 (☎ 541/493-2612).

Steens Mountain, a different sort of desert oasis, is 30 miles southeast of Frenchglen on a gravel road that's usually open only between July and October. Even then the road is not recommended for cars with low clearance, but if you have the appropriate vehicle, the mountain is well worth a visit. Rising to 9,733 feet high, Steens Mountain, a fault-block mountain, was formed when the land on the west side of a geological fault line rose in relationship to the land on the east side of the fault. This geologic upheaval caused the east slope of Steens Mountain to form a precipitous escarpment that falls away to the Alvord Desert a mile below. The panorama out across southeastern Oregon is spectacular. The mountain rises so high that it creates its own weather, and on the upper slopes the sagebrush of the high desert gives way to juniper and aspen forests. From Frenchglen, there's a 66-mile loop road that leads to the summit and back down by a different route.

More wildlife-viewing opportunities are available at the **Hart Mountain National Antelope Refuge,** which is a refuge for both pronghorns, the fastest land mammal in North America and not really an antelope at all, and California bighorn sheep. The most accessible location for viewing antelope is the refuge headquarters, 49 miles southwest of Frenchglen on gravel roads. Bighorn sheep are harder to spot, but tend to keep to the steep cliffs west of the refuge headquarters. Primitive camping is available near the headquarters at **Hot Springs Campground.** For more information, contact the **Hart Mountain National Antelope Refuge,** P.O. Box 111, Lakeview, OR 97630 (☎ **541/947-3315**).

WHERE TO STAY & DINE

Frenchglen Hotel. Frenchglen, OR 97736. ☎ **541/493-2825.** Fax 541/493-2825. 8 rms, none with bath. $48–$50 double. DISC, MC, V. Closed Nov 16–Mar 14.

Frenchglen is in the middle of nowhere, so for decades the Frenchglen Hotel (now owned by the Oregon State Parks) has been an important way station for travelers passing through this remote region. The historic two-story hotel is 60 miles south of Burns on the edge of Malheur National Wildlife Refuge. Though the historic setting will appeal to anyone with an appreciation for pioneer days, the hotel is most popular with bird watchers. The guest rooms are on the second floor and are small and simply furnished. This hotel is often booked up months in advance. Three meals a day will cost $20 to $25 per person, and the hearty dinners are quite good.

Hotel Diamond. Diamond Lane, Diamond, OR 97722. ☎ **541/493-1898.** 6 rms (1 with private bath). A/C. $50–$70 double. MC, V.

Located 54 miles south of Burns off Ore. 205, the Hotel Diamond is on the opposite side of the Malheur Wildlife Refuge from Frenchglen. Built in 1898, this hotel serves as lodging, general store, post office, and gas station for the remote community of Diamond. Completely restored in the late 1980s, the hotel is now open year-round. There's a big screened porch across the front and a green lawn complete with a croquet court and horseshoe pits. Bicycles are also available. Inexpensive meals are served to guests only.

✪ McCoy Creek Inn. McCoy Creek Ranch, HC 72, Box 11, Diamond, OR 97722. ☎ **541/ 493-2131.** Fax 541/493-2131. 4 rms. $75 double. Rates include full breakfast. DC, MC, V.

Of the three lodges in this area, the McCoy Creek Inn is the most remote and most luxurious. Set on a working cattle ranch that has been run by the same family for five generations, the inn consists of three rooms in the main house plus one more in the bunkhouse. McCoy Creek runs right through the property and its canyon is full of wildlife. You can hike the trails, splash in the stream, or feed the farm animals (if you're so inclined). Steens Mountain rises up from the ranch and the Malheur National Wildlife Refuge is nearby. A hot tub provides the perfect end to a long day of exploring the high desert.

Index

FROMMER'S® COMPLETE TRAVEL GUIDES

*(Comprehensive guides to destinations around the world, with
selections in all price ranges—from deluxe to budget)*

Acapulco, Ixtapa &
   Zihuatenejo
Alaska
Amsterdam
Arizona
Atlanta
Australia
Austria
Bahamas
Barcelona, Madrid &
   Seville
Belgium, Holland &
   Luxembourg
Bermuda
Boston
Budapest & the Best of
   Hungary
California
Canada
Cancún, Cozumel & the
   Yucatán
Cape Cod, Nantucket &
   Martha's Vineyard
Caribbean
Caribbean Cruises & Ports
   of Call
Caribbean Ports of Call
Carolinas & Georgia
Chicago
China
Colorado
Costa Rica
Denver, Boulder &
   Colorado Springs
England

Europe
Florida
France
Germany
Greece
Hawaii
Hong Kong
Honolulu, Waikiki & Oahu
Ireland
Israel
Italy
Jamaica & Barbados
Japan
Las Vegas
London
Los Angeles
Maryland & Delaware
Maui
Mexico
Miami & the Keys
Montana & Wyoming
Montréal & Québec City
Munich & the Bavarian Alps
Nashville & Memphis
Nepal
New England
New Mexico
New Orleans
New York City
Northern New England
Nova Scotia, New
   Brunswick
   & Prince Edward Island
Oregon
Paris

Philadelphia & the Amish
   Country
Portugal
Prague & the Best of the
   Czech Republic
Provence & the Riviera
Puerto Rico
Rome
San Antonio & Austin
San Diego
San Francisco
Santa Fe, Taos &
   Albuquerque
Scandinavia
Scotland
Seattle & Portland
Singapore & Malaysia
South Pacific
Spain
Switzerland
Thailand
Tokyo
Toronto
Tuscany & Umbria
USA
Utah
Vancouver & Victoria
Vienna & the Danube
   Valley
Virgin Islands
Virginia
Walt Disney World &
   Orlando
Washington, D.C.
Washington State

FROMMER'S® DOLLAR-A-DAY GUIDES

(The ultimate guides to comfortable low-cost travel)

Australia from $50 a Day
California from $60 a Day
Caribbean from $60 a Day
Costa Rica & Belize
   from $35 a Day
England from $60 a Day
Europe from $50 a Day
Florida from $50 a Day
Greece from $50 a Day
Hawaii from $60 a Day
India from $40 a Day

Ireland from $50 a Day
Israel from $45 a Day
Italy from $50 a Day
London from $60 a Day
Mexico from $35 a Day
New York from $75 a Day
New Zealand from $50 a Day
Paris from $70 a Day
San Francisco from $60 a Day
Washington, D.C., from
   $60 a Day

FROMMER'S® PORTABLE GUIDES

(Pocket-size guides for travelers who want everything in a nutshell)

Bahamas
California Wine Country
Charleston & Savannah
Chicago

Dublin
Las Vegas
London
Maine Coast
New Orleans

Puerto Vallarta, Manzanillo
   & Guadalajara
San Francisco
Venice
Washington, D.C.

FROMMER'S® NATIONAL PARK GUIDES

(Everything you need for the perfect park vacation)

Grand Canyon
National Parks of the American West
Yellowstone & Grand Teton

Yosemite & Sequoia/
   Kings Canyon
Zion & Bryce Canyon

FROMMER'S® IRREVERENT GUIDES

(Wickedly honest guides for sophisticated travelers)

Amsterdam
Chicago
London

Manhattan
New Orleans
Paris

San Francisco
Santa Fe

Walt Disney World
Washington, D.C.

FROMMER'S® BY NIGHT GUIDES

(The series for those who know that life begins after dark)

Amsterdam
Chicago
Las Vegas
London

Los Angeles
Madrid
   & Barcelona
Manhattan

Miami
New Orleans
Paris

Prague
San Francisco
Washington, D.C.

THE COMPLETE IDIOT'S TRAVEL GUIDES

(The ultimate user-friendly trip planners)

Cruise Vacations
Las Vegas
New Orleans

New York City
Planning Your Trip
   to Europe

San Francisco
Walt Disney World

SPECIAL-INTEREST TITLES

Arthur Fommer's New World of Travel
The Civil War Trust's Official Guide to
   the Civil War Discovery Trail
Frommer's Caribbean Hideaways
Frommer's Complete Hostel Vacation
   Guide to England, Scotland & Wales
Frommer's Europe's Greatest
   Driving Tours
Frommer's Food Lover's Companion
   to France
Frommer's Food Lover's Companion to
   Italy
Israel Past & Present
New York City with Kids
New York Times Weekends

Outside Magazine's Adventure Guide
   to New England
Outside Magazine's Adventure Guide
   to Northern California
Outside Magazine's Adventure Guide
   to the Pacific Northwest
Outside Magazine's Adventure Guide
   to Southern California & Baja
Outside Magazine's Guide to Family Vacations
Places Rated Almanac
Retirement Places Rated
Washington, D.C., with Kids
Wonderful Weekends from New York City
Wonderful Weekends from San Francisco
Wonderful Weekends from Los Angeles

WHEREVER
YOU TRAVEL,
*H*ELP IS NEVER
FAR AWAY.

From planning your trip to providing travel assistance
along the way, American Express® Travel Service Offices
are always there to help you do more.

Oregon

Triangle Travel (R)
4836 S.W. Western Avenue
Beaverton
503-626-4645

Jackson Travel Agency (R)
2933 Bullock Road
Medford
541-779-5525

Ambassador Travel (R)
239 Coburg Road
Eugene
541-484-1325

American Express Travel Service
Standard Plaza Building
1100 S.W. Sixth Avenue
Portland
503-226-2961

Ambassador Travel Downtown (R)
190 East 11th Avenue
Eugene
541-686-1234

Southern Oregon Travel (R)
122 Depot Street
Rogue River
503-582-0591

Southern Oregon Travel (R)
740 N.W. 6th Street
Grants Pass
503-476-4495

Sather Travel, Inc. (R)
2290 Commercial Street S.E.
Suite 108
Salem
503-588-0834

do more

Travel

http://www.americanexpress.com/travel

**American Express Travel Service Offices are
found in central locations throughout Oregon.**